THE BARBOUR COLLECTION
OF CONNECTICUT TOWN
VITAL RECORDS

THE BARBOUR COLLECTION OF CONNECTICUT TOWN VITAL RECORDS

DANBURY 1685–1847

DARIEN 1820–1851

DERBY 1655–1852

Compiled by

Lorraine Cook White

GENEALOGICAL PUBLISHING Co., Inc.

INTRODUCTION

As early as 1640 the Connecticut Court of Election ordered all magistrates to keep a record of the marriages they preformed. In 1644 the registration of births and marriages became the official responsibility of town clerks and registrars, with deaths added to their duties in 1650. From 1660 until the close of the Revolutionary War these vital records of birth, marriage, and death were generally well kept, but then for a period of about two generations until the mid-nineteenth century, the faithful recording of vital records declined in some towns.

General Lucius Barnes Barbour was the Connecticut Examiner of Public Records from 1911 to 1934 and in that capacity directed a project in which the vital records kept by the towns up to about 1850 were copied and abstracted. Barbour previously had directed the publication of the Bolton and Vernon vital records for the Connecticut Historical Society. For this new project he hired several individuals who were experienced in copying old records and familiar with the old script.

Barbour presented the completed transcriptions of town vital records to the Connecticut State Library where the information was typed onto printed forms. The form sheets were then cut, producing twelve small slips from each sheet. The slips for most towns were then alphabetized and the information was then typed a second time on large sheets of rag paper, which were subsequently bound into separate volumes for each town. The slips for all towns were then interfiled, forming a statewide alphabetized slip index for most surviving town vital records.

The dates of coverage vary from town to town, and of course the records of some towns are more complete than others. Altogether the entire Barbour Collection--one of the great genealogical manuscript collections and one of the last to be published--covers 137 towns and comprises 14,333 typed pages.

TABLE OF CONTENTS

ABBREVIATIONS

ae.------------age
b. ------------born, both
bd.------------buried
B. G.---------Burying Ground
d. ------------died, day, or daughter
decd.---------deceased
f.--------------father
h.--------------hour
J. P.-----------Justice of Peace
m.-------------married or month
res.------------resident
s.--------------son
st.-------------stillborn
w. ------------wife
wid.----------widow
wk.-----------week
y. ------------year

THE BARBOUR
COLLECTION
OF CONNECTICUT TOWN
VITAL RECORDS

DANBURY VITAL RECORDS

1685 - 1847

	Vol.	Page

ABBOT, ABBOTT, ABOT, Abijah, of Ridgebury, m. Mrs. Hannah
CROFUT, of Danbury, Mar. 26, 1823, by Rev. Oliver
Tuttle — 3, 16

Asenath, d. John, of Ridgefield, m. Ebenezer **BENEDICT,**
3rd, May 5, 1783 — 1, 403

Augustus H., m. Harriette E. **DANN,** July 24, 1849, by Rev.
A. Perkins — 3, 160

David P., m. Sally O. **BANKS,** [Dec.] 27, [1826], by G. Benedict — 3, 37

Ezra, m. Mary A. **FOOT,** b. of Danbury, Dec. 1, 1845, by Rev.
Fitch Read — 3, 137

John, a foreigner, m. Harriet **HOYT,** this day [Dec. 27, 1835],
by Levi Bosbom — 3, 84

Joseph, m. Esther O. **BANKS,** Nov. 27, 1823, by George
Benedict — 3, 19

Mary E., m. Amos J. **STONE,** Sept. 26, 1849, by Rev. A. Perkins — 3, 160

Mary Jane, m. Daniel **WHITE,** b. of Danbury, Nov. 28, 1849,
by Nathan Burton, P. T. — 3, 145

Nancy, d. Amos, b. July 9, 1810 — 2, 100

Silas, s. [Amos], b. Mar. 1, 1822 — 2, 100

ABERNETHY, John, of Woodbury, m. Susan T. **BULL,** of Danbury,
this day, Sept. 11, 1845, by Rev. Rollin S. Stone — 3, 136

ADAMS, Betsey, m. Ezra **PATCH,** b. of Danbury, Oct. 22, 1828, by
John Nickerson — 3, 49

Bradley, of Redding, m. Olive **WHITLOCK,** of Danbury, Nov.
10, 1826, by Rev. John G. Lowe — 3, 38

Deborah, d. Samuel, of Fairfield, m. John **McLEAN,** s. Nail
& grandson of Hector, of Scotland, Oct. 12, 1759 — 1, 483

Deborah, w. Samuel, m. Deborah **McLEAN,** d. Feb. 2, 1796 — 1, 483

John, m. Adaline **WILDMAN,** b. of Danbury, Dec. 24, 1820,
by William Cooke, J. P. — 3, 5

Lemuel, of Redding, m. Rebekah **HOYT,** of Danbury, Sept. 13,
1825, by Marvin Richardson — 3, 28

Louisa, of Lawrence, N. Y., m. Silliman B. **PECK,** of Danbury,
June 22, 1831, by Rev. Erastus Cole — 3, 63

Lucy, d. David, of Weston, m. Joshua **CHAPMAN,** Nov. 26,
1788 — 1, 484

Lynda, m. Joel **TAYLOR,** b. of Danbury, Oct. 18, 1820, by
William Cooke, J. P. — 3, 5

Mary M., of Danbury, m. Nathaniel **BARNUM,** of New York,

1

	Vol.	Page
ADAMS, (cont.)		
May 20, 1846, by Thomas T. Guion	3	140
Polly, of Danbury, m. Anthony WYGANT, of Newtown, this		
day, [Sept. 4, 1831], by Rev. Lemuel B. Hull	3	64
Samuel, late of Fairfield, f. Deborah, w. John McLEAN,		
d. Feb. 13, 1782	1	483
Samuel, of Dutchess Co., N. Y., m. Anna GRIFFIN, of Danbury,		
Dec. 25, 1842, by James Floy	3	118
Sarah E., m. John* E. ELLIS, Sept. 22, 1836, by Rev. A. Rood		
*(E. uncertain)	3	87
Susanna, of Weston, m. Timothy FOSTER, Sept. 28, 1788	1	462
ADKINS, Abby, d. Alfred, of South East, N. Y., b. June 6, 1822	2	178
ALLEN, ALLIN, Hannah, m. Errich B. JONES, [Dec.] 1, [1830], by		
Rev. A. Rood	3	58
Hester, m. Jesse OLMSTED, June 13, 1824, by Nathan Burton	3	22
John, of Fairfield, m. Eunice CORBIN, of Danbury, July		
12, 1799	1	370
Loiza, m. Walter MOORE, Nov. 27, 1823, by Nathan Burton	3	19
Mary Ann, m. Charles A. BRUSH, b. of Danbury, Aug. 30,		
1846, by R. K. Bellamy	3	140
Silence, m. Reuben CURTISS, Oct. 4, 1775	1	419
AMBLER, Alfred S., m. Martha P. HOLMES, Apr. 15, [1846], by		
Rev. R. H. Bellamy	3	139
Alfred Segar, [s. Benjamin & Polly], b. June 7*, 1824		
*(or "1st")	2	180
Apphia, d. [Benjamin & Polly], b. Jan. 17, 1816	2	180
Aphia, m. Waters Furman OLMSTED, Jan. 22, 1837, by Rev.		
J. G. Collom	3	99
Augustin Irie, [s. Irie & Lucinda], b. Dec. 27, 1818	1	392
Benjamin, s. [Peter & Hannah], b. Nov. 20, 1787	1	486
Benjamin, b. Nov. 20, 1787; m. Polly [ ], Apr. 13, 1806	2	180
Benjamin Shove, s. [Benjamin & Polly], b. May 6, 1814	2	180
Betty, [w. Fairchild], d. June 6, 1810	2	175
Betty Maria, d. [Fairchild & Sally], b. Sept. 22, 1811	2	175
Caroline Eliza, [d. Fairchild & Sally], b. June 26, 1814	2	175
Charles, s. [Squire & Elizabeth], b. Jan. 29, 1791	1	406
Chloe, d. [Thomas & Elizabeth], b. Oct. 13, 1813	2	179
Chloe, m. Edward S. HULL, Sept. 14, 1831, by Rev. Thomas		
Larcombe	3	63
David, s. [Peter & Hannah], b. [ ]	1	486
David Augustus, s. David, b. Aug. 19, 1821	2	134
David Augustus, m. Martha COBURN, Mar. 18, 1844, by James		
Floy	3	125
Deborah, [d. Fairchild & Sally], b. Oct. 29, 1812	2	175
Edward, [s. David], b. Nov. 17, 1827	2	134
Edward Crosby, s. [Benjamin & Polly], b. Feb. 24, 1807	2	180
Elizabeth, [d. Benjamin & Polly], b. [ ], 1826	2	180
Eunice, [d. Fairchild & Sally], b. Nov. 20, 1816	2	175

Vol. Page

AMBLER, (cont.)

Eunice, m. David S. **WILDMAN**, b. of Danbury, Oct. 30, 1836,
    by Rev. Salmon C. Bulkley   3   88

Ezra Hoyt, s. [Gilead & Anne], b. Oct. 29, 1796   1   371

Ezra Hoyt, m. Paulina **CROFUT**, June 6, 1821, by Rev.
    W[illia]m Andrews   3   7

Fairchild, s. [Peter & Hannah], b. Nov. 22, 1785   1   486

Fairchild, m. Betty **SEGAR**, Apr. 13, 1806   2   175

Fairchild, m. Sally **CROFUT**, Nov. 11, 1810   2   175

Franklin Picket, s. [Squire & Elizabeth], b. Jan. 3, 1797   1   406

George, [s. David], b. Feb. 22, 1826   2   134

Gilead, 6th s. John, of Danbury, b. Apr. 15, 1773; m. Anne
    HOYT, d. Jonathan, of Norwalk, Jan. 1, 1795   1   371

Hannah, d. [Peter & Hannah], b. Nov. 18, 1789   1   486

Hannah, d. [Benjamin & Polly], b. Aug. 10, 1810   2   180

Hannah, m. Stebbins **BAXTER**, b. of Danbury, May 2, 1832,
    by Thomas Larcombe   3   70

Hannah, of Bethel, m. Abel J. **STILSON**, of Newtown, this
    day, [Sept. 26, 1839], by John Greenwood   3   99

Hannah E., m. Charles **HULL**, b. of Danbury, Nov. 18, 1840,
    by Addison Parker   3   107

Harriot, d. [Squire & Elisabeth], b. Mar. 2, 1794; d. Aug.
    22, 1795   1   406

Henry Fairchild, s. [Fairchild & Sally], b. Oct. 14, 1822   2   175

Henry Granvill, s. [Thomas & Elizabeth], b. Sept. 1, 1822   2   179

Hyram, s. [Gilead & Anne], b. Dec. 4, 1798 (Hiram)   1   371

Huldah, [d. Stephen & Rachel], b. Sept. 4, 1788   1   429

Irel, m. Rebecca Jane **PHILLIPS**, b. of Danbury, Oct. 6, 1839,
    by Rev. Z. Cook   3   100

Irie, b. Oct. 6, 1793; m. Lucinda **PERKINS**, Feb. 11, 1818,
    by Rev. William Andrews   1   392

Jerusha, of Danbury, m. Phineas **BEERS**, of New Milford,
    July 11, 1830, by Rev. Solomon Glover   3   57

John Linus, m. Anna **LOBDEN***, June 8, 1823, by Rev.
    [Willia]m Andrews *(**LOBDELL**?)   3   17

Joseph, s. [Peter & Hannah], b. Feb. 18, 1792   1   486

Joseph Legran, [s. Benjamin & Polly], b. Nov. 18, 1808;
    d. Feb. 19, 1848   2   180

Julius, s. [David], b. Aug. 15, 1823   2   134

Lucia Ruggles, [d. Benjamin & Polly], b. Aug. 5, 1812;
    d. June 14, 1818   2   180

Lucia Ruggles, [d. Benjamin & Polly], b. May 25, 1818; d. [   ]   2   180

Marthia, [d. Benjamin & Polly], b. Mar. 23, 1822   2   180

Mary, [d. Benjamin & Polly], b. July 9, 1820   2   180

Mary, m. William R. **FIELD**, b. of Danbury, [Apr.] 22, [1840],
    by Addison Parker   3   103

Mary Luzern, [d. Irie & Lucinda], b. July 2, 1821   1   392

Nancy, of Danbury, m. William **ANDRUS**, of Huntington, July 1,

	Vol.	Page
AMBLER, (cont.)		
[1822], by Nathan Seelye, J. P.	3	12
Peter, m. Hannah **SHOVE,** d. Benjamin, Oct. 21, 1784	1	486
Peter, s. [Thomas & Elizabeth], b. Apr. 2, 1816*; d. Apr. 5, 1816 *(Dates rewritten)	2	179
Peter Wildman, s. [Thomas & Elizabeth], b. July 23, 1817	2	179
Polly, [d. Stephen & Rachel], b. May 20, 1785	1	429
Rachel, d. [Peter & Hannah], b. [ ]	1	486
Rachel, wid., of Danbury, m. Solomon **GLOVER,** of Newtown, June 25, 1826, by Josiah Dikeman	3	33
Russel Perkins, [s. Irie & Lucinda], b. Oct. 2, 1827	1	392
Sarah, m. Ira **KELLOGG,** Nov. 10, 1824, by George Benedict, M. B.	3	25
Sarah, d. [Peter & Hannah], b. [ ]	1	486
Sarah Crofut, d. [Fairchild & Sally], b. July 26, 1825	2	175
Sarah E., m. Nathan **MILLER,** Nov. 22, 1843, by Rev. William R. Webb	3	124
Silas, s. [Peter & Hannah], b. [ ]	1	486
Squire, m. Elisabeth **PICKET,** d. Ebenezer, Feb. 5, 1784	1	406
Squire, m. Jerusha **HOYT,** b. of Danbury, June 11, 1820, by Phineas Taylor, J. P.	3	1
Stephen, b. Apr. 27, 1758; m. Rachel **MUNSON,** Apr. 15, 1783	1	429
Thomas, s. [Peter & Hannah], b. Nov. 20, 1793	1	486
Thomas, m. Elizabeth **BARBER,** Nov. 23, 1812	2	179
William Hart, s. [Fairchild & Betty], b. Oct. 19, 1807	2	175
AMERMAN, John W., of Norwalk, m. Mary **BARNUM,** of Danbury, Feb. 4, 1835, by Oliver N.* Amerman *(N or V)	3	82
AMES, Flavius, s. Everit, b. July 31, 1821; d. Jan. 18, 1823	2	170
ANDERSON, Albert, m. Mary **HITCHCOCK,** Oct. 15, 1844, by Thomas T. Guion	3	132
Cynthia, of Danbury, m. William W. **PADDOCK,** of South East, N. Y., Oct. 3, 1842, by Rev. James Floy	3	117
Harris, m. Cynthia **BARTRIM,** b. of Danbury, [Sept.] 24, [1837], by Jacob Shaw	3	92
ANDREWS, ANDRUS, Aaron, m. Polly Maria **BENEDICT,** b. of Danbury, Dec. 16, 1825, by Rev. John G. Lowe	3	35
Andrew P., m. Margarett **HAWLEY,** b. of Danbury, Apr. 27, [1845], by John L. Ambler, C. M.	3	134
Anson Siely, [d. John, Jr. & Eunice], b. Aug. 2, 1786	1	410
Betsey Ann, m. Lewis **OSBORN,** [Jan.] 1, [1832], by Rev. A. Rood	3	66
Charles, m. Susan **TALMAGE,** b. of Danbury, June 7, 1848, by John Crawford	3	142
Eliakim, m. Annice **NICKESON,** Sept. 28, 1786	1	463
Eliakim, s. [Eliakim & Annice], b. Feb. 16, 1787	1	463
Eliza, m. Augustus M. **GREGORY,** [May] 11, [1831], by Rev. A. Rood	3	62
Ezra, m. Clarissa **TAYLOR,** b. of Danbury, this day [Nov.		

	Vol.	Page
ANDREWS, ANDRUS, (cont.)		
21, 1824], by Rev. Lemuel B. Hull	3	25
Frances E., m. Benedict **STARR**, b. of Danbury, Apr. 7, 1846, by Rev. Fitch Read	3	139
George, m. Catharine **MONTGOMERY**, Oct. 31, 1832, by Thomas Larcombe	3	74
George A., m. Lucy Jane **TAYLOR**, b. of Danbury, this day, [Sept. 23, 1840], by Rev. S. H. Clark	3	105
Hannah, b. Jan. 13, 1745; m. Benajah **BENEDICT**, June 28, 1787	1	442
Hannah, w. Thaddeus, decd., d. May 3, 1806	1	478
Hannah, m. John **TURKINGTON**, Feb. 17, 1822, by Rev. Ambrose S. Todd	3	11
Harriet L., m. Ezra H. **WHITE**, Nov. 24, [1839], by Rev. Z. Cook	3	100
Harriet T*. m. Rev. Salmon C. **BULKLEY**, b. of Danbury, June 29, 1837, by Rev. Shaler J. Hillyer, of North Salem, N. Y. & Long Ridge, Conn. *(Possibly "S")	3	90
Israel W., of Marietta, O., m. Mariann S. **CLARK**, of Danbury, this day [Aug. 24, 1842], by Rev. Rollin S. Stone	3	116
Israel Ward, of Marietta, O., m. Sarah H. **CLARKE**, of Danbury, Aug. 8, 1839, by Rev. Rollin S. Stone	3	99
James, [d. Eliakim & Annice], b. Jan. 15, 1789	1	463
John, Jr., m. Eunice **SIELY**, d. Seth, Oct. 21, 1785	1	410
John Liman, [s. John, Jr. & Eunice], b. Dec. 24, 1787	1	410
Julia, [d. John, Jr. & Eunice], b. July 24, 1792	1	410
Julia Maria, m. William H. **CLARK**, b. of Danbury, Sept. 9, 1841, by S. B. Britton	3	112
Lucy, m. Levi **TAYLOR**, Jan. 6, 1805	1	432
Mary, of Bethel, m. Azariel **SMITH**, of Bridgewater, Dec. 29, 1823, by Rev. John G. Lowe	3	23
Mary, m. Hiram **JUDD**, b. of Danbury, Oct. 31, 1825, by Rev. John G. Lowe	3	34
Naomi, d. Thaddeus, m. Benj[ami]n **BARNUM**, Jr., Oct. 30, 1788	1	441
Nathanael, [s. Eliakim & Annice], b. Nov. 1, 1791	1	463
Rebeckah, m. Ezra **FROST**, Sept. 7, 1785	1	478
Rebecca, m. Abel **BENEDICT**, Feb. 22, 1791	1	442
Seth, [s. John, Jr. & Eunice], b. Feb. 17, 1790	1	410
William, of Huntington, m. Nancy **AMBLER**, of Danbury, July 1, [1822], by Nathan Seelye, J. P.	3	12
APPLEBY, Lewis C., of New York State, m. Betsey Ann **DOBBS**, of Danbury, Dec. 20, 1827, by John Nickerson	3	43
ARCHER, Elisabeth, m. Stephen B. **PECK**, Feb. 18, 1838, by Rev. Rollin S. Stone	3	93
ARMSTRONG, [see also **URMSTON**], Margaret, of New York, m. Henry S. **SIGNOR**, of Danbury, June 28, 1847, by Thomas T. Guion	3	163

	Vol.	Page

ARMSTRONG, (cont.)
W[illia]m H., m. Betsey JENNINGS, Nov. 19, 1834, by Rev.
    A. Rood   **3**   **86**

ARNOLD, Harriet, m. David PARSONS, b. of Danbury, July 1, 1840,
    by Addison Parker   **3**   **104**

ASA, Anne, d. Elizabeth GUTHRIE, b. Aug. 7, 1778; father,
    Jacob ASA   **1**   **376**

ATWATER, Lucius, Rev., m. Mary BULKLEY, b. of Danbury, Sept.
    30, 1840, by Addison Parker   **3**   **105**

AVERIL[L], Roger, of Salisbury, m. Maria D. WHITE, of Danbury,
    this day [ ], by Rev. Rollin S. Stone, Recorded Oct. 31,
    1844   **3**   **129**

AVERY, Orrin, m. Mary ROBERTS, Nov. 20, 1825, by Rev.
    W[illia]m Andrews   **3**   **29**

BABBS, Hariet E., m. David FRY, Apr. 11, 1840, by Thomas P.
    White, J. P.   **3**   **102**

BACON, Mary, b. Feb. 20, 1797; m. Daniel WILLIAMS, Sept. [ ],
    1820   **2**   **101**

BAILEY, BAILY, BALLEY, Amme, [d. Benjamin & Hannah], b.
    May 14, 1780   **1**   **433**

Amme, d. Benj[ami]n, m. Abel HOYT, May 15, 1799   **1**   **371**

Andrew Jackson, [s. William W.], b. June 19, 1813   **1**   **411**

Anson, [s. Benjamin & Hannah], b. Aug. 1, 1798   **1**   **433**

Benjamin, s. [Samuel & Lydia], b. Dec. 9, 1756   **1**   **409**

Benjamin, m. Hannah DIBBLE, d. Eleazer, June 5, 1777   **1**   **433**

Caroline, d. [Lemuel B. & Abbey], b. July 12, 1802   **1**   **356**

Caroline, [d. William W.], b. Apr. 1, 1806   **1**   **411**

Clary, d. [Ebenezer & Anne], b. May 27, 1779   **1**   **427**

David, of Cherryvalley, m. Rebecca Evelina EARL, of Danbury,
    [Nov.] 10, [1822], by John Nickerson   **3**   **13**

Deborah, [d. Benjamin & Hannah], b. [ ]   **1**   **433**

Ebenezer, [s. Samuel & Lydia], b. June 24, 1759   **1**   **409**

Ebenezer, m. Anne STARR, Dec. 9, 1778   **1**   **427**

Ebenezer G., m. Polly Ann KEELER, Jan. 1, 1851, by John
    Abbot, Elder   **3**   **153**

Edmond, [s. Benjamin & Hannah], b. [ ]   **1**   **433**

Eli, [s. Benjamin & Hannah], b. Nov. 12, 1786   **1**   **433**

Eliza, [d. William W.], b. June 15, 1808   **1**   **411**

George Washington, [s. William W.], b. Feb. 1, 1811   **1**   **411**

Hannah, [w. Benjamin], d. Nov. 6, 1800   **1**   **433**

Hannah Luvana, [d. Lemuel B. & Abbey], b. June 14, 1804   **1**   **356**

Henry Starr, [s. William W.], b. July 7, 1819   **1**   **411**

John, m. Elizabeth CONNOR, [ ] 25, [1851], by Rev.
    Michael O'Farrell   **3**   **159**

Lemuel B., 4th s. Samuel, m. Abbey GREGORY, 2nd d.
    Abraham, decd., of Norwalk, Sept. 20, 1801   **1**   **356**

Lemuel Beebe, [s. Samuel & Lydia], b. Nov. 2, 1779   **1**   **409**

Lucy, [d. Ebenezer & Anne], b. Apr. 2, 1782   **1**   **427**

	Vol.	Page

BAILEY, BAILY, BALLEY, (cont.)

Lucy Ann, of Danbury, m. William **STEVENS**, of New York,
July 14, 1840, by Nathaniel Bishop — 3 — 105

Lydia, [d. Samuel & Lydia], b. May 8, 1769 — 1 — 409

Lydia, w. Samuel, d. May 21, 1784 — 1 — 409

Lydia, d. Samuel, m. Edmond **BEEBE**, Sept. 27, 1787 — 1 — 433

Lydia, [d. Ebenezer & Anne], b. June 11, 1788 — 1 — 427

Major, [s. Benjamin & Hannah], b. May 21, 1783 — 1 — 433

Mary, m. Oliver **HAMLIN**, b. of Danbury, Oct. 23, 1837, by
Rev. Salmon C. Bulkley — 3 — 92

Mary Ann, of South East, m. Nachan C. **SHERWOOD**, of
Reading, Mar. 11, 1838, by Rev. John Greenwood, of
Bethel — 3 — 92

Nabbe, [d. Benjamin & Hannah], b. Apr. 4, 1778; d. July 1, 1788 — 1 — 433

Nabbe, 2nd, [d. Benjamin & Hannah], b. July 20, 1791 — 1 — 433

Noah I., [s. Ebenezer & Anne], b. July 16, 1790 — 1 — 427

Samuel, m. Lydia **BEEBE**, d. Capt. Lemuel, Feb. 20, 1756 — 1 — 409

Samuel, [s. Samuel & Lydia], b. Sept. 25, 1766 — 1 — 409

Samuel, m. wid, Mary **DIBBLE**, Oct. 23, 1786 — 1 — 409

Warren, m. Mary **TREADWELL**, Dec. 27, 1846, by R. K.
Bellamy — 3 — 161

Xoe, [child of Ebenezer & Anne], b. July 13, 1784 — 1 — 427

------, m. Emily B. **SEGAR**, b. of Danbury, Aug. 18, 1844,
by Elder E. M. Jackson — 3 — 126

BAKER, Heman, m. Abigail **BARNUM**, b. of Danbury, this day
[Sept. 25, 1825], by Rev. Lemuel B. Hull — 3 — 28

BALDWIN, Caleb, m. Martha **BROWN**, d. Joseph, Feb. 21, 1745 — 1 — 438

Caleb, s. [Samuel & Hannah], b. Dec. 1, 1785 — 1 — 471

Chloe, [d. Caleb & Martha], b. July 24, 1756 — 1 — 438

Eliakim, s. [Samuel & Hannah], b. July 8, 1790 — 1 — 471

Henry, s. [Samuel & Hannah], b. July 4, 1792 — 1 — 471

James, s. [Samuel & Hannah], b. May 16, 1780 — 1 — 471

Leman, [s. Caleb & Martha], b. Feb. 7, 1758 — 1 — 438

Mary, d. [Caleb & Martha], b. Mar. 8, 1746; d. Sept. 11, 1781 — 1 — 438

Mary E., m. Thomas G. **BARBER**, Feb. 14, 1844, by Rev.
William R. Webb — 3 — 124

Mary E., m. Ezra B. **STEVENS**, b. of Danbury, July 27, 1851,
by Rev. F. N. Barlow, of Mill Plain — 3 — 156

Rachel, d. [Samuel & Hannah], b. May 18, 1788 — 1 — 471

Rebecca, d. [Samuel & Hannah], b. Mar. 14, 1774 — 1 — 471

Roxey, d. [Samuel & Hannah], b. Mar. 18, 1783 — 1 — 471

Samuel, [s. Caleb & Martha], b. May 22, 1753 — 1 — 438

Samuel, m. Hannah **NORTHROP**, d. James, of Ridgbury, Dec. 9,
1772 — 1 — 471

Samuel, of Newark, N. J., m. Sylvia Ann **STEVENS**, of
Danbury, this day [Jan. 11, 1843], by Rev. Rollin S. Stone — 3 — 119

Sam[ue]l Smith, s. [Samuel & Hannah], b. July 5, 1777 — 1 — 471

Sarah J., m. Thomas S. **STONE**, July 9, 1851, by Rev. A.

	Vol.	Page

BALDWIN, (cont.)

Perkins 3 160

BALL, Ferris D., of Brookfield, m. Harriet C. **BARNUM**, of Danbury, this day [Nov. 24, 1841], by Rev. Rollin S. Stone 3 113

George, m. Electa Minerva **POLLY**, b. of Danbury, Feb. 9, 1846, by Rev. Fitch Read 3 138

BALLEY, [see under **BAILEY**]

BANKS, Abraham O., m. Mary G. **CORNWELL**, b. of Danbury, Jan. 3, 1846, by Thomas T. Guion 3 140

Alva O., m. Eliza **GAGE**, Jan. 1, 1829, by Nathan Bulkley 3 50

Cordelia O., m. William **SILLICK**, b. of Danbury, May 4, 1831, by John Nickerson 3 61

Esther C., m. Joseph **ABBOTT**, Nov. 27, 1823, by George Benedict 3 19

Hannah H., m. John **HALL**, b. of Danbury, July 29, 1823, by John Nickerson 3 18

Mary, m. James H. **TROWBRIDGE**, Aug. 7, 1820, by Laban Clark 3 2

Rebecca S., m. Henry A. **HOYT**, Nov. 1, 1836, by Rev. A. Rood 3 87

Sally O., m. David P. **ABBOTT**, [Dec.] 27, [1826], by G. Benedict 3 37

Sam O., m. Burritt **SCRIBNER**, b. of Danbury, Oct. 15, 1834, by J. Nickerson 3 81

W[illia]m R., of Redding, m. Emiline **MORGAN**, of Bethel, Oct. 5, [1845], by Thomas T. Guion 3 137

BARACO, Angeline Hortencia, of West Milford, N. J., m. Ezra P. **HURD**, of Danbury, this day [Feb. 8, 1842], by Rev. Rollin S. Stone 3 114

BARBER, Adah B., m. Asa **HOYT**, b. of Danbury, Apr. 15, 1840, by Rev. Philetus Roberts 3 103

Almira, of Danbury, m. Anson **COMSTOCK**, of New York, Oct. 8, 1834, by John Nickerson 3 81

Ama, [d. Benjamin & Ruth], b. Oct. 4, 1773; d. Sept. 28, 1781 1 411

Angeline, of Danbury, m. Nathaniel S. **HULL**, of Redding, Sept. 1, 1841, by George N. Kelton 3 111

Benjamin, b. Jan. 23, 1729; m. [ ], Apr. 15, 1751 1 411

Benjamin, his 1st w. [ ], d. Nov. 6, 1753 1 411

Benjamin, m. 2nd w. Ruth **STEVENS**, Mar. 16, 1755 1 411

Benj[ami]n, [s. Benjamin & Ruth], b. Apr. 9, 1757 1 411

[Benjamin], m. 3rd w. Susanna **HORTON**, May 31, 1790 1 411

Elizabeth, m. Thomas **AMBLER**, Nov. 23, 1812 2 179

George, m. Lavinna(?) **PLATT**, b. of Danbury, Nov. 10, 1827, by John G. Stone 3 44

Harriet N., of Danbury, m. Oliver F. **HURLBURT**, of Brookfield, Sept. 1, 1847, by Rev. Rollin S. Stone 3 164

Jakin M., m. Abigail M. **SHERMAN**, b. of Danbury, Mar. 31, 1841, by Addison Parker 3 108

Lydia, [d, Benjamin & Ruth], b. Dec. 19, 1769 1 411

	Vol.	Page

BARBER, (cont.)

Lydia, m. Elnathan **KNAP**, Jr., Sept. 25, 1788 — 1 — 387

Matthew L., m. Betsey E. **PAYNE**, Nov. 21, 1824, by Nathan Bulkley — 3 — 25

Nathan, [s. Benjamin & Ruth], b. Jan. 3, 1763 — 1 — 411

Nathaniel, [s. Benjamin & Ruth], b. Dec. 21, 1767 — 1 — 411

Orris, m. Emeline **DOCONS**, July 13, [1828], by George Benedict — 3 — 48

Patience, [d. Benjamin & Ruth], b. Mar. 24, 1786*
*(Written possibly for "1776") — 1 — 411

Patience, m. Seth **SHOOVE**, Jr., Nov. 28, 1792 — 1 — 420

Ruth, w. [Benjamin], d. Dec. 25, 1788 — 1 — 411

Sarah, d. John, m. Samuel **CURTISS**, June 20, 1753 — 1 — 455

Simeon, [s. Benjamin & Ruth], b. June 6, 1771 — 1 — 411

Solomon, [s. Benjamin], b. Dec. 10, 1752 — 1 — 411

Stephen, [s. Benjamin & Ruth], b. Sept. 9, 1759 — 1 — 411

Thomas G., m. Mary E. **BALDWIN**, Feb. 14, 1844, by Rev. William R. Webb — 3 — 124

Zacheus, [s. Benjamin & Ruth], b. May 3, 1764 — 1 — 411

BARBURY, Eliza, m. Fred[eric]k **GILLETT**, Oct. 18, 1827, by George Benedict — 3 — 46

BARD, John, m. Lois Ann **WILDMAN**, June 12, 1826, by Rev. William Andrews — 3 — 33

BARKER, Martha, d. Joseph, of Long Island, m. Niram **DIKEMAN**, Oct. 19, 1805 — 1 — 467

BARLOW, Betsey, m. Reuben **WOOD**, Nov. 5, 1820 — 2 — 181

Daniel P., m. Lucy J. **MALLERY**, b. of Danbury, [Nov.] 8, [1847], by Nathaniel Bishop — 3 — 164

John, m. Julia Ann **JARVIS**, Dec. 28, 1825, by Rev. W[illia]m Andrews — 3 — 30

Laura, m. Philo **HOYT**, b. of Danbury, Mar. 8, 1840, by John Nickerson — 3 — 102

Morris*, m. Mary Ann **FLOYD**, Apr. 21, 1831, by Levi Brunson
*(Written "Morris **BARTOW**") — 3 — 61

Phebe, of Ridgefield, m. Nathaniel **WOOD**, Nov. 4, 1809 — 2 — 118

Rachel, m. Harmon **KNAPP**, Jan. 1, 1852, by Rev. A. Perkins — 3 — 160

W[illia]m Henry, m. Hariet E. **SIGNOR**, b. of Danbury, Oct. 18, 1840, by A. Parker — 3 — 106

BARNES, Eliza, m. John S. **BRADLEY**, b. of Danbury, Jan. 21, 1845, by Thomas T. Guion — 3 — 132

Mary A., m. John D. **LACY**, b. of Danbury, this day [ ], by Rev. Lemuel B. Hull. Recorded Nov. 26, 1835 — 3 — 83

Sarah M., of Danbury, m. Zar **JOICE**, of Brookfield, Sept. 24, 1839, by Rev. Z. Cook — 3 — 100

BARNUM, Abel, [s. Elijah], b. Nov. 20, 1764 — 1 — 426

Abel, m. Annis **TURNER**, Nov. 15, 1787 — 1 — 429

Abigael, d. [Eleazer & Keziah], b. Dec. 2, 1776 — 1 — 457

Abigail, [d. John, Jr. & Betty], b. June 27, 1780 — 1 — 427

BARNUM, (cont.)

Abigail, d. [Eliakim & Mercy], b. July 17, 1803	1	362
Abigail, m. Heman **BAKER,** b. of Danbury, this day [Sept. 25, 1825], by Rev. Lemuel B. Hull	3	28
Abigail, m. Ammon **WILLIAMS,** b. of Danbury, Oct. 20, 1826, by Rev. John G. Lowe	3	38
Abigail, of Danbury, m. Minor R. **DEMING,** of Cincinnati, O., Aug. 2, 1836, by Rev. Jonathan G. Collom	3	85
Abijah, m. Orpha **HAMILTON,** d. Capt. Silas, Oct. 20, 1763	1	388
Abijah, [s. Abijah & Orpha], b. Apr. 14, 1766	1	388
Abijah, Jr., m. Sibel [　　], Feb. 5, 1789	1	393
Adelia, d. [Daniel, Jr. & Rana], b. Jan. 29, 1808	2	61
Albacinda, m. John **KNAPP,** b. of Danbury, Feb. 19, 1829, by [　　]	3	51
Alethene, [d. Abel & Annis], b. Feb. 23, 1792	1	429
Almon, m. Almyria **TROWBRIDGE,** Jan. 8, 1823, by Rev. John G. Lowe	3	14
Almon, m. Almira **TROWBRIDGE,** b. of Danbury, Jan. 15, 1823, by Rev. John G. Lowe	3	22
Alva, [s. Noah & Catey], b. Jan. 8, 1788	1	436
Amelia, w. Zera, d. Nov. 15, 1822	2	178
Amos, s. [Joseph, Jr. & Temperance], b. Oct. 22, 1775	1	401
Andrew, [s. Daniel & Joanna], b. Jan. 3. 1790	1	452
Ann, of Danbury, m. Everit **CLARK,** of Brookfield, Feb. 20, 1822, by Abner Brundage	3	10
Anna, d. [David & Rachel], b. Mar. 8, 1771	1	475
Anna, d. Benj[ami]n, m. Noah **HUBBEL,** May 1, 1788	1	454
Anna, [d. Josiah & Abigail], b. Nov. 18, 1790	1	425
Anna M., of Danbury, m. George **LEAVENWORTH,** of Monroe, June 25, 1851, by Rev. Charles Bartlett	3	154
Anne, [d. Matthew, Jr. & Mary], b. Aug. 26, 1792	1	452
Annis, m. David **CURTIS,** b. of Danbury, [Oct.] 12, [1828], by Rev. Thomas Robbins	3	49
Annis, m. Amos **BISHOP,** Dec. 23, 1838, by Rev. L. Cook	3	96
Asel, [s. Matthew & Jane], b. Nov. 15, 1776	1	452
Augustus, m. Delia **HOYT,** Apr. 30, 1848, by Lucius Atwater	3	142
Beecher, of Kent, m. Sophia **COMES,** of Danbury, Oct. 11, 1827, by John Nickerson	3	42
Benjamin, Jr., m. Dorcas **RICE,** July 24, 1757	1	440
Benj[ami]n, Jr., m. Naomi **ANDRUS,** d. Thaddeus, Oct. 30, 1788	1	441
Betsey, [d. Nathanael & Eunice], b. July 27, 1777	1	454
Betsy, [d. Abijah & Orpha], b. Mar. 8, 1783	1	388
Betsey, d. [Justus & Mary], b. Aug. 20, 1784	1	501
Bettsey, [d. Levy & Joanna], b. Dec. 11, 1788	1	423
Betsey, of Danbury, m. Charles **CHURCH,** of Kent, Dec. 5, 1829, by Nathan Bulkley	3	54
Betsey, m. Lewis **RAYMOND,** Feb. 2, 1833, by Timothy B. Hickock, J. P.	3	74

Vol. Page

BARNUM, (cont.)

Betsey, m. Israel H. **WILSON**, b. of Danbury, Feb. 12, 1845,
    by John L. Ambler, M. G.   3   133
Betty, [d. Matthew & Jane], b. Nov. 1, 1780   1   452
Beulah, d. Benj[ami]n, m. Ithuriel **CLARK**, June 24, 17[ ]   1   503
Beulah, d. [Abijah & Orpha], b. July 16, 1764   1   388
Caroline, m. Anson **ODLE**, b. of Danbury, Jan. 15, 1822, by
    Phineas Taylor, J. P.   3   10
Caroline, m. Adam **WILLIAMS**, this day [Feb. 25, 1829], by
    Nathan Seelye, J. P.   3   51
Caty, d. [Stephen & Sarah], b. Oct. 23, 1792   1   461
Catie M., of Danbury, m. Russel **SLOCUM**, of Sherman, Jan.
    1, 1826, by Nathan Bulkley   3   31
Charles, m. Laura **BENEDICT**, b. of Danbury, Mar. 15, 1825,
    by Rev. John G. Lowe   3   38
Charles Parmer, [s. Eliphalet & Mary], b. Sept. 8, 1788   1   454
C[h]loe, [d. Ephraim & Keziah], b. July 30, 1774;
    d. Aug. 7, 1775   1   460
Chloe Ann, of Danbury, m. Henry **HULL**, of Brookfield,
    this day, [Feb. 1, 1827], by Rev. Lemuel C. Hull   3   39
Clarissa, d. [Justus & Mary], b. Mar. 18, 1790   1   501
Clarissa, m. Nelson **BROCKINGTON**, May 24, 1843, by Rev.
    William R. Webb   3   124
Clarissa H., m. Starr **FERRY**, b. of Danbury, this day [Dec.
    29, 1832], by Rev. Lemuel B. Hull   3   77
Cordelia, m. John **BENEDICT**, b. of Bethel, Jan. 2, 1842,
    by John Greenwood   3   113
Daniel, s. [Matthew & Jane], b. Oct. 6, 1761   1   452
Daniel, [s. Abijah & Orpha], b. Sept. 28, 1772   1   388
Daniel, s. [David & Rachel], b. Nov. 12, 1778   1   475
Daniel, m. Joanna **DIBBLE**, d. John, Jr., Jan. 22, 1783   1   452
Daniel, [s. Daniel & Joanna], b. Oct. 5, 1791   1   452
Daniel, Jr., m. Rana **HOYT**, Apr. 9, 1807   2   61
Daniel, m. Sarah **BARNUM**, b. of Bethel, Feb. 21, 1824, by
    John G. Lowe   3   24
Dan[ie]l, m. Charlotte **SHEPARD**, b. of Danbury, Jan. 17,
    1827, by Rev. John G. Lowe   3   39
Daniel Segar, s. [Gabriel & Sarah], b. Sept. 8, 1794   1   399
Daniel T., m. Polly Ann **TOMLINSON**, Nov. 23, 1820, by
    W[illia]m Andrews   3   4
David, m. Rachel **BENEDICT**, d. Ebenezer, Apr. 14, 1760   1   475
David, s. [David & Rachel], b. Jan. 12, 1761; d. July 30, 1764   1   475
David, s. [David & Rachel], b. Sept. 23, 1768   1   475
David, [s. Abijah & Orpha], b. Apr. 26, 1770   1   388
Dorcas, [d. Ephraim & Keziah], b. Jan. 13, 1766   1   460
Dorcas, d. Benj[ami]n, m. Amos **HOYT**, July 6, 1788   1   400
Drewphila, [child of Matthew & Jane], b. May 20, 1783   1   452
Earl, [s. Noah & Catey], b. Apr. 28, 1792; d. Nov. 4, 1792   1   436

	Vol.	Page
BARNUM, (cont.)		
Ebenezer, s. [David & Rachel], b. Apr. 8, 1781	1	475
Eder, [child of Ephraim & Rachel], b. Jan. 12, 1780	1	460
Eleazer, m. Keziah **STARR**, d. Thomas, Jr., Dec. 13, 1775	1	457
Eleazer Starr, [s. Eleazer & Keziah], b. Sept. 5, 1789	1	457
Eli, [s. Elijah], b. Aug. 17, 1771; d. Feb. [ ], 1772	1	426
Eli, [s. Elijah], b. Mar. 6, 1774	1	426
Eli, s. [Judah & Lois], b. Feb. 7, 177[ ]	1	390
Eli, [s. Judah & Lois], b. Aug. 24, 177[ ]	1	390
Eli, s. [Judah & Lois], b. Nov. 19, 177[ ]	1	390
Eli H., m. Mrs. **ELWELL**, b. of Danbury, Apr. 23, [1829], by Daniel Crocker	3	51
Eli Starr, [s. Eliphalet & Mary], b. Mar. 8, 1783	1	454
Eliakim, s. [David & Rachel], b. Aug. 27, 1772	1	475
Eliakim, 4th, s. David, m. Mercy **BENEDICT**, eldest d. Seth, Oct. 20, 1799	1	362
Elijah, b. Feb. 1, 1738; m. [ ], July [ ], 1760	1	426
Elijah, [s. Elijah], b. Oct.* 16, 1760; d. [ ], 1770 *("Aug." crossed out]	1	426
Elijah, [s. Elijah], b. Mar. 9, 1769; d. Feb. 1, 1769	1	426
Elijah, [s. Joseph, Jr. & Temperance], b. July 7, 1782	1	401
Elijah, m. Clarissa **LOBDELL**, Dec. 22, 1839 (b. of Danbury), by John Nickerson	3	101
Eliphalet, b. Dec. 10, 1750; m. Mary [ ], June 4, 1777	1	454
Eliud, [s. Gabriel & Sarah], b. May 4, 1789	1	399
Eliza Maria, of Danbury, m. George **SHUTE**, of Wilton, Aug. 3, 1839, by Reuben Booth, J. P.	3	98
Elisabeth, d. Capt. John, m. James **KNAP**, Apr. 7, 1755* *(Corrected from "1760")	1	404
Elizabeth A., of Danbury, m. John F. **REMMEY**, of New York, May 20, 1846, by Rev. Rollin S. Stone	3	140
Emily, m. John **SCHENCH**, b. of Danbury, July 4, 1847, by Rev. John Crawford	3	163
Emily A., m. David **LYON**, Oct. 26, 1851, by Rev. Charles Bartlett	3	158
Ephraim, m. Keziah [ ], May 2, 1753	1	460
Ephraim, [s. Elijah], b. Oct. 14, 1766	1	426
Ephraim, Sr., d. Aug. [ ], 1775	1	460
Ephraim, m. 2nd w. Rachel **BEEBE**, Feb. 1, 1776	1	460
Ephraim, Jr., m. Sarah **SEELY**, Nov. 11, 1790	1	425
Esther, d. John, b. July 9, 1749; m. David **BISHOP**, Oct. 23, 1774	1	487
Esther, [d. Josiah & Abigail], b. Oct. 19, 1782	1	425
Esther, d. Josiah, of Danbury, m. Joseph Bennit **OSBORN**, s. Jonathan, of New Fairfield, Aug. 15, 1801	1	358
Eunice, [d. Nathanael & Eunice], b. July 4, 1782	1	454
Ezra, s. [David & Rachel], b. Mar. 2, 1762	1	475
Ezra, s. [Justus & Mary], b. Mar. 22, 1779	1	501

	Vol.	Page

BARNUM, (cont.)

	Vol.	Page
Ezra, [s. John, Jr. & Betty], b. Sept. 12, 1781	1	427
Ezra, m. Jerusha SMITH, d. Henry,of Huntington, Nov. 25, 1784	1	456
Ezra Smith, [s. Ezra & Jerusha], b. June 21, 1792	1	456
Fairchild, m. Sally TAYLOR, b. of Danbury, Oct. 16, 1827, by John G. Lowe	3	44
Fanna, [d. Levy & Joanna], b. Aug. 25, 1787	1	423
Fanny, m. Platt HUSTED, Dec. 25, 1807	2	62
Forward, s. [Stephen & Sarah], b. Dec. 18, 1789	1	461
Forward, d. May 23, 1792	1	456
Freelove, d. [Gabriel & Sarah], b. Aug. 6, 1782	1	399
Gabriel, b. Mar. 24, 1760; m. Sarah SEGER, Dec. 6, 1781	1	399
George, [s. Samuel & Beckah], b. Feb. 17, 1791	1	448
George, m. Ophelia SMITH, Sept. 6, 1831, by Rev. Erastus Cole	3	65
Grandison M., m. Keziah B. BOUGHTON, b. of Danbury, this day, [Oct. 12, 1834], by Rev. Lemuel B. Hull	3	84
Hannah, [d. Elijah], b. Feb. 19, 1762	1	426
Hannah, [d. Ephraim & Keziah], b. Nov. 5, 1771; d. July 5, 1775	1	460
Hannah, [d. Abijah & Orpha], b. Mar. 8, 1780; d. Dec. 6, 1792	1	388
Hannah, d. [Josiah & Abigail], b. Aug. 3, 1780	1	425
Hannah, d. Elijah, m. Thomas DIBBLE, Oct. 26, 1780	1	469
Hannah, [d. Benjamin, Jr. & Naomi], b. Aug. 10, 1789	1	441
Harriet C., of Danbury, m. Ferris D. BALL, of Brookfield, this day [Nov. 24, 1841], by Rev. Rollin S. Stone	3	113
Huldah, [d. Elijah], b. Feb. 1, 1769	1	426
Huldah, [d. Matthew & Jane], b. Nov. 16, 1778	1	452
Ira, s. [Justus & Mary], b. Mar. 3, 1782; d. May 23, 1787	1	501
Ira, s. [Abel & Annis], b. June 20, 1788	1	429
Irena, [d. Elijah], b. Aug. 25, 1789	1	426
Irena, of Bethel, m. Darius C. NEWELL, of Sing Sing, this day [July 22, 1839], by John Greenwood	3	98
Isaac, [s. Eleazer & Keziah], b. Aug. 31, 1784	1	457
Isaac, m. Emma CAMP, [Apr.] 14, [1830], by Rev. A. Rood	3	55
James Harvey, s. [Stephen & Sarah], b. Jan. 12, 1788	1	461
Jane, [d. Matthew & Jane], b. Oct. 17, 1771	1	452
Jane, [d. Abijah, Jr. & Sibel], b. Apr. 27, 1789	1	393
Jane, d. Matthew, m. Matthew TAYLOR, Oct. 14, 1792	1	430
Jane, m. Eliphalet GREGORY, b. of Danbury, Mar. 19, [1829], by J. Nickerson	3	51
Jemima, m. Seth SHOVE, Nov. 16, 1757	1	421
Jerusha, [d. Levy & Joanna], b. Sept. 24, 1786	1	423
Joanna, d. [Justus & Mary], b. Mar. 29, 1777	1	501
Joanna, [d. Levy & Joanna], b. Jan. 18, 1790	1	423
Joanna, d. [Justus & Mary], d. Aug. 12, 1798	1	501
John, Jr., b. Mar. 7, 1756; m. Betty [ ], July 7, 1779	1	427
John, Jr., m. Catren KELBY, d. Eben[eze]r, of Weathersfield, Aug. [ ], 178[ ]* *(Edge of leaf off)	1	496
John, s. [John, Jr. & Betty], b. July 1, 1797	1	427

	Vol.	Page

BARNUM, (cont.)

Joseph, Jr., b. Dec. 3, 1751; m. Temperance **NICHOLS**, Apr.
16, 1772 — 1 — 401

Joseph, s. [Ephraim & Keziah], b. Aug. 14, 1761 — 1 — 460

Joseph C., m. Cynthia **TAYLOR**, b. of Danbury, this day,
[ ], by Rev. Lemuel B. Hull. Recorded Dec. 5, 1825 — 3 — 30

Josiah, m. Abigail **CURTISS**, d. Stephen, Mar. 4, 1779 — 1 — 425

Judah, m. Lois **HOYT**, d. John, Jan. 6, 177[ ] — 1 — 390

Jus[tus], s. Joseph, m. Mary **BENEDICT**, d. Sam[ue]l, Jr.,
May 4, 1775 — 1 — 501

Keziah, d. [Ephraim & Keziah], b. Jan. 28, 1756 — 1 — 460

Keziah, w. Ephraim, d. Aug. 4, 1775 — 1 — 460

Keziah, d. [Eleazer & Keziah], b. Oct.* 26, 1779 *(First
written "Dec." and crossed out) — 1 — 457

Larcy, [child of Noah & Catey], b. Mar. 31, 1790 — 1 — 436

Laury, d. [Justus & Mary], b. July 7, 1793 — 1 — 501

Lemira, m. Lemuel **SHEPARD**, of Newtown, Jan. 26, 1830, by
Reuben Booth, J. P. — 3 — 55

Levi, s. [David & Rachel], b. Mar. 25, 1769 — 1 — 475

Levy, m. Joanna **STOCKER**, Jan.* 11, 178[ ] *("July, March"
crossed out) — 1 — 423

Levi, [s. Levy & Joanna], b. July 15, 1791 — 1 — 423

Libbeus, m. Phebe Ann **BARNUM**, b. of Danbury, Jan. 26, 1840,
by Rev. D. H. Short — 3 — 107

Lois, d. [Judah & Lois], b. June 28, 178[ ] — 1 — 390

Luis, [child Matthew, Jr. & Mary], b. May 30, 1788 — 1 — 452

Luis, [child of Abijah, Jr. & Sibel], b. Oct. 23, 1790 — 1 — 393

Lois, m. Amos **JACKSON**, Nov. 27, 1805 — 2 — 66

Lucinda, [d. John, Jr. & Betty], b. May 6, 1785 — 1 — 427

Lucinda, [d. Daniel & Joanna], b. July 8, 1787 — 1 — 452

Lucy, [d. Ephraim & Keziah], b. Nov. 9, 1757 — 1 — 460

Lucy, d. [Stephen & Sarah], b. May 19, 1786 — 1 — 461

Lucy, m. Levi **HANFORD**, Oct. 14, [1844], by R. K. Bellamy — 3 — 130

Lucy, m. Selleck **BOOTH**, Sept. 30, 1849, by Rev. John Purves,
of Bethel — 3 — 151

Luis, [see under Lois]

Moriah*, d. [Justus & Mary], b. July 1, 1796 *(Maria) — 1 — 501

Maria, 2nd d. [Daniel, Jr. & Rana], b. Feb. 20, 1811 — 2 — 61

Maria, m. Abel Beers **BLACKMAN**, b. of Bethel, [May] 14,
[1828], by Rev. Thomas Robbins — 3 — 47

Mariah, m. Thomas **HOYT**, b. of Danbury, Dec. 19, 1829, by
Nathan Bulkley — 3 — 54

Mary, m. Matthew **WILKES**, Jan. 2, 1753 — 1 — 396

Mary, d. [David & Rachel], b. June 30, 1765 — 1 — 475

Mary, m. Eleazer **BENEDICT**, Feb. 1, 1770 — 1 — 504

Mary, m. Nathan **STARR**, May 21, 1778 — 1 — 424

Mary, [d. Elijah], b. July 13, 1779 — 1 — 426

Mary, [d. Gabriel & Sarah], b. May 29, 1784 — 1 — 399

	Vol.	Page

BARNUM, (cont.)

Mary, [w. Eliphalet], d. July 3, 1799 — 1 454

Mary, of Danbury, m. John W. **AMERMAN**, of Norwalk, Feb. 4,
1835, by Oliver N.* Amerman *(V?) — 3 82

Matthew, m. Jane **DIBBLE**, d. Lieut. John, Nov. 27, 1760 — 1 452

Matthew, [s. Matthew & Jane], b. Dec. 27, 1764 — 1 452

Matthew, Jr., m. Mary **STARR**, d. Samuel, Oct. 17, 1784 — 1 452

Matthew, his grand son Joshua **STEVENS**, b. May 2, 1785 — 1 452

Mercy, [d. Matthew & Jane], b. Mar. 9, 1763 — 1 452

Mercy, [d. Nathanael & Eunice], b. Mar. 13, 1780 — 1 454

Mercy, d. Matthew, m. Nathaniel **STEVENS**, Aug. 28, 1783 — 1 450

Milo, s. [Benjamin, Jr. & Naomi], b. June 14, 1808 — 1 41

Milo, m. Rebecca **BOUGHTON**, [Jan.] 4, [1830], by Rev. A.
Rood — 3 54

Molly, [d. Matthew, Jr. & Mary], b. Nov. 16, 1787 — 1 452

Moses, s. [Eleazer & Keziah], b. Dec. 13, 1778 — 1 457

Naby, [d. Abijah & Orpha], b. Dec. 2, 1776 — 1 388

Nancy C., of Danbury, m. Joseph **CONVERSE**, of Norwalk,
Jan. 1, 1826, by Nathan Bulkley — 3 31

Naomi, [d. Matthew & Jane], b. Nov. 18, 1766 — 1 452

Naomy, d. Matthew, m. Ethel **BEEBE**, Apr. 26, 1789 — 1 430

Nathanael, m. Eunice **BOSTICK**, Nov. 8, 1769 — 1 454

Nathanael, [d. Nathanael & Eunice], b. Jan. 7, 1785 — 1 454

Nathanael, d. June 17, 1786 — 1 454

Nathaniel, of New York, m. Mary M. **ADAMS**, of Danbury, May
20, 1846, by Thomas T. Guion — 3 140

Nathaniel Brisco, s. [Nathanael & Eunice], b. Sept. 27, 1773;
d. Dec. 31, 1773 — 1 454

Noah, [s. Ephraim & Keziah], b. July 5, 1768; d. July 25, 1775 — 1 460

Noah, [s. Abijah & Orpha], b. Nov. 10, 1778 — 1 388

Noah, m. Catey* **BISHOP**, Feb. 9, 1784 *(Letter crossed out) — 1 436

Noah, Jr., s. Seth, m. Sally **SHERWOOD**, d. John, of Reading,
Mar. 1, 1801 — 1 364

Noah S., s. [Ephraim & Rachel], b. Aug. 28, 1776 — 1 460

Olive, m. Asa **HOYT**, Dec. 2, 1784 — 1 423

Olive, m. James **PICKET**, Apr. 3, 1791 — 1 461

Orpha, d. [Silas & Rane], b. Mar. 19, 1792 — 1 405

Orra, m. Darius H. **DIKEMAN**, b. of Danbury, Jan. 9, 1831,
by J. Nickerson — 3 60

Pamela, m. Russel **SMITH**, b. of Danbury, Jan. 2, 1825, by
Oliver Shepard, J. P. — 3 26

Peter, [s. Ephraim & Rachel], b. Mar. 7, 1784 — 1 460

Phebe, [d. Gabriel & Sarah], b. Mar. 6, 1786 — 1 399

Phebe Ann, m. Libbeus **BARNUM**, b. of Danbury, Jan. 26, 1840,
by Rev. D. H. Short — 3 107

Philander S., m. Fidelia M. **FERRY**, b. of Danbury, Oct. 2,
1845, by Rev. Fitch Reed — 3 136

Philo, s. [Ephraim & Rachel], b. Apr. 4, 1778 — 1 460

	Vol.	Page
BARNUM, (cont.)		
Platt, [s. Matthew, Jr. & Mary], b. Nov. 19, 1790	1	452
Polly, [d. Matthew & Jane], b. July 31, 1774	1	452
Polly, [d. Eleazer & Keziah], b. May 10, 1782	1	457
Polly, d. [Ezra & Jerusha], b. Dec. 20, 1785	1	456
Polly, [d. Eliphalet & Mary], b. Apr. 11, 1791	1	454
Polly, 4th d. Matthew, m. Ezra HAMILTON, 5th s. Joseph, Sept. 15, 1793	1	357
Priscilla, [d. Eleazer & Keziah], b. Feb. 5, 1788	1	457
Rachel, d. [David & Rachel], b. Aug. 10, 1763	1	475
Rachel, [s. Eliphalet & Mary], b. Sept. 24, 1785	1	454
Rachel, of Bethel, m. Asahel DUNNING, of Brookfield, Mar. 26, 1823, by John G. Lowe	3	24
Rachel, m. Thomas BELL, Nov. 13, 1836, by Levi Osborn	3	88
Rane, d. Joseph, m. Silas BARNUM, Oct. 9, 1791	1	405
Rebekah, [d. Ephraim & Keziah], b. May 13, 1759; d. Aug. 2, 1775	1	460
Rebecca, d. [Eliphalet & Mary], b. Sept. 24, 1780	1	454
Rebecca, [d. Ephraim & Rachel], b. July 8, 1781	1	460
Rebecca, [d. Josiah & Abigail], b. Feb. 22, 1785	1	425
Rebeca, d. [John, Jr. & Catren], b. Aug. 27, 1787	1	496
Rebecca, d. [Ezra & Jerusha], b. Mar. 26, 1788	1	456
Reine, [d. Gabriel & Sarah], b. Feb. 4, 1788; d. Feb. 14, 1788	1	399
Rhoda, d. [Judah & Lois], b. Jan. 9, 177[ ]	1	390
Rhoda, d. [Nathanael & Eunice], b. Aug. 31, 1775	1	454
Richard, [s. John, Jr. & Betty], b. Dec. 18, 1788	1	427
Roxey, d. [Noah & Catey], b. Dec. 7, 1784; d. Mar. 12, 1785	1	436
Ruth, [d. Ephraim & Keziah], b. Nov. 20, 1763	1	460
Ruth, m. Abel LACY, Jan. 9, 1783	1	426
Sabra Stocker, [d. Levy & Joanna], b. Jan. 14, 1782	1	423
Sally, m. Edward TAYLOR, Sept. 17, 1820, by W[illia]m Andrews	3	3
Samantha, [d. Ezra & Jerusha], b. Mar. 29, 1790	1	456
Samuel, [s. Matthew & Jane], b. Aug. 20, 1769	1	452
Sam[ue]ll, d. Mar. [ ], 1775	1	457
Samuel, m. Beckah TROWBRIDGE, d. Isaac, Mar. 10, 1790	1	448
Samuel B., s. [Justus & Mary], b. Apr. 25, 1787	1	501
Sarah, d. [Nathanael & Eunice], b. Oct. 30, 1770	1	454
Sarah, m. Daniel BARNUM, b. of Bethel, Feb. 21, 1824, by John G. Lowe	3	24
Seely, s. [Ephraim, Jr. & Sarah], b. Sept. 28, 1791	1	425
Silas, [s. Abijah & Orpha], b. Mar. 25, 1768	1	388
Silas, m. Rane BARNUM, d. Joseph, Oct. 9, 1791	1	405
Stephen, m. Sarah BENEDICT, d. Josiah, Sept. 4, 1785	1	461
Thomas, s. [David & Rachel], b. Mar. 25, 1775	1	475
Thomas, [s. Eleazer & Keziah], b. Apr. 28, 1792	1	457
Timothy F., [s. John, Jr. & Betty], b. Sept. 23, 1790	1	427
Tirze, [child of Matthew, Jr. & Mary], b. Sept. 5, 1784	1	452

	Vol.	Page

BARNUM, (cont.)

William, [s. Abijah, Jr. & Sibel], b. Apr. 11, 1792 — 1 — 393

Zar, [child Abijah & Orpha], b. Jan. 17, 1775 — 1 — 388

Zar, [s. David & Rachel], b. Oct. 24, 1789 — 1 — 475

BARR, Mary Ann, of Danbury, m. Samuel MURWIN, of Fairfield, Sept. 7, 1823, by Nathan Bulkley — 3 — 18

BARRETT, Thomas, m. Mary DOLYN, [, 1851?], by Thomas Ryan. Witnesses: Michael Deen* & Catharine Kearney *(Perhaps "Deere") — 3 — 156

BARTLEY, Charles, m. Cordelia BENEDICT, Dec. 1, 1820, by W[illia]m Andrews — 3 — 3

BARTON, John, m. Cynthia STEVENS, b. of Danbury, May 9, 1838, by Rev. Rollin S. Stone — 3 — 94

BARTOW*, Morris, m. Mary Ann FLOYD, Apr. 21, 1831, by Levi Brunson *(BARLOW) — 3 — 61

BARTRAM, BARTRIM, BARTRUM, Cynth[i]a, m. Harris ANDERSON, b. of Danbury, [Sept.] 24, [1837], by Jacob Shaw — 3 — 92

Emila, m. Thomas STUDWELL, b. of Danbury, Dec. 14, 1845, by Rev. Fitch Read — 3 — 137

Emily J., see Emily J. HARRIS, — 3 — 158

Horace, m. Amanda Elizabeth BEVANS, b. of Danbury, Aug. 27, 1845, by Rev. Fitch Reed — 3 — 135

Ira, m. Urarana WEED, Nov. 12, 1821, by Rev. W[illia]m Andrews — 3 — 9

James, m. Polly BEVANS, b. of Danbury, Nov. 20, 1844, by Rev. Fitch Reed — 3 — 129

Lucy M., m. Joel B. SANFORD, b. of Danbury, Jan. 27, 1833, by Rev. Nicholas White — 3 — 73

Mary, m. George J. CROFUT, b. of Danbury, this day [Nov. 25, 1841], by Rev. S. H. Clark — 3 — 113

Susan, of Danbury, m. Nathan F. HARRIS, of South Salem, West Chester Co., N. Y., Dec. 14, 1845, by Rev. Fitch Reed — 3 — 137

BARTS, John, m. Eunice TRUBY, Dec. 7, 1783 — 1 — 492

BASS*, Zaruah, d. Benj[ami]n, of Fairfield, m. [Jos]eph BOUGHTON, Nov. 20, 1778 *(BEERS?) — 1 — 502

BATES, George, of Danbury, m. Deborah Ann DAVIS, of Mill Plain, Dec. 30, 1849, by Rev. George H. Deere — 3 — 145

Sarah, m. Daniel OLMSTED, Apr. 5, 1786 — 1 — 424

Stephen, m. Deborah TAYLOR, b. of Danbury, June 29, 1837, by Rev. Salmon C. Bulkley — 3 — 90

Walter, m. Lorany WOOD, [Sept.] 4, [1833], by Rev. A. Rood — 3 — 76

BAXTER, B., m. F. L. BOGARDUS, b. of Danbury, Nov. 27, 1844, by Thomas T. Guion — 3 — 132

Daniel, m. Laura STEVENS, Nov. 23, 1825, by George Benedict — 3 — 30

Rebecca, m. Levi BURN, Sr., Mar. 20, 1830, by Levi Brunson — 3 — 55

Samuel, m. Paulina* DOWNS, May 17, 1843, by Rev. William R. Webb *(Should be "Purlina" added in later hand) — 3 — 124

	Vol.	Page

BAXTER, (cont.)

Stebbins, m. Hannah **AMBLER**, b. of Danbury, May 2, 1832, by Thomas Larcombe — 3 — 70

Thomas, m. Sarah **WILDMAN**, wid. of Nathan, Feb. 4, 1798 — 1 — 370

Thomas, s. [Thomas & Sarah], b. May 1, 1799 — 1 — 370

BEACH, Gilbert, of Waterbury, m. Caroline **DOBBS**, of Danbury, Aug. 18, 1833, by John Nickerson — 3 — 77

John B., of Weston, m. Mary Ann **COLE**, of Bethel, Nov. 26, 1845, by Thomas T. Guion — 3 — 137

Sarah, m. David **BEEBE**, June 8, 1780 — 1 — 456

BEACHAM, George B., m. Elmyra **FENNER**, b. of Danbury, Oct. 27, 1839, by Rev. D. H. Short — 3 — 107

BEANDIHEN*, Jonne, s. Elizabeth **GUTHRIE**, & father John **BEANDIHEN***, b. Mar. 26, 1785; d. Mar. 6, 1787 *(Last three letters uncertain) — 1 — 376

BEARD, Catharine I., m. Levi **HOPKINS**, [Oct.] 3, [1831], by Rev. A. Rood — 3 — 65

Elisabeth F., m. William **WILDMAN**, Sept. 29, [1829], by Rev. A. Rood — 3 — 53

BEARDSLEY, BEARDSLEE, Fanny, of Redding, m. Jacob **BURR**, of Ridgefield, Sept. [ ], 1831, by John Nickerson — 3 — 63

Herman, m. Lucy **STONE**, b. of Danbury, Apr. 26, 1848, by Rev. Rollin S. Stone — 3 — 141

Walter, of New Fairfield, m. Julia **PAINE**, of Danbury, [Nov.] 22, [1829], by Rev. Daniel Crocker — 3 — 54

BEARSE, BEARSS, [see also **BEERS & BASS**], Abigail, [d. Newcomb & Martha], b. Nov. 29, 1784 — 1 — 406

Anna, m. Eleazer **WEED**, May 24, 1781 — 1 — 446

Barrett, [s. Newcomb & Martha], b. Mar. 18, 1790 — 1 — 406

David Picket, s. [Newcomb & Martha], b. Oct. 17, 1779 — 1 — 406

Enoch Comstock, [s. Newcomb & Martha], b. Aug. 13, 1781 — 1 — 406

Newcomb, m. Martha **PICKET**, d. David, Dec. 17, 1778 — 1 — 406

Prudy, d. Joseph, of New Fairfield, m. Thomas **PICKET**, s. Ebenezer, Sept. 7, 1797 — 1 — 363

William, of New Fairfield, m. Sarah **STEVENS**, of Danbury, Apr. 26, 1831, by Nathan Burton — 3 — 61

Zeruah, m. Joseph **BOUGHTON**, Nov. 12, 1778 — 1 — 442

BEATY, Anne, d. [James & Ruhana], d. Dec. 12, 1751 — 1 — 368

Anne, d. [James & Ruhana], b. Aug. 30, 1754 — 1 — 368

Anne, d. [James & Ruhana], b. Aug. 30, 1754 — 1 — 368

Catherine, d. [James & Ruhana], b. Jan. 20, 1761 — 1 — 368

Daniel, twin with Sarah, s. [James & Ruhana], b. Aug. 23, 1767 — 1 — 368

James, s. [James & Ruhana], b. Sept. 2, 1749 — 1 — 368

James, m. Ruhana **STURGES**, [ ], 1784* *(Probably 1748) — 1 — 368

James, m. Elizabeth **NORTHROP**, of Ridgefield, (2nd w.), Jan. [ ], 1798 — 1 — 368

Ruhama, d. [James & Ruhana], b. Oct. 17, 1758 — 1 — 368

Ruhana, w. [James], d. Mar. 9, 1797 — 1 — 368

	Vol.	Page
BEATY, (cont.)		
Sarah, twin with Daniel, d. [James & Ruhana], b. Aug. 23, 1767	1	368
BECK, Deborah, m. Riley **FENNER,** Sept. 11, 1842, by Rev. Charles		
Chittenden	3	117
Joseph F., m. Sarah M. **NICKERSON,** b. of Danbury, June 4,		
1843, by James Floy	3	121
BECKET, Henry, m. Eliza **BELL,** July 29, [1849], by Rev. A. Perkins	3	160
BEDIENT, Charles Augustus, [s. William W. & Juliett], b. Feb.		
2, 1836; d. Dec. 11, 1841	2	181
Eleazer, m. Rachel **HOYT,** d. John, May 25, 1788	1	388
Eleazer, d. [ ]	1	388
John, [twin with Phene, s. Eleazer & Rachel], b. Apr. 14, 1791	1	388
John H., d. July 11, 1842	1	388
Phene, [twin with John, child of Eleazer & Rachel], b. Apr.		
14, 1791	1	388
Rachel, w. [Eleazer], d. [ ]	1	388
Sarah, of Danbury, m. Orange **KINNEY,** of New Milford, July		
24, 1830, by Reuben Booth, J. P.	3	57
Sophia, [d. Eleazer & Rachel], b. Oct. 28, 1792	1	388
Stephen S., m. Deborah **HODGES,** b. of Danbury, May 7, 1844,		
by James Floy	3	126
William W., b. Aug. 14, 1814; m. Juliett **DOBBS,** Sept. 29, 1835	2	181
Zadock, s. [Eleazer & Rachel], b. Feb. 27, 1789	1	388
BEEBE, Abel, [s. Lemuel & Hannah], b. Jan. 26, 1772; d. Aug.		
21, 1775	1	434
Abel, [s. Lemuel & Hannah], b. Dec. 18, 1775	1	434
Abigail, d. Lemuel, m. Benj[ami]n **HOYT,** Oct. 1, 1768	1	434
Ann L., m. John H. **DART,** Nov. 3, 1842, by Rev. Thomas T.		
Guion	3	117
Anne, d. [Jonathan & Charity], b. July 3, 1792	1	386
Clarissa M., of Waterbury, m. Samuel N. **BOTSFORD,** of		
Danbury, Sept. 1, 1834, by Reuben Booth, J. P.	3	80
David, m. Sarah **BEACH,** June 8, 1780	1	456
Edmond, m. Lydia **BAILY,** d. Samuel, Sept. 27, 1787	1	433
Ethel, [s. Lemuel & Hannah], b. Mar. 23, 1765	1	434
Ethel, m. Naomy **BARNUM,** d. Matthew, Apr. 26, 1789	1	430
Ethel Augustus, m. Jane Elizabeth **CROFUT,** b. of Danbury,		
Oct. 19, 1837, by Rev. D. H. Short	3	106
Eunice, [d. David & Sarah], b. May 23, 1787	1	456
Ezra, of Brookfield, m. Tamer **BENEDICT,** of Danbury, May 11,		
1831, by Elias Birchard, J. P.	3	62
Hannah, [d. Lemuel & Hannah], b. July 24, 1768; d. Aug.		
18, 1775	1	434
Hannah, [d. Lemuel & Hannah], b. July 10, 1783	1	434
Hiram, m. Rebecca **HICKOK,** b. of Bethel, May 10, 1848,		
by E. O. Dunning	3	143
James, [s. Lemuel & Hannah], b. Apr. 25, 1781	1	434
James Hawley, s. [Joseph, Jr. & Rebecca], b. Dec. 28, 1785	1	472

	Vol.	Page
BEEBE, (cont.)		
Jonathan, [s. David & Sarah], b. Apr. 21, 1791	1	456
Jonathan, m. Charity **SHUTE**, d. Capt. Richard, Sept. 7, 1791	1	386
Joseph, Jr., m. Rebecca **BENEDICT**, d. Sam[ue]l, Jr., Sept. 10, 1778	1	472
Joseph, f. of Joseph, Jr., d. Dec. 16, 1803	1	472
Joseph B., of Brookfield, m. Betsey **KNAPP**, of Danbury, Dec. 7, 1830, by Joseph S. Covell	3	59
Joseph Benedict, s. [Joseph, Jr. & Rebecca], b. June 8, 1779	1	472
Lemuel, m. Hannah **DIBBLE**, d. John, July 19, 1764	1	434
Lydia, d. Capt. Lemuel, m. Samuel **BAILEY**, Feb. 20, 1756; d. May 21, 1784	1	409
Lydia, [d. Lemuel & Hannah], b. Sept. 27, 1766; d. Aug. 23, 1775	1	434
Lydia, [d. Lemuel & Hannah], b. Oct. 30, 1777	1	434
Mary, [d. Lemuel & Hannah], b. June 2, 1774; d. Aug. 11, 1775	1	434
Mary Jennet, of Danbury (Bethel Soc.), m. Albert B. **STEBBINS**, of Springfield, Mass., this day [Aug. 31, 1836], by Rev. David H. Short	3	85
Olive, m. John **CALVIN**, Nov. 2, 1820, by W[illia]m Andrews	3	3
Phebe, d. [Joseph, Jr. & Rebecca], b. June 15, 1781	1	472
Polly, d. [Joseph, Jr. & Rebecca], b. Jan. 21, 1784	1	472
Polly, of Danbury, m. James **DeFOREST**, of Woodbury, [June] 4, [1828], by Rev. Thomas Robbins	3	47
Rachel, m. Ephraim **BARNUM**, Feb. 1, 1776	1	460
Rachel, [d. David & Sarah], b. Dec. 23, 1784	1	456
Rachel, d. Jonathan, d. Apr. 16, 1823	1	386
Rebecca, d. [Joseph, Jr. & Rebecca], b. Jan. 3, 1794	1	472
Rebecca, m. Ezra P. **BENEDICT**, b. of Danbury, Apr. 2, 1828, by Levi Osborn	3	47
Ruth Anna, d. [David & Sarah], b. Sept. 11, 1781	1	456
Sally, d. [Joseph, Jr. & Rebecca], b, Aug. 1, 1789	1	472
Sarah, [d. David & Sarah], b. June 25, 1789	1	456
Sarah, mother of Joseph, Jr., d. Feb. 7, [ ]	1	472
Tamar, [d. Lemuel & Hannah], b. Apr. 4, 1770; d. Aug. 14, 1775	1	434
Tamar, [d. Ethel & Naomy], b. Oct. 18, 1789; d. July 12, 1790	1	430
Tamar, 2nd, [d. Ethel & Naomy], b. Apr. 9, 1791	1	430
BEERS, [see also **BEARSE**], Eleazer, Dea. of Reading, m. Mrs. Rebecca **SMITH**, of Danbury, Apr. 22, 1838, by Rev. J. G. Collom	3	93
Julia A., of Redding, m. Andrew I. **JAMES**, of Danbury, Jan. 21, 1849, by Rev. Asahel Bronson	3	144
Phineas, of New Milford, m. Jerusha **AMBLER**, of Danbury, July 11, 1830, by Rev. Solomon Glover	3	57
Sukey*, m. Levi **CROFUT**, Dec. 31, 1789 *(Erasure with name written in)	1	468
BELDEN, Charlotte E., of Wilton, m. Eli **OSBORNE**, of Redding, July 4, 1847, by Rev. R. S. Stone	3	162

	Vol.	Page

BELDEN, (cont.)

Elizabeth S. C., of Wilton, m. Edgar S. **TWEEDY**, of Danbury,
this day [June 4, 1834], by Rev. Lemuel B. Hull — 3 — 79

Jane, m. Reuben **BOOTH**, June 4, 1821 — 2 — 171

BELL, Eliza, m. Henry **BECKET**, July 29, 1849, by Rev. A. Perkins — 3 — 160

Joseph, of Washington, N. Y., m. Mary Ann **HISCOCK**, of
Danbury, this day [Dec. 7, 1840], by Rev. D. H. Short — 3 — 107

Thomas, m. Rachel **BARNUM**, Nov. 13, 1836, by Levi Osborn — 3 — 88

BENEDICT, Aaron J., d. Oct. 18, 1822 — 2 — 176

Abel, s. [[ ]saac & Mary], b. Oct. 1, 1748 — 1 — 501

Abel, s. [Benajah & Hannah], b. Dec. 10, 1767; d. Jan. 25, 1768 — 1 — 442

Abel, 2nd, s. [Benajah & Hannah], b. Aug. 20, 1769 — 1 — 442

Abel, s. [Nathaniel, Jr.], b. Nov. 3, 1789 — 1 — 373

Abel, m. Rebecca **ANDRUS**, b. Feb. 22, 1791 — 1 — 442

Abel, s. [John, Jr. & Lydia], b. Dec. 14, 1800 — 1 — 463

Abel, m. Eunice **BOUGHTON**, b. of Danbury, Dec. 28, 1831,
by John Nickerson — 3 — 66

Abigail, d. [Thaddeus & Abigail], b. Apr. 29, [   ] — 1 — 498

Abigail, d. [[ ]saac & Mary], b. Sept. 30, 1745 — 1 — 501

Abigail, [d. Samuel, Jr. & Phebe], b. July 31, 1746 — 1 — 444

Abigail, w. [Thaddeus], d. Apr. 6, 175[ ] — 1 — 498

Abigail, d. Samuel, Jr., m. David **KNAP**, May 16, 1765 — 1 — 386

Abigale, m. Eliakim **STARR**, Oct. 2, 1771* *(First written
"May 1790", changed to "1788" then written "1771") — 1 — 414

Abigail, d. [Peter & Anne], b. Jan. 26, 1789 — 1 — 360

Abigail, of Danbury, m. Seeley **HARRIS**, of Norwalk, this
day, [Apr. 12, 1834], by Rev. Lemuel B. Hull — 3 — 83

Abijah, s. Matthew, b. May 18, 1735; m. Betey **STUART**, of
Fredericksborough, d. Charles, May 10, 1785 — 1 — 485

Abraham, [s. Jonah & Betsey], b. Dec. 30, 1787; d. Jan. 1, 1788 — 1 — 413

Adah, d. Caleb, m. Eleasaph **KELLOGG**, Dec. 12, 1771 — 1 — 436

Alfred, m. Clarinda **DIKEMAN**, b. of Danbury, Dec. 5, 1827,
by John Nickerson — 3 — 43

Almon, s. [Cyrus & Penelope], b. Aug. 27, 1799 — 1 — 480

Ammon, [s. James & Roda], b. Apr. 27, 1792 — 1 — 430

Amos, s. [Thaddeus & Abigail], b. May 14, 1775 — 1 — 498

Amos, 2nd s. Theophilus, b. Nov. 11, 1778; m. Sarah
BENEDICT, d. Jonas, Mar. 12, 1800 — 1 — 356

Andrew, s. [Lewis & Elizabeth], b. Apr. 1, 1802 — 1 — 490

Andrew Burr, s. [Ezra & Mabel], b. July 28, 1788 — 1 — 480

An[n]a, d. David, b. Mar. 19, 1752; m. Jonathan **TAYLOR**,
Apr. 26, 1770 — 1 — 438

Anna, m. James **STEVENS**, Mar. 15, 1774 — 1 — 433

Anna, d. Timothy, m. David **JUDD**, Nov. 3, 1774 — 1 — 450

Anna, d. Josiah, m. [Edmo]nd **WASHBURN**, Oct. 3, 1781 — 1 — 499

Anna, d. [Ezra & Mabel], b. Aug. 8, 1783 — 1 — 480

Anna, [d. Eleazer & Jerusha], b. Apr. 16, 1784 — 1 — 504

Anna, d. Joseph, m. Noah **KNAP**, June 14, 1792 — 1 — 459

BENEDICT, (cont.)   Vol.   Page

Anne, [d. Joseph & Elisabeth], b. Apr. 9, 1774

Anne, [d. Benajah & Hannah], b. Jan. 13, 1777   1   465

Anne, [d. Levi & Hannah], b. Oct. 23, 1792   1   442

Anne, d. [Peter & Anne], b. Jan. 9, 1794   1   432

Annis, [d. Eleazer & Jerusha], b. [   ]* 8, [   ] *(faded out)   1   360

Annis, 6th d. Eleazer, m. James HODGES, eldest s. Ezra,   1   504
    Sept. 14, 1803

Archie, [s. Capt. Noble & Eunice], b. Feb. 17, 1782   1   356

Asa, [s. Samuel, Jr. & Phebe], b. Aug. 22, 1762   1   403

Asahel, m. Lydia DIBBLE, Nov. 25, 1773   1   444

Benajah, m. Hannah SEELY, May 28, 1767   1   434

Benajah, m. 2nd w. Hannah ANDRUS, June 28, 1787   1   442

Benjamin, s. [Nathaniel, Jr.], b. Mar. 7, 1794   1   442

Betsey, d. [Eleazer & Jerusha], b. Dec. [   ]* *(Faded out)   1   373

Betsey, d. [Peter & Anne], b. Dec. 16, 1782   1   504

Betsey, d. [Ephraim & Betty], b. Apr. 7, 1796   1   360

Betty, [d. Daniel & Rhoda], b. Mar. 9, 1790   1   478

Betty, [d. Joshua & Ruth], b. Feb. 23, 1792; d. Apr. 2, 1792   1   437

Betty, d. [Joshua & Ruth], b. Sept. 14, 1793   1   457

Billy, [s. Hezekiah, Jr. & Huldah], b. May 5, 1791*   1   457
    *(Possibly "1790")

Caleb, m. Ruth BENEDICT, d. Eben[eze]r, Mar. 28, 1763   1   406

Caleb, s. [Caleb & Ruth], b. Aug. 6, 1764   1   488

Caleb, Jr., m. Anne GREGORY, d. Ephraim, decd., Oct. 28,   1   488
    1784

Charles, m. Angeline SILLICK, Oct. 8, 1828, b. of Danbury,   1   488
    by John Nickerson

Charles, m. Sally Botsford DIBBLE, Sept. 12, 1832, by   3   49
    Thomas Larcombe

C[h]loe, d. [Ezra & Rachel], b. [   ], 1772; d. Nov. 17, 1788   3   71

Clare, [d. Levi & Hannah], b. Jan. 17, 1786   1   480

Clara Ann, of Danbury, m. Elizur W. KEELER, of Newtown,   1   432
    yesterday [July 14, 1847], by Rev. Rollin S. Stone

Clarisca*, [d. David & Deborah], b. Mar. 29, 1783 *(Line   3   163
    drawn through)

Clary, [d. Joshua & Ruth], b. Apr. 4, 1790   1   414

Clarry, d. [Lewis & Elizabeth], b. Oct. 21, 1799   1   457

Comfort, [s. Joseph & Elisabeth], b. Jan. 13, 1769   1   490

Comfort, [s. Joseph & Elisabeth], d. Sept. 25, 1783   1   465

Cordelia, m. Charles BARTLEY, Dec. 1, 1820, by W[illia]m   1   465
    Andrews

Cornelia, m. Almon HICKOK, [May] 23, [1838], by Rev. J. G.   3   3
    Collom

Cornelius, of Danbury, m. Rachel HAMLIN, of New Milford,   3   94
    Apr. 16, 1828, by John Nickerson

Cyril H., m. Angeline JUDD, b. of Bethel, Nov. 9, 1837,   3   47
    by E. Cole

                                                                 3   92

	Vol.	Page
BENEDICT, (cont.)		
Cyrus, s. [Caleb & Ruth], b. Apr. 16, 1771	1	488
Cyrus, m. Penelope **DUNING**, Jan. 3, 1793	1	480
Daniel, [s. Hezekiah, Jr. & Huldah], b. Feb. 1, 1782	1	406
Daniel, s. [Jonas & Mercy], b. Jan. 3, 1783	1	481
Daniel, m. Rhoda **BENEDICT**, d. Theophilus, Apr. 4, 1785	1	437
Darius, s. [Lewis & Elizabeth], b. Nov. 4, 1797	1	490
David, m. Deborah **DIBBLE**, Oct. 17, 1782	1	414
David M., m. Mary B. **BOUGHTON**, this day [Sept. 24, 1832], by Rev. Lemuel B. Hull	3	76
Deborah, d. [Thaddeus & Abigail], b. Apr. 19, 175[ ]	1	498
Debory, d. Thaddeus, m. Samuel **WILDMAN**, Jr., Sept. 14, 1785	1	410
Deborah, d. [Peter & Anne], b. Jan. 23, 1804	1	360
Deborah A., of Danbury, m. James W. **SIMMONS**, of New York, Nov. 26, 1830, by John Nickerson	3	59
Delilah, d. [Nathaniel, Jr.], b. Nov. 23, 1791	1	373
Drucilla, [d. James & Roda], b. June 28, 1788	1	430
Ebenezer, b. Sept. 4, 1764	1	403
Ebenezer, Jr., m. Elisabeth **BENEDICT**, d. Nathan, Oct. 31, 1770	1	393
Ebenezer, s. [Hezekiah, Jr. & Huldah], b. Aug. 3, 1779	1	406
Ebenezer, 3rd, m. Asenath **ABBOT**, d. John, of Ridgefield, May 5, 1783	1	403
Ebenezer, Jr., d. Nov. 17, 1803	1	393
Ebenezer, s. [Cyrus & Penelope], b. Jan. 15, 1808	1	480
Eder, [d. Joseph & Elisabeth], b. Apr. 17, 1764	1	465
Eder, [child of Joseph & Elisabeth], d. Dec. 26, 1778	1	465
Edear, [child of Levi & Hannah], b. Feb. 5, 1779	1	432
Edwin, [s. John, Jr. & Lydia], b. Feb. 7, 1803	1	463
Eleazer*, d. [ ] *(Written above in pencil "Eleazer **BEDIENT**")	1	388
Eleazer, [s. Samuel, Jr. & Phebe], b. Dec. 27, 1747	1	444
Eleazer, b. Dec. 27, 1747; m. Mary **BARNUM**, Feb. 1, 1770	1	504
Eleazer, m. Jerusha **CROSBY**, Apr. 24, 1777	1	504
Eleazer, [& w. Jerusha, had child b.] July 2, 1788* *(Faded out)	1	504
Elizer, s. [John, Jr. & Lydia], b. Jan. 1, 1799	1	463
Elem, s. [Benajah & Hannah], b. May 7, 1772	1	442
Eli, s. [John, Jr. & Lydia], b. Sept. 18, 1787; d. Dec. 17, 1788	1	463
Eli, s. [Jonas & Mercy], b. Jan. 9, 1789	1	481
Eli, 2nd, s. [John, Jr. & Lydia], b. Feb. 7, 1789	1	463
Eli Starr, [s. Peter & Anne], b. Sept. 14, 1791	1	360
Eliakim, s. [Thaddeus & Abigail], b. Sept. 26, 175[ ]	1	498
Eliakim, Jr., m. Hannah **BENEDICT**, d. Joseph, May 22, 1783	1	497
Eliakim Starr, s. [Eliakim, Jr. & Hannah], b. May 3, 1799; d. Nov. 9, 1803	1	497
Elias, [s. Benajah & Hannah, his 2nd w.] b. Oct. 9*, 1773* *(Fig. "26" crossed out) *(Year corrected)	1	442
Elihu, s. [Thaddeus & Abigail], b. Aug. 1, 176[ ]	1	498

	Vol.	Page
BENEDICT, (cont.)		
Hannah, d. [Eliakim, Jr. & Hannah], b. Sept. 22, 1802	1	497
Hannah, m. John H. **WHITING**, Jan. 1, 1828, by Rev. L. P. Hickok	3	43
Heman, [s. John, Jr. & Lydia], b. Feb. 17, 1792	1	463
Henry, m. Elizabeth **MOREHOUSE**, b. of Danbury, this day [Sept. 12, 1832], by Rev. Lemuel B. Hull	3	76
Henry, of New York, m. Lorany Ann **GREGORY**, of Danbury, Mar. 26, 1834, by Timothy B. Hickok, J. P.	3	79
Hezekiah, Jr., b. Mar. 16, 1754; m. Huldah **HALL**, Jan. 30, 1777	1	406
Huldah, [d. Hezekiah, Jr. & Huldah], b. July 29, 1783	1	406
Ira, [s. Asahel & Lydia], b. Apr. 5, 1782	1	434
Ira, s. [Cyrus & Penelope], b. July 18, 1803	1	480
Ira, m. Sarah Ophelia **BUCKLEY**, of Danbury, Oct. 18, 1823, by Rev. Ambrose S. Todd	3	15
Irene, [d. Asahel & Lydia], b. Nov. 14, 1777	1	434
Isaac Hoyt, s. [Peter & Anne], b. Dec. 24, 1786; d. Dec. 8, 1793	1	360
Isaac Hoyt, s. [Peter & Anne], b. Dec. 12, 1795	1	360
Jabesz, s. [Ephraim & Betty], b. Jan. 10, 1791	1	478
James, [s. Benajah & Hannah], b. Sept. 18, 1774	1	442
James, [s. Jonah & Betsey], b. Sept. 20, 1784	1	413
James, m. Roda **DIBBLE**, d. Samuel, Dec. 11, 1784	1	430
James, m. Lucy **GREGORY**, June 1, 1828, by George Benedict	3	48
Jane, m. Lewis T. **PRICE**, Dec. 31, 1844, by Rev. J. K. Ingalls	3	131
Jere, [s. Capt. Noble & Eunice], b. Mar. 23, 1775; d. July 26, 1775	1	403
Jerusha, d. Zadock, m. Isaac **IVES**, Mar. 14, 1792	1	407
Jesse, s. [Thaddeus & Abigail], b. June 11 N. S., 175[ ]	1	498
Jesse, [s. Hezekiah, Jr. & Huldah], b. May 5, 1787	1	406
Joanna, [d. Samuel, Jr. & Phebe], b. Nov. 21, 1754	1	444
Joanna, [d. Samuel, Jr. & Phebe], d. Oct. 1, 1776	1	444
Joanna, d. [Elijah & Tamar], b. Sept. 28, 1794	1	444
John, [s. Samuel, Jr. & Phebe], b. Feb. 4, 1760; d. Feb. 4, 1780	1	444
John, s. [Eleazer & Jerusha], b. Dec. 14, 1780	1	504
John, Jr., m. Lydia **PECK**, Sept. 18, 1786	1	463
John, [s. Ebenezer, 3rd & Asenath], b. Mar. 13, 1790	1	403
John, s. [John, Jr. & Lydia], b. June 10, 1790	1	463
John, m. Cordelia **BARNUM**, b. of Bethel, Jan. 2, 1842, by John Greenwood	3	113
John Curtiss, s. [Ephraim & Betty], b. Apr. 27, 1785	1	478
Jonah*, m. Betsey **ENGLISH**, Jan. 6, 1781 *("Governor" crossed out)	1	413
Jonas, m. Mercy **BOUGHTON**, d. Benj[ami]n, Jan. 14, 1767	1	481
Jonas, s. [Jonas & Mercy], b. Mar. 18, 1773; d. May 31, 1776	1	481
Joseph, m. Elisabeth **HALL**, Oct. 24, 1750	1	465
Joshua, m. Ruth **WESTCOAT**, d. Nathaniel, of Norwalk, Apr. 13, 1774	1	457
Laura, m. Charles **BARNUM**, b. of Danbury, Mar. 15, 1825,		

	Vol.	Page
BENEDICT, (cont.)		
by Rev. John G. Lowe	3	38
Lemuel, [s. Stephen Brownson & Eunice], b. Oct. 12, 1792	1	441
Levi, s. [Joseph & Elisabeth], b. Nov. 28, 1752; d. Dec. 30, 1754	1	465
Levi, 2nd, [s. Joseph & Elisabeth], b. Mar. 12, 1755	1	465
Levy, [s. Benajah & Hannah, his 2nd, w.], b. Oct. 26, 1769	1	442
Levi, m. Hannah HALBUT, July 29, 1773	1	432
Levi, [s. Levi & Hannah], b. Mar. 18, 1783	1	432
Levi, [s. Hezekiah, Jr. & Huldah], b. Jan. 3, 1786	1	406
Levi, s. [Caleb, Jr. & Anne], b. July 23, 1795	1	488
Levi, m. Alice **GREGORY**, Oct. 26, 1823, by Rev. W[illia]m Andrews	3	19
Levi S., m. Mary **GREGORY**, Oct. 7, [1829], by George Benedict	3	53
Lewis, s. [Caleb & Ruth], b. Mar. 1, 1780	1	488
Lewis, b. Mar. 1, 1780	1	490
Lewis, m. Elizabeth **CROFUT**, Dec. 22, 1796	1	490
Lois, d. [Theophilus & Mary], b. July [ ], 1740	1	370
Lois, d. [Joshua & Ruth], b. Dec. 14, 1776; d. Oct. *20, 1778 *("Dec. 14" crossed out)	1	457
Lois, 2nd, d. [Joshua & Ruth], b. Mar. 4, 1779	1	457
Lucinda, d. [Michael, 2nd & Rachel], b. Nov. 15, 1791	1	462
Lucy, [d. Ebenezer, Jr. & Elisabeth], b. July 18, 1775; d. Oct. 4, 1777	1	393
Lucy, [d. Joshua & Ruth], b. June 23, 1786	1	457
Lucy, m. Franklin **PAYNE**, b. of Danbury, Feb. 19, [1826], by John Nickerson	3	32
Lucy, m. Jonathan **CROFUT**, Apr. 13, 1826, by George Benedict	3	32
Lucy Ann, of Danbury, m. W[illia]m Monson **KEELER**, of Bethel, Aug. 28, [1839], by Rev. Rollin S. Stone	3	99
Luman, s. [Caleb, Jr. & Anne], b. June 4, 1788	1	488
Mabel, d. June 23, 1822, ae 65	2	101
Mabel, m. Joshua **HOYT**, Oct. 22, 1829, by Levi Osborn	3	53
Maria, m. Winthrop **FAIRCHILD**, b. of Danbury, Jan. 21, 1827, by Rev. John G. Lowe	3	39
Mary, see Mary **BOUGHTON**	1	377
Mary, d. Thomas, m. Joseph **STARR**, [ ]	1	467
Mary, [d. Theophilus & Mary], b. June 20, 1744	1	370
Mary, 2nd, d. Theophilus & Mary, b. June [ ], 1744; m. Miles **BOUGHTON**, 2nd, s. Benjamin & Lydia, Dec. 3, 1761	1	374
Mary, 2nd, d. [Thaddeus & Abigail], b. Feb. 19, 175[ ]; d. June 9, [ ]	1	498
Mary, d. [Thaddeus & Abigail], b. Oct. [ ], 175[ ]; d. Oct. [ ], 175[ ]	1	498
Mary, d. [[ ]saac & Mary], b. Nov. 21, 1750	1	501
Mary, [d. Samuel, Jr. & Phebe], b. Apr. 15, 1752	1	444
Mary, d. Abraham, m. Ebenezer **HICKOK**, Feb. 15, 1770	1	394

	Vol.	Page

BENEDICT, (cont.)

Mary, w. [Eleazer], d. Oct. 24, 1774 — 1 504

Mary, d. Sam[ue]l, Jr., m. Jus[tus] **BARNUM**, s. Joseph,
May 4, 1775 — 1 501

Mary, d. [Eleazer & Jerusha], b. Mar. 15, 1778 — 1 504

Mary, [d. Daniel & Rhoda], b. Sept. 17, 1785 — 1 437

Mary, [w. Theophilus], d. May 15, 1796 — 1 370

Mary, m. Forward **STEVENS**, b. of Danbury, Oct. 28, 1823,
by Nathan Bulkley — 3 19

Mary Babcock, [d. Thaddeus & Abigail], see Mary **BENEDICT**,
2nd — 1 498

Mary H., of Bethel, m. Amos **WOODMAN**, of New York, Feb.
9, 1842, by J. Greenwood — 3 114

Matthew, [s. Jonah & Betsey], b. Apr. 24, 1781 — 1 413

Mehetabel, d. Caleb, of Norwalk, m. Jonathan **STEVENS**, Nov.
23, 1778* *(Date corrected from Apr. 20, 1752) — 1 459

Mercy, [d. Seth & Abigail], b. June 10, 1778 — 1 475

Mercy, d. Abraham, m. Ebenezer **JUDD**, July 14, 1791 — 1 397

Mercy, eldest d. Seth, m. Eliakim **BARNUM**, 4th s. David,
Oct. 20, 1799 — 1 362

Micajah, s. [Lewis & Elizabeth], b. Apr. 24, 1804 — 1 490

Michael, 2nd, m. Rachel **PROUT**, of New Milford, Aug. 31,
1788 — 1 462

Najah, [s. Benajah & Hannah], b. Mar. 19, 1782 — 1 442

Nancy, d. Amos & Sarah, b. June 3, 1801 — 1 356

Nathan Dunning, s. [Cryus & Penelope], b. Nov. 26, 1797 — 1 480

Nath[anie]l, [f. of [ ]saac], d. Oct. 9, 1767 — 1 501

Nathaniel, Jr., b. Jan. 1, 1768; m. [ ], Aug. 24, 1787 — 1 373

Nathaniel, 3rd, s. [Nathaniel, Jr.], b. May 8, 1796 — 1 373

Nathaniel M., of Ridgefield, m. Malinda **WILLIAMS**, of
Danbury, Oct. 2, 1823, by Nathan Seelye, J. P. — 3 18

Noble, Capt., b. Jan. 25, 1735; m. Eunice **GREGORY**, d.
Sam[ue]l, July 6, 1763* *(Corrected from "1773") — 1 403

Olive, d. Nathaniel, Jr., decd., b. [ ], 1765 — 1 373

Olive, [d. Joseph & Elisabeth], b. Sept. 5, 1766 — 1 465

Orra, [child of Ebenezer, 3rd & Asenath], b. Aug. 7, 1787 — 1 403

Orrilla, d. [Michael, 2nd & Rachel], b. Nov. 4, 1789 — 1 462

Orrin, m. Julia Maria **STARR**, b. of Danbury, Oct. 11, 1840,
by Rev. D. H. Short — 3 107

Orville, d. [John, Jr. & Lydia], b. Apr. 7, 1797 — 1 463

Patience, d. [Eleazer & Jerusha], b. Apr. 5, 1779 — 1 504

Peter, s. [Thaddeus & Abigail], b. Dec. 11, 175[ ] — 1 498

Peter, 4th, s. Thaddeus, m. Anne **PECK**, eldest d. Abijah,
b. of Danbury, Dec. 22, 1779 — 1 360

Phebe, m. Samuel **BENEDICT**, Jr., Dec. 9, 1742 — 1 444

Phebe, [d. Samuel, Jr. & Phebe], b. Jan. 22, 1750 — 1 444

Phebe, m. Samuel **DIBBLE**, Aug. 5, 1774 — 1 464

Philer*, s. [David & Deborah], b. Apr. 14, 1790 *("Deborah"

	Vol.	Page
BENEDICT, (cont.)		
crossed out)	1	414
Platt, s. [Jonas & Mercy], b. Mar. 18, 1775	1	481
Polly, d. [Jonas & Mercy], b. Oct. 25, 1785	1	481
Polly, d. [Cyrus & Penelope], b. Aug. 3, 1795	1	480
Polly Maria, m. Aaron ANDREWS, b. of Danbury, Dec. 16, 1825, by Rev. John G. Lowe	3	35
Priscilla, d. [[ ]saac & Mary], b. July 6, 1755	1	501
Rachel, d. [Theophilus & Mary], b. Aug. 4, 1746	1	370
Rachel, 3rd d. Theophilus, b. Aug. 15, 1746; m. Joshua HOYT, eldest s. Thomas, decd., Aug. 22, 1764	1	371
Rachel, d. Ebenezer, m. David BARNUM, Apr. 14, 1760	1	475
Rachel, d. [Ebenezer, Jr. & Elisabeth], b. Aug. 25, 1771; d. Oct. 6, 1777	1	393
Rachel, d. Lieut. John, m. John MATTHEWS, Oct. 28, 1772	1	464
Rachel, [w. Ezra], d. Oct. 15, 1773	1	480
Rachel, d. [Ezra & Mabel], b. Jan. 6, 1781; d. Feb. 14, 1785	1	480
Rachel, d. [Peter & Anne], b. Feb. 20, 1801	1	360
Rebec[c]a, [d. Samuel, Jr. & Phebe], b. May 22, 1757	1	444
Rebe[c]kah, d. [[ ]saac & Mary], b. Nov. 20, 1771	1	501
Rebe[c]kah, [d. [ ]saac & Mary], d. Sept. 2, 1775	1	501
Rebecca, [d. Benajah & Hannah, his 2nd w.], b. Nov. 26, 1776	1	442
Rebe[c]kah, d. [Sam[ue]l, 4th & Sarah], b. Jan. 8, 1778	1	504
Rebecca, d. Sam[ue]l, Jr., m. Joseph BEEBE, Jr., Sept. 10, 1778	1	472
Rhoda, d. Theophilus, m. Daniel BENEDICT, Apr. 4, 1785	1	437
Rossel, s. [Ephraim & Betty], b. Aug. 4, 1798	1	478
Russel, m. Marietta MALLORY, b. of Danbury, Aug. 20, 1837, by Rev. D. H. Short	3	106
Ruth, d. Eben[eze]r, m. Caleb BENEDICT, Mar. 28, 1763	1	488
Ruth, d. [Caleb & Ruth], b. Sept. 19, 1769	1	488
Ruth, d. [Seth & Abigail], b. Sept. 15, 1780	1	475
Ruth, d. Jakin, m. Samuel DIBBLE, 3rd, Sept. 20, 1791	1	468
Ruth, d. [Ephraim & Betty], b. Feb. 19, 1794	1	478
Ruth, of Danbury, m. Abraham MUFFET, of Phillips, N. Y., Jan. 15, 1826, by John Nickerson	3	31
Sally, d. Daniel & Rhoda], b. Feb. 6, 1787	1	437
Sally, [d. Joshua & Ruth], b. July 11, 1788	1	457
Sally, d. Joseph, Jr., m. Ephraim Gregory STEVENS, s. Thomas, decd., Nov. 20, 1802	1	359
Sally Betey, d. [Abijah & Betey], b. May 24, 1789	1	485
Samuel, Jr., m. Phebe BENEDICT, Dec. 9, 1742	1	444
Sam[ue]l, s. [Samuel, Jr. & Phebe], b. July 28, 1744	1	444
Sam[ue]l,3rd, b. July 28, 1744; m. Betty WESCOT, Apr. 7, 1768	1	504
Sam[ue]l, s. [[ ]saac & Mary], b. July 29, 1753	1	501
Samuel, 3rd, m. Betty WESCOT, Apr. 7, 1768	1	443
Sam[ue]l, 4th, m. Sarah WEED, d. Reuben, of Stanford, Oct. 25, 1774	1	504
Sam[ue]l, d. May 19, 1792, ae 70 y. 5 m.	1	444

	Vol.	Page

BENEDICT, (cont.)

	Vol.	Page
Samuel, d. Aug. 18, 1803	1	443
Samuel Baldwin, s. [John, Jr. & Lydia], b. Sept. 18, 1794	1	463
Samuel Ward, s. [Peter & Anne], b. Mar. 12, 1798	1	360
Sarah, d. [Samuel, 3rd & Betty], b. Mar. 10, 1774;		
d. Aug. 5, 1775	1	443
Sarah, d. [Samuel, 3rd & Betty], b. Mar. 10, 1774;		
d. Aug. 5, 1775	1	504
Sarah, d. Ens. Thomas, m. Christopher GLOVER, June 10, 1774	1	492
Sarah, [d. Samuel, 3rd & Betty], b. Mar. 14, 1780	1	443
Sarah, d. [Jonas & Mercy], b. Nov. 23, 1780	1	481
Sarah, d. Jonas, b. Nov. 23, 1780; m. Amos BENEDICT, 2nd,		
s. Theophilus, Mar. 12, 1800	1	356
Sarah, d. Jakin, m. Nathan DIBBLE, Jr., Dec. 7, 1781	1	485
Sarah, d. Josiah, m. Stephen BARNUM, Sept. 4, 1785	1	461
Sarah, d. [Ephraim & Betty], b. Sept. 20, 1787	1	478
Sarah, [twin with Susanna], [d. Stephen Brownson & Eunice],		
b. Apr. 23, 1790	1	441
Seth, [s. Joseph & Elisabeth], b. Oct. 22, 1757	1	465
Seth, m. Abigail OLMSTED, Feb. 13, 1777	1	475
Seth, m. Ann STARR, b. of Bethel, July 4, 1824, by Rev.		
John G. Lowe	3	24
Stephen, s. [Ebenezer, 3rd & Asenath], b. Aug. 12, 1785	1	403
Stephen Brownson, m. Eunice WILDMAN, d. Comfort, May 24,		
1789	1	441
Stodard, [s. Samuel, 3rd & Betty], b. Feb. 2, 1787	1	443
Susan Jane, m. William I. SCHOONMAKER, b. of Danbury,		
Feb. 2, 1845, by Rev. Fitch Reed	3	132
Susanna, d. [Ezra & Rachel], b. Aug. 27, 1769; d. July 8, 1791	1	480
Susanna, [twin with Sarah, d. Stephen Brownson & Eunice],		
b. Apr. 23, 1790	1	441
Talmage, [s. Levi & Hannah], b. Jan. 22, 1776	1	432
Tamer, of Danbury, m. Ezra BEEBE, of Brookfield, May 11,		
1831, by Elias Birchard, J. P.	3	62
Thaddeus, m. Abigail S*. STARR, d. Lieut. Benjamin, Feb.		
[,]* *(faded out)	1	498
Thaddeus, s. [Thaddeus & Abigail S.], b. Aug. 14, [ ]	1	498
Thaddeus, m. 2nd w. Catha[rine] DIBBLE, wid. Nehemiah,		
Nov. [ ]	1	498
Thankfull, m. Nathan GREGORY, Apr. 2, 1760	1	428
Theophilus, 3rd s. Daniel, 1st. b. [ ], 1711; m. Mary		
STARR, d. John, b. of Danbury, [ ], 1737	1	370
Theophilus, s. [Theophilus & Mary], b. [ ], 1738	1	370
Theophilus, d. Dec. 4, 1786	1	370
Thomas, s. Ens. Thomas, had negro Enoch, s. Rhoda, b. Feb.		
28, 1784	1	487
Thomas, Jr., 2nd s. Thomas, m. Mercy ROCKWELL, eldest		
child of Dr. Elihud, decd., Oct. 10, 1787	1	362

	Vol.	Page

BENEDICT, (cont.)

Thomas Brrigham, s. [Amos & Sarah], b. Sept. 25, 1803 — 1 — 356

Trowbridge, s. [Samuel, 3rd & Betty], b. Aug. 7, 1776 — 1 — 443

Trowbridge, s. [Samuel, 3rd & Betty], b. Aug. 7, 1776 — 1 — 504

Urius, [child of Jonah & Betsey], b. May 14, 1783 — 1 — 413

Zadock, s. [Abijah & Betey], b. June 4, 1786; d. June 14, 1787 — 1 — 485

Zadoc R., m. Mary Ann **WHITE**, Aug. 16, 1825, by Rev. W[illia]m Andrews — 3 — 28

Zadock R., m. Mariett **TWEEDY**, Sept. 1, 1830, by Rev. A. Rood — 3 — 57

Zar, s. [Samuel, 3rd & Betty], b. Jan. 7, 1769 — 1 — 443

Zar, s. [Samuel, 3rd & Betty], b. Jan. 7, 1769 — 1 — 504

Zera, [child of James & Roda], b. Nov. 10, 1785 — 1 — 430

Ziba, [child Benajah & Hannah], b. July 9, 1784 — 1 — 442

[ ]saac*, s. Nathaniel, m. Mary **VIDETS**, d. John, May 24, 1744 *(Worn off) — 1 — 501

BENJAMIN, Eliza, of Bethel, m. Thomas **DALLORY**, of Woodbury, June 15, 1842, by J. Greenwood — 3 — 115

George, of Danbury, m. Susan **JONES**, of Norwalk, Jan. 1, 1850, by Rev. Rollin S. Stone — 3 — 147

Harriet, m. David **GILLET**, Sept. 11, 1836, by Rev. Jonathan G. Collom — 3 — 86

Martha, of Bethel, m. William A. **WHITING**, of Bridgeport, May 9, 1849, by Rev. Rollin S. Stone — 3 — 147

Sarah, m. Orlando **WILCOX**, b. of Danbury, Oct. 19, 1841, by Addison Parker — 3 — 112

Sarah, m. Henry B. **STONE**, b. of Danbury, Nov. 30, 1848, by Rev. Rollin S. Stone — 3 — 146

BENNETT, BENNET, Daniel, m. Harriet **DISBROW**, Mar. 23, 1821, by Oliver Tuttle — 3 — 6

Elvira, of Monroe, m. George **FAIRCHILD**, of Newtown, Jan. 1, 1837, by Rev. Salmon C. Bulkley — 3 — 89

Hanford, N., M. D., m. Clarinda **WILLIAMS**, b. of Bethel, Apr. 18, 1838, by Rev. J. G. Collom — 3 — 93

Mary, m. Edmund **PRICE**, b. of Danbury, Aug. 2, 1820, by William Andrews — 3 — 1

Polly, m. Nathaniel S. **STARR**, b. of Danbury, Feb. 7, 1821, by William Cooke, J. P. — 3 — 5

Sally Ann, m. Calvin **JENKINS**, May 21, 1823, by Reuben Booth, J. P. — 3 — 17

BETTS, Philo, m. Betsey **TAYLOR**, b. of Danbury, Apr. 25, 1838, by Rev. D. H. Short — 3 — 107

Susan Electa, d. Philo & Betsey, b. June 10, 1839 — 3 — 158

BETTYS, Betsey Ann, m. Harvey **KNAPP**, b. of Danbury, Dec. 30, 1832, by Levi Brunson — 3 — 73

BEVANS, BEVENS, Amanda Elizabeth, m. Horace **BARTRAM**, b. of Danbury, Aug. 27, 1845, by Rev. Fitch Reed — 3 — 135

Edward Starr, twin with Edwin Akerly, s. Benj[amin],

	Vol.	Page

BEVANS, BEVENS, (cont.)

    b. Feb. 26, 1822 — 2 — 100

    Edwin Akerly, twin with Edward Starr, s. Benj[ami]n, b.
Feb. 26, 1822 — 2 — 100

    Frederick S.*, m. Jennett **GRIFFIN,** b. of Danbury, Oct. 24,
1841, by Addison Parker *(Possibly "T") — 3 — 112

    John, of Trumbull, m. Samantha **COLE,** of Danbury, Nov. 19,
1843, by James Floy — 3 — 123

    Lorana, m. Beach T. **WILSON,** b. of Danbury, June 10, 1845,
by Rev. Fitch Reed — 3 — 135

    Polly, m. James **BARTRAM,** b. of Danbury, Nov. 20, 1844, by
Rev. Fitch Reed — 3 — 129

    Polly Ann, of Danbury, m. Anson **SLY,** of Huntington, July
6, 1828, by John Nickerson — 3 — 48

    Russel, of Danbury, m. Amanda **GOULD,** of Wilton, Jan. 1,
1829, by Josiah Dikeman — 3 — 50

    Sarah Maria, m. Henry **CROFUT,** b. of Danbury, this day [May
4, 1841], by S. H. Clark — 3 — 109

BICKER, Henry K., m. Mary C. **STARR,** July 18, 1831, by Rev. A.
Rood — 3 — 63

BIFFIELD, William, m. Elizabeth B. **LOBDELL,** b. of Danbury,
Nov. 10, 1844, by Rev. Fitch Reed — 3 — 129

BIGLOW, Franklin H., m. Catherine V. **PERKINS,** Sept. 4, 1849,
by Rev. A. Perkins — 3 — 160

BIRCH, Marcus, of New York, m. Polly **MUNROE,** of Danbury, Oct.
3, 1831, by John Nickerson — 3 — 63

BIRDSELL, BIRDSALL, Mary Caroline, m. Gilbert **SHUTE,** b. of
Danbury, Dec. 26, 1832, by John Mitchel — 3 — 73

    Sheldon, m. Eunice **KNAPP,** Dec. 25, 1847, by Lucius Atwater — 3 — 142

BISHOP, Amelia, of Danbury, m. Hosea **OTIS,** of Mass., Jan. 5,
1823, by Rev. Ambrose S. Todd — 3 — 15

    Amos, m. Mary **MUNROW,** May 23, 1831, by John Nickerson — 3 — 62

    Amos, m. Annis **BARNUM,** Dec. 23, 1838, by Rev. L. Cook — 3 — 96

    Ann, m. Edgar S. **TWEEDY,** [Jan.] 24, [1832], by Rev. A. Rood — 3 — 66

    Annis, d.* [David & Esther], b. July 22, 1775 *("s." crossed out) — 1 — 487

    Betsey, m. John C. **BLACKMAN,** b. of Danbury, this day
[May 5, 1830], by Rev. Lemuel B. Hull — 3 — 56

    Catey*, m. Noah **BARNUM,** Feb. 9, 1784 *(Letter crossed out) — 1 — 436

    David, m. Esther **BARNUM,** d. John, Oct. 23, 1774 — 1 — 487

    David, s. [David & Esther],. b. Jan. 26, 1780 — 1 — 487

    David, d. Apr. 17* 1781 *("30" marked out) — 1 — 487

    Enos, s. [David & Esther], b. Feb. 12, 1777 — 1 — 487

    Esther, m. Malancton **STARR,** b. of Danbury, this day [Nov.
21, 1824], by Rev. Lemuel B. Hull — 3 — 25

    Fanny, m. David D. **WILDMAN,** b. of Danbury, May 19, 1829,
by Rev. A. Rood — 3 — 52

    Hannah, wid., m. Joseph P. **COOKE,** Jr., June 8, 1814 — 1 — 487

    Martha, m. Thomas W. **SPRAGUE,** May 25, 1835, by Rev. A.

	Vol.	Page
BISHOP, (cont.)		
Rood	3	87
BLACKMAN, Abel Beers, m. Maria **BARNUM,** b. of Bethel, [May] 14, [1828] by Rev. Thomas Robbins	3	47
Edwin, m. Sarah H. **SEIGNIOR,** b. of Danbury, Dec. 21, 1845, by Rev. Rollin S. Stone	3	138
Frederick S., m. Sarah A. **MORRIS,** June 5, 1850, by William W. Bronson	3	149
Harriet Sophia, m. Edward Arthur **NICHOLS,** b. of Danbury, Sept. 30, 1840, by Rev. D. H. Short	3	107
Isaac, of Newtown, m. Betsey **MORGAN,** of Danbury, Jan. 2, 1837, by Rev. Salmon C. Bulkley	3	90
John C., m. Betsey **BISHOP,** b. of Danbury, this day [May 5, 1830], by Rev. Lemuel B. Hull	3	56
BLISS, Abraham, of New York, m. Mary **DIKEMAN,** of Danbury, Nov. 17, 1829, by John Nickerson	3	53
BLISSARD, BLISARD, George H., m. Caroline **SQUIRES,** b. of Danbury, May 20, 1847, by Rev. Rollin S. Stone	3	162
Peter, of Pokapsie, m. Rebecca **PATCH,** of Danbury, Apr. 27, 1832, by John Nickerson	3	70
BODWELL, Horace, s. Joseph, b. Dec. 6, 1821; d. May 8, 1822	2	120
BOGARDUS, Ephraim P., of Cooksakie, N. Y., m. Harriet **WOOD,** of Danbury, Apr. 4, 1827, by Josiah Dikeman	3	40
F. L., m. B. **BAXTER,** b. of Danbury, Nov. 27, 1844, by Thomas T. Guion	3	132
BONNEY, Mary W., of Danbury, m. Russel R. **PRATT,** of Cornwall, Jan. 23, 1850, by Rollin S. Stone	3	147
BOOTH, Ann, d. Dea. Ephraim, of Stratford, m. Thomas P. **WHITE,** Jan. 29, 1769	1	393
Aurinda B., m. William R. **WHITE,** Sept. 2, 1851, by Rev. W. White Bronson	3	156
Cornelia E., m. George W. **FERRY,** Sept. 11, 1851, by Rev. W. White Bronson	3	156
Nathaniel, s. Abner, of Reading, d. Mar. 22, 1793, at the house of Thaddeus Morehouse	1	412
Phebe, b. Apr. 24, 1757; m. Stiles **NICHOLS,** Nov. 12, 1787	1	496
Phebe, d. Abel, of Newtown, m. Ebenezer **GREGORY,** July 12, 1768	1	480
Rachel, d. Ephraim, of Stratford, b. May 19, 1741; m. Joseph Moss **WHITE,** Jan. 15, 1766	1	473
Reuben, m. Jane **BELDEN,** June 4, 1821	2	171
Sarah, m. Levi **PECK,** Apr. 17, 1786	1	396
Sarah, of Danbury, m. E. LeRoy **FERRY,** of Bethel, Sept. 14, 1842, by Thomas T. Guion	3	117
Sarah Hull, d. [Reuben & Jane], b. June 29, 1822	2	171
Selleck, m. Lucy **BARNUM,** Sept. 30, 1849, by Rev. John Purves, of Bethel	3	161
BOSTWICK, BOSTICK, Azariel, m. S[ ]iano **CLARK,** b. of		

BOSTWICK, BOSTICK, (cont.)

	Vol.	Page
Danbury, Sept. 30, 1846, by Nathaniel Bishop	3	140
Eunice, m. Nathanael **BARNUM**, Nov. 8, 1769	1	454
BOTSFORD, Samuel N., of Danbury, m. Clarissa M. **BEEBE**, of		
Waterbury, Sept. 1, 1834, by Reuben Booth, J. P.	3	80
BOUGHTON, Abijah, m. Rebecca **SHUTE**, Dec. 18, 1788	1	405
Archibald, of New York State, m. Nancy **WILLIAMS**, of		
Danbury, Nov. 19, 1826, by John Nickerson	3	37
Betty, d. [Miles & Mary, 2nd], b. Mar. 3, 1764	1	374
Betty, d. Miles, m. Filor **MYGATT**, Mar. 15, 1787	1	455
David, Jr., m. Rachel **STARR**, d. Capt. Josiah, May 8, 1777	1	385
David H., m. Mary B. **STARR**, b. of Danbury, this day [Aug.		
8, 1826], by Rev. Lemuel B. Hull	3	34
Deborah, [d. Abijah & Rebecca], b. Feb. 10, 1790	1	405
Dorcas, d. [Miles & Mary, 2nd], b. Dec. 17, 1762	1	374
Edward Morris, [s. Ezra & Sarah], b. Aug. 29, 1822	2	99
Eli Henry, [s. Ezra & Sarah], b. Feb. 9, 1820	2	99
Elisabeth, d. Capt. Samuel, m. Daniel **TAYLOR**, June 1, 1742	1	489
Elizabeth B., m. Myron **MORE**, b. of Danbury, Apr. 17, 1839,		
by Rev. Willis Lord	3	98
Elizabeth Benedict, [d. Ezra & Sarah], b. Mar. 30, 1816	2	99
Eunice, m. Abel **BENEDICT**, b. of Danbury, Dec. 28, 1831,		
by John Nickerson	3	66
Ezra Wildman, [s. Ezra & Sarah], b. May 20, 1814	2	99
Hannah, [d. Ezra & Sarah], b. Aug. 4, 1810	2	99
Hannah, Mrs., m. Niram **WILDMAN**, Mar. 27, 1838, by Rev.		
Rollin S. Stone	3	93
[Jos]eph, b. Jan. 22, 1751; m. Zaruah **BASS**, d. Benj[ami]n,		
of Fairfield, Nov. 20, 1778	1	502
Joseph, m. Zeruah **BEARSS**, Nov. 12, 1778	1	442
Kezia, m. Thaddeus **HOYT**, Feb. 18, 1780	1	463
Keziah B., m. Grandison M. **BARNUM**, b. of Danbury, this day,		
[Oct. 12, 1834], by Rev. Lemuel B. Hull	3	84
Knap, s. [David, Jr. & Rachel], b. Oct. 31, 1779	1	385
Lois, d. Miles & Mary, 2nd], b. Apr. 5, 1766	1	374
Lucius H., m. Emily **COMSTOCK**, [June] 4, [1833], by Rev.		
A. Rood	3	75
Margaret, m. Oliver **STONE**, Oct. 12, 1775	1	395
Mary, wid. Miles, 2nd d. Theophilus **BENEDICT**, m. Eli		
MYGATT, Mar. 20, 1784	1	377
Mary, d. [Ezra & Sarah], b. Sept. 12, 1806	2	99
Mary, m. George **FRY**, Sept. 27, 1825, by Rev. W[illia]m		
Andrews	3	29
Mary B., m. David M. **BENEDICT**, this day [Sept. 24, 1832],		
by Rev. Lemuel B. Hull	3	76
Mercy, d. Benj[mi]n, m. Jonas **BENEDICT**, Jan. 14, 1767	1	481
Miles, 2nd s. Benjamin & Lydia, b. [ ], 1740; m. Mary		
BENEDICT, 2nd, d. Theophilus & Mary, Dec. 3, 1761	1	374

	Vol.	Page

BROAS, Adelia, m. Benedict **TROWBRIDGE**, Aug. 6, 1848, by Rev.
A. Perkins — 3 — 160
BROCKINGTON, Nelson, m. Clarissa **BARNUM**, May 24, 1843, by
Rev. William R. Webb — 3 — 124
BROCKLETON, Stephen, m. Abiga[i]l **WHITNEY**, Aug. 26, 1821,
by Rev. Aaron Hunt — 3 — 8
BRODERICK, Jane, m. John B. **KEELER**, Oct. 14, 1851, by Rev.
Charles Bartlett — 3 — 158
BRONSON, BRUNSON, Amelia, of Danbury, Starrs Plain, m. Isaac
SARINE, of Danbury, Bethel Society, [Oct.] 10, [1821], by
Rev. Oliver Tuttle — 3 — 8
Ann, m. Richard **OSBORN**, Nov. 20, 1823, by Levi Bronson — 3 — 20
Barlow B., m. Mary A. **HICKOK**, b. of Danbury, Sept. 15, 1840,
by Addison Parker — 3 — 105
Betsey A., m. Truman **JUDD**, Oct. 15, 1851, by Rev. Charles
Bartlett — 3 — 158
Lucinda, d. Thaddeus, of Danbury, m. Phinehas **LOBDELL**, of
Ridgefield, May 6, 1793 — 1 — 358
Mary Ann, of Danbury, m. Hiram K. **SCOTT**, of Ridgefield,
Oct. 4, 1843, by Levi Bronson — 3 — 122
Ovra, of Danbury, m. Edwin **MILLS**, of Ridgefield, Oct. 1,
1830, by Levy Bronson — 3 — 58
Thaddeus, m. Sally **CRARY**, Dec. 15, 1823, by Levi Bronson — 3 — 20
BROOKS, Anna, m. Ezra **CROFUT**, Feb. 17, 1781 — 1 — 422
Benjamin, of Norwalk, m. Mercy **STARR**, of Danbury, [June]
2, [1830], by Rev. A. Rood *(Possibly "Mary") — 3 — 56
BROTHINGTON, Charles, m. Mary M. **FENNER**, Sept. 29, 1847, by
Rev. John Purves, of Bethel — 3 — 151
BROWN, Christy Ann, m. George **GAUL**, b. of Danbury, Mar. 10,
1847, by Edward Taylor, J. P. — 3 — 162
Hannah E., of Danbury, m. Joseph **ROOT**, of Redding, Nov.
11, 1846, by Rev. John Crawford — 3 — 161
Har[r]iet, m. William **OSBORN**, Sept. 21, 1843, by Rev. J.
K. Inalls — 3 — 122
Jane [   ]*, of Wilton, m. John **LOCKWOOD**, of Reading,
Oct. 6, 1839, by James Beebe, J. P. *(Word crossed out) — 3 — 100
John, m. Sophia **SHEPARD**, b. of Danbury, May 28, 1843, by
Levi Osborn — 3 — 120
Martha, d. Joseph, m. Caleb **BALDWIN**, Feb. 21, 1745 — 1 — 438
Roswell, m. Amelia A. **WHITTLESEY**, [Sept.] 25, [1833], by
Rev. A. Rood — 3 — 76
BROWNELL, Grove L., Rev., m. Mary A. **WHITTLESEY**, [Apr.],
25, [1832], by Rev. A. Rood — 3 — 70
BROWNSON, Alfred, s. [Ira & Amelia], b. Feb. 9, 1793 — 1 — 490
Bets[e]y, d. [Ira & Amelia], b. Dec. 17, 1794 — 1 — 490
Hiram, s. [Ira & Amelia], b. June 24, 1796 — 1 — 490
Ira, m. Amelia **COZIER**, d. Benjamin, Feb. 2, 1792 — 1 — 490
BRUNSON, [see under **BRONSON**]

	Vol.	Page
BRUSH, Charles A., m. Mary Ann **ALLEN**, b. of Danbury, Aug. 30, 1846, by R. K. Bellamy	3	140
BUCHUM, Mary*, m. Ira **TROWBRIDGE**, b. of Danbury, Nov. 1, 1831, by Rev. Lemuel B. Hull *(Possibly "Meny")	3	67
Meny, see Mary **BUCHUM**	3	67
BUCK, Phebe A., m. Zalmon H. **HULL**, Feb. 26, 1840, by Rev. Z. Cook	3	102
Sarah, d. Ezekiel, of New Milford, m. Matthew **CROFUT**, Jr., Dec. 25, 1765	1	488
BULKLEY, BUCKLEY, Amelia, of Greenfield, m. Marcus **NOBLE**, of New Milford, Nov. 2, 1831, by Rev. Lemuel B. Hull	3	67
Eunice, m. John **RIDER**, b. of Danbury, Dec. 2, 1844, by Rev. Rollin S. Stone	3	130
Lucy A., m. Hiram **SHEPARD**, Nov. 27, 1839, by John Crawford	3	101
Mary, m. Rev. Lucius **ATWATER**, b. of Danbury, Sept. 30, 1840, by Addison Parker	3	105
Peter W., m. Clarinda **NONEY**, b. of Danbury, this day [Sept. 12, 1841], by S. H. Clark	3	111
Salmon C., Rev., m. Harriet T.* **ANDREWS**, b. of Danbury, June 29, 1837, by Rev. Shaler J. Hillyer, of North Salem, N. Y. & Long Ridge, Conn. *(Possibly "S")	3	90
Sarah Ophelia, m. Ira **BENEDICT**, Oct. 18, 1823, by Rev. Ambrose S. Todd	3	15
Turney, m. Lucy **SHERMAN**, Jan. 1, 1843, by Lucius Atwater	3	120
BULL, Elizabeth, d. Asa, of Litchfield, m. David **FOOT**, Dec. 29, 1792	1	389
Elizabeth G., of Danbury, m. Oliver S. **ST. JOHN**, of Ridgebury, this day [Sept. 21, 1841], by Rev. Rollin S. Stone	3	111
Ezra D., m. Sarah Mariah **WHITE**, b. of Danbury, Oct. 30, 1832, by Rev. Nicholus White	3	71
Serina, of Danbury, m. Charles F. **THURSTON**, of New York, May 11, 1847, by Rev. Rollin S. Stone	3	162
Susan T., of Danbury, m. John **ABERNETHY**, of Woodbury, this day, Sept. 11, 1845, by Rev. Rollin S. Stone	3	136
BURCH, Silas, of Patterson, N. Y., m. Lucy Maria **SKIDMORE**, of Danbury, this day [Oct. 14, 1840], by Rev. Rollin S. Stone	3	106
BURCHARD, Daniel, [s. Elijah & Ruth], b. Aug. 7, 1781	1	407
Eden, [child of Elijah & Ruth], b. Apr. 4, 1777	1	407
Elijah, m. Ruth **MOREHOUSE**, Dec. 1, 1764	1	407
Elijah, s. [Elijah & Ruth], b. Oct. 9, 1765	1	407
Hannah, [d. Elijah & Ruth], b. May 13, 1767; d. Sept. 5, 1781	1	407
Lydia, [d. Elijah & Ruth], b. May 6, 1771	1	407
Sarah, [d. Elijah & Ruth], b. Dec. 11, 1774; d. Oct. 6, 1775	1	407
BURNS, Levi, Sr., m. Rebecca **BAXTER**, Mar. 20, 1830, by Levi Brunson	3	55
BURR, BURS, Andrew, s. [Oliver & Mary], b. Mar. 23, 1789	1	477
David, of Saugatuck, m. Anna M. **HEACOCK**, of Danbury,		

	Vol.	Page

BURR, BURS, (cont.)

Oct. 5, 1821, by Rev. Oliver Tuttle — 3 — 8

Elisabeth, d. Oliver, m. Joseph Fairchild **WHITE**, June 22, 1790 — 1 — 474

Jacob, of Ridgefield, m. Fanny **BEARDSLEE**, of Redding,
Sept. [ ], 1831, by John Nickerson — 3 — 63

John, s. [Oliver & Mary], d. July 26, 1789, ae 13 y. 20 d.
(drowned at New Haven) — 1 — 477

John, s. [Oliver & Mary], b. Jan. 13, 1791; d. [   ] — 1 — 477

Leander S., m. Esther **WHITLOCK**, Jan. 24, 1830, by Levi
Bronson — 3 — 55

Oliver, s. [Oliver & Mary], b. Mar. 15, 1787 — 1 — 477

Sarah, d. Oliver & Mary, b. Nov. 21, 1784 — 1 — 477

Susanna, d. Oliver, m. Russel **WHITE**, Apr. 4, 1792 — 1 — 458

Willys, of Reading, m. Zuba **MORGAN**, of Danbury, [May] 16,
[1822], by Rev. Daniel Crocker — 3 — 12

BURRIT, BURRET, Aaron, [s. Philip & Rachel], b. Mar. 12, 1781 — 1 — 389

Abijah, [s. Philip & Rachel], b. Feb. 8, 1779 — 1 — 389

Betty, [d. Philip & Rachel], b. Mar. 6, 1777 — 1 — 389

Iaulent, [child of Philip & Rachel], b. Mar. 9, 1783 — 1 — 389

Moses, [s. Philip & Rachel], b. Nov. 1, 1784 — 1 — 389

Philip, m. Rachel **READ**, d. William, Mar. 1, 1774 — 1 — 389

Polly, [d. Philip & Rachel], b. Aug. 16, 1792 — 1 — 389

Rachel, m. Ezra **BENEDICT**, Nov. 30, 1768 ; d. Oct. 15, 1773 — 1 — 480

Read, [s. Philip & Rachel], b. Apr. 16, 1787 — 1 — 389

Sarah, [d. Philip & Rachel], b. Aug. 3, 1789 — 1 — 389

William, s. [Philip & Rachel], b. Jan. 15, 1775 — 1 — 389

BURTON, Hannah, m. Aulbert D. **SLOSON**, Mar. 15, 1840, by
Nathan Burton — 3 — 103

BUSH, Catharine, m. Abraham **GAUL**, Oct. 14, 1827, by John S.
Blackman, J. P. — 3 — 42

BUXTON, Ann, m. Embre A. **STEVENS**, b. of Danbury, Mar. 15,
[1829], by J. Nickerson — 3 — 51

CABLE, John, m. Mary E. **STEPHENS**, Apr. 9, 1851, by Rev. A.
Perkins — 3 — 160

CALHOON, Nancy, d. [Philo & Sarah], b. Feb. 19, 1803 — 1 — 450

Philo, m. Sarah **McLEAN**, Mar. 7, 1802 — 1 — 450

CALVIN, John, m. Olive **BEEBE**, Nov. 2, 1820, by W[illia]m
Andrews — 3 — 3

CAMP, Calvin Brunson, m. Mary Elizabeth **COBURN**, Mar. 18, 1844,
by James Floy — 3 — 125

Daniel, of Brookfield, m. Betsey **STURGES**, of Danbury,
Apr. 4, 1821, by Rev. Benjamin Benham, of New Milford
& Brookfield — 3 — 6

Emma, m. Isaac **BARNUM**, [Apr.] 14, [1830], by Rev. A. Rood — 3 — 55

CANFIELD, C[h]loe, d. Lecretia, b. Feb. 12, 1801 — 1 — 379

Daniel, s. [Samuel & Mehitabel], b. May 17, 1761 — 1 — 499

Lecretia, had d. C[h]loe, b. Feb. 12, 1801 & s. Nathan
Clark **GRIFFEN**, b. May 1, 1804 — 1 — 379

	Vol.	Page

CHAPPELL, CHAPPEL, (cont.)

6, 1825], by Rev. Lemuel B. Hull — 3 30

Sally, m. John McLEAN, Jr., Mar. 26, 1797 — 1 484

William, m. Lilly McLEAN, d. John, Mar. 6, 1793 — 1 384

William Ogden, s. [William & Lilly], b. Oct. 30, 1796 — 1 384

CHASE, Alanson, of Danbury, m. Harriet GRIFFEN, of Redding,
Oct. 12, [1825], by John Nickerson — 3 29

Charles, of New Fairfield, m. Sarah Ann GRIFFIN, of Danbury,
Dec. 9, 1849, by Rev. Geo[rge], H. Deere — 3 145

CHATFIELD, George, of Newtown, m. Mary GRAY, of Danbury,
Nov. 28, 1844, by Thomas T. Guion — 3 132

CHICHESTER, Samuel, m. Fanny SHERMAN, b. of Danbury,
[June], 15, [1838], by J. Shaw — 3 92

CHURCH, Asa, [s. Thomas & Elisabeth], b. Mar. 5, 1770 — 1 439

Charles, of Kent, m. Betsey BARNUM, of Danbury, Dec. 5,
1829, by Nathan Bulkley — 3 54

Daniel, b. Apr. 18, 1707, in Honingtown; m. Eunice WINTER,
of Killingsworth, in the 24th y. of his age; by this marriage
he had 15 children — 1 475

Daniel, m. 2nd w. Elizabeth MYGATT, wid. Joseph, Sept.
[ ], 1751 — 1 475

Daniel, [s. Thomas & Elisabeth], b. Nov. 20, 1767 — 1 439

Elisabeth, [d. Thomas & Elisabeth], b. Jan. 30, 1776 — 1 439

Elizabeth, w. Daniel, d. Oct. 4, 1777 — 1 475

Eunice, w. Daniel, d. [ ], in the 40th y. of her age — 1 475

Thomas, m. Elisabeth [ ], Mar. 1, 1765 — 1 439

Thomas, d. Apr. 6, 1782 — 1 439

W[illia]m, [s. Thomas & Elisabeth], b. May 4, 1774 — 1 439

CLAPP, Edmund B., m. Fanny E. CRAWFORD, Sept. 8, 1847, by
Rev. John Purves, of Bethel — 3 151

John, of Hartford, m. Maria HICKOK, Jan. 1, 1823, by Rev.
I. G. Lowe — 3 14

John, m. Maria HICKOK, b. of Bethel, Jan. 1, 1823, by Rev.
John G. Lowe — 3 23

CLARK, CLARKE, Abigail, d. Sallec P. & Hannah, b. June 20, 1822 — 2 120

Abigail S., m. W[illia]m O. KEELER, b. of Danbury, Apr. 26,
[1843], by Thomas T. Guion — 3 120

Edward, m. Sally Anne BRADLEY, b. of Danbury, Sept. 24,
1848, by Rev. William Biddlee, of Brookfield — 3 143

Elisha, of Farmington, m. [ ]*, May 27, [ ].
*(Faded out) — 1 503

Elizabeth P., of Danbury, m. George R. ROSSITER, of Marietta,
O., Sept. 20, 1849, by Rev. Rollin S. Stone — 3 147

Everit, of Brookfield, m. Ann BARNUM, of Danbury, Feb. 20,
1822, by Abner Brundage — 3 10

Ezra, of Newtown, m. Maria CORIN, of Danbury, Mar. 18,
1840, by James Beebe, J. P. — 3 103

Hannah, m. Eli H. MALLORY, b. of Danbury, Feb. 27, 1837,

	Vol.	Page

CLARK, CLARKE, (cont.)

by Rev. D. H. Short — 3 — 106

Horace, [s. Joseph & Anna], b. May 21, 1792 — 1 — 387

Ithuriel, m. Beulah **BARNUM,** d. Benj[ami]n, June 24, 17[ ]*
  *(Bound in) — 1 — 503

Joseph, m. Anna **STEDMAN,** June 21, 1787 — 1 — 387

Levi, m. Fanny **STEVENS,** b. of Danbury, this day [Oct. 6,
  1824], by Rev. Lemuel B. Hull — 3 — 24

Mariann S., of Danbury, m. Israel W. **ANDREWS,** of
  Marietta, O., this day [Aug. 24, 1842], by Rev. Rollin S.
  Stone — 3 — 116

Olive, d. Capt. James, m. Dr. Joseph **TROWBRIDGE,** Sept.
  [ ], 1791 — 1 — 479

Oliver, of Brookfield, m. Huldah **LACEY,** of Danbury, Jan.
  25, 1821, by Ebenezer Russel White — 3 — 5

Oliver P., m. Sarah **PATCH,** b. of Danbury, Aug. 31, 1837,
  by Rev. Salmon C. Bulkley — 3 — 91

Olivia, m. Thomas **STEVENS,** Feb. 22, 1836*, by Rev. Lemuel
  B. Hull *(First written "1832") — 3 — 83

Peter B., s. S[allec] P., d. Nov. 30, 1822 — 2 — 120

Rufus, s. Timothy, of New Haven, m. Sarah **GLOVER,** d.
  Christopher, of Danbury, Oct. 8, 1797 — 1 — 367

[Rufus], [& w. Sarah], had d. [ ], b. Jan. 19, 1801 — 1 — 367

Sarah H., of Danbury, m. Israel Ward **ANDREWS,** of Marietta,
  O., Aug. 8, 1839, by Rev. Rollin S. Stone — 3 — 99

S[ ]iano, m. Azariel **BOSTWICK,** b. of Danbury, Sept. 30,
  1846, by Nathaniel Bishop — 3 — 140

Sophia, d. [Joseph & Anna], b. June 20, 1788 — 1 — 387

Stedman, [s. Joseph & Anna], b. Feb. 17, 1790 — 1 — 387

William H., m. Julia Maria **ANDREWS,** b. of Danbury, Sept.
  9, 1841, by S. B. Britton — 3 — 112

William Loins, 1st s. [Rufus & Sarah], b. Jan. 29, 1799 — 1 — 367

CLIFFORD, Sarah, m. Ralph **MANSFIELD,** July 3, 1850, by Rev.
  John Purves, of Bethel — 3 — 151

CLINE, Mary, of Philadelphia, m. Hiram **WEED,** of Danbury, Aug.
  29, 1826, by Rev. J. G. Lowe — 3 — 36

CLOSSON, Elisabeth, d. Jonathan, of Stanford, m. Thomas **STARR,**
  Jr., Mar. 27, 1745* *("1745" a correction) — 1 — 436

COAN, Thomas I., of Guilford, m. Betsey **TROWBRIDGE,** Jan. 8,
  [1823], by Rev. J. G. Lowe — 3 — 14

COBURN, Martha, m. David Augustus **AMBLER,** Mar. 18, 1844, by
  James Floy — 3 — 125

Mary Elizabeth, m. Calvin Brunson **CAMP,** Mar. 18, 1844, by
  James Floy — 3 — 125

CODWISE, Elizabeth, d. Capt. George, of New York, b. Aug. 23,
  1762; m. Ezra **STARR,** Apr. 24, 1781 — 1 — 366

COGSWELL, Sarah E., m. Gerrace **HOTCHKISS,** b. of Woodbury,
  Apr. 25, 1848, by Rev. Rollin S. Stone — 3 — 141

Vol.   Page

COLE, [see also COWLES], Esther, of Danbury, m. Garry B.
    NORTON, of Southbury, Nov. 26, 1824, by John Nickerson   3   26
    George, m. Esther Mary SQUIRES, b. of Danbury, Mar. 31,
        1844, by Thomas P. White, J. P.   3   125
    Hiram, m. Catharine Olivia ROBINSON, b. of Danbury, Jan.
        29, 1826, by Rev. Lemuel B. Hull   3   32
    Mary Ann, of Bethel, m. John B. BEACH, of Weston, Nov. 26,
        1845, by Thomas T. Guion   3   137
    Nathan, m. Sarah KINNEY, b. of Danbury, Nov. 20, 1836, by
        Rev. Salmon C. Bulkley   3   89
    Samantha, of Danbury, m. John BEVANS, of Trumbull, Nov.
        19, 1843, by James Floy   3   123
    Sarah, d. Nath[anie]l, of New Milford, m. Daniel PICKET,
        Nov. 25, 1792   1   469
COLEMAN, Amelia, m. Nathan PRICE, Dec. 31, 1844, by Rev. J. K.
    Ingalls   3   131
COLEY, Mary M., m. Matthew W. STARR, Jr., b. of Bethel, Nov.
    4, 1841, by John Greenwood   3   113
COLLAR, Moses J., m. Eunice KEELER, b. of Danbury, Dec. 31,
    1846, by Rev. John Crawford   3   161
COMBS, COMES, Abigale, [d. William & [E]unice], b. Sept. 24,
    1776   1   416
    Clarinda, m. Lemon CURTIS, July 19, [1837], by Jacob Shaw   3   91
    Elemuel, [s. William & [E]unice], b. Oct. 3, 1785   1   416
    Eluid, s. John, b. July 28, 1779; m. Dinah STEVENS, d.
        Jonathan, Nov. [ ], 1799   1   365
    Eluid, s. [John & Mary], b. July 28, 1779   1   502
    [John], m. Mary BROADBROOKS, d. [J]oseph], Mar. 24, 1776   1   502
    John, s. [Eliud & Dinah], b. Sept. 6, 1800   1   365
    John, m. Polly RUSSICO, b. of Danbury, Sept. 13, [1825],
        by John Nickerson   3   29
    Lucy, [d. William & [E]unice], b. Dec. 1, 1778   1   416
    Merry, of Danbury, m. Heman DEPW, of Goshen, Oct. 6, 1834,
        by Orlando Starr   3   81
    Olive, [d. William & [E]unice], b. Jan. 10, 1790   1   416
    Rachel, d. [John & Mary], b. July 29, 1777   1   502
    Sophia, of Danbury, m. Beecher BARNUM, of Kent, Oct. 11,
        1827, by John Nickerson   3   42
    William, [s. William & [E]unice], b. Apr. 10, 1781   1   416
    William, m. [E]unice TOWNER, [ ]   1   416
COMSTOCK, Andrew, m. Mercy STARR, d. Capt. Joseph, May 27,
    1773   1   449
    Andrew, d. Mar. 7, 1789   1   449
    Anson, of New York, m. Almira BARBER, of Danbury, Oct. 8,
        1834, by John Nickerson   3   81
    Betsey, Mrs., d. Sept. 22, 1807   1   484
    Betsey Maria*, [d. Seth & Betsey], b. July 26, 1800
        *("Maria" written over erasure)   1   484

	Vol.	Page
COMSTOCK, (cont.)		
Billy, [s. Andrew & Mercy], b. June 17, 1776	1	449
Daniel, b. Mary 30, 1748; m. Adra **FROST**, d. Jabez, Nov. 15, 1770	1	447
David N., [s. Seth & Betsey], b. Feb. 6, 1804	1	484
Emily, m. Lucius H. **BOUGHTON**, [June] 4, [1833], by Rev. A. Rood	3	75
Evetina, [child of Seth & Betsey], b. Sept. 7, 1796	1	484
Evelina, m. Nathanul M. **URMSTON**, Sept. 28, 1826, by W[illia]m C. Kniffin, M. G.	3	36
Hannah, [d. Seth & Betsey], b. Apr. 8, 1794	1	484
Hannah, [d. Seth & Betsey], d. Sept. [ ], 1805	1	484
Juliana, m. Hezekiah **NICHOLS**, June 7, 1821, by Rev. W[illia]m Andrews	3	7
Mary, of Danbury, m. Charles Gorham, Dr., of Reading, Apr. 4, 1826, by Rev. W[illia]m C. Kniffin	3	32
Mercy Laurana, [d. Andrew & Mercy], b. Aug. 25, 1787	1	449
Polly, d. [Daniel & Adra], b. Aug. 3, 1771; d. Dec. 13, 1774	1	447
Polly, [d. Andrew & Mercy], b. June 18, 1774; d. July 18, 1775	1	449
Polly, [d. Andrew & Mercy], b. June 19, 1778	1	449
Rebecca, [d. Andrew & Mercy], b. Sept. 2, 1784	1	449
Sarah, m. Noah **HOYT**, Oct. 30, 1760	1	417
Sarah W., [w. W[illia]m P.], d. Nov. 11, 1838	2	65
Sarah W., d. Nov. 11, 1838	2	65
Seth, b. Jan. 21, 1772; m. Betsey **GREGORY**, Sept. 15, 1793	1	484
Seth, m. Rebecca **TAYLOR**, Oct. 23, 1822, by Rev. W[illia]m Andrews	3	13
William King, [s. Daniel & Adra], b. Dec. 2, 1772	1	447
W[illia]m P., b. Feb. 23, 1808; m. Sarah W. **STARR**, Nov. 26, 1833	2	65
William P., [s. Seth & Betsey], b. Feb. 23, 1808	1	484
CONDIT, Rob[er]t W., Rev., m. Harriet **WHITTLESEY**, Dec. 21, 1820, by W[illia]m Andrews	3	5
CONGAR, Maria, of Brookfield, m. Bennett **ROSWELL**, of Southbury, [, 1830 (?)], by Levi Osborn	3	57
CONGO, Sally, of New Milford, m. Uz **WILDMAN**, of Danbury, Oct. 23, 1828, by John Nickerson	3	49
CONNOR, Elizabeth, m. John **BALLEY**, [ ] 25, [1851], by Rev. Michael O'Farrell	3	159
CONVERSE, Elijah, s. Demmon R. & Sarah, b. Aug. 16, 1789	1	369
Joseph, of Norwalk, m. Nancy C. **BARNUM**, of Danbury, Jan. 1, 1826, by Nathan Bulkley	3	31
COOKE, Abigail, d. [Sam[ue]l & Rebecca], b. Nov. 13, 1779	1	496
Amos Shove, s. [Joseph P. Jr., & Annis], b. Dec. 1, 1810	1	487
Anna, d. [Sam[ue]l & Rebecca], b. Mar. 10, 1790	1	496
Annis, w. [Joseph P., Jr.], d. Feb. 5, 1813	1	487
Betsey, 2nd w. of Ebenezer Booth **WHITE**, b. Dec. 30, 1779	1	474
Betsey, d. William, m. Ebenezer Booth **WHITE**, Aug. 24, 1800	1	474

	Vol.	Page
COOKE, (cont.)		
Catharine, d. [Thomas & Catharine], b. May 13, 1790;		
d. May 17, 1791	1	477
Catharine, w. Thomas, d. June 18, 1790	1	477
Catherine, d. [Joseph P. Jr. & Annis], b. Dec. 21, 1791	1	487
Catharine, d. [Joseph P. Jr. & Annis], d. Jan. 24, 1824	1	487
E. W., Rev. of Haddam, m. Martha M. SMITH, of Danbury,		
June 2, 1847, by Rev. Rollin S. Stone	3	162
Elisabeth, d. Col. Joseph P., m. Capt. Timothy TAYLOR,		
Dec. 12, 1784	1	493
Elisabeth, d. [Joseph P. Jr. & Annis], b. Mar. 13, 1789	1	487
Elizabeth, d. [Joseph P., Jr. & Annis], d. Oct. 24, 1803	1	487
Horace, s. [Joseph P. Jr. & Annis], b. Sept. 7, 1786	1	487
Horace, d. Feb. 7, 1837	2	119
Horace Davis, s. Horace, b. Oct. 12, 1820	2	119
James H., m. Hannah P. HATCH, Apr. 8, 1823, by Rev.		
W[illia]m Andrews	3	16
Joseph P. Jr., m. Annis STARR, d. Capt. Thomas, Sept. 16, 1785	1	487
Joseph P. Jr., m. 2nd w. wid. Hannah BISHOP, June 8, 1814	1	487
Joseph Platt, s. [Joseph P. Jr. & Annis], b. July 3, 1794;		
d. Jan. 9, 1797	1	487
Joseph Platt, 2nd, [s. Joseph P. Jr. & Annis], b. July 30,		
1800; d. Dec. 3, 1802	1	487
Mary, d. [Joseph P. Jr. & Annis], b. Nov. 11, 1797	1	487
Mary E., m. Timothy B. KEELER, Oct. 2, 1822, by Rev.		
William Andrews	3	12
Mary Esther, m. Elisha W. HUBBELL, b. of Norwalk, this		
day, [Oct. 4, 1840], by S. H. Clark	3	105
Polly, d. [Thomas & Catharine], b. Feb. 11, 1783	1	477
Rebeccah, d. [Sam[ue]l & Rebecca], b. May 26, 1785	1	496
Rebecca, m. James WAKELEY, Feb. 10, 1805	2	61
Sam[ue]l, m. Rebecca DICKINSON, d. Dr. Sam[ue]l, Dec.		
[ ], 1778	1	496
Sarah, d. [Joseph P. Jr. & Annis], b. Jan. 26, 1805	1	487
Sarah, wid. Joseph P., d. Oct. 31, 1822	2	180
Sarah A., m. Rev. Chancy WILCOX, [Dec.] 8, [1831], by Rev.		
A. Rood	3	68
Thomas, s. [Thomas & Catharine], b. Aug. 4, 1735*		
*(Probably "1785")	1	477
Thomas, m. Catharine DIBBLE, d. Daniel, Oct. 24, 1782	1	477
Thomas, m. 2nd w. Betty HOYT, d. Capt. Elijah, Jan. 11, 1792	1	477
CORBIN, Eunice, of Danbury, m. John ALLIN, of Fairfield, July		
12, 1799	1	370
Hannah, d. Philip, b. June 21, 1771	1	439
Hannah, d. Philip, decd., m. Matthew CROFUT,Jr., Dec. 6, 1795	1	380
Sarah, d. Philip, decd., m. Sam[uel]ll JINNINS, Feb. 3, 1793	1	379
Tamezin, m. Nathan GREGORY, Jr., Mar. 27, 1782	1	428
CORIN, Maria, of Danbury, m. Ezra CLARK, of Newtown, Mar. 18,		

Vol. Page

CRAFTS, CRAFTE, (cont.)
    by James Beebe, J. P.   3   95
CRAIGE, Grisorl, d. [Robert & Elizabeth], b. Sept. 26, 1794   1   376
    Robert, m. Elizabeth **GUTHRIE,** Dec. 1, 1793   1   376
CRANE, George P., of New York, m. Anne Jenette **SMITH,** of
    Bethel, Mar. 16, 1846, by Rev. Lent S. Hough   3   139
CRARY, Esther, [d. James & Esther], b. June 20, 1784   1   437
    Esther, w. [James], d. Sept. 8, 1784   1   437
    Hannah, [d. James & Esther], b. June 1, 1778   1   437
    James, m. Esther **STONE,** d. W[illia]m, June 24, 1769   1   437
    James, m. 2nd w. Rachel **ROBERTS,** d. Comfor[t] **RAIMOND,**
    Dec. 28, 1786   1   437
    James, [s. James & Rachel], b. Sept. 13, 1787   1   437
    Mary, [d. James & Esther], b. Mar. 5, 1773   1   437
    Phebe, [d. James & Esther], b. June 18, 1775   1   437
    Raymond, [s. James & Rachel], b. Mar. 9, 1790   1   437
    Sally, m. Thaddeus **BRONSON,** Dec. 15, 1823, by Levi Bronson   3   20
CRAWFORD, [see also **CROFUT**], Fanny, m. George **PECK,** this
    day [Feb. 4, 1824], by Rev. Lemuel B. Hull   3   21
    Fanny E., m. Edmund B. **CLAPP,** Sept. 8, 1847, by Rev. John
    Purves, of Bethel   3   151
    Sarah J., of Danbury, m. George S. **HARE,** of Milford, Sept. 1,
    1847, by Rev. John Crawford   3   164
CROCKER, William A., m. Mary **MONTGOMERY,** this day [Nov.
    3, 1834], by James H. Linsley   3   82
CROFUT, CROFUTT, CRAWFAUT, [see also **CRAWFORD**],
    Abel, s. [Levi & Sukey], b. Feb. 19, 1791   1   468
    Abigail, d. [Matthew, Jr. & Hannah], b. July 27, 1796   1   380
    Abigail, of Danbury, m. Truman Bennet **JUDSON,** of Newtown,
    Feb. 24, 1828, by John G. Lowe   3   45
    Anna, [d. Ezra & Anna], b. Sept. 4, 1790   1   422
    Anna U., m. Burr **ROWLAND,** Aug. 24, 1842, by Lucius
    Atwater   3   120
    Aurila, of Newtown, m. Ezra **PLATT,** of Danbury, July 9,
    [1824], by Rev. John G. Lowe   3   22
    Benjamin, b. Mar. 24, 1750; m. Abigail **WOOD,** d. Sam[ue]l,
    Mar. 24, 1773   1   486
    Benjamin, s. [Benjamin & Abigail], b. June 15, 1789   1   486
    Benjamin, m. Esther **PICKETT,** b. of Danbury, Jan. 14, 1844,
    by James Floy   3   123
    Bennit, s. [Samuel, Jr. & Susanna], b. Sept. 15*, 1791;
    d. Dec. 4, 1793 *(Date written after erasure)   1   431
    Bennit, 2nd, s. [Samuel, Jr. & Susanna], b. Dec. 11, 1795   1   431
    Cloa, [d. Samuel & Sarah], b. Apr. 7, 1773; d. Jan. 13, 1788   1   431
    Chloe, d. [Samuel, Jr. & Susanna], b. Oct. 27, 1792   1   431
    Comfort, [child of Seth & Sarah], b. June 29, 1783   1   428
    Daniel, m. Eliza D. **REED,** b. of Danbury, Jan. 23, 1843,
    by Israel A. Beardslee, J. P.   3   119

	Vol.	Page

CROFUT, CROFUTT, CRAWFAUT, (cont.)

Eben, of Danbury, m. Fanny **PLATT**, of Reading, Feb. 19, 1826,
by [   ]   3   35

Ebenezer, of Danbury, m. Fanny **PLATT**, of Redding, Mar. 18,
1826, by Rev. John G. Lowe   3   38

Eli, [s. Ezra & Anna], b. Dec. 27, 1783   1   422

Elijah, s. [Benjamin & Abigail], b. Dec. 20, 1773   1   486

Eliza, of Danbury, m. Ezra Wheeler **DIBBLE**, of Brookfield,
this day [Nov. 9, 1825], by Rev. Lemuel B. Hull   3   30

Elizabeth, d. Mathew, m. [John] **STONE**, Apr*. 19, 1770
*(Crossed out)   1   505

Elizabeth, b. Aug. 25, 1773   1   490

Elisabeth, d. [Josiah & Rebecca], b. July 4, 1790   1   430

Elizabeth, m. Lewis **BENEDICT**, Dec. 22, 1796   1   490

Ephraim, of Middletown, m. Lois **ROBBINSON**, of Danbury,
Nov. 25, 1779   1   503

Eri, of Danbury, m. Betsey **DAVARIN**, of Reading, Nov. 29,
1798   1   378

Ery, [child of Samuel & Sarah], b. May 28, 1778   1   431

Eunice, [d. Samuel & Sarah], b. Aug. 22, 1775; d. Aug. 16, 1788   1   431

Eunice, [d. Seth & Sarah], b. Dec. 5, 1785   1   428

Eunice, d. [Samuel, Jr. & Susanna], b. May 11, 1794   1   431

Ezra, m. Anna **BROOKS**, Feb. 17, 1781   1   422

Frederick, of Redding, m. Jerusha **MORGAN**, of Danbury,
Apr. 22, 1822, Phineas Taylor, J. P.   3   11

George J., m. Mary **BARTRAM**, b. of Danbury, this day [Nov.
25, 1841], by Rev. S. H. Clark   3   113

George S., of Bethel, m. Mary Ann **FOSTER**, of Redding, June
6, 1847, by Rev. I. D. Marshall, of Redding   3   141

Hannah, [d. Ezra & Anna], b. Nov. 22, 1792   1   422

Hannah, m. Zalmon **SHERMAN**, b. of Danbury, Aug. 19, 1821,
by Zach Clark, Jr. J. P.   3   7

Hannah, Mrs. of Danbury, m. Abijah **ABOT**, of Ridgebury,
Mar. 26, 1823, by Rev. Oliver Tuttle   3   16

Henry, m. Sarah Maria **BEVANS**, b. of Danbury, this day,
[May 4, 1841], by S. H. Clark   3   109

Hiram, s. [Samuel, Jr. & Susanna], b. July 3, 1797   1   431

Horrace(?), m. Phebe Maria **SCOFIELD**, b. of Danbury, Aug.
23, 1846, by R. K. Bellamye   3   140

Hulda, [d. Josiah & Rebecca], b. Sept. 24, 1792   1   430

Ira, s. [Mathew, Jr. & Sarah], b. Sept. 16, 1778   1   488

James H., m. Mary **MORRIS**, Jan. 14, 1824, by George
Benedict, Jr.   3   21

James Seely, s. [Seely & Hannah], b. Mar. 11, 1791   1   431

Jane E., m. W[illia]m E. **HITCHCOCK**, b. of Danbury, Nov.
23, 1831, by Rev. James Young   3   65

Jane Elizabeth, m. Ethel Augustus **BEEBE**, b. of Danbury,
Oct. 19, 1837, by Rev. D. H. Short   3   106

Vol. Page

CROFUT, CROFUTT, CRAWFAUT, (cont.)

Jerusha, [d. Ezra & Anna], b. Mar. 13, 1788   1   422

Jerusha, m. Charles **PECK,** b. of Danbury, Jan. 26, 1828,
by John G. Lowe   3   45

Jesse, s. [Seth & Sarah], b. Nov. 19, 1781   1   428

Jesse, s. [Levi & Sukey], b. Apr. 24, 1793   1   468

Jonathan, m. Lucy **BENEDICT,** Apr. 13, 1826, by George
Benedict   3   32

Joseph, Jr., of Danbury, m. Charlotte **WEED,** of Ridgebury,
[July] 5, [1835], by Rev. Orson Spencer   3   83

Josiah, m. Rebecca **GREGORY,** d. Daniel, Mar. 25, 1790   1   430

Laura, of Danbury, m. Josiah **LAUTON,** of Brookfield, Feb.
19, 1832, by Levi Brunson   3   68

Levi, s. [Matthew, Jr. & Sarah], b. Apr. 25, 1768   1   488

Levi, m. Sukey **BEERS*,** Dec. 31, 1789   *(Erasure with name
written in)   1   468

Lois, d. [Levi & Sukey], b. Dec. 16, 1794   1   468

Lois, d. [Eri & Betsey], b. July 31, 1799   1   378

Lucy, [d. Seth & Sarah], b. Nov. 9, 1779   1   428

Lucy, d. [Samuel, Jr. & Susanna], b. Nov. 26, 1801   1   431

Lucy, of Danbury, m. James **MILLER,** of Roxbury, [Oct.] 15,
[1826], by John Nickerson   3   36

Luzon, of Newtown, m. Calister **HOYT,** of Danbury, Dec. 4,
1821, by Medad Rogers   3   9

Lydia, m. Stephen **TROWBRIDGE,** May 27, 174[ ]   1   466

Lydia, d. [Matthew, Jr. & Sarah], b. Aug. 13, 1775;
d. Aug. 8, 1798   1   488

Lydia, d. [Matthew, Jr. & Hannah], b. Aug. 21, 1798   1   380

Lydia, mother of Lydia **TROWBRIDGE,** w. of Stephen, b. Nov.
1, 1701; d. Feb. 24, 1799   1   466

Lydia, m. Charles **COUCH,** b. of Danbury, May 15, 1828, by
John Nickerson   3   47

Lyman, s. [Levi & Sukey], b. Apr. 24, 1797   1   468

Madison, s. [Samuel, Jr. & Susanna], b. Sept. 25, 1809   1   431

Mary, d. [Benjamin & Abigail], b. Apr. 13, 1779   1   486

Mary A., m. Zadoc B. **STONE,** May 2, 1849, by Rev. A. Perkins   3   160

Mary Ann, of Danbury, m. Henry D. **WHEELER,** of Wilton,
Nov. 7, 1838, by Rev. D. H. Short   3   107

Mary W., m. Eli W. **STONE,** b. of Bethel, Feb. 23, 1842,
by J. Greenwood   3   114

Matthew, Jr., m. Sarah **BUCK,** d. Ezekiel, of New Milford,
Dec. 25, 1765   1   488

Matthew, s. [Matthew, Jr. & Sarah], b. Nov. 15, 1773   1   488

Mathew, f. Benjamin, d. Sept. 23, 1782, ae 71 y. 8 m. 2 d.   1   486

Matthew, Jr., m. Hannah **CORBIN,** d. Philip, decd., Dec. 6, 1795   1   380

Nanna, d. [Samuel, Jr. & Susanna], b. Jan. 4, 1807   1   431

Paulina, m. Ezra Hoyt **AMBLER,** June 6, 1821, by Rev.
W[illia]m Andrews   3   7

	Vol.	Page

CROFUT, CROFUTT, CRAWFAUT, (cont.)

Phebe Gregory, m. Isaac M. LOCKWOOD, Feb. 16, 1834, at
the home of Hoyt Gregory, by Rev. John D. Smith — 3 — 79

Plebeann, [child of Samuel, Jr. & Susanna], b. Aug. 19, 1803 — 1 — 431

Pollina, d. [Eri & Betsey], b. Mar. 17, 1801 — 1 — 378

Preston, m. Sally Ann JUDSON, May 31, 1829, by Rev. A. Rood — 3 — 52

Rachel, d. [Benjamin & Abigail], b. Apr. 19, 1784 — 1 — 486

Rachel, d. Benjamin, m. Levi WEED, s. Asa, b. of Danbury,
Apr. 12*, 1803 *(13th?) — 1 — 357

Rebecah, d. [Matthew, Jr. & Sarah], b. Mar. 19, 1772 — 1 — 488

Rebecca, of Danbury, m. Isaac LAKE, of Newtown, this day
[May 30, 1830], by Rev. Lemuel B. Hull — 3 — 56

Russel, s. [Samuel, Jr. & Susanna], b. May 18, 1800 — 1 — 431

Ruth, d. [Matthew, Jr. & Sarah], b. Sept. 29, 1786 — 1 — 488

Ruth, [d. Matthew, Jr. & Sarah], d. May 2, 1774 — 1 — 488

Ruth, m. Burritt JENNINGS, Nov. 26, 1790 — 1 — 382

Sally, [d. Seth & Sarah], b. Sept. 24, 1790 — 1 — 428

Sally, m. Fairchild AMBLER, Nov. 11, 1810 — 2 — 175

Sally, of Danbury, m. Justice PERRY, of Brookfield, Oct.
6, 1844, by Elder E. M. Jackson — 3 — 128

Sally Maria, m. James HUNT, b. of Bethel, July 11, 1841,
by John Greenwood — 3 — 110

Samuel, m. Sarah CROFUT, May 28, 1767 — 1 — 431

Samuel, [s. Samuel & Sarah], b. Dec. 4, 1770 — 1 — 431

Samuel, m. Abigail SEELY, Aug. 2, 1781 — 1 — 431

Samuel, Jr., m. Susanna SUMMERS, Feb. 17, 1791* *(Date
written after erasure) — 1 — 431

Samuel, [twin with Susanna, s. Samuel, Jr. & Susanna], b.
Feb. 29, 1812 — 1 — 431

Sam[ue]l Wood, s. [Benjamin & Abigail], b. Oct. 27, 1776 — 1 — 486

Sarah, m. Samuel CROFUT, May 28, 1767 — 1 — 431

Sarah, d. [Matthew, Jr. & Sarah], b. Nov. 28, 1769 — 1 — 488

[Sarah, w. Samuel], d. Nov. 28, 1780 — 1 — 431

Sarah, w. [Matthew, Jr.], d. Oct. 20, 1805 — 1 — 488

Sarah, of Danbury, m. John SKIDMORE, of Newtown, this day,
[Mar. 27, 1827], by Rev. Lemuel B. Hull — 3 — 40

Seely, [s. Samuel & Sarah], b. Mar. 13, 1768 — 1 — 431

Seely, m. Hannah HOLCOMB, of Berkhempstead, Apr. 12, 1790 — 1 — 431

Seth, m. Sarah PECK, Oct. 14, 1778* *(Corrected from
"1788") — 1 — 428

Seth, [s. Seth & Sarah], b. Apr. 11, 1788 — 1 — 428

Sophia, Mrs., m. Daniel ODELL, b. of Bethel, this day [Mar. 14,
1841], by Rev. S. H. Clark — 3 — 109

Summers, s. [Samuel, Jr. & Susanna], b. Dec. 28, 1798 — 1 — 431

Susanna, [twin with Samuel, d. Samuel, Jr. & Susanna], b.
Feb. 29, 1812 — 1 — 431

Thankful, [d. Ezra & Anna], b. Dec. 6, 1785 — 1 — 422

Thomas, m. Abigael PECK, b. of Danbury, Jan. 8, 1834,

Vol. Page

CROFUT, CROFUTT, CRAWFAUT, (cont.)

by John Nickerson 3 79

William, of Dover, Dutchess Co., N. Y., m. Loisa **PEIRCE,**
of Danbury, Aug. 3, [1834], by Elias Birchard, J. P. 3 80

William E., of Redding, m. Mary E. **WOOD,** of Danbury, Nov.
5, 1845, by Rev. William F. Collins 3 136

CROSBY, [see also **CROSLY**], Eliza, of Danbury, m. Philander R.
JARVIS, of New Milford, this day [Apr. 11, 1843], by Rev.
Rollin S. Stone 3 119

Jerusha, b. June 29, 1754; m. Eleazer **BENEDICT,** Apr. 24, 1777 1 504

Judah P., m. Catharine **STEVENS,** b. of Danbury, Feb. 27,
1839, by Rev. Rollin S. Stone 3 96

Phineas D., m. Rebecca E. **NICHOLS,** b. of Danbury, this day
[Sept. 1, 1840], by Rev. Rollin S. Stone 3 105

CROSLY*, [see also **CROSBY**], Maria, m. W[illia]m **SMITH,** Nov.
28, 1849, by Rev. A. Perkins   *(CROSBY?) 3 160

CROSSMAN, Mary, m. Jairus L. **STEWART,** [Nov.] 17*, [1830], by
Rev. A. Rood *(Possibly [Dec.] 7) 3 59

CUMMINS, Lucy, m. Charles **DIXON,** Sept. 11, 1791 1 384

CUNTAG*, Betsey, m. Cornelius **GUINEE,** Aug. 11, 1844, by R. K.
Bellamy *("t" inserted in pencil) 3 127

CURTIS, CURTISS, Abigail, m. Noah **HOYT,** Jan. 8, 1760;
d. May 20, 1760 1 417

Abigail, [d. Stephen & Esther], b. Apr. 10, 1763 1 429

Abigail, d. Stephen, m. Josiah **BARNUM,** Mar. 4, 1779 1 425

Abigail, d. [Asa & Elisabeth], b. June* 21, 1780
*(First written "July") 1 448

Abner, s. [Reuben & Silence], b. Dec. 15, 1776 1 149

Abner, s. Ruben & Silence, m. Mary **OSBORN,** d. Moses &
Sarah, Nov. 20, 1796 1 419

Abner & w. Mary, had d. [   ], b. Dec. 13, 1797 1 419

Allen, [s. Reuben & Silence], b. [ ]; d. [   ] 1 419

Asa, m. Elisabeth **MUNSON,** d. Ebenezer, June 7, 1775 1 448

Asa, s. [Asa & Elisabeth], b. Feb. 24, 1776 1 448

Betsey, d. [Eliphalet & Elizabeth Deborah], b. Jan. 29, 1792 1 468

Betty, d. [Samuel & Sarah], b. June 16, 1764 1 455

Betty, d. Samuel, m. Ephraim **BENEDICT,** Sept. 30, 1784 1 478

Betey, [d. Asa & Elisabeth], b. Jan. 5, 1791 1 448

Caroline, of Danbury, m. Edmund **PULFORD,** of New Town,
Aug. 13, 1837, by Oliver Shepard, J. P. 3 91

Cezar, m. Mary **WILLY,** Dec. 25, 1821, by Rev. Oliver Tuttle 3 10

David, [twin with Phebe, s. Reuben & Silence], b. Dec. 31, 1786 1 419

David, m. Annis **BARNUM,** b. of Danbury, [Oct.] 12, 1828],
by Rev. Thomas Robbins 3 49

Edmon, of Danbury, m. Sally Ann **LEWIS,** of New Milford,
Aug. 9, 1842, by James Beebe, J. P. 3 116

Eliphalet, [s. Stephen & Esther], b. Oct. 3, 1768 1 429

Eliphalet*, m. Elizabeth Deborah **WHITLOCK,** d. Abraham,

	Vol.	Page
CURTIS, CURTISS, (cont.)		
of Ridgefield, Aug. 5, 1790 *(Word crossed out)	1	468
Hannah, [d. Reuben & Silence], b. June 28, 1792	1	419
Hannah, m. Benjamin **LOBDELL**, b. of Danbury, Dec. 30, 1832, by John Nickerson	3	72
Jesse, s. [Asa & Elisabeth], b. Feb. 17, 1778	1	448
Joseph, [s. Reuben & Silence], b. Feb. 3, 1781; d. Feb. 12, 1781	1	419
Joseph, 2nd, [s. Reuben & Silence], b. Sept. 19, 1782	1	419
Joshua, [s. Asa & Elisabeth], b. July 28, 1782	1	448
Julia, m. Major **WOOD**, b. of Danbury, Nov. 6, 1842, by James Beebe, J. P.	3	117
Keziah, of Sharon, m. John **GREGORY**, Nov. 22, 1763	1	420
Lemon, m. Clarinda **COMES**, July 19, [1837], by Jacob Shaw	3	91
Lucy, m. Augustus **TAYLOR**, b. of Danbury, Oct. 31, 1827, by John G. Lowe	3	44
Martha, [d. Stephen & Esther], b. Sept. 18, 1776	1	429
Mary, [d. Stephen & Esther], b. July 24, 1771	1	429
Mary, [d. Reuben & Silence], b. Sept. 4, 1790	1	419
Mary, m. Zadock B. **STONE**, b. of Danbury, Jan. 3, 1829, by John Nickerson	3	50
Matthew, [s. Reuben & Silence], b. Sept. 9, 1784	1	419
Nabbe, [d. Reuben & Silence], b. Nov. 1, 1778	1	419
Noah, [s. Stephen & Esther], b. Apr. 17, 1774	1	429
Phebe, [twin with David, d. Reuben & Silence], b. Dec. 31, 1786	1	419
Phinehas, [s. Stephen & Esther], b. Jan. 5, 1783	1	429
Polly, m. Prosper **PRATT**, Aug. 13, 1820, by W[illia]m Andrews	3	2
Rebec[c]a, [d. Stephen & Esther], b. Jan. 17, 1765; d. Aug. 11, 1769	1	429
Reuben, m. Silence **ALLEN**, Oct. 4, 1775	1	419
R[e]uben, [s. Reuben & Silence], b. [ ]; d. [ ]	1	419
Reuben Judson, [twin with Silene White, s. Reuben & Silence], b. Mar. 11, 1797	1	419
Ruth, [d. Asa & Elisabeth], b. May 23, 1784	1	448
Ruth, [w. Stephen], d. Apr. 26, 1798	1	455
Ruth, m. Joseph **ROBINSON**, Mar. 23, 1803; d. Aug. 4, 1824	2	179
Samuel, m. Sarah **BARBER**, d. John, June 20, 1753	1	455
Sam[ue]l, s. [Samuel & Sarah], b. Dec. 16, 1762	1	455
Sarah, [d. Samuel & Sarah], b. Dec. 2, 1769	1	455
Sarah, d. Samuel, m. Meneah **PORTER**, June 1, 1789	1	478
Silene White, [twin with Reuben Judson, d. Reuben & Silence], b. Mar. 11, 1797	1	419
Stephen, m. Esther **PECK**, Apr. 2, 1760	1	429
Stephen, [s. Stephen & Esther], b. May 29, 1780	1	429
Stephen, [s. Samuel & Sarah], b. Sept. 30, 1787	1	455
Stephen, m. Ruth **HOYT**, d. Caleb, Dec. 4, 1787	1	455
Stephen, m. Lois **WOOD**, d. James, May 27, 1798	1	455
Stephen, d. Mar. 1, 1799	1	455

Vol.   Page

CURTIS, CURTISS, (cont.)

Thomas, [s. Reuben & Silence], b. Oct. 31, 1788   1   419

Thomas Gould, [s. Asa & Elisabeth], b. June 15, 1786   1   448

Walter Munson, [s. Asa & Elisabeth], b. June 14, 1789   1   448

CUSHING, Milton F., b. Sept. 7, 1787; m. Fanny **NICHOLS,** Sept.
26, 1807   1   429

DAILEY, Isaac, of Sherman, m. Lucy **GRIFFIN,** of Danbury,
yesterday, [Mar. 1, 1846], by Rev. Rollin S. Stone   3   139

DALLORY, Thomas, of Woodbury, m. Eliza **BANJAMIN,** of Bethel,
June 15, 1842, by J. Greenwood   3   115

DANN, DAN, Anne, [d. Isaac], b. Aug. 27, 1759   1   412

Edward, m. Amarillis **GALE,** b. of Danbury, Jan. 13, 1850,
by Rev. John S. Whittlesey   3   146

Esther, [d. Isaac], b. Dec. 12, 1755   1   412

Harriet E., m. Delos **GREGORY,** Nov. 13, [1844], by R. K.
Bellamy   3   130

Harriette E., m. Augustus H. **ABBOTT,** July 24, 1849, by Rev.
A. Perkins   3   160

Henry S., m. Achsah **WOOD,** Feb. 10, 1828, by Levi Brunson   3   46

Isaac, m. May 13, 1752   1   412

Isaac, [s. Isaac], b. July 20, 1765   1   412

John, m. Elisabeth **TAYLOR,** Nov. 5, 1828, by Nathan Burton   3   50

Mary, [d. Isaac], b. May 6, 1756   1   412

Puter, [child of Isaac], b. Apr. 7, 1769   1   412

Sarah, [d. Isaac], b. Dec. 30, 1752   1   412

DART, John H., m. Ann L. **BEEBE,** Nov. 3, 1842, by Rev. Thomas
T. Guion   3   117

Lodowick, m. Sally **MORGAN,** b. of Danbury, Dec. 31, 1820,
by Phineas Taylor, J. P.   3   4

Lucy A., of Bethel, m. Henry B. **MEEKER,** of Reading, Dec.
23, 1840, by J. Greenwood. Int. Pub.   3   108

Mary, m. Harry **HOYT,** Dec. 25, 1833, at the house of Charles
Dart, by Rev. John D. Smith   3   77

Susan M., of Redding, m. Ethel B. **SHERMAN,** of Bethel, Nov.
23, 1845, by Thomas T. Guion   3   137

DAVARIN, Betsey, of Reading, m. Eri **CROFUT,** of Danbury, Nov.
29, 1798   1   378

DAVIS, Abigail, m. James **TROWBRIDGE,** Jan. 1, 1771   1   421

Deborah Ann, of Mill Plain, m. George **BATES,** of Danbury,
Dec. 30, 1849, by Rev. George H. Deere   3   145

Lucy, m. Zar **DIBBLE,** Sept. 14, 1785* *("5" indistinct)   1   450

William, of New York, m. Julia **STURGES,** of Danbury, Nov.
19, 1833, by John Nickerson   3   77

DEACON*, George, m. Mary **HAWLEY,** b. of Danbury, this day
[Dec. 8, 1833], by Levi Osborn *(Or **DEAVON**")   3   78

DEAN, [see also **DEERE**], Jeremiah, m. Ann* **WICKSON,** b. of
Bethel, May 15, 1831, by Rev. Erastus Cole *(Possibly
"Ame")   3   62

	Vol.	Page
DEAVON, George, see George **DEACON**	3	78
DECKERMAN, [see also **DIKEMAN**], Anne, d. [Thomas & Sarah],		
b. Apr. 12, 1795	1	467
Hannah, d. [Thomas & Sarah], b. Aug. 28, 1798	1	467
Joseph, s. [Thomas & Sarah], b. Dec. 14, 1796	1	467
Polly, d. [Thomas & Sarah], b. Oct. 22, 1790	1	467
Salomy, d. [Thomas & Sarah], b. Aug. 28, 1792	1	467
Thomas, m. Sarah **WASHBORN**, d. Joseph, Mar. 23, 1790	1	467
DEERE, [see also **DEAN**], Alvira Jane, m. Charles **WHITE**, May 27,		
1850, by George H. Deere	3	148
George H., Rev., m. Louisa **DOWNING**, Dec. 24, 1850, by Rev.		
Henry Lyon	3	153
DeFOREST, James, of Woodbury, m. Polly **BEEBE**, of Danbury,		
[June] 4, [1828], by Rev. Thomas Robbins	3	47
Mary Ann, m. David **KEYS**, b. of Danbury, this day [June 14,		
1842], by Rev. Rollin S. Stone	3	116
Sabra, d. Thaddeus **MEAD**, m. John **TAYLOR**, Mar. 24, 1790	1	438
DeLAVAN, DELEVAN, Betsey, m. Elisha C. **STEVENS**, b. of		
Danbury, Oct. 30, 1831, by Elias Birchard, J. P.	3	65
George, of Danbury, m. Elizabeth **HODGE**, of New Fairfield,		
Oct. 26, 1827, by John Nickerson	3	42
DELLICOR, Leonard N., of New York, m. Julia E. **WILDMAN**, of		
Danbury, this day [Nov. 7, 1842], by Rev. Rollin S. Stone	3	118
DEMING, Minor R., of Cincinnati, O., m. Abigail **BARNUM**, of		
Danbury, Aug. 2, 1836, by Rev. Jonathan G. Collom	3	85
DEMON, Ann, m. Samuel **JUDD**, 2nd, b. of Danbury, this day [Oct.		
22, 1826], by Rev. Lemuel B. Hull	3	36
DENBY, Richard, m. Mary **PATCHEN**, b. of Danbury, Jan. 20, 1843,		
by James Floy	3	118
DENTON, Gilbert, m. Susan M. **JENNINGS**, b. of Danbury, May 30,		
1841, by Addison Parker	3	109
DEPW, Heman, of Goshen, m. Merry **COMES**, of Danbury, Oct. 6,		
1834, by Orlando Starr	3	81
DIBBLE, Abigail, d. [Nathan & Abigail], b. Jan. 9, 1765	1	495
Abigail, [d. Ezra & Griswould], b. Mar. 31, 1782; d. July 7, 1789	1	418
Adah, [d. Samuel & Phebe], b. Nov. 13, 1779	1	464
Ame, d. [Thomas & Hannah], b. Nov. 5, 1782	1	469
Amerillas, d. Daniel, b. Dec. 23, 1763; m. Moses **HOYT**, s.		
Noah, Dec. 13, 1784	1	368
Amme, d. [Nathan & Abigail], b. June 28, 1782	1	495
Betsey, d. [Nathan & Abigail], b. Aug. 6, 1772; d. July 25, 1773	1	495
Betsey, 2nd, d. [Nathan & Abigail], b. June 10, 1773	1	495
Betsey, d. [Zar & Lucy], b. July 21, 1787; d. Jan. 5, 1790	1	450
Catharine, d. Daniel, m. Thomas **COOKE**, Oct. 24, 1782	1	477
Catha[rine], wid. Nehemiah, m. Thaddeus **BENEDICT**, Nov. [ ]	1	498
Daniel S., m. Mary **PLATT**, b. of Bethel, Dec. 16, 1830, by		
Rev. Erastus Cole	3	59
Deborah, m. David **BENEDICT**, Oct. 17, 1782	1	414

	Vol.	Vol.
DIBBLE, (cont.)		
Edwin, m. Elizabeth **WARNER,** Oct. 4, 1843, by Rev. William R. Webb	3	124
Eleazer, s. [Thomas & Hannah], b. Apr. 13, 1792	1	469
Eli, s. [Nathan & Abigail], b. Nov. 17, 1757	1	495
Eli, m. Rachel **LOCKWOOD,** Mar. 25, 1779	1	455
Eli Lockwood, [s. Eli & Rachel], b. Aug. 1, 1785	1	455
Ezra, m. Griswould **FROST,** Oct. 31, 1771	1	418
Ezra, s. [Ezra & Griswould], b. Feb. 3, 1775; d. [ ]* 28, Sept., 1796 *("July 1" crossed out)	1	418
Ezra, s. [Nehemiah & Rebecca], b. May 27, 1785	1	458
Ezra Wheeler, of Brookfield, m. Eliza **CROFUTT,** of Danbury, this day [Nov. 9, 1825], by Rev. Lemuel B. Hull	3	30
Hannah, d. John, m. Lemuel **BEEBE,** July 19, 1764	1	434
Hannah, d. Eleazer, m. Benjamin **BAILY,** June 5, 1777	1	433
Jane, d. Lieut. John, m. Matthew **BARNUM,** Nov. 27, 1760	1	452
Joanna, d. John, Jr., m. Daniel **BARNUM,** Jan. 22, 1783	1	452
John, [s. Samuel & Phebe], b. June 19, 1784	1	464
John, m. Loretty **WARNER,** d. William, May 29, 1791	1	451
Joseph, b. Aug. 14, 1749	1	458
Lockwood, [s. Eli & Rachel], d. May 10, 1784	1	455
Lorinda, m. W[illia]m B. **ELY,** June 29, 1814	2	177
Lorral, [child of Eli & Rachel], b. July 15, 1788	1	455
Lucinda, d. [Thomas & Hannah], b. Feb. 15, 1786	1	469
Lucy, [d. Eli & Rachel], b. July 12, 1790	1	455
Lydia, m. Asahel **BENEDICT,** Nov. 25, 1773	1	434
Lydia, w. Eli, d. Apr. 15, 1822	2	66
Mabel, d. [Samuel & Sarah], b. June 15, 1763	1	464
Mary, d. [Nathan & Abigail], b. Sept. 19, 1766; d. Nov. 26, 1767	1	495
Mary, 2nd, d. [Nathan & Abigail], b. May 30, 1769	1	495
Mary, d. [Samuel & Phebe], b. Apr. 20, 1776	1	464
Mary, wid., m. Samuel **BAILEY,** Oct. 23, 1786	1	409
Mary, d. Nathan, m. Jonathan **STARR,** Jr., Mar. 29, 1787	1	385
Mary B., d. [Nehemiah & Rebecca], b. Feb. 12, 1776	1	458
Mela, [d. Samuel & Phebe], b. Apr. 23, 1781	1	464
Miriam, d. John, m. Levi **OSBORN,** Mar. 10, 1784	1	469
Nathan, s. John, b. Aug. 17, 1736; m. Abigail **STEVENS,** Mar. 17, 1757	1	495
Nathan, s. [Nathan & Abigail], b. July 25, 1760	1	495
Nathan, Jr., m. Sarah **BENEDICT,** d. Jakin, Dec. 7, 1781	1	485
Nathan, d. Nov. 30, 1784	1	495
Nathan B., m. Hannah **WOOD,** Jan. 22, 1826, by Reuben Booth, J. P.	3	31
Nehemiah, b. Dec. 21, O.S., 1741; m. Rebecca **HUTTON,** d. Samuel, of Stanford, Dec. 21, 1768	1	458
Nehemiah, Sr., d. Sept. 23, 1774	1	458
Noah, s. [Nathan & Abigail], b. Nov. 3, 1771	1	495
Oran H*., s. [Nehemiah & Rebecca], b. Aug. 9, 1771 *("H"		

	Vol.	Page
DIBBLE, (cont.)		
crossed out)	1	458
Phebe, d. [Nathan & Abigail], b. Jan. 31, 1779	1	495
Phebe, [d. Samuel & Phebe], b. Nov. 20, 1787	1	464
Polly, d. [Nathan & Abigail], b. Mar. 11, 1777	1	495
Polly, [d. Ezra & Griswould], b. Mar. 27, 1790	1	418
Polly, [d. Zar & Lucy], b. Oct. 11, 1790	1	450
Polly M., m. Fred[eric]k SEELEY, Jan. 20, 1819	2	176
Rachel, d. John, Jr., m. Solomon WEED, Nov. 30, 1779	1	451
Rachel, d. [Eli & Rachel], b. Apr. 27, 1782	1	455
Rane, d. [Samuel & Phebe], b. Feb. 28, 1778	1	464
Rhoda, d. [Samuel & Sarah], b. Apr. 18, 1765	1	464
Roda, d. Samuel, m. James BENEDICT, Dec. 11, 1784	1	430
Rue, d. [Eli & Rachel], b. Apr. 6, 1780	1	455
Sallomy, d. [Samuel & Sarah], b. June 5, 1767	1	464
Sally Botsford, m. Charles BENEDICT, Sept. 12, 1832, by		
Thomas Larcombe	3	71
Samuel, m. Sarah TROWBRIDGE, July 21, 1762	1	464
Samuel, s. [Samuel & Sarah], b. Nov. 6, 1769	1	464
Samuel, m. 2nd w. Phebe BENEDICT, Aug. 5, 1774	1	464
Samuel, 3rd, m. Ruth BENEDICT, d. Jakin, Sept. 20, 1791	1	468
Samuel C., s. [Nehemiah & Rebecca], b. Oct. 15, 1769	1	458
Samuel I*., m. Rebecca STARR, d. Capt. Joseph, Nov. 21, 1790		
*(Possibly "C")	1	458
Sarah*, d. Lieut. John, m. Benjamin FERRY, Jan. 22, 1763		
*(This entry in pencil)	1	451
Sarah, w. [Samuel], d. July 15, 1772 [?]	1	464
Sarah, d. [Samuel & Sarah], b. July 19, 1772	1	464
Sarah, d. [Nehemiah & Rebecca], b. June 12, 1780	1	458
Sarah, m. Russel LACEY, May 17, 1821, by Rev. Amborse S.		
Todd	3	6
Squire, s. [Thomas & Hannah], b. Mar. 1, 1790	1	469
Susa, [d. Samuel & Phebe], b. Jan. 30, 1790	1	464
Thomas, m. Hannah BARNUM, d. Elijah, Oct. 26, 1780	1	469
Timothy I., m. Hester TAYLOR, June 8, 1823, by Rev. William		
Andrews	3	17
Walter, s. [Nehemiah & Rebecca], b. Apr. 27, 1788	1	458
William, m. Livonia STEVENS, b. of Danbury, Dec. 19, 1826,		
by Rev. John G. Lowe	3	39
William N., s. [Nehemiah & Rebecca], b. Aug. 4, 1773	1	458
Zar, m. Lucy DAVIS, Sept. 14, 1785* *(Fig. "5" indistanct)	1	450
DICKINSON, Rebecca, d. Dr. Sam[ue]l, m. Sam[ue]l COOKE, Dec.		
[ ], 1778	1	496
DIKEMAN, DITEMAN, DYKIMAN, DYKEMAN, [see also		
DECKERMAN], Betsey M., of Danbury, m. Ebenezer **DIKEMAN**,		
of Newtown, Jan. 20, 1833, by John Nickerson	3	74
Clarinda, m. Alfred BENEDICT, b. of Danbury, Dec. 5, 1827,		
by John Nickerson	3	43

	Vol.	Page
DIKEMAN, DITEMAN, DYKIMAN, DYKEMAN, (cont.)		
Darius H., m. Orra **BARNUM**, b. of Danbury, Jan. 9, 1831, by J. Nickerson	3	60
Ebenezer, of Newtown, m. Betsey M. **DIKEMAN**, of Danbury, Jan. 20, 1833, by John Nickerson	3	74
Eunice, m. Daniel **JUDD**, May 27, 1772	1	470
Frederick B., m. Hannah **MORGAN**, b. of Danbury, Dec. 21, 1842, by Rev. Morris Hill	3	118
Harriet, m. Ezra **SCOFIELD**, Sept. 7, 1828, by George Benedict	3	49
Huldah, m. Charles **HOYT**, b. of Danbury, May 11, 1831, by John Nickerson	3	61
Ira W., m. Eliza **WILDMAN**, Jan. 9, 1822, by Rev. W[illia]m Andrews	3	10
Josiah, of Danbury, m. Phebe **PUTE***, of Pawlings, N. Y., Nov. 4, 1832, by John Mitchel *(Possibly "JUTE")	3	72
Laura, of Danbury, m. Ezra **CARTER**, of Reading, Dec. 29, 1841, by Morris Hill	3	114
Leander, s. [Niram & Martha], b. May 21, 1806	1	467
Leander, m. Betsey M. **OSBORN**, b. of Danbury, Jan. 14, [1829], by John Nickerson	3	50
Lois, m. Elihu **JUDD**, June 15, 1782	1	470
Major, m. Maria **VAIL**, Oct. 31, 1827, by Reuben Booth, J. P.	3	42
Martha, m. James E. **PLATT**, b. of Danbury, Feb. 25, 1845, by Rev. W. P. Collins	3	133
Mary, of Danbury, m. Abraham **BLISS**, of New York, Nov. 17, 1829, by John Nickerson	3	53
Niram, m. Martha **BARKER**, d. Joseph, of Long Island, Oct. 19, 1805	1	467
Susan, of Danbury, m. James H. **HOYT**, of Ridgefield, Mar. 29, 1848, by Rev. I. D. Marshall, of Redding	3	141
DISBROW, Gould S., m. Fanny S. **HAWLEY**, b. of Danbury, Mar. 7, 1843, by S. B Britton	3	119
Harriet, m. Daniel **BENNET**, Mar. 23, 1821, by Oliver Tuttle	3	6
Mary, Mrs., m. Hiram **PAYNE**, b. of Danbury, Nov. 21, 1821, by Nathan Bulkley	3	9
Mary, m. Alexander **KNAPP**, June 19, 1850, by Rev. George H. Deere	3	149
DITTS? [see also **DOBBS**], Philander, m. Jane Elizabeth **WILCOX**, this day [Mar. 26, 1835], by Rev. Lemuel B. Hull	3	84
DIXON, Charles, m. Lucy **CUMMINS**, Sept. 11, 1791	1	384
John, s. [Charles & Lucy], b. Apr. 1, 1794	1	384
Timothy Grim, s. [Charles & Lucy], b. July 4, 1792	1	384
DOBBS, [see also **DITTS**], Betsey Ann, of Danbury, m. Lewis C. **APPLEBY**, of New York State, Dec. 20, 1827, by John Nickerson	3	43
Caroline, of Danbury, m. Gilbert **BEACH**, of Waterbury, Aug. 18, 1833, by John Nickerson	3	77
David, m. Maria **HULL**, Dec. 21, 1823, by Reuben Booth, J. P.	3	20

Vol. Page

DOBBS, (cont.)

David, m. Eliza **PHILLIPS**, b. of Danbury, Sept. 16, 1838,
    by Rev. D. H. Short   3   107

Elizabeth, [d. William & Urania], b. Dec. 11, 1782   1   416

John, [s. William & Urania], b. Nov. 4, 1784   1   416

Joseph, [s. William & Urania], b. Jan. 18, 1781   1   416

Juliett, b. June 2, 1815; m. William W. **BEDIENT**, Sept. 29,
    1835   2   181

Louisa, m. Edwin B. **WHITNEY**, Dec. 29, 1850, by W. White
    Bronson   3   153

Mary Ann, m. George C. **MEEKER**, [Apr.] 3, [1831], by Rev.
    A. Rood   3   60

Oliver, [s. William & Urania], b. Feb. 8, 1787   1   416

Rachel, [d. William & Urania], b. Dec. 22, 1791   1   416

Russel, [s. William & Urania], b. Mar. 29, 1789   1   416

Sally M., m. Hubbel W. **WILDMAN**, Aug. 1, 1821, by Rev.
    W[illia]m Andrews   3   7

William, m. Urania **HOYT**, June 17, 1777   1   416

William, [s. William & Urania], b. Sept. 17, 1778   1   416

William, Sr., d. May 30, 1802   1   416

W[illia]m, m. Emeline **GREGORY**, [Sept.] 9, [1832], by Rev.
    A. Rood   3   73

DOCONS, Emeline, m. Orris **BARBER**, July 13, [1828], by George
    Benedict   3   48

DODD, Elisa, d. [John & Ann], b. Apr. 22, 179[ ]   1   497

Frederick, s. [John & Ann], b. Sept. 22, 180[ ]   1   497

James, 2nd, s. [John & Ann], b. June 1, 179[ ]   1   497

James, eldest s. [John & Ann], b. Sept. 10, 179[ ];
    d. May 10, 1794   1   497

John, m. Ann **McLEAN**, Sept. 26, 179[ ]*   *(Last fig. bound in)   1   497

John McLean, s. [John & Ann], b. Oct. 22, 1800   1   497

Sarah, [d. John & Ann], b. Aug. 30, 179[ ]   1   497

DOLAN, DOLYN, Mary, m. Thomas **BARRET**, [, 1851?], by
    Thomas Ryan. Witnesses: Michael Deen* & Catharin
    Kearney *("Dean" or Deere")   3   156

Patrick, m. Ann **McDERMOTT**, [   ], by Thomas Ryan.
    Witnesses: John McDermott & Margaret McDermott.
    Recorded Aug. 1851   3   156

DORN, Mary, m. Michael **KERNEY**, b. of Danbury, Oct. 9, 1851, by
    Michael O'Farrell   3   157

DOUGLASS, Nathan, s. Capt. Nathan, of New London, m. Elisabeth
    WHEELER, d. Eliphalet, of Long Island, Sept. 8, 1782   1   384

DOWNING, Louisa, m. Rev. George H. **DEERE**, Dec. 24, 1850, by
    Rev. Henry Lyon   3   153

DOWNS, Hannah, m. Miles **HINES**, May 31, 1826, by Marvin
    Richardson   3   33

Paulina*, m. Samuel **BAXTER**, May 17, 1843, by Rev. William
    R. Webb *(Changed to "Purlina" in later hand)   3   124

	Vol.	Page

DOWNS, (cont.)

William W., m. Mary Ann **KELLOGG**, June 3, 1839, by Rev.
J. G. Collom — 3, 97

DOYLE, Andrew, m. Alice **ROURK**, Oct. 26, 1851, by Rev. Michael
O'Farrell — 3, 157

DUFFEE, David, of Philadelphia, m. Julia **HAWLEY**, of Danbury,
Aug. 27, last [1820], by Phineas Taylor, J. P. — 3, 2

DUNCOMBE, Jesse Q.(?), m. Maria Loisa **NOBLE**, b. of Danbury,
Nov. 5, 1847, by R. K. Bellamy — 3, 164

DUNHAM, Peter, of New Jersey, m. Mariah **SURINE**, of Weston,
Jan. 26, 1823, by Levi Brunson — 3, 15

Sarah Ann, of Greenfield, m. Oliver **WOOD**, of Danbury,
July 16, 1849, by Rev. Rollin S. Stone — 3, 147

DUNNING, DUNING, Annis, m. William H. **GREEN**, b. of Danbury,
this day, [Oct. 21, 1840], by Rev. S. H. Clark — 3, 106

Asahel, of Brookfield, m. Rachel **BARNUM**, of Bethel, Mar.
26, 1823, by John G. Lowe — 3, 24

Calvin R., m. Susana **FURGUSON**, b. of Danbury, Jan. 6, 1847,
by Rev. John Crawford — 3, 161

Mary, m. James **WEBB**, b. of Danbury, Sept. 20, 1843, by
John L. Ambler — 3, 121

Penelope, m. Cyrus **BENEDICT**, Jan. 3, 1793 — 1, 480

DUNSKAM, Lydia, m. Eli **HOYT**, b. of Danbury, Aug. 6, 1820, by
Phineas Taylor, J. P. — 3, 1

DURANT, Preston B., m. Harriet P. **HOLISTER**, b. of Bethel, Apr.
29, 1846, by Rev. Fitch Read — 3, 139

EAGAN, Alice, m. Edward **LEAHEY**, Nov. 9, 1851, by Rev.
Michael O'Farrell — 3, 159

EAMES, Barret, s. [Everit & Phebe], b. Apr. 5, 1784 — 1, 494

Charles, s. [Everit & Phebe], b. Oct. 2, 1780 — 1, 494

Everit, m. Phebe **TROWBRIDGE**, d. John, Nov. 11, 1778 — 1, 494

Polly, d. [Everit & Phebe], b. Dec. 9, 1788 — 1, 494

Salle, d. [Everit & Phebe], b. Aug. 10, 1779 — 1, 494

EARL, EARLE, Betsey Ann, m. William **MASSEY**, of New York,
Oct. 2, 1831, by John Nickerson — 3, 64

John T*. of Danbury, m. Margaret A. **MASSY**, of New York,
Apr. 13, 1834, by John Nickerson *(Possibly "I") — 3, 80

Rebecca Evelins, of Danbury, m. David **BAILEY**, of
Cherryvalley, [Nov.] 10, [1822], by John Nickerson — 3, 13

EDDIE, William H., m. Mary E. **JUDD**, Apr. 28, 1850, by Rev. John
Purves, of Bethel — 3, 151

EDMOND, EDMON, EDMONDS, Braley L., m. Marinda B.
KELLOGG, Nov. 28, [1844], by R. K. Bellamy — 3, 130

James, m. Amanda **WILDMAN**, Nov. 2, 1823, by Russel Hoyt,
J. P. — 3, 19

Mary Elizabeth, m. Elias **STARR**, Nov. 14, 1804 — 2, 62

Stephen C., of Kent, Litchfield Co., m. Lois **SCOFIELD**, of
Danbury, Apr. 4, 1824, by Levi Brunson — 3, 22

	Vol.	Page
EDWARDS, Frederick, m. Dorcas **HODGES**, Oct. 25, 1819	2	62
Mary Amelia, d. [Frederick & Dorcas], b. Dec. 6, 1820	2	62
Mercia, of Bethel, m. Elijah B. **WHEELER**, of New Town, Dec.		
25, 1838, by J. Greenwood	3	95
ELLIS, John E. (?), m. Sarah E. **ADAMS**, Sept. 22, 1836, by Rev.		
A. Rood	3	87
ELMER, Andrew, [s. Hezekiah & Elisabeth], b. Feb. 2, 1782	1	426
Bushnell, [s. Hezekiah & Elisabeth], b. Nov. 10, 1787	1	426
Eliakim, [s. Hezekiah & Elisabeth], b. July 15, 1785	1	426
Elisabeth, [d. Hezekiah & Elisabeth], b. Nov. 1, 1790	1	426
Hezekiah, m. Elisabeth **BENEDICT**, [ ]	1	426
Lucy, d. [Hezekiah & Elisabeth], b. Nov. 28, 1780	1	426
ELWELL, Lucius C., d. Dec. 30, 1822	2	176
Rebecca, m. Allen **STANLEY**, b. of Danbury, Dec. 3, 1827,		
by John G. Lowe	3	44
------, Mrs., m. Eli H. **BARNUM**, b. of Danbury, Apr. 23,		
[1829], by Daniel Crocker	3	51
ELWOOD, Mary A., m. Alonzo **WHITEHEAD**, Dec. 25, 1849, by		
Rev. A. Perkins	3	160
ELY, Abijah Peck, s. [Edward & Rachel], b. June 11, 1799	1	481
Caroline C., m. Charles W. **LAMB**, of New York, Sept. 23,		
1849, by Rev. Rollin S. Stone	3	146
Catharine, [d. William B. & Lorinda], b. Apr. 8, 182[ ];		
d. Aug. 29, 1821	2	177
Catharine Issabella, m. Horace T. **WILDMAN**, b. of Danbury,		
May 11, 1830, by Rev. Lemuel B. Hull	3	56
Clarissa, d. [Edward & Rachel], b. Oct. 17, 1794	1	481
Clarissa, [d. William B. & Lorinda], b. Jan. 24, 1818	2	177
Clarissa, m. Jonathan **STEVENS**, b. of Danbury, Feb. 4, 1846,		
by Nathaniel Bishop	3	139
Drusilla, d. [Edward & Rachel], b. May 4, 1797	1	481
Drusilla, [d. William B. & Lorinda], b. July 5, 1822	2	177
Drusilla, m. Silvester S. **SCRIBNER**, b. of Danbury, Jan.		
1, 1845, by Nathaniel Bishop	3	131
Edward, m. Rachel **PECK**, d. Abijah, Dec. 28, 1791	1	481
John, Rev. m. Mary **LORD**, d. Abner, of Lyme, Jan. 26, 1791	1	383
John, s. [Rev. John & Mary], b. Aug. 25, 1795; d. Dec. 18, 1795	1	383
John, s. [Rev. John & Mary], b. June 10, 1797	1	383
John Edwards, s. [Edward & Rachel], b. Aug. 20, 1801; d. [ ]	1	481
John Edwards, 2nd, s. [Edward & Rachel], b. Nov. 20, 1804	1	481
Lucy Maria, d. [William B. & Lorinda], b. June 25, 1815	2	177
Lydia, d. [Rev. John & Mary], b. June 26, 1792	1	383
Lydia, d. [Rev. John & Mary], d. Jan. 18, 1793	1	383
Thomas Lord, s. [Rev. John & Mary], b. Apr. 1, 1794	1	383
W[illia]m B., m. Lorinda **DIBBLE**, June 29, 1814	2	177
W[illia]m Brewster, s. [Edward & Rachel], b. Nov.* Oct.		
11, 1792 *("Nov. 2nd" Partly erased)	1	481
ENGLISH, Betsey, m. Jonah* **BENEDICT**, Jan. 6, 1781		

Vol. Page

ENGLISH, (cont.)

    *("Governor" crossed out)   1   413

FAIRCHILD, Adoniram, of Newtown, m. Sarah **CHANDLER,** of
    Danbury, Jan. 10, 1846, by Thomas T. Guion   3   140

    Dinah, d. Alexander, m. Samuel **WILDMAN,** Mar. 22, 1758   1   453

    Eunice E., m. Joshua L. **TAYLOR,** b. of Bethel, Mar. 1, 1838,
    by Rev. John Greenwood, of Bethel   3   93

    Eveline, of Newtown, m. William **OLIVER,** of [Horseneck]*,
    July 5, 1840, by James Beebe, J. P. *(Written in pencil)   3   105

    George, of Newtown, m. Elvira **BENNETT,** of Monroe, Jan. 1,
    1837, by Rev. Salmon C. Bulkley   3   89

    Josiah, of Newtown, m. Ruth **LACEY,** of Danbury, this day
    [Apr. 27, 1825], by Nathan Seelye, J. P.   3   26

    Lewis, of Roxbury, m. Rheuna **JUDD,** of Bethel, Mar. 30, 1845,
    by John L. Ambler   3   134

    Sarah, m. Orrin **ROCKWELL,** b. of Bethel, Dec. 26, 1830, by
    Rev. Erastus Cole   3   59

    Sarah, m. Asahel B. **TAYLOR,** b. of Bethel, May 23, 1839,
    by John Greenwood   3   97

    Sarah B., m. Niram J. **STONE,** b. of Danbury, Nov. 27, [1850],
    by Rev. J. B. Merwin   3   155

    Walter, of New Town, m. Narbby **JENNINGS,** of Danbury, Nov.
    28, 1820, by Nathan Seeley, J. P.   3   4

    Winthrop, m. Maria **BENEDICT,** b. of Danbury, Jan. 21, 1827,
    by Rev. John G. Lowe   3   39

FAIRMAN, Jerusha, of Newtown, m. John W. **STARR,** Sept. 18,
    1810   2   65

FANTON, Arata, m. Ezra B. **STEVENS,** Feb. 3, 1814   2   119

    Bradley, of New Fairfield, m. Lucy **GREGORY,** of Danbury,
    Nov. 7, 1832, by John Nickerson   3   72

    Bradley B., m. Eleanor A. **NOBLE,** Apr. 7, 1850, by Rev. A.
    Perkins   3   160

    Harriet H., m. Charles W. **FRY,** b. of Danbury, Mar. 29,
    1843, by James Floy   3   119

FARNAM, Catharine, m. John **GREENWOOD,** b. of Bethel, June 9,
    1841, by John Greenwood   3   109

    Ethel T., m. Mary J. **SUMMERS,** b. of Bethel, Jan. 26, 1840, by
    John Greenwood   3   101

FENNER, Abigail, m. Caleb S. **STONE,** Jan. 13, 1822, by Rev.
    W[illia]m Andrews   3   10

    Elmyra, m. George B. **BEACHAM,** b. of Danbury, Oct. 27,
    1839, by Rev. D. H. Short   3   107

    George H., m. Mary A. **PERRY,** b. of Danbury, July 6, 1845,
    by Rev. F. Reed.   3   135

    Mary, Mrs., m. John **FLOYD,** b. of Danbury, Feb. 17, 1825,
    by Josiah Dikeman   3   26

    Mary M., m. Charles **BROTHINGTON,** Sept. 29, 1847, by Rev.
    John Purves   3   151

	Vol.	Page
FENNER, (cont.)		
Riley, m. Deborah **BECK**, Sept. 11, 1842, by Charles Chittenden	3	117
FENNING, James, m. Sarah **HICKOK**, Oct. 19, 1843, by Rev. William R. Webb	3	124
FERGUSON, FURGUSON, FURGISON, Charles Edward, m. Hannah **JENNINGS**, Oct. 10, 1831, by Thomas Larcombe	3	64
Daniel H., m. Jeanette **KEELER**, b. of Danbury, June 21, 1838, by J. G. Collom	3	94
Eloina L., m. James P. **SANDERS**, b. of Danbury, Nov. 19, 1840, by Addison Parker	3	107
Susana, m. Calvin R. **DUNNING**, b. of Danbury, Jan. 6, 1847, by Rev. John Crawford	3	161
William, m. Sarah **TAYLOR**, b. of Danbury, this day [Nov. 15, 1826], by Levi Osborn	3	37
FERRIS, Mary, d. Zachary, of Newtown, m. Seth **WHITLOCK**, Aug. 20, 1789	1	410
FERRY, Abigail, [d. Benjamin & Sarah], b. Nov. 16, 1766	1	451
Amelia, [d. Benjamin], b. Mar. 19, 1777	1	451
Bailey, m. Lucy **HOYT**, b. of Danbury, Jan. 1, 1824, by Samuel Cochran	3	21
Benjamin, m. [Sarah **DIBBLE**, d. Lieut. John]*, Jan. 22, 1763 *(In Pencil)	1	451
Benjamin, [s. Benjamin & Sarah], b. Feb. 15, 1769	1	451
Benjamin, m. [ ], July 3, 1769	1	451
E. LeRoy, of Bethel, m. Sarah **BOOTH**, of Danbury, Sept. 14, 1842, by Thomas T. Guion	3	117
Eleanor, m. Hiram **KNAPP**, b. of Danbury, June 12, 1821, by Zachariah Clark, Jr. J. P.	3	7
Fidelia M., m. Philander S. **BARNUM**, b. of Danbury, Oct. 2, 1845, by Rev. Fitch Reed	3	136
Frederick, of Danbury, m. Mary Jane **PATRICK**, of Wilton, Apr. 20, 1845, by Rev. John L. Ambler	3	134
George, m. Mary W. **STARR**, b. of Danbury, June 26, 1838, by Rev. D. H. Short	3	107
George W., m. Cornelia E. **BOOTH**, Sept. 11, 1851, by Rev. W. White Bronson	3	156
Jerusha, [d. Benjamin & Sarah], b. Nov. 27, 1763	1	451
Joseph, [s. Benjamin], b. Feb. 2, 1772	1	451
Joshua B., m. Anna **WELLS**, Dec. 24, 1822, by Adonirum Fairchild, J. P.	3	14
Lorinda, m. Belial **SMITH**, [Oct.] 9, [1831], by Rev. A. Rood	3	64
Lydia, [d. Benjamin], b. Aug. 1, 1773; d. Dec. 11, 1774	1	451
Lydia, [d. Benjamin], b. Aug. 6, 1775	1	451
Lydia, b. Aug. 9, 1775; m. Isaac **WILLIAMS**, July 9, 1795	2	63
Philander, m. Harriett H. **SCOFIELD**, b. of Danbury, June 4, 1843, by James Floy	3	121
Polly M., of Bethel, m. David C. **PERRY**, Rev. of New Fairfield, Sept. 21, 1841, by John Greenwood	3	111

Vol.Page

FERRY, (cont.)

[Sarah], w. [Benjamin], d. Mar. 5, 1769 1 451

Sarah*, d. Benjamin & Sarah (d. Lieut. John **DIBBLE**),
m. Closen **HAWLEY**, Nov. 6, 1777   *(Inserted in pencil) 1 416

Sary*, m. Samuel S. **TWEEDY**, b. of Danbury, Apr. 20, 1845,
by Rev. John L. Ambler   *(Possibly "Seny"?) 3 134

Solomon, [s. Benjamin], b. Apr. 21, 1770 1 451

Starr, m. Clarissa H. **BARNUM**, b. of Danbury, this day
[Dec. 29, 1832], by Rev. Lemuel B. Hull 3 77

Walker, m. Lois **WILDMAN**, Nov. 3, 1847, by Rev. John
Purves, of Bethel 3 151

William H. H., m. Harriet **MAYHEW**, b. of Bethel, Oct. 16,
1839, by John Greenwood 3 100

FIELD, Deborah B., of South East, m. Harry **STONE**, of Danbury,
this day [Mar. 27, 1844], by Rev. Rollin S. Stone 3 125

William R., m. Mary **AMBLER**, b. of Danbury, [Apr.] 22,
[1840], by Addison Parker 3 103

FITCH, Molly, m. Benjamin **NAMES**, (colored), Sept. 2*, 1820, by
W[illia]m Andrews   *(Day crossed out) 3 2

FLINN, Harriet, m. Real **GUN**, b. of Danbury, June 25, [1826],
by John Nickerson 3 33

FLOYD, John, m. Mrs. Mary **FENNER**, b. of Danbury, Feb. 17, 1825,
by Josiah Dikeman 3 26

Mary Ann, m. Morris **BARTOW**, Apr. 21, 1831, by Levi
Brunson 3 61

FLUGLER, Alfred, m. Sarah E. **ODELL**, b. of Danbury, May 17,
1847, by R. K. Bellamy 3 162

FOOT, Betsey, Mrs., m. Samuel W. **JENNINGS**, b. of Danbury, Feb.
18, 1845, by Rev. Fitch Reed 3 133

David, [s. John & Huldah], b. June 15, 1785 1 405

David, m. Elizabeth **BULL**, d. Asa, of Litchfield, Dec. 29, 1792 1 389

David A., m. Eliza M. **TROWBRIDGE**, Dec. 25, 1846, by R. H.
Bellamy 3 138

Elijah, [s. John & Huldah], b. May 2, 1789 1 405

Grandison D., m. Mercy Ann **PORTER**, b. of Danbury, this
day, [Nov. 5, 1843], by J. K. Ingalls 3 122

John, m. Huldah **STONE**, Nov. 28, 1781 1 405

John, [s. John & Huldah], b. [ ] 13, 1791 1 405

John, s. John, d. May 10, 1822, ae 1 y. 2 129

Joseph B., of Danbury, m. Maria L. **TAYLOR**, of New York,
May 18, 1834, by John Nickerson 3 81

Lucy, d. John, m. Robert **McMEIHN**, Sept. 14, 1785 1 491

Mary A., m. Ezra **ABBOTT**, b. of Danbury, Dec. 1, 1845, by
Rev. Fitch Read 3 137

Phile, [child of John & Huldah], b. Apr. 11, 1787 1 405

Sally, [d. John & Huldah], b. Aug. 31, 1783 1 405

FORD, Clarissa, of Bridgewater, m. Nathan **GREGORY**, of Danbury,
Mar. 27, 1831, by John Nickerson 3 60

	Vol.	Page

FOSTER, Alanson, of Danbury, m. Polly STONE, of Redding, Dec.
 17, 1823, by John Nickerson — 3 — 20

 Cornell, s. [Timothy & Susanna], b. Jan. 10, 1791 — 1 — 462

 David Adams, s. [Timothy & Susanna], b. July 19, 1792 — 1 — 462

 Mary Ann, of Redding, m. George S. CROFUT, of Bethel, June
 6, 1847, by Rev. I. D. Marshall, of Redding — 3 — 141

 Timothy, m. Susanna ADAMS, of Weston, Sept. 28, 1788 — 1 — 462

FOYLE, Margaret, m. Thomas SWIFT, b. of Danbury, Jan. 28, 1844,
 by Thomas T. Guion — 3 — 123

FRENCH, Mary, of Weymouth, b. May 20, 1726; m. Ebenezer
 WHITE, Mar. [ ], 1747; d. Aug. 24, 1807 in 82 y. of her
 age — 1 — 473

FROST, Adra, d. Jabez, b. Jan. 21, 1748; m. Daniel COMSTOCK,
 Nov. 15, 1770 — 1 — 447

 Daniel Andrus, eldest s. [Ezra & Rebeckah], b. May 23, 1787 — 1 — 478

 Ezra, m. Rebeckah ANDRUS, Sept. 7, 1785 — 1 — 478

 Griswould, m. Ezra DIBBLE, Oct. 31, 1771 — 1 — 418

 Hannah, b. Apr. 24, 1761, in Reading; m. Samuel Henly
 PHILLIPS, Jan. 2, 1785 — 1 — 477

 Henry King, 2nd, s. [Ezra & Rebeckah], b. July 21, 1789 — 1 — 478

 Jacob, of New Fairfield, m. Angeline STEVENS, of Danbury,
 Apr. 14, 1839, by Rev. L. Atwater — 3 — 98

 Lucy, m. Thomas STOCKER, Feb. [ ], 1814 — 2 — 120

 Phebe Ann, m. Charles H. LAKE, b. of Danbury,*, Jan. 13,
 1842, by Addison Parke *(Crossed out) — 3 — 115

 Stoddard Jabez, s. [Ezra & Rebeckah], b. Nov. 14, 1791 — 1 — 478

FRY, Charles W., m. Harriet H. FANTON, b. of Danbury, Mar. 29,
 1843, by James Floy — 3 — 119

 David, m. Hariet E. BABBS, Apr. 11, 1840, by Thomas P.
 White, J. P. — 3 — 102

 George, m. Mary BOUGHTON, Sept. 27, 1825, by Rev.
 [Willia]m Andrews — 3 — 29

 Jane, m. Walter C. SPARKS, b. of Danbury, this day [July
 3, 1842], by Rev. Rollin S. Stone — 3 — 116

 Jemima, of Bethel, m. Roswell REYNOLDS, of New Haven,
 July 9, 1848, by Oliver Shepard, J. P. — 3 — 143

 Mary E., of Danbury, m. Charles N. LOCKWOOD, of Troy,
 Nov. 26, 1844, by Rev. Rollin S. Stone — 3 — 130

 Sally, m. Zarel WHEELER, of Newtown, Sept. 12, 1830, by
 John Nickerson — 3 — 58

 W[illia]m B., m. Caroline GREGORY, b. of Danbury, July 1,
 1828, by Rev. Lemuel B. Hull — 3 — 48

GAGE, Ann D., m. William WOOD, b. of Danbury, Aug. 20, 1843,
 by John L. Ambler — 3 — 122

 Eliza, m. Alva O. BANKS, Jan. 1, 1829, by Nathan Bulkley — 3 — 50

 Maria, Mrs., m. George E. STEVENS, Sept. 7, 1846, by R. K.
 Bellamy — 3 — 161

 Romanzo, of Danbury, m. Mary NEALY, of Orange, N. J., Mar.

	Vol.	Page

GAGE, (cont.)

2, 1851, by John L. Ambler — 3 — 154

William, m. Sarah M. SININE, Nov. 10, 1844, by Levi Brunson — 3 — 130

GALE, Amarillis, m. Edward DANN, b. of Danbury, Jan. 13, 1850, by Rev. John S. Whittlesey — 3 — 146

GALIHER, Patrick, m. Catherine KENNY, Oct. 26, 1851, by Rev. Michael O'Farrell — 3 — 157

GALL, [see under GAUL]

GAN, [see also GAUL & GUNN], Abraham, m. Dilley HAWLEY, b. of Danbury, May 14, 1822, by Phineas Taylor, J. P. — 3 — 12

GANUNG, Lewis, m. Betsey A. WHITE, b. of Danbury, Jan. 11, 1846, by Morris Hill — 3 — 138

Peter, m. Rachel NICHOLS, Nov. 8, 1843, by Rev. William R. Webb — 3 — 124

GARDNER, Louisa Ann, m. Prosper PATCH, Nov. 22, 1849, by Rev. A. Perkins — 3 — 160

GATES*, Stephen, of Ridgefield, m. Lucy KNAPP, of Danbury, June 24, 1834, by John Nickerson *(Letter "G" uncertain) — 3 — 81

GAUL, GALL, [see also GAN & GAULT], Abraham, m. Catharine BUSH, Oct. 14, 1827, by John S. Blackman, J. P. — 3 — 42

Daniel, of Danbury, m. Harsey BRISCOE, of Newtown, Nov. 7, 1821, by Phineas Taylor, J. P. — 3 — 9

George, m. Christy Ann BROWN, b. of Danbury, Mar. 10, 1847, by Edward Taylor, J. P. — 3 — 162

GAULT, [see also GAUL & GAN], Abner C., of Patterson, N. J., m. Eliza STEVENS, of Danbury, Dec. 2, 1850, by Rev. George H. Deere — 3 — 153

GAY, Phebe, m. Elijah JANES, Feb. 4, 1785 — 1 — 491

[GAYLORD], GAILORD, Julius, of Watertown, m. Frances NICHOLS, of Waterbury, Nov. 16, 1846, by Thomas T. Guion — 3 — 161

GILBERT, Charlotty, d. Hezekiah, m. Noah ROBERTS, Oct. 20, 1790 — 1 — 407

James, m. Mary H. RIDER, May 18, 1825, by Rev. William Andrews — 3 — 26

Matthew K., m. Abigail TROWBRIDGE, b. of Danbury, this day, [May 29, 1825], by Rev. Lemuel B. Hull — 3 — 27

GILLETT, GILLET, David, m. Harriet BENJAMIN, Sept. 11, 1836, by Rev. Jonathan G. Collom — 3 — 86

Elizabeth Ann, Mrs., m. Ezra B. STEVENS, May 17, 1835, by Rev. A. Rood — 3 — 86

Fred[eric]k, m. Eliza BARBURY, Oct. 18, 1827, by George Benedict — 3 — 46

John, [s. Joseph], b. Feb. 21, 1825 — 2 — 171

Nancy, d. Joseph, d. July 7, 1822 — 2 — 171

Phineas Judd, s. Joseph, b. Jan. 1, 1823 — 2 — 171

Susan, m. Simeon M. STEWART, b. of Danbury, Oct. 10, 1825, by Reuben Booth, J. P. — 3 — 29

	Vol.	Page
GLOVER, Amelia, d. [Christopher & Sarah], b. Feb. 21, 1784	1	492
Benj[ami]n, s. [Christopher & Sarah], b. Feb. 19*, 1780		
*(First written "20th or 25th")	1	492
Chloe, d. [Christopher & Sarah], b. Mar. 4, 1793	1	492
Christopher, m. Sarah BENEDICT, d. Ens. Thomas, June 10, 1774	1	492
Daniel, s. [Christopher & Sarah], b. Sept. 12, 1787	1	492
Ezra, s. [Christopher & Sarah], b. Apr. 17, 1777	1	492
Henry, s. [Christopher & Sarah], b. Sept. 21, 1785	1	492
Isaac Beach, s. [Christopher & Sarah], b. May 25, 1775	1	492
John, s. [Christopher & Sarah], b. Dec. 5, 1789	1	492
Sarah, d. [Christopher & Sarah], b. Jan. 7, 1782	1	492
Sarah, w. [Christopher], d. Oct. [ ], 1794	1	492
Sarah, d. Christopher, of Danbury, m. Rufus CLARK, s. Timothy, of New Haven, Oct. 8, 1797	1	367
Solomon, of Newtown, m. wid. Rachel AMBLER, of Danbury, June 25, 1826, by Josiah Dikeman	3	33
Suckie*, d. [Christopher & Sarah], b. Jan. 5, 1792 *(Almost faded out, name uncertain)	1	492
GORHAM, Charles, Dr. of Reading, m. Mary COMSTOCK, of Danbury, Apr. 4, 1826, by Rev. W[illia]m C. Kniffin	3	32
GOULD, Amanda, of Wilton, m. Russel BEVENS, of Danbury, Jan. 1, 1829, by Josiah Dikeman	3	50
Urana, Mrs., m. George A. WINSLOW, Sept. 8, 1827, by Josiah Dikeman	3	41
GRAAM, Adam, of New York State, m. Sally LITTLE, of Danbury, Oct. 9, 1821, by Phineas Taylor, J. P.	3	8
GRANNESS, Sydney, m. Mary STARR, b. of Danbury, Dec. 4, [1850], by Rev. J. B. Merwin	3	155
GRAY, Abigail, d. John, m. Eliphalet STEVENS, Dec. 7, 1767	1	432
John C., m. Esther BENEDICT, Oct. 25, 1807	1	364
John Noble, 2nd, s. [John C. & Esther], b. Aug. 23, 1810	1	364
Mary, of Danbury, m. George CHATFIELD, of Newtown, Nov. 28, 1844, by Thomas T. Guion	3	132
Oliver Benedict, s. [John C. & Esther], b. Sept. 3, 1808	1	364
Temperance, Mrs., m. Hezekiah STEVENS, July 11, 1820, at the house, of Elijah Barnum, by Daniel Foot, J. P.	3	1
W[illia]m B., m. Mercy* WILDMAN, [May] 23, [1832], by Rev. A. Rood *(Perhaps "Mary"?)	3	70
GREANLEAF, [see under GREENLEAF]		
GREEN, Ammon, m. Catharine A. TROWBRIDGE, Jan. 9, 1849, by Rev. John Purves, of Bethel	3	151
Anna, [d. Dorastus & Hannah], b. May 18, 1787	1	395
Dorastus, m. Hannah PORTER, d. John, June 1, 1783	1	395
Eli, s. [Dorastus & Hannah], b. Oct. 8, 1783	1	395
Eli, [s. Dorastus & Hannah], d. May 19, 1784	1	395
Eli, 2nd, s. [Dorastus & Hannah], b. Oct. 23, 1790	1	395
Henry, of West Springfield, Mass., m. Almira JENKINS, of		

	Vol.	Page

GREGORY, (cont.)

Knoles, of Ridgefield, Nov. 13, 1796	1	358
Caroline, m. W[illia]m B. FRY, b. of Danbury, July 1, 1828, by Rev. Lemuel B. Hull	3	48
Catharine, d. Nathaniel, m. David WOOD, Feb. 3, 1772* *(Perhaps "1774"?)	1	476
Chary Ann, d. [Isaac & Phebee], b. Oct. 1, 1800	1	369
Cordilia, m. Andrew HICKOK, b. of Danbury, Oct. 14, 1822, by Rev. John G. Low	3	22
Delia, m. Sam[ue]l G. SHERWOOD, b. of Reading, Nov. 16, 1825, by Rev. John G. Lowe	3	35
Delos, m. Harriet E. DANN, Nov. 13, [1844], by R. K. Bellamy	3	130
Dolly, wid. of Norwalk, d. of Dea. Peter LOCKWOOD, m. Comfort HOYT, Jr., Jan. 16, 1793	1	465
Ebenezer, m. Phebe BOOTH, d. Abel, of Newtown, July 12, 1768	1	480
Edgar, s. [Ephraim & Rachel], b. July 11, 1819	2	146
Edward, of Danbury, m. Betsey STONE, of Redding, Nov. 30, 1831, by John Nickerson	3	66
Eli, [s. Nathan & Thankfull], b. Oct. 11, 1772	1	428
Elijah, of Danbury, m. Polly MORSE, of Danbury, this day, [,1836(?)], by Rev. David H. Short	3	85
Eliphalet, m. Jane BARNUM, b. of Danbury, Mar. 19, [1829], by J. Nickerson	3	51
Eliza Ann, d. [Isaac & Phebee], b. Sept. 21, 1799	1	369
Emeline, m. W[illia]m DOBBS, [Sept.] 9, [1832], by Rev. A. Rood	3	73
Ephraim, m. Rachel STEVENS, Jan. 4, 1815	2	146
Esther, d. [Ebenezer & Phebe], b. Nov. 23, 1772	1	480
Easther, m. Timothy HICKOK, Nov. 30, 1820, by W[illia]m Andrews	3	4
Eunice, d. Sam[ue]l, b. Jan. 29*, 1738; m. Capt. Noble Benedict, July 6, 1763* *("Aug. 13" crossed out) *(Corrected from "1773")	1	403
Ezra, [s. John & Keziah], b. Sept. 2, 1764	1	420
Ezra, m. Mary MYGATT, d. Thomas, of Oblong, Mar. 3, 1789	1	420
Ezra, m. Lucy STARR, d. Caleb, decd., Feb. 12, 1804	1	420
Ferdinand M., of Danbury, m. Harriet OLMSTED, [Jan. 1, 1840], by Addison Parker	3	101
Hannah, m. Enos SCHOFIELD, Mar. 4, 1778	1	445
Hannah, d. John & Philena, b. May 15, 1825	2	475
Hannah, m. Timothy W. ST. JOHN, July 24, 1825, by George Benedict	3	27
Harriott, d. [Ezra & Mary], b. Mar. 2, 1790	1	420
Henry, m. Betsey STEVENS, this day [Dec. 8, 1824], by Levi Osborn	3	25
Horris, s. [Ezra & Mary], b. Aug. 26, 1795	1	420
Huldah, d. [Ebenezer & Phebe], b. Apr. 9, 1769	1	480

	Vol.	Page

GREGORY, (cont.)

Huldah, d. [Ebenezer & Phebe], d*. Jan. 12, 1774

    *("b." crossed out)   1   480

Huldah, 2nd, d. [Ebenezer & Phebe], b. Aug. 19, 1776;

    d. Oct. 12, 1778   1   480

Ira, m. Maria GREGORY, Oct. 14, [1829], by George Benedict   3   53

Isaac, of Danbury, m. Phebee WHEELER, of Newtown, Oct. 10,

    1798   1   369

Jemima, d. Daniel, m. Will[ia]m GRIFFETH, Nov. 19, 1787   1   484

John, m. Keziah CURTISS, of Sharon, Nov. 22, 1763   1   420

John, [s. John & Keziah], b. July 15, 1766   1   420

John, m. 2nd w. Ruth ST. JOHN, of Sharon, July 6, 1788   1   420

John, m. Jerusha WILDMAN, b. of Danbury, June 16, 1830,

    by John Nickerson   3   57

John, m. Lois STONE, b. of Danbury, May 8, 1850, by Rev.

    Rollin S. Stone   3   148

John, Jr., m. Philina HOYT, Nov. 28, 1822, by Reuben Booth,

    J. P.   3   13

John A., m. Betsey OSBORN, Nov. 13, 1825, by Rev. W[illia]m

    Andrews   3   29

John Sears, s. [Caleb Curtis & Desire], b. Oct. 3, 1797   1   358

Joseph, m. Lavinia W. HATCH, [Apr.] 23, [1832], by Rev. A.

    Rood   3   70

Julia, m. John WHITTLESEY, June 8, 1823, by Rev. W[illia]m

    Andrews   3   17

Keziah, [w. John], d. Mar. 17, 1787   1   420

Keziah, d. [Ezra & Mary], b. Nov. 5, 1797   1   420

Keziah, [d. Ezra & Mary], d. June 4, 1804   1   420

Lois, m. Munson GREGORY, [ur] 31, 1767   1   391

Lorany Ann, of Danbury, m. Henry BENEDICT, of New York,

    Mar. 26, 1834, by Timothy B. Hickok, J. P.   3   79

Lucy, [d. Nathan & Thankfull], b. Oct. 21, 1770;

    d. Nov. 14, 1771   1   428

Lucy, [d. John & Keziah], b. Jan. 17, 1776   1   420

Lucy, [d. Nathan, Jr. & Tamezin], b. Feb. 26, 1783   1   428

Lucy, m. James BENEDICT, June 1, 1828, by George Benedict   3   48

Lucy, of Danbury, m. Bradley FANTON, of New Fairfield,

    Nov. 7, 1832, by John Nickerson   3   72

Maria, m. Ira GREGORY, Oct. 14, [1829], by George Benedict   3   53

Mary, d. Nathaniel, b. Nov. 18, 1752; m. Benjamin WOOD,

    3rd s. Capt. John, Apr. 16, 1771   1   372

Mary, [w. Ezra], d. June 29, 1803   1   420

Mary, m. Levi S. BENEDICT, Oct. 7, [1829], by George

    Benedict   3   53

Matthew, d. Jan. 13, 1823   2   171

Meba, d. [Thomas & Rachel], b. Oct. 3, 1789   1   476

Munson, m. Lois GREGORY, [ur] 31, 1767   1   391

Nathan, m. Thankfull BENEDICT, Apr. 2, 1760   1   428

	Vol.	Page

GREGORY, (cont.)

Nathan, [s. Nathan & Thankfull], b. Jan. 23, 1761 — 1 428

Nathan, Jr., m. Tamezin **CORBIN**, Mar. 27, 1782 — 1 428

Nathan, of Danbury, m. Clarissa **FORD**, of Bridgewater,
Mar. 27, 1831, by John Nickerson — 3 60

Olburt, s. [Caleb Curtis & Desire], b. June 7, 1799 — 1 358

Patty, d. Selah, m. Eli **WILDMAN**, June 2, 1790 — 1 453

Phebe, m. Matthew **LINDSLEY**, Mar. 6, 1781 — 1 397

Rachel, d. [Thomas & Rachel], b. Apr. 18, 1792 — 1 476

Rebecca, d. Daniel, m. Josiah **CROFUT**, Mar. 25, 1790 — 1 430

Sam[ue]l, d. Apr. 9, 1783 — 1 443

Samuel [C.]*, m. Mary Ann **STEVENSON**, b. of Danbury, Apr.
21, 1846, by Rev. Fitch Reed *(Crossed out) — 3 139

Sarah, d. [Thomas & Rachel], b. Oct. 7, 1787 — 1 476

Sarah, d. John & Philena], b. May 11, 1828 — 2 175

Sarah M., of Danbury, m. Levi E. **JUD[D]**, of Roxbury, May
1, 1845, by Rev. Fitch Reed — 3 135

Stephen Townsend, s. [Caleb & Fanny], b. Oct. 5, 1800 — 1 367

Susanna, d. Caleb C., b. Aug. 27, 1822; d. Dec. 9, 1822 — 2 179

Thankful, m. Ebenezer **MUNSON**, Oct. 6, 1757 — 1 391

Thankfull, [d. Nathan & Thankfull], b. Feb. 13, 1766 — 1 428

Thomas, m. Rachel **TAYLOR**, d. Abn[ ]*, Apr. 8, 1783
*(Edge of leaf missing) — 1 476

Thomas M., m. Lucy **STARR**, b. of Danbury, this day [Aug. 4,
1828], by Rev. Lemuel B. Hull — 3 48

Thomas Mygatt, s. [Ezra & Mary], b. May 6, 1801 — 1 420

[ ]bert, [child of Munson & Lois], b. Apr. 2, 1785 — 1 391

[ ]tephen, [child of Munson & Lois], b. June 15, 1775 — 1 391

GRIDLY, Sally, d. Luke, of Bristol, m. Bennet **PEPPER**, of Danbury,
Oct. 19, 1801 — 1 359

GRIFFETH, Edwin M., m. Melissa O. **SEGAR**, b. of Danbury, Dec.
31, [1850], by Rev. J. B. Merwin — 3 155

Gershom, s. [William & Jemima], b. Mar. 27, 1789 — 1 484

Lucy, d. [William & Jemima], b. Jan. 7, 1793 — 1 484

Molly, d. [William & Jemima], b. Jan. 2, 1791 — 1 484

Will[ia]m, m. Jemima **GREGORY**, d. Daniel, Nov. 19, 1787 — 1 484

GRIFFIN, GRIFFEN, GRIFFING, Anna, of Danbury, m. Samuel
ADAMS, of Dutchess Co., N. Y., Dec. 25, 1842, by James
Floy — 3 118

Harriet, of Redding, m. Alanson **CHASE**, of Danbury, Oct.
12, [1825], by John Nickerson — 3 29

Jennett, m. Frederick S*. **BEVANS**, b. of Danbury, Oct. 24,
1841, by Addison Parker *(Possibly "T") — 3 112

Lucy, of Danbury, m. Isaac **DAILEY**, of Sherman, yesterday,
[Mar. 1, 1846], by Rev. Rollin S. Stone — 3 139

Martin H., m. Mariette **HOYT**, b. of Danbury, May 27, 1846,
by Rev. Rollin S. Stone — 3 140

Mary Ann, m. William **HURLBURT**, b. of Danbury, Nov. 2,

	Vol.	Page

GRIFFIN, GRIFFEN, GRIFFING, (cont.)

1844, by Rev. J. K. Ingalls — 3 — 129

Nathan Clark, s. Lecretia **CANFIELD**, b. May 1, 1804 — 1 — 379

Sarah Ann, of Danbury, m. Charles **CHASE**, of New Fairfield,
Dec. 9, 1849, by Rev. Geo[rge] H. Deere — 3 — 145

William, d. May [ ], 1795 — 1 — 484

GRLOOLY, Bernard, m. Julia **McESPREL**, May 11, 1851, by
Thomas Ryan. Witnesses: Thomas Kenny, Julia English — 3 — 154

GUINEE, Cornelius, m. Betsey **CUNTAG***, Aug. 11, 1844, by R. K.
Bellamy ("t" inserted in pencil) — 3 — 127

GUNN, GUN,[see also **GAN**], Anna, m. Daniel **HOYT**, May 20, 1779 — 1 — 435

Hannah, of Waterbury, m. Moses **WOOD**, s. Benjamin & Mary,
of Danbury, Nov. 19, 1803 — 1 — 372

Real, m. Harriet **FLINN**, June 25, [1826], b. of Danbury,
by John Nickerson — 3 — 33

GUTHRIE, Elizabeth, d. John, b. Jan. 17, 1752 — 1 — 376

Elizabeth, had d. Anne **ASA**, b. Aug. 7, 1778; father Jacob **ASA**
d. Deborah **SCOTT**, b. Aug. 13, 1781; father Elijah
SCOTT s. Jonne **BEANDIHEN***, b. Mar. 26, 1785; d. Mar.
6, 1787; father John **BEANDIHEN***   *(Last three letters
uncertain) — 1 — 376

Elizabeth, had s. Lewis **LEE**, b. Mar. 5, 1787; f. Abraham **LEE** — 1 — 376

Elizabeth, m. Robert **CRAIGE**, Dec. 1, 1793 — 1 — 376

HACK, Hannah, m. Epaphrus H. **WILDMAN**, b. of Danbury, June 9,
1839, by Reuben Booth, J. P. — 3 — 97

Maria, of Danbury, m. W[illia]m **TRUMBULL**, of Milford,
[Dec.] 27, [1840], by Addison Parker — 3 — 107

Mary Ann, m. William **SCHOFIELD**, b. of Danbury, Oct. 17,
1824, by John Nickerson — 3 — 24

Millinda, m. Agur B. **HOYT**, Nov. 18, 1823, by Rev. W[illia]m
Andrews — 3 — 19

HADDON, Daniel, m. Mary A. **LANIGAN**, May 22, 1850, by Rev.
George H. Deere — 3 — 148

HALBUT, [see under **HURLBURT**]

HALL, [see also **HULL**], Amos, m. Mary **PORTER**, Apr. 2, 1843, by
Rev. William R. Webb — 3 — 124

Elisabeth, m. Joseph **BENEDICT**, Oct. 24, 1750 — 1 — 465

Huldah, b. Nov. 17, 1753; m. Hezekiah **BENEDICT**, Jr., Jan.
30, 1777 — 1 — 406

John, m. Hannah H. **BANKS**, b. of Danbury, July 29, 1823,
by John Nickerson — 3 — 18

Jonathan W., m. Esther W. **NONEY**, b. of Bethel, May 4,
1842, by J. Greenwood — 3 — 115

Mary, m. Eliud **TAYLOR**, Apr. 13, 1780 — 1 — 401

Rachel Ann, d. Amaziah, b. May 9, 1822 — 2 — 67

HALLIDAY, HALLADAY, Ann, m. Enoch **MORE**, Sept. 26, 1821,
by Rev. W[illia]m Andrews — 3 — 8

Betsey Ann, m. Horace S. **BRADLEY**, [June] 15, [1829], by

	Vol.	Page

HALLIDAY, HALLADAY, (cont.)

Rev. A. Rood — 3 52

Susan, m. William **MONTGOMERY,** b. of Danbury, Jan. 18, 1832, by Thomas Larcombe — 3 67

HAMILTON, Ame, m. Ebenezer **WHITLOCK,** May 21, 1760 — 1 398

Anne, d. Capt. Paul, m. Jesse **HOYT,** Jr., Dec. 31, 1794 — 1 484

Daniel Ezra, s. [Ezra & Polly], b. Aug. 31, 1794 — 1 357

Elizabeth, d. Capt. Silas, m. Lemuel **LINDSLEY,** May 27, 1773 — 1 390

Ezra, 5th s. Joseph, b. Dec. 3, 1768; m. Polly **BARNUM,** 4th d. Matthew, Sept. 15, 1793 — 1 357

George, m. Laura **KNAPP,** June 18, 1843, by Lucius Atwater — 3 120

Joseph, Jr., m. Elizabeth **WILKES,** d. Matthew, Mar. 16, 1780 — 1 394

Lucy, m. Ransom **SHERWOOD,** [Jan.] 30, [1833], by Rev. A. Rood — 3 73

Orpha, d. Capt. Silas, m. Abijah **BARNUM,** Oct. 20, 1763 — 1 388

Philander, m. Betsey Ann **STONE,** b. of Danbury, Nov. 24, 1844, by Rev. Rollin S. Stone — 3 130

Zenas, [s. Joseph, Jr. & Elizabeth], b. Nov. 6, 1782 — 1 394

HAMLIN, Betsey Sophia, [d. Russel & Sally], b. Feb. 16, 1824 — 2 100

Julia, of Danbury, m. Orman **BRADLY,** of Brookfield, Nov. 17, 1839, by John Nickerson — 3 101

Oliver, m. Mary **BAILEY,** b. of Danbury, Oct. 23, 1837, by Rev. Salmon C. Bulkley — 3 92

Rachel, of New Milford, m. Cornelius **BENEDICT,** of Danbury, Apr. 16, 1828, by John Nickerson — 3 47

Sally, w. Russel, d. Apr. 23, 1822 — 2 100

Sally Arline, d. Russel & Sally, b. Aug. 10, 1816 — 2 100

HANFORD, Apollus, s. Joseph Whitman & Mercy, b. Jan. 24, 1795 — 1 475

Levi, m. Lucy **BARNUM,** Oct. 14, [1844], by R. K. Bellamy — 3 130

HARE, George S., of Milford, m. Sarah J. **CRAWFORD,** of Danbury, Sept. 1, 1847, by Rev. John Crawford — 3 164

HARRIS, Emily J., m. Benjamin **TIMPSON,** b. of Danbury, June 1, [ ], at her father's house (Eri **BARTRAM**), by Rev. J. B. Merwin. Recorded Aug. 1854 — 3 158

Nathan F., of South Salem, West Chester Co., N. Y., m. Susan **BARTRAM,** of Danbury, Dec. 14, 1845, by Rev. Fitch Read — 3 137

Seeley, of Norwalk, m. Abigail **BENEDICT,** of Danbury, this day, [Apr. 12, 1834], by Rev. Lemuel B. Hull — 3 83

Susan, m. Amos **RAYMOND,** July 15, 1850, by Rev. Charles Mead — 3 149

HARRISON, James, of Montpelier, Vt., m. Mary Ann **LAWTON,** of Danbury, Dec. 15, 1844, by Rev. Fitch Reed — 3 130

HARVEY, Henry S., m. Abigail A. **HOLMAN,** Oct. 3, 1838, by Rev. J. G. Collom — 3 95

Henry S., m. Adelaide R. **RAYMOND,** Aug. 12, 1844, by R. K. Bellamy — 3 127

Mary, m. William **HOYT,** June 14*, 1843, by Rev. John Mitchell

	Vol.	Page
HARVEY, (cont.)		
*(First written "18th")	3	121
HATCH, Hannah P., m. James H. COOKE, Apr. 8, 1823, by Rev. W[illia]m Andrews	3	16
Julia P., of Danbury, m. P. HENDERSON, of New York, July 5, 1836, by Rev. A. Rood	3	87
Lavinia W., m. Joseph GREGORY, [Apr.] 23, [1832], by Rev. A. Rood	3	70
HAWKSLY, [see also HAWLEY], George, m. Abigail WOOD, Oct. 6, 1840, by Edward Taylor, J. P.	3	106
HAWLEY, [see also HAWKSLY, Angelina, [d. Closen & Sarah], b. June 17, 1790	3	416
Closon, m. [Sarah FERRY, d. Benjamin & Sarah (d. Lieut. John DIBBLE)]*, Nov. 6, 1777 *(Inserted in Pencil)	1	416
Daniel, [s. Closen & Sarah], b. Mar. 16, 1785	1	416
Dilley, m. Abraham GAN, b. of Danbury, May 14, 1822, by Phineas Taylor, J. P.	3	12
Emmond, of Brookfield, m. Hancy OBRION, of Danbury, Sept. 12, 1830, by Rev. E. Washburn	3	58
Fanny S., m. Gould S. DISBROW, b. of Danbury, Mar. 7, 1843, by S. B. Britton	3	119
Hulday, d. Elijah, of New Fairfield, b. Jan. 24, 1775; m. Stephen HOYT, 2nd s. Jonathan, Mar. 2, 1796	1	374
James, of Brookfield, m. Rachel SHADBOTT, of Danbury, July 5, 1829, by John Nickerson	3	52
John, of Brookfield, m. Polly SLOCUM, of New York, Oct. 21, 1832, by John Nickerson	3	71
Julia, of Danbury, m. David DUFFEE, of Philadelphia, Aug. 27, last, [1820], by Phineas Taylor, J. P.	3	2
Julia A., of Danbury, m. Marcus B. SHERMAN, of Newtown, Apr. 30, 1848, by Rev. J. D. Marshall, of Redding	3	142
Lally, [child of Closen & Sarah], b. Jan. 8, 1788	1	416
Lucy, [d. Closen & Sarah], b. Jan. 6, 1779	1	416
Marcy, [d. Closen & Sarah], b. May 16, 1782	1	416
Margarett, m. Andrew P. ANDREWS, b. of Danbury, Apr. 27, [1845], by John L. Ambler, C. M.	3	134
Mary, m. George DEACON*, b. of Danbury, this day [Dec. 8, 1833], by Levi Osborn *(DEAVON?)	3	78
Phebe, m. James W. NICHOLS, b. of Danbury, July 6, 1845, by Rev. F. Reed	3	135
Sally, m. Amos HICKOK, May 18, 1806	2	61
HAYES, HAY, Homer L., of Brookfield, m. Sarah L. TAYLOR, of Danbury, this day [Oct. 23, 1836], by Rev. D. H. Short	3	87
John, of New Fairfield, m. Clarissa WILDMAN, of Danbury, Sept. 9, 1828, by S. S. Burdett	3	48
Lewis, m. Melinda TURNEY, Sept. 5, 1847, by Lucius Atwater	3	142
Maria, [d. Dr. Peter & Mary], b. Mar. 8, 1785	1	415
Peter, Dr., m. wid. Mary ROCKWELL, Feb. 6, 1777	1	415

	Vol.	Page

HAYES, HAY, (cont.)

Peter Perrit, [s. Dr. Peter & Mary], b. July 9, 1788	1	415
Polly, [d. Dr. Peter & Mary], b. Apr. 4, 1782	1	451
Rhoda, m. Peter **STARR**, Aug. 21, [1837], by Jacob Shaw	3	91
Thomas Starr, s. [Dr. Peter & Mary], b. Nov. 29, 1778	1	415

HAYNES, Chauncey, of Pawlings, N. Y., m. Mrs. Martha
   HOLLISTER, of Danbury, this day [Aug. 9, 1841], by
   Rev. Rollin S. Stone .... 3 ... 110

HAYT, [see under **HOYT**]

HEACOCK, [see also **HITCHCOCK, HICKOK & HISCOCK**],

| Anna M., of Danbury, m. David **BURR**, of Saugatuck, Oct. 5, 1821, by Rev. Oliver Tuttle | 3 | 8 |
| William, m. Betsey **HOLLY**, Oct. 17, 1833, by John Nickerson | 3 | 77 |

HENDERSON, P., of New York, m. Julia P. **HATCH**, of Danbury,
   July 5, 1836, by Rev. A. Rood .... 3 ... 87

HENDRICK, Eli F., M. D., of N. Y., m. Maria B. **STEVENS**, of Mill
   Plain, Nov. 27, 1851, by Rev. F. N. Barlow .... 3 ... 157

HIBBARD, Nathaniel, m. Mary Ann **WILLIAMS**, b. of Danbury,
   Nov. 12, 1834, by Edward Taylor, J. P. .... 3 ... 82

HICKOK, [see also **HITCHCOCK, HISCOCK & HEACOCK**],

Aaron Hawley, s. [Amos & Sally], b. Apr. 17, 1807	2	61
Almon, m. Cornelia **BENEDICT**, [May 23, [1838], by Rev. J. G. Collom	3	94
Amos, [s. Capt. Daniel & Lucy], b. Dec. 17, 1781	1	401
Amos, m. Sally **HAWLEY**, May 18, 1806	2	61
Andrew, m. Cordilia **GREGORY**, b. of Danbury, Oct. 14, 1822, by Rev. John G. Low	3	22
Caroline, of Danbury, m. William **McDOLE**, of New York City, Dec. 20, 1829, by Oliver Shepard, J. P.	3	54
Caroline Maria, d. [Amos & Sally], b. Oct. 4, 1808	2	61
Charles, s. [Amos & Sally], b. July 1, 1810	2	61
Daniel, Capt., m. Lucy **STARR**, d. Capt. Thomas, Nov. 23, 1769	1	401
Daniel, s. [Capt. Daniel & Lucy], b. Feb. 4, 1771	1	401
Ebenezer, m. Mary **BENEDICT**, d. Abraham, Feb. 15, 1770	1	394
Ebenezer, s. [Ebenezer & Mary], b. Jan. 1, 1774	1	394
Esther, [d. Capt. Daniel & Lucy], b. Aug. 28, 1772	1	401
Esther, m. Cyrus **SMITH**, Nov. 14, 1821, by Rev. W[illia]m Andrews	3	9
Henry, m. Mary E. **HOYT**, b. of Danbury, Oct. 28, 1847, by John Crawford	3	164
Horace E., m. Amelia **TROWBRIDGE**, Oct. 23, 1842, by Rev. Thomas T. Guion	3	117
Julia J., of Danbury, m. Edward **STAPLETON**, of Sandusky, O., Sept. 17, 1844, by Rev. George T. Todd	3	128
Laurens, m. Elisabeth **TAYLOR**, b. of Bethel, Oct. 8, 1822, by Rev. John G. Lowe	3	22
Lucy, [d. Capt. Daniel & Lucy], b. Nov. 26, 1777	1	401
Maria, m. John **CLAPP**, of Hartford, Jan. 1, 1823, by Rev.		

	Vol.	Page
HICKOK, (cont.)		
I. G. Lowe	3	14
Maria, m. John **CLAPP**, b. of Bethel, Jan. 1, 1823, by Rev. John G. Lowe	3	23
Mary, [d. Ebenezer & Mary], b. July 29, 1778; d. June 6, 1792	1	394
Mary A., m. Barlow B. **BRONSON**, b. of Danbury, Sept. 15, 1840, by Addison Parker	3	105
Noah, [s. Capt. Daniel & Lucy], b. Dec. 6, 1774	1	401
Rebecca, [d. Ebenezer & Mary], b. Jan. 20, 1781	1	394
Rebecca, m. Hiram **BEEBE**, b. of Bethel, May 10, 1848, by E. O. Dunning	3	143
Sally, m. Harvey **HOYT**, this day [Mar. 20, 1821], by Nathan Seelye, J. P.	3	6
Sarah, d. Ebenezer, of Canaan, m. Joel **KELLOGG**, Nov. 4, 1792	1	392
Sarah, m. James **FENNING**, Oct. 19, 1843, by Rev. William R. Webb	3	124
Silas, [s. Ebenezer & Mary], b. May 7, 1776	1	394
Timothy, m. Easther **GREGORY**, Nov. 30, 1820, by W[illia]m Andrews	3	4
William C., m. Sarah E. **TAYLOR**, b. of Danbury, Sept. 16, 1844, by Rev. George T. Todd	3	128
William Thomas, [s. Amos & Sally], b. May 13, 1812	2	61
HIGLY, Abiah, of Granby, m. Benjamin **WHITLOCK**, Aug. 19, 1796	1	398
HILL, Sarah, m. Thomas **STOCKER**, Dec. 22, 1844, by John Nickerson	3	131
HINES, HINS, Cordelia, m. Darius S. **WEBB**, Apr. 12, 1840, by Thomas P. White, J. P.	3	103
Miles, m. Hannah **DOWNS**, May 31, 1826, by Marvin Richardson	3	33
HISCOCK, [see also **HITCHCOCK, HEACOCK & HICKOK**],		
Elizabeth J., m. Ezra B. **OSBORNE**, Feb. 26, 1850, by W. W. Bronson	3	148
Mary Ann, of Danbury, m. Joseph **BELL**, of Washington, N. Y., this day, [Dec. 7, 1840], by Rev. D. H. Short	3	107
HITCHCOCK, [see also **HEACOCK, HICKOK & HISCOCK**],		
Eliza A., m. George **HOYT**, b. of Danbury, this day [Dec. 4, 1825], by Rev. Lemuel B. Hull	3	30
Fordyce, m. Caroline **JENNINGS**, June 12, 1834, by Rev. Albert Case	3	80
Mary, m. Albert **ANDERSON**, Oct. 15, 1844, by Thomas T. Guion	3	132
Sallu Pell, m. Esther **STANLEY**, Nov. 5, 1828, by Nathan Burton	3	50
Susan, of Danbury, m. Wyllys **LYON**, of Bridgeport, Aug. 5, 1840, by Rev. D. H. Short	3	107
W[illia]m E., m. Jane E. **CROFUT**, b. of Danbury, Nov. 23, 1831, by Rev. James Young	3	65

	Vol.	Page

HOYT, HAYT, (cont.)

	Vol.	Page
Anna, [twin with Lucy, d. Nathaniell & Anna], b. Sept. 14, 1772	1	386
Anna, [d. Daniel & Anna], b. Apr. 4, 1783	1	435
Anne, d. [Comfort, Jr. & Eunice], b. Apr. 27, 1777;		
d. Sept. 19, 1778	1	465
Anne, 2nd, d. [Comfort, Jr. & Eunice], b. Apr. 19, 1779	1	465
Anne, d. Jonathan, of Norwalk, Jan. 1, 1795	1	371
Any, [d. Benj[ami]n & Abigail], b. May 26, 1789	1	434
Asa, m. Olive BARNUM, Dec. 2, 1784	1	423
Asa, m. Adah B. BARBER, b. of Danbury, Apr. 15, 1840, by		
Rev. Philetus Roberts	3	103
Avis, d. Harvy, d. July 24, 1822	2	170
Beach, [s. Daniel & Anna], b. Mar. 24, 1780	1	435
Benj[ami]n, m. Abigail BEEBE, d. Lemuel, about Oct. 1, 1768	1	434
Benjamin, s. [Benj[ami]n & Abigail], b. Sept. 9, 1778	1	434
Betsey, eldest d. [Agur & Lois], b. Nov. 3, 1786	1	497
Betsey, d. [Moses & Amerillus], b. Mar. 18, 1790	1	368
Betsey, m. David WOOD, Sept. 23, 1805	2	65
Betsey, of Danbury, m. Peter HURD, of Brookfield, Nov. 20,		
1831, by Rev. Lemuel B. Hull	3	67
Betey, d. [Thaddeus & Kezia], b. Apr. 3, 1790	1	463
Betty, d. Capt. Elijah, m. Thomas COOKE, Jan. 11, 1792	1	477
Billy, s. [Moses & Amerillus], b. Apr. 17, 1798	1	368
Calister, of Danbury, m. Luzon CROFUT, of Newtown, Dec.		
4, 1821, by Medad Rogers	3	9
Catharine C., m. George S. O'BANKS, Oct. 18, 1838, by Rev.		
J. G. Collom	3	95
Charles, m. Huldah DITEMAN, b. of Danbury, May 11, 1831,		
by John Nickerson	3	61
Clary, [d. Daniel & Anna], b. Dec. 16, 1781	1	435
Clary, [d. Daniel, Jr. & Sarah], b. Nov. 22, 1791	1	449
Comfort, Jr., s. Capt. Comfort, b. May 4, 1751; m. Eunice		
MALLERY, d. Aaron, of Woodbury, May 15, 1776	1	465
Comfort, Jr., m. wid. Dolly GREGORY, of Norwalk, d. Dea.		
Peter Lockwood, Jan. 16, 1793	1	465
Comfort, f. Comfort, Jr., d. May 19, 1812, in the 89th y.		
of his age	1	465
Comfort, m. Ann HUBBELL, [Nov.] 24, [1831], by Rev. A.		
Rood	3	65
Comfort, d. Mar. 11, 1836, ae 86 y.	1	465
Daniel, [s. Noah & Sarah], b. Nov. 3, 1761	1	417
Daniel, [s. Jonathan, Jr. & Sarah], b. July 27, 1765	1	449
Daniel, m. Anna GUN, May 20, 1779	1	435
Daniel, Jr., m. Sarah HOYT, d. Ezra, Sept. 8, 1785	1	449
Daniel A., m. Emily HULL, b. of Danbury, Feb. 13, [1845],		
by Thomas T. Guion	3	133
Daniel Augustin, s. [Daniel, Jr. & Sarah], b. Feb. 11, 1803	1	449
Dan[iel]l Augustin, m. Julia M. HOYT, b. of Danbury, Oct.		

	Vol.	Page
HOYT, HAYT, (cont.)		
24, 1825, by Rev. John G. Lowe	3	35
Daniel Drake, [s. Noah & Sarah], b. Apr. 14, 1765	1	417
Daniel Drake, m. Hannah **WOOD**, Oct. 12, 1786	1	418
David Holmes, [s. Nathan & Rebeckah], b. Mar. 12, 1778?	1	413
David Picket, [s. Noah & Sarah], b. Nov. 16, 1772	1	417
Deborah, d. [Thaddeus & Kezia], b. Dec. 18, 1785	1	463
Delia, m. Augustus **BARNUM**, Apr. 30, 1848, by Lucius Atwater	3	142
Doctor Drak, [s. Nathan & Rebeckah], b. Apr. 15, 1775;		
d. Oct. 15, 1778	1	413
Dorcas, [d. Nathan & Dorcas], b. Oct. 10, 1790	1	413
Edwin B., m. Martha[ ]*, b. of Danbury, Feb. 5, [1831],		
by Levi Osborn *(No last name given)	3	60
Eli, s. [Joshua & Rachel], b. [ ], 1766; d. Apr. 8, 1782	1	371
Eli, [s. James & Rebecah], b. Oct. 6, 1781	1	423
Eli, s. [Theophilus & Hannah], b. May 30, 1791	1	371
Eli, m. Lydia **DUNSKAM**, b. of Danbury, Aug. 6, 1820, by		
Phineas Taylor, J. P.	3	1
Eli Boughton, s. [Agur & Lois], b. Aug. 28, 1808	1	497
Eli T., m. Mary M. **WHITE**, b. of Danbury, this day [Apr.		
23, 1827], by Rev. Daniel Crocker	3	44
Eli Thatcher, s. [Enos & Sarah], b. Sept. 25, 1793	1	439
Elias, [s. Daniel & Anna], b. Oct. 6, 1784	1	435
Eliza Ann, m. Joseph W. **ROBINSON**, Mar. 23, 1828, by John		
Nickerson	3	46
Elizabeth, m. Theodore C. **SEARS**, Oct. 27, 1850, by Rev.		
A. Perkins	3	160
Enoch, [s. Noah & Sarah], b. Sept. 18, 1788	1	417
Enoch Comstock, s. [Moses & Amerillus], b. Sept. 28, 1792	1	368
Enos, m. Sarah **PENFIELD**, d. Capt. Peter, of New Fairfield,		
Mar. 30, 1785	1	439
Eunice, w. Comfort, Jr., d. Dec. 6, 1791	1	465
Ezra, [s. Nathaniell & Anna], b. Nov. 8, 1782	1	386
Ezra, s. [Amos & Dorcas], b. Apr. 16, 1789	1	400
Ezra, s. [Daniel, Jr. & Sarah], b. Mar. 30, 1796	1	449
Ezra, s. Lewis, b. Aug. 12, 1822	2	129
Ezra, m. Mrs. Sophia **HOYT**, Oct. 11, 1826, by Josiah Dikeman	3	36
George, m. Eliza A. **HITCHCOCK**, b. of Danbury, this day,		
[Dec. 4, 1825], by Rev. Lemuel B. Hull	3	30
Hannah, [d. Daniel, Jr. & Sarah], b. June 27, 1789	1	449
Hannah, of Danbury, m. David **POTTER**, of Bridgeport, this		
eve, [Dec. 7, 1823], by Nathan Seelye, J. P.	3	20
Hannah M., of Danbury, m. Charles B. **MASON**, of Penn.,		
June 2, 1833, by John Nickerson	3	75
Harriot, d. [Stephen & Hulday], b. Jan. 28, 1809	1	374
Harriet, m. John **ABBOTT**, a foreigner, this day [Dec. 27,		
1835], by Levi Bosbom	3	84
Harriet E., of Danbury, m. Olover H. **PERRY**, of Southport,		

	Vol.	Page

HOYT, HAYT, (cont.)

Sept. 9, 1846, by Rev. Rollin S. Stone — 3 — 140

Harry, m. Mary **DART**, Dec. 25, 1833, at the house of Charles
Dart, by Rev. John D. Smith — 3 — 77

Harvey, m. Sally **HICKOCK**, this day [Mar. 20, 1821], by
Nathan Seelye, J. P. — 3 — 6

Henry A., m. Rebecca S. **BANKS**, Nov. 1, 1836, by Rev. A.
Rood — 3 — 87

Horatio C., m. Anna **KNAPP**, b. of Danbury, Feb. 19, 1824,
by Josiah Dikeman — 3 — 21

Huldah, d. [Nathaniell & Anna], b. Oct. 8, 1774 — 1 — 386

Hulday, d. [Moses & Amerillus], b. Nov. 27, 1787 — 1 — 368

Ira, [s. Comfort, Jr. & Eunice], b. July 30, 1785 — 1 — 465

Ira, d. Nov. 17, 1822 — 2 — 478

Jeames, m. Rebecah **TAYLOR**, Sept. 8, 1773 — 1 — 423

James H., of Ridgefield, m. Susan **DYKEMAN**, of Danbury,
Mar. 29, 1848, by Rev. I. D. Marshall, of Redding — 3 — 141

Jeames Taylor, [s. Jeames & Rebecah], b. June 27, 1777 — 1 — 423

James Taylor, s. James, m. Rachel **STARR**, d. Samuel, Jan.
11, 1798 — 1 — 369

Jamymer, [s. Nathan & Dorcas], b. May 5, 1784 — 1 — 413

Jeray, [s. Nathan & Dorcas], b. Oct. 9, 1779 — 1 — 413

Jerusha, m. Squire **AMBLER**, b. of Danbury, June 11, 1820,
by Phineas Taylor, J. P. — 3 — 1

Jesse, [s. Noah & Sarah], b. Feb. 5, 1771 — 1 — 147

Jesse, Jr., m. Anne **HAMILTON**, d. Capt. Paul, Dec. 31, 1794 — 1 — 484

John Comstock, [s. Noah & Sarah], b. Nov. 17, 1778 — 1 — 417

Jonathan, Jr., m. Sarah **WOOD**, d. Capt. John, Aug. 13, 1761 — 1 — 449

Jonathan, [s. Noah & Sarah], b. Aug. 13, 1780 — 1 — 417

Jonathan, d. Dec. 30, 1821 — 1 — 449

Jonathan S., [s. Nathan & Rebeckah], b. July 28, 1762 — 1 — 413

Joseph, [s. Nathan & Rebeckah], b. Nov. 3, 1773 — 1 — 413

Joseph Dibble, [s. Moses & Amerillus], b. Dec. 23, 1785 — 1 — 368

Joshua, eldest s. Thomas, decd., b. Apr. [ ], 1740;
m. Rachel **BENEDICT**, 3rd d. Theophilus, Aug. 22, 1764 — 1 — 371

Joshua, d. Dec. 22, 1794 — 1 — 371

Joshua, 2nd child [Abel & Amme], b. Jan. 15, 1801 — 1 — 371

Joshua, m. Mabel **BENEDICT**, Oct. 22, 1829, by Levi Osborn — 3 — 53

Julia, m. William **LACEY**, M. D., Oct. 11, 1847, by Rev.
John Purves, of Bethel — 3 — 151

Julia M., m. Dan[ie]l Augustin **HOYT**, b. of Danbury, Oct.
24, 1825, by Rev. John G. Lowe — 3 — 35

Levi, [s. Nathaniell & Anna], b. [ ] 17, [ ] — 1 — 386

Levy, [s. Nathan & Dorcas], b. Dec. 6, 1781 — 1 — 413

Levi, [s. Daniel & Anna], b. Dec. 28, 1791 — 1 — 435

Lewis, s. [Jesse, Jr. & Anne], b. Dec. 23, 1795 — 1 — 484

Lois, d. John, m. Judah **BARNUM**, Jan. 6, 177[ ] — 1 — 390

Lois, m. Stephen **SCHOFIELD**, Feb. 1, 1776* *(First written

	Vol.	Page

HOYT, HAYT, (cont.)

"1766")	1	422
Lois, d. [Theophilus & Hannah], b. Apr. 12, 1794	1	371
Lois, w. [Agur], d. Aug. 28, 1808	1	497
Lucy, [twin with Anna, d. Nathaniell & Anna], b. Sept. 14, 1772	1	386
Lucy, [d. Jeames & Rebecah], b. Apr. 6, 1775	1	423
Lucy, m. Jabez TROWBRIDGE, s. James, Sept. 27, 1797	1	389
Lucy, m. Bailey FERRY, b. of Danbury, Jan. 1, 1824, by Samuel Cochran	3	21
Mariette, m. Martin H. GRIFFING, b. of Danbury, May 27, 1846, by Rev. Rollin S. Stone	3	140
Mary, [d. Nathaniell & Anna], b. Mar. 31, 1791	1	386
Mary E., m. Henry HICKOK, b. of Danbury, Oct. 28, 1847, by John Crawford	3	164
Mary Madelia, d. Harvy, b. June 25, 1822	2	170
Matilda, m. Hiram PLATT, [May] 25, [1831], by Rev. A. Rood	3	62
Mehetibal, m. Lyman HOLISTER, b. of Danbury, Sept. 13, 1827, by John Nickerson	3	41
Micajah, s. [Nathaniell & Anna], b. Dec. 12, 1770	1	386
Micajah, m. Esther TROWBRIDGE, Nov. 1, 1792	1	421
Mitchel, [s. Comfort, Jr. & Eunice], b. Sept. 24, 1782	1	465
Molly, d. [Daniel, Jr. & Sarah], b. Apr. 15, 1786	1	449
Moses, s. Noah, b. July 2, 1763; m. Amerillus DIBBLE, d. Daniel, Dec. 13, 1784	1	368
Moses, [s. Noah & Sarah], b. July 2, 1763	1	417
Naomy, [d. Jeames & Rebecah], b. Nov. 17, 1783	1	423
Nathan, m. Rebeckah STARR, Sept. 5, 1758	1	413
Nathan, m. 2nd, w. Dorcas PICKIT, Dec. 31, 1778	1	413
Nathan, [s. Nathan & Dorcas], b. May 5, 1787	1	413
Nath[anie]ll, m. Anna WHITE, d. Israel, decd., May 24, 1770	1	386
Nathaniel, [s. Nathaniell & Anna], b. Feb. 21, 1777	1	386
Noah, m. Abigal CURTIS, Jan. 8, 1760	1	417
Noah, m. 2nd w. Sarah COMSTOCK, Oct. 30, 1760	1	417
Noah, [s. Noah & Sarah], b. Feb. 21, 1767	1	417
Noah, Jr., m. Roda WATERS, of Richmond, Nov. 29, 1792	1	447
Norman, m. Alvira STEVENS, b. of Danbury, Feb. 24, 1828, by John G. Lowe	3	45
Olive, d. [Joshua & Rachel], b. July 30, 1785	1	371
Phebe, [d. Noah & Sarah], b. Oct. 13, 1789	1	417
Philena, [d. Daniel Drake & Hannah], b. Oct. 8, 1787	1	418
Philina, m. John GREGORY, Jr., Nov. 28, 1822, by Reuben Booth, J. P.	3	13
Phile, [child of Amos & Dorcas], b. Mar. 9, 1791	1	400
Philo, s. [Agur & Lois], b. Sept. 30, 1794	1	497
Philo, m. Laura BARLOW, b. of Danbury, Mar. 8, 1840, by John Nickerson	3	102
Philo W., m. Clarissa STEVENS, this day [June 6, 1833], by Levi Osborn	3	75

	Vol.	Page

HOYT, HAYT, (cont.)

Polly, d. [Agur & Lois], b. Aug. 15, 1792 — 1 / 497

Polly, m. Horace Reed QUICK, Dec. 18, [probably 1833], at
the house of wid. Abel Hoyt, by Rev. John D. Smith — 3 / 78

Rachel, d. [Joshua & Rachel], b. Dec. [ ], 1764; d. Jan. [ ], 1766 — 1 / 371

Rachel, 2nd, d. [Joshua & Rachel], b. May 17, 1781 — 1 / 371

Rachel, d. John, m. Eleazer BEDIENT, May 25, 1788 — 1 / 388

Rane, d. [Thaddeus & Kezia], b. Dec. 16, 1781 — 1 / 463

Rana, m. Daniel BARNUM, Jr., Apr. 9, 1807 — 2 / 61

Rebeckah, [w. Nathan], d. Oct. 15, 1777 — 1 / 413

Rebekah, [d. Jeames & Rebecah], b. June 2, 1788 — 1 / 423

Rebicca, d. [Daniel, Jr. & Sarah], b. Oct. 26, 1799 — 1 / 449

Rebekah, of Danbury, m. Lemuel ADAMS, of Redding, Sept. 13,
1825, by Marvin Richardson — 3 / 28

Rebecca, m. Abram A. MAFFET, b. of Danbury, Sept. 25, 1844,
by Rev. W. F. Collins — 3 / 127

Rebeccah, d. Thomas, decd., m. Nath[anie]l Stevens, [ ] — 1 / 490

Ruey, [d. Daniel & Anna], b. Feb. 14, 1786 — 1 / 435

Russel, s. [Enos & Sarah], b. Jan. 25, 1786 — 1 / 439

Russel, m. Caroline MORGAN, b. of Bethel, June 16, 1841,
by John Greenwood — 3 / 110

Russel W., m. Henrietta STEVENS, b. of Danbury, Jan. 11,
1843, by David C. Perry — 3 / 118

Russel Wheeler, s. [William B. & Ann Maria], b. Jan. 21, 1821 — 2 / 63

Ruth, [d. Nathaniell & Anna], b. Nov. 3, 1780 — 1 / 386

Ruth, d. Caleb, m. Stephen CURTISS, Dec. 4, 1787;
d. Apr. 26, 1798 — 1 / 455

Sally, d. [Moses & Amerillus], b. July 11, 1794 — 1 / 368

Samuel, m. Mrs. Rebecca KNAPP, [Apr.] 5, [1831], by Rev.
A. Rood — 3 / 61

Sarah, [d. Noah & Sarah], b. Dec. 14, 1774 — 1 / 417

Sarah, d. Ezra, m. Daniel HOYT, Jr., Sept. 8, 1785 — 1 / 449

Sarah E., m. Lyman PLATT, b. of Danbury, Sept. 25, 1850,
by Rev. Rollin S. Stone — 3 / 150

Simeon, [s. Comfort, Jr. & Eunice], b. Sept. 26, 1780 — 1 / 465

Sophia, Mrs., m. Ezra HOYT, Oct. 11, 1826, by Josiah Dikeman — 3 / 36

Stephen, [s. Nathan & Rebeckah], b. Aug. 18, 1766 — 1 / 413

Stephen, 2nd, s. Jonathan, b. Aug. 27, 1767; m. Hulday
HAWLEY, d. Elijah, of New Fairfield, Mar. 2, 1796 — 1 / 374

Stephen, [s. Jonathan, Jr. & Sarah], b. Aug. 27, 1767 — 1 / 449

Tamer, d. John, decd., b. Mar. 10, 1754; m. Thaddeus
MOREHOUSE, Mar. 12, 1772 — 1 / 412

Tamisan, [s. Benj[ami]n & Abigail], b. Oct. 20, 1780 — 1 / 434

Thaddeus, m. Kezia BOUGHTON, Feb. 18, 1780 — 1 / 463

Theophilus, s. [Joshua & Rachel], b. Oct. 16, 1769 — 1 / 371

Theophilus, s. Joshua & Rachel, m. Hannah STARR, 5th d.
Capt. Joseph, July 25, 1789 — 1 / 371

Thomas, m. Mariah BARNUM, b. of Danbury, Dec. 19, 1829,

Vol.   Page

HYATT, HAYT, (cont.)

Apr. 19, 1840, by John Greenwood   3   103

Oliver H. P., m. Eliza **STEVENS**, May 16, 1848, by Rev.
W[illia]m W. Bronson   3   142

Samuel*, m. Mrs. Rebecca **KNAPP**, [Apr.] 5, [1831], by Rev.
A. Rood *(Probably "Samuel **HYATT**"?)   3   61

IVES, George White, s. [Isaac & Jerusha], b. Feb. 28, 1798   1   407

Isaac, m. Jerusha **BENEDICT**, d. Zadock, Mar. 14, 1792   1   407

Jerusha Russel, d. [Isaac & Jerusha], b. May 18, 1793   1   407

JACKSON, Amos, m. Lois **BARNUM**, Nov. 27, 1805   2   66

Barnum P., s. [Amos & Lois], b. June 8, 1819   2   66

Betsey A., of Brookfield, m. Frederick **RICHARDSON**, of
Danbury, Oct. 20, 1850, by Rev. Joseph L. Morse.
Witnesses: Peter McFarlan & Huldah E. McFarlan   3   151

Eli M., s. [Amos & Lois], b. Apr. 26, 1813   2   66

Mary, d. [Amos & Lois], b. Mar. 16, 1809   2   66

Mary E., m. W[illia]m Henry **SANFORD**, b. of Danbury, this
day, [Jan. 6, 1845], by Rev. Rollin S. Stone   3   131

Rachel, b. Jan. [ ], 1784; m. Thomas **SHUTE**, Nov. 24, 1803   1   444

JAMES, Andrew I., of Danbury, m. Julia A. **BEERS**, of Redding,
Jan. 21, 1849, by Rev. Asahel Bronson   3   144

JANES, Elijah, m. Phebe **GAY**, Feb. 4, 1785   1   491

JARVIS, Abigail, d. [Stephen & Rachel], b. Aug. 16, 1764   1   460

Betsey, d. [Stephen & Rachel], b. Aug. 11, 1766   1   460

Betsey, d. Stephen, m. Jedediah **WELLMAN**, Sept. 23, 1792   1   381

Eli, s. [Stephen & Rachel], b. May 23, 1768   1   460

Hannah, d. [Stephen & Rachel], b. June 14, 1774   1   460

Julia Ann, m. John **BARLOW**, Dec. 28, 1825, by Rev. W[illia]m
Andrews   3   30

Mary, d. [Stephen & Rachel], b. Nov. 20, 1760   1   460

Mary, d. Stephen, m. John **RIDER**, s. John, of South East,
Dec. 1, 1783   1   493

Philander R., of New Milford, m. Eliza **CROSBY**, of Danbury,
this day [Apr. 11, 1843], by Rev. Rollin S. Stone   3   119

Rachel, d. [Stephen & Rachel], b. Oct. 12, 1762   1   460

Samuel, s. [Stephen & Rachel], b. Oct. 20, 1758   1   460

Stephen, m. Rachel **STARR**, Feb. 6, 1756   1   460

Stephen, s. [Stephen & Rachel], b. Nov. 6, 1756   1   460

JENKINS, Almira, of Danbury, m. Henry **GREEN**, of West
Springfield, Mass., Aug. 13, 1837, by James Beebe, J. P.   3   95

Almyra, of Danbury, m. Henry **GREEN**, of West Springfield,
Mass., Aug. 13, 1837, by James Beebe, J. P.   3   99

Calvin, m. Sally Ann **BENNETT**, May 21, 1823, by Reuben
Booth, J. P.   3   17

JENNINGS, JINNINS, Bennett, of Newtown, m. Marila **MORGAN**,
of Danbury, Dec. 30, 1828, by John G. Lowe   3   45

Betsey, m. W[illia]m H. **ARMSTRONG**, Nov. 19, 1834, by Rev.
A. Rood   3   86

Vol. Page

JENNINGS, JINNINS, (cont.)

Burritt, m. Ruth CROFUT, Nov. 26, 1790   1   382

Caroline, m. Fordyce HITCHCOCK, June 12, 1834, by Rev.
Albert Case   3   80

Eli, m. Almira MALLORY, b. of Danbury, May 21, 1826, by
Reuben Booth, J. P.   3   33

Eliza, of Reading, m. Augustus THATCHER, of Hartford, Apr.
15, 1834, by Rev. W[illia]m L. Strong   3   79

George, s. [Sam[ue]ll & Sarah], b. Mar. 8, 1803   1   379

Hannah, m. Charles Edward FERGUSON, Oct. 10, 1831, by
Thomas Larcombe   3   64

Lavinia P., m. Bradley WEED, b. of Danbury, Apr. 6, 1845,
by Rev. Fitch Reed   3   133

Levina, d. [Burritt & Ruth], b. Nov. 25, 1791   1   382

Marietta, d. Samuel, d. Oct. 18, 1822   2   178

Marietta, d. [Zebulon I. & Evelina], b. Jan. 20, 1823   2   118

Mariette, of Bridgewater, m. Dudley SQUIRE, of Redding,
Nov. 10, 1826, by Rev. John G. Lowe   3   38

Marinda, d. [Sam[ue]ll & Sarah], b. Jan. 17, 1799   1   379

Michael, of Redding, m. Mrs. Catharine TAYLOR, [Jan.] 26,
[1830], by Rev. A. Rood   3   54

Narbby, of Danbury, m. Walter FAIRCHILD, of New Town,
Nov. 28, 1820, by Nathan Seeley, J. P.   3   4

Orlando, m. Ann Eliza MORRIS, July 28, 1850, by Rev. George
H. Deere   3   149

Paulina, d. [Burritt & Ruth], b. May 3, 1793   1   382

Sam[ue]ll, m. Sarah CORBIN, d. Philip, decd., Feb. 3, 1793   1   379

Samuel, s. [Sam[ue]ll & Sarah], b. Sept. 22, 1794   1   379

Samuel W., m. Mrs. Betsey FOOT, b. of Danbury, Feb. 18,
1845, by Rev. Fitch Reed   3   133

Sarah, d. [Sam[ue]ll & Sarah], b. Oct. 21, 1796   1   379

Susan M., m. Gilbert DENTON, b. of Danbury, May 30, 1841,
by Addison Parker   3   109

Zebulon I*., m. Evelina KNAPP, Mar. 18, 1822 *(Probably
"Zebulon J.")   2   118

Zebulon I., m. Evelina KNAPP, b. of Danbury, Mar. 18, 1822,
by Asa Bronson   3   11

Zebulon Jackson, s. [Sam[ue]ll & Sarah], b. Feb. 8, 1801   1   379

[JEWELL], see under JUEL]

JINKS, Hannah, m. Thaddeus WILLIAMS, Aug. 25, 1774   1   422

JOHNSON, Charles, of South Brittan, m. Almeda TROWBRIDGE,
of Danbury, [Jan.] 18, [1829], by John Nickerson   3   50

John, formerly of Newtown, m. Sally MORGAN, of Danbury,
May 12, 1835, by Edward Taylor, J. P.   3   82

Reuben, m. Achsah PEARCE, b. of Danbury, Sept. 4, 1842,
by Rev. George N. Kelton   3   116

JONES, Errich B., m. Hannah ALLEN, [Dec.] 1, [1830], by Rev.
A. Rood   3   58

	Vol.	Page

JUDD, JUD, (cont.)

Fila, [child of David & Anna], b. Jan. 12, 1783 — 1 — 450

Flora, [d. David & Anna], b. July 27, 1785 — 1 — 450

Frank, m. Mary **MORGAN**, b. of Bethel, June 1, 1841, by John
Greenwood — 3 — 109

Hiram, m. Mary **ANDREWS**, b. of Danbury, Oct. 31, 1825, by
Rev. John G. Lowe — 3 — 34

Levi E., of Roxbury, m. Sarah M. **GREGORY**, of Danbury, May
1, 1845, by Rev. Fitch Reed — 3 — 135

Lydea M., of Danbury, m. James M. **SMITH**, of Brookfield,
Aug. 21, 1842, by Rev. Tho[ma]s T. Guion — 3 — 116

Mary, d. [Elihu & Lois], b. May 5, 1786 — 1 — 470

Mary E., m. William H. **EDDIE**, Apr. 28, 1850, by Rev. John
Purves, of Bethel — 3 — 151

Parla, [child of David & Anna], b. Oct. 25, 1787;
d. June 19, 1788 — 1 — 450

Parla, [child of David & Anna], b. Nov. 21, 1789 — 1 — 450

Phinehas, s. [Daniel & Eunice], b. Apr. 4, 1773 — 1 — 470

Polly M., of Ridgebury, m. Silas **MEEKER**, of Greens Farms,
[June] 7, [1820], by Oliver Tuttle — 3 — 1

Rebecca, w. Ebenezer, d. Apr. 17, 1791 — 1 — 397

Reumah, d. [Elihu & Lois], b. Aug. 8, 1791 — 1 — 470

Rheuna, of Bethel, m. Lewis **FAIRCHILD**, of Roxbury, Mar.
30, 1845, by John L. Ambler — 3 — 134

Samuel, 2nd, m. Ann **DEMON**, b. of Danbury, this day [Oct.
22, 1826], by Rev. Lemuel B. Hull — 3 — 36

Sherman, [s. David & Anna], b. Sept. 4, 1777 — 1 — 450

Sturges M., m. Aphia **STURDEVANT**, [Feb.] 9, [1830], by Rev.
A. Rood — 3 — 55

Taylor, s. [Elihu & Lois], b. Apr. 25, 1789 — 1 — 470

Truman, m. Betsey A. **BRONSON**, Oct. 15, 1851, by Rev.
Charles Bartlett — 3 — 158

JUDSON, Addison, of Roxbury, m. Clarissa **WILDMAN**, of Danbury,
Nov. 27, 1831, by Levi Osborn — 3 — 65

Hannah, d. Rev. David, of Newtown, m. Ebenezer Russell
WHITE, Nov. 18, 1767 — 1 — 479

Phebe, d. David, of Newtown, m. Eli **MYGATT**, July 6, 1769 — 1 — 377

Phebe, m. Daniel **CHAPMAN**, [June] 10, [1838], by J. Shaw — 3 — 92

Sally Ann, m. Preston **CROFUT**, May 31, 1829, by Rev. A.
Rood — 3 — 52

Truman Bennet, of Newtown, m. Abigail **CROFUT**, of Danbury,
Feb. 24, 1828, by John G. Lowe — 3 — 45

William, of Monroe, m. Emeline **JUDD**, of Bethel, Nov. 9,
1849, by Rev. Rollin S. Stone — 3 — 147

JUEL, John V., of Poughkeepsie, N. Y. m. Huldah **PLATT**, of
Danbury, Apr. 27, 1843, by James Floy — 3 — 119

JUTE, Phebe, see Phebe **PUTE** — 3 — 72

KEELER, Barret B., see Vanet B. **KEELER** — 3 — 51

	Vol.	Page

KEELER, (cont.)

Elizur W., of Newtown, m. Clara Ann **BENEDICT,** of Danbury, yesterday, [July 14, 1847], by Rev. Rollin S. Stone — 3 — 163

Eunice, m. Moses J. **COLLAR,** b. of Danbury, Dec. 31, 1846, by Rev. John Crawford — 3 — 161

Hiram, m. Sally Ann **ROCKWELL,** b. of Danbury, Apr. 30, 1843, by James Floy — 3 — 119

Ira, m. Sally **WILDMAN,** Oct. 1, 1820, by W[illia]m Andrews — 3 — 2

Jeanette, m. Daniel H. **FERGUSON,** b. of Danbury, June 21, 1838, by J. G. Collom — 3 — 94

John B., m. Jane **BRODERICK,** Oct. 14, 1851, by Rev. Charles Bartlett — 3 — 158

Mary A., m. Henry **SELLECK,** Sept. 21, 1820, by W[illia]m Andrews — 3 — 2

Polly Ann, m. Ebenezer G. **BAILEY,** Jan. 1, 1851, by John Abbot, Elder — 3 — 153

Sally, of Ridgefield, m. Richard **BOUGHTON,** of Danbury, Nov. 23, 1831, by John Nickerson — 3 — 6

Samuel C., m. Lydia **WILLIAMS,** b. of Bethel, Apr. 2, 1851, by Rev. J. B. Merwin — 3 — 155

Street Hall*, m. Lucy **TROWBRIDGE,** Jan. 5, 1834, at the house of Eliakim Trowbridge, of Bethel, by Rev. John D. Smith *(Or "HULL") — 3 — 78

Timothy B., m. Mary E. **COOKE,** Oct. 2, 1822, by Rev. William Andrews — 3 — 12

Vanet* B., of Brookfield, m. Syntha **WHITLOCK,** of Danbury, Feb. 25, 1829, by J. Nickerson *(Possibly "Barret") — 3 — 51

W[illia]m Monson, of Bethel, m. Lucy Ann **BENEDICT,** of Danbury, Aug. 28, [1839], by Rev. Rollin S. Stone — 3 — 99

W[illia]m O., m. Abigail S. **CLARK,** b. of Danbury, Apr. 26, [1843], by Thomas T. Guion — 3 — 120

KELBRIDE, Margaret, m. Patrick **CAVANAGH,** [ ] 25, [1851], by Rev. Michael O'Farrell — 3 — 159

KELBY, Catren, d. Eben[eze]r, of Weathersfield, m. John **BARNUM,** Jr., Aug. [ ], 178[ ]* *(Edge of leaf off) — 1 — 496

KELLOGG, KELOGG, Ann, m. Elnathan **KNAP,** Mar. 10, 1752* *(Possibly "1750") — 1 — 435

Eleasaph, m. Adah **BENEDICT,** d. Caleb, Dec. 12, 1771 — 1 — 436

Elizabeth, [d. Eleasaph & Adah], b. Nov. 13, 1785 — 1 — 436

Esther, [d. Eleasaph & Adah], b. Mar. 4, 1777 — 1 — 436

Ezra, [s. Eleasaph & Adah], b. Aug. 29, 1791 — 1 — 436

Ira, s. [Eleasaph & Adah], b. Mar. 12, 1795 — 1 — 436

Ira, m. Sarah **AMBLER,** Nov. 10, 1824, by George Benedict, M. B. — 3 — 25

Ira, m. Mrs. Sally **SEARS,** Feb. 5, 1839, by J. G. Collom — 3 — 96

Joel, [s. Eleasaph & Adah], b. Oct. 17, 1772 — 1 — 436

Joel, m. Sarah **HICKOK,** d. Ebenezer, of Canaan, Nov. 4, 1792 — 1 — 392

Marinda B., m. Braley L. **EDOM,** Nov. 28, [1844], by R. K.

	Vol.	Page
KELLOGG, KELOGG, (cont.)		
Bellamy	3	130
Mary Ann, m. William W. **DOWNS**, b. of Danbury, June 3, 1839, by Rev. J. G. Collom	3	97
Mehetabel, [d. Eleasaph & Adah], b. Mar. 23, 1780	1	436
Melesant, [d. Eleasaph & Adah], b. Mar. 4, 1788	1	436
Rachel, [d. Eleasaph & Adah], b. Oct. 9, 1782	1	436
Sarah B., m. Henry **SCRIBNER**, b. of Danbury, Nov. 5, 1845, by Rev. R. K. Bellamy	3	138
KENNY, [see under **KINNEY**]		
KENT, Henry, m. Nancy C. **SPEAR**, b. of Springfield, Bradford Co., Penn., this day [Sept. 21, 1825], by Rev. Lemuel B. Hull	3	28
KERNEY, Michael, m. Mary **DORN**, b. of Danbury, Oct. 9, 1851, by Michael O'Farrell	3	157
KETCHAM, Betey*, d. [Nathanael & Ruth], b. Aug. 25, 1770 *(Betsey)	1	486
Betsey, d. Nathaniel, m. Siemour **PICKET**, July 24, 1791	1	385
Eli, s. [Nathanael & Ruth], b. Sept. 14, 1772	1	486
Irenah, d. [Nathanael & Ruth], b. Nov. 8, 1783	1	486
Nathanael, m. Ruth **TAYLOR**, d. Capt. Daniel, Aug. 10, 1769	1	486
Rebecca, d. [Nathanael & Ruth], b. Aug. 19, 1774	1	486
KEYS, David, m. Mary Ann **DeFOREST**, b. of Danbury, this day [June 14, 1842], by Rev. Rollin S. Stone	3	116
KINNEY, KINNEE, KENNY, Catherine, m. Patrick **GALIHER**, Oct. 26, 1851, by Rev. Michael O'Farrell	3	157
Mary A., m. Samuel B. **PECK**, Nov. 17, [1844], by R. K. Bellamy	3	130
Orange, of New Milford, m. Sarah **BEDIENT**, of Danbury, July 24, 1830, by Reuben Booth, J. P.	3	57
Sarah, m. Nathan **COLE**, b. of Danbury, Nov. 20, 1836, by Rev. Salmon C. Bulkley	3	89
KINSMAN, Margaret, m. Gamaliel **ST. JOHN**, Nov. 16, 1788	1	440
KNAPP, KNAP, Abigail, [d. Bracy], b. Feb. 21, 1772	1	446
Abigail, m. Alfred **MANSFIELD**, b. of Danbury, Oct. 9, 1832, by John Mitchel	3	71
Abijah, [s. Elnathan & Ann], b. Oct. 15, 1757	1	435
Adah, [d. James & Elisabeth], b. Feb. 14, 1763	1	404
Alanson, s. [David & Hannah], b. Sept. 10, 1799	1	407
Alexander, m. Mary **DISBROW**, June 19, 1850, by Rev. George H. Deere	3	149
Alfred R., m. Nancy P. **NORTON**, Feb. 24, 1828, by George Benedict	3	46
Anna, [d. Bracy], b. Dec. 5, 1765	1	446
Anna, [d. Elnathan & Ann], d. Sept. 10, 1777	1	435
Anna, [d. Elnathan & Ann], b. July 29, 1781	1	435
Anna, [d. Elnathan, Jr. & Lydia], b. Aug. 28, 1792	1	387
Anna, m. Horatio C. **HOYT**, b. of Danbury, Feb. 19, 1824, by Josiah Dikeman	3	21

Vol. Page

KNAPP, KNAP, (cont.)

Anna, m. Robert J. **VANDUSEN,** Oct. 19, 1851, by Rev. A.
Perkins — 3 160

Azor, [s. James & Elisabeth], b. Nov. 14, 1771;
d. July 25, 1777 — 1 404

Azor B., m. Lucy **PEARCE,** June 8, 1825, by Nathan Bulkley — 3 27

Barnum, m. Hannah A. **MANSFIELD,** b. of Danbury, Mar. 11,
[1849], by Elder E. M. Jackson — 3 144

Benjamin, m. Mercy **WILDMAN,** d. Jacob, Aug. 17, 1764 — 1 402

[Benjamin], m. wid. Rachel **WILDMAN,** Jan. 4, 1787 — 1 402

Betsey, of Danbury, m. Joseph B. **BEEBE,** of Brookfield,
Dec. 7, 1830, by Joseph S. Covell — 3 59

Bracy, m. [ ], May 5, 1762 — 1 446

Brazilla, m. Ruth Ann **ROBERTS,** Nov. 20, 1842, by Lucius
Atwater — 3 120

C[h]loe, [d. James & Elisabeth], b. Apr. 14, 1766 — 1 404

Cynthia, d. [David & Hannah], b. Sept. 21, 1801 — 1 407

David, m. Abigail **BENEDICT,** d. Samuel, Jr., May 16, 1765 — 1 386

David, s. [David & Abigail], b. Jan. 15, 1777 — 1 386

David, m. Hannah **PECK,** d. Ezra, Oct. 7, 1798 — 1 407

David P., [s. David & Hannah], b. Aug. 13, 1806 — 1 407

David P.* m. Betsey **PECK,** b. of Danbury, Dec. 28, 1836,
by Rev. Salmon C. Bulkley *(Possibly "I") — 3 89

Davis, s. [Noah], b. Sept. [ ], 1791 — 1 446

Deborah, [d. Bracy], b. Mar. 28, 1776 — 1 446

Eli, [s. Bracy], b. Apr. 17, 1774 — 1 446

Eli, [s. Elnathan & Ann], d. Sept. 18, 1777 — 1 435

Eli, s. Mrs. Lucinda **ST. JOHN,** b. of Danbury, Apr. 2,
1832, by Levi Brunson — 3 69

Elisabeth, [twin with James, d. James & Elisabeth], b. Mar.
10, 1769 — 1 404

Elnathan, m. Ann **KELLOGG,** Mar. 10, 1752* *(Possibly
"1750") — 1 435

Elnathan, Jr., m. Lydia **BARBER,** Sept. 25, 1788 — 1 387

Eunice, m. Sheldon **BIRDSALL,** Dec. 25, 1847, by Lucius
Atwater — 3 142

Evelina, m. Zebulon I. **JENNINGS,** Mar. 18, 1822 — 2 118

Evelina, m. Zebulon I. **JENNINGS,** b. of Danbury, Mar. 18,
1822, by Asa Bronson — 3 11

Ezra, [s. Bracy], b. Sept. 13, 1781 — 1 446

Hannah, [d. Elnathan & Ann], d. Sept. 2, 1777 — 1 435

Hannah, [d. Elnathan, Jr. & Lydia], b. Jan. 12, 1790 — 1 387

Harmon, m. Rachel **BARLOW,** Jan. 1, 1852, by Rev. A. Perkins — 3 160

Harvey, m. Betsey Ann **BETTYS,** b. of Danbury, Dec. 30, 1832,
by Levi Brunson — 3 73

Hiram, m. Eleanor **FERRY,** b. of Danbury, June 12, 1821, by
Zachariah Clark, Jr., J. P. — 3 7

James, m. Elisabeth **BARNUM,** d. Capt. John, Apr. 7, 1755*

	Vol.	Page
KNAPP, KNAP, (cont.)		
*(First written "1760")	1	404
James, [twin with Elisabeth, s. James & Elisabeth], b.		
Mar. 10, 1769	1	404
James, Jr., s. James, m. Abigail **SHUTE**, d. of Richard, b.		
of Danbury, Dec. 18, 1796	1	373
Joanna, [d. Bracy], b. Dec. 3, 1783	1	446
John, [s. Elnathan & Ann], d. Aug. 29, 1777	1	435
John, m. Albacinda **BARNUM**, b. of Danbury, Feb. 19,		
1829, by [ ]	3	51
John Barnum, s. [James & Elisabeth], b. Jan. 22, 1756*		
*(First written "1761"]	1	404
Laura, m. George **HAMILTON**, June 18, 1843, by Lucius		
Atwater	3	120
Leon, m. Nancy Jane **PYERZ**, June 2, 1839, by Reuben Booth,		
J. P.	3	98
Lucy, d. Joshua, b. Aug. 17, 1766; m. Comfort S. **MYGATT**,		
Oct. 26, 1783	1	380
Lucy, d. [David & Abigail], b. May 10, 1770	1	386
Lucy, of Danbury, m. Stephen **GATES***, of Ridgefield, June		
24, 1834, by John Nickerson *(Letter "G" uncertain)	3	81
Mary, [d. Bracy], b. Sept. 23, 1786	1	466
Mercy, d. [Benjamin & Mercy], b. Sept. 19, 1767	1	402
Mercy, w. Benjamin, d. Oct. 4, 1786	1	402
Nathan, [s. Elnathan & Ann], b. Mar. 10, 1753	1	435
Noah, [s. Bracy], b. Sept. 13, 1769	1	446
Noah, s. [Benjamin & Mercy], b. Mar. 22, 1770	1	402
Noah, m. [ ], Dec. 11, 1789	1	446
Noah, m. Anna **BENEDICT**, d. Joseph, June 14, 1792	1	459
Orrin, m. Hester **HOMES**, b. of Danbury, Jan. 13, 1828, by		
Nathan Bulkley	3	46
Permelia, of Danbury, m. Hamon **LACY**, of Harpersfield, N.		
Y. Dec. 17, 1829, by Josiah Dikeman	3	53
Phebe A.,m. Henry **SHERWOOD**,Dec.8, 1842,by Lucius Atwater	3	120
Philander, s. [David & Hannah], b. Feb. 16, 1804	1	407
Rachel, d. [David & Abigail], b. June 6*, 1766 *(First		
written "May 10, 1776")	1	386
Rachel, [d. Bracy], b. Nov. 18, 1767	1	446
Rachel, d. David, m. Forward **STEVENS**, Apr. 11, 1782	1	399
Rachel, m. Norman **PAYNE**, b. of Danbury, Nov. 24, 1836, by		
Rev. Salmon C. Bulkley	3	89
Rebecca, Mrs., m. Samuel **HAYT**, [Apr.] 5, [1831], by Rev.		
A. Rood	3	61
Rue, d. [Benjamin & Mercy], b. Mar. 19, 1776	1	402
Ruth, d. [Elnathan, Jr. & Lydia], b. Nov. 2, 1788	1	387
Salmon W., m. Anna **PLATT**, b. of Danbury, Feb. 1, 1832, by		
Thomas Larcombe	3	67
Samuel, [s. James & Elisabeth], b. June 2, 1759; d. Jan. 4, 1777	1	404

	Vol.	Page
KNAPP, KNAP, (cont.)		
Sarah, d. [Benjamin & Mercy], b. Oct. 11, 1765	1	402
Sarah, [d. Elnathan & Ann], d. Sept. 13, 1777	1	435
Sarah, [d. Elnathan & Ann], b. Oct. 14, 1778	1	435
Susan, of Danbury, m. Jessy **MOREHOUSE**, of Ridgefield, Dec. 12, 1832, by John Nickerson	3	72
Tamma, d. Uriah, of Greenwich, m. Noah **TAYLOR**, Apr. 12, 1780	1	408
Thomas, [s. Bracy], b. Sept. 19, 1779	1	446
William, m. Eunice **WEBB**, May 22, 1831, by Reuben Booth, J. P.	3	61
LACEY, LACY, Abel, m. Ruth **BARNUM,** Jan. 9, 1783	1	426
Hamon, of Harpersfield, N. Y., m. Permelia **KNAPP**, of Danbury, Dec. 17, 1829, by Josiah Dikeman	3	53
Huldah, of Danbury, m. Oliver **CLARKE**, of Brookfield, Jan. 25, 1821, by Ebenezer Russel White	3	5
Irenea, [d. Abel & Ruth], b. June 28, 1783	1	426
John D., m. Mary A. **BARNES**, b. of Danbury, this day [ ], by Rev. Lemuel B. Hull. Recorded Nov. 26, 1835	3	83
Noah Anson, [s. Abel & Ruth], b. May 26, 1786	1	426
Russel, m. Sarah **DIBBLE**, May 17, 1821, by Rev. Ambrose S. Todd	3	6
Ruth, of Danbury, m. Josiah **FAIRCHILD**, of Newtown, this day, [Apr. 27, 1825], by Nathan Seelye, J. P.	3	26
William, M. D., m. Julia **HOYT**, Oct. 11, 1847, by Rev. John Purves, of Bethel	3	151
LAKE, Charles, H., m. Phebe Ann **FROST**, b. of Danbury*, Jan. 13, 1842, by Addison Parke *(Crossed out)	3	115
Isaac, of Newtown, m. Rebecca **CROFUT**, of Danbury, this day, [May 30, 1830], by Rev. Lemuel B. Hull	3	56
Joseph, of Newtown, m. Emeline **WEBB**, of Danbury, [Sept.] 10, [1837], by F. C. Taylor, J. P.	3	91
LAMB, Charles W., of New York, m. Caroline C. **ELY**, Sept. 23, 1849, by Rev. Rollin S. Stone	3	146
LANDERS, Polly, had s. Oliver **SMITH**, b. Mar. 16, 1791	1	466
LANE, Ebenezer T., m. Sarah B. **WILDMAN**, b. of Danbury, Sept. 12, 1850, by Rev. John Purves, of Bethel	3	152
LANGDON, Betsey, d. [Rev. Timothy & Lucy], b. Dec. 9, 1793	1	482
John, s. [Rev. Timothy & Lucy], b. Feb. 12, 1790	1	482
Lucy, d. [Rev. Timothy & Lucy], b. Jan. 25, 1792	1	482
Lucy, [w. Rev. Timothy], d. Mar. 7, 1794, ae 35 y.	1	482
Timothy, Rev., m. Lucy **TRUMBULL**, d. Rev. John, of Watertown, Jan. 8, 1787	1	482
Timothy, s. [Rev. Timothy & Lucy], b. May 19, 1788	1	482
LANIGAN, Mary A., m. Daniel **HADDON**, May 22, 1850, by Rev. George H. Deere	3	148
LANLEY, Margaret, m. Jacob Gooster **STONE**, b. of Danbury, Oct. 14, 1844, by Rev. George T. Todd	3	129

	Vol.	Page
LAWRENCE, Daniel Starr, s. [Oliver & Rebecca], b. Mar. 31, 1783	1	495
Daniel Starr, [s. Oliver & Rebecca], d. Apr. 25, 1784	1	495
George M., of Newtown, m. Mabel MORGAN, of Danbury, Mar. 27, 1844, by John L. Ambler	3	125
Oliver, m. Rebecca STARR, d. Maj. Daniel, May 12, 1782	1	495
LAWTON, LAUTON, Josiah, of Brookfield, m. Laura CROFUT, of Danbury, Feb. 19, 1832, by Levi Brunson	3	68
Mary Ann, of Danbury, m. James HARRISON, of Montpelier, Vt., Dec. 15, 1844, by Rev. Fitch Reed	3	130
LEACH, Abigail, w. [Christopher], d. Aug. 11, 1785	1	491
Christopher, m. Abigail TAYLOR, d. Tho[ma]s, Dec. 11, 1783	1	491
Eli, b. Dec. 20, 1784	1	440
Eli* Taylor, s. [Christopher & Abigail], b. Dec. 20, 1784 *(First written "Elizur" and last three letters crossed out)	1	491
LEAHEY, Edward, m. Alice EAGAN, Nov. 9, 1851, by Rev. Michael O'Farrell	3	159
LEAVENWORTH, Charles D., m. Ursula MORROW, Apr. 30, 1849, by Rev. John Purves, of Bethel	3	151
George, of Monroe, m. Anna M. BARNUM, of Danbury, June 25, 1851, by Rev. Charles Bartlett	3	154
LEE, Lewis, s. Elizabeth GUTHRIE & reputed f. Abraham LEE, b. Mar. 5, 1787	1	376
Mary, m. John WHITLOCK, Jan. 12, 1737/8	1	409
LEONARD, Charles H., of Kent, m. Patty WILKES, of Danbury, Dec. 31, 1828, by Nathan Bulkley	3	50
Cuylor, of Sandusky, O., m. Julia A. SEELEY, of Danbury, Oct. 25, 1849, by Rev. Rollin S. Stone	3	146
LEWIS, Ann Maria, of Patterson, m. George STARR, of Danbury, Dec. 28, 1825, by [ ]	3	35
Betsey, of New Milford, m. Ery WOOD, of Danbury, Apr. 9, 1843, by Levi Bronson	3	119
Eowar*, of Danbury, m. Jane JONES, from Wales, Sept. 13, 1836, by Rev. Salmon C. Bulkeley *(Last three letters uncertain)	3	86
Frederick A., of Brookfield, m. Lucy A. WILDMAN, of Danbury, Oct. 17, 1847, by John Crawford	3	164
Hanford, m. Mina WEBB, Aug. 16, 1829, by John S. Blackman, J. P.	3	53
Huldah, of Danbury, m. Jonathan H. REED, of Brookfield, Apr. 11, 1832, by John Nickerson	3	69
Sally Ann, of New Milford, m. Edmon CURTIS, of Danbury, Aug. 9, 1842, by James Beebe, J. P.	3	116
LINDLEY, [see also LINDSLEY], Clarinda C., of Danbury, m. William PERRY, of Reading, Mar. 14, 1833, by Rev. Nicholus White	3	74
LINDSLEY, LINSLEY, [see also LINDLEY], Daniel, [s. Lemuel & Elizabeth], b. June 24, 1786	1	390
Deborah, [d. Matthew & Lois], b. Apr. 20, 1769	1	397

	Vol.	Page

LINDSLEY, LINSLEY, (cont.)

Eliud, [s. Matthew & Lois], b. Oct. 20, 1773	1	397
Elisabeth, [d. Matthew & Lois], b. Apr. 10, 1772;		
d. Sept. 10, 1775	1	397
Elisabeth, [d. Matthew & Lois], b. Mar. 6, 1776; d. Oct. 1, 1776	1	397
Elum, [child of James & Phebe], b. Jan. 14, 1788	1	390
Hannah, d. [Lemuel & Elizabeth], b. Apr. 8, 1774;		
d. Dec. 12, 1775	1	390
Hannah, 2nd, d. [Lemuel & Elizabeth], b. Feb. 4, 1781	1	390
Ira, m. Polly Geline SMITH, Dec. 25, 1823, by Reuben Booth, J. P.	3	21
James, m. Phebe BOUGHTON, d. Joseph, June 10, 1777	1	390
Lemuel, m. Elizabeth HAMILTON, d. Capt. Silas, May 27, 1773	1	390
Lois, d. [Matthew & Lois], b. Oct. 15, 1768	1	397
Lois, w. Matthew, d. Aug. 15, 1780	1	397
Lois, d. Matthew, m. Joshua PERCE, Oct. 15, 1784	1	400
Lucas, [s. James & Phebe], b. Aug. 31, 1791	1	390
Lucy, [d. Matthew & Lois], b. Aug. 11, 1780	1	397
Mary, [d. Matthew & Ruth], b. Apr. 14, 1764	1	397
Mary, [d. James & Phebe], b. Dec. 28, 1780	1	390
Matthew, m. Ruth BOUGHTON, d. Matthew, Feb. 20, 1760	1	397
Matthew, s. [Matthew & Ruth], b. May 12, 1762	1	397
Matthew, m. Lois PICKET, Dec. 25, 1767	1	397
Matthew, m. 2nd w. Phebe GREGORY, Mar. 6, 1781	1	397
Noah, [s. Lemuel & Elizabeth], b. Oct.* 2, 1776		
*("10th" crossed out)	1	390
Rebecca, [d. Matthew & Lois], b. Sept. 19, 1770	1	397
Ruth, [w. Matthew], d. June 30, 1765	1	397
Salmon, [s. James & Phebe], b. Oct. 6, 1789	1	390
Tamar, d. [James & Phebe], b. Nov. 26, 1778	1	390
Zilla, d. [Matthew & Ruth], b. Jan. 8, 1761	1	397

LITTLE, Sally, of Danbury, m. Adam GRAAM, of New York State,
Oct. 9, 1821, by Phineas Taylor, J. P.   3   8

LLOYD, Amelia, w. John, d. Aug. 1, 1818   1   473

Angelina, d. [John & Amelia], b. Sept. 12, 1785	1	473
John, m. Amelia WHITE, Apr. 1, 1783	1	473
John Nelson, s. [John & Amelia], b. Dec. 30, 1783	1	473
Mary Amelia, d. [John & Amelia], b. Feb.* 19, 1791;		
d. Jan. 20, 1806, in New York *(Word crossed out)	1	473

LOBDELL, Benjamin, m. Hannah CURTIS, b. of Danbury, Dec. 30,
1832, by John Nickerson   3   72

Clarissa, m. Elijah BARNUM, b. of Danbury, Dec. 22, 1839,
by John Nickerson   3   101

Elizabeth B., m. William BIFFIELD, b. of Danbury, Nov. 10,
1844, by Rev. Fitch Reed   3   129

Harriet, of Danbury, m. John N. WHITE, of New York, July
9, 1843, by John L. Ambler   3   121

Huldah, m. Jutson WHITE, Nov. 3, 1824, by Rev. W[illia]m

	Vol.	Page
LOBDELL, (cont.)		
Andrews	3	24
Phinehas, of Ridgefield, m. Lucinda **BRUNSON**, of Danbury, d. of Thaddeus, May 6, 1793	1	358
Sillick, m. Lucy **WOOD**, Mar. 17, 1822, by Levi Brunson	3	11
LOBDEN*, Ann, m. John Linus **AMBLER**, June 8, 1823, by Rev. W[illia]m Andrews *(**LOBDELL**?)	3	17
LOCKWOOD, Charles N., of Troy, m. Mary E. **FRY**, of Danbury, Nov. 26, 1844, by Rev. Rollin S. Stone	3	130
Dolly, see Dolly **GREGORY**	1	465
Isaac M., m. Phebe Gregory **CROFUT**, Feb. 16, 1834, at the house of Hoyt Gregory, by Rev. John D. Smith	3	79
John, of Reading, m. Jane [ ]* **BROWN**, of Wilton, Oct. 6, 1839, by James Beebe, J. P. *(Word crossed out)	3	100
Rachel, m. Eli **DIBBLE**, Mar. 25, 1779	1	455
LOGLEN, Edward, m. Harriet **SCOFIELD**, b. of Danbury, May 17, 1841, by Addison Parker	3	109
LORD, Mary, d. Abner, of Lyme, m. Rev. John **ELY**, Jan. 26, 1791	1	383
LOVELESS, Mary Ann, m. Levi K. **WILDMAN**, b. of Danbury, Oct. 31, 1836, by Rev. Salmon C. Bulkley	3	88
LYON, Chloa Ann, m. George **PLATT**, Apr. 3, 1848, by Lucius Atwater	3	142
David, Jr., of Danbury, m. Julia **MORGAN**, of Bethel, this day, [Mar. 28, 1844], by Rev. Rollin S. Stone	3	125
David, m. Emily A. **BARNUM**, Oct. 26, 1851, by Rev. Charles Bartlett	3	158
Eliza Ann, m. Frederick **STARR***, this day [Feb. 2, 1842], by Rev. Rollin S. Stone *(Possibly **STOTT**"?)	3	114
Elizabeth S., m. Peter **STARR**, b. of Danbury, June 1, 1847, by Rev. Rollin S. Stone	3	162
Emily A., m. George **MANSFIELD**, b. of Danbury, Sept. 4, 1850, by E. M. Jackson	3	150
Lucy, m. Eli **STARR**, Nov. 14, 1804	1	383
Mariette, m. Azor H. **THOMAS**, b. of Danbury, this day [ ], by Rev. Rollin S. Stone. Recorded May 9, 1842	3	115
Mary*, of Danbury, m. Ira **MORSE**, of Bridgeport, May 19, 1847, by Thomas T. Guion *(Posssibly "Mercy"?)	3	163
Mercy, see Mary **LYON**	3	163
Noble, m. Eliza **TAYLOR**, [May] 22, [1838], by Rev. J. C. Collom	3	94
Orva E., m. Chloe A. **MANSFIELD**, Aug. 10*, 1841, by Edward C. Ambler *("10th" crossed out)	3	111
Wyllys, of Bridgeport, m. Susan **HITCHCOCK**, of Danbury, Aug. 5, 1840, by Rev. D. H. Short	3	107
McCLOSKY, Charles C., m. Mary A. **SANFORD**, b. of Danbury, Sept. 9, 1850, by Rev. E. S. Huntington	3	150
McDERMOTT, Ann, m. Patrick **DOLAN**, [ ], by Thomas Ryan. Witnesses: John McDermott & Margaret McDermott.		

	Vol.	Page
McDERMOTT, (cont.)		
Recorded Aug. 1851	3	156
Bridget, m. Patrick HUGHES, [ ] 10, [1851], by Rev.		
Michael O'Farrell	3	159

McDOLE, William, of New York City, m. Caroline **HICKOK**, of
Danbury, Dec. 20, 1829, by Oliver Shepard, J. P.   3   54

McESPREL, Julia, m. Bernard **GRLOOLY**, May 11, 1851, by
Thomas Ryan. Witnesses: Thomas Kenny & Julia English   3   154

McLEAN, Alexander, s. [John & Deborah], b. Dec. 19, 1768   1   483

Ann, m. John **DODD**, Sept. 26, 179[ ]   1   497

Anna, d. [John & Deborah], b. Dec. 3, 1761   1   483

Deborah, d. [John & Deborah], b. Nov. 3, 1763   1   483

Hugh, s. [John & Deborah], b. June 10, 1781   1   483

John, s. Nail & grandson of Hector, of Balafedrys and of
the House of Bororack, b. [   ] in the Island of Tyree,
Argyleshire, Scotland. Left Scotland May 20, 1757; arrived
in America, Aug. 14, 1757; m. Deborah **ADAMS**, d.
Samuel of Fairfield, Oct. 12, 1759   1   483

[John & w. Deborah], had twin sons, b. Mar. 16, 1766;
d. same day   1   483

John, s. [John & Deborah], b. Feb. 27, 1773   1   483

John, had negroes Cato, b. Sept. [ ], 1780, in New York;
Letty, b. Nov. 10, 1783; Samuel, b. Mar. 1787, in the family
of Frederick J. **WHITING**; James, b. Dec. 1789; Betsey b.
Oct. 16, 1792. All children of Cato & Viny. Affidavit
made Dec. 13, 1792, by John **McLEAN**   1   483

John, Jr., m. Sally **CHAPPELL**, Mar. 26, 1797   1   484

John, d. Apr. 7, 1805   1   483

Lanne, twin with Lilly, d. [John & Deborah], b. Oct. 27,
1765; d. 10 days after   1   483

Lanne, d. [John & Deborah], b. Apr. 9, 1776   1   483

Laura, m. John **HURLBUT**, b. of Danbury, Aug. 18, 1844, by
Edward Taylor, J. P.   3   126

Lilly, twin with Lanne, d. [John & Deborah], b. Oct. 27,
1765; d. 10 days after   1   483

Lilly, d. [John & Deborah], b. Feb. 17, 1771   1   483

Lilly, d. John, m. William **CHAPPEL**, Mar. 6, 1793   1   384

Mary, d. [John & Deborah], b. July 25, 1760   1   483

Sarah, d. [John & Deborah], b. Sept. 4, 1778   1   483

Sarah, m. Philo **CALHOON**, Mar. 7, 1802   1   450

McMEIHN, Robert, m. Lucy **FOOT**, d. John, Sept. 14, 1785   1   491

McNAMARA, Martin, m. Margaret **BREADY**, Nov. 11, 1851, by
Rev. Michael O'Ferrell   3   159

McNAMEE, Thomas, m. Mary **MALLON**, Nov. 23, 1851, by Rev.
Michael O'Farrell   3   159

MAFFET, Abram A., m. Rebecca **HOYT**, b. of Danbury, Sept. 25,
1844, by Rev. W. F. Collins   3   127

MALLON, Mary, m. Thomas **McNAMEE**, Nov. 23, 1851, by Rev.

	Vol.	Page

MALLON, (cont.)

Michael O'Farrell — 3 159

MALLORY, MALLERY, Almira, m. Eli **JENNINGS**, b. of Danbury, May 21, 1826, by Reuben Booth, J. P. — 3 33

Betsey, of Danbury, m. Homer **SMITH**, of Brookfield, June 1, 1823, by Samuel H. Philliips, J. P. — 3 17

Eli H., m. Hannah **CLARK**, b. of Danbury, Feb. 27, 1837, by Rev. D. H. Short — 3 106

Eliza, m. William S. **PECK**, b. of Danbury, Feb. 2, 1834, by Levi Osborn — 3 78

Eunice, d. Aaron, of Woodbury, b. Mar. 23, 1756; m. Comfort **HOYT**, Jr., s. Capt. Comfort, May 15, 1776 — 1 465

Grace, m. John **WHITLOCK**, July 21, 1761 — 1 409

Horace, m. Fanny **WOOD**, b. of Danbury, Mar. 24, 1839, by Levi Osborn — 3 96

Jane Anne, m. Aaron E. **HOYT**, b. of Danbury, Sept. 12, 1841, by Levi Osborn — 3 111

John, of Redding, m. Sally **MORRIS**, of Danbury, this day [Jan. 15, 1823], by Nathan Seelye, J. P. — 3 14

John D., m. Fansy E. **SCOTT**, Sept. 11, 1850, by Rev. A. Perkins — 3 160

Lucy J., m. Daniel P. **BARLOW**, b. of Danbury, [Nov.] 8, [1847], by Nathaniel Bishop — 3 164

Marietta, m. Russsel **BENEDICT**, b. of Danbury, Aug. 20, 1837, by Rev. D. H. Short — 3 106

Mary, of Dan[ ], m. Elisha **HUIT**, Dec. 9, 1779 — 1 503

Walter, m. Sophia **SMITH**, of Bethel, Sept. 13, 1830, by Rev. Erastus Cole — 3 59

MANION, Bridget, m. Francis **HURGEN**, Nov. 16, 1851, by Rev. Michael O'Farrell — 3 159

MANLY, Daniel B., m. Lucy M. **STEWART**, b. of Danbury, Sept. 11, 1850, by Rev. John S. Whittlesey — 3 150

MANSFIELD, Alfred, m. Abigail **KNAPP**, b. of Danbury, Oct. 9, 1832, by John Mitchel — 3 71

Chloe A., m. Orva E. **LYON**, Aug. 10*, 1841, by Edward C. Ambler, *("10th" crossed out) — 3 111

David, m. Sally B. **THOMAS**, Apr. 21, 1822, by Josiah Dikeman — 3 11

George, m. Emily A. **LYON**, b. of Danbury, Sept. 4, 1850, by E. M. Jackson — 3 150

Hannah A., m. Barnum **KNAPP**, b. of Danbury, Mar. 11, [1849], by Elder E. M. Jackson — 3 144

Julia, m. John **PLOUGH**, May 8, 1843, by Lucius Atwater — 3 120

Ralph, m. Sarah **CLIFFORD**, July 3, 1850, by Rev. John Purves, of Bethel — 3 151

MARSHALL, Horace, m. Mary **CHAPPELL**, b. of Danbury, this day [Nov. 6, 1825], by Rev. Lemuel B. Hull — 3 30

MASON, Caroline, m. Peter **HOLMES**, b. of Danbury, May 19, 1844, by John Nickerson — 3 126

	Vol.	Page

MASON, (cont.)

Charles B., of Penn., m. Hannah M. **HOYT**, of Danbury, June 2, 1833, by John Nickerson — 3, 75

MASSEY, Margaret A., of New York, m. John T*. **EARLE**, of Danbury, Apr. 13, 1834, by John Nickerson *(Possibly "I") — 3, 80

William, of New York, m. Betsey Ann **EARL**, Oct. 2, 1831, by John Nickerson — 3, 64

MATTHEWS, Billy, [s. John & Rachel], b. May 8, 1789 — 1, 464

Eli, s. [John & Rachel], b. Feb. 15, 1744; d. Aug. 30, 1775 — 1, 464

Eli, [s. John & Rachel], b. Mar. 6, 1779 — 1, 464

Hannah, [d. John & Rachel], b. Apr. 2, 1787 — 1, 464

John, m. Rachel **BENEDICT**, d. Lieut. John, Oct. 28, 1772 — 1, 464

John, [s. John & Rachel], b. July 14, 1776 — 1, 464

Limon, [s. John & Rachel], b. Oct. 6, 1791 — 1, 464

Samuel, [s. John & Rachel], b. May 9, 1781 — 1, 464

Thomas, [s. John & Rachel], b. Mar. 15, 1783 — 1, 464

William, of Philadelphia, m. Joanna **WILLIAMS**, of Danbury, Oct. 31, 1825, by Rev. John G. Lowe — 3, 34

Zebah, [child of John & Rachel], b. Mar. 16, 1785 — 1, 464

MAXFIELD, Chloe, of Danbury, m. Manoah **PORTER**, of Brookfield, [   ], by Nathan Bulkley. Recorded July 8, 1830 — 3, 57

MAXWELL, Polly, m. Squire **MUNROWE**, Nov. 29, 1812 — 2, 62

MAY, Anseline, m. Walter **RYLEES**, Sept. 13, 1821, by Rev. W[illia]m Andrews — 3, 8

Elijah, m. Polly **STANLEY**, May 26, 1831, by Rev. John Boyden, Jr. — 3, 62

MAYHEW, Harriet, m. William H. H. **FERRY**, b. of Bethel, Oct. 16, 1839, by John Greenwood — 3, 100

Theodore, m. Betsey **SHERMAN**, b. of Bethel, Oct. 11, 1843, by John L. Ambler — 3, 122

MEAD, David, of Ohio, m. Ann **NICKIRSON**, Oct. 13, 1822, by John Nickerson — 3, 13

Henry, of Danbury*, m. Hannah Amelia **SQUIRES**, of Weston, Dec. 26, 1839, by S. A. Brown *(Or "Cranbury") — 3, 101

Martin, m. Polly Maria **SHEPARD**, b. of Danbury, this day [May 29, 1825], by Rev. Lemuel B. Hull — 3, 27

Sabra, see Sabra **DeFOREST** — 1, 438

MEEKER, George C., m. Mary Ann **DOBBS**, [Apr.] 3, [1831], by Rev. A. Rood — 3, 60

Henry B., of Reading, m. Lucy A. **DART**, of Bethel, Dec. 23, 1840, by J. Greenwood. Int. Pub. — 3, 108

Silas, of Greens Farms, m. Polly M. **JUDD**, of Ridgebury, [June] 7, [1820], by Oliver Tuttle — 3, 1

MERRITT, Charles G., m. Ann Maria **WHITE**, [July] 22, [1833], by Rev. A. Rood — 3, 75

Charles H., m. Mary Amelia **WHITE**, July 18, 1826, by Nathan

	Vol.	Page

MERRITT, (cont.)

Burton | 3 | 34

MERWIN, MURWIN, Philo C., of Brookfield, m. Julia A.
SHEPARD, of Danbury, May 14, 1850, by Rev. D. C.
Curtiss | 3 | 153

Samuel, of Fairfield, m. Mary Ann **BARR**, of Danbury, Sept.
7, 1823, by Nathan Bulkley | 3 | 18

Timothy T., m. Hannah B. **WHITE**, [Sept.] 2, [1830], by Rev.
A. Rood | 3 | 58

MILLER, James, of Roxbury, m. Lucy **CROFUT**, of Danbury, [Oct.]
15, [1826], by John Nickerson | 3 | 36

Nathan, m. Sarah E. **AMBLER**, Nov. 22, 1843, by Rev. William
R. Webb | 3 | 124

MILLS, Edwin, of Ridgefield, m. Ovra **BRUNSON**, of Danbury, Oct.
1, 1830, by Levy Bronson | 3 | 58

Henry, m. Elizabeth **WOOD**, Dec. 4, 1845, by Rev. I. W.
Alvord, of Stamford | 3 | 137

MILSON, Ebenezer Platt, twin with William Andrews, s. Eli, b.
Mar. 10, 1822; d. Mar. 16, 1822 | 2 | 66

William Andrews, twin with Ebenezer Platt, s. Eli, b. Mar.
10, 1822 | 2 | 66

MITCHELL, Elisabeth, d. John, of Woodbury, m. Major **TAYLOR**,
Apr. 26, 1771 | 1 | 492

MONGER, Ezias W., of Litchfield, m. Hulda **CHAMBERS**, of
Danbury, Oct. 24, 1841, by John Nickerson | 3 | 113

MONROE, MONROW, MUNROE, MUNROWE, MANROW,
Henry H., m. Eliza **SANFORD**, June 12, [1837], by Jacob
Shaw | 3 | 91

John H., m. Sally **CARLE**, b. of Danbury, Mar. 2, 1823, by
Matthew Wilkes | 3 | 15

Marietta Elizabeth, m. Orsen* **POLLY**, b. of Danbury, Apr.
2, 1843, by James Floy *(Name rewritten and doubtful) | 3 | 119

Mary, d. Joseph, of Sharon, m. Daniel **WOOD**, Jan. 9, 1746 | 1 | 499

Mary, m. Amos **BISHOP**, May 23, 1831, by John Nickerson | 3 | 62

Polly, of Danbury, m. Marcus **BIRCH**, of New York, Oct. 3,
1831, by John Nickerson | 3 | 63

Squire, m. Polly **MAXWELL**, Nov. 29, 1812 | 2 | 62

Wealthy, d. Noah, of Sharon, m. Daniel **WOOD**, Jr., May 13,
1777 | 1 | 494

Willis*, of Derby, m. Sarah **POTTER**, of Hamden, Feb. 18,
1847, by Timothy Hol[l]ister, J. P. *(Willis **MONSON**?) | 3 | 161

Zachary, m. Rachel **SWALLOW**, Apr. 24, 1821, by Nathan
Bulkley | 3 | 6

MONTGOMERY, Catharine, m. George **ANDREWS**, Oct. 31, 1832,
by Thomas Larcombe | 3 | 74

Laura, wid., m. Daniel **SHARPE**, b. of Danbury, Sept. 11,
1823, by Josiah Dikeman | 3 | 18

Mary, m. William A. **CROCKER**, this day [Nov. 3, 1834],

	Vol.	Page

MONTGOMERY, (cont.)

by James H. Linsley — 3 — 82

William, m. Susan **HALLIDAY**, b. of Danbury, Jan. 18, 1832, by Thomas Larcombe — 3 — 67

MOON, Mary A., see Mary A. **MOORE** — 3 — 162

MOORE, MOOR, MORE, Alfred, m. Amelia **OSBORN**, Nov. 6, 1822, by Rev. W[illia]m Andrews — 3 — 13

Eliza, m. Warren **TAYLOR**, Feb. 12, 1824, by Rev. W[illia]m Andrews — 3 — 21

Enoch, m. Ann **HOLLIDAY**, Sept. 26, 1821, by Rev. W[illia]m Andrews — 3 — 8

Mary A*. m. Samuel A. **TROWBRIDGE**, b. of Danbury, June 1, 1847, by Rev. Rollin S. Stone *(Or "MOON?") — 3 — 162

Myron, m. Elizabeth B. **BOUGHTON**, b. of Danbury, Apr. 17, 1839, by Rev. Willis Lord — 3 — 98

Walter, m. Loiza **ALLEN**, Nov. 27, 1823, by Nathan Burton — 3 — 19

MOREHOUSE, Elizabeth, m. Henry **BENEDICT**, b. of Danbury, this day, [Sept. 12, 1832], by Rev. Lemuel B. Hull — 3 — 76

Jessy, of Ridgefield, m. Susan **KNAPP**, of Danbury, Dec. 12, 1832, by John Nickerson — 3 — 72

Mabel, m. Ezra **BENEDICT**, Nov. 2, 1775 — 1 — 480

Ruth, m. Elijah **BURCHARD**, Dec. 1, 1764 — 1 — 407

Thaddeus, b. Oct. 25, 1748; m. Tamer **HOYT**, d. John, decd., Mar. 12, 1772 — 1 — 412

MORGAN, Adaline, of Danbury, m. Henry **SHEPARD**, of Newtown, Oct. 25, 1848, by Rev. I. Atwater — 3 — 144

Betsey, of Danbury, m. Isaac **BLACKMAN**, of Newtown, Jan. 2, 1837, by Rev. Salmon C. Bulkley — 3 — 90

Caroline, m. Russel **HOYT**, b. of Bethel, June 16, 1841, by John Greenwood — 3 — 110

Emiline, of Bethel, m. [Willia]m R. **BANKS**, of Redding, Oct. 5, [1845], by Thomas T. Guion — 3 — 137

Hannah, m. Frederick B. **DIKEMAN**, b. of Danbury, Dec. 21, 1842, by Rev. Morris Hill — 3 — 118

Jerusha, of Danbury, m. Frederick **CRAWFAUT**, of Redding, Apr. 22, 1822, by Phineas Taylor, J. P. — 3 — 11

John, of New Fairfield, m. Clorinda **TAYLOR**, of Danbury, this day [Jan. 1, 1821], by Nathan Seeley, J. P. — 3 — 4

John Newton, of Wilton, m. Estella Jane **MORRIS**, of Danbury, Nov. 11, 1849, by Rev. George H. Deere — 3 — 145

Julia, of Bethel, m. David **LYON**, Jr., of Danbury, this day [Mar. 28, 1844], by Rev. Rollin S. Stone — 3 — 125

Mabel, of Danbury, m. George M. **LAWRENCE**, of Newtown, Mar. 27, 1844, by John L. Ambler — 3 — 125

Marila, of Danbury, m. Bennett **JENNINGS**, of Newtown, Dec. 30, 1828, by John G. Lowe — 3 — 45

Mary, m. Frank **JUDD**, b. of Bethel, June 1, 1841, by John Greenwood — 3 — 109

	Vol.	Page

MORGAN, (cont.)

Sally, m. Lodowick **DART**, b. of Danbury, Dec. 31, 1820, by
Phineas Taylor, J. P. — 3 — 4

Sally, of Danbury, m. John **JOHNSON**, formerly of Newtown,
May 12, 1835, by Edward Taylor, J. P. — 3 — 82

Zuba, of Danbury, m. Willys **BURR**, of Reading, [May] 16,
[1822], by Rev. Daniel Crocker — 3 — 12

MORRIS, **MORRICE**, Ann Eliza, m. Orlando **JENNINGS**, July 28,
1850, by Rev. George H. Deere — 3 — 149

Clarissa, m. Thomas P. **WHITE**, b. of Danbury, Mar. 9, 1828,
by Levi Osborn — 3 — 46

Elijah, s. Shadrack, m. Olive **STEVENS**, d. Eliphatee, Apr.
8, 1798 — 1 — 359

Estella Jane, of Danbury, m. John Newton **MORGAN**, of Wilton,
Nov. 11, 1849, by Rev. George H. Deere — 3 — 145

Frederick, of Poughkeepsie, m. Caroline **STEVENS**, of Mill
Plain, this day [Oct. 16, 1833], by Levi Osborn — 3 — 76

George, m. Hannah **STEVENS**, b. of Danbury, Feb. 5, [probably
1834], by Levi Osborn — 3 — 78

Jachin, s. [Elijah & Olive], b. Jan. 12, 1799 — 1 — 359

John Stevens, s. [Elijah & Olive], b. Jan. 14, 1801 — 1 — 359

Mary, m. James H. **CROFUT**, Jan. 14, 1824, by George
Benedict, Jr. — 3 — 21

Sally, of Danbury, m. John **MALLORY**, of Redding, this day
[Jan. 15, 1823], by Nathan Seelye, J. P. — 3 — 14

Samuel, of Danbury, m. Phebe **STARR**, of Brookfield, Jan.
17, 1821, by William Cooke, J. P. — 3 — 5

Sarah A., m. Frederick S. **BLACKMAN**, June 5, 1850, by
William W. Bronson — 3 — 149

William D., m. Clarissa **STEVENS**, b. of Danbury, [Nov.] 1,
[1826], by John Nickerson — 3 — 37

MORROW, John, m. Elvira **ODELL**, b. of Bethel, Sept. 29, 1845,
by Thomas T. Guion — 3 — 137

Ursula, m. Charles D. **LEAVENWORTH**, Apr. 30, 1849, by
Rev. John Purves, of Bethel — 3 — 151

MORSE, **MOSS**, Harriet, m. John **ROWAN**, Nov. 5, 1839, by John
Crawford — 3 — 101

Ira, of Bridgeport, m. Mary* **LYON**, of Danbury, May 19,
1847, by Thomas T. Guion   *(Possibly "Mercy") — 3 — 163

Mary, d. Joseph, of Derby, m. Ebenezer **WHITE**, [   ] — 1 — 473

Polly, of Danbury, m. Elijah **GREGORY**, of Danbury, this
day, [, 1836(?)], by Rev. David H. Short — 3 — 85

MUFFET, Abraham, of Phillips. N. Y., m. Ruth **BENEDICT**, of
Danbury, Jan. 15, 1826, by John Nickerson — 3 — 31

MUNSON, **MONSON**, Betsey, [d. Ebenezer & Thankful], b. Feb. 19,
1772 — 1 — 391

David, [s. Ebenezer & Thankful], b. Feb. 11, 1766;
d. June [   ], 1776 — 1 — 391

	Vol.	Page
MUNSON, MONSON, (cont.)		
David, [s. Ebenezer & Thankful], b. Dec. 3, 1776	1	391
Ebenezer, m. Thankful **GREGORY,** Oct. 6, 1757	1	391
Ebenezer, [s. Ebenezer & Thankful], b. Jan. 9, 1764	1	391
Eli, [s. Ebenezer & Thankful], b. Sept. 29, 1774	1	391
Eliakim, [s. Ebenezer & Thankful], b. Feb. 19, 1762;		
d. Oct. [ ], 1782* *(Perhaps 1792?)	1	391
Elisabeth, d. Ebenezer, m. Asa **CURTISS,** June 7, 1775	1	448
Ira, [s. Ebenezer & Thankful], b. Jan. 24, 1778	1	391
Johannah, [d. Ebenezer & Thankful], b. July 16, 1758	1	391
Levy, [s. Ebenezer & Thankful], b. Jan. 24, 1760	1	391
Lydia, [d. Ebenezer & Thankful], b. Jan. 29, 1770	1	391
Patience, [d. Ebenezer & Thankful], b. Apr. 22, 1768	1	391
Rachel, m. Stephen **AMBLER,** Apr. 15, 1783	1	429
Willis*, of Derby, m. Sarah **POTTER,** of Hamden, Feb. 18,		
1847, by Timothy Holister, J. P. *("Willis **MONROW**"?)	3	161
MURPHY, Patrick, m. Ellen **TROPHY,** May 25, 1851, by Thomas		
Ryan. Witnesses: James Kernain & Mary Whelan	3	154
MYERS, Cornelius, m. Abigail H. **STARR,** b. of Danbury, Oct. 10,		
1841, by D. H. Short	3	112
MYGATT, Abigail, d. Jos., b. May 6, 1744; m. John **TAYLOR,** Dec.		
16, 1762	1	438
Abigail, s. [Eli], d. Nov. 27, 1767, ae 25 y.	1	377
Abigail, d. [Comfort S. & Lucy], b. Apr. 16, 1785	1	380
Amerilas, d. [Eli & Abigail], b. May [ ], 1762; d. Sept. [ ], 1762	1	377
Anna Maria, d. [Comfort S. & Lucy], b. Dec. 30, 1799	1	380
Betsy, d. [Comfort S. & Lucy], b. Feb. 20, 1790	1	380
Betty, d. [Eli & Phebe], b. June 21, 1771	1	377
Betty, d. Col. Eli, m. Ebenezer Booth **WHITE,** Mar. 23, 1791	1	474
Comfort, s. [Comfort S. & Lucy], b. Dec. 25, 1792	1	380
Comfort S., b. Aug. 23, 1763; m. Lucy **KNAP,** d. Joshua,		
Oct. 26, 1783	1	380
Comfort Starr, s. [Eli & Abigail], b. Aug. 23, 1763	1	377
David Judson, s. [Eli & Phebe], b. Feb. 21, 1773;		
d. Aug. 20, 1775	1	377
David Judson, 2nd, s. [Eli & Phebe], b. Oct. 1, 1777	1	377
Eli, 2nd, s. Joseph, b. Jan. 25, 1742 O. S.; m. Abigail		
STARR, d. Samuel, [ ], 1759	1	377
Eli, m. 2nd w. Phebe **JUDSON,** d. David, of Newtown, July 6,		
1769	1	377
Eli, s. [Eli & Phebe], b. Mar. 24, 1770	1	377
Eli, m. 3rd w. Mary **BOUGHTON,** wid. Miles, 2nd d.		
Theophilus **BENEDICT,** Mar. 20, 1784	1	377
Eli, Col., d. Oct. 26, 1807, at New Haven	1	377
Elizabeth, wid. Joseph, m. Daniel **CHURCH,** Sept. [ ], 1751;		
d. Oct. 4, 1777	1	475
Filor, s. [Eli & Abigail], b. Dec. 24, 1765	1	377
Filor, m. Betty **BOUGHTON,** d. Miles, Mar. 15, 1787	1	455

	Vol.	Page

MYGATT, (cont.)

Georg[e]*, s. [Comfort S. & Lucy], b. June 14, 1797

*("e" added in pencil | 1 | 380

Joseph, d. Apr. [ ], 1749 | 1 | 475

Julia, d. [Comfort S. & Lucy], b. May 2, 1789 | 1 | 380

Laury, [child of Filor & Betty], b. Dec. 9, 1788 | 1 | 455

Lucy, d. [Comfort S. & Lucy], b. July 28, 1794 | 1 | 380

Lucy, w. Comfort, d. Mar. 8, 1804 | 1 | 380

Mary, d. Thomas, of Oblong, m. Ezra **GREGORY**, Mar. 3, 1789 | 1 | 420

Miles Benedict, s. [Eli & Mary], b. Feb. 27, 1787 | 1 | 377

Noadiah, s. [Eli & Abigail], b. Feb. 15, 1760 | 1 | 377

Phebe, [w. Eli], d. Aug. 13, 1783, ae 36 y. 11 m. 28 d. | 1 | 377

Phebe Judson, d. [Eli & Mary], b. Mar. 17, 1785 | 1 | 377

Polly, d. [Comfort S. & Lucy], b. Jan. 8, 1787 | 1 | 380

Rachel, d. [Filor & Betty], b. June 29, 1787 | 1 | 455

Rebekea, d. [Eli & Mary], b. Aug. 31, 1789 | 1 | 377

NAMES, Benjamin, m. Molly **FITCH** (colored), Sept. 2*, 1820, by
W[illia]m Andrews *(Day crossed out) | 3 | 2

NEALY, Mary, of Orange, N. J., m. Romanzo **GAGE**, of Danbury,
Mar. 2, 1851, by John L. Ambler | 3 | 154

NELSON, Thomas, m. Sarah **TAYLOR**, d. Abner, Dec. 24, 1796 | 1 | 381

NEWELL, Darius C., of Sing Sing, m. Irena **BARNUM**, of Bethel,
this day [July 22, 1839], by John Greenwood | 3 | 98

NICHOLS, Betsey, m. Sherwood **OSBORN**, Mar. 21, 1819 | 2 | 146

Bettey, d. [Stiles & Phebe], b. Dec. 22, 1798 | 1 | 496

David Beach, s. [Stiles & Phebe], b. May 14, 179[2(?)]*
*(Last fig. faded out) | 1 | 496

Edward Arthur, m. Harriet Sophia **BLACKMAN**, b. of Danbury,
Sept. 30, 1840, by Rev. D. H. Short | 3 | 107

Ephraim Fairchild, s. [Stiles & Phebe], b. June 18, 1789 | 1 | 496

Fanny, d. [Stiles & Phebe], b. July 24, 1788 | 1 | 496

Fanny, b. July 24, 1788; m. Milton F. **CUSHING**, Sept. 26, 1807 | 1 | 429

Frances, of Waterbury, m. Julius **GAILORD**, of Watertown,
Nov. 16, 1846, by Thomas T. Guion | 3 | 161

Frederick m. Emily **WILCOX**, b. of Danbury, this day [Oct.
20, 1841], by Rev. S. H. Clark | 3 | 112

George, m. Susan **THOMPSON**, Nov. 14, 1842, by Rev. Thomas
T. Guion | 3 | 117

Harriet L., m. John R. **STRATTON**, June 15, 1848, by Rev.
William W. Bronson | 3 | 143

Hezekiah, m. Juliana **COMSTOCK**, June 7, 1821, by Rev.
W[illia]m Andrews | 3 | 7

James W., m. Phebe **HAWLEY**, b. of Danbury, July 6, 1845,
by Rev. F. Reed | 3 | 135

Lowell M., m. Lydia A. **TROBRIDGE**, Nov. 19, 1851, by Rev.
Charles Bartlett | 3 | 158

Rachel, m. Peter **GANUNG**, Nov. 8, 1843, by Rev. William R.
Webb | 3 | 124

	Vol.	Page
NOBLE, (cont.)		
Maria Loisa, m. Jesse Q*(?) **DUNCOMBE**, b. of Danbury, Nov. 5, 1847, by R. K. Bellamy	3	164
NONEY, Clarinda, m. Peter W. **BUCKLEY**, b. of Danbury, this day [Sept. 12, 1841], by S. H. Clark	3	111
Esther W., m. Jonathan W. **HALL**, b. of Bethel, May 4, 1842, by J. Greenwood	3	115
NORRIS, Mary, m. Bradley **SEARS**, Jan. 17, 1832, by Nathan Burton	3	66
NORTHROP, Elizabeth, of Ridgefield, m. James **BEATY**, Jan. [ ], 1798	1	368
Hannah, d. James, of Ridgbury, m. Samuel **BALDWIN**, Dec. 9, 1772	1	471
Norman, of Bridgeport, m. Eliza **SELLICK**, of Brookfield, Feb. 26, 1822, by Abner Brundage	3	10
Thomas I., of Newtown, m. Ruth Ann **HULL**, of Danbury, Mar. 13, 1833, by Abram Stow, J. P.	3	74
NORTON, Cyprian C., of Chicago, m. Laura Ann **HUSTED**, of Danbury, July 29, 1846, by Rev. Rollin S. Stone	3	140
Garry B., of Southbury, m. Esther **COLE**, of Danbury, Nov. 26, 1824, by John Nickerson	3	26
Nancy P., m. Alfred R. **KNAPP**, Feb. 24, 1828, by George Benedict	3	46
Russel, of Danbury, m. Emily **POLLY**, of Bridgeport, July 13, 1851, by Rev. J. L. Gilder, of Redding	3	155
O'BANKS, George S., m. Catharine C. **HOYT**, Oct. 18, 1838, by Rev. J. G. Collom	3	95
OBRION, Hancy, of Danbury, m. Emmond **HAWLEY**, of Brookfield, Sept. 12, 1830, by Rev. E. Washburn	3	58
ODELL, ODLE, Anson, m. Caroline **BARNUM**, b. of Danbury, Jan. 15, 1822, by Phineas Taylor, J. P.	3	10
Daniel, m. Mrs. Sophia **CROFUT**, b. of Bethel, this day, [Mar. 14, 1841], by Rev. S. H. Clark	3	109
Elvira, m. John **MORROW**, b. of Bethel, Sept. 29, 1845, by Thomas T. Guion	3	137
Mary E., of Danbury, m. John G. **ROFF**, of New Jersey, Dec. 28, 1846, by R. K. Bellamy	3	161
Sarah E., m. Alfred **FLUGLER**, b. of Danbury, May 17, 1847, by R. K. Bellamy	3	162
OHARO, Jesse, b. Sept. 1, 1772	1	412
OLIVER, William, of [Horse Neck]*, m. Eveline **FAIRCHILD**, of Newtown, July 5, 1840, by James Beebe, J. P. *(Written in pencil)	3	105
OLMSTEAD, OLMSTED, Abigail, m. Seth **BENEDICT**, Feb. 13, 1777	1	475
Betsey, d. [Daniel & Sarah], b. Aug. 15, 1801	1	424
Daniel, m. Sarah **BATES**, Apr. 5, 1786	1	424
Daniel, s. [Daniel & Sarah], b. Dec. 30, 1795	1	424
Esther, [d. Daniel & Sarah], b. Mar. 2, 1787	1	424

	Vol.	Page

OLMSTEAD, OLMSTED, (cont.)

George, of New Milford, m. Julia Ann **RICHARDSON,** of
    Danbury, Nov. 27, 1844, by Thomas T. Guion   3   132

Harriet, m. Ferdinand M. **GREGORY,** [Jan. 1, 1840], by
    Addison Parker   3   101

Jesse, m. Hester **ALLEN,** June 13, 1824, by Nathan Burton   3   22

Mary E., of Redding, now of Bethel, m. George R. **WEED,** of
    Burlington, Vt., Oct. 17, 1850, by Rev. John S. Whittlesey   3   152

Waters Furman, m. Aphia **AMBLER,** Jan. 22, 1837, by Rev. J.
    G. Collom   3   99

OSBORN, OSBORNE, Amelia, m. Alfred **MORE,** Nov. 6, 1822, by
    Rev. W[illia]m Andrews   3   13

Betsey, m. John A. **GREGORY,** Nov. 13, 1825, by Rev.
    W[illia]m Andrews   3   29

Betsey M., m. Leander **DIKEMAN,** b. of Danbury, Jan. 14,
    [1829], by John Nickerson   3   50

Eli, of Redding, m. Charlotte E. **BELDEN,** of Wilton, July
    4, 1847, by Rev. R. S. Stone   3   162

Ezra B., m. Elizabeth J. **HISCOCK,** Feb. 26, 1850, by W. W.
    Bronson   3   148

George Nichols, s. [Sherwood & Betsey], b. Feb. 8, 1820   2   146

Hannah, of Danbury, m. Edwin S. **RAY,** of Litchfield, this
    day, [Nov. 29, 1843], by Rev. Rollin S. Stone   3   123

Hannah Nichols, d. [Sherwood & Betsey], b. Jan. 3, 1825   2   146

Hiram, s. [Joseph Bennit & Esther], b. Jan. 15, 1802   1   358

Ira, s. [Levi & Miriam], b. Mar. 26, 1786   1   469

Joseph Bennit, s. Jonathan, of New Fairfield, m. Esther
    BARNUM, d. Josiah, of Danbury, Aug. 15, 1801   1   358

Julia, d. [Sherwood & Betsey], b. Mar. 1, 1823   2   146

Julia, m. Abraham **STOW,** b. of Danbury, July 18, 1831, by
    Rev. Erastus Cole   3   64

Levi, m. Miriam **DIBBLE,** d. John, Mar. 10, 1784   1   469

Lewis, m. Betsey Ann **ANDREWS,** [Jan.] 1, [1832], by Rev. A.
    Rood   3   66

Martin, of Brookfield, m. Lois **VAIL,** of Danbury, Jan. 15,
    [1840], by Addison Parker   3   101

Mary, d. Moses & Sarah, m. Abner **CURTIS,** s. Ruben &
    Silence, Nov. 20, 1796   1   419

Mary, of Bethel, m. Anson **TAYLOR,** of New York, Mar. 6,
    1843, by Rev. Thomas T. Guion   3   120

Mary El[i]zebeth, d. [Sherwood & Betsey], b. June 1, 1821   2   146

Phebe, m. Russel **WOOD,** b. of Danbury, Feb. 24, 1841, by
    Levi Osborn   3   108

Richard, m. Ann **BRONSON,** Nov. 20, 1823, by Levi Bronson   3   20

Sarah, m. Thomas W*. **SHEPARD,** Oct. 8, 1823, by Rev.
    W[illia]m Andrews *(Possibly "N"?)   3   18

Sherwood, m. Betsey **NICHOLS,** Mar. 21, 1819   2   146

White, s. [Levi & Miriam], b. Nov. 11, 1787   1   469

	Vol.	Page
PATCHEN, (cont.)		
1843, by James Floy	3	118
Sarah, m. James **WELLS**, b. of Danbury, Nov. 28, 1844, by		
Thomas T. Guion	3	132
Zalmon, of Saugatuck, m. Ann M. **HODGE**, of Danbury, May 3,		
1835, by Elias Birchard, J. P.	3	82
PATRICK, Mary Jane, of Wilton, m. Frederick **FERRY**, of Danbury,		
Apr. 20, 1845, by Rev. John L. Ambler	3	134
PAYNE, [see under **PAINE**]		
PEARCE, PERCE, PERCER, [see also **PIERCE**], Aaron, s. [David		
& Phebe], b. Mar. 13, 1763; d. May 17, 1788	1	424
Achsah, m. Reuben **JOHNSON**, b. of Danbury, Sept. 4, 1842,		
by Rev. George N. Kelton	3	116
Caleb, [s. David & Phebe], b. Sept. 15, 1788	1	424
David, m. Phebe **STEVENS**, Apr. 28, 1762	1	424
David, [s. David & Phebe], b. Feb. 11, 1774	1	424
David, Jr., m. Caroline **SILLECK**, Nov. 21, 1838, by Rev.		
John Crawford	3	95
Elisabeth, [d. David & Phebe], b. Oct. 7, 1766	1	424
Eunice, [d. Joshua & Lois], b. Apr. 12, 1788	1	400
Hannah, d. Aaron, b. Nov. 1, 1824	2	118
Joshua, [s. David & Phebe], b. Sept. 25, 1764	1	424
Joshua, m. Lois **LINDSLEY**, d. Matthew, Oct. 15, 1784	1	400
Lewis, s. [Joshua & Lois], b. Dec. 28, 1785	1	400
Lowis, m. David **WEED**, July 8, 1821, by Nathan Bulkley	3	7
Lucy, m. Azor B. **KNAPP**, June 8, 1825, by Nathan Bulkley	3	27
Lurana Ann, m. Hiram **PULLING**, b. of Danbury, Aug. 28,		
[1844], by Elder E. M. Jackson	3	127
Nath[anie]l S., s. [David & Phebe], b. Feb. 23, 1781	1	424
Phebe, [d. David & Phebe], b. Mar. 21, 1775	1	424
Phebe, [d. Joshua & Lois], b. Dec. 15, 1792	1	400
Tamar, [d. David & Phebe], b. Mar. 12, 1769	1	424
Tamar, m. Elijah **BENEDICT**, Apr. 12, 1787	1	444
Wilson, s. Aaron, b. Jan. 27, 1823	2	118
PECK, Abigael, m. Thomas **CROFUT**, b. of Danbury, Jan. 8, 1834,		
by John Nickerson	3	79
Abijah, Jr., 2nd s. Abijah, of Danbury, b. Sept. 30, 1768;		
m. Clarissa **STEDMAN**, d. Thomas, of Hampton, Oct. 4,		
1790	1	357
Abijah, s. [Abijah, Jr. & Clarissa], b. Mar. 9, 1800	1	357
Abijah, d. Feb. 5, 1804	1	357
Adoniram, [s. Stephen], b. Aug. 1, 1792	1	445
Ammirilus, d. [Eliakim & Polly], b. Nov. 26, 1797	1	360
Amaryllis, m. Alfred **GREGORY**, Oct. 10, 1820, by Ambrose		
S. Todd	3	3
Ammon T., m. Harriet **TAYLOR**, b. of Bethel, Nov. 8, 1843,		
by J. K. Ingalls	3	122
Ana, [d. Levi & Jerusha], b. May 29, 1783	1	396

	Vol.	Page

PECK, (cont.)

Angeline, d. [Eli & Matha], b. Nov. 12, 1804 — 1 — 425

Anne, eldest d. Abijah, m. Peter **BENEDICT**, 4th s. Thaddeus,
b. of Danbury, Dec. 22, 1779 — 1 — 360

Anne, d. Ephraim, of Newtown, m. John **PORTER**, Jr., Feb.
12, 1784 — 1 — 476

Benjamin, s. Jesse, m. Elizabeth **NICKERSON**, d. William,
June 10, 1783 — 1 — 362

Benjamin Williams, s. [Daniel & Phebe], b. Nov. 20, 1791 — 1 — 399

Betsey, m. David P*. **KNAPP**, b. of Danbury, Dec. 28, 1836,
by Rev. Salmon C. Bulkley *(Possibly "I") — 3 — 89

Bulah, d. [Eliakim & Polly], b. Oct. 15, 1789 — 1 — 360

Charles, s. [Eliakim & Polly], b. Sept. 4, 1787 — 1 — 360

Charles, m. Jerusha **CROFUT**, b. of Danbury, Jan. 26, 1828,
by John G. Lowe — 3 — 45

Charles, m. Hannah M. **TAYLOR**, b. of Danbury, this day
[Nov. 6, 1836], by Rev. D. H. Short — 3 — 88

Clarice, [d. Stephen], b. Nov. 15, 1787 — 1 — 445

Daniel, [s. Levi & Sarah], b. June 29, 1787 — 1 — 396

Daniel, m. Phebe **WHITLOCK**, Feb. 2, 1791* *(Possibly
"1790"?) — 1 — 399

David, [s. Levi & Jerusha], b. Feb. 18, 1781 — 1 — 396

Edwin, s. [Abijah, Jr. & Clarissa], b. Mar. 18, 1798 — 1 — 357

Ekana, s. Phinehas, m. Hannah **PARKER**, d. Elisha, of Lower
Salem, N. Y., June 8, 1800, by Mr. McNeu — 1 — 363

Eli, [s. Levi & Jerusha], b. Aug. 23, 1778 — 1 — 396

Eli, m. Matha **ROGERS**, Feb. 1, 1804 — 1 — 425

Eliakim, eldest s. Abijah, m. Polly **STARR**, 2nd d. Caleb,
Nov. 8, 1786 — 1 — 360

Elizabeth A., d. William, of Danbury, m. Clark S. **WILSON**,
of New Fairfield, June 17, 1840, by Rev. George Nelson
Kelton — 3 — 104

Elkanah, s. Phinehas, b. Feb. 3, 1779 — 1 — 445

Esther, m. Stephen **CURTISS**, Apr. 2, 1760 — 1 — 429

Frederick, s. [Abijah, Jr. & Clarissa], b. Sept. 18, 1793 — 1 — 357

George, s. [Eliakim & Polly], b. Aug. 11, 1800 — 1 — 360

George, m. Fanny **CRAWFORD**, this day [Feb. 4, 1824], by
Rev. Lemuel B. Hull — 3 — 21

Hannah, d. Ezra, m. David **KNAPP**, Oct. 7, 1798 — 1 — 407

Henry, s. [Abijah, Jr. & Clarissa], b. Nov. 21, 1791 — 1 — 357

James Stedman, s. [Abijah, Jr. & Clarissa], b. Apr. 19, 1802 — 1 — 357

Jerusha, [w. Levi], d. Dec. 14, 1785 — 1 — 396

Jerusha, [d. Levi & Sarah], b. Jan. 29, 1792* *(Originally
written "1782") — 1 — 396

Jesse, s. [Stephen], b. Sept. 10, 1781 — 1 — 445

John W., of New York, m. Caroline **SEELEY**, of Danbury, Dec.
13, 1840, by James Beebe, J. P. — 3 — 108

Joseph, [s. Levi & Sarah], b. Jan. 21, 1796 — 1 — 396

	Vol.	Page

PECK, (cont.)

Levi, m. Jerusha **STARR,** d. Thomas, Jr., Nov*. 7, 1771
*("Dec." crossed out) | 1 | 396

[Levi], m. Sarah **BOOTH,** Apr. 17, 1786 | 1 | 396

Lewis, [s. Stephen], b. Sept. 14, 1783 | 1 | 445

Lucy, [d. Stephen], b. June 5, 1790 | 1 | 445

Lydia, m. John **BENEDICT,** Jr., Sept. 18, 1786 | 1 | 463

Noah, s. [Levi & Jerusha], b. Dec. 12, 1772 | 1 | 396

Phinehas Parker, s. [Ekana & Hannah], b. June 23, 1801 | 1 | 363

Rachel, d. Abijah, m. Edward **ELY,** Dec. 28, 1791 | 1 | 481

Rebecca, d. Dea. Joseph, m. Isaac **TROWBRIDGE,** Feb. 17, 1767 | 1 | 448

Rebecca, [d. Levi & Sarah], b. Feb. 15, 1800 | 1 | 396

Rebeca, m. Thomas P. **STEVENS,** b. of Danbury, Oct. 25, 1826, by Zadock Stevens, J. P. | 3 | 37

Sally, d. [Eliakim & Polly], b. Mar. 21, 1792 | 1 | 360

Samuel, [s. Stephen], b. Nov. 17, 1785 | 1 | 445

Samuel B., m. Mary A. **KINNEE,** Nov. 17, [1844], by R. K. Bellamy | 3 | 130

Sarah, m. Seth **CROFUT,** Oct. 14, 1778* *(First written "1788") | 1 | 428

Silliman B., of Danbury, m. Louisa **ADAMS,** of Lawrence, N. Y., June 12, 1831, by Rev. Erastus Cole | 3 | 63

Sophia, d. [Abijah, Jr. & Clarissa], b. Jan. 16, 1796 | 1 | 357

Starr, s. [Eliakim & Polly], b. Apr. 2, 1795 | 1 | 360

Stephen, m. [   ], Oct. 15, 1780 | 1 | 445

Stephen B., m. Elisabeth **ARCHER,** Feb. 18, 1838, by Rev. Rollin S. Stone | 3 | 93

Stephen S., m. Sarah **HURD,** this day [Oct. 2, 1831], by Rev. Lemuel B. Hull | 3 | 64

Tirzah, m. Matthew **WILKES,** Jr., Oct. 8, 1783 | 1 | 427

William*, [s. Levi & Sarah], b. Dec. 12, 1789 *("Billa" crossed out) | 1 | 396

William S., m. Eliza **MALLORY,** b. of Danbury, Feb. 2, 1834, by Levi Osborn | 3 | 78

William Starr, s. [Eli & Matha], b. Oct. 30, 1806 | 1 | 425

PEET, Sarah, m. Stephen **HURLBUT,** Apr. 9, 1823, by Rev. W[illia]m Andrews | 3 | 16

PENFIELD, Many, see Mary **PENFIELD** | 1 | 381

Mary*, m. Abraham **WILLY,** Oct. 22, 1794 *(Many?) | 1 | 381

Sarah, d. Capt. Peter, of New Fairfield. m. Enos **HOYT,** Mar. 30, 1785 | 1 | 439

PEPPER, Bennet, of Danbury, m. Sally **GRIDLY,** d. Luke, of Bristol, Oct. 19, 1801 | 1 | 359

Gridly, s. [Bennet & Sally], b. July 22, 1802 | 1 | 359

PERCER, [see under **PEARCE**]

PERKINS, Catherine V., m. Franklin H. **BIGLOW,** Sept. 4, 1849, by Rev. A. Perkins | 3 | 160

	Vol.	Page

PERKINS, (cont.)

Lucinda, b. Mar. 17, 1795; m. Irie **AMBLER**, Feb. 11, 1818,
by Rev. William Andrews 1   392

PERRY, Anna, d. Solomon, of Ridgfield, m. James **SIEL***, of
Belfast, Ireland, Nov. 1, 1787 *("**SHIELDS**" crossed out) 1   485

David C., Rev. of New Fairfield, m. Polly M. **FERRY**, of Bethel,
Sept. 21, 1841, by John Greenwood 3   111

George, of Redding, m. Eliza **WHITLOCK**, of Danbury, Mar.
27, 1831, by Rev. E. Washburn 3   60

Justice, of Brookfield, m. Sally **CROFUT**, of Danbury, Oct.
6, 1844, by Elder E. M. Jackson 3   128

Mary A., m. George H. **FENNER**, b. of Danbury, July 6, 1845,
by Rev. F. Reed 3   135

Olover H., of Southport, m. Harriet E. **HOYT**, of Danbury,
Sept. 9, 1846, by Rev. Rollin S. Stone 3   140

William, of Reading, m. Clarinda C. **LINDLEY**, of Danbury,
Mar. 14, 1833, by Rev. Nicholus White 3   74

PETERS, Lyman H., m. Nancy **CAR**, [Jan.] 20, [1831], by Rev. A.
Rood 3   59

PHILLIPS, PHILIPS, Abial, m. Rebecah **BOUGHTON**, d. John,
Sept. 17, [   ] 1   392

Eleazer, s. [Samuel Henly & Hannah], b. Feb. 16, 1788 1   477

Eliza, m. David **DOBBS**, b. of Danbury, Sept. 16, 1838, by
Rev. D. H. Short 3   107

Levi, [s. Abial & Rebecah], b. Dec. 29, 1777 1   392

Rebecca Jane, m. Irel **AMBLER**, b. of Danbury, Oct. 6, 1839,
by Rev. Z. Cook 3   100

Sam[ue]ll, s. Samuel Henly & Hannah, b. May 1, 1786 1   477

Samuel Henly, b. Jan. 16, 1760, in Charlestown, Mass.,
m. Hannah **FROST**, Jan. 2, 1785 1   477

Seymour, s. [Abial & Rebecah], b. June 29, 1767 1   392

PICKETT, PICKET, PICKIT, Betsey, d. [Siemour & Betsey], b.
Nov. 26, 1797 1   385

Betsey, d. [Thomas & Prudy], b. Jan. 27, 1801 1   363

Caleb, s. Ebenezer, m. Sally **STEWART**, d. Nathan, of
Litchfield, Sept. 16, 1801 1   363

Daniel, m. Sarah **COLE**, d. Nath[anie]l, of New Milford,
Nov. 25, 1792 1   469

Dorcas, m. Nathan **HOYT**, Dec. 31, 1778 1   413

Eliza Ann, of Danbury, m. Jason **WHITLOCK**, of Ridgefield,
Jan. 1, 1840, by Addison Parker 3   101

Elisabeth, d. Ebenezer, m. Squire **AMBLER**, Feb. 5, 1784 1   406

Ely, s. [Siemour & Betsey], b. May 7, 1792 1   385

Esther, m. Benjamin **CROFUT**, b. of Danbury, Jan. 14, 1844,
by James Floy 3   123

Harriot, d. [Thomas & Prudy], b. Aug. 4, 1808 1   363

James, m. Olive **BARNUM**, Apr. 3, 1791 1   461

Levi Bearss, s. [Thomas & Prudy], b. July 15, 1803 1   363

	Vol.	Page
PICKETT, PICKET, PICKIT, (cont.)		
Lois, m. Matthew **LINDSLEY**, Dec. 25, 1767	1	397
Lois, d. Daniel, m. Simmons **STURGES**, Mar. 12, 1786	1	394
Moriah, d. [Thomas & Prudy], b. Apr. 6, 1799 *(Maria)	1	363
Martha, d. David, m. Newcomb **BEARSS**, Dec. 17, 1787	1	406
Martha, m. Joseph **PRESBEY**, July 9, 1790	1	461
Pollina, d. [Thomas & Prudy], b. Feb. 21, 1806	1	363
Rozil, s. [James & Olive], b. Mar. 1, 1792	1	461
Siemour, m. Betsey **KETCHAM**, d. Nathaniel, July 24, 1791	1	385
Thomas, s. Ebenezer, m. Prudy **BEARSS**, d. Joseph, of New Fairfield, Sept. 7, 1797	1	363
Warren, m. Mary Jane **TAYLOR**, b. of Danbury, Dec. 1, 1841, by Rev. D. H. Short	3	113
[PIERCE], PEIRCE, [see also **PEARCE**], Loisa, of Danbury, m. William **CROFUT**, of Dover, Dutchess Co., N. Y., Aug. 3, [1834], by Elias Birchard, J. P.	3	80
PITMAN, Thomas, m. Sarina **SANFORD**, Sept. 18, 1822, by Rev. William Andrews	3	12
PLATT, Alfred L., of Waterbury, m. Jane* **SHERMAN**, of Danbury, July 28, 1847, by R. K. Bellamy *(Incorrect. Should be "Sarah")	3	163
Anna, m. Salmon W. **KNAPP**, b. of Danbury, Feb. 1, 1832, by Thomas Larcombe	3	67
Betsey, m. Azra G*. **SCOTT**, [Apr.] 14, [1830], by Rev. A. Rood *(Possibly "L"?)	3	55
Deborah, m. Noah **WOOD**, eldest s. Daniel, Jr., Apr. 16, 1797	1	365
Emily E., m. Harrison **WEED**, Nov. 29*, 1851, by Rev. A. Perkins *(Possibly "27th")	3	160
Ezra, of Danbury, m. Aurila **CROFUT**, of Newtown, July 9, [1824], by Rev. John G. Lowe	3	22
Fanny, of Reading, m. Eben **CROFUT**, of Danbury, Feb. 19, 1826, by [ ]	3	35
Fanny, of Redding, m. Ebenezer **CROFUT**, of Danbury, Mar. 18, 1826, by Rev. John G. Lowe	3	38
George, m. Chloa Ann **LYON**, Apr. 3, 1848, by Lucius Atwater	3	142
Hiram, m. Matilda **HOYT**, [May] 25, [1831], by Rev. A. Rood	3	62
Huldah, of Danbury, m. John V. **JUEL**, of Poughkeepsie, N. Y., Apr. 27, 1843, by James Floy	3	119
James E., m. Martha **DIKEMAN**, b. of Danbury, Feb. 25, 1845, by Rev. W. P. Collins	3	133
Lavinna*, m. George **BARBER**, b. of Danbury, Nov. 10, 1827, by John G. Stone *("La" and some letters uncertainn)	3	44
Le L*., m. Jane **SHERMAN**, Oct. 1, 1844, by R. K. Bellamy *(Should be "Lorin L. PLATT")	3	130
Lorin L., see Le L. **PLATT**	3	130
Lyman, of South East, N. Y., m. Sarah Ann **STEPHENS**, of Danbury, this day [Oct. 11, 1840}, by S. H. Clark	3	106
Lyman, m. Sarah E. **HOYT**, b. of Danbury, Sept. 25, 1850,		

	Vol.	Page

PLATT, (cont.)

by Rev. Rollin S. Stone   3   150

Mary, m. Daniel S. **DIBBLE,** b. of Bethel, Dec. 16, 1830,
by Rev. Erastus Cole   3   59

Samuel D., m. Mary A. **WHITE,** May 18, 1840, by John
Crawford   3   104

William, m. Fanny **SHERMAN,** b. of Stoney **HILL,** Danbury,
[Apr.] 2, [1839], by Rev. J. G. Collom   3   97

PLOUGH, John, m. Julia **MANSFIELD,** May 8, 1843, by Lucius
Atwater   3   120

POLLY, POLLEY, Clark, m. Eunice M. **COUCH,** Nov. 20, 1833, by
John Nickerson   3   77

Electa Minerva, m. George **BALL,** b. of Danbury, Feb. 9,
1846, by Rev. Fitch Read   3   138

Emily, of Bridgeport, m. Russel **NORTON,** of Danbury, July
13, 1851, by Rev. J. L. Gilder, of Redding   3   155

James, m. Sarah A. **SMITH,** b. of Danbury, Jan. 19, 1845,
by Rev. Fitch Reed   3   131

Orseh*, m. Marietta Elizabeth **MONROE,** b. of Danbury,
Apr. 2, 1843, by James Floy *(Name rewritten and
doubtful)   3   119

Rebecca, m. William W. **STEVENS,** b. of Danbury, July 18,
1827, by John Nickerson   3   41

PORTER, Anna, d. [John, Jr. & Anne], b. Oct. 28, 1791   1   476

Barry Peck, s. [John, Jr. & Anne], b. Aug. 22, 1787   1   476

Hannah, d. John, m. Dorastus **GREEN,** June 1, 1783   1   395

Hoyt, m. Maria **STEWART,** Dec. 16, 1839, by Rev. Z. Cook   3   96

John, Jr., m. Anne **PECK,** d. Ephrain, of Newtown, Feb. 12,
1784   1   476

Levi Goodwin, of Watertown, m. Betsey **GREANLEAF,** of
Danbury, Aug. 20, 1821, by Ambrose S. Todd   3   7

Lewis, s. [John, Jr. & Anne], b. Dec. 16, 1784   1   476

Liman, s. [John, Jr. & Anne], b. Apr. 25, 1789   1   476

Manoah, of Brookfield, m. Chloe **MAXFIELD,** of Danbury
[   ], by Nathan Bulkley. Recorded July 8, 1830   3   57

Monoah, see also Meneah

Mary, m. Amos **HALL,** Apr. 2, 1843, by Rev. William R. Webb   3   124

Meneah, m. Sarah **CURTIS,** d. Samuel, June 1, 1789   1   478

Meneah, see also Manoah

Mercy Ann, m. Grandison D. **FOOT,** b. of Danbury, this day
[Nov. 5, 1843], by J. K. Ingalls   3   122

Susannah, [d. Meneah & Sarah], b. Sept. 7, 1789*
*(Perhaps "1799"?)   1   478

POST, Benjamin, m. Belinda **COUCH,** b. of Danbury, Aug. 1, 1847 ,
by Rev. John Crawford   3   163

POTTER, David, of Bridgeport, m. Hannah **HOYT,** of Danbury, this
eve, [Dec. 7, 1823], by Nathan Seelye, J. P.   3   20

Sarah, of Hamden, m. Willis **MONSON*,** of Derby, Feb. 18,

Vol.   Page

POTTER, (cont.)

    1847, by Timothy Holister, J. P. *(MONROW ?)   3   161

PRATT, Prosper, m. Polly **CURTIS,** Aug. 13, 1820, by W[illia]m
    Andrews   3   2

    Russel R., of Cornwall, m. Mary W. **BONNEY,** of Danbury,
    Jan. 23, 1850, by Rev. Rollin S. Stone   3   147

PRESBEY, Joseph, m. Martha **PICKET,** July 9, 1790   1   461

PRICE, Edmund, m. Mary **BENNET,** b. of Danbury, Aug. 2, 1820, by
    William Andrews   3   1

    Lewis T., m. Jane **BENEDICT,** Dec. 31, 1844, by Rev. J. K.
    Ingalls   3   131

    Lydia, m. Oliver **STONE,** Nov. 30, 1788   1   395

    Nathan, m. Amelia **COLEMAN,** Dec. 31, 1844, by Rev. J. K.
    Ingalls   3   131

PRINDLE, Damaris, of Newtown, m. James **SARINE,** of Danbury,
    Aug. 23, 1821, by Phineas Taylor, J. P.   3   8

PROUT, Rachel, of New Milford, m. Michael **BENEDICT,** 2nd,
    Aug. 31, 1788   1   462

PROVOST, Christopher T., of New York, m. Susan **RAYMOND,** of
    Danbury, July 4, 1848, by Rev. William White Bronson   3   143

PULFORD, Edmund, of New Town, m. Caroline **CURTIS,** of
    Danbury, Aug. 13, 1837, by Oliver Shepard, J. P.   3   91

PULLING, Hiram, m. Lurana Ann **PEARCE,** b. of Danbury, Aug. 28,
    [1844], by Elder E. M. Jackson   3   127

    Smith, of Ridgefield, m. Wealthy Ann **STONE,** of Danbury,
    this day, Sept. 24, 1845, by Rev. Rollin S. Stone   3   136

PURDY, Abigail, of New York, m. Thomas **BRAMON,** of Rhode
    Island, Aug. 3, 1831, by John Nickerson   3   63

    Harvy, of South East, m. Mary Ann **WOOD,** of Danbury,
    Nov. 24, 1836, by Rev. H. Humphreys   3   89

PUTE*, Phebe, of Pawlings, N. Y., m. Josiah **DIKEMAN,** of
    Danbury, Nov. 4, 1832, by John Mitchel   *(Possibly
    "JUTE")   3   72

PYERZ, Nancy Jane, m. Leon **KNAPP,** June 2, 1839, by Reuben
    Booth, J. P.   3   98

QUICK, Horace Reed, m. Polly **HOYT,** Dec. 18, [probably 1833],
    at the house of wid. Abel Hoyt, by Rev. John D. Smith   3   78

RAND, Munson, m. Polly **STONE,** b. of Danbury, June 1, 1838,
    by J. Shaw   3   92

RANS, Abigail, d. Timothy N., b. May 1, 1789   1   445

RAY, Edwin S., of Litchfield, m. Hannah **OSBORN,** of Danbury,
    this day [Nov. 29, 1843], by Rev. Rollin S. Stone   3   123

RAYMOND, RAIMOND, RAMOND, Adelaide R., m. Henry S.
    HARVEY, Aug. 12, 1844, by R. K. Bellamy   3   127

    Amos, m. Susan **HARRIS,** July 15, 1850, by Rev. Charles Mead   3   149

    Charles, m. Harriet **NICKERSON,** b. of Trumbull, Apr. 29,
    1834, by John Nickerson   3   81

    Isaac, m. Cara **NICKERSON,** b. of Danbury, Jan. 13, 1828,

	Vol.	Page
RAYMOND, RAIMOND, RAMOND, (cont.)		
by John G. Lowe	3	45
Lewis, m. Betsey **BARNUM**, Feb. 2, 1833, by Timothy B.		
Hickok, J. P.	3	74
Rachel, see Rachel **ROBERTS**	1	437
Susan, of Danbury, m. Christopher T. **PROVOST**, of New York,		
July 4, 1848, by Rev. William White Bronson	3	143
READ, REED, Benjamin B., of Redding, m. Catharine **SELLICK,**		
of Danbury, Jan. 1, 1831, by Rev. J. B. Merwin [1851?]	3	155
Charles A. H., m. Evelina **STEVENS**, Oct. 16, 1833, by Rev.		
A. Rood	3	86
Eliza D., m. Daniel **CROFUT**, b. of Danbury, Jan. 23, 1843,		
by Israel A. Beardslee, J. P.	3	119
Elisabeth, d. [Isaac & Sarah], b. Nov. 15, 1774	1	494
Isaac, s. Isaac & Sarah, b. Feb. 1, 1773	1	494
Jonathan H., of Brookfield, m. Huldah **LEWIS**, of Danbury,		
Apr. 11, 1832, by John Nickerson	3	69
Nathan H., s. [Isaac & Sarah], b. July 28, 1776	1	494
Rachel, d. William, m. Philip **BURRIT**, Mar. 1, 1774	1	389
REMMEY, John F., of New York, m. Elizabeth A. **BARNUM**, of		
Danbury, May 20, 1846, by Rev. Rollin S. Stone	3	140
REYNOLDS, Roswell, of New Haven, m. Jemima **FRY**, of Bethel,		
July 9, 1848, by Oliver Shepard, J. P.	3	143
RICE, Dorcas, m. Benjamin **BARNUM**, Jr., July 24, 1757	1	440
RICHARDSON, Frederick, of Danbury, m. Betsey A. **JACKSON**, of		
Brookfield, Oct. 20, 1850, by Rev. Joseph L. Morse.		
Witnesses: Peter McFarlan & Huldah E. McFarlan	3	151
Julia Ann, of Danbury, m. George **OLMSTEAD**, of New		
Milford, Nov. 27, 1844, by Thomas T. Guion	3	132
RIDER, Charles, s. [John & Mary], b. Jan. 24, 1801	1	493
George, s. [John & Mary], b. June 9, 1796	1	493
Jane C., m. Orrin **COWLES**, Aug. 30, 1836, by Rev. A. Rood	3	87
Jane Caroline, d. [John, Jr. & Ann], b. June 14, 1814	2	134
John, s. John, of South East, b. Mar. 28, 1760; m. Mary		
JARVIS, d. Stephen, Dec. 1, 1783	1	493
John, s. [John & Mary], b. Dec. 2, 1784	1	493
John, m. Eunice **BULKLEY**, b. of Danbury, Dec. 2, 1844, by		
Rev. Rollin S. Stone	3	130
Julia, m. John **TWENAIR**, b. of Danbury, this day [Aug. 31,		
1843], by Rev. Rollin S. Stone	3	121
Mary, d. [John & Mary], b. Sept. 21, 1786	1	493
Mary, m. Russel **WILDMAN**, Apr. 20, 1823, by Samuel Cochran	3	16
Mary H., m. James **GILBERT**, May 18, 1825, by Rev. William		
Andrews	3	26
Mary Hannah, twin with William Hervey, [d. John & Mary],		
b. Aug. 4, 1798	1	493
Oliver Roberts, s. [John, Jr. & Ann], b. June 2, 1811	2	134
Rachel, d. [John & Mary], b. Sept. 11, 1790	1	493

	Vol.	Page

RIDER, (cont.)

Ralph, s. [John & Mary], b. July 11, 1793 — 1 493

Sarah Noble, [d. John, Jr. & Ann], b. Jan. 20, 1820 — 2 134

Stephen Jarvis, s. [John & Mary], b. Nov. 1, 1788 — 1 493

William Hervey, twin with Mary Hannah, [s. John & Mary], b. Aug. 4, 1798 — 1 493

ROBERTS, Isaac, [s. W[illia]m & Ann], b. May 12, 1763; d. July 7, 1784 — 1 408

Lora, d. [Noah & Charlotty], b. Dec. 18, 1791 — 1 407

Mary, m. Orrin **AVERY,** Nov. 20, 1825, by Rev. W[illia]m Andrews — 3 29

Matilda, m. Charles L. **STEVENS,** b. of Danbury, May 9, 1841, by Rev. Shaler J. Hillyer — 3 109

Noah, [s. W[illia]m & Ann], b. Dec. 31, 1766 — 1 408

Noah, m. Charlotty **GILBERT,** d. Hezekiah, Oct. 20, 1790 — 1 407

Rachel, d. Comfor[t] **RAIMOND,** m. as 2nd w. James **CRARY,** Dec. 28, 1786 — 1 437

Ruth Ann, m. Brazilla **KNAPP,** Nov. 20, 1842, by Lucius Atwater — 3 120

Sarah, [d. W[illia]m & Ann], b. Mar. 17, 1770; d. Sept. 7, 1777 — 1 408

Sibel, [d. W[illia]m & Ann], b. Feb. 13, 1765 — 1 408

W[illia]m, m. Ann **SHERWOOD,** Mar. 23, 1762 — 1 408

Willis S., of South East Put Co., N. Y., m. Phebe S. **STEVENS,** of Danbury, Mar. 15, 1837, by Rev. Salmon C. Bulkley — 3 90

ROBINSON, ROBBINSON, Alexander Benedict, [twin with Charles Augustus, s. Joseph & Ruth], b. July 7 & 8, 1819 — 2 179

Anne, d. [Zelotus & Anna], b. Oct. 19, 1792 — 1 383

Billy, s. [Zelotus & Anna], b. Dec. 17, 1784 — 1 383

Billy, s. [Zelotus & Anna], d. Oct. 31, 1800 — 1 383

Catharine Olivia, m. Hiram **COLE,** b. of Danbury, Jan. 29, 1826, by Rev. Lemuel B. Hull — 3 32

Charles Augustus, [twin with Alexander Benedict, s. Joseph & Ruth], b. July 7 & 8, 1819 — 2 179

George, s. [Zelotus & Anna], b. May 21, 1787 — 1 383

Hannah Elizabeth, [d. Joseph & Ruth], b. Apr. 26, 1811*; d. June 3, 1814 *(Corrected) — 2 179

Hannah Elizabeth, [d. Joseph & Ruth], b. Apr. 13, 1821; d. Sept. 9, 1822 — 2 179

Henry, [s. Joseph & Ruth], b. Dec. 26, 1814 — 2 179

Hulday, d. [Zelotus & Anna], b. Aug. 3, 1794 — 1 383

James, [s. Joseph & Ruth], b. May 4, 1817 — 2 179

John, s. [Zelotus & Anna], b. Feb. 11, 1782 — 1 383

Joseph, s. [Zelotus & Anna], b. Oct. 16, 1779 — 1 383

Joseph, m. Ruth **CURTIS,** Mar. 23, 1803 — 2 179

Joseph W., m. Eliza Ann **HOYT,** Mar. 23, 1828, by John Nickerson — 3 46

	Vol.	Page
ROBINSON, ROBBINSON, (cont.)		
Joseph Waller, s. [Joseph & Ruth], b. Feb. 9, 1806	2	179
Lois, of Danbury, m. Ephraim **CROFUT,** of Middletown, Nov. 25, 1779	1	503
Lovisee, d. [Zelotus & Anna], b. Apr. 4, 1777	1	383
Ruth, [s. Joseph], d. Aug. 4, 1824	2	179
Thomas Gould, [s. Joseph & Ruth], b. Aug. 10, 1808	2	179
Waller, s. [Zelotus & Anna], b. May 27, 1790	1	383
William Curtis, s. [Joseph & Ruth], b. Mar. 21, 1804	2	179
Zelotus, m. Anna **WALLER,** Jan. 25, 1776	1	383
ROCK[ ]*, Rachel, d. John, of Ridgefield, m. Comfort **WILDMAN,** July 12, 1764 *(Worn off)	1	500
ROCKWELL, Abigail, wid. Daniel, of Ridgbury, m. Samuel **WILDMAN,** May 22, 1801	1	453
Benj[ami]n S., m. Triphena **STARR,** d. Jonathan, May 14, 1785	1	497
Benjamin Sperry, [s. Jabez & Elizabeth], b. May 17, 1762	1	415
Burr, m. Nancy **WOOD,** b. of Danbury, June 9, 1833, by John Nickerson	3	75
Doshe Belden, [s. Jabez & Phebe], b. Sept. 26, 1779	1	415
Eli, [s. Jabez & Elizabeth], b. Apr. 26, 1778	1	415
Elisabeth, m. Daniel **WILDMAN,** Oct. 28, 1762	1	502
Elisabeth, [d. Jabez & Elizabeth], b. Feb. 20, 1774	1	415
Eluid, Dr., m. Mary **STARR,** Nov. 17, 1768; d. Dec. 9, 1774	1	415
Ezra Bedent, [s. Jabez & Phebe], b. Apr. 12, 1782	1	415
Jabez, m. Elizabeth **SPERRY,** June 30, 1759	1	415
Jabez, m. Phebe **BEDENT,** [ ], 1778	1	415
Laurinda, m. Harvey **COUCH,** b. of Bethel, Feb. 15, 1823, by Rev. John G. Lowe	3	23
Levi, [s. Jabez & Elizabeth], b. May 2, 1769	1	415
Martha Ann, m. John **NICKERSON,** July 21, 1812	2	177
Mary, wid., m. Dr. Peter **HAYES,** Feb. 6, 1777	1	415
Mercy, [d. Dr. Eluid & Mary], b. June 17, 1770	1	415
Mercy, eldest Child of Dr. Elihud, decd., m. Thomas **BENEDICT,** Jr., 2nd s. Thomas, Oct. 10, 1787	1	362
Noah, [s. Dr. Eluid & Mary], b. Mar. 24, 1772	1	415
Orrin, m. Sarah **FAIRCHILD,** b. of Bethel, Dec. 26, 1830, by Rev. Erastus Cole	3	59
Orrin, m. Catharine **HOLLISTER,** b. of Bethel, Sept. 5, 1838, by Rev. John Greenwood, of Bethel	3	94
Sally Ann, m. Hiram **KEELER,** b. of Danbury, Apr. 30, 1843, by James Floy	3	119
ROFF, John G., of New Jersey, m. Mary E. **ODELL,** of Danbury, Dec. 28, 1846, by R. K. Bellamy	3	161
ROGERS, Matha, m. Eli **PECK,** Feb. 1, 1804	1	425
ROOT, Joseph, of Redding, m. Hannah E. **BROWN,** of Danbury, Nov. 11, 1846, by Rev. John Crawford	3	161
ROSSITER, George R., of Marietta O., m. Elizabeth P. **CLARK,** of Danbury, Sept. 20, 1849, by Rev. Rollin S. Stone	3	147

	Vol.	Page
ROSSWELL, Bennett, of Southbury, m. Maria **CONGAR**, of Brookfield, [, 1830(?)], by Levi Osborn	3	57
ROURK, Alice, m. Andrew **DOYLE**, Oct. 26, 1851, by Rev. Michael O'Farrell	3	157
ROWAN, John, m. Harriet **MORSE**, Nov. 5, 1839, by John Crawford	3	101
Peter C., m. Polly **SCOFIELD**, Mar. [ ], 1840, by John Crawford	3	104
ROWLAND, Burr, m. Anna U. **CROFUT**, Aug. 24, 1842, by Lucius Atwater	3	120
RUGGLES, Elisabeth, d. Joseph of New Milford, m. Eli **SEGAR**, Apr. 15, 17[ ]* *(Worn off)	1	500
Lucy, m. Jonathan **STARR**, Oct. 1, 1760	1	417
RUSSEL, Submit, d. Ithiel, of Branford, m. Rev. Noah **WETMORE**, July 9, 1761	1	489
RUSSICO, Polly, m. John **COMBS**, b. of Danbury, Sept. 13, [1825], by John Nickerson	3	29
RYAN, Ann, m. John **HUGHS**, [, 1851(?)], by Thomas Ryan. Witnesses: Thomas Ryan & Mary Kenny	3	156
RYLEES, Walter, m. Anseline **MAY**, Sept. 13, [1821], by Rev. W[illia]m Andrews	3	8
ST. JOHN, Charles of Ridgefield, m. Sarah I. **STONE**, of Danbury, this day, [Oct. 27, 1841], by Rev. Rollin S. Stone	3	112
Elijah, [s. Gamaliel & Margaret], b. Aug. 20, 1789	1	440
Gamaliel, m. Margaret **KINSMAN**, Nov. 16, 1788	1	440
George, m. Emeline **SMITH**, b. of Danbury, May 9, 1843, by Thomas T. Guion	3	120
James, m. Adeline **GREGORY**, Sept. 6, 1825, by George Benedict	3	28
James H., of Ridgefield, m. Anna **STONE**, d. Francis, of Danbury, this day [Sept. 4. 1842], by Rev. Rollin S. Stone	3	117
Lucinda, Mrs., m. Eli **KNAPP**, b. of Danbury, Apr. 2, 1832, by Levi Brunson	3	69
Mary Ann, m. Edwin **STONE**, b. of Danbury, this day [Aug. 11, 1841], by Rev. Rollin S. Stone	3	110
Moriah, [d. Gamaliel & Margaret], b. May 13, 1791	1	440
Oliver S., of Ridgebury, m. Elizabeth G. **BULL**, of Danbury, this day [Sept. 21, 1841], by Rev. Rollin S. Stone	3	111
Ruth, of Sharon, m. John **GREGORY**, July 6, 1788	1	420
Timothy W., m. Hannah **GREGORY**, July 24, 1825, by George Benedict	3	27
SANDERS, James P., m. Eloina L. **FERGUSON**, b. of Danbury, Nov. 19, 1840, by Addison Parker	3	107
SANFORD, **SANDFORD**, Charles H., [s. Elias S.], b. Mar. 14, 1826	2	272
Edward W., s. Elias S., b. Jan. 6, 1817	2	272
Eliza, m. Henry H. **MUNROE**, June 12, [1837], by Jacob Shaw	3	91
Frederick, [s. Elias S.], b. Dec. 17, 1827	2	272
Hannah, m. Edmond **WHEELER**, b. of Danbury, Mar. 4, 1838,		

	Vol.	Page
SCOTT, (cont.)		
A. Perkins	3	160
Hiram K., of Ridgefield, m. Mary Ann **BRUNSON**, of Danbury, Oct. 4, 1843, by Levi Bronson	3	122
Maria, of Ridgefield, m. Ira **WOOD**, Nov. 28, 1816	2	181
SCRIBNER, Burritt, m. Sam O. **BANKS**, b. of Danbury, Oct. 15, 1834, by J. Nickerson	3	81
Charles, m. Mary **SMITH**, b. of Danbury, Oct. 22, 1844, by Thomas T. Guion	3	132
George*, of Danbury, m. Amarillus **STARR**, of Bethel, Mar. 28, 1849, by Rev. Rollin S. Stone *(Should be "Henry")	3	147
Henry, m. Sarah B. **KELOGG**, b. of Danbury, Nov. 5, 1845, by Rev. R. K. Bellamy	3	138
Priscilla, m. Lewis **SILLICK**, Mar. 25, 1827, by George Benedict	3	40
Silvester S., m. Drusilla **ELY**, b. of Danbury, Jan. 1, 1845, by Nathaniel Bishop	3	131
SEARS, Bradley, m. Mary **NORRIS**, Jan. 17, 1832, by Nathan Burton	3	66
Desire, d. Knoles, of Ridgefield, m. Caleb Curtis **GREGORY**, s. John, of Danbury, Nov. 13, 1796	1	358
Sally, Mrs., m. Ira **KELLOGG**, Feb. 5, 1839, by J. G. Collom	3	96
Theodore C., m. Elizabeth **HOYT**, Oct. 27, 1850, by Rev. A. Perkins	3	160
SEELEY, SEELY, SEELYE, SIELY, [see also **SEIL**], Abigail, m. Samuel **CROFUT**, Aug. 2, 1781	1	431
Alonzo, s. Aaron, d. Sept. 29, 1822	2	178
Caroline, of Danbury, m. John W. **PECK**, of New York, Dec. 13, 1840, by James Beebe, J. P.	3	108
Elizabeth Benedict, d. [Seth & Abigal], b. Sept. 14, 1820; d. June 10, 1822	2	63
Eunice, d. Seth, m. John **ANDREWS**, Jr., Oct. 21, 1785	1	410
Eunice, d. James, m. Joshua **TAYLOR**, s. Matthew, [ ]	1	498
Fred[eric]k, m. Polly M. **DIBBLE**, Jan. 20, 1819	2	176
Hannah, m. Benajah **BENEDICT**, May 28, 1767	1	442
Harry, m. Melinda **TAYLOR**, b. of Danbury, May 15, 1827, by Rev. John G. Lowe	3	40
Horace Alonzo, s. [Frederick & Polly M.], b. Oct. 24, 1826	2	176
Jane, d. [Frederick & Polly M.], b. Aug. 8, 1822	2	176
Julia A., of Danbury, m. Cuylor **LEONARD**, of Sandusky, O., Oct. 25, 1849, by Rev. Rollin S. Stone	3	146
Mariette, m. Charles F. **STARR**, b. of Danbury, June 30, 1841, by Rev. Rollin S. Stone	3	110
Philander, m. Hetty Elizabeth **TOWN**, Dec. 12, 1832, by Rev. Joseph S. Covell, of Brookfield	3	76
Samuel Taylor, s. [Seth & Abigail], b. Oct. 24, 1822	2	63
Sarah, m. Ephraim **BARNUM**, Jr., Nov. 11, 1790	1	425
Sarah Maria, d. [Frederick & Polly M.], b. May 27, 1820	2	176
Seth, m. Abigal **TAYLOR**, Oct. 11, 1815	2	63
Tho[ma]s Taylor, s. [Seth & Abigail], b. Aug. 23, 1818	2	63

	Vol.	Page
SEGAR, SEGER, Alfred, twin with Elbert, s. Eli, b. Nov. 27, 1788;		
d. Feb. 16, 1789	1	412
Betty, m. Fairchild **AMBLER,** Apr. 13, 1806; d. June 6, 1810	2	175
Betty, d. [Eli & Elisabeth], b. Sept. 22, [ ]	1	500
Elbert, twin with Alfred, s. Eli, b. Nov. 27, 1788	1	412
Eli, m. 2nd w. Elisabeth **RUGGLES,** d. Joseph, of New Milford,		
Apr. 15, 17[ ]	1	500
Eli, m. Mercy **WEED,** d. J[ ], Oct. 27, 17[ ]	1	500
Eli, s. [Eli & Mercy], b. Sept. 3, 177[ ]	1	500
Eli, d. Aug. 24, 1822, ae 75 y.	2	180
Emily B., m. [ ] **BAILEY,** b. of Danbury, Aug. 18, 1844,		
by Elder E. M. Jackson	3	126
Melissa O., m. Edwin M. **GRIFFETH,** b. of Danbury, Dec. 31,		
[1850], by Rev. J. B. Merwin	3	155
Mercy, d. [Eli & Elisabeth], b. Feb. 28, [ ]	1	500
Mercy, w. [Eli], d. Oct. 19, 177[ ]	1	500
Polly, d. [Eli & Elisabeth], b. Sept. 22, [ ]	1	500
Sarah, b. Dec. 18, 1763; m. Gabriel **BURNUM,** Dec. 6, 1781	1	399
SEIGNIOR, [see also **SIGNOR**], Sarah H., m. Edwin **BLACKMAN,**		
b. of Danbury, Dec. 21, 1845, by Rev. Rollin S. Stone	3	138
[SEIL], SIEL, [see also **SEELEY**], Daniel Rockwell, s. [James],		
b. July 26, 1821	2	272
David Wildman, [s. James], b. Apr. 12, 1825	2	272
Henry Perry, [s. James], b. May 4, 1818	2	272
James*, of Belfast, Ireland, m. Anna **PERRY,** d. Solomon, of		
Ridgefield, Nov. 1, 1787 *("Shields" crossed out)	1	485
James, s. [James & Anna], b. July 16, 1795	1	485
James, d. Mar. [ ], 1797	1	485
Jane, d. James, b. Oct. 13, 1816	2	272
Jenny, d. [James & Anna], b. Jan. 24, 1790	1	485
Martha Merrill, [d. James], b. June 30, 1823	2	272
Oliver, [s. James], b. Jan. 22, 1820	2	272
Sally, d. [James & Anna], b. Sept. 15, 1792	1	485
Sarah Ann, [d. James], b. Oct. 15, 1827	2	272
SELLECK, SELLICK, SILLECK, SILLICK, Angeline, m. Charles		
BENEDICT, b. of Danbury, Oct. 8, 1828, by John		
Nickerson	3	49
Benjamin, m. Phebe **WOOD,** b. of Danbury, Apr. 27, 1842, by		
Rev. Morris Hill	3	115
Caroline, m. David **PEARCE,** Jr., Nov. 21, 1838, by Rev.		
John Crawford	3	95
Catharine, of Danbury, m. Benjamin B. **READ,** of Redding, Jan.		
1, 1831, by Rev. J. B. Merwin [1851?]	3	155
Darius, m. Maria **TERRY,** Sept. 25, 1850, by Rev. A. Perkins	3	160
Eliza, of Brookfield, m. Norman **NORTHROP,** of Bridgeport,		
Feb. 26, 1822, by Abner Brundage	3	10
Henry, m. Mary A. **KEELER,** Sept. 21, 1820, by W[illia]m		
Andrews	3	2

	Vol.	Page

SELLECK, SELLICK, SILLECK, SILLICK, (cont.)

Lewis, m. Priscilla **SCRIBNER**, Mar. 25, 1827, by George
Benedict ... 3 ... 40

Mary Ann, of Danbury, m. John **WHITLOCK**, of Ridgefield,
May 25, 1842, by John Nickerson ... 3 ... 115

William, m. Cordelia O. **BANKS**, b. of Danbury, May 4, 1831,
by John Nickerson ... 3 ... 61

William, of Ridgefield, m. Mary **PARSONS**, of Danbury, Mar.
15, 1840 ... 3 ... 102

SHADBOTT, Rachel, of Danbury, m. James **HAWLEY**, of
Brookfield, July 5, 1829, by John Nickerson ... 3 ... 52

SHARPE, Daniel, m. wid. Laura **MONTGOMERY**, b. of Danbury,
Sept. 11, 1823, by Josiah Dikeman ... 3 ... 18

SHEPARD, SHEPHERD, Charlotte, m. Dan[ie]l **BARNUM**, b. of
Danbury, Jan. 17, 1827, by Rev. John G. Lowe ... 3 ... 39

Frederick, m. Eliza M. **SMITH**, b. of Bethel, Nov. 10, 1839,
by J. Greenwood ... 3 ... 100

Henry, of Newtown, m. Adaline **MORGAN**, of Danbury, Oct.
25, 1848, by Rev. I. Atwater ... 3 ... 144

Henry, of Carmel, m. Emeline **TAYLOR**, Dec. 3, 1849, by
Rev. John Purves, of Bethel ... 3 ... 151

Hiram, m. Lucy A. **BUCKLEY**, Nov. 27, 1839, by John
Crawford ... 3 ... 101

Julia A., of Danbury, m. Philo C. **MERWIN**, of Brookfield,
May 14, 1850, by Rev. D. C. Curtiss ... 3 ... 153

Lemuel, of Newtown, m. Lemira **BARNUM**, Jan. 26, 1830, by
Reuben Booth, J. P. ... 3 ... 55

Polly Maria, m. Martin **MEAD**, b. of Danbury, this day
[May 29, 1825], by Rev. Lemuel B. Hull ... 3 ... 27

Sophia, m. John **BROWN**, b. of Danbury, May 28, 1843, by
Levi Osborn ... 3 ... 120

Stephen, m. Betsey Ann **GREGORY**, b. of Bethel, June 4, 1840,
by J. Greenwood ... 3 ... 104

Thomas W*, m. Sarah **OSBORN**, Oct. 8, 1823, by Rev.
W[illia]m Andrews   *(Possibly "N") ... 3 ... 18

W[illia]m C., m. Emily **TROWBRIDGE**, b. of Danbury, Nov.
23, 1831, by Rev. Lemuel B. Hull ... 3 ... 68

SHERMAN, Abigail M., m. Jakin M **BARBER**, b. of Danbury, Mar.
31, 1841, by Addison Parker ... 3 ... 108

Betsey, m. Theodore **MAYHEW**, b. of Bethel, Oct. 11, 1843,
by John L. Ambler ... 3 ... 122

Ethel B., of Bethel, m. Susan M. **DART**, of Redding, Nov.
23, 1845, by Thomas T. Guion ... 3 ... 137

Fanny, m. Samuel **CHICHESTER**, b. of Danbury, [June] 15,
[1838], by J. Shaw ... 3 ... 92

Fanny, m. William **PLATT**, b. of Stony Hill, Danbury,
[Apr.] 2, [1839], by Rev. J. G. Collom ... 3 ... 97

Hannah P., m. Daniel **HYATT**, b. of Bethel, Apr. 19, 1840,

	Vol.	Page
SHERMAN, (cont.)		
by John Greenwood	3	103
Harriet, d. Oman, b. Feb. 3, 1822	2	100
Jane, d. [Oman], b. May 31, 1824	2	100
Jane, m. Le L*. PLATT, Oct. 1, 1844, by R. K. Bellamy		
*(Should be "Lorin L. PLATT")	3	130
Jane*, of Danbury, m. Alfred L. PLATT, of Waterbury, July 28, 1847, by R. K. Bellamy *(Incorrect. Should be "Sarah")	3	163
Lucy, m. Tumey BULKLEY, Jan. 1, 1843, by Lucius Atwater	3	120
Marcus B., of Newtown, m. Julia A. HAWLEY, of Danbury, Apr. 30, 1848, by Rev. J. D. Marshall, of Redding	3	142
Sarah, d. [Oman], b. Feb. 10, 1827	2	100
Sarah, see Jane SHERMAN	3	163
Zalmon, m. Hannah CROFUT, b. of Danbury, Aug. 19, 1821, by Zach Clark, Jr., J. P.	3	7
SHERWOOD, Andrew, m. Sally JOICE, Feb. 2, 179[ ]* *(Edge of leaf missing)	1	424
Ann, m. W[illia]m ROBERTS, Mar. 23, 1762	1	408
Flora, d. [Andrew & Sally], b. Oct. 28, 1792	1	424
Henry, m. Phebe A. KNAPP, Dec. 8, 1842, by Lucius Atwater	3	120
James H., m. Mary Ann PATCH, Dec. 21, 1823, by Rev. W[illia]m Andrews	3	20
Lucinda, of Danbury, m. Samuel PARDY, of New York, Sept. 22, 1844, by John Nickerson	3	127
Molly, m. Phinehas TAYLOR, Sept. 11, 1783	1	387
Nachan C., of Reading, m. Mary Ann BAILEY, of South East, Mar. 11, 1838, by Rev. John Greenwood, of Bethel	3	92
Ransom, m. Lucy HAMILTON, [Jan.] 30, [1833], by Rev. A. Rood	3	73
Sally, d. John, of Reading, m. Noah BARNUM, Jr., s. Seth, Mar. 1, 1801	1	364
Sam[ue]l G., m. Delia GREGORY, b. of Reading, Nov. 16, 1825, by Rev. John G. Lowe	3	35
SHOVE, SHOOVE, Anna, [d. Seth & Jemima], b. May 23, 1765	1	421
Hannah, d. Benjamin, m. Peter AMBLER, Oct. 21, 1784	1	486
Jemima, wid. Seth, d. June 15, 1822	2	171
Levi, [s. Seth & Jemima], b. Mar. 22, 1761	1	421
Lois, [d. Seth & Jemima], b. Mar. 6, 1779	1	421
Lorana, [d. Seth & Jemima], b. July 22, 1782	1	421
Lorana, d. Seth, m. Nathan WOOD, Jr., s. Nathan, b. of Danbury, Nov. 27, 1799	1	364
Lucy, d. [Seth & Jemima], b. June 27, 1759; d. Mar. [ ], 1783	1	421
Mary, m. [Da]niel WILDMAN, Apr. 14, 1757* *(Faded out)	1	502
Mary, [d. Seth & Jemima], b. Apr. 10, 1763	1	421
Phebe, d. [Seth, Jr. & Patience], b. July 19, 1793	1	420
Sam[ue]l, [s. Seth & Jemima], b. July 2, 1769	1	421
Sarah, wid. Benj[amin], d. Feb. 17, 1823	2	171

	Vol.	Page

SHOVE, SHOOVE, (cont.)

Seth, m. Jemima **BARNUM**, Nov. 16, 1757 — 1 — 421

Seth, [s. Seth & Jemima], b. June 8, 1772 — 1 — 421

Seth, Jr., m. Patience **BARBER**, Nov. 28, 1792 — 1 — 420

SHUTE, Abigail, d. Richard, m. James **KNAPP**, Jr., s. James, b.
of Danbury, Dec. 18, 1796 — 1 — 373

Charity, d. Capt. Richard, m. Jonathan **BEEBE**, Sept. 7, 1791 — 1 — 386

George, of Wilton, m. Eliza Maria **BARNUM**, of Danbury, Aug.
3, 1839, by Reuben Booth, J. P. — 3 — 98

Gilbert, m. Mary Caroline **BIRDSELL**, b. of Danbury, Dec. 26,
1832, by John Mitchel — 3 — 73

Henry, m. Maria **STONE**, b. of Danbury, July 15, 1838, by
Rev. Rollin S. Stone — 3 — 94

Lucy Ann, d. [Thomas & Rachel], b. June 27, 1804 — 1 — 444

Lucy Ann, m. Anson **GREGORY**, [Apr.] 14, [1833], by Rev.
A. Rood — 3 — 75

Rebecca, m. Abijah **BOUGHTON**, Dec. 18, 1788 — 1 — 405

Thomas, b. Mar. 22, 1782; m. Rachel **JACKSON**, Nov. 24, 1803 — 1 — 444

SIEL, [see under **SEIL**]

SIGNOR, [see also **SEIGNIOR**], Hariet E., m. W[illia]m Henry
BARLOW, b. of Danbury, Oct. 18, 1840, by A. Parker — 3 — 106

Henry S., of Danbury, m. Margaret **ARMSTRONG**, of New
York, June 28, 1847, by Thomas T. Guion — 3 — 163

SILLECK, [see under **SELLECK**]

SIMMONS, James W., of New York, m. Deborah A. **BENEDICT**, of
Danbury, Nov. 26, 1830, by John Nickerson — 3 — 59

SININE, Sarah M., m. William **GAGE**, Nov. 10, 1844, by Levi
Brunson — 3 — 130

SIRRINE, Abbey J., m. Demond F. **STOCKER**, Jan. 7, 1844, by Levi
Brunson — 3 — 123

SKIDMORE, SKEDMER, John, of Newtown, m. Sarah **CROFUTT**,
of Danbury, this day, [Mar. 27, 1827], by Rev. Lemuel B.
Hull — 3 — 40

Lucy Maria, of Danbury, m. Silas **BURCH**, of Petterson, N. Y.,
this day [Oct. 14, 1840], by Rev. Rollin S. Stone — 3 — 106

Many, m. Jabez **TAYLOR**, Jr., Nov. 12, 1778 — 1 — 425

SLOCUM, Polly, of New York, m. John **HAWLEY**, of Brookfield,
Oct. 21, 1832, by John Nickerson — 3 — 71

Russel, of Sherman, m. Catie M. **BARNUM**, of Danbury, Jan.
1, 1826, by Nathan Bulkley — 3 — 31

SLOSON, Aulbert D., m. Hannah **BURTON**, Mar. 15, 1840, by
Nathan Burton — 3 — 103

SLY, Anson, of Huntington, m. Polly Ann **BEVENS**, of Danbury,
July 6, 1828, by John Nickerson — 3 — 48

SMITH, Anna, d. Reuben, of Nine Partners, m. Samuel **TWEEDY**,
Nov. 18, 1769 — 1 — 402

Anne Jenette, of Bethel, m. George P. **CRANE**, of New York,
Mar. 16, 1846, by Rev. Lent S. Hough — 3 — 139

	Vol.	Page

SMITH, (cont.)

Azariel, of Bridgewater, m. Mary **ANDREWS**, of Bethel, Dec.
29, 1823, by Rev. John G. Lowe — 3 — 23

Belial, m. Lorinda **FERRY**, [Oct. 9, [1831], by Rev. A. Rood — 3 — 64

Charles S., m. Anne **TAYLOR**, Nov. 21, 1821, by Rev.
W[illia]m Andrews — 3 — 9

Cyrus, m. Esther **HICKOCK**, Nov. 14, 1821, by Rev. W[illia]m
Andrews — 3 — 9

Eliza M., m. Frederick **SHEPARD**, b. of Bethel, Nov. 10, 1839,
by J. Greenwood — 3 — 100

Emilinee, m. Amzi **WHEELER**, b. of Danbury, Nov. 29, 1827,
by John G. Lowe — 3 — 44

Emeline, m. George **ST. JOHN**, b. of Danbury, May 9, 1843,
by Thomas T. Guion — 3 — 120

Homer, of Brookfield, m. Betsey **MALLORY**, of Danbury, June
1, 1823, by Samuel H. Phillips, J. P. — 3 — 17

James M., of Brookfield, m. Lydea M. **JUDD**, of Danbury,
Aug. 21, 1842, by Rev. Tho[ma]s T. Guion — 3 — 116

Jerusha, d. Henry, of Huntington, m. Ezra **BARNUM**, Nov. 25,
1784 — 1 — 456

Martha M., of Danbury, m. E. W. **COOK** (Rev.), of Haddam,
June 2, 1847, by Rev. Rollin S. Stone — 3 — 162

Mary, m. Charles **SCRIBNER**, b. of Danbury, Oct. 22, 1844,
by Thomas T. Guion — 3 — 132

Mary Amelia, m. Samuel Shetton **HURD**, this day [Oct. 7,
1841], by Rev. D. H. Short — 3 — 112

Mary E., m. Oliver S. **STONE**, Apr. 17, 1850, by Rev. A.
Perkins — 3 — 160

Oliver, s. Polly **LANDERS**, b. Mar. 16, 1791 — 1 — 466

Ophelia, m. George **BARNUM**, Sept. 6, 1831, by Rev. Erastus
Cole — 3 — 65

Polly Geline, m. Ira **LINSLEY**, Dec. 25, 1823, by Reuben
Booth, J. P. — 3 — 21

Rebecca, Mrs. of Danbury, m. Dea. Eleazer **BEERS**, of
Reading, Apr. 22, 1838, by Rev. J. G. Collom — 3 — 93

Robert, m. Hannah **BRENON**, Nov. [ ], 1792 — 1 — 404

Russel, m. Pamela **BARNUM**, b. of Dan¹ ¹ry, Jan. 2, 1825, by
Oliver Shepard, J. P. — 3 — 26

Samuel B., of Richmond, Mass., m. Rebecca **STANLEY**, of
Bethel, Mar. 23, 1831, by Rev. Erastus Cole — 3 — 60

Sarah A., m. James **POLLEY**, b. of Danbury, Jan. 19, 1845,
by Rev. Fitch Reed — 3 — 131

Sophia, of Bethel, m. Walter **MALLORY**, Sept. 13, 1830, by
Rev. Erastus Cole — 3 — 59

William, of Bridge Water, m. Annis **TAYLOR**, of Danbury,
Dec. 20, 1826, by Rev. John G. Lowe — 3 — 39

W[illia]m, m. Maria **CROSLY**, Nov. 28, 1849, by Rev. A.
Perkins — 3 — 160

	Vol.	Page
SPARKS, Walter C., m. Jane FRY, b. of Danbury, this day [July 3, 1842], by Rev. Rollin S. Stone	3	116
SPEAR, Nancy C., m. Henry KENT, b. of Springfield, Bradford Co., Penn., this day [Sept. 21, 1825], by Rev. Lemuel B. Hull	3	28
SPELLMAN, Eliza, of Danbury, m. Burr WARREN, of Ridgefield, this day, Oct. 15, 1845, by Levi Brunson	3	136
SPERRY, Elizabeth, m. Jabez ROCKWELL, June 30, 1759	1	415
SPRAGUE, Thomas W., m. Martha BISHOP, May 25, 1835, by Rev. A. Rood	3	87
SQUIRES, SQUIRE, Caroline, m. George H. BLISSARD, b. of Danbury, May 20, 1847, by Rev. Rollin S. Stone	3	162
David, m. Betsey HODGES, b. of Danbury, Apr. 22, 1845, by Rev. Fitch Reed	3	134
Dudley, of Redding, m. Mariette JENNINGS, of Bridgewater, Nov. 10, 1826, by Rev. John G. Lowe	3	38
Esther Mary, m. George COLE, b. of Danbury, Mar. 31, 1844, by Thomas P. White, J. P.	3	125
Hannah Amelia, of Weston, m. Henry MEAD, of Danbury*, Dec. 26, 1839, by S. A. Brown *(Or "Cranbury")	3	101
STANLEY, Allen, m. Rebecca ELWELL, b. of Danbury, Dec. 3, 1827, by John G. Lowe	3	44
Esther, m. Sallu Pell HITCHCOCK, Nov. 5, 1828, by Nathan Burton	3	50
Polly, m. Elijah MAY, May 26, 1831, by Rev. John Boyden, Jr.	3	62
Rebecca, of Bethel, m. Samuel B. Smith, of Richmond, Mass., Mar. 23, 1831, by Rev. Erastus Cole	3	60
STAPLETON, Edward, of Sandusky City, O., m. Julia J. HICKOK, of Danbury, Sept. 17, 1844, by Rev. George T. Todd	3	128
STARR, Abigail, d. Samuel, m. Eli MYGATT, 2nd, s. Joseph, [ ], 1759	1	377
Abigail, w. Matthew W., d. Sept. 10, 1821	2	129
Abigail H., m. Cornelius MYERS, b. of Danbury, Oct. 10, 1841, by D. H. Short	3	112
Abigail, S*., d. Lieut. Benjamin, m. Thaddeus BENEDICT, Feb. [ ]* *(Worn off) *(Years faded out)	1	498
Abijah, [s. Eliakim & Abigale], b. Dec. 27, 1778	1	414
Altania, [child of Eliakim & Abigale], b. Aug. 2, 1788	1	414
Ammirillis, d. [Caleb & Bulah], b. Jan. 19, 1766	1	443
Amarillus, of Bethel, m. George* SCRIBNER, of Danbury, Mar. 28, 1849, by Rev. Rollin S. Stone *(Should be "Henry")	3	147
Angeline, m. Sylvester STEVENS, b. of Danbury, Jan. 16, 1827, by Rev. John G. Lowe	3	39
Ann, m. Seth BENEDICT, b. of Bethel, July 4, 1824, by Rev. John G. Lowe	3	24
Anne, m. Ebenezer BAILEY, Dec. 9, 1778	1	427
Annis, d. Capt. Thomas, m. Joseph P. COOKE, Jr., Sept. 16, 1785	1	487

	Vol.	Page

STARR, (cont.)

Lucy, [d. Jonathan & Lucy], b. May 15, 1779 — 1 417

Lucey, [d. Eliakim & Abigale], b. May 20, 1787 — 1 414

Lucey, d. [Jonathan, Jr. & Mary], b. Aug. 25, 1797 — 1 385

Lucy, d. Caleb, decd., m. Ezra **GREGORY,** Feb. 12, 1804 — 1 420

Lucy, m. Thomas M. **GREGORY,** b. of Danbury, this day [Aug. 4, 1828], by Rev. Lemuel B. Hull — 3 48

Lure, d. [Jonathan, Jr. & Mary], b. Mar. 9, 1795 — 1 385

Lydia, d. [Thaddeus & Lydia], b. July 27, 1784 — 1 466

Lynda, d. [Jube & Sarah], b. July 30, 1787 — 1 381

Maria, [d. Ezra & Elizabeth], b. Feb. 22, 1784 — 1 366

Maria, of Bethel, m. Isaac **STURGES,** of Westport, this day, [July 17, 1843], by Rev. Rollin S. Stone — 3 121

Martha E., m. Joseph **TAYLOR,** Jr., Nov. 26, 1845, by Rev. R. K. Bellamy — 3 138

Mary, d. John, b. Dec. [ ], 1714; m. Theophilus **BENEDICT,** 3rd s. Daniel, 1st, b. of Danbury, [ ], 1737 — 1 370

Mary, d. [Joseph & Mary], b. Jan. 5, 1753 — 1 467

Mary, [d. Thomas, Jr. & Elisabeth], b. Feb. 25, 1756* *("6" a correction) — 1 436

Mary, m. Dr. Eluid **ROCKWELL,** Nov. 17, 1768 — 1 415

Mary, [d. Matthew & Elisabeth], b. Aug. 22, 1774; d. June 4, 1776 — 1 418

Mary, 2nd, [d. Matthew & Elisabeth], b. Dec. 19, 1776 — 1 418

Mary, d. [Jube & Sarah], b. Sept. 22, 1782 — 1 381

Mary, d. Samuel, m. Matthew **BARNUM,** Jr., Oct. 17, 1784 — 1 452

Mary, m. Sydney **GRANNESS,** b. of Danbury, Dec. 4, [1850], by Rev. J. B. Merwin — 3 155

Mary B., m. David H. **BOUGHTON,** b. of Danbury, this day [Aug. 8, 1826], by Rev. Lemuel B. Hull — 3 34

Mary C., m. Henry K. **BICKER,** July 18, 1831, by Rev. A. Rood — 3 63

Mary Chandler, 2nd, d. [Elias & Mary Elizabeth], b. July 3, 1808 — 2 62

Mary W., m. George **FERRY,** b. of Danbury, June 26, 1838, by Rev. D. H. Short — 3 107

Matthew, m. Elisabeth **WHITE,** Apr. 15, 1766 — 1 418

Matthew, [s. Matthew & Elisabeth], b. Jan. 16, 1785 — 1 418

Matthew W., m. Martha T. **TAYLOR,** this day [Dec. 16, 1821], by Nathaniel Freeman — 3 9

Matthew W., Jr., m. Mary M. **COLEY,** b. of Bethel, Nov. 4, 1841, by John Greenwood — 3 113

Malancton*, m. Esther **BISHOP,** b. of Danbury, this day [Nov. 21, 1824], by Rev. Lemuel B. Hull *(Melancton) — 3 25

Mercy, d. [Joseph & Mary], b. Sept. 26, 1750 — 1 467

Mercy, d. Capt. Joseph, m. Andrew **COMSTOCK,** May 27, 1773 — 1 449

Mercy*, of Danbury, m. Benjamin **BROOKS,** of Norwalk, [June] 2, [1830], by Rev. A. Rood   *(Possibly "Mary"?) — 3 56

Nahum, s. [Jonathan, Jr. & Mary], b. Jan. 24, 1790 — 1 385

	Vol.	Page

STARR, (cont.)

Nathan, m. Mary **BARNUM**, May 21, 1778 — 1 — 424

Nathan, of New York, m. Mary **WILDMAN**, of Danbury, this
day, [June 23, 1829], by Rev. Lemuel B. Hull — 3 — 52

Nathaniel S., m. Polly **BENNET**, b. of Danbury, Feb. 7, 1821,
by William Cooke, J. P. — 3 — 5

Nathaniel Winthrop, s. [Elias & Mary Elizabeth], b. May 6,
1811 — 2 — 62

Orman, s. [Jonathan, Jr. & Mary], b. Nov. 13, 1791 — 1 — 385

Peter, m. Rhoda **HAY**, Aug. 21, [1837], by Jacob Shaw — 3 — 91

Peter, m. Elizabeth S. **LYON**, b. of Danbury, June 1, 1847, by
Rev. Rollin S. Stone — 3 — 162

Phebe, of Brookfield, m. Samuel **MORRICE**, of Danbury, Jan.
17, 1821, by William Cooke, J. P. — 3 — 5

Polly, [d. Caleb & Bulah], b. Dec. 30, 1768 — 1 — 443

Polly, [d. Nathan & Mary], b. Dec. 22, 1780 — 1 — 424

Polly, 2nd d. Caleb, m. Eliakim **PECK**, eldest s. Abijah,
Nov. 8, 1786 — 1 — 360

Polley, d. [Jonathan, Jr. & Mary], b. Nov. 12, 1793 — 1 — 385

Priscilla, [d. Thomas, Jr. & Elisabeth], b. Apr. 2, 1767 — 1 — 436

Rachel, d. John, m. Daniel **TAYLOR**, June 10, 1739 — 1 — 489

Rachel, m. Stephen **JARVIS**, Feb. 6, 1756 — 1 — 460

Rachel, [d. Jonathan & Lucy], b. Oct. 12, 1765 — 1 — 417

Rachel, d. Capt. Josiah, m. David **BOUGHTON**, Jr.,May 8, 1777 — 1 — 385

Rachel, [d. Matthew & Elisabeth], b. Mar. 30, 1779 — 1 — 418

Rachel, d. the late Major Daniel, m. Frederick Jones
WHITING, May 18, 1783 — 1 — 358

Rachel, [d. Ezra & Elizabeth], b. Feb. 13, 1786 — 1 — 366

Rachel, d. Samuel, m. James Taylor, **HOYT**, s. James, Jan. 11,
1798 — 1 — 369

Rebeckah, m. Nathan **HOYT**, Sept. 5, 1758 — 1 — 413

Rebecca, [d. Joseph & Mary], b. Nov. 4, 1766 — 1 — 467

Rebeckah, [d. Eliakim & Abigale], b. Jan. 31, 1777 — 1 — 414

Rebecca, d. Maj. Daniel, m. Oliver **LAWRENCE**, May 12, 1782 — 1 — 495

Rebecca, d. Capt. Joseph, m. Samuel I*. **DIBBLE**, Nov. 21, 1790
*(Possibly "C"?) — 1 — 458

Rebecca, [d. Ezra & Elizabeth], b. Feb. 28, 1792 — 1 — 366

Rebecca, m. Timothy **HOLLISTER**, Feb. 15, 1821, by Rev.
W[illia]m Andrews — 3 — 5

Salmon, [s. Jonathan & Lucy], b. Jan. 9, 1770 — 1 — 417

Sam[ue]l Gregory, [s. Caleb & Bulah], b. July 19, 1785 — 1 — 443

Sarah, [d. Thomas, Jr. & Elisabeth], b. Jan. 12, 1750 — 1 — 436

Sarah, [d. Thomas, Jr. & Elisabeth], d. July 20, 1752 — 1 — 436

Sarah, [d. Thomas, Jr. & Elisabeth], b. Apr. 12, 1760 — 1 — 436

Sarah, d. [Matthew & Elisabeth], b. Feb. 14, 1767 — 1 — 418

Sarah, [w. Jube], d. Nov. 2, 1801 — 1 — 381

Sarah, 3rd d. [Elias & Mary Elizabeth], b. Dec. 2, 1863*
*(Probably "1813") — 2 — 62

	Vol.	Page
STARR, (cont.)		
Sarah W., b. Sept. 23, 1811; m. W[illia]m P. COMSTOCK,		
Nov. 26, 1833; d. Nov. 11, 1838	2	65
Sarah Wood, d. [John W. & Jerusha], b. Sept. 23, 1811	2	65
Sherman, [s. Matthew & Elisabeth], b. Mar. 19, 1772;		
d. Aug. 7, 1775	1	418
Sherman, 2nd, [s. Matthew & Elisabeth], b. Sept. 22, 1787;		
d. Sept. 6, 1790	1	418
Stephen, [s. Caleb & Bulah], b. Jan. 28, 1778; d. Dec. 16, 1779	1	443
Stephen, 2nd, [s. Caleb & Bulah], b. Feb. 7, 1780	1	443
Susan M., m. George **WARREN**, Jan. 22, 1832, by Rev. Lemuel		
B. Hull	3	68
Thaddeus, [s. Joseph & Mary], b. Dec. 14, 1759	1	467
Thaddeus, m. Lydia **TROWBRIDGE**, May 22, 1783	1	466
Thomas, Jr., m. Elisabeth **CLOSSON**, d. Jonathan, of Stanford,		
Mar. 27, 1745* *("1745" a correction)	1	436
Thomas, s. [Thomas, Jr. & Elisabeth], b. Mar. 6, 1748	1	436
Thomas, Lieut., m. Lois **WOOD**, d. Dr. John, Mar. 3, 1784	1	411
Trypena, d. [Jonathan & Lucy], b. May 12, 1762	1	417
Triphena, d. Jonathan, m. Benj[ami]n S. **ROCKWELL**, May 14,		
1785	1	497
Walter, [s. Caleb & Bulah], b. May 20, 1783	1	443
STEBBINS, Albert B., of Springfield, Mass., m. Mary Jennet		
BEEBE, of Danbury, (Bethel Soc.), this day [Aug. 31,		
1836], by Rev. David H. Short	3	85
STEDMAN, Anna, m. Joseph **CLARK**, June 21, 1787	1	387
Clarissa, d. Thomas, of Hampton, b. Jan. 23, 1772;		
m. Abijah **PECK**, Jr., 2nd s. Abijah, of Danbury, Oct. 4,		
1790	1	357
STEVENS, **STEVEN**, **STEPHENS**, Abigail, b. Nov. 17, 1738;		
m. Nathan **DIBBLE**, s. John, Mar. 17, 1757	1	495
Abigail, [d. Eliphalet & Abigail], b. Aug. 10, 1786	1	432
Abraham, [s. Eliphalet & Abigail], b. Nov. 12, 1779	1	432
Alvira, m. Norman **HOIT**, b. of Danbury, Feb. 24, 1828,		
by John G. Lowe	3	45
Angelina, d. [Zadock & Phebe], b. Mar. 5, 1809	1	362
Angeline, of Danbury, m. Jacob **FROST**, of New Fairfield,		
Apr. 14, 1839, by Rev. L. Atwater	3	98
Anna, d. [Nathaniel & Rebeccah], b. Jan. 12, 1773	1	490
Aniss, [d. James & Anna], b. Aug. 29, 1784	1	433
Annis, m. Benjamin **TOWNSEND**, [Apr.] 20, [1826], by George		
Benedict	3	32
Antoinett, of New York, m. Hezekiah **STONE**, Apr. 9, 1832,		
by John Nickerson	3	69
Any, [d. James & Anna], b. Mar. 21, 1782	1	433
Asahel, s. [Nathaniel & Rebeccah], b. July 15, 1764	1	490
Barnum, of New Fairfield, m. Hannah **WEBB**, of Danbury,		
Feb. 22, 1829, by John S. Blackman, J. P.	3	51

Vol.   Page

STEVENS, STEVEN, STEPHENS, (cont.)

Bekke, d. [Nathaniel & Rebeccah], b. Dec. 1, 1784	1	490
Benjamin, [s. James & Anna], b. Sept. 9, 1777	1	433
Betsey, m. Henry **GREGORY**, this day [Dec. 8, 1824], by Levi Osborn	3	25
Betty, d. [Thomas & Abigail], b. Oct. 17, 1768	1	472
Betty, d. [Thomas & Abigail], d. June 25, 1777	1	472
Betty, d. [Jonathan & Mehetabel], b. Nov. 16, 1779	1	459
Caroline, of Mill Plain, m. Frederick **MORRIS**, of Poughkeepsie, this day [Oct. 16, 1833], by Levi Osborn	3	76
Catharine, m. Judah P. **CROSBY**, of Danbury, Feb. 27, 1839, by Rev. Rollin S. Stone	3	96
Charles, of Brookfield, m. Lucy **STEVENS**, of Danbury, Sept. 17, 1832, by John Nickerson	3	71
Charles L., m. Matilda **ROBERTS**, b. of Danbury, May 9, 1841, by Rev. Shaler J. Hillyer	3	109
Charles Lewis, s. [Zadock & Phebe], b. Nov. 21, 1816	1	362
Clarissa, m. William D. **MORRIS**, b. of Danbury, [Nov.] 1, [1826], by John Nickerson	3	37
Clarissa, m. Philo W. **HOYT**, this day [June 6, 1833], by Levi Osborn	3	75
Cynthia, m. John **BARTON**, b. of Danbury, May 9, 1838, by Rev. Rollin S. Stone	3	94
David Benedict, twin with Ezra Barnum, [s. Forward & Rachel], b. Mar. 16, 1794	1	399
Dinah, [d. Jonathan & Mehetabel], b. Aug. 10, 1781	1	459
Dinah, d. Jonathan, m. Eluid **COMES**, s. John, Nov. [ ] , 1799	1	365
Eli, s. [Nathaniel & Rebeccah], b. Nov. 3, 1782	1	490
Eliphalet, m. Abigail **GRAY**, d. John, Dec. 7, 1767	1	432
Eliphalet, [s. Eliphalet & Abigail], b. Sept. 23, 1771	1	432
Eliphalet, d. Mar. 7, 1807	1	432
Elisha C., m. Betsey **DELEVAN**, b. of Danbury, Oct. 30, 1831, by Elias Birchard, J. P.	3	65
Eliza, d. [Ezra B. & Arata], b. Jan. 29, 1818	2	119
Eliza, m. Oliver H. P. **HYATT**, May 16, 1848, by Rev. W[illia]m W. Bronson	3	142
Eliza, of Danbury, m. Abner C. **GAULT**, of Patterson, N. J., Dec. 2, 1850, by Rev. George H. Deere	3	153
Embre A., m. Ann **BUXTON**, b. of Danbury, Mar. 15, [1829], by J. Nickerson	3	51
Emeline, of Bethel, m. Horace **WARNER**, of New Milford, Nov. 20, 1823, by Rev. John G. Lowe	3	23
Epaphrass Bull, s. [Zadock & Phebe], b. June 24, 1812	1	362
Ephraim Gregory, s. [Thomas & Abigail], b. Sept. 25, 1776	1	472
Ephraim Gregory, s. Thomas, decd., m. Sally **BENEDICT**, d. Joseph Jr., Nov. 20, 1802	1	359
Erastus, [s. David B.], b. Oct. 7, 1821	2	146
Esther, d. [Thomas & Abigail], b. July 30, 1764	1	472

	Vol.	Page
STEVENS, STEVEN, STEPHENS, (cont.)		
Esther, [d. James & Anna], b. Nov. 5, 1786	1	433
Evelina, m. Charles A. H. **REED**, Oct. 16, 1833, by Rev. A. Rood	3	86
Ezra B., m. Arata **FANTON**, Feb. 3, 1814	2	119
Ezra B., m. Mrs. Elizabeth Ann **GILLET**, May 17, 1835, by Rev. A. Rood	3	86
Ezra B., of New Fairfield, m. Mary **WHEELER**, of Bethel, Mar. 22, 1849, by Rev. Rollin S. Stone	3	147
Ezra B., m. Mary E. **BALDWIN**, b. of Danbury, July 27, 1851, by Rev. F. N. Barlow, of Mill Plain	3	156
Ezra Barnum, twin with David Benedict, [s. Forward & Rachel], b. Mar. 16, 1794	1	399
Fanny, m. Levi **CLARK**, b. of Danbury, this day [Oct. 6, 1824], by Rev. Lemuel B. Hull	3	24
Forward, m. Rachel **KNAP**, d. David, Apr. 11, 1782	1	399
Forward, m. Mary **BENEDICT**, b. of Danbury, Oct. 28, 1823, by Nathan Bulkley	3	19
George, [s. Jonathan & Mehetabel], b. Sept. 2, 1785	1	459
George, of Brookfield, m. Sarah **CASY**, of Poughkeepsie, Mar. 19, 1848, by Rev. William White Bronson	3	141
George E., m. Mrs. Maria **GAGE**, Sept. 7, 1846, by R. K. Bellamy	3	161
Hannah, [d. Eliphalet & Abigail], b. Dec. 3, 1774	1	432
Hannah, [d. James & Anna], b. Mar. 27, 1775* *("5" uncertain)	1	433
Hannah, [d. David B.], b. Apr. 18, 1819	2	146
Hannah, m. George **MORRIS**, b. of Danbury, Feb. 5, [probably 1834], by Levi Osborn	3	78
Hannah, of Danbury, m. William **WASHBURN**, of Moulton, Mass., Nov. 11, 1850, by Rev. J. B. Merwin	3	155
Henrietta, [d. David B.], b. Oct. 5, 1823	2	146
Henrietta, m. Russel W. **HOYT**, b. of Danbury, Jan. 11, 1843, by David C. Perry	3	118
Hezekiah, m. Mrs. Temperence **GRAY**, July 11, 1820, at the house of Elijah Barnum, by Daniel Foot, J. P.	3	1
Ira, [s. James & 1st w. [ ]], b. Nov. 21, 1770	1	433
James, m. Anna **BENEDICT**, Mar. 15, 1774	1	433
James, [s. James & Anna], b. May 6, 1789	1	433
Jerusha, d. [Zadock & Phebe], b. Sept. 24, 1806	1	362
Jerusha, m. Alva **WHEELER**, b. of Danbury, Oct. 25, 1826, by Rev. John G. Lowe	3	38
John, [s. Eliphalet & Abigail], b. Oct. 9, 1782	1	432
John, s. Amos, d. June 15, 1822, ae 18 y.	2	129
Jonathan, m. Mehetabel **BENEDICT**, d. Caleb, of Norwalk, Nov. 23, 1778* *(Date first written "Apr. 20, 1752")	1	459
Jonathan, m. Clarissa **ELY**, b. of Danbury, Feb. 4, 1846, by Nathaniel Bishop	3	139
Joseph Frederick, [s. Zadock & Phebe], b. Aug. 24, 1814	1	362

	Vol.	Page
STEVENS, STEVEN, STEPHENS, (cont.)		
Joshua, s. [Nathaniel & Rebeccah], b. Nov. 10, 1762	1	490
Joshua, grandson of Matthew BARNUM, b. May 2, 1785	1	452
Laura, m. Daniel BAXTER, Nov. 23, 1825, by George Benedict	3	30
Levi, s. [Nathaniel & Rebeccah], b. Apr. 4, 1771	1	490
Livonia, m. William DIBBLE, b. of Danbury, Dec. 19, 1826, by Rev. John G. Lowe	3	39
Lois, d. [Thomas & Abigail], b. Mar. 25, 1770	1	472
Lucy, [twin with Phebe, d. Nathaniel & Rebeccah], b. Aug. 17, 1777	1	490
Lucy, [d. Forward & Rachel], b. Apr. 20, 1788	1	399
Lucy, of Danbury, m. Charles STEVENS, of Brookfield, Sept. 17, 1832, by John Nickerson	3	71
Lydia, d. Capt. Tho[ma]s, b. May 13, 1752* *(Fig. "2" uncertain)	1	472
Lydia, [d. Eliphalet & Abigail], b. July 12, 1784	1	432
Maria B., of Mill Plain, m. Eli F. HENDRICK, M. D., of N. Y., Nov. 27, 1851, by Rev. F. N. Barlow	3	157
Marietta, m. Legrand STOCKER, b. of Danbury, Mar. 3, 1840, by John Nickerson	3	102
Mary, d. [Nathaniel & Rebecca], b. Nov. 15, 1766	1	490
Mary Ann, d. [Zadock & Phebe], b. Sept. 27, 1801	1	362
Mary Ann, of Danbury, m. Morris BRADLEY, of New Fairfield, Sept. 8, [1822], by Josiah Dikeman	3	12
Mary E., m. John CABLE, Apr. 9, 1851, by Rev. A. Perkins	3	160
Matthew B., of Brookfield, m. Diadema WILDMAN, of Danbury, Nov. 6, 1844, by Rev. J. K. Ingalls	3	129
Mehetabel, [d. Jonathan & Mehetabel], b. Jan. 16, 1790	1	459
Molly, [d. James & Anna], b. Aug. 17, 1779	1	433
Moses, [s. Eliphalet & Abigail], b. Aug. 21, 1768	1	432
Nathaniel, s. [Nathaniel & Rebeccah], b. Apr. 10, 1780	1	490
Nathaniel, m. Mercy BARNUM, d. Matthew, Aug. 28, 1783	1	450
Nath[anie]l, m Rebeccah HOYT, d. Thomas, decd. [ ]	1	490
Ollive, [d. Eliphalet & Abigail], b. Oct. 18, 1776	1	432
Olive, d. Eliphatee, m. Elijah MORRIS, s. Shadrack, Apr. 8, 1798	1	359
Oliver, [s. James & Anna], b. Oct. 16, 1791	1	433
Phebe, m. David PERCE, Apr. 28, 1762	1	424
Phebe, twin with Lucy, [d. Nathaniel & Rebeccah], b. Aug. 17, 1777	1	490
Phebe, d. [Forward & Rachel], b. Jan. 31, 1785	1	399
Phebe S., of Danbury, m. Willis S. ROBERTS, of South East Put Co., N. Y., Mar. 15, 1837, by Rev. Salmon C. Bulkley	3	90
Phebe Sturges, [d. David B.], b. Jan. 25, 1817	2	146
Philander, s. [Ezra B. & Arata], b. Dec. 26, 1815	2	119
Rachel, d. [Thomas & Abigail], b. Mar. 19, 1766	1	472
Rachel, d. [Nathaniel & Rebeccah], b. June 4, 1769	1	490
Rachel, [d. Jonathan & Mehetabel], b. Oct. 15, 1787	1	459

	Vol.	Page

STEVENS, STEVEN, STEPHENS, (cont.)

Rachel, [d. Forward & Rachel], b. July 27, 1790 — 1 — 399

Rachel, m. Ephraim **GREGORY**, Jan. 4, 1815 — 2 — 146

Rachel, d. [Ezra B. & Arata], b. Mar. 18, 1820 — 2 — 119

Ruth, m. Benjamin **BARBER**, Mar. 16, 1755 — 1 — 411

Sally, [d. Ezra B. & Arata], b. Aug. 11, 1823 — 2 — 119

Sarah, d. [Thomas & Abigail], b. Jan. 4, 1772 — 1 — 472

Sarah, of Danbury, m. William **BEARSE**, of New Fairfield,
  Apr. 26, 1831, by Nathan Burton — 3 — 61

Sarah Ann, of Danbury, m. Lyman **PLATT**, of South East,
  N. Y., this day [Oct. 11, 1840], by S. H. Clark — 3 — 106

Silvester, s. [Zadock & Phebe], b. Sept. 12, 1804 — 1 — 362

Sylvester, m. Angeline **STARR**, b. of Danbury, Jan. 16, 1827,
  by Rev. John G. Lowe — 3 — 39

Sylvia Ann, of Danbury, m. Samuel **BALDWIN**, of Newark, N.
  J., this day [Jan. 11, 1843], by Rev. Rollin S. Stone — 3 — 119

Thomas, m. Abigail **GREGORY**, d. Ephraim, Jan. 12, 1763 — 1 — 472

Thomas, Capt., d. July 20, 1791 — 1 — 472

Thomas, d. Dec. 15, 1801 — 1 — 472

Thomas, m. Olivia **CLARK**, Feb. 22, 1836*, by Rev. Lemuel
  B. Hull   *(First written "1832) — 3 — 83

Thomas P., m. Rebeca **PECK**, b. of Danbury, Oct. 25, 1826, by
  Zadock Stevens, J. P. — 3 — 37

Thomas Phillips. [s. Zadock & Phebe], b. Jan. 22, 1803 — 1 — 362

Wait, [child of Jonathan & Mehetabel], b. July 24, 1783 — 1 — 459

William, of New York, m. Lucy Ann **BAILEY**, of Danbury,
  July 14, 1840, by Nathaniel Bishop — 3 — 105

William W., m. Rebecca **POLLY**, b. of Danbury, July 18, 1827,
  by John Nickerson — 3 — 41

Zadock, s. Ezra, m. Phebe **WHITE**, d. Thomas, b. of Danbury,
  Oct. 5, 1800 — 1 — 362

Zadock White, s. [Zadock & Phebe], b. Sept. 26, 1810 — 1 — 362

STEVENSON, Mary Ann, m. Samuel [C.]* **GREGORY**, b. of
  Danbury, Apr. 21, 1846, by Rev. Fitch Reed   *("C" crossed
  out) — 3 — 139

STEWART, [see also STUART], Alexander H., m. Eliza **HULL**,
  Nov. 21, 1824, by Reuben Booth, J. P. — 3 — 25

Emily J., m. Miles H. **WILDMAN**, Sept. 21, 1843, by Rev.
  J. K. Inalls — 3 — 122

Jairus L., m. Mary **CROSSMAN**, [Nov.] 17*, [1830], by
  Rev. A. Rood   *(Possibly [Dec.] 7) — 3 — 59

Lucy M., m. Daniel B. **MANLY**, b. of Danbury, Sept. 11, 1850,
  by Rev. John S. Whittlesey — 3 — 150

Maria, m. Hoyt **PORTER**, Dec. 16, 1839, by Rev. Z. Cook — 3 — 96

Sally, d. Nathan, of Litchfield, m. Caleb **PICKET**, s. Ebenezer,
  Sept. 16, 1801 — 1 — 363

Simeon M., m. Susan **GILLETT**, b. of Danbury, Oct. 10,
  1825, by Reuben Booth, J. P. — 3 — 29

	Vol.	Page
STILSON, Abel J., of Newtown, m. Hannah **AMBLER**, of Bethel,		
this day, [Sept. 26, 1839], by John Greenwood	3	99
Mehitabel, d. Joseph, of Newtown, m. Samuel **CANFIELD**,		
Sept. 10, 1760	1	499
STOCKER, Almira, [twin with Elmira, d. Thomas & Lucy], b. Aug.		
17, 1830	2	120
Cornelius, s. [Thomas & Lucy], b. Sept. 4, 1823	2	120
Demmon, s. [Thomas & Lucy], b. Dec. 25, 1819	2	120
Demond F., m. Abbey J. **SIRRINE**, Jan. 7, 1844, by Levi		
Brunson	3	123
Elmira, [twin with Almira, d. Thomas & Lucy], b. Aug. 17, 1830	2	120
Joanna, m. Levy **BARNUM**, Jan*. 11, 178[ ] *("July, March"		
crossed out)	1	423
Legrand, s. [Thomas & Lucy], b. Apr. 24, 1817	2	120
Legrand, m. Marietta **STEVENS**, b. of Danbury, Mar. 3, 1840,		
by John Nickerson	3	102
Lucy Ann, d. [Thomas & Lucy], b. Jan. 4, 1816	2	120
Thomas, m. Lucy **FROST**, Feb. [ ], 1814	2	120
Thomas, m. Sarah **HILL**, Dec. 22, 1844, by John Nickerson	3	131
STONE, Abigail, Mrs., m. Eli **WILDMAN**, [May] 1, [1833], by Rev.		
A. Rood	3	75
Alanson, m. Anna **WOOD**, Nov. 1, 1820, by W[illia]m Andrews	3	3
Amos J., m. Mary E. **ABBOTT**, Sept. 26, 1849, by Rev. A.		
Perkins	3	160
Anna, d. Francis, of Danbury, m. James H. **ST. JOHN**, of		
Ridgefield, this day [Sept. 4, 1842], by Rev. Rollin S. Stone	3	117
Anne, d. [John & Elizabeth], b. Apr. 10, 1784	1	505
Asa, [s. Levi & Mary], b. May 20, 1781	1	445
Betsey, [d. Levi & Mary], b. Dec. 14, 1788	1	445
Betsey, of Redding, m. Edward **GREGORY**, of Danbury, Nov.		
30, 1831, by John Nickerson	3	66
Betsey Ann, m. Philander **HAMILTON**, b. of Danbury, Nov. 24,		
1844, by Rev. Rollin S. Stone	3	130
Billy, [s. Oliver & Lydia], b. Aug. 30, 1789	1	395
Caleb S., m. Abigail **FENNER**, Jan. 13, 1822, by Rev.		
W[illia]m Andrews	3	10
Daniel, [s. Oliver & Lydia], b. Jan. 22, 1791	1	395
Daniel, m. Mary Ann **WILDMAN** , Dec. 20, 1820, by W[illia]m		
Andrews	3	4
Dolla, [d. Levi & Mary], b. June 20, 1783	1	445
Edwin, m. Mary Ann **ST. JOHN**, b. of Danbury, this day [Aug.		
11, 1841], by Rev. Rollin S. Stone	3	110
Eli, s. [John & Elizabeth], b. July 5, 1771; d. Jan. 27, 1774	1	505
Eli, s. [John & Elizabeth], b. May 16, 1775	1	505
Eli W., m. Mary W. **CROFUT**, b. of Bethel, Feb. 23, 1842,		
by J. Greenwood	3	114
Esther, d. W[illia]m, m. James **CRARY**, June 24, 1769	1	437
Eunice, [d. Oliver & Margaret], b. July 31, 1777	1	395

	Vol.	Page
STONE, (cont.)		
Francis, [s. Oliver & Margaret], b. Nov. 15, 1783	1	395
Hannah, d. [John & Elizabeth], b. Oct. 26, 1777	1	505
Harry, m. Ruth Ann **WILKES**, [Jan.] 25, [1832], by Rev. A. Rood	3	66
Harry, of Danbury, m. Deborah B. **FIELD**, of South East, this day, [Mar. 27, 1844], by Rev. Rollin S. Stone	3	125
Henry B., m. Sarah **BENJAMIN**, b. of Danbury, Nov. 30, 1848, by Rev. Rollin S. Stone	3	146
Hezekiah, m. Antoinett **STEVENS**, of New York, Apr. 9, 1832, by John Nickerson	3	69
Huldah, d. [John & Elizabeth], b. Apr. 1, 1781	1	505
Huldah, m. John **FOOT**, Nov. 28, 1781	1	405
Ira, s. [John & Elizabeth], b. May 27, 1773	1	505
Jacob Gooster, m. Margaret **LANLEY**, b. of Danbury, Oct. 14, 1844, by Rev. George T. Todd	3	129
[John], m. Elizabeth **CROWFUT**, d. Mathew, Apr.* 19, 1770 *(Crossed out)	1	505
John, s. [John & Elizabeth], b. Oct. 3, 1787	1	505
John, d. May 23, 1790, ae 42	1	505
Levi, m. Mary **WILDMAN**, July 4, 1776	1	445
Levi, [s. Oliver & Margaret], b. Sept. 2, 1781	1	395
Lois, m. John **GREGORY**, b. of Danbury, May 8, 1850, by Rev. Rollin S. Stone	3	148
Lucy, m. Herman **BEARDSLEY**, b. of Danbury, Apr. 26, 1848, by Rev. Rollin S. Stone	3	141
Margaret, [w. Oliver], d. May 27, 1788	1	395
Maria, m. Henry **SHUTE**, b. of Danbury, July 15, 1838, by Rev. Rollin S. Stone	3	94
Mary Ann, m. Benedict **HUSTED**, b. of Danbury, Apr. 21, 1844, by James Floy	3	126
Mary B., m. W[illia]m **WHITE**, b. of Danbury, Apr. 1*, 1832, by Rev. Lemuel B. Hull *(Perhaps"5th")	3	69
Nancy, [d. Levi & Mary], b. Oct. 31, 1785	1	445
Niram J., m. Sarah B. **FAIRCHILD**, b. of Danbury, Nov. 27, [1850], by Rev. J. B. Merwin	3	155
Oliver, m. Margaret **BOUGHTON**, Oct. 12, 1775	1	395
Oliver, m. 2nd w. Lydia **PRICE**, Nov. 30, 1788	1	395
Oliver, m. Sephronia **WILDMAN**, Mar. 12, 1823, by Rev. W[illia]m Andrews	3	16
Oliver, m. Abigail **WOOD**, [Nov.] 16, [1830], by Rev. A. Rood	3	58
Oliver S., m. Mary E. **SMITH**, Apr. 17, 1850, by Rev. A. Perkins	3	160
Orson, of Redding, m. Sally **WOOD**, of Danbury, Sept. 19, 1827, by Levi Brunson	3	42
Polly, [d. Oliver & Margaret], b. July 16, 1779	1	395
Polly, of Redding, m. Alanson **FOSTER**, of Danbury Dec. 17, 1823, by John Nickerson	3	20

Vol.   Page

STONE, (cont.)

Polly, m. Munson **RAND,** b. of Danbury, June 1, 1838, by
J. Shaw   3   92

Rebecca, m. Truman **TROWBRIDGE,** Dec. 5, 1822, by Rev.
W[illia]m Andrews   3   14

Russel, [s. Levi & Mary], b. May 3, 1779   1   445

Sally M., Mrs., m. Daniel B. **WOOD,** b. of Danbury, Sept.
7, 1845, by Morris Hill   3   138

Samuel W., [s. Levi & Mary], b. July 24, 1791   1   445

Sarah, d. William, m. Nathan **WILDMAN,** Dec. 13, 1792   1   370

Sarah I., of Danbury, m. Charles **ST. JOHN,** of Ridgefield,
this day, [Oct. 27, 1841], by Rev. Rollin S. Stone   3   112

Thomas S., m. Sarah J. **BALDWIN,** July 9, 1851, by Rev. A.
Perkins   3   160

Wealthy Ann, of Danbury, m. Smith **PULLING,** of Ridgefield,
this day, Sept. 24, 1845, by Rev. Rollin S. Stone   3   136

Zadock B., m. Mary **CURTIS,** b. of Danbury, Jan. 3, 1829,
by John Nickerson   3   50

Zadoc B., m. Mary A. **CROFUT,** May 2, [1849], by Rev. A.
Perkins   3   160

STOTT, Frederick, see Frederick **STARR**   3   114

STOW, Abraham, m. Julia **OSBORN,** b. of Danbury, July 18, 1831,
by Rev. Erastus Cole   3   64

Polly, m. Moses **PARSONS,** May 23, 1821, by Rev. W[illia]m
Andrews   3   6

STRATTON, John R., m. Harriet L. **NICHOLS,** June 15, 1848, by
Rev. William W. Bronson   3   143

STUART, [see also **STEWART**], Betey, of Fredericksborough, d.
Charles, m. Abijah **BENEDICT,** s. Matthew, May 10, 1785   3   485

STUDWELL, Thomas, m. Emila **BARTRAM,** b. of Danbury, Dec.
14, 1845, by Rev. Fitch Read   1   137

STURDEVANT, Aphia, m. Sturges M. **JUDD,** [Feb.] 9, [1830], by
Rev. A. Rood   3   55

STURGES, Anna, d. [Simmons & Lois], b. Oct. 15, 1787   1   394

Betsey, of Danbury, m. Daniel **CAMP,** of Brookfield, Apr. 4,
1821, by Rev. Benjamin Benham, of New Milford &
Brookfield   3   6

Clary, [d. Simmons & Lois], b. Sept. 11, 1792   1   394

Esther, [d. Simmons & Lois], b. June [ ], 1790; d. June 29, 1791   1   394

Isaac, of Westport, m. Maria **STARR,** of Bethel, this day
[July 17, 1843], by Rev. Rollin S. Stone   3   121

Julia, of Danbury, m. William **DAVIS,** of New York, Nov. 19,
1833, by John Nickerson   3   77

Ruhana, m. James **BEATY,** [ ], 1784* *("1748"?)   1   368

Simmons, m. Lois **PICKET,** d. Daniel, Mar. 12, 1786   1   394

Stephen B., m. Eliza **TAYLOR,** b. of Danbury, this day
[Mar. 7, 1841], by Rev. D. H. Short   3   108

SUMMERS, Hannah, of Bethel, m. Thomas **WATT,** Oct. 5, 1851,

	Vol.	Page

TAYLOR, (cont.)

Clorinda, of Danbury, m. John **MORGAN**, of New Fairfield,
this day [Jan. 1, 1821], by Nathan Seeley, J. P. — 3 — 4

Cynthia, m. Joseph C. **BARNUM**, b. of Danbury, this day [ ],
by Rev. Lemuel B. Hull. Recorded Dec. 5, 1825 — 3 — 30

Daniel, m. Rachel **STARR**, d. John, June 10, 1739 — 1 — 489

Daniel, m. 2nd w. Elisabeth **BOUGHTON**, d. Capt. Samuel, June
1, 1742 — 1 — 489

Daniel, s. [Daniel & Elizabeth], b. Oct. 18, 1748;
d. Dec. 14, 1773 — 1 — 489

Daniel, s. [Major & Elisabeth], b. Mar. 28, 1787 — 1 — 492

Daniel, [s. Zalmon & Hannah], b. Nov. [ ], 1787 — 1 — 437

Daniel, d. Sept. 23, 1791, in the 77th y. of his age — 1 — 489

Deborah, d. [Eliud & Mary], b. Mar. 28, 1782 — 1 — 401

Deborah, m. Stephen **BATES**, b. of Danbury, June 29, 1837,
by Rev. Salmon C. Bulkley — 3 — 90

Edward, m. Sally **BARNUM**, Sept. 17, 1820, by W[illia]m
Andrews — 3 — 3

Eleazer, [s. Jonathan & Anna], b. Sept. 30, 1785 — 1 — 438

Eliakim, m. Aug. 18, 1784 — 1 — 439

Elias, [s. Jabez, Jr. & Many], b. Oct. 17, 1789 — 1 — 425

Elias Gage, [s. Gilead & Jenny], b. Oct. 28, 1781 — 1 — 419

Eliud, m. Mary **HALL**, Apr. 13, 1780 — 1 — 401

Eliza, m. Nobel **LYON**, [May] 22, [1838], by Rev. J. G. Collom — 3 — 94

Eliza, m. Stephen B. **STURGES**, b. of Danbury, this day [Mar. 7,
1841], by Rev. D. H. Short — 3 — 108

Elisabeth, d. [Daniel & Elisabeth], b. Dec. 5, 1745 — 1 — 489

Elisabeth, w. Daniel, d. Nov. [ ], 1793 — 1 — 489

Elisabeth, [w. Major], d. Aug. 31, 1796, in the 45th y. of
her age — 1 — 492

Elizabeth, wid, James, d. Jan. 25, 1798, in the 72 y. of
her age — 1 — 423

Elisabeth, m. Laurens **HICKOK**, b. of Bethel, Oct. 8, 1822, by
Rev. John G. Lowe — 3 — 22

Elisabeth, m. John **DAN**, Nov. 5, 1828, by Nathan Burton — 3 — 50

Elnathan Hall, [s. Eliud & Mary], b. Aug. 18, 1791 — 1 — 401

Emeline, m. Henry **SHEPHERD**, of Carmel, Dec. 3, 1849, by
Rev. John Purves, of Bethel — 3 — 151

Emily B., of Danbury, m. Edward B. **WILSON**, of Easton, Oct.
3, 1850, by Rev. John S. Whittlesey — 3 — 152

Esther, [d. Noah & Tamma], b. Oct. 9, 1787 — 1 — 408

Eugene, s. Leve & [grandson] of Levi & Lucy *(Entry in pencil) — 1 — 432

Ezra, [s. Jonathan & Anna], b. June 3, 1778 — 1 — 438

Ezra, s. [Zalmon & Hannah], b. Feb. 26, 1785 — 1 — 437

George, of Saugatuck, m. Rebecca **HODGE**, of Danbury, Sept. 2,
1832, by Elias Birchard, J. P. — 3 — 70

Gilead, m. Jenny **HOPKINS**, Oct. 4, 1764 — 1 — 419

Hannah, d. [Daniel & Rachel], b. Jan. 21, 1741; d. Feb. 7*,

	Vol.	Page

TAYLOR, (cont.)

	Vol.	Page
1741 *(Possibly "1st")	1	489
Hannah, d. [Daniel & Elisabeth], b. June 18, 1758: d. Mar. 14, 1778	1	489
Hannah, d. John & Abigail, b. Nov. 7, 1765	1	438
Hannah, [d. Noah & Tamma], b. Jan. 6, 1785	1	408
Hannah, d. John*, m. Nathan **WHITNEY**, Dec. 16, 1787 *("Levi" crossed out. "John TAYLOR" written over)	1	435
Hannah, d. [Eliakim], b. Jan. 22, 1788	1	439
Hannah, [d. Eliud & Mary], b. Jan. 8, 1789	1	401
Hannah M., m. Charles **PECK**, b. of Danbury, this day [Nov. 6, 1836], by Rev. D. H. Short	3	88
Harriet, m. Ammon T. **PECK**, b. of Bethel, Nov. 8, 1843, by J. K. Ingalls	3	122
Harriet, m. Reuben·[ ], b. of Danbury, Oct. 30, 1844, by Rev. J. K. Ingalls	3	129
Harry, s. [Lemuel & Ada], b. June 1, 1789	1	462
Hester, m. Timothy I. **DIBBLE**, June 8, 1823, by Rev. William Andrews	3	17
Horrace, s. [John & Sabra], b. July 20, 1798	1	438
Huldah, [d. Jabez, Jr. & Many], b. June 2, 1787	1	425
Ira, [s. Gilead & Jenny], b. June 4, 1771	1	419
Irene, d. [Phinehas & Molly], b. Oct. 7, 1784	1	387
Jabez, Jr., m. Many **SKEDMER**, Nov. 12, 1778	1	425
James, [d. Eliakim], b. Apr. 16, 1789	1	439
Joel, m. Lynda **ADAMS**, b. of Danbury, Oct. 18, 1820, by William Cooke, J. P.	3	5
John, b. Oct. 13, 1743; m. Abigail **MYGATT**, d. Jos., Dec. 16, 1762	1	438
John, [s. John & Abigail], b. Aug. 22, 1779	1	438
John, s. [Jabez, Jr. & Many], b. Nov. 1, 1780	1	425
John, m. Sabra **DeFOREST**, d. Thaddeus **MEAD**, Mar. 24, 1790	1	438
Jonathan, b. Oct. 25, 1752; m. An[n]a **BENEDICT**, d. David, Apr. 26, 1770	1	438
Joseph, had Richard, s. Patience, b. Dec. 5, 1779 (negro); Richard, m. Isabella, May 1, 1802. Their s. Isaac Sydney, b. Nov. 2, 1803	1	361
Joseph, had negro **RICHARD**, s. Dorcas, b. Dec. 5, 1779	1	369
Joseph, had servant Billy, s. Zimri & Peg (servant of Dr. John **WOOD**, b. Mar. 7, 1788, also Eliphibe, b. Apr. 4, 1790, Joanne, b. Aug. 4, 1792; Peg d. Aug. 3, 1792	1	487
Joseph, 2nd, b. 1703, d. Nov. 7, 1793	1	361
Joseph, Jr., m. Martha E. **STARR**, Nov. 26, 1845, by Rev. R. K. Bellamy	3	138
Joseph Platt, s. [Timothy & Elisabeth], b. [ ]	1	493
Joshua, s. Matthew, m. Eunice **SEELY**, d. James, [ ]	1	498
Joshua L., m. Eunice E. **FAIRCHILD**, b. of Bethel, Mar. 1, 1838, by Rev. John Greenwood, of Bethel	3	93

	Vol.	Page
TAYLOR, (cont.)		
Laura, d. [Lemuel & Ada], b. Nov. 6, 1791	1	462
Limuel, [s. Gilead & Jenny], b. Mar. 24, 1765	1	419
Lemuel, m. Ada CORNWELL, of Middletown, Mar. 6, 1787	1	462
Leve, only s. [Leve & Lucy], & father of Eugene	1	432
Levi, b. Jan. 19, 1762; m. Lucy ANDREWS June 6, 1805	1	432
Levi, [s. Jonathan & Anna], b. May 16, 1771	1	438
Lora, [d. Phinehas & Molly], b. Aug. 19, 1791	1	387
Lucy, d. [Levi & Lucy], b. Dec. 7, 1805	1	432
Lucy Jane, m. George A. ANDREWS, b. of Danbury, this day, [Sept. 23, 1840], by Rev. S. H. Clark	3	105
Major, s. [Daniel & Elisabeth], b. Apr. 17, 1743	1	489
Major, m. Elisabeth MITCHELL, d. John, of Woodbury, Apr. 26, 1771	1	492
Maria, d. [Lemuel & Ada], b. June 14, 1790	1	462
Maria, m. Charles HUBBELL, b. of Danbury, Dec. 20, 1842, by S. B. Britton	3	118
Maria L., of New York, m. Joseph B. FOOT, of Danbury, May 18, 1834, by John Nickerson	3	81
Martha T., m. Matthew W. STARR, this day [Dec. 16, 1821], by Nathaniel Freeman	3	9
Mary, m. William TWEEDY, Jr., b. of Danbury, this day, [June 19, 1825], by Rev. Lemuel B. Hull	3	27
Mary Jane, m. Warren PICKET, b. of Danbury, Dec. 1, 1841, by Rev. D. H. Short	3	113
Matthew, m. Jane BARNUM, d. Matthew, Oct. 14, 1792	1	430
Melinda, m. Harry SEELYE, b. of Danbury, May 15, 1827, by Rev. John G. Lowe	3	40
Mynenda, [child of Eliakim], b. May 18, 1791	1	439
Najah, [child of John & Abigail], b. Oct. 31, 1769	1	438
Nathan, [s. Eliud & Mary], b. July 15, 1784	1	401
Noah, m. Tamma KNAPP, d. Uriah, of Greenwich, Apr. 12, 1780	1	408
Oliver, [s. Jabez, Jr. & Many], b. Nov. 3, 1791	1	425
Philo, s. [Major & Elisabeth, b. Apr. 13, 1790	1	492
Phinehas, m. Molly SHERWOOD, Sept. 11, 1783	1	387
Rachel, [w. Daniel], d. July 3, 1741	1	489
Rachel, d. [Daniel & Elisabeth], b. June 16, 1754	1	489
Rachel, d. Abn[ ], m. Thomas GREGORY, Apr. 8, 1783	1	476
Rebecah, m. Jeames HOYT, Sept. 8, 1773	3	423
Rebecca, m. Seth COMSTOCK, Oct. 23, 1822, by Rev. W[illia]m Andrews	3	13
Russel, m. Laura WALLIN, b. of Bethel, Aug. 15, 1822, by Rev. John G. Lowe	3	23
Ruth, d. [Daniel & Elisabeth], b. Sept. 4, 1750; d. May 8, 1795	1	489
Ruth, d. Capt. Daniel, m. Nathanael KETCHAM, Aug. 10, 1769	1	486
Ruth, [d. Noah & Tamma], b. Oct. 25, 1789	1	408
Sally, m. Fairchild BARNUM, b. of Danbury, Oct. 16, 1827, by John G. Lowe	3	44

	Vol.	Page

TAYLOR, (cont.)

Samuel, m. Lurana **CORNELL,** d. Capt. John, Apr. 3, 1788 — 1 — 440

Sarah, [d. Jonathan & Anna], b. Jan. 25, 1776 — 1 — 438

Sarah, d. Abner, m. Thomas **NELSON,** Dec. 24, 1796 — 1 — 381

Sarah, m. William **FURGISON,** b. of Danbury, this day [Nov. 15, 1826], by Levi Osbom — 3 — 37

Sarah E., m. William C. **HICKOK,** b. of Danbury, Sept. 16, 1844, by Rev. George T. Todd — 3 — 128

Sarah L., of Danbury, m. Homer L. **HAYES,** of Brookfield, this day, [Oct. 23, 1836], by Rev. D. H. Short — 3 — 87

Sarane, d. [Major & Elisabeth], b. Sept. 12, 1774 — 1 — 492

Silas, b. June 24, 17[ ]; m. Jerusha [ ], May 7, 1778 — 1 — 500

Susan, Mrs., m. William S. **TAYLOR,** b. of Danbury, Sept. 29, 1844, by Rev. Fitch Reed — 3 — 128

Tamma, [d. Noah & Tamma], b. Apr. 3, 1792 — 1 — 408

Timothy, Capt. m. Elisabeth **COOKE,** d. Col. Joseph P., Dec. 12, 1784 — 1 — 493

Timothy, d. May 3, 1802, in the 49th y. of his age — 1 — 493

Warren, m. Eliza **MOOR,** Feb. 12, 1824, by Rev. W[illia]m Andrews — 3 — 21

W[illia]m Lewis, s. Lewis, b. Jan. 28, 1822 — 2 — 66

William S., m. Mrs. Susan **TAYLOR,** b. of Danbury, Sept. 29, 1844, by Rev. Fitch Reed — 3 — 128

Zalmon, m. Hannah **BENEDICT,** d. Theophilus, Oct. 26, 1780 — 1 — 437

TERRY, Maria, m. Darius **SELLECK,** Sept. 25, 1850, by Rev. A. Perkins — 3 — 160

THATCHER, Augustus, of Hartford, m. Eliza **JENNINGS,** of Reading, Apr. 15, 1834, by Rev. W[illia]m L. Strong — 3 — 79

THOMAS, Azor H., m. Mariette **LYON,** b. of Danbury, this day [ ], by Rev. Rollin S. Stone. Recorded May 9, 1842 — 3 — 115

Sally B., m. David **MANSFIELD,** Apr. 21, 1822, by Josiah Dikeman — 3 — 11

THOMPSON, [see also **TIMPSON**], Edward, m. Maria **CORNWALL,** b. of Danbury, May 29, 1842, by Rev. Thomas P. Guion — 3 — 115

Susan, m. George **NICHOLS,** Nov. 14, 1842, by Rev. Thomas T. Guion — 3 — 117

THURSTON, Charles F., of New York, m. Serina **BULL,** of Danbury, May 11, 1847, by Rev. Rollin S. Stone — 3 — 162

TIMMANUS, Phebe, m. John **WILLIAMS,** b. of Danbury, May 5, 1829, by Rev. A. Rood — 3 — 52

TIMPSON, [see also **THOMPSON**], Benjamin, m. Emily J. **HARRIS,** b. of Danbury, June 1, [ ], at her father's house. (Eri **BARTRAM**), by Rev. J. B. Merwin. Recorded Aug. 1854 — 3 — 158

TOMLINSON, Polly Ann, m. Daniel T. **BARNUM,** Nov. 23, 1820, by W[illia]m Andrews — 3 — 4

TOWN, Hetty Elizabeth, m. Philander **SEELEY,** Dec. 12, 1832,

	Vol.	Page
TOWN, (cont.)		
by Rev. Joseph S. Covell, of Brookfield	3	76
TOWNER, [E]unice, m. William **COMES**, [ ]	1	416
TOWNSEND, Benjamin, m. Annis **STEVENS**, [Apr]. 20, [1826], by George Benedict	3	32
TREADWELL, Mary, m. Warren **BAILEY**, Dec. 27, 1846, by R. K. Bellamy	3	161
TREET, Mary Jane, of Danbury, m. George **WELLS**, of Newtown, [Apr.] 20, [1845], by Rev. John L. Ambler	3	134
TROWBRIDGE, TROBRIDGE, Abigail, m. Matthew K. **GILBERT**, b. of Danbury, this day, [May 29, 1825], by Rev. Lemuel B. Hull	3	27
Almeda, of Danbury, m. Charles **JOHNSON**, of South Brittan, [Jan.] 18, [1829], by John Nickerson	3	50
Almyria, m. Almon **BARNUM**, Jan. 8, 1823, by Rev. John G. Lowe	3	14
Almira, m. Almon **BARNUM**, b. of Danbury, Jan. 15, 1823, by Rev. John G. Lowe	3	22
Amelia, m. Horace E. **HICKOK**, Oct. 23, 1842, by Rev. Thomas T. Guion	3	117
Beckah, d. [Isaac & Rebecca], b. Dec. 17, 1770	1	448
Beckah, d. Isaac, m. Samuel **BARNUM**, Mar. 10, 1790	1	448
Benedict, m. Adelia **BROAS**, Aug. 6, 1848, by Rev. A. Perkins	3	160
Betsey, m. Thomas I. **COAN**, of Guilford, Jan. 8, [1823], by Rev. J. G. Lowe	3	14
Catharine A., m. Ammon **GREEN**, Jan. 9, 1849, by Rev. John Purves, of Bethel	3	151
Dilla, [d. James & Abigail], b. July 25, 1778	1	421
Eli T., m. Eliza **JUDD**, b. of Danbury, this day [Oct. 4, 1843], by Rev. Rollin S. Stone	3	122
Eliakim D., [s. James & Abigail], b. June 21, 1776	1	421
Eliza M., m. David A. **FOOT**, Dec. 25, 1846, by R. H. Bellamy	3	138
Elisabeth, [d. James & Abigail], b. Apr. 6, 1782	1	421
Elisabeth, of Danbury, m. Thomas **CORVAN***, of New York, Jan. 15, 1823, by Rev. John G. Lowe *(Perhaps **CORRAN**"?)	3	23
Emily, m. W[illia]m C. **SHEPARD**, b. of Danbury, Nov. 23, 1831, by Rev. Lemuel B. Hull	3	68
Esther, [d. James & Abigail], b. Oct. 22, 1774	1	421
Esther, m. Micajah **HOYT**, Nov. 1, 1792	1	421
Hannah, d. [Dr. Joseph & Olive], b. Mar. 24, 1792	1	479
Ira, [s. James & Abigail], b. Aug. 4, 1783; d. Jan. 22, 1808	1	421
Ira, m. Mary* **BUCHUM**, b. of Danbury, Nov. 1, 1831, by Rev. Lemuel B. Hull *(Possibley "Meny"?)	3	67
Isaac, m. Rebecca **PECK**, d. Dea. Joseph, Feb. 17, 1767	1	448
Jabez, s. [James & Abigail], b. Mar. 2, 1772	1	421
Jabez, s. James, m. Lucy **HOYT**, Sept. 27, 1797	1	389
James, s. [Stephen & Lydia], b. Aug. 28, 1749	1	466

	Vol.	Page
TROWBRIDGE, TROBRIDGE, (cont.)		
James, m. Abigail **DAVIS**, Jan. 1, 1771	1	421
James H., m. Mary **BANKS**, Aug. 7, 1820, by Laban Clark	3	2
Jerusha, of Danbury, m. William H. **HUSTED**, of New York, Jan. 12, 1840, by John Nickerson	3	102
Joseph, [s. Isaac & Rebecca], b. May 19, 1780	1	448
Joseph, Dr., m. Olive **CLARK**, d. Capt. James, Sept. [ ], 1791	1	479
Laura, m. Rufus L. **COUCH**, May 12, 1840, by John Crawford	3	104
Lucy, m. Street Hall* **KEELER**, Jan. 5, 1834, at the house of Eliakim Trowbridge, of Bethel, by Rev. John D. Smith *(Or "Hull"?)	3	78
Lydia, d. [Stephen & Lydia], b. Feb. 25, 1761	1	466
Lydia, m. Thaddeus **STARR**, May 22, 1783	1	466
Lydia, w. of Stephen, d. Feb. 24, 1799. Entered by Stephen **TROWBRIDGE**, son-in-law of said deceased	1	466
Lydia A., m. Lowell M. **NICHOLS**, Nov. 19, 1851, by Rev. Charles Bartlett	3	158
Phebe, d. John, m. Everit **EAMES**, Nov. 11, 1778	1	494
Polly, d. [Isaac & Rebecca], b. July 12, 1769; d. Jan. 19, 1770	1	448
Polly, [d. Isaac & Rebecca], b. Aug. 7, 1775; d. Dec. 3, 1775	1	448
Sally Lorana, d. [Dr. Joseph & Olive], b. May 11, 1794	1	479
Sam[ue]l, s. [Stephen & Lydia], b. Mar. 19, 1752	1	466
Samuel A., m. Mary A. **MOORE***, b. of Danbury, June 1, 1847, by Rev. Rollin S. Stone *(Or **MOON**"?)	3	162
Sarah, m. Samuel **DIBBLE**, July 21, 1762	1	464
Stephen, m. Lydia **CROFUT**, May 27, 174[ ]* *(Last fig. blotted)	1	466
Stephen, s. [Stephen & Lydia], b. Jan. 18, 1756	1	466
Stephen, [s. Isaac & Rebecca], b. June 17, 1773	1	448
Stephen, s. Eliekim D., b. Jan. 15, 1822	2	65
Truman, m. Rebecca **STONE**, Dec. 5, 1822, by Rev. W[illia]m Andrews	3	14
TRUBY, Eunice, m. John **BARTS**, Dec. 7, 1783	1	492
TRUMBULL, Lucy, d. Rev. John, of Watertown, m. Rev. Timothy **LANGDON**, Jan. 8, 1787	1	482
W[illia]m, of Milford, m. Maria **HACK**, of Danbury, [Dec.] 27, [1840], by Addison Parker	3	107
TUCKER, Charity, d. Major Thomas, m. Ephraim Moss **WHITE**, May 6, 1798	1	474
Mary, of Danbury, m. Elisha **WHITTLESEY**, of Danbury, s. Eliphalet, May 29, 1788	1	378
TURKINGTON, John, m. Hannah **ANDREWS**, Feb. 17, 1822, by Rev. Ambrose S. Todd	3	11
TURNER, Ambrose B., m. Mary Ann **WILLIAMS**, Oct. 16, 1827, by Benaiah Y. Morse	3	43
Annis, m. Abel **BARNUM**, Nov. 15, 1787	1	429
TURNEY, Melinda, m. Lewis **HAYES**, Sept. 5, 1847, by Lucius Atwater	3	142

	Vol.	Page
TWEEDY, Anna, [d. Samuel & Anna], b. Oct. 18, 1778	1	402
David B., m. Comelia A. WARNER, b. of Danbury, June 26, 1844, by Thomas T. Guion	3	126
Edgar S., m. Ann BISHOP, [Jan.] 24, [1832], by Rev. A. Rood	3	66
Edgar S., of Danbury, m. Elizabeth S. C. BELDEN, of Wilton, this day [June 4, 1834], by Rev. Lemuel B. Hull	3	79
John, [s. Samuel & Anna], b. Mar. 16, 1774	1	402
Mariett, m. Zadock R. BENEDICT, Sept. 1, 1830, by Rev. A. Rood	3	57
R[e]uben, s. [Samuel & Anna], b. Aug. 8, 1770	1	402
Samuel, m. Anna SMITH, d. Reuben, of Nine Partners, Nov. 18, 1769	1	402
Sam[ue]l, [s. Samuel & Anna], b. Mar. 8, 1776	1	402
Samuel S., m. Sary* FERRY, b. of Danbury, Apr. 20, 1845, by Rev. John L. Ambler *(Possibly "Seny")	3	134
Smith, [s. Samuel & Anna], b. Sept. 22, 1784	1	402
William, [s. Samuel & Anna], b. Mar. 18, 1772	1	.402
William, Jr., m. Mary TAYLOR, b. of Danbury, this day [June 19, 1825], by Rev. Lemuel B. Hull	3	27
TWENAIR, John, m. Julia RIDER, b. of Danbury, this day [Aug. 31, 1843], by Rev. Rollin S. Stone	3	121
URMSTON, [see also ARMSTRONG], Nathanul M., m. Evelina COMSTOCK, Sept. 28, 1826, by W[illia]m C. Kniffin, M.G.	3	36
VAIL, VEAL, Hannah, wid. Moses, m. Benjamin WOOD, Jan. 7, 1798	1	372
Huldah, m. Alanson GREGORY, Nov. 6, 1822, by Reuben Booth, J. P.	3	13
Lois, of Danbury, m. Martin OSBORN, of Brookfield, Jan. 15, [1840], by Addison Parker	3	101
Maria, m. Major DIKEMAN, Oct. 31, 1827, by Reuben Booth, J. P.	3	42
VANDUSEN, Robert J., m. Anna KNAPP, Oct. 19, 1851, by Rev. A. Perkins	3	160
VIDETS, Mary, d. John, m. [ ]saac* BENEDICT, s. Nathaniel, May 24, 1744 *(Wom off)	1	501
WAKELEY, James, m. Rebecca COOKE, Feb. 10, 1805	2	61
Joseph Burton, s. [James & Rebecca], b. Feb. 18, 1809	2	61
Samuel Dickenson, s. [James & Rebecca], b. Nov. 22, 1805	2	61
William Andrews, s. [James & Rebecca], b. Oct. 28, 1815	2	61
WALLER, [see also WELLER], Abigail, mother of Caleb STARR, d. July 24, 1791, in the 88th y. of her age	1	443
Anna, m. Zelotus ROBINSON, Jan. 25, 1776	1	383
WALLIN, Laura, m. Russel TAYLOR, b. of Bethel, Aug. 15, 1822, by Rev. John G. Lowe	3	23
WARNER, Comelia A., m. David B. TWEEDY, b. of Danbury, June 26, 1844, by Thomas T. Guion	3	126
Cynthia Maria, b. Feb. 18, 1811	1	482

	Vol.	Page

WEED, (cont.)

David, [s. Eleazer & Anna], b. Jan. 1, 1785 — 1 — 446

David, m. Lowis **PEARCE,** July 8, 1821, by Nathan Bulkley — 3 — 7

Eleazer, [twin with Ithemar, s. Samuel & Hannah], b. Jan. 28, 1756 — 1 — 446

Eleazer, m. Anna **BEARSS,** May 24, 1781 — 1 — 446

Eli, [s. Eleazer & Anna], b. Apr. 11, 1788 — 1 — 446

Ezra, [s. Asa], b. July 15, 1788 — 1 — 414

George R., of Burlington, Vt., m. Mary E. **OLMSTEAD,** of Redding, now of Bethel, Oct. 17, 1850, by Rev. John S. Whittlesey — 3 — 152

Harrison, m. Emily E. **PLATT,** Nov. 29*, 1851, by Rev. A. Perkins *(Possibly "27th"?) — 3 — 160

Hiram, of Danbury, m. Mary **CLINE,** of Philadelphia, Aug. 29, 1826, by Rev. J. G. Lowe — 3 — 36

Ithemar, [twin with Eleazer, s. Samuel & Hannah], b. Jan. 28, 1756 — 1 — 446

John, s. [Solomon & Rachel], b. Sept. 25, 1783 — 1 — 451

Joseph Bearss, [s. Eleazer & Anna], b. Nov. 11, 1790 — 1 — 446

Levy, [s. Asa], b. July 4, 1784 — 1 — 414

Levi, [s. Solomon & Rachel], b. Sept. 22, 1787 — 1 — 451

Levi, s. Asa, m. Rachel **CROFUT,** d. Benjamin, b. of Danbury, Apr. 12*, 1803   *(May be "13th"?) — 1 — 357

Lucy, [d. Eleazer & Anna], b. Sept. 5, 1782 — 1 — 446

Mercy, d. J[   ]*, m. Eli **SEGAR,** Oct. 27, 17[ ] *(Worn off) — 1 — 500

Phebe Lucina Livinna, d. Zar. b. Mar. 2, 1825 — 2 — 101

Philo, [s. Asa], b. June 15, 1786 — 1 — 414

Samuel, m. Hannah **HUBBELL,** Apr. 15, 1745 — 1 — 446

Sarah, d. Reuben, of Stanford, m. Sam[ue]l **BENEDICT,** 4th, Oct. 25, 1774 — 1 — 504

Solomon, m. Rachel **DIBBLE,** d. John, Jr., Nov. 30, 1779 — 1 — 451

Tho[ma]s, m. Susan **HOLDMAN,** July 26, 1829, by George Benedict — 3 — 53

Urarana, m. Ira **BARTRUM,** Nov. 12, 1821, by Rev. W[illia]m Andrews — 3 — 9

Zar, [child of Asa], b. July 12, 1792 — 1 — 414

Zerah, [child of Solomon & Rachel], b. Feb. 19, 1788 — 1 — 451

WELLER, [see also **WALLER**], Justus, of New Milford, m. Susanna **PATCH,** of Danbury, [Apr.] 2, [1826], by John Nickerson — 3 — 32

WELLMAN, Jedediah, m. Betsey **JARVIS,** d. Stephen, Sept. 23, 1792 — 1 — 381

William Watson, s. [Jedediah & Betsey], b. Aug. 5, 1793 — 1 — 381

WELLS, Anna, m. Joshua B. **FERRY,** Dec. 24, 1822, by Adonirum Fairchild, J. P. — 3 — 14

George, of Newtown, m. Mary Jane **TREET,** of Danbury, [Apr.] 20, [1845], by Rev. John L. Ambler — 3 — 134

James, m. Sarah **PATCHEN,** b. of Danbury, Nov. 28, 1844, by Thomas T. Guion — 3 — 132

	Vol.	Page
WESCOT, WESTCOAT, Betty, b. Aug. 2, 1745; m. Samuel		
BENEDICT, 3rd, Apr. 7, 1768	1	443
Betty, b. Aug. 2, 1745; m. Sam[ue]l BENEDICT, 3rd, Apr. 7, 1768	1	504
Ruth, d. Nathaniel, of Norwalk, m. Joshua BENEDICT, Apr. 13, 1774	1	457
WETMORE, Apollos, s. [Rev. Noah & Submit], b. Dec. 14, 1771	1	489
Hannah, d. [Rev. Noah & Submit], b. Jan. 22, 1765	1	489
Irene, d. [Rev. Noah & Submit], b. Sept. 11, 1762	1	489
Noah, Rev., m. Submit RUSSEL, d. Ithiel, of Branford, July 9, 1761	1	489
Noah, s. [Rev. Noah & Submit], b. May 4, 1767	1	489
Sam[ue]l Ithiel, s. [Rev. Noah & Submit], b. Sept. 30, 1774	1	489
Submit, d. [Rev. Noah & Submit], b. Mar. 1, 1769; d. same day	1	489
WHEELER, Alva, m. Jerusha STEVENS, b. of Danbury, Oct. 25, 1826, by Rev. John G. Lowe	3	38
Amos, s. [Philip & Jerusha], b. May 29, 1784	1	471
Amzi, m. Emilinee SMITH, b. of Danbury, Nov. 29, 1827, by John G. Lowe	3	44
Ann Maria, m. William B. HOYT, Jan. 5, 1819	2	63
Edmond, m. Hannah SANDFORD*, b. of Danbury, Mar. 4, 1838, by Rev. D. H. Short	3	106
Elijah B., of New Town, m. Mercia EDWARDS, of Bethel, Dec. 25, 1838, by J. Greenwood	3	95
Elisabeth, d. Eliphalet, of Long Island, m. Nathan DOUGLASS, s. Capt. Nathan, of New London, Sept. 8, 1782	1	384
Fanney, d. [Philip & Jerusha], b. Aug. 17, 1788	1	471
Henry D., of Wilton, m. Mary Ann CROFUT, of Danbury, Nov. 7, 1838, by Rev. D. H. Short	3	107
Jerusha, d. [Philip & Jerusha], b. Apr. 26, 1786	1	471
Mary, of Bethel, m. Ezra B. STEVENS, of New Fairfield, Mar. 22, 1849, by Rev. Rollin S. Stone	3	147
Phebe, d. [Philip & Jerusha], b. July 25, 1791	1	471
Phebee, of Newtown, m. Isaac GREGORY, of Danbury. Oct. 10, 1798	1	369
Philip, m. Jerusha STARR, d. Capt. Thomas, May 22, 1783	1	471
Ruana*, m. Horace COUCH, Apr. 4, 1845, by John Nickerson *(Last letters doubtful; may be "er")	3	134
Zarel, of Newtown, m. Sally FRY, Sept. 12, 1830, by John Nickerson	3	58
WHITE, Alexander, s. [Ephraim Moss & Charity], b. July 26, 1815	1	474
Amelia, d. [Ebenezer & Mary], b. May 7, 1760	1	473
Amelia, d. [Joseph Moss & Rachel], b. May 17, 1773	1	473
Amelia, m. John LLOYD, Apr. 1, 1783	1	473
Amelia, d. [Joseph Fairchild & Elisabeth], b. June* 29, 1809 *(First written "Aug.")	1	474
Ann B., of Danbury, m. Thomas WHITE, of Bridgeport, this		

	Vol.	Page

WHITE, (cont.)

day, [Sept. 29, 1835], by Rev. Orson Spencer — 3 — 83

Ann Maria, d. [Ephraim Moss & Charity], b. May 8, 1804 — 1 — 474

Ann Maria, m. Charles G. **MERRITT,** [July] 22, [1833], by
Rev. A. Rood — 3 — 75

Anna, d. Israel, decd., m. Nath[anie]ll **HOYT,** May 24, 1770 — 1 — 386

Anne, d. [Ebenezer Russel & Hannah], b. Oct. 20, 1779 — 1 — 479

Augustus, s. [Ephraim Moss & Charity], b. Dec. 19, 1799 — 1 — 474

Benjamin, m. Rodah H. **BOUGHTON,** b. of Danbury, Sept. 8,
1845, by Nathan Burton — 3 — 136

Betsey, d. [Ebenezer Russel & Hannah], b. Jan. 27, 1777 — 1 — 479

Betsey, see Betsey **COOKE** — 1 — 474

Betsey A., m. Lewis **GANUNG,** b. of Danbury, Jan. 11, 1846,
by Morris Hill — 3 — 138

Betty, w. [Ebenezer **BOOTH**], d. June 21, 1800 — 1 — 474

Charles, m. Alvira Jane **DEERE,** May 27, 1850, by George H.
Deere — 3 — 148

Charles Lewis, [s. Thomas P. & Ann], b. Jan. 6, 1784 — 1 — 393

Daniel, m. Mary Jane **ABBOTT,** b. of Danbury, Nov. 28, 1849,
by Nathan Burton, P. T. — 3 — 145

David, s. [Ebenezer Russel & Hannah], b. Sept. 23, 1781 — 1 — 479

Ebenezer, m. Mary **MOSS,** d. Joseph, of Derby, [   ] — 1 — 473

Ebenezer, s. [Ebenezer & Mary], b. Sept. 6, 1739;
d. Mar. 6, 1742 — 1 — 473

Ebenezer, m. 2nd w. Mary **FRENCH,** of Weymouth, Mar. [ ],
1747 — 1 — 473

Ebenezer, d. Sept. 11, 1779 — 1 — 473

Ebenezer Booth, s. [Joseph Moss & Rachel], b. Sept. 11, 1771 — 1 — 473

Ebenezer Booth, m. Betty **MYGATT,** d. Col. Eli, Mar. 23, 1791 — 1 — 474

Ebenezer Booth, m. 2nd w. Betsey **COOKE,** d. William, Aug.
24, 1800 — 1 — 474

Ebenezer Booth, s. Joseph Moss & Rachel, d. Apr. 15, 1817 — 1 — 473

Ebenezer Booth, d. Apr. 15, 1817 — 1 — 474

Ebenezer Judson, [s. Ebenezer Russel & Hannah], b. Aug.
23, 1768 — 1 — 479

Ebenezer R., had negro Prince, b. Mar. 3, 1784; d. Nov. 24, 1801 — 1 — 479

Ebenezer Russel, s. [Ebenezer & Mary], b. Dec. 22, 1743 — 1 — 473

Ebenezer Russel, m. Hannah **JUDSON,** d. Rev. David, of
Newtown, Nov. 18, 1767 — 1 — 479

Eli, s. [Ebenezer Booth & Betty], b. Sept. 26, 1791 — 1 — 474

Elisabeth, m. Matthew **STARR,** Apr. 15, 1766 — 1 — 418

Elizabeth, [d. Thomas P. & Ann], b. Sept. 6, 1774 — 1 — 393

Ephraim Moss, s. [Joseph Moss & Rachel], b. Mar. 9, 1775 — 1 — 473

Ephraim Moss, m. Charity **TUCKER,** d. Major Thomas, May 6,
1798 — 1 — 474

Ezra H., m. Harriet L. **ANDREWS,** Nov. 24, [1839], by Rev. Z.
Cook — 3 — 100

George, s. [Ebenezer Russel & Hannah], b. Sept. 24, 1786 — 1 — 479

	Vol.	Page

WHITE, (cont.)

Granvill, s. [Ephraim Moss & Charity], b. Mar. 10, 1801 — 1 / 474

Hannah, d. [Ebenezer Russel & Hannah], b. Sept. 13, 1772 — 1 / 479

Hannah, d. Ebenezer R., m. Matthew B. **WHITTLESEY**, Dec. 28, 1794 — 1 / 379

Hannah B., m. Timothy T. **MERWIN**, [Sept.] 2, [1830], by Rev. A. Rood — 3 / 58

Hannah Bartow, d. [Ephraim Moss & Charity], b. Jan. 3, 1809 — 1 / 474

Harriott, d. [Joseph Fairchild & Elisabeth], b. Sept. 27, 1792 — 1 / 474

Hart Howard, s. [Ebenezer Booth & Betsey], b. June* 15, 1809 *("Aug." crossed out) — 1 / 474

Jane, b. June 5, 1768; m. Peter **WOODBRIDGE**, Sept. 11, 1797 — 1 / 403

Jane, m. Peter **WOODBRIDGE**, Sept. 11, 1797 — 1 / 403

John N., of New York, m. Harriet **LOBDELL**, of Danbury, July 9, 1843, by John L. Ambler — 3 / 121

John Phillips, s. [Thomas P. & Ann], b. Sept. 3, 1778 — 1 / 393

Joseph Fairchild, s. [Joseph Moss & Rachel], b. Mar. 7, 1769 — 1 / 473

Joseph Fairchild, m. Elisabeth **BURR**, d. Oliver, June 22, 1790 — 1 / 474

Joseph Frederick, [s. Thomas P. & Ann], b. June 2, 1786 — 1 / 393

Joseph Moss, s. [Ebenezer & Mary], b. Sept. 13, 1741 — 1 / 473

Joseph Moss, m. Rachel **BOOTH**, d. Ephraim, of Stratford, Jan. 15, 1766 — 1 / 473

Joseph Moss, s. [Ebenezer Booth & Betsey], b. Feb. 4, 1806 — 1 / 474

Joseph Moss, d. July 10, 1822 — 1 / 473

Jutson, m. Huldah **LOBDELL**, Nov. 3, 1824, by Rev. W[illia]m Andrews — 3 / 24

Maria, d. [Ebenezer Russel & Hannah], b. Mar. 18, 1789 — 1 / 479

Maria D., of Danbury, m. Roger **AVERIL**, of Salisbury, this day [ ], by Rev. Rollin S. Stone. Recorded Oct. 31, 1844 — 3 / 129

Marian Amelia, d. [Ebenezer Booth & Betsey], b. Oct. 18, 1816 — 1 / 474

Mary, 2nd w. Ebenezer, b. May 20, 1726; d. Aug. 24, 1807, in the 82nd y. of her age — 1 / 473

Mary, d. [Ebenezer & Mary], b. Oct. 3, 1737 — 1 / 473

Mary, w. [Ebenezer], d. Aug. 5, 1746 — 1 / 473

Mary, d. [Ebenezer & Mary], b. June 3, 1748 — 1 / 473

Mary, 2nd, d. [Ebenezer & Mary], b. Aug. 3, 1751; d. [ ] — 1 / 473

Mary A., m. Samuel D. **PLATT**, May 18,p1240, by John Crawford — 3 / 104

Mary Amelia, d. [Ephraim Moss & Charity], b. Dec. 8, 1805 — 1 / 474

Mary Amelia, m. Charles H. **MERRITT**, July 18, 1826, by Nathan Burton — 3 / 34

Mary Ann, d. [Joseph Moss & Rachel], b. Oct. 14, 1767 — 1 / 473

Mary Ann, m. Niram **WILDMAN**, Mar. 17, 1811 — 1 / 461

Mary Ann, d. [Joseph Moss & Rachel], m. Niram **WILDMAN**, Mar. 17, 1811 — 1 / 473

Mary Ann, m. Zadoc R. **BENEDICT**, Aug. 16, 1825, by Rev. W[illia]m Andrews — 3 / 28

	Vol.	Page
WHITE, (cont.)		
Mary **(FRENCH)**, had mother Silence **WHITE**, who d. Oct. 29, 1755, ae 72	1	473
Mary M., m. Eli T. **HOYT**, b. of Danbury, this day [Apr. 23, 1827], by Rev. Daniel Crocker	3	44
Melancton Lloyd, s. [Joseph Fairchild & Elisabeth], b. Oct. 7*, 1794 *(First written "Oct. 6")	1	474
Nelson, s. [Eprhaim Moss & Charity], b. Apr. 7, 1812	1	474
Oliver, [s. Ebenezer Russel & Hannah], b. Sept. 25, 1784	1	479
Oliver Burr, s. [Joseph Fairchild & Elisabeth], b. Aug. 12, 1802	1	474
Patty, d. [Joseph Moss & Rachel], b. July 27, 1778; d. Sept. 10, 1778	1	473
Phebe, [d. Thomas P. & Ann], b. July 30, 1776	1	393
Phebe, d. Thomas, m. Zadock **STEVENS**, s. Ezra, b. of Danbury, Oct. 5, 1800	1	362
Philander, s. [Ebenezer Booth & Betty], b. Apr. 6, 1796	1	474
Philo Booth, [s. Thomas P. & Ann], b. June 5, 1789	1	393
Rachel, d. [Joseph Moss & Rachel], b. Nov. 14, 1782; d. Dec. 8, 1782	1	473
Rebecca French, d. [Joseph Moss & Rachel], b. Oct. 22, 1779	1	473
Roswell, s.*. [Ebenezer Russel & Hannah], b. Mar. 26, 1791 *("d." crossed out)	1	479
Russell, s. [Ebenezer Russel & Hannah], b. Mar. 31, 1770	1	479
Russel, m. Susanna **BURR**, d. Oliver, Apr. 4, 1792	1	458
Russel, m. Betsey **WOOD**, Dec. 17, 1827, by Levy Brunson	3	43
Samuel French, s. [Ebenezer & Mary], b. Sept. 8, 1755; d. Sept. 6, 1779	1	473
Samuel French, [s. Thomas P. & Ann], b. June 9, 1781	1	393
Sarah, d. [Thomas P. & Ann], b. May 18, 1771; d. Aug. 13, 1790	1	393
Sarah, d. [Thomas P. & Ann], d. Aug. 13, 1790	1	393
Sarah Mariah, m. Ezra D. **BULL**, b. of Danbury, Oct. 30, 1832, by Rev. Nicholus White	3	71
Silence, mother of Mary **(FRENCH) WHITE**, d. Oct. 29, 1755, ae 72	1	473
Theodore, s. [Joseph Fairchild & Elisabeth], b. June 29, 1812	1	474
Thomas, of Bridgeport, m. Ann B. **WHITE**, of Danbury, this day, [Sept. 29, 1835], by Rev. Orson Spencer	3	83
Thomas P., m. Ann **BOOTH**, d. Dea. Ephraim, of Stratford, Jan. 29, 1769	1	393
Tho[ma]s P., had negro Benhadaa, s. Jenny, b. May 10, 1789	1	488
Thomas P., m. Clarissa **MORRIS**, b. of Danbury, Mar. 9, 1828, by Levi Osbom	3	46
Thomas Phillips, s. [Ebenezer & Mary], b. Apr. 26, 1746	1	473
Tho[ma]s Prosper, [s. Thomas P. & Ann], b. June 3, 1792	1	393
William, s. [Ebenezer Russel & Hannah], b. Mar. 11, 1775	1	479
W[illia]m, m. Mary B. **STONE**, b. of Danbury, Apr. 1*, 1832, by Rev. Lemuel B. Hull *(Or "5th")	3	69

	Vol.	Page
WHITE, (cont.)		
William Cooke, s. [Ebenezer Booth & Betsey], b. Aug. 7, 1803	1	474
William R., m. Aurinda B. **BOOTH,** Sept. 2, 1851, by Rev. W. White Bronson	3	156
WHITEHEAD, Alonzo, m. Mary A. **ELWOOD,** Dec. 25, 1849, by Rev. A. Perkins	3	160
WHITING, Frederick Augustus, s.* [Frederick Jones & Rachel], b. Feb. 24, 1788 *(Word erased)	1	358
Frederick Jones, m. Rachel **STARR,** d. the late Major Daniel, May 18, 1783	1	358
Henry Starr, s. [Frederick Jones & Rachel], b. Mar. 20, 1785	1	358
John H., m. Hannah **BENEDICT,** Jan. 1, 1828, by Rev. L. P. Hickok	3	43
William A., of Bridgeport, m. Martha **BENJAMIN,** of Bethel, May 9, 1849, by Rev. Rollin S. Stone	3	147
WHITLOCK, Anna, d. [Squire & Mary], b. June 22, 1788	1	398
Benj[ami]n, [s. Ebenezer & Ame], b. May 12, 1775	1	398
Benjamin, m. Abiah **HIGLY,** of Granby, Aug. 19, 1796	1	398
Betsey, [d. Ebenezer & Ame], b. July 13, 1779	1	398
Syntha, of Danbury, m. Vanet* B. **KEELER,** of Brookfield, Feb. 25, 1829, by J. Nickerson *(Possibly "Barret"?)	3	51
Ebenezer, s. [John & Mary], b. Mar. 21, 1738/9	1	409
Ebenezer, m. Ame **HAMILTON,** May 21, 1760	1	398
Ebenezer, [s. Ebenezer & Ame], b. June 10, 1764	1	398
Eliza, of Danbury, m. George **PERRY,** of Redding, Mar. 27, 1831, by Rev. E. Washburn	3	60
Elizabeth Deborah, d. Abraham, of Ridgefield, m. Eliphalet* **CURTISS,** Aug. 5, 1790 *(Word crossed out)	1	468
Esther, [d. Ebenezer & Ame], b. Aug. 21, 1772	1	398
Esther, m. Leander S. **BURS,** Jan. 24, 1830, by Levi Bronson	3	55
Ezekiel, [s. Ebenezer & Ame], b. Apr. 2, 1777	1	398
Hannah, [d. John & Mary], b. Oct. 2, 1743	1	409
Hezekiah, [s. John & Mary], b. Apr. 5, 1741	1	409
Hiram Higley, [s. Benjamin & Abiah], b. Mar. 5, 1799	1	398
Jason, of Ridgefield, m. Eliza Ann **PICKET,** of Danbury, Jan. 1, 1840, by Addison Parker	3	101
John, m. Mary **LEE,** Jan. 12, 1737/8	1	409
John, [s. John & Mary], b. Nov. 14, 1745	1	409
John, m. Grace **MALLERY,** July 21, 1761	1	409
John, of Ridgefield, m. Mary Ann **SILLECK,** of Danbury, May 25, 1842, by John Nickerson	3	115
Joseph, [s. John & Mary], b. Aug. 20, 1752	1	409
Joseph, [s. John & Mary], d. [ ], 1777	1	409
Mary, [d. John & Mary], b. Aug. 28, 1748	1	409
Mary, [d. Ebenezer & Ame], b. July 4, 1762	1	398
Mary, w. [John], d. [ ]	1	409
Olive, of Danbury, m. Bradley **ADAMS,** of Redding, Nov. 10, 1826, by Rev. John G. Lowe	3	38

	Vol.	Page
WHITLOCK, (cont.)		
Phebe, [d. Ebenezer & Ame], b. Sept. 5, 1767	1	398
Phebe, m. Daniel **PECK,** Feb. 2, 1791* *(Possibly "1790"?)	1	399
Rebecca, [d. Squire & Mary], b. Feb. 28, 1792	1	398
Sarah, [d. John & Grace], b. Mar. 12, 1763; d. July 3 or 4, 1772 .	1	409
Sarah Ann, [d. Seth & Mary], b. May 30, 1790	1	410
Seth, [s. John & Grace], b. July 5, 1766	1	409
Seth, m. Mary **FERRIS,** d. Zackary, of Newtown, Aug. 20, 1789	1	410
Squire, m. Mary **HODGE,** Mar. 13, 1788	1	398
Zalmon, s. [Ebenezer & Ame], b. Dec. 13, 1760	1	398
WHITNEY, Abigal, m. Stephen **BROCKLETON,** Aug. 26, 1821, by Rev. Aaron Hunt	3	8
Edward, [s. Nathan & Hannah], b. Aug. 1, 1788	1	435
Edwin B., m. Louisa **DOBBS,** Dec. 29, 1850, by W. White Bronson	3	153
Elias B., m. Catharine **CRAFTS,** July 12, 1847, by Nathan Burton	3	163
Mary, of Danbury, m. Hiram H. **CARLEY,** of Sharon, Feb. 3, 1842, by Levi Bronson	3	114
Nathan, m. Hannah **TAYLOR,** d. John*, Dec. 16, 1787 *(First written "Levi")	1	435
WHITTLESEY, Amelia A., m. Roswell **BROWN,** [Sept.] 25, [1833], by Rev. A. Rood	3	76
Elisha, of Danbury, s. Eliphalet, m. Mary **TUCKER,** of Danbury, May 19, 1788	1	378
Elisha, d. Nov. [ ]. 1802	1	378
Elisha Dana, s. [Elisha & Mary], b. Feb. 10, 1792	1	378
Hannah, d. [Elisha & Mary], b. Aug. 3, 1796; d. May 26, 1798	1	378
Harriet, d. [Elisha & Mary], b. May 12, 1794	1	378
Harriet, m. Rev. Rob[er]t W. **CONDIT,** Dec. 21, 1820, by W[illia]m Andrews	3	5
John, m. Julia **GREGORY,** June 8, 1823, by Rev. W[illia]m Andrews	3	17
Julia A., m. Platt T. **HOLLY,** [Nov.] 21, [1832], by Rev. A. Rood	3	73
Mary A., m. Rev. Greve L. **BROWNELL,** [Apr.] 25, [1832], by Rev. A. Rood	3	70
Matthew B., m. Hannah **WHITE,** d. Ebenezer R., Dec. 28, 1794	1	379
Thomas, [s. Elisha & Mary], b. Dec. 8, 1798	1	378
William, s. [Elisha & Mary], b. Dec. 13, 1789; d. Mar. 10, 1794	1	378
William Augustus, s. [Matthew B. & Hannah], b. July 14, 1796	1	379
WICKSON, Ann*, m. Jeremiah **DEAN,** b. of Bethel, May 15, 1831, by Rev. Erastus Cole *(Possibly "Ame"?)	3	62
WILCOX, Chancy, Rev., m. Sarah A. **COOKE,** [Dec.] 8, [1831], by Rev. A. Rood	3	68
Emily, m. Frederick **NICHOLS,** b. of Danbury, this day [Oct. 20, 1841], by Rev. S. H. Clark	3	112
Jane Elizabeth, m Philander **DITTS** (?), this day [Mar. 26,		

	Vol.	Page
WILCOX, (cont.)		
1835], by Rev. Lemuel B. Hull	3	84
Margaret K., m. Morris C. HULL, Jan. 29, 1849, by Rev. A. Perkins	3	160
Orlando, m. Sarah BENJAMIN, b. of Danbury, Oct. 19, 1841, by Addison Parker	3	112
WILDMAN, Abraham, f. Samuel, d. May 3, 1761	1	453
Abraham, Jr., m. Rebekah NICKESON, Oct. 16, 1791	1	459
Abraham, Jr., d. Apr. 4, 182[ ]* *(Possibly "1822")	2	100
Adaline, m. John ADAMS, b. of Danbury, Dec. 24, 1820, by William Cooke, J. P.	3	5
Adenirim, s. [Comfort & Rachel], b. May 7, 1771	1	500
Amanda, m. James EDMOND, Nov. 2, 1823, by Russel Hoyt, J. P.	3	19
Asa, [s. Samuel & Dinah], b. Feb. 12, 1771; d. Nov. 26, 1774	1	453
Asa. [twin with Ezra, s. Samuel & Dinah], b. Apr. 28, 1775; d. Apr. 24, 1776	1	453
Benajah, s. [Comfort & Rachel], b. Jan. 7, 1776	1	500
Benjamin K.*, of Danbury, m. Sarah WILLIS, of Monroe, Nov. 16, 1845, by Thomas T. Guion *(Perhaps "R"?)	3	137
Betsey, [d. Samuel & Dinah], b. Apr. 11, 1768; d. Sept. 21, 1774	1	453
Betty, d. [Daniel & Elisabeth], b. Sept. 19, 1765	1	502
Clarissa, of Danbury, m. John HAYES, of New Fairfield, Sept. 9, 1828, by S. S. Burdett	3	48
Clarissa, of Danbury, m. Addison JUDSON, of Roxbury, Nov. 27, 1831, by Levi Osborn	3	65
Comfort, m. Rachel ROCK[ ]*, d. John, of Ridgefield, July 12, 1764 *(Worn off)	1	500
[Da]niel, m. Mary SHOVE, Apr. 14, 1757* *(Faded out)	1	502
[Daniel], m. 2nd w. Elisabeth ROCKWELL, Oct. 28, 1762	1	502
Daniel, [s. Daniel & Elisabeth], b. Dec. 10, 1763	1	502
David D., m. Fanny BISHOP, b. of Danbury, May 19, 1829, by Rev. A. Rood	3	52
David S., m. Eunice AMBLER, b. of Danbury, Oct. 30, 1836, by Rev. Salmon C. Bulkley	3	88
Demas, m. Elizabeth HURD, b. of Danbury, Mar. 6, 1836, by Joel Taylor, J. P.	3	85
Diadema, of Danbury, m. Matthew B. STEVENS, of Brookfield, Nov. 6, 1844, by Rev. J. K. Ingalls	3	129
Dinah, w. Samuel, d. Feb. 1, 1790	1	453
Dorcas, d. [Comfort & Rachel], b. Oct. 17, 1777	1	500
Eli, [twin with Sam[ue]l, s. Samuel & Dinah], b. May 15, 1760; d. May 22 & 31, 1760	1	453
Eli, [s. Samuel & Dinah], b. June 1, 1765	1	453
Eli, m. Patty GREGORY, d. Selah, June 2, 1790	1	453
Eli, m. Mrs. Abigail STONE, [May] 1, [1833], by Rev. A. Rood	3	75
Eliakim, s. [Comfort & Rachel], b. Jan. 5, 1767	1	500

	Vol.	Page

WILDMAN, (cont.)

Eliza, m. Ira W. **DYKIMAN**, Jan. 9, 1822, by Rev. W[illia]m
Andrews — 3 — 10

Elisabeth, [w. Abraham], d. Mar. 10, 1770 — 1 — 453

Emily Augusta, d. [Fairchild & Mary P.], b. Sept. 6, 1814*
*(Rewritten and corrected) — 2 — 67

Epaphrus H., m. Hannah **HACK**, b. of Danbury, June 9, 1839,
by Reuben Booth, J. P. — 3 — 97

Esther, [d. Samuel & Dinah], b. Nov. 16, 1778 — 1 — 453

Esther, d. Samuel, m. Samuel **HUSTEAD**, s. Andrew, Nov. 25,
1799 — 1 — 368

Eunice, d. [Comfort & Rachel], b. May 11, 1769 — 1 — 500

Eunice, d. Comfort, m. Stephen Brownson **BENEDICT**, May 24,
1789 — 1 — 441

Ezra, [twin with Asa, s. Samuel & Dinah], b. Apr. 28, 1775 — 1 — 453

Fairchild, [s. Samuel, Jr. & Debory], b. Feb. 3, 1787 — 1 — 410

Fairchild, m. Mary P. **CANFIELD**, of New Milford, Nov. 30,
189[ ]* *(1809?) — 2 — 67

Frederick S., m. Julia Ann **STARR**, b. of Danbury, this day,
[June 21, 1827], by Rev. Lemuel B. Hull — 3 — 41

Grace, [d. Samuel & Dinah], b. June 15, 1761 — 1 — 453

Hannah, d. [Daniel & Mary], b. Apr. 26, 1758* *(Faded out) — 1 — 502

Hannah, d. Capt. Daniel, m. Nathan **WOOD**, Apr. 23, 1777 — 1 — 395

Harriot, m. Ezra M. **STARR**, Sept. 27, 1820, by John T. Peters,
Judge of S. C. — 3 — 3

Harriet, see Harriet **STARR** — 2 — 119

Henry Fairchild, s. [Fairchild & Mary P.], b. Nov. 9, 1826*
*(Rewritten and corrected) — 2 — 67

Hiram, of Danbury, m. Rebecca **BRADLEY**, of Bridgeport,
Mar. 4, 1832, by John Nickerson — 3 — 69

Horace T., m. Catharine Issabella **ELY**, b. of Danbury,
May 11, 1830, by Rev. Lemuel B. Hull — 3 — 56

Horatio, s. Zalmon & Mary, d. Nov. 8, 1816, ae 18 y.
10 m. 12 d. "Member of senior class in Union College
Schenectaday, N. Y." — 2 — 119

Hubbel W., m. Sally M. **DOBBS**, Aug. 1, 1821, by Rev.
W[illia]m Andrews — 3 — 7

Jerusha, m. John **GREGORY**, b. of Danbury, June 16, 1830,
by John Nickerson — 3 — 57

John Rockwell, s. [Comfort & Rachel], b. Apr. 9, 1773 — 1 — 500

Julia E., of Danbury, m. Leonard N. **DELLICOR**, of New York,
this day, [Nov. 7, 1842], by Rev. Rollin S. Stone — 3 — 118

Julia Elvira, d. [Fairchild & Mary P.], b. May 16, 1822*
*(Rewritten and corrected) — 2 — 67

Levi K., m. Mary Ann **LOVELESS**, b. of Danbury, Oct. 31,
1836, by Rev. Salmon C. Bulkley — 3 — 88

Lois, m. Walker **FERRY**, Nov. 3, 1847, by Rev. John Purves, of
Bethel — 3 — 151

	Vol.	Page

WILDMAN, (cont.)

Lois Ann, m. John **BARD,** June 12, 1826, by Rev. William
Andrews . . . . 3 . . . 33

Lucy A., of Danbury, m. Frederick A. **LEWIS,** of Brookfield,
Oct. 17, 1847, by John Crawford . . . . 3 . . . 164

Mary, d. [Samuel & Dinah], b. Dec. 18, 1758 . . . . . . 1 . . . 453

Mary, w. [Daniel], d. Nov. 26, 1759 . . . . 1 . . . 502

Mary, d. [Daniel & Elisabeth], b. Feb. 28, 1767 . . . . 1 . . . 502

Mary, m. Levi **STONE,** July 4, 1776 . . . . 1 . . . 445

Mary, of Danbury, m. Nathan **STARR,** of New York, this day,
[June 23, 1829], by Rev. Lemuel B. Hull . . . . . . 3 . . . 52

Mary, see Mercy **WILDMAN** . . . . 3 . . . 70

Mary Ann, m. Daniel **STONE,** Dec. 20, 1820, by W[illia]m
Andrews . . . . 3 . . . 4

Mercy, d. Jacob, m. Benjamin **KNAP,** Aug. 17, 1764 . . 1 . . . 402

Mercy*, m. W[illia]m B. **GRAY,** [May] 23, [1832], by Rev.
A. Rood   *(Perhaps "Mary"?) . . . . 3 . . . 70

Miles H., m. Emily J. **STEWART,** Sept. 21, 1843, by Rev.
J. K. Inalls . . . . 3 . . . 122

Nathan, s. [Daniel & Elisabeth], b. Oct. 25, 1769 . . . 1 . . . 502

Nathan, m. Sarah **STONE,** d. William of Danbury, Dec. 13, 1792 . 1 . . . 370

Nathan, s. [Nathan & Sarah], b. Aug. 5, 1794 . . . . . 1 . . . 370

Nathan, d. July 12, 1796 . . . . 1 . . . 370

Niram, m. Mary Ann **WHITE,** Mar. 17, 1811 . . . . . . 1 . . . 461

Niram, m. Mary Ann **WHITE,** d. [Joseph Moss & Rachel], Mar.
17, 1811 . . . . 1 . . . 473

Niram, m. Mrs. Hannah **BOUGHTON,** Mar. 27, 1838, by Rev.
Rollin S. Stone . . . . 3 . . . 93

Polly, [d. Samuel, Jr. & Debory], b. Dec. 21, 1792 . . 1 . . . 410

Rachel, wid., m. Benjamin **KNAP,** Jan. 4, 1787 . . . . 1 . . . 402

Rachel, [d. Thomas & Hannah], b. Nov. 13, 1790 . . . . 1 . . . 441

Rebecca, w. Sam[ue]ll, d. Nov. 14, 1795 . . . . 1 . . . 453

Russel, m. Mary **RIDER,** Apr. 20, 1823, by Samuel Cochran . 3 . . . 16

Sally, m. Ira **KEELER,** Oct. 1, 1820, by W[illia]m Andrews . 3 . . . 2

Samuel, m. Dinah **FAIRCHILD,** d. Alexander, Mar. 22, 1758 . 1 . . . 453

Sam[ue]l, [twin with Eli, s. Samuel & Dinah], b. May 15,
1760; d. 22 & 31 May 1760 . . . . 1 . . . 453

Samuel, [s. Samuel & Dinah], b. Jan. 30, 1763 . . . . . 1 . . . 453

Samuel, Jr., m. Debory **BENEDICT,** d. Thaddeus, Sept. 14, 1785 . 1 . . . 410

Samuel, m. Rebecca **NICHOLS,** wid. Sam[ue]ll, Jan. 22, 1795 . 1 . . . 453

Samuel, m. Abigail **ROCKWELL,** wid. Daniel, of Ridgbury,
May 22, 1801 . . . . 1 . . . 453

Sam[ue]l C., s. [Fairchild & Mary P.], b. Mar. 16, 1811*
*(Rewritten and corrected) . . . . 2 . . . 67

Sarah, d. [Thomas & Hannah], b. Apr. 11, 1787 . . . . . 1 . . . 441

Sarah, wid. of Nathan, m. 2nd h. Thomas **BAXTER,** Feb. 4, 1798 . 1 . . . 370

Sarah B., m. Ebenezer T. **LANE** b. of Danbury, Sept. 12, 1850,
by Rev. John Purves, of Bethel . . . . 3 . . . 152

	Vol.	Page
WILLIAMS, (cont.)		
Deborah, [d. Thaddeus & Hannah], b. Sept. 2, 1787	1	422
Henry, [s. Isaac & Lydia], b. July 22, 1812	2	63
Ira, [s. Isaac & Lydia], b. May 11, 1804	2	63
Isaac, s. [Thaddeus & Hannah], b. Mar. 10, 1775	1	422
Isaac, b. Mar. 10, 1775; m. Lydia **FERRY**, July 9, 1795	2	63
Isabel Catharine, [d. Isaac & Lydia], b. Mar. 23, 1820;		
d. Aug. 17, 1822	2	63
Jane, d. [Daniel & Mary], b. June 25, 1821	2	101
Jinks, [s. Thaddeus & Hannah], b. Jan. 25, 1781	1	422
Joanna, of Danbury, m. William **MATTHEW**, of Philadelphia,		
Oct. 31, 1825, by Rev. John G. Lowe	3	34
John, [s. Thaddeus & Hannah], b. Jan. 30, 1785	1	422
John, [s. Isaac & Lydia], b. Dec. 11, 1810	2	63
John, m. Phebe **TIMMANUS**, b. of Danbury, May 5, 1829,		
by Rev. A. Rood	3	52
Lydia, [d. Thaddeus & Hannah], b. Jan. 18, 1783	1	422
Lydia, m. Samuel C. **KEELER**, b. of Bethel, Apr. 2, 1851,		
by Rev. J. B. Merwin	3	155
Malinda, d. [Isaac & Lydia], b. Dec. 24, 1805	2	63
Malinda, of Danbury, m. Nathaniel M. **BENEDICT**, of		
Ridgefield, Oct. 2, 1823, by Nathan Seelye, J. P.	3	18
Mary Ann, d. [Isaac & Lydia], b. Feb. 14, 1817	2	63
Mary Ann, m. Ambrose B. **TURNER**, Oct. 16, 1827, by Benaiah		
Y. Morse	3	43
Mary Ann, m. Nathaniel **HIBBARD**, b. of Danbury, Nov. 12,		
1834, by Edward Taylor, J. P.	3	82
Nancy, of Danbury, m. Archibald **BOUGHTON**, of New York,		
Nov. 19, 1826, by John Nickerson	3	37
Olive, [d. Thaddeus & Hannah], b. Jan. 1, 1779	1	422
Sarah, d. [Isaac & Lydia], b. Jan. 22, 1797	2	63
Thaddeus, m. Hannah **JINKS**, Aug. 25, 1774	1	422
Thaddeus, [s. Thaddeus & Hannah], b. Aug. 14, 1790	1	422
Warre Jenks, [s. Isaac & Lydia], b. Sept. 26, 1802	2	63
Welcome, [s. Thaddeus & Hannah], b. Aug. 11, 1800	1	422
Whipple, [s. Thaddeus & Hannah], b. May 2, 1798	1	422
WILLIS, Sarah, of Monroe, m. Benjamin K.* **WILDMAN**, of		
Danbury, Nov. 16, 1845, by Thomas T. Guion *("R"?)	3	137
WILLY, Abraham, m. Mary* **PENFIELD**, Oct. 22, 1794		
*(Perhaps "Many")	1	381
Mary, m. Cezar **CURTIS**, Dec. 25, 1821, by Rev. Oliver Tuttle	3	10
WILSON, Beach T., m. Lorana **BEVANS**, b. of Danbury, June 10,		
1845, by Rev. Fitch Reed	3	135
Clark S., of New Fairfield, m. Elizabeth A. **PECK**, of Danbury;		
d. William, June 17, 1840, by Rev. George Nelson Kelton	3	104
Edward B., of Easton, m. Emily B. **TAYLOR**, of Danbury, Oct.		
3, 1850, by Rev. John S. Whittlesey	3	152
Israel H., m. Betsey **BARNUM**, b. of Danbury, Feb. 12, 1845,		

	Vol.	Page
WOOD, (cont.)		
Daniel, Jr., had grandson Arza G. **SCOTT,** b. Jan. 4, 1804	1	494
Daniel B., m. Mrs. Sally M. **STONE,** b. of Danbury, Sept. 7, 1845, by Morris Hill	3	138
Daniel Barlow, s. [Philo], b. Mar. 18*, 1811 *(Possibly ("10"?)	2	175
Darius S., [s. Abijah & Submit], b. Oct. 4, 1807* *(Date corrected)	2	181
Darius S., m. Nancy **JONES,** b. of Danbury, [Oct.] 23, [1828], by Rev. Thomas Robbins	3	49
David, b. Dec. 26, 1747; m. Catharine **GREGORY,** d. Nathaniel, Feb. 3, 1772* *(Perhaps "1774"?)	1	476
David, s. [David & Catharine], b. Dec. 23, 1781	1	476
David, d. Feb. 15, 1796	1	476
David, s. [Nathan, Jr. & Lorana], b. Mar. 10, 1801	1	364
David, m. Betsey **HOYT,** Sept. 23, 1805	2	65
David Augustus, s. [David & Betsey], b. May 22, 1807	2	65
Deborah, d. [Daniel, Jr. & Wealthy], b. May 8, 1791	1	494
Eli, s. [Daniel, Jr. & Wealthy], b. Mar. 22, 1794	1	494
Elijah, Capt., m. Hannah **STARR,** d. Capt. Thomas, Jan. 9, 1766	1	482
Elijah, s. [Capt. Elijah & Hannah], b. Feb. 22, 1771	1	482
Eliza Ann, [d. Abijah & Submit], b. Mar. 5, 1811	2	181
Elisabeth, [d. David & Betsey], b. Apr. 3, 1820	2	65
Elizabeth, m. Henry **MILLS,** Dec. 4, 1845, by Rev. I. W. Alvord, of Stamford	3	137
Ery, of Danbury, m. Betsey **LEWIS,** of New Milford, Apr. 9, 1843, by Levi Bronson	3	119
Ezra, s. [David & Catharine], b. Aug. 14, 1791	1	476
Fanny, m. Horace **MALLORY,** b. of Danbury, Mar. 24, 1839, by Levi Osborn	3	96
Frederick, s. [David & Betsey], b. Aug. 22, 1815	2	65
Grizzel, [child of Nathan & Hannah], b. Oct. 23, 1789	1	395
Hannah, [twin with Sarah, d. Daniel & Mary], b. Sept. 9, 1748	1	499
Hannah, d. [Capt. Elijah & Hannah], b. Dec. 3, 1768	1	482
Hannah, m. Daniel Drake **HOYT,** Oct. 12, 1786	1	418
Hannah, m. Nathan B. **DIBBLE,** Jan. 22, 1826, by Reuben Booth, J. P.	3	31
Harlow, s. Sherman, d. Oct. 3, 1822	2	176
Harriet, of Danbury, m. Ephraim P. **BOGARDUS,** of Cooksakie, N. Y., Apr. 4, 1827, by Josiah Dikeman	3	40
Harvey, 2nd, s. [Noah & Deborah], b. Mar. 29, 1799	1	365
Henriett, d. [Nathaniel & Phebe], b. Sept. 29, 1810(?)* *(Conflicts with date of Catharine's birth. Possibly "1812" or "1813"?)	2	118
Henry, m. Caroline **WEBB,** Apr. 24, 1839, by George Andrews, Jr.	3	97
Ira, s. [Daniel, Jr. & Wealthy], b. Aug. 29, 1796	1	494
Ira, m. Maria **SCOTT,** of Ridgefield, Nov. 28, 1816	2	181

	Vol.	Page

WOOD, (cont.)

Entry	Vol.	Page
Jesse Scott, s. [Ira & Maria], b. Oct. 17, 1817	2	181
John, s. [Capt. Elijah & Hannah], b. Oct. 2, 1779	1	482
John, Dr., had servant Ned, s. Peg, b. Feb. 15, 1786	1	487
John B., s. [Nathaniel & Phebe], b. Mar. 7, 1819	2	118
Jonah Starr, s.* [Capt. Elijah & Hannah], b. Apr. 15, 1787		
*(First written "d.")	1	482
Joseph, d. May 20, 1822	2	101
Joseph Platt, eldest s.* [Noah & Deborah], b. June 29, 1797		
*(Word crossed out)	1	365
Laura E., d. [Reuben & Betsey], b. Sept. 18, 1827;d. Oct. 3, 1828	2	181
Lemuel, d. May 31, 1795	1	505
Lois, b. June 5, 1778	1	455
Lois, d. James, b. June 5, 1778; m. Stephen CURTISS, May 27, 1798	1	455
Lois, d. Dr. John, m. Lieut. Thomas STARR, Mar. 3, 1784	1	411
Lois, d. James, m. Stephen CURTISS, May 27, 1798	1	455
Lois Ann, d. [David & Betsey], b. Dec. 20, 1811	2	65
Lorana, d. Philo, b. Nov. 15, 1808	2	175
Lorany, m. Walter BATES, [Sept.] 4, [1833], by Rev. A. Rood	3	76
Loretta, m. Augustus M. GREGORY, b. of Danbury, Feb. 28, 1836, by Rev. Orson Spencer	3	84
Lorry, d. [Capt. Elijah & Hannah], b. Sept. 12, 1784	1	482
Lucy, d. [Benjamin & Mary], b. Apr. 30, 1772; d. Oct. 29, 1774	1	372
Lucy, 2nd, d. [Benjamin & Mary], b. Dec. 23, 1777	1	372
Lucy, d. [Daniel, Jr. & Wealthy], b. Mar. 26, 1782	1	494
Lucy, d. [Noah & Deborah], b. July 28, 1802	1	365
Lucy, m. Sillick LOBDELL, Mar. 17, 1822, by Levi Brunson	3	11
Lyman, s. [Ira & Maria], b. Apr. 9, 1819	2	181
Major, m. Julia CURTIS, b. of Danbury, Nov. 6, 1842, by James Beebe, J. P.	3	117
Maria Ann, [d. Philo], b. Feb. 7, 1816	2	175
Mary, d. [Daniel & Mary], b Oct. 19, 1746	1	499
Mary, d. [Benjamin & Mary], b. Aug. 14, 1775	1	672
Mary, [d. Nathan & Hannah], b. Mar. 23, 1780	1	395
Mary, w. Benj[ami]n, d. Jan. 10, 1791	1	372
Mary Ann, d. [Nathaniel & Phebe], b. Dec. 29, 1821	2	118
Mary Ann, of Danbury, m. Harvy PURDY, of South East, Nov. 24, 1836, by Rev. H. Humphreys	3	89
Mary Catharine, d. [David & Betsey], b. Aug. 31, 1817	2	65
Mary E., of Danbury, m. William E. CROFUT, of Redding, Nov. 5, 1845, by Rev. William F. Collins	3	136
Mary Emma, [d. Philo], b. Aug. 2, 1822	2	175
Moses, s. [Benjamin & Mary], b. Oct. 18, 1782	1	372
Moses, s. Benjamin & Mary, of Danbury, m. Hannah GUNN, of Waterbury, Nov. 19, 1803	1	372
Moses, d. June [ ], 1824	2	101
Moses Minor, s. Moses, d. Apr. 25, 1822, ae 15 y.	2	101

	Vol.	Page
WOOD, (cont.)		
Nancy, m. Burr **ROCKWELL,** b. of Danbury, June 9, 1833, by John Nickerson	3	75
Nathan, m. Hannah **WILDMAN,** d. Capt. Daniel, Apr. 23, 1777	1	395
Nathan, s. [Nathan & Hannah], b. Dec. 13, 1777	1	395
Nathan, Jr., s. Nathan, m. Lorana **SHOVE,** d. Seth, b. of Danbury, Nov. 27, 1799	1	364
Nathanael, s. [David & Catharine], b. Apr. 14, 1786	1	476
Nathaniel, m. Phebe **BARLOW,** of Ridgefield, Nov. 4, 1809	2	118
Nath[an]iel Erastus, s. [David & Betsey], b. Apr. 22, 1809	2	65
Noah, s. [Daniel, Jr. & Wealthy], b. Feb. 24, 1780	1	494
Noah, eldest s. Daniel, Jr., m. Deborah **PLATT,** Apr. 16, 1797	1	365
Oliver, of Danbury, m. Sarah Ann **DUNHAM,** of Greenfield, July 16, 1849, by Rev. Rollin S. Stone	3	147
Phebe, d. [Nathaniel & Phebe], b. Jan. 14, 1815	2	118
Phebe, m. Benjamin **SILLECK,** b. of Danbury, Apr. 27, 1842, by Rev. Morris Hill	3	115
Philo, s. [Daniel, Jr. & Wealthy], b. Dec. 7, 1788	1	494
Philo, [s. Philo], b. May 13, 1820	2	175
Reuben, s. [Benjamin & Tamer], b. Feb. 26, 1794	1	372
Reuben, m. Betsey **BARLOW,** Nov. 5, 1820	2	181
Roxanna, of Danbury, m. Jesse **CARNES,** of Penn., July 16, [1826], by John Nickerson	3	34
Russel, m. Phebe **OSBORN,** b. of Danbury, Feb. 24, 1841, by Levi Osborn	3	108
Sally, of Danbury, m. Orson **STONE,** of Redding, Sept. 19, 1827, by Levi Brunson	3	42
Samantha, d. [Reuben & Betsey], b. Nov. 11, 1821; d. Nov. 12, 1825	2	181
Samuel, f. Abigail, [w. Benjamin **CROFUT**], d. July 24, 1797 ae 76 y. 11 m.	1	486
Sarah, [twin with Hannah, d. Daniel & Mary], b. Sept. 9, 1748	1	499
Sarah, d. Capt. John, m. Jonathan **HOYT,** Jr., Aug. 13, 1761	1	449
Sarah, d. [David & Catharine], b. Oct. 1, 1778	1	476
Sarah, d. [David & Catharine], d. Aug. 25, 1806	1	476
Sarah, [d. Abijah & Submit], b. Nov. 15, 1821* *(Year corrected)	2	181
Sarah Maria, d. [David & Betsey], b. May 5, 1813* *(Corrected after erasure)	2	65
Sherman, s. [Capt. Elijah & Hannah], b. Apr. 3, 1781	1	482
Submit, [w. Abijah], d. Nov. 15, 1822, ae 34 y.	2	181
Tamer, w. [Benjamin], d. Sept. 7, 1797	1	372
Thankful, d. [Daniel & Mary], b. Dec. 7, 1754	1	499
Uriah H., m. Rebecca **NICHOLS,** Oct. 17, 1821, by Rev. W[illia]m Andrews	3	8
Wealthy, [w. Daniel, Jr.], d. July 10, 1820* *(Entered "1819" marked over to read "1820")	1	494
William, s. [Daniel, Jr. & 2nd w.], b. Sept. 10, 1822	1	494

	Vol.	Page
WOOD, (cont.)		
William, m. Ann D. **GAGE**, b. of Danbury, Aug. 20, 1843, by John L. Ambler	3	122
Zadock, s. [Benjamin & Mary], b. Feb. 22, 1786	1	372
WOODBRIDGE, Cate, d. [Peter & Jane], b. Mar. 11, 1798	1	403
Hannah, colored d. Peter, b. Sept. 14, 1818	2	67
Jane, d. [Peter & Jane], b. June 25, 1803	1	403
Oliver, s. [Peter & Jane], b. Feb. 23, 1808	1	403
Peter, m. Jane **WHITE**, Sept. 11, 1797	1	403
WOODMAN, Amos, of New York, m. Mary H. **BENEDICT**, of Bethel, Feb. 9, 1842, by J. Greenwood	3	114
WOOSTER, Laura S., m. William H. **WEBB**, Feb. 16, 1834, by Nathan Burton, D. T.	3	79
WYGANT, Anthony, of Newtown, m. Polly **ADAMS**, of Danbury, this day, [Sept. 4, 1831], by Rev. Lemuel B. Hull	3	64
YOUNG, W[illia]m H., m. Mary A. **HOLMES**, Apr. 25, [1849], by Rev. A. Perkins	3	160
YROPHY, Ellen, m. Patrick **MURPHY**, May 25, 1851, by Thomas Ryan. Witnesses: James Kernain & Mary Whelan	3	154
NO SURNAME		
Benjamin, s. Samson & Rhoda (free negros), b. July 20, 1803	1	487
Betty, b. July 5, 1760, m. John **BARNUM,** Jr., July 7, 1779	1	427
Billy, negro, b. Mar. 27, 1788	1	414
Dorcas, colored b. Mar. 11, 1777	1	361
Elisabeth, m. Thomas **CHURCH,** Mar. 1, 1765	1	439
Horrace, s. Saul & Dorcas (colored), b. Apr. 18, 1800	1	361
Jerusha, b. July 11, 1753; m. Silas **TAYLOR,** May 7, 1778	1	500
Jerusha, b. [ ]; m. Zar **JOYCE,** Sept. 24, 1806	2	61
Judith, m. Luther **HOLCOMB,** [ ]	1	470
Keziah, m. Ephraim **BARNUM,** May 2, 1753; d. Aug. 4, 1775	1	460
Lois, b. Apr. 5, 1766*; m. Agur **HOYT,** Dec. 11, 1783 *(Original entry changed to "1766")	1	497
Martha, m. Edwin B. **HOYT,** b. of Danbury, Feb. 5, [1831], by Levi Osborn	3	60
Mary, b. Oct. 27, 1750; m. Eliphalet **BARNUM,** June 4, 1777	1	454
Polly, [b.] Sept. 22, 1784; m. Benjamin **AMBLER,** Apr. 13, 1806	2	180
Reuben, m. Harriet **TAYLOR,** b. of Danbury, Oct. 30, 1844, by Rev. J. K. Ingalls	3	129
Sarah, b. Apr. 14, 1748; m. Benjamin **CROZIER,** June 17, 1766	1	447
Saul, negro, m. Dorcas, [ ]	1	361
Sibel, m. Abijah **BARNUM,** Jr., Feb. 5, 1789	1	393
Tack, negro, b. Aug. 28, 1772	1	414

DARIEN VITAL RECORDS
1820 - 1851

JESSUP, (cont.)

Peter, m. Adaline **WATERBURY,** Feb. 13, 1825, by Rev. Daniel Smith,
of Stamford   7

JONES, John H., m. Sally **JENNINGS,** Feb. 24, 1822, in Darien, by Rev. John
Noyes   3

Susan Ann, m. Henry **PRINCE,** b. of Darien, Oct. 5, 1845, by Rev.
Ezra D. Kinney. Int. Pub.   24

JUDSON, Samuel, m. Finetta Jane **WEED,** b. of New Canaan, May 16, 1841,
by Rev. E. D. Kinney   21

KELLEY, William, of Troy, N. Y., m. Mary Ann **WATERBURY,** of Darien,
this day, [, 1837?], by Rev. William Biddle   14

LAURIE, Julia, m. Alexander **ROGERS,** b. of New York, Apr. 10, 1842,
by Abram Clark, J. P.   21

LEE, Elizabeth, of New York, m. Charles **WELL,** of Darien, Feb. 14, 1843,
by Rev. Ezra D. Kinney   22

LEEDS, John R., of Stamford, m. Julia M. **WEED,** of Darien, Jan. 4, 1837,
by Rev. Daniel Smith, of Stamford   15

Lavina, of Darien, m. Benire **BROWN,** of Norwalk, Nov. 23, 1836,
by Rev. Ambrose S. Todd   25

LITTLE, Benjamin, m. Sarah **ANDRUS,** b. of Darien, Apr. 26, 1841, by
Rev. E. D. Kinney   20

Jacob, m. Nancy **LOCKWOOD,** b. of Darien, Feb. 25, 1821, by John
Noyce. V. D. M.   2

LOCKWOOD, Daniel, m. Hannah **STEVENS,** b. of Darien, Dec. 21, 1828,
by Jonathan Bates, J. P.   9

Hannah M., of Darien, m. Benjamin A. **STARR,** of New York, Aug. 19,
1827, by Rev. Ebenezer Platt   8

Jacob, Jr., m. Mary **HANFORD,** b. of Darien, Feb. 4, 1821, by John
Noyce, V. D. M.   1

Jacob, of Norwalk, m. Fanny **RAYMOND,** of Darien, Feb. 11, 1822,
by Absolom Day, in Darien   3

Nancy, m. Jacob **LITTLE,** b. of Darien, Feb. 25, 1821, by John Noyce,
V. D. M.   2

Nathan, of Norwalk, m. Mrs. Betsey **BELL,** of Darien, Mar. 6, 1821, by
Sylvester Eaton   2

Robert H., m. Mary L. **WATERBURY,** Oct. 22, 1845, by Rev. Ambrose
S. Todd   27

LODER, Henry Harvey, m. Hannah Maria **STEVENS,** b. of Darien, Nov. 30,
1842, by Abram Clark, J. P.   21

LOUNSBURY, Angeline, of Stamford, m. Eliasph **WHITNEY,** of Darien,
Dec. 12, 1824, by Rev. Ebenezer Platt   6

McINTIRE, James, m. Sally **WATERBURY,** b. of Darien, Jan. 16, 1825,
by Rev. Daniel Smith   6

McKENZIE, Elizabeth, m. John C. **CONLEY,** Sept. 8, 1745, by Rev.
P. C. Oakley   24

MARVIN, Betsey, m. Allen H. **BETTS,** b. of Wilton, Nov. 16, 1847, by Rev.
E. D. Kinney, at the house of George Homan   29

MATHER, Betsey, m. David L. **FERRIS,** b. of Darien, Apr. 8, 1844, by

Page

PARMAN, (cont.)
    N. Y., Nov. 18, 1838, by Abram Clark, J. P.   16

PATTERSON, Giles, of Greens Farms, m. Abigail WALMSLEY, of Darien,
    Apr. 7, 1824, by Rev. Daniel Smith   5

PERDERN, John, m. Eliza SLAWSON, b. of Darien, Dec. 29, 1842, by Rev.
    George Brown   22

PERRY, Rosanna M., m. William H. MILLS, b. of Darien, Oct. 12, 1842,
    by Rev. E. D. Kinney   21

    Thaddeus, m. Hannah W. FINCHLY, b. of Darien, May 31, 1840, by
    Abram Clark, J. P.   20

PLUMB, David H., Rev. of Berlin, m. Hellen M. WALLACE, of Darien,
    Dec. 6, 1843, by Rev. J. K. Ingalls   23

PRINCE, Henry, m. Susan Ann JONES, b. of Darien, Oct. 5, 1845, by
    Rev. Ezra D. Kinney. Int. Pub.   24

QUIGLEY, John, of Scriba, Otsego Cty., N. Y., m. Mary Jane SLAWSON,
    of Darien, Feb. 23, 1834, by Jesse Whiting, J. P.   11

RAYMOND, Ann E., of Darien, m. W[illia]m B. JELLIFF, of Norwalk,
    Nov. 1, 1829, by E. Platt   9

    Fanny, of Darien, m. Jacob LOCKWOOD, of Norwalk, Feb. 11, 1822, by
    Absolom Day, in Darien   3

    Jane Esther, m. Ferdinand GREFFIN, b. of Norwalk, Dec. 2, 1849, by
    Rev. E. D. Kinney   29

    Mary Jane, of Darien, m. Edward R. FANSHAW, of New York City,
    Dec. 25, 1838, by Rev. E. D. Kenney   17

    Sarah Ann, m. Nathan ROBERTS, b. of Norwalk, Nov. 18, 1840,
    by Rev. Ezree D. Kinney   20

REED, George, of Norwalk, m. Harriet STURGES, of Darien, [Jan.] 14,
    [1830], by E. Platt, at the house of Mr. Sturges   9

    Harriet, m. George J. BOWLER, b. of Darien, Feb. 21, 1841, by
    Rev. E. D. Kinney   20

RICHARDS, Charlotte, m. John DINGEE, Apr. 3, 1834, by B. Y.
    Messenger   11

    Esther, m. Ebenezer WEED, b. of Darien, Oct. 17, 1824, by
    Rev. Ebenezer Platt   5

    Lewis, m. Almira WATERBURY, Oct. 7, 1821, by John B. Matthias   2

    Mary, of Darien, m. Daniel GIDNEY, of Rye, N. Y., Nov. 2, 1829,
    by E. Platt   9

RITCHIE, Rebecca, of Darien, m. John HAMILTON, of Norwalk, July 23,
    1848, by Rev. E. D. Kinney. Witnesses: family of E. D. Kinney,
    Daniel Fitzgerald   29

ROBERTS, Nathan, m. Sarah Ann RAYMOND, b. of Norwalk, Nov. 18,
    1840, by Rev. Ezree D. Kinney   20

ROGERS, Alexander, m. Julia LAURIE, b. of New York, Apr. 10, 1842,
    by Abram Clark, J. P.   21

    Benj[ami]n, m. Mary HOYT, [Jan.] 23, [1838], by Rev. Ulric Maynard   15

    Mary, Mrs., of Darien, m. Seymour COMSTOCK, of New Canaan, May
    6, 1851, by Rev. E. D. Kinney   31

ST. JOHN, Abraham W., m. Maria M. WHITING, Jan. 28, 1849, by Rev. E.

Page

SELLECK, (cont.)

Nov. 28, 1822, by Rev. John Noyes   3

Henry, of South Norwalk, m. Phebe Ann H. **HANFORD**, of Darien, Feb.
21, 1844, by Rev. Harvey Husted   23

Isaac, of Norwalk, m. Deborah Ann **MATHER**, of Darien, Oct. 14, 1846,
by Rev. E. D. Kinney   27

Kilbown, of Salisbury, m. Catharine **SELLECK**, of Stamford, Oct. 19,
1816, by Rev. W[illia]m Fisher, of Stamford   7

Lewis, m. Polly **SELLECK**, b. of Norwalk, Oct. 5, 1823, in Darien,
by Rev. Daniel Smith, of Stamford   4

Mary, m. Leonidus **STEVENS**, b. of Darien, Dec. 30, 1839, by
Rev. Cyrus Foss   18

Polly, m. Lewis **SELLECK**, b. of Norwalk, Oct. 5, 1823, in Darien, by
Rev. Daniel Smith, of Stamford   4

Sands, m. Eliza Jane **FOWLER**, b. of Darien, Feb. 25, 1849, by Rev.
Ezra D. Kinney   29

Theodosia, m. Joseph A. **GRAY**, b. of Darien, Feb. 12, 1840, by Abram
Clark, J. P.   18

SHARP, Samuel N., m. Amanda Fitzallen **STODDARD**, May 16, 1824, by
Rev. Ambrose S. Todd   24

SHAW, Hannah, m. W[illia]m **WATERBURY**, b. of Darien, Apr. 20, 1851, by
Rev. Ezra D. Kinney   30

Mary E., m. Charles H. **WEED**, Sept. 29, 1841, by Rev. Ambrose S. Todd   26

Nancy, m. Capt. Lewes C. **WATERBURY**, b. of Darien, Nov. 11,
[1844], by Rev. E. D. Kinney   24

Phebe, m. Stephen **HUESTED**, b. of Darien, Oct. 7, 1846, by Rev.
E. D. Kenney   27

SLASON, [see also **SLAWSON**], Daniel B., m. Emma **STEVENS**, b. of
Darien, May 20, [1851], by Rev. E. D. Kinney   32

Henry, m. Bemetta J. **STEVENS**, b. of Darien, May 23, 1841, by
Abram Clark, J. P.   21

SLAWSON, [see also **SLASON**], Eliza, m. John **PERDERN**, b. of Darien,
Dec. 29, 1842, by Rev. George Brown   22

George N., of Darien, m. Eliza **TURNEY**, of Bridgeport, Feb. 24,
1828, at the house of Capt. Slawson, by Rev. Ebenezer Platt   8

Lewis, m. Nancy **HOLMES**, b. of Darien, Oct. 5, 1823, by Rev. Daniel
Smith, of Stamford   4

Mary Jane, of Darien, m. John **QUIGLEY**, of Scriba Otsego Cty, N. Y.,
Feb. 23, 1834, by Jesse Whitney, J. P.   11

STARR, Benjamin A., of New York, m. Hannah M. **LOCKWOOD**, of Darien,
Aug. 19, 1827, by Rev. Ebenezer Platt   8

STEVENS, Bemetta J., m. Henry **SLASON**, b. of Darien, May 23, 1841, by
Abram Clark, J. P.   21

Emma, m. Daniel B. **SLASON**, b. of Darien, May 20, [1851], by
Rev. E. D. Kinney   32

George R., m. Nancy **WATERBURY**, Apr. 12, 1837, by Rev. Ambrose
S. Todd   25

Hannah, m. Daniel **LOCKWOOD**, b. of Darien, Dec. 21, 1828, by

STEVENS, (cont.)

    Jonathan Bates, J. P. 9

    Hannah Maria, m. Henry Harvey **LODER**, b. of Darien, Nov. 30, 1842,
        by Abram Clark, J. P. 21

    Leonidus, m. Mary **SELLECK**, b. of Darien, Dec. 30, 1839, by Rev.
        Cyrus Foss 18

    Samuel, m. Emma **WATERBURY**, b. of Darien, Nov. 24, 1825, by Rev.
        Ebenezer Platt 7

    Sarah A., m. W[illia]m H. **HOWE**, Mar. 17, 1846, by Ira Scofield, J. P. 28

STODDARD, Amanda Fitzallen, m. Samuel N. **SHARP**, May 16, 1824, by
    Rev. Ambrose S. Todd 24

STREET, Chauncey, of Norwalk, m. Eliza **HOYT**, of Darien, Feb. 25, 1840,
    by Rev. E. D. Kinney 19

    George, m. Hannah **WOOLSEY**, May 11, [1828], by Rev. N. C. Saxton 8

    Harvey H., m. Susan A. **WEED**, b. of Darien, Mar. 13, 1848, by Rev.
        E. D. Kinney 29

    Nathaniel Jarvis, of Norwalk, m. Catharine **SCOFIELD**, of Darien,
        Oct. 16, 1838, by Rev. E. D. Kinney 16

STURGES, Harriet, of Darien, m. George **REED**, of Norwalk, [Jan.] 14,
    [1830], by E. Platt, at the house of Mr. Sturges 9

    Henrietta E., of Darien, m. Whitmore **NICHOLS**, of Weston, Jan. 10,
        1826, by Rev. Ebenezer Platt 8

THOMAS, Augustus, of New York, m. Anne **HOYT**, of Darien, Dec. 25,
    1843, at the house of her uncle Epenetus W. **WALMESLEY**, by
    Rev. Ezra D. Kinney 22

TILLE, John, m. Catharine **MILLS**, b. of Darien, Oct. 16, 1825, by Rev.
    Ebenezer Platt 7

TOOKER, Hannah M., m. Frederick S. **FLIPPER**, b. of Stamford, July 28,
    1839, by Abram Clark, J. P. 17

TURNEY, Eliza, of Bridgeport, m. George N. **SLAWSON**, of Darien, Feb.
    24, 1828, at the house of Capt. Slawson, by Rev. Ebenezer Platt 8

TUTTLE, TUTHILL, Mary R., m. Samuel B. **GORHAM**, b. of Darien, Mar.
    23, 1852, by Rev. E. D. Kinney 31

    Morris, of Walkill, N. Y., m. Catharine **SELLECK**, of Darien, Nov. 28,
        1822, by Rev. John Noyes 3

    Nelson, of Norwalk, m. Mary **ST. JOHN**, of Darien, Nov. 2, 1847,
        by Rev. E. D. Kinney 28

    Polly, m. Charles A. **BATES**, b. of Darien, Aug. 1, [1830], by Ebenezer
    Platt 10

VAIL, Silas J., of New York City, m. Sarah J. **MATHER**, of Darien, Dec.
    18, 1839, by Rev. Ezra D. Kinney 18

VAN GASBECK, Abraham H., of Collicoon, N. Y., m. Mary **WARRING**, of
    Darien, Apr. 18, 1852, by Rev. E. D. Kinney 31

WALLACE, Hellen M., of Darien, m. David H. **PLUMB** (Rev.), of Berlin,
    Dec. 6, 1843, by Rev. J. K. Ingalls 23

WALMSLEY, Abigail, of Darien, m. Giles **PATTERSON**, of Greens Farms,
    Apr. 7, 1824, by Rev. Daniel Smith 5

WARREN, [see also **WARRING**], Edmund, of Ridgefield, m. Mary Jane

Page

WARREN, (cont.)

WEED, of Darien, Nov. 10, 1839, by Rev. E. D. Kinney   17

Hannah, of Darien, m. Theodore WILMOT, of Greenwich, Feb. 24, 1840,
by Rev. Edward Aldrin, of Stamford   19

WARRING, [see also WARREN], Henry F., of Stamford, m. Amelia F.
WEED, of Darien, Oct. 21, 1844, by Rev. Adison Parker   23

Mary, of Darien, m. Abraham H. VAN GASBECK, of Collicoon, N. Y.,
Apr. 18, 1852, by Rev. E. D. Kinney   31

WATERBURY, Adaline, m. Peter JESSUP, Feb. 13, 1825, by Rev. Daniel
Smith, of Stamford   7

Almira, m. Lewis RICHARDS, Oct. 7, 1821, by John B. Matthias   2

Amey E., m. W[illia]m W. WEED, June 18, 1835, by Rev. Ambrose
S. Todd   25

Catharine, m. Ezra A. BISHOP, b. of Darien, Mar. 25, 1832, at
the house of Azariah Waterbury, by Abram Clark, J. P.   11

Charles, m. Caroline L. HARMON, b. of Darien, June 10, 1838, by
Rev. E. D. Kenney   16

Eliza Ann, m. Alvah WILMOT, Jan. 3, 1821, by G. S. Webb   1

Emma, m. Samuel STEVENS, b. of Darien, Nov. 24, 1825, by Rev.
Ebenezer Platt   7

Hannah Maria, of Darien, m. Charles DARNLEY, of Troy, N. Y.,
Oct. 29, 1833, by Rev. Ambrose S. Todd   25

John W., m. Hannah E. GRAY, Nov. 25, 1844, by Rev. Ambrose
S. Todd   26

Lewes C., Capt., m. Nancy SHAW, b. of Darien, Nov. 11, [1844], by
Rev. E. D. Kinney   24

Mary, m. Benjamin WEED, Jr., b. of Darien, [   ], 4, 1845, by
Rev. J. W. Alvord, of Stamford   24

Mary Ann, of Darien, m. William KELLEY, of Troy, N. Y., this day,
[, 1837?], by Rev. William Biddle   14

Mary L., m. Robert H. LOCKWOOD, Oct. 22, 1845, by Rev. Ambrose
S. Todd   27

Nancy, m. George R. STEVENS, Apr. 12, 1837, by Rev. Ambrose S.
Todd   25

Peter L., of Darien, m. Emeline CRABB, of Norwalk, Mar. 8, 1841,
by Rev. E. D. Kinney   20

Polly, m. Rev. Samuel B. HULL, Oct. 18, 1824, by Rev. Ambrose S.
Todd   25

Sally, m. James McINTIRE, b. of Darien, Jan. 16, 1825, by Rev.
Daniel Smith   6

Sally, m. Josiah WHETNEY, b. of Darien, Nov. 4, 1829, by E. Platt   9

Sally, m. Isaac WEED, b. of Darien, Apr. 3, 1832, by Rev. Daniel
Smith, of Stamford   11

W[illia]m, m. Hannah SHAW, b. of Darien, Apr. 20, 1851, by Rev.
Ezra D. Kinney   30

WEBB, George, of Darien, m. Azuba WILMOT, of Greenwich, Feb. 19, 1846,
by Rev. E. D. Kinney   27

Pilsey, of New York, m. Hannah BISHOP, of Darien, Mar. 24, 1823,

WEED, (cont.)
    Ebenezer Platt   6
    Rufus, m. Phebe **CLARK**, b. of Darien, Feb. 23, 1831, by Rev.
        Daniel Smith, of Stamford   10
    Sally, m. Darius K. **SCOFIELD**, b. of Darien, Nov. 14, 1824, by Rev.
        Ebenezer Platt   5
    Sarah, of Darien, m. Jonathan **JESSUP**, of Greenwich, Nov. 25, 1821,
        by Rev. Daniel Smith, of Stamford   2
    Susan A., m. Harvey H. **STREET**, b. of Darien, Mar. 13, 1848,
        by Rev. E. D. Kinney   29
    W[illia]m M., m. Amey E. **WATERBURY**, June 18, 1835, by Rev.
        Ambrose S. Todd   25
WELL, Charles, of Darien, m. Elizabeth **LEE**, of New York, Feb. 14,
    1843, by Rev. Ezra D. Kinney   22
WHITING, Maria M., m. Abraham W. **ST. JOHN**, Jan. 28, 1849, by Rev.
    E. D. Kinney   30
WHITNEY, WHETNEY, Charles E., m. Rosanna **MATHER**, Nov. 5, 1833,
    by B. Y. Messenger, V. D. M.   11
    Cornelia, m. Henry **MOREHOUSE**, b. of Darien, Nov. 8, 1841, by
        Rev. E. D. Kinney   21
    Eliasph, of Darien, m. Angeline **LOUNSBURY**, of Stamford, Dec. 12,
        1824, by Rev. Ebenzer Platt   6
    Josiah, m. Sally **WATERBURY**, b. of Darien, Nov. 4, 1829, by E.
        Platt   9
    Marian, m. George **MATHER**, b. of Darien, Oct. 22, 1826, by Rev.
        Ebenezer Platt   8
WICKS, John A., of Long Island, m. Caroline **SCOFIELD**, of Darien,
    Nov. 14, 1836, by Rev. Ulric Maynard   13
WILCOXSON, Harriet, of Darien, m. Henry **DEAN**, of Poundridge, N. Y.,
    [Jan.] 22, [1829], by E. Platt, at his house   9
WILMOT, Abigail A., m. Jonathan N. **HUSTED**, Oct. 6, 1823, by Rev.
    Eli Denniston   5
    Alvah, m. Eliza Ann **WATERBURY**, Jan. 3, 1821, by G. S. Webb   1
    Angeline, m. Aaron B. **BRADLEY**, b. of Darien, Apr. 4, 1857*, by
        Rev. Ulric Maynard   *(Probably "1837")   14
    Azuba, of Greenwich, m. George **WEBB**, of Darien, Feb. 19, 1846, by
        Rev. E. D. Kinney   27
    James, m. Betsey H. **WOOD**, b. of Darien, Aug. 20, 1843, by
        Abram Clark, J. P.   22
    Julia Ann B., m. George S. **BATES**, b. of Darien, Apr. 19, 1840, by
        Rev. E. D. Kinney   19
    Theodore, of Greenwich, m. Hannah **WARREN**, of Darien, Feb. 24, 1840,
        by Rev. Edward Aldrin, of Stamford   19
WISEMAN, Mary, of Providence, R. I., m. Nathan R. **BYXBEE**, of Darien,
    Feb. 14, 1843, by Rev. Ezra D. Kinney   22
WOOD, Betsey H., m. James **WILMOT**, b. of Darien, Aug. 20, 1843, by
    Abram Clark, J. P.   22
    Frances Amanda, m. W[illia]m H. **BULL** (?), b. of Darien, Sept.

DERBY VITAL RECORDS
1655 - 1852

	Vol.	Page
ABBOTT, Caroline, of Middlebury, m. Nathan N. **BRADLEY**, of Waterbury, [Dec.] 19, [1847], by Rev. N. S. Richardson	1	208
ABEL, Ann C., of Humphreysville, m. Abraham B. **KINGSLAND**, of New York, Nov. 20, 1843, by Rev. W[illia]m Bliss Ashley, in St. James Church	1	333
ACKLEY, W[illia]m B., of N. Y., m. Sarah J. **LUM**, of Derby, Oct. 13, 1852, by Rev. Thomas T. Guion	1	194
ADAMS, John, m. Julia Ann **THOMPSON**, b. of Derby, Nov. 26, 1849, by Rev. S. Howland	1	193
Sarah, m. Moses **JOHNSON**, Apr. 15, 1703	2	13
ADDIS, William, of Litchfield, m. Julia Ann **BROWN**, of Milford, May 27, 1828, by John T. Wheeler, J. P.	1	83
ADEE, ADYE, Dorcas, d. John & Hannah, b. Mar. 13, 1785	TM1	108
John, m. Hannah **JOHNSON**, Mar. 22, 1775	TM1	108
Sarah, d. John & Hannah, b. Jan. 2, 1775* *(Overwritten in pencil to read "Aug. 6, 1775")	TM1	108
Sarah, m. John **CRAWFORD**, Dec. 13, 1795	TM1	215
Sarah Jane, m. Stephen H. **CULVER**, b. of Derby, Nov. 7, 1847, by Rev. Sylvester Smith	1	234
William, s. John & Hannah, b. Jan. 2, 1780	TM1	108
ADYE, [see under **ADEE**]		
ALABY, Emiline Jane, m. David P. **BELDEN**, Feb. 1, 1847, by Rev. George L. Fuller	1	208
ALDEN, Austen, m. Nancy **OCOM**, Sept. 8, 1839, by John D. Smith	1	145
ALLEN, ALLIEN, ALLIN, [see also **ALLING**], Austin, of Woodbury, m. Sarah **CLARK**, of Derby, Nov. 10, [1839], by Rev. J. B. Beach	1	192
Betsey, m. Josiah **SMITH**, Nov. 7, 1836, by Rev. L. D. Howell	1	179
Charlotte M., m. Charles H. **BASSETT**, Oct. 16, 1844, by Rev. W[illia]m Bliss Ashley	1	206
Clarissa, m. David W. **PLUMP**, Mar. 14, 1841, by Rev. Joseph Scott	1	173
David, m. Ellender **SMITH**, Dec. 27, 1769, by Richard Mansfield	TM1	40
David, s. David & Ellener, b. Feb. 12, 1789	TM1	163
Denzel, of Orange, m. Elizabeth **HOTCHKISS**, of Derby, June 21, 1829, in Humphreysville	1	106
Eliner. d. David & Eliner, b. Sept. 20, 1780	TM1	96
Elisabeth, d. David & Elener, b. Aug. 1, 1773	TM1	61
Ephraim, s. David & Eliner, b. Dec. 26, 1775	TM1	92

	Vol.	Page
ALLEN, ALLIEN, ALLIN, (cont.)		
Esther, m. Gedion **WASHBOND**, Oct. 6, 1743	LR4	A4
Esther, m. Gedion **WASHBOND**, Oct. 6, 1743	LR5	4
Fitch, s. Samuel & Susannah, b. Sept. 25, 1782	TM1	213
Hannah, d. David & Elender, b. Mar. 8, 1771	TM1	40
Isaac, m. Grace **BOTSFORD**, Oct. 9, 1825, by Rev. Abner Smith	1	105
Isaac Noyes, m. Mrs. Elenor **JOHNSON**, of Oxford, Mar. 1, 1832, by Rev. Stephen Jewett	1	108
Jennett, of Humphreysville, m. John **DAVIS**, of Naugatuck, Oct. 11, 1847, by N. L. Richardson	1	248
Levi, m. Delia **FREEMAN**, Sept. 21, 1843, by Rev. W[illia]m Bliss Ashley	1	193
Lucius, of Woodbridge, m. Harriet **HOTCHKISS**, of Derby, Nov. 12, 1829, by P. Jewett	1	82
Mathew, m. Jane **CAMP**, June 28, 1847, by Rev. W[illia]m B. Curtiss	1	193
Nancy, m. Nehemiah **ANDREW**, May 9, 1848, by Rev. W[illia]m B. Curtiss, at Humphreysville	1	193
Rebeckah, see Rebeckah **NOYCE**	TM1	123
Sidney, m. Eliza Ann **BEMER**, b. of Derby, Sept. 12, 1830, by Rev. Zepheniah Swift	1	107
ALLING, [see also **ALLEN**], Eugenia H., of Ansonia, m. William H. **PLUMMER**, of New Haven, Oct. 11, 1852, by Rev. Owen Street	1	407
ALLIS, Caroline, m. Rev. Oliver **HOPSON**, Sept. 9, 1833, by Rev. S. Jewett	1	161
Frances E., m. David H. **GRANGER**, June 1, 1846, by Rev. W[illia]m B. Curtiss	1	279
Lucius, m. Emily **WARNER**, b. of Derby, [ ], by Rev. N. S. Richardson. Recorded Dec. 2, 1845	1	193
Lucius, m. Emily **WARNER**, b. of Derby, [ ], by Rev. N. S. Richardson. Recorded Dec. 2, 1845	1	325
ANDREWS, ANDREW, [see also **ANDRUS**], Elizabeth, m. Merrit **NICKOLS**, b. of Waterbury, Apr. 26, 1837, by Rev. John E. Bray	1	169
Harriet, of Bethany, m. Joseph **REYNOLDS**, of New Haven, June 26, 1843, by Rev. Sylvester Smith	1	425
Hiram, m. Grace **TERREL**, b. of Bethany, Sept. 17, 1837, by Sylvester Smith	1	145
Jeremiah, m. Hannah **COOPER**, b. of Derby, Sept. 13, 1840, by Rev. John B. Beach	1	192
Mary Ann, m. Peter **WAITH**, b. of Humphreysville, July 1, 1849, by Rev. W[illia]m Denison	1	482
Nehemiah, m. Nancy **ALLEN**, May 9, 1848, by Rev. W[illia]m B. Curtiss, at Humphreysville	1	193
ANDRUS, [see also **ANDREW**], Ame, m. Gideon **CANDEE**, b. of Derby, May 14, 1772	TM1	75a
Desire, d. Ephraim & Sarah, b. Mar. 18, 1747	LR5	232

	Vol.	Page
ANDRUS, (cont.)		
Desire, m. John **DURAND**, Jr., b. of Derby, Oct. 3, 1769,		
by Timothy Russell	TM1	92
Ephraim, m. Sarah **HUMPHRIS**, Mar. 21, 1745	LR5	4
--annah, d. Ephraim & Sarah, b. June 22, 174[ ]	LR5	2
ARMITAGE, Angeline, m. Andrew McIntyre **GARDNER**, b. of		
Ansonia, June 12, 1853, by Rev. Daniel W[illia]m Havens,		
at Ansonia	1	280
ARNOLD, Edwin, of Haddam, m. Maria **THOMPSON**, Aug. 15,		
1833, by Zepheniah Swift	1	147
ARTHUR, Duncan M., m. Mary **FURGUSON**, b. of Derby, Aug.		
[ ], 1850, by Rev. Jno Morrison Reid	1	211
ASKNITH, John, m. Margaret **NICHOLSON**, b. of Derby, Apr. 1,		
1851, by Rev. Thomas T. Guion	1	193
ATWATER, Henry Charles, of New Haven, m. Marianne		
KIMBERLY, of Derby, Sept. 19, 1831, by Rev. Stephen		
Jewett	1	92
Richard, of New Haven, m. Anna Ritta **MORRISS**, of Derby,		
July 12, 1829, by Rev. Stephen Jewett	1	124
ATWOOD, Sarah, of Derby, m. S. B. P. **HIGGINS**, of New York,		
May 7, 1851, by Rev. Thomas T. Guion	1	292
AUGUST, Horace Augustus, m. Elizabeth **HANSON**, b. of New		
Haven, June 13, 1831, by Rev. Charles Thompson, of		
Humphreyville	1	121
AUGUSTUS, Eliza, of Derby, m. John **BARTIS**, of Oxford, Jan.		
8, 1830, by Wait Bassett, J. P., at the house of Mrs.		
Augustus	1	88
Nancy C., of New Haven, m. William **PECK**, of Newtown,		
May 15, 1838, by Rev. Joseph Scott	1	172
AUSTIN, Moses, Hon. of Durham, N. Y., m. Sarah **HUMPHREY**, of		
Derby, Feb. 26, 1829, by Rev. P. Jewett	1	82
Sarah M., m. William **BEACH**, May 20, 1847, by Rev.		
W[illia]m B. Curtiss	1	208
BABBIT, Samuel Tillotson, of Huntington, m. Elisabeth **SMITH**,		
of Derby, Apr. 17, 1821, by Rev. Abner Smith	1	85
BACON, Nathaniel, of New Haven, m. Mrs. Sophia **MOULTON**, of		
Derby, Apr. 11, 1838, by Rev. Lewis D. Howell	1	168
BAGDEN, Lois, m. Nelson **WESTON**, Sept. 30, 1834, by Rev.		
Joseph Scott	1	187
BAGLEY, Joseph, of Humphreysville, m. Jane **NORTHROP**, of		
Sherman, Apr. 19, 1840, by Rev. Sylvester Smith	1	189
BALDWIN, **BALDWEN**, Abigail, d. Josiah & Mary, b. June 5, [ ]	LR3	3
Abner S., m. Mary A. **CAMP**, May 26, 1833, by Zepheniah		
Swift	1	147
Alletha, m. Smith **CLARK**, of Litchfield, Dec. 26, 1830, by		
Rev. Charles Thompson	1	90
Andrew M., m. Martha A. **CHATFIELD**, b. of Woodbridge,		
[July] 24, 1836, by L. D. Howell	1	168

	Vol.	Page
BALDWIN, BALDWEN, (cont.)		
Anne, d. Timothy & Sarah, b. Feb. 24, 1757	LR6	443
Betsey Jane, of Woodbridge, m. William **DANULS**, of Grove, Alegany County, N. Y., [Oct.] 9, [1836], by Rev. L. D. Howells	1	151
Charles, s. Siluanus & Mary, b. May 8, 1751	LR6	2
Deb[o]rah, d. Dr. Silas & Mary, b. Aug. 22, 1782	TM1	111
Dorcus, d. Siluanus & Mary, b. Aug. 18, 1738	LR5	2
Elisha, s. Siluanus & Mary, b. Mar. 7, 1741	LR5	2
Eunice, d. Dr. Silas & Mary, b. Nov. 12, 1768	TM1	43
George, of Huntington, m. Mary **CAMP**, of Orange, Sept. 18, 1842, by Zephaniah Swift	1	205
Hannah, d. Dr. Silas & Mary, b. Mar. 10, 1766	TM1	14
Harriet, of Derby, m. Merrit **WOOSTER**, of Oxford, Jan. 28, 1829, by Eli Barnett, Elder	1	124
Henrietta, m. Augustus **FELCH**, Nov. 29, 1837, by Rev. Joseph Scott	1	155
Hezekiah, s. Josiah & Mary, b. Aug. 20, [ ]	2	13
Hezekiah, s. Josiah & Mary, d. Aug. 29, 170[ ]?	2	27
Hezekiah, s. Josiah & Mary, b. Jan. 15, 1710/11	LR3	0
Hezekiah, s. Josiah & Mary, d. [ ], 1712/13	LR3	6
Hezekiah, s. Siluanus & Mary, b. Jan. 21, 1746/7	LR5	232
Hezkekiah, s. Siluanus & Mary, d. Mar. 2, 1746/7	LR5	1
Hezekiah, s. Silvames & Mary, b. Aug. 24, 1756	LR6	440
Huldah, m. David H. **MONSON**, b. of Woodbridge, Sept. 18, 1836, by Rev. S. D. Howell	1	166
Isaac, d. Jan. 4, 1799	TM1	367
Jabez, m. Jane **BOTSFORD**, b. of Derby, Sept. 19, [ ]	1	106
James, d. Aug. 27, 1760	LR6	447
James, s. Silas & Mary, b. Dec. 1, 1763	LR7	252
Jane E., of Woodbridge, m. David **NATHAN**, of Derby, Sept. 16, 1841, by Rev. Joseph Scott	1	170
Jared, s. Josiah & Mary, b. Mar. 23, 1706/7	2	23
Jared, s. Josiah, d. Nov. 6, 1707	2	27
Jenette, of Humphreysville, m. James Sheldon **GREEN**, of Coventry, Jan. 9, 1831, by Rev. Stephen Jewett	1	102
Jesse, s. Dr. Silas & Mary, b. Feb. 15, 1771	TM1	40
Josiah, m. Mary **PERSON**, Sept. 19, 1700	2	25
Josiah, s. Josiah & Mary, b. Sept. 17, 1701	2	12
Judson, m. Charity Mary **BLACKMAN**, of Huntington, Jan. 29, 1837, by Rev. Joseph Scott	1	168
Julia M., m. Elisha **BLACKMAN**, b. of Derby, Dec. 22, 1839, by H. Read	1	171
Julius, of New Hartford, m. Hannah Maria **CAMP**, of Woodbridge, Sept. 23, 1838, by Rev. Zepheniah Swift	1	153
Lewis, s. Isaac & Philena, b. Nov. 17, 1780	TM1	111
Louisa, m. Harry **ENGLISH**, Mar. 14, 1834, by Rev. Charles William Bradley	LR5	153

	Vol.	Page

BALWIN, BALDWEN, (cont.)

Lucy Ann, m. Amos Benham **BLAKELEY**, of New Haven, Oct.
    11, 1832, by Rev. Zepheniah Swift — 1 — 147

Marcy, d. Josiah & Mary, b. Jan. 10, 1714 — LR3 — 2

Maria, m. John William **BASSETT**, b. of Derby, Mar. 3, 1836,
    by John D. Smith — 1 — 148

Mary, d. Josiah & Mary, b. Oct. 11, [   ] — 2 — 13

Mary, d. Josiah & Mary, d. Oct. 28, 170[ ] — 2 — 27

Mary, d. Siluanus & Mary, b. Oct. 16, 1735 — LR5 — 2

Merrit P., m. Eliza **PECK**, of Woodbridge, Apr. 18, 1830,
    by Rev. Stephen Jewett — 1 — 88

Patty, m. Samuel **FELCH**, May 8, 1836, by Rev. L. D. Howell — 1 — 155

Sarah, d. Siluanus & Mary, b. Mar. 16, 1743/4 — LR5 — 2

Sarah, d. Siluanus & Mary, d. Jan. 23, 1745/6 — LR5 — 1

Sarah, d. Siluanus & Mary, b. Feb. 1, 1747/8 — LR6 — 2

Sarah, m. Simeon **WHE[E]LER**, b. of Derby, Oct. 10, 1764,
    by Rev. Mr. Humphry — TM1 — 31

Sarah, d. Dr. Silas & Mary, d. Jan. 1, 1774 — TM1 — 52

Sarah, d. Dr. Silas & Mary, b. Feb. 4, 1780 — TM1 — 128

Sarah, m. William **BURRITT**, Apr. 24, 1784 — TM1 — 155

Sarah, had d. Tuly Ann, b. Sept. 3, 1802 — TM1 — 368

Sarah, of Derby, m. Dan F. **BEACH**, of Hartland, Mar. 17, 1840,
    by Rev. J. B. Beach — 1 — 192

Sarah A., of Derby, m. Oliver **CUSHMAN**, of Becket, Mass.,
    Nov. 27, 1837, by Sylvester Smith — 1 — 152

Silas, m. Mrs. Mary **PLUMB**, Feb. 12, 1755 — LR6 — 7

Silas, s. Silas & Mary, b. Aug. 25, 1774 — TM1 — 109

Siluanus, m. Mary **FRENCH**, Apr. 18, 1734 — LR5 — 4

Star, of Derby, m. Emily **NEWELL**, of New Haven, June 28,
    1835, by Rev. Zephaniah Swift — 1 — 146

Stephen, of Oxford, m. Betsey Ann **HUBBELL**, of Derby,
    Dec. 16, 1820, by Rev. Zephaniah Swift — 1 — 85

Stiles, m. Mary **JOHNSON**, June 2, 1834, by Zepheniah Swift — 1 — 147

Thadeus, s. Timothy & Sarah, b. June 22, 1751 — LR6 — 2

Timothy, m. Sarah **BEACHER**, Jan. 15, 1744/5 — LR5 — 4

Timothy, d. Aug. 30, 1822, ae 74 — 1 — 511

Tuly Ann, d. Sarah, b. Sept. 3, 1802 — TM1 — 368

William, m. Sarah M. **HOTCHKISS**, b. of Derby, Nov. 22,
    1835, by Rev. John E. Bray — 1 — 148

Willis B.,, of Woodbridge, m. Jane **BASSETT**, of
    Humphreysville, Feb. 21, 1847, by Rev. John Purves — 1 — 207

Willis B., m. Almira A. **HUNTLY**, Aug. 18, 1850, by Rev.
    Jno Morrison Reid — 1 — 211

Zuriel, s. Dr. Silas & Mary, b. Jan. 6, 1758 — LR6 — 443

----, m. Samuel **RIG[G]S**, June 14, [   ] — 2 — 1

BALL, Chauncey, m. Eleanor **SMITH**, b. of Derby, Nov. 28, 1852,
    by Rev. Thomas T. Guion — 1 — 212

BANKS, David A., m. Julia N. **WAKELEY**, b. of Derby, Mar. 3,

	Vol.	Page

BANKS, (cont.)

    1845, by Rev. W[illia]m Bliss Ashley   1   207

BARCLIN, John W., of Dutton, Mass., m. Emma M. **GAY**, of Derby,

    Sept. 20, 1840, by Rev. W[illia]m Denison   1   209

BARKER, John G., of New York City, m. Margarett **LOCKWOOD**,

    of Derby, June 22, 1847, by Rev. W[illia]m Bliss Ashley   1   208

BARLOW, Mary, of Stratford, m. Abiel **CANFIELD**, of Derby, Dec.

    23, 1779   TM1   76

BARNES, BARNS, Aseneth, Mrs. of Woodbury, m. John **SMITH**, of

    New York, Nov. 17, 1830, by Bennet Lum, J. P.   1   112

    Lelia E., m. Hiram G. **KELBOURNE**, July 2, 1851, by Rev.

    Jno Morrison Reid   1   330

    Lucy, Mrs., of Waterbury, m. Ebnezer **JOHNSON**, of Derby,

    Mar. 19, 1754, by M. Leuenworth   LR6   6

    Lucy, of Plymouth, m. Alva **BUNNEL**, of Derby, Feb. 28, 1836,

    By Rev. John E. Bray   1   148

    Willard, m. Elizabeth **BUNNEL**, Jan. 2, 1823, by Rev. Abner

    Smith   1   84

BARNUM, James H., m. Deborah **HORTON**, b. of Bethel, Nov. 7,

    1847, by Rev. Nathan E. Shailer   1   208

BARRET, Dennis, m. Johanna **FITZGIBBONS**, Aug. 17, 1851, by

    Rev. James Lynch, of Birmingham   1   213

BARTHOLOMEW, George, m. Ann Eliza **SISSON**, Oct. 14, 1829,

    by P. Jewett   1   82

    Hannah, m. Abijah **HAWKINS**, b. of Derby, [Feb.] 16,

    [1823], by Rev. Stephen Jewett   1   96

    Sophronia A., of Ansonia, m. Theodore P. **TERRY**, of

    Terrysville, Nov. 6, 1854, by Rev. O. Street, at Ansonia   1   249

    Sophronia A., of Ansonia, m. Theodore P. **TERRY**, of

    Terrysville, Nov. 6, 1854, by Rev. O. Street, at Ansonia   1   461

BARTIS, BARTUSS, John, s. John & Mary, b. June 24, 1761   TM1   11

    John, of Oxford, m. Eliza **AUGUSTUS**, of Derby, Jan. 8,

    1830, by Wait Bassett, J. P., at the house of Mrs. Augustus   1   88

    Samuel, s. John & Mary, b. Oct. 19, 1763   TM1   11

BASSETT, BASSIT, BASSITT, Abigail, m. John **POOL**, [   ], 1783   TM1   162

    Abraham, s. Sam[ue]ll & Deborah, b. Feb. 27, 1725   LR4   A3

    Abraham, s. Sam[ue]ll & Sarah, b. Mar. 21, 1753   LR6   3

    Abram, of Oxford, m. Harriet L. **STILES**, of Southbury, Feb.

    27, 1831, by Rev. John Lovejoy   1   100

    Amos, s. Sam[ue]ll & Deborah, b. Jan. 7, 1734   LR4   A3

    Amos, m. Keziah **ROWE**, Sept. 7, 1845, by Rev. John D. Smith   1   207

    Betsey, m. Talmage **BEARDSLEE**, b. of Derby, Jan. 1, 1826,

    by Rev. Zepheniah Swift   1   83

    Calsina Jennet, of Derby, m. Thomas **SPENCE**, of Oxford,

    Nov. 15, 1835, by Rev. Joseph Scott   1   179

    Carroline, m. David Daniel **WOOSTER**, 2nd, b. of Derby,

    Apr. 9, 1835, by Sylvester Smith   1   186

    Catharine, m. Isaac **BREWSTER**, of New York, June 4, 1834,

	Vol.	Page
BASSETT, BASSIT, BASSITT, (cont.)		
by Zepheniah Swift	1	147
Charles, m. Jane E. **STONE,** Oct. 22, 1843, by Rev. John D. Smith	1	206
Charles H., m. Charlotte M. **ALLEN,** Oct. 16, 1844, by Rev. W[illia]m Bliss Ashley	1	206
Charles L., of Derby, m. Angeline C. **SALSBURY,** of Long Meadow, Mass., Oct. 30, 1848, by Rev. Joseph Scott	1	209
David, m. Nab[b]e **TOMLINSON,** b. of Derby, Oct. 21, 1773, by John Davis	TM1	94
Deborah, d. Sam[ue]ll & Deb[o]rah, b. Mar. 22, 1726	LR4	A3
Deborah, m. John **TOMLINSON,** Apr. 28, 1748	LR5	4
Deborah, m. John **TOMLINSON,** Apr. 28, 1748	LR6	450
Dickerman M., m. Mary **SMITH,** Nov. 17, 1852, by Rev. Cha[rle]s Dickinson	1	212
Eben[e]zer, s. Sam[ue]ll & Deb[o]rah, b. June 19, 1731	LR4	A3
Ebenezer, m. Sarah **TOMLINSON,** Feb. 2, 1742/3	LR4	A4
Ebenezer, of Derby, m. Hannah **SMITH,** of Milford, Mar. 17, 1756	LR6	450
Ebenezer, d. May 24, 1760	LR6	445
Ebenezer, s. John & Naomy, b. Dec. 12, 1760	LR7	252
Electa, m. Ebner **WHITE,** b. of Derby, Dec. 2, 1849, by Rev. S. Howland	1	482
--liphaz, s. Thomas & Sarah, b. Jan. 11, 1729/30	LR3	11
Eliza A., m. Sydney A. **DOWNS,** b. of Derby, Oct. 6, 1840, by Rev. Hollis Read	1	151
Elizabeth, d. Sam[ue]ll & Deb[o]rah, b. Mar. 15, 1728	LR4	A3
Elizabeth, m. Abraham **HAWKINS,** Apr. 20, 1748	LR5	4
Elisabeth, d. John & Naomi, b. Mar. 3, 1750	LR5	414
Elisabeth, m. Ransom **SMITH,** b. of Derby, Apr. 7, 1844, by Rev. Ezra Jagger	1	439
Ellen H., of Derby, m. George H. **NORTON,** of N[ew] H[aven], Sept. 4, 1849, by Rev. Thomas T. Guion	1	381
Ellen Sophia, [d. Sheldon & Harriet], b. Jan. 24, 1832	1	3
Enos, of Oxford, m. Jane **LEES,** of Derby, May 13, 1821, by Rev. David Miller	1	85
Ephraim, s. Sam[ue]ll & Deborah, b. Feb. 7, 1738	LR4	A3
Esther, d. John & Naomy, b. June 17, 1753	LR6	3
Esther, m. Ebenezer **PLANT,** b. of Derby, Aug. 17, 1774	TM1	82
Eunice, d. Samuel & Sarah, b. Jan. 9, 1759	LR6	440
George, of Oxford, m. Sally **RUSSELL,** of Derby, Nov. 2, 1824, by Rev. Abner Smith	1	83
George, m. Laura **TOMLINSON,** Dec. 24, 1844, by Rev. John D. Smith	1	206
Glover, m. Nancy **GILYARD,** b. of Derby, t. 21, 1839, by Rev. Sam[ue]l R. Hickcox. Witnesses: Jared Bassett, Sally B. Bassett	1	167
Hannah, d. Sam[ue]ll & Sarah, b. June 30, 1756	LR6	441

	Vol.	Page
BASSETT, BASSIT, BASSITT, (cont.)		
Hepzibah, of Derby, m. Walker **LAKE**, of Oxford, Apr. 4, 1838, by Rev. David Miller	1	164
Isaac, Jr., m. Pemelia **FRENCH**, b. of Derby, Sept. 8 , 1822, by Eli Barnett	1	87
Isaac, m. Mary **BASSETT**, b. of Derby, Sept. 9, 1830, by Rev. S. Jewett, of St. James	1	83
James, s. Ebenzer & Hannah, b. Sept. 16, 1757	LR6	443
James, m. Betty **CANFIELD**, b. of Derby, Mar. 28, 1780	TM1	129
Jane, of Humphreysville, m. Willis B. **BALDWIN**, of Woodbridge, Feb. 21, 1847, by Rev. John Purves	1	207
Joel, s. Thomas & Sarah, b. Oct. 15, 1734	LR3	11
John, s. Sam[ue]ll & Deborah, b. Feb. 15, 1721/2	LR4	A3
John, m. Naomi **WOOSTER**, Dec. 15, 1746	LR5	4
John, s. Samuel & Sarah, b. Nov. 14, 1751	LR6	2
John, Jr., m. Catherine Sophia **GILBERT**, Jan. 7, 1838, by John D. Smith	1	174
John William, m. Maria **BALDWIN**, b. of Derby, Mar. 3, 1836, by John D. Smith	1	148
John William, of New York, m. Sarah B. **COGSWELL**, of Derby, Sept. 13, 1849, by Rev. C. S. Putman. Int. Pub.	1	209
Joseph, s. Sam[ue]ll & Deborah, b. Aug. 31, 1722	LR4	A3
Joseph, s. Sam[ue]ll, b. Aug. 31, 1722	LR3	4
Joseph, m. Sarah **HAWKINS**, Nov. 16, 1748	LR5	4
Joseph, m. Molly **HENMAN**, Mar. 18, 1779	TM1	156
Julia Ann, m. Rockwell M. **DAN**, b. of Derby, Apr. 4, 1844, by Rev. Sylvester Smith	1	247
Julius, m. Ann Augusta **LAKE**, Sept. 13, 1841, by John D. Smith	1	189
Laurey, d. Joseph & Molly, b. Mar. 13, 1784	TM1	156
Lavinia Hull, [d. Sheldon & Harriet], b. Apr. 17, 1834	1	3
Lorenzo M., m. Sarah T. **SCOTT**, b. of Derby, May 7, 1848, by Rev. Sylvester Smith	1	208
Lucy, d. Sheldon & Harriet, b. May 10, 1837	1	3
Lucy, m. William **CANFIELD**, b. of Derby, Nov. 30, 1841 by Rev. Joseph Scott	1	154
Lury* Matilda, [d. Sheldon & Harriet], b. May 20, 1830 *(Lucy)	1	3
Lucy Matilda, d. Sheldon & Harriet, d. Aug. 28, 1831, ae 15 m. 8 d.	1	511
Maria, of Derby, m. Robert **MAY**, of Apilachicola, Fla., Oct. 3, 1839, by Rev. Hollis Reed	1	167
Maria L., m. Isaac H. **DAVIS**, Mar. 26, 1842, by John D. Smith	1	247
Mary, d. Sam[ue]ll & Deborah, b. Nov. 29, 1736	LR4	A3
Mary, m. Samuel **CANFIELD**, Apr. 3, 1754	LR6	6
Mary, m. Isaac **BASSETT**, b. of Derby, Sept. 9, 1830, by Rev. S. Jewett of St. James	1	83
Mary, m. Ambrose **BEARDSLEY**, b. of Derby, Apr. 30, 1837, by Rev. E. Edward Beardsley	1	168

	Vol.	Page
BASSETT, BASSIT, BASSITT, (cont.)		
Mary Jane, m. Edward C. LUM, b. of Derby, Mar. 2, 1845, by		
Rev. W[illia]m Bliss Ashley	1	341
Miranda, m. Timothy HITCHCOCK, b. of Derby, Aug. 2, 1843,		
by Rev. Sylvester Smith	1	289
Nancy, d. Joseph & Molly, b. Mar. 22, 1782	TM1	156
Rebecca Ann, of Oxford, m. William BUTLER, of Derby, Mar.		
28, 1841, by Rev. Samuel R. Hickcox	1	174
Rhode, d. Joseph & Sarah, b. Feb. 12, 1769	LR7	252
Robert N., m. Elizabeth S. DOWNS, b. of Derby, Oct. 5, 1842,		
by Rev. H. Read	1	205
Royal Moulton, [s. Sheldon & Harriet], b. Oct. 22, 1828	1	3
Sam[ue]ll, m. Mrs. Deborah BENNIT, Jan. 1, 1719	LR4	A4
Samuel, s. Samuel, b. Nov. 29, 1719	LR3	3
Sam[ue]ll, s. Sam[ue]ll & Deborah, b. Nov. 29, 1719	LR4	A3
Samuel, Jr., m. Sarah BOCHFORD, Oct. 26, 1748	LR5	4
Samuel, s. Joseph & Sarah, b. June 25, 1751	LR6	2
Samuel, Rev., m. Fanny JOHNSON, Oct. 6, 1828, by		
Sam[ue]l R. Hickcox. Witnesses: Isaac Basssett, Joseph		
Johnson, Isaac Bassett, Jr.	1	88
Sarah, d. Samuel & Sarah, b. Feb. 14, 1761	LR7	249
Sarah, of Humphreysville, m. Sylvester T. Smith, of		
Birmingham, Sept. 21, 1845, by Rev. John Parvies	1	440
Sheldon, s. Joseph & Molly, b. Feb. 14, 1780	TM1	156
Sheldon, m. Harriet HULL, Mar. 4, 1827, by Rev. Zepheniah		
Swift	1	86
Tafeenes, d. Joseph & Sarah, b. Jan. 12, 1762	LR7	252
Thomas, m. Sarah PEIRSON, Aug. 24, 1727	LR3	10
William, s. James & Betty, b. Jan. 18, 1781	TM1	129
William Hull, s. Sheldon & Harriet, b. Oct. 21, 1827	1	3
BATES, Benjamin, m. Abigail HINE, Apr. 2, 1751	LR6	450
Betty, d. Benjamin & Abigail, b. Oct. 10, 1757	LR6	443
Betty, m. Luke BUNNEL, b. of Derby, Mar. 31, 1785	TM1	158
Elihu, s. Benjamin & Abigail, b. May 2, 1752	LR6	450
Elihu, s. Benjamin & Abigail, b. Apr. 26, 1754	LR6	443
Mary, m. Jonathan PEIRSON, Mar. 5, 1739	LR4	A4
Sarah, d. Benj[ami]n & Abigail, b. Apr. 26, 1754	LR6	450
BEACH, Abigail, wid. Rev. John, of New Town, d. Feb. 7, 1783,		
in the 76th y of her age	TM1	129
Dan F., of Hartland, m. Sarah BALDWIN, of Derby, Mar.		
17, 1840, by Rev. J. B. Beach	1	192
Jesse, m. Sally WHE[E]LER, July 30, 1792	TM1	210
John, s. Hubbard, b. May 20, 1831, at Humphreysville	1	3
Louisa, m. Samuel MORGAN, b. of Woodbridge, Apr. 27, 1840,		
by Rev. John E. Bray	1	167
Lucretia, m. Isaac NATHANIEL, b. of Derby, Oct. 8, 1837,		
by Rev. Abraham Brown	1	169
Lucy Mariah, d. Jesse & Lucy, b. Feb. 23, 1794	TM1	210

	Vol.	Page
BEACH, (cont.)		
Mary Jennet, d. Hubbard, b. May 28, 1838	1	3
Nelson M., m. Elizabeth M. **DURAND,** b. of Derby, Nov. 4, 1838, by Rev. Orlando Starr	1	167
Sally Keziah, d. Jesse & Sally, b. Sept. 9, 1796	TM1	210
Samuel, M. D., of Stanford, m. Mary **SWIFT,** of Derby, Apr. 13, 1829, by Rev. Zephiniah Swift	1	82
Sarah, m. Samuel **WASHBON,** May 19, 1741	LR5	4
Sharon, of North Haven, m. Adaline **SPERRY,** of North Milford, Oct. 3, 1832, by Rev. C. Thompson	1	179
Uriah M., m. Angeline **HUBBLE,** Sept. 5, 1827, by Rev. Zepheniah Swift	1	86
William, m. Sarah M. **AUSTIN,** May 20, 1847, by Rev. W[illia]m B. Curtiss	1	208
BEAMANT, [see under **BEMAN**]		
BEARD, Amelia, d. James & Ruth, b. Mar. 21, 1756	LR6	13
Amelia, m. Levi **TOMLINSON,** b. of Derby, Dec. 29, 1774, by Rev. Daniel Humphrys	TM1	101
James, m. Mrs. Ruth **HOLBROOK,** Oct. 31, 1754	LR6	7
James, of Derby, m. Mary **HOBARD,** of Guilford, Dec. 10, 1781, by Rev. Mr. Ells, of Branford	TM1	36
Samuel, s. James & Ruth, b. Oct. [ ], 1757	LR6	442
Samuel, s. James & Ruth, d. Jan. 7, 1758	LR6	440
Sarah, m. Levi **CHATFIELD,** b. of Derby, May 27, 1781	TM1	111
BEARDSLEY, BEARDSLEE, Ambrose, m. Mary **BASSETT,** b. of Derby, Apr. 30, 1837, by Rev. E. Edward Beardsley	1	168
Edward, of Stratford, m. Priscilla **WALLACE,** of Derby, Dec. 31, 1852, by Rev. Thomas T. Guion	1	212
James, of Huntington, m. Charity **VOSE,** of Oxford, Sept. 7, 1822, by Rev. Abner Smith	1	85
Rachel, of Stratford, m. William **MOSS,** of Derby, Sept. 20, 1759	LR7	250
Talmage, m. Betsey **BASSETT,** b. of Derby, Jan. 1, 1826, by Rev. Zepheniah Swift	1	83
BEEBE, BEEBEE, Joel, m. Mary **HALE,** Feb. 1, 1823, by Rev. Stephen Jewett, of St. James Church	1	84
Ursula, of Waterbury, m. Walter **WOOSTER,** of Derby, Nov. 15, 1780	TM1	130
BEECHER, BEACHER, Abigail, m. Jonathan **HICHCOCK,** Jan. 21, 1746/7	LR5	4
Burr, of Oxford, m. Jane **HAWKINS,** of Derby, Nov. 10, 1830, by Rev. Stephen Jewett	1	91
Eliza S., m. Morrison **HULL,** Sept. 7, 1847, by Rev. W[illia]m Bliss Ashley	1	289
Henry Beers, m. Betsey Ann **WHITNEY,** Sept. 27, 1840, by John D. Smith	1	171
Julia E., of New Haven, m. Joseph N. **RIGGS,** of Oxford, Apr. 2, 1835, by Zepheniah Swift	1	177

	Vol.	Page
BEECHER, BEACHER, (cont.)		
Laura B., of N[ew] H[aven], m. Jonathan COLLINS, of		
Branford, Nov. 17, 1852, by Rev. Thomas T. Guion	1	236
Lowes, m. Nathan FAIRCHILD, Apr. 24, 1765	TM1	9
Lydia, of New Haven, m. Gideon JOHNSON, of Derby,		
Mar. 24, 1749	LR6	6
Milo, m. Mary A. TOLLES, b. of Bethany, May 5, 1833, by		
Rev. Stephen Jewett	1	147
Philo, m. Sally Maria MOSHER, Jan. 27, 1840, by John		
D. Smith	1	189
Polly, m. Nehemiah TOLLES, Dec. 4, 1836, by John D. Smith	1	181
Sarah, m. Timothy BALDWIN, Jan. 15, 1744/5	LR5	4
Sarah, m. Edwin BUCKINGHAM, Oct. 4, 1835, by John D.		
Smith	1	148
BEERS, Abel, of Newtown, m. Harriet LOSEE, of Derby, Sept.		
11, 1836, by Rev. John E. Bray	1	168
Abigail, m. Noah TOMLINSON, July 2, 1747	LR5	4
Charles C., m. Henrietta G. GILBERT, b. of Derby, Jan.		
18, 1835, by Rev. Z. Swift	1	146
Jonathan, m. Darcos WISEBURY, b. of Derby, Apr. 6, 1768,		
by Rev. Mr. Daniel Humphry	TM1	37
Sarah, m. Joseph TOMLINSON, May 24, 1743	LR4	A4
Sarah M., m. Conrad STEUCKMAN, b. of Derby, Oct. 15, 1848,		
by Rev. W[illia]m Denison	1	441
William P., m. Jane M. HOLBROOK, Mar. 15, 1848, by Rev.		
W[illia]m B. Curtiss	1	208
BELDEN, David P., m. Emiline Jane ALABY, Feb. 1, 1847, by		
Rev. George L. Fuller	1	208
BEMAN, BEAMAN, BEAMANT, George, m. [ ], Aug. 28, 1679,		
by Mr. W[illia]m Jon[e]s	A1	9
George, s. George, b. Jun[e], 1, 1683	2	2
Martha, d. Georg[e] & Mary, b. July 21, 1697	2	31
Martha, m. Joseph SMITH, Oct. 11, 1722	LR3	9
Mary, m. John WEED, Dec. 17, 1702	2	13
Mary, d. June 15, 1724	LR3	6
Mary, d. George, [ ]	2	1
Young, s. Georg[e], d. Dec. 20, 1692	2	27
-----, s. George, b. Feb. 11, 1685	2	2
BEMER, Eliza Ann, m. Sidney ALLEN, b. of Derby, Sept. 12, 1830,		
by Rev. Zepheniah Swift	1	107
BENEDICT, Sherwood Blair, m. [ ], Sept. 19, 1833, by		
Zepheniah Swift	1	147
BENHAM, Daniel, Rev. of Newtown, m. Mrs. Hannah BLAKESLEE,		
of Derby, Nov. 19, 1823, by Rev. Stephen Jewett	1	100
Jarius N., of Woodbridge, m. Elizabeth Ann CURTISS,		
of Derby, May 18, 1843, by Rev. W[illia]m Bliss Ashley	1	205
BENJAMINE, [S]amuell, s. wid. Mary, d. Dec. 29, 1684	2	2
BENNIT, Deborah, Mrs., m. Sam[ue]ll BASSITT, Jan. 1, 1719	LR4	A4

	Vol.	Page

BENTLY, Ellen, m. Jesse **MOORE**, b. of Ansonia, Nov. 27, 1851,
by David Osborn   1   358

BERDEM, Daniel S., m. Clary **LEWIS**, Oct. 14, 1822, by Rev.
Stephen Jewett   1   85

BIRCH, George, m. Phebe Ann **TOWNSEND**, of Fishkill, N. Y.
(colored) [   ], by Rev. N. S. Richardson. Recorded Dec.
2, 1845   1   207

BIRDSEY, BIRDSEYE, Caroline, m. David **NATHANS**, Mar. 24,
1850, by Rev. Cha[rle]s Dickinson   1   358

Caroline, m. David **NATHANS**, Mar. 24, 1850, by Rev.
Cha[rle]s Dickinson   1   381

Eunice, m. Nathan **BOOTH**, Jr., s. Nathan & Comfort, Nov.
7, 1770, (Book of Marriages, page 77, Huntington Rec.)   1   215

Philo C., m. Sarah **TUCKER**, Dec. 25, 1843, by Rev. W[illia]m
Bliss Ashley   1   205

BISHOP, Charles L., of Meriden, m. Emily M. **COCHRANE**, of
Derby, Nov. 29, 1849, by Rev. W[illia]m Denison   1   210

BIZELL, Abigail, m. Joseph **TOWNER**, Jan. 4, 1743/4   LR5   4

BLACHLY, Benjamin, of Norwalk, m. Mrs. Lydia **DEPLANK**,
of Derby, Sept. 15, 1757   LR6   451

BLACKMAN, Anne, m. Thomas **SILBY**, Oct. 12, 1756   LR6   445

Charity Mary, of Huntington, m. Judson **BALDWIN**, Jan. 29,
1837, by Rev. Joseph Scott   1   168

Elisha, m. Julia M. **BALDWIN**, b. of Derby, Dec. 22, 1839,
by H. Read   1   171

George, m. Julia Ann **TOMLINSON**, Jan. 6, 1823, by Rev.
Zephiniah Swift   1   84

Gershom, s. Ann **CHATFIELD**, d. Sept. 14, 1751   LR6   5

BLAKE, David, s. Jeremiah & Mary, b. Apr. 9, 1759   LR6   440

Esther, of Derby, m. Henry **TUTTLE**, of New Haven, Dec. 25,
1832, by Rev. S. Jewett   1   181

Harriet, of Derby, m. Isaac H. **TYRREL**, of Newtown, Dec.
5, 1830, by Rev. S. Jewett   1   104

Isaac, m. Marmre **CLARK**, Feb. 3, 1843, by John D. Smith   1   205

Jennette Minnerva, m. Lyman Albert **CLINTON**, b. of Derby,
Apr. 6, 1837, by John D. Smith   1   150

Mary, of New Preston, now of Derby, m. William **GREEN**,
of Sharon, May 13, 1832, by Prince Hawes   1   157

Mary Ann, m. Isaiah Smith **CLINTON**, b. of Derby, Aug. 2,
1838, by Rev. Joseph Scott   1   152

William, m. Elizabeth **CLARK**, Mar. 8, 1842, by John D. Smith   1   205

BLAKELELY, Amos Benham, of New Haven, m. Lucy Ann
BALDWIN, Oct. 11, 1832, by Rev. Zepheniah Swift   1   147

BLAKEMAN, Birdseye, m. Anna M. **TOMLINSON**, Jan. 29, 1850,
by Cha[rle]s Dickinson, Bishop   1   211

Julia A., m. Isaac P. **JACOBS**, July 13, 1846, by Rev.
George Thacher   1   325

Marcus A., m. Polly Maria **HUBBEL**, Apr. 13, 1851, by

	Vol.	Page

BLAKEMAN, (cont.)

Rev. Ja[me]s N. Mershon — 1 — 211

BLAKESLEE, BLAKESLY, Betsey, of North Haven, m. Isaac
FREDON, of New Preston, Sept. 8, 1832, by Rev. Charles
Thompson — 1 — 154

Daniel, of Roxbury, m. Myra SMITH, of Derby, June 19, 1844,
by Rev. George Thacher — 1 — 206

Hannah, Mrs. of Derby, m. Rev. Daniel BENHAM, of Newtown,
Nov. 19, 1823, by Rev. Stephen Jewett — 1 — 100

Henry, of Plymouth, m. Betsey GILLET, of Roxbury, Apr.
6, 1837, by Rev. John E. Bray — 1 — 166

Sally Mansfield, m. Dr. Pearl CRAFTS, Dec. 24, 1812, by Rev.
Richard Mansfield — 1 — 87

BLAND, John A., m. Elizabeth TERREL, Dec. 2, 1841, by John D.
Smith — 1 — 190

John A., m. Mrs. Caroline E. JOYCE, Dec. 19, 1844, by Rev.
John D. Smith — 1 — 206

BLANNETT, Jane, of Humphreysville, m. Robert HITCHCOCK, of
Springfield, Mass., Mar. 24, 1850, by Rev. S. Howland — 1 — 291

BLISS, Lemuel, of West Springfield, Mass., m. Emeline FRENCH,
of Derby, June 10, 183[ ], by Rev. John E. Bray — 1 — 146

BLONCY, John, m. Catherine ROCHE, Feb. 15, 1[8]52, by Rev.
James Lynch of Birmingham — 1 — 213

BLOOMFIELD, Mary, of Derby, m. Samuel KIDD, of England, Mar.
18, 1821, by Rev. Zephaniah Swift — 1 — 101

Rebecca, m. Andrew JOHNSON, b. of Derby, Sept. 15, 1821, by
Rev. Abner Smith — 1 — 99

BOARDMAN, BOADMAN, Hannah M., of Humphreyville, m.
Alonzo M. CROSBY, of Litchfield, July 16, 1848, by Rev.
W[illia]m Denison — 1 — 234

James L., of Humphreysville, m. Harriet L. JOYCE, of
Huntington, July 16, 1848, by Rev. W[illia]m Denison — 1 — 209

William L., m. Marietta SCOTT, Apr. 2, 1840, by John D. Smith — 1 — 189

BODGE, John, m. Huldah ROWE, b. of Humphreysville, Sept. 10,
1845, by Samuel R. Hickcox — 1 — 207

BOOTH, Abell, s. Zachariah & Sarah, b. Feb. 6, 1742/3 (vol. 5,
page 31, Stratford Rec.) — 1 — 215

Abijah, s. Zechariah & Sarah, b. Jan. 12, 1744/5 (vol. 5,
page 31, Stratford Rec.) — 1 — 215

Agur, s. Zachariah & Sarah, b. [ ] 3, 1749, (vol. 5, page
31, Stratford Rec.) — 1 — 215

Agur, s. Nathan & Eunice, b. Dec. 12, 1779 (Book of
Marriages, page 77, Huntington Rec.) — 1 — 216

Anna, d. Richard, b. Sept. 14, 1643 (Stratford Rec., vol. 1,
page 24 — 1 — 214

Anna, d. Richard of Stratford, b. Sept. 14, 1643 — 1 — 218

Anna, d. Zachariah & Sarah, b. Feb. 13, 1737/8 (vol. 5,
page 31, Stratford Rec.) — 1 — 215

	Vol.	Page

BOOTH, (cont.)

Bethia, d. Richard, b. Aug. 18, 1658 (vol. 1, page
24, Stratford Rec.) — 1 — 214

Bethia, d. Richard of Stratford, b. Aug. 18, 1658 — 1 — 218

Charity, d. Nathan & Eunice, b. July 9, 1773 (Book of
Marriages, page 77, Huntington Rec.) — 1 — 215

Charity, d. Nathan & Eunice, m. Nathan LEWIS, s. Abel &
Hannah (CLARK), Sept. [ ], 1793 — 1 — 216

Charity, see Charity (BOOTH) LEWIS — 1 — 217

Comfort, w. Nathan, d. Jan. 19, 1772, ae 53 y. (vol. 5,
Stratford Rec.) — 1 — 215

Daniel, s. Zachariah & Anna, b. Feb. 6, 1723/4 (vol. 2,
page 487, Stratford Rec.) — 1 — 214

Deborah, of Stratford, m. John PRINGLE, of Derby, May 31,
1709, by Joseph Curtiss — 3 — 451

Eben, s. Nathan & Eunice, b. Jan. 1, 1782, (Book of
Marriages, page 77, Huntington Rec.) — 1 — 216

Ebenezer, s. Richard, b. Nov. 19, 1651 (Stratford Rec.
vol. 1, page 24) — 1 — 214

Ebenezer, s. Richard of Stratford, b. Nov. 19, 1681 — 1 — 218

Elijah, s. Nathan & Comfort, b. June 14, 1746; d. Sept.
14, 1747 (vol. 5, Stratford Rec.) — 1 — 215

Elijah, s. Nathan & Comfort, b. Feb. 7, 1759; d. Nov.
5, 1778 (vol. 5, Stratford Rec.) — 1 — 215

Elizabeth, d. Richard, b. Sept. 10, 1641 (Stratford Rec.
vol. 1, page 24) — 1 — 214

Elizabeth, d. Richard of Stratford, b. Sept. 10, 1641 — 1 — 218

Ephraim, s. Richard, b. Aug. 1, 1648, (Stratford Rec.
vol 1, page 24) — 1 — 214

Ephraim, s. Richard of Stratford, b. Aug. 1, 1648 — 1 — 218

Hezekiah, s. Zachariah & 2nd w. Sarah, b. July 27, 1736;
d. Dec. 27, 1737, (vol. 5, page 31, Stratford Rec.) — 1 — 215

Hilkiah, s. Zachariah & Sarah, b. Dec. 19, 1739 (vol. 5,
page 31, Stratford Rec.) — 1 — 215

Johannah, d. Richard of Stratford, b. Mar. 21, 1661 — 1 — 218

John, s. Richard, b. Nov. 5, 1653 (Stratford Rec. Vol.
1, page 24) — 1 — 214

John, s. Richard of Stratford, b. Nov. 5, 1653 — 1 — 218

Joseph, s. Richard, b. Mar. 8, 1656 (Stratford Rec. vol.
1, page 24) — 1 — 214

Joseph, s. Richard of Stratford, b. Mar. 8, 1656 — 1 — 218

Joseph, Sr., d. Aug. 31, 1703 (vol. 2, page 485, Stratford Rec.) — 1 — 214

Joseph, s. Richard, had sons, James, Joseph, Robert, Nathan,
Zechariah & David, b. [ ] (vol. 2, page 406-7 Stratford
Rec.) — 1 — 214

Lucius, s. Nathan & Eunice, b. Nov. 1, 1790 (Book of
Marriages, page 77, Huntington Rec.) — 1 — 216

Nathan, s. Zachariah & Anna, b. Feb. 27, 1719/20 (vol.

	Vol.	Page
BOTCHFORD, (cont.)		
[ ]er, d. Sam[ue]ll & Hannah, b. Jan. 7, 1737/8	LR3	11
BOTSFORD, [see also BOTCHFORD & BOXFORD], Abby		
Minerva, m. Perry **CADWELL**, b. of Derby, Jan. 22, 1837,		
by John D. Smith	1	150
Betsey, m. Lucius **BOTSFORD**, b. of Derby, Oct. 6, 1836, by		
Rev. John E. Bray	1	168
Diantha, m. Isaac **FOOT**, b. of Derby, Apr. 30, 1837, by John		
D. Smith	1	155
Experience, of Derby, m. Timothy **SCOVILLE**, of Oxford, Dec.		
3, 1820, by Rev. Abner Smith	1	117
Frederic T., of Woodbury, m. Augusta B. **CANFIELD**, of		
Derby, Dec. 24, 1841, by Rev. Joseph Scott	1	189
Grace, m. Isaac **ALLEN**, Oct. 9, 1825, by Rev. Abner Smith	1	105
Isaac, Jr., m. Mary Jenett **MILES**, b. of Derby, Dec. 21, 1828		
by Rev. Stephen Jewett	1	88
Lucinda, m. Leverett **SCHOVIL**, Mar. 11, 1822, by Rev.		
Abner Smith	1	117
Lucius, m. Betsey **BOTSFORD**, b. of Derby, Oct. 6, 1836, by		
Rev. John E. Bray	1	168
Maria, of Woodbridge, m. Daniel M. **LYONS**, of Derby, May		
9, 1847, by Rev. Sylvester Smith	1	341
Mary S., m. Charles R. **MOWREN**, Feb. 10, 1840, by John D.		
Smith	1	167
Samuel, of Derby, m. Jane **DAVIS**, of Newtown, Aug. 20, 1845,		
by Rev. W[illia]m Bliss Ashley	1	207
Sarah, m. Abraham **COLLINS**, Nov. 2, 1847, by Rev. W[illia]m		
B. Curtiss	1	234
Treat, m. Caroline **CANFIELD**, Jan. 5, 18[ ], by John D. Smith	1	146
BOUGHTON, Eliza, of Waterbury, m. Horace **RANFORD**, of Derby,		
Nov. 9, 1834, by Sylvester Smith	1	177
Emily, m. Andrew **HARTSHORN**, Jan. 5, 1840, by John D.		
Smith	1	158
Lucy, of Waterbury, m. Lewis **SPENCER**, of Derby, Dec. 28,		
1835, by Sylvester Smith	1	179
Maria, of Waterbury, m. Pearl **HUBBLE**, of Derby, Nov. 27,		
1834, by Sylvester Smith	1	159
Mary, of Waterbury, m. Jerome **TUCKER**, of Oxford, July 30,		
1837, by Sylvester Smith	1	182
BOUTWELL, George B., m. Emerette **ROOT**, Apr. 4, 1852, by Rev.		
J. Guernsey	1	210
BOWERS, Anna, m. Ffrances **FFRENCH**, Sept. 2, 1703	2	13
Barbery, m. Samuell **MOSS**, Dec. 3, 1713	LR3	9
Bridget, Mrs., d. May 19, 1720	LR3	6
Jemima, d. Samuel & Lde (Lydia?), b. Nov. 30, 1696	2	26
John, d. Sept. 23, 1708	2	27
John, d. Jan. 26, 173[ ]	LR3	12
John, m. Sarah **RIGGS**, Nov. 22, 1732	LR3	10

	Vol.	Page

BOWERS, (cont,)

John & w. Sarah had d. [ ], b. Aug. 18, 1736	LR3	11
Josiah, d. Dec. 14, 1712	LR3	6
Kezziah, d. Sam[ue]l & Lydia, b. Mar. 2, 1698/9	2	12
Kezia, d. Samuel & Lidde, b. Mar. 2, 1699	2	31
Leddy, d. Samuel, b. Aug. 1, 1692	2	26
Lidia, m. Israeil MOSS, Dec. 31, 1717	LR3	9
Mary, Mrs., m. Samuell NICHOLS, May [ ], 1682, by Major Trea[ ]	2	1
Miriam, d. Sam[ue]l & Lydia, b. Apr. 5, 1703	2	12
Merriam, m. Ephraim WASHBON, Oct. 7, 1722	LR3	9
Nathaniel, d. Dec. 14, 1712	LR3	6
Nathaniel, s. Jno & Sarah, d. May 6, [ ]	LR3	12
Rebeckah, d. Samuel, b. Mar. 9, 1694	2	26
Rebecah, d. Dec. 7, 1712	LR3	6
Rebecka, d. Sam[ue]ll & Sarah, b. July 8, 1729	LR3	11
Sam[ue]l, m. Lydia FFRENCH, Nov. 4, 1691	2	13
Samuell, s. Samuell & Lydia, b. Dec. 22, [ ]	2	13
Sarah, m. Timothy WOOSTER, Mar. 22, 1737	LR5	4
Sarah, Mrs., m. Rev. Daniel HUMPHRY, Apr. 18, 1739	LR4	A4
Sarah, d. John & Sarah, d. Dec. 3, [ ]	LR3	12
Sarah, m. Agar TOMLINSON, Dec. 4, [ ]	LR3	10
-----, d. June 14, 1687	2	2
---ell, m. Ruth WO[O]STER, b. of [ ]	2	2

BOXFORD, [see also BOTCHFORD & BOTSFORD], Hannah, m.

John PRINGLE, Dec. 21, 1699	2	25

BOYCE, BOICE, Elisabeth S., m. Marvin WARNER, b. of Derby,

May 16, 1847, by Rev. W[illia]m Bliss Ashley	1	481
Jane, m. Jarvis RENODE, June 29, 1841, by Rev. Joseph Scott	1	184
Mary C., of Derby, m. Daniel H. WHEELER, of Huntington, Apr. 2, 1843, by Rev. I. B. Beach	1	481

BOYD, David W., m. Rebecca SMITH, b. of Derby, Nov. 20, 1848,

by Rev. Thomas T. Guion	1	212
David Willis, m. Rebecca SMITH, b. of Derby, Nov. 30, 1848, by Rev. Tho[ma]s T. Guion	1	209

BOYLE, Patrick, m. Mary Ann HEATER, Jan. 28, 1844, by George

Thacher	1	206

BRADLEY, BRADLY, Abijah, s. Enos & Hannah, b. Mar. 23, 1769

	TM1	41
Anna, d. Enos & Hannah, b. May 12, 1757	TM1	41
Burwell A., of New York, m. Emma NORTH, of Birmingham, Oct. 11, 1852, by Rev. Thomas G. Osborn, of Birmingham	1	211
David, s. Enos & Hannah, b. Feb. 25, 1771	TM1	41
Edward E., m. Grace TUCKER, b. of Derby, Nov. 18, 1838, by Rev. Orlando Starr	1	171
Elisha, s. Enos & Hannah, b. Nov. 13, 1760	TM1	41
Enos, m. Hannah PERSON, Nov. 7, 1751	LR6	6
Enos, m. Hannah PERSON, b. of Derby, Nov. 9, 1751, by Mr. Dickinson, of Norwalk	TM1	41

	Vol.	Page
BRADLEY, BRADLY, (cont.)		
Enos, s. Enos & Hannah, b. Jan. 14, 1759	TM1	41
Eunice, d. Enos & Hannah, b. Nov. 21, 1762	TM1	41
Hannah, d. Enos & Hannah, b. Jan. 14, 1754	LR6	4
Hannah, d. Enos & Hannah, b. Jan. 14, 1754	TM1	41
Hannah, of [Laneboro, Mass.], m. Sheldon C. **CURTISS**, Oct. 11, 1812, by Rev. Amos Pardee, of Laneboro, Mass.	1	87
Henry, m. Mary E. **UMBERFIELD**, Apr. 17, 1848, by Rev. W[illia]m B. Curtiss	1	209
Jane, of Derby, m. Alfreda **DAN**, of Oneida, N. Y., July 8, 1832, by Rev. Charles Thompson	1	149
Jane, of Derby, m. Alfred **DAN**, of Oneida, N. Y., July 8, 1832, by Charles Thompson	1	180
Jarius, m. Hannah **BUNNELL**, Feb. 23, 1853, by Rev. Charles Dickinson	1	212
Mabel, m. Samuel **CANDE**, Mar. 20, 1777	TM1	108
Maranda, of Derby, m. Merit **BROWN**, of East Haven, Nov. 25, 1830, by rev. Charls Thompson	1	90
Maria, of Derby, m. Dan **FENN**, of Milford, Mar. 26, 1834, by Zepheniah Swift	1	155
Maria, of Derby, m. Horace **CATERLINE**, of Newark, N. Y., Oct. 15, 1835, by Rev. Zepheniah Swift	1	150
Mary A., m. Edwin A. **PRATT**, Apr. 14, 1845, by Rev. George Thacher	1	407
Mary Ann, m. Henry **RIGGS**, Sept. 24, 1837, by John D. Smith	1	176
Nancy, d. Eldad & Charity (**HAWLEY**), b. Apr. 2, 1818; m. Thomas A. **WOOSTER**, s. Thomas R. & Lenonera (**MALLORY**), Sept. 27, 1840, by Rev. George Fuller; recorded Nov. 19, 1860	1	484
Nancy A., m. Ransom R. **MUNSON**, b. of Naugatuck, Mar. 13, 1850, by Rev. Sylvester Smith	1	358
Nathan, s. Enos & Hannah, b. May 15, 1767	TM1	41
Nathan N., of Waterbury, m. Caroline **ABBOTT**, of Middlebury, [Dec.] 19, [1847], by Rev. N. S. Richardson	1	208
Ruth, d. Enos & Hannah, b. Oct. 3, 1755	TM1	41
Samuel, s. Enos & Hannah, b. Jan. 23, 1765	TM1	41
Sarah, d. Enos & Hannah, b. July 27, 1752	LR6	5
Sarah, d. Enos & Hannah, b. July 27, 1752	TM1	41
BREWSTER, BRUSTER, Abigail, m. [ ], Feb. 21, 1725	LR3	9
Cyrus, Rev. of Montreal, L. C., m. Sarah Eliza **MILLS**, of Huntington, Aug. 29, 1842, by H. Read	1	205
Isaac, of New York, m. Catharine **BASSET**, June 4, 1834, by Zepheniah Swift	1	147
Sarah, m. Joseph **HAWKINS**, Nov. 17, 1720	LR3	9
BRIGDEN, Mary, of New Haven, m. David **HINE**, of Derby, Dec. 29, 1820, by Rev. Zephaniah Swift	1	97
BRINSMEAD, John, m. Abigail **WHEELER**, July 28, 1703	2	13
BRISTOL, BRISTOLL, Charles, of Milford, m. Harriet **BRADLEY,**		

	Vol.	Page
BRISTOL, BRISTOLL, (cont.)		

BRISTOL, BRISTOLL, (cont.)

of Derby, Sept. 12, 1830 — 1 — 106

George, m. Caroline **HULL**, b. of Derby, Sept. 30, [1835], by Rev. Joseph Scott — 1 — 148

Mark, m. Emma **DIS**-----, b. of Derby, Jan. 18, 1835, by Rev. Z. Swift — 1 — 146

Moses, s. Moses & Rachel, b. Sept. 3, 1753 — LR6 — 3

Nancy M., m. James H. **GRIFFEN**, Dec. 26, 1838, by Rev. Joseph Scott — 1 — 157

Nathan, m. Mary Ann **HAWLEY**, b. of Derby, Dec. 2, 1838, by Rev. Orlando Starr — 1 — 171

Sarah, d. Moses & Rachel, b. June 26, 1751 — LR6 — 3

Sarah, m. Ransom **WHEELER**, b. of Humphreyville, Jan. 29, 1832, by Rev. Stephen Jewett — 1 — 121

BROADBENT, John, m. Elizabeth **TIFFNY**, b. of Leeds, England, May 22, 1848, by Edward Wright — 1 — 209

BROADWELL, Elizabeth H., of Derby, m. John **SCOTT**, of Warsing, Ulster Co., N. Y., Mar. 23, 1843, by Rev. Sylvester Smith — 1 — 439

Harriet, m. Walter I. **MERRICK**, b. of Derby, Mar. 3, 1847, by Rev. Sylvester Smith — 1 — 357

BROCK, Amelia A., of Birmingham, m. Beach **HALL**, of Trumbull, Feb. 11, 1852, by Rev. Thomas G. Osborn — 1 — 292

BROCKWAY, Nicholas, m. Jane **SHEY**, Jan. 8, [18]52, by Rev. James Lynch, of Birmingham — 1 — 213

BRONSON, [see under **BRUNSON**]

BROWNSON, [see under **BRUNSON**]

BRUNSON, BROWNSON, BRONSON, Anna, d. David & Anna, b. Mar. 13, 1768 — TM1 — 10

Betsey, of New Milford, m. Abram **HAWKINS**, Jr., of Derby, Jan. 17, 1836, by Rev. Joseph Scott — 1 — 160

Betty, d. David & Anna, b. Aug. 4, 1772 — TM1 — 87

Betty, d. David & Anne, d. Nov. 27, 1776 — TM1 — 96

Billy Augustus, s. David & Anne, b. Sept. 25, 1776 — TM1 — 96

Clarissa, m. Sylvester **REDFIELD**, Jan. 23, 1837, by Sheldon Bassett, J. P. Witnesses: Jos[eph] P. Canfield, Isaac S. Gilbert, Elisha Hotchkiss — 1 — 176

David, Rev., of Derby, m. Mrs. Anna **CAMP**, of New Milford, June 4, 1765, by Rev. Nathaniel Tayler — TM1 — 19

David, s. David & Anna, b. Mar. 22, 1766 — TM1 — 14

David, s. David & Anne, b. Mar. 23, 1779 — TM1 — 97

David, s. David & Anne, d. Nov. 29, 1776 — TM1 — 96

Harvey D., of Derby, m. Elizabeth Ann **WADSWORTH**, of Hartford, Jan. 26, 1842, by Joseph Scott — 1 — 174

Martha, d. David & Anna, b. Apr. 4, 1770 — TM1 — 40

Martha, d. David & Anne, d. Nov. 18, 1776 — TM1 — 96

Mary J., of Derby, m. William J. **PATCHEN**, of Danbury, Sept. 15, 1839, by Sam[ue]l R. Hickcox. Witnesses: Samuel Hickcox, Hannah Oxborn — 1 — 173

	Vol.	Page

BRUNSON, BROWNSON, BRONSON, (cont.)

Miles L., m. Eunice **WARNER**, b. of Derby, Dec. 3, 1843, by
Rev. Zephaniah Swift — 1 — 205

Susan L., of Derby, m. Eli **RIGGS**, of Oxford, Sept. 31, 1835,
by Rev. John E. Bray — 1 — 177

BROOKS, BROOK, Daniel, m. Margaret **HUGHS**, Feb. 26, 1837, by
Rev. Joseph Scott — 1 — 168

Eunice, m. Jared **BUCKINGHAM**, May 1, 1764 — TM1 — 15

William, m. Hannah **LEDDLE**, Oct. 3, 1844, by Rev. W[illia]m
Bliss Ashely in Birmingham — 1 — 206

BROWN, Caroline, m. Francis **TUCKER**, Jan. 12, 1851, by Rev.
Cha[rle]s Dickinson — 1 — 462

Eunice, of Bethany, m. Byram **TUCKER**, of Oxford, Apr. 23,
1837, by Rev. John E. Bray — 1 — 182

Julia Ann, of Milford, m. William **ADDIS**, of Litchfield,
May 27, 1828, by John T. Wheeler, J. P. — 1 — 83

Merit, of East Haven, m. Maranda **BRADLEY**, of Derby, Nov.
25, 1830, by Rev. Charles Thompson — 1 — 90

BRUSTER, [see under **BREWSTER**]

BRYANT, Ezekiel D., of Sheffield, Mass., m. Lucy T. **MATHEWS**,
of Derby, Sept. 5, 1841, by Rev. Nathaniel Mead, of
Birmingham — 1 — 189

Martin, of New York, m. Sally **HARDYEAR**, of Derby, Sept. 19,
1824, by Rev. Stephen Jewett — 1 — 83

BRYSON, Leslie, Capt., m. Sarah E. **GILBERT**, Aug. 25, 1844,
by Rev. John D. Smith — 1 — 206

Maxwell, m. Mrs. Elizabeth **CHILSON**, July 9, 1815, by
Levi Tomlinson, J. P. — 1 — 89

BUCHANAN, Robert, m. Mary J. **OVIATT**, Oct. 27, 1851, by Rev. J.
Guernsey — 1 — 211

BUCK, Zepheniah, of East Guilford, m. Ruth **FOOT**, of Derby, May
11, 1823, by Rev. Abner Smith — 1 — 84

BUCKINGHAM, Edwin, m. Sarah **BEECHER**, Oct. 4, 1835, by John
D. Smith — 1 — 148

Eunice, d. Jared & Eunice, b. Mar. 1, 1765 — TM1 — 10

Isaac, s. Jared & Eunice, b. June 23, 1766 — TM1 — 10

Jared, m. Eunice **BROOK**, May 1, 1764 — TM1 — 15

Sally M., of Derby, m. Isaac **ROODE**, of Milford, Jan. 22, 1843,
by Rev. Nathaniel Mead — 1 — 425

Samuel, s. Jared & Eunice, b. Nov. 25, 1768 — TM1 — 10

William, m. Nancy **SMITH**, b. of New Haven, Nov. 10, 1835,
by Rev. Zepheniah Swift — 1 — 148

BUCKLEY, Catherine, m. Patrick **COLLINS**, June 22, 1851, by
Rev. James Lynch — 1 — 236

Charles, [s. Thomas & Betty], b. Oct. 29, 1819; recorded
Jan. 10, 1831 — D B — 152

Elizabeth Jane, [d. Thomas & Betty], b. Feb. 20, 1822;
recorded Jan. 10, 1831 — D B — 152

	Vol.	Page

BUCKLEY, (cont.)

Thomas, [s. Thomas & Betty], b. Sept. 22, 1814;
recorded Jan. 10, 1831 — DB 152

William, [s. Thomas & Betty], b. Oct. 6, 1817;
recorded Jan. 10, 1831 — DB 152

BUNNELL, BUNNEL, BUNEL, Alva, of Derby, m. Lucy **BARNES,**
of Plymouth, Feb. 28, 1836, by Rev. John E. Bray — 1 148

Amos N., of Plainville, m. Emma **STEPHENSON,** of Ansonia,
Sept. 12, 1852, by Rev. Owen Street, in Ansonia — 1 213

Amos O. N., of Plainville, m. Emma **STEPHENSON,** of
Ansonia, Sept. 12, 1852, by Rev. Owen Street — 1 212

Anne, m. David **WEBSTER,** Mar. 13, 1826, by Rev. Abner
Smith — 1 122

Benjamin, Jr., m. Ruth **SMITH,** b. of Derby, Oct. 10, 1752,
by Rev. Jonathan Lyman — LR6 444

Benjamin, s. Benjamin & Ruth, b. July 19, 1763 — LR7 252

Benjamin, of Waterbury, late of Derby, d. Nov. 5, 1770 — TM1 48

Caroline E., m. Lorenzo **TRUESDALE,** b. of Derby, Nov. 10,
1844, by Rev. Samuel R. Hickcox, of Humphreysville — 1 461

Catherine, m. Samuel **KNAPP,** b. of Derby, Nov. 10, [1839],
by Rev. J. B. Beach — 1 192

Catharine C., m. Sheldon **CHATFIELD,** b. of [Oxford], Jan.
4, 1835, by Rev. Samuel R. Hickox. Witnesses: Samuel
Hickox, Sarah Hickox — 1 146

Charles, s. Benjamin & Mehtebell, d. July 26, 1758,
in the 20th y. of his age, between Fort Edward & Lake
George in the Kings Seruice — LR6 440

Charles, s. Benjamin & Ruth, b. Jan. 19, 1759 — LR6 451

Elizabeth, m. Willard **BARNS,** Jan. 2, 1823, by Rev.
Abner Smith — 1 84

Elisabeth Ann, d. Benjamin & Ruth, b. Apr. 12, 1771 — TM1 63

Hannah, m. Jarius **BRADLEY,** Feb. 23, 1853, by Rev. Charles
Dickinson — 1 212

Horace, m. Fanny **SPERRY,** Nov. 16, 1840, by John D. Smith — 1 189

Isaac, s. Isaac & Ann, b. May 11, 1759 — TM1 59

Jane E., m. Isaac **LOSEE,** b. of Humphreysville, Oct. 15,
1848, by Rev. Charles Stearns, at Humphreysville — 1 342

Lucinda, m. Christopher **SMITH,** Jan. 4, 1823, by Rev.
Abner Smith — 1 117

Luke, s. Benjamin & Mehetabel, d. Oct. 23, 1756, at
Cannan, "in the Kings Service" — LR6 440

Luke, s. Isaac & Ann, b. Feb. 28, 1758 — TM1 59

Luke, m. Betty **BATES,** b. of Derby, Mar. 31, 1785 — TM1 158

Mehethebel, d. Isaac & Ann, b. Feb. 6, 1765 — TM1 59

Philemon, s. Isaac & Ann, b. Sept. 27, 1767 — TM1 59

Ruben, s. Benjamin & Ruth, b. Dec. 24, 1765 — TM1 11

Russel R., m. Alesia W. **KING,** b. of Derby, June 6, 1841,
by Rev. Hollis Read — 1 174

	Vol.	Page
BUNNELL, BUNNEL, BUNEL, (cont.)		
Sarah A., of Oxford, m. William H. **THORNTON**, of Baltimore, Md., Nov. 21, 1842, by Rev. Nathaniel Mead	1	461
William, s. Isaac & Ann, b. Dec. 16, 1761	TM1	59
BURGES, Maria, of Derby, m. John **MEAD**, of Albany, N. Y., Sept. 16, 1838, by Rev. Joseph Scott	1	167
BURK, Michael, m. Bridget **MACKEY,** July 13, 1851, by Rev. James Lynch of Birmingham	1	213
BURNER (?)*, Lucretia Ann, m. Frederick W. **PARRIOTT,** Apr. 8, 1827, by Rev. Zepheniah Swift *(Perhaps "BURNES")	1	111
BURNS, BURNES, Diana, m. Nicholas **PENFIELD,** Oct. 12, 1840, by John D. Smith	1	156
Lucretia Ann*, m. Frederick W. **PARRIOTT,** Apr 8. 1827, by Rev. Zepheniah Swift *(Perhaps "Lucretia Ann **BURNER")**	1	111
Nancy S., m. Thomas **GAORDON,** b. of Milford, Nov. 30, 1837, by Thomas Ellis	1	157
BURR, Hildah, of Trumble, m. Elias **CLARK,** of Woodbury, Mar. 27, 1834, by Rev. Luther Meed	1	149
BURRITT, BURRETT, BURRIT, Abel, s. William & Mary, b. June 17, 1777	TM1	155
Becky, d. William & Sarah, b. June 9, 1789; d. Aug. 4, 1790	TM1	155
Ely, m. Charlotte C. **HAWKINS,** Nov. 7, 1841, by John D. Smith	1	174
Eunice, d. William & Mary, b. Mar. 13, 1773	TM1	155
Eunice, d. William & Mary, d. Aug. 17, 1794	TM1	155
Isaac, s. William & Mary, b. Dec. 15, 1775	TM1	155
John, s. William & Mary, b. Sept. 18, 1782	TM1	155
Lewis, s. William & Mary, b. Aug. 6, 1772	TM1	155
Lewis, d. May 17, 1776, in the 31st y. of his age	TM1	123
Mary, w. William, d. Mar. 7, 1784	TM1	155
Mary, d. William & Sarah, b. July 16, 1785	TM1	155
Patte, d. William & Mary, b. Apr. 15, 1766	TM1	155
Samuel, s. William & Mary, b. Apr. 8, 1780	TM1	155
Sarah, m. Leveret **HOTCHKISS,** Aug. 14, 1785, by Rev. Martin Tuller	TM1	164
Sarah Lewis, d. William & Mary, b. Jan. 3, 1763	LR7	256
Sarah Lewis, d. William & Mary, b. Jan. 3, 1763	TM1	155
William, m. Mary **FRENCH,** Apr. 22, 1762	TM1	155
William m. Mary **FRENCH,** b. of Derby, Apr. 22, 1762, by Rev. Richard Mansfield	LR7	256
William, s. William & Mary, b. Oct. 24, 1764	TM1	155
William, m. Sarah **BALDWIN,** Apr. 24, 1784	TM1	155
BURROUGHS, Daniel I., m. Almira **FOOT,** b. of Derby, Mar. 12, 1843, by Rev. H. Read	1	205
Daniel I., m. Almira **FOOT,** b. of Derby, Mar. 12, 1843, by Rev. H. Read	1	439
BURTON, Comfort, d. Judson & Comfort, b. July 3, 1768	TM1	74

Vol.   Page

BURTON, (cont.)

	Vol.	Page
Comfort, w. Judson, d. May 2, 1771	TM1	74
Judson, s. Judson & Eunice, b. Sept. 14, 1730, in Stratford	TM1	74
Judson, m. Comfort **KEENEY**, Nov. 23, 1758, by Rev. Daniel Humphry	TM1	74
Judson, m. Comfort **KEENEY**, Nov. 23, 1758	LR7	248
Judson, s. Judson & Comfort, b. Jan. 5, 1764	TM1	74
Judson, s. Judson & Comfort, d. Apr. 12, 1765	TM1	74
Lewis, s. Judson & Comfort, b. Apr. 14, 1762	TM1	74
Nathaniel, s. Judson & Comfort, b. Mar. 15, 1760	TM1	74
Nathaniel, s. Judson & Comfort, d. June 27, 1764	TM1	74
Nathaniel, d. Judson & Comfort, b. Jan. 18, 1766	TM1	74

BURWELL, Eunice, d. Stephen & Sibillah, b. Jan. 28, 1765 — TM1 — 30
Luce, d. Stephen & Sibillah, b. Feb. 28, 1763 — TM1 — 30
Samuel, s. Stephen & Sibillah, b. Apr. 28, 1767 — TM1 — 30
Stephen, m. Sibbillah **TOMLINSON**, Aug. 12, 1754 — LR6 — 451
Stephen, s. Stephen & Sibillah, b. Dec. 31, 1760 — TM1 — 30
Sibbillah, d. Stephen & Sibillah, b. Mar. 10, 1756 — LR6 — 442

BUSTER, [see under **BREWSTER**]

BUTLER, Eunice M., m. Newel **WARNER**, Aug. 2, 1840, by Rev. Sm[ue]l R. Hickox — 1 — 186
William, of Derby, m. Rebbecca Ann **BASSETT**, of Oxford, Mar. 28, 1841, by Rev. Samuel R. Hickcox — 1 — 174

CADWELL, Perry, m. Abby Minerva **BOTSFORD**, b. of Derby, Jan. 22, 1837, by John D. Smith — 1 — 150

CAINE, Charlotte D., m. Merrit **CLARK**, b. of Derby, Jan. 2, 1841, by Rev. Sylvester Smith — 1 — 153
Hannah, Mrs., m. John **TOWNER**, June 26, 1759 — LR6 — 445

CAMP, Anna, Mrs. of New Milford, m. Rev. David **BROWNSON**, of Derby June 4 , 1765, by Rev. Nathaniel Tayler — TM1 — 19
Hannah Maria, of Woodbridge, m. Julius **BALDWIN**, of New Hartford, Sept. 23, 1838, by Rev. Zepheniah Swift — 1 — 153
Jane, m. Mathew **ALLEN**, June 28, 1847, by Rev. W[illia]m B. Curtiss — 1 — 193
Mary, of Orange, m. George **BALDWIN**, of Huntington, Sept. 18, 1842, by Zephaniah Swift — 1 — 205
Mary A., m. Abner S. **BALDWIN**, May 26, 1833, by Zepheniah Swift — 1 — 147
Olive, m. Francis **FRENCH**, b. of Derby, Dec. 19, 1779 — TM1 — 130

CAMPION, Ellen, m. Pat **DUTTON**, Sept. 18, 1851, by Rev. James Lynch — 1 — 248
Margaret, m. James **HOLLARON**, Aug. 3, 1851, by Rev. James Lynch — 1 — 292

CAN----, Anna Addaline, m. Samuel **HINE**, b. of Oxford, Jan. 20, 1828, by Rev. Stephen Jewett — 1 — 122

CANDEE, CANDE, Amos, s. Samuel & Mabel, b. Oct. 18, 1777 — TM1 — 108
Benjamin, s. Samuel & Mabel, b. Feb. 18, 1779 — TM1 — 108
Gideon, m. Ame **ANDRUSS**, b. of Derby, May 14, 1772 — TM1 — 75a

	Vol.	Page
CANDEE, CANDE, (cont.)		
Gideon, s. Gideon & Amy, b. July 7, 1784	TM1	161
Hulday, d. Gideon & Amy, b. May 16, 1782	TM1	161
Jennett, m. Luther **MOTHROP**, Dec. 19, 1830, by Rev. Charles		
Thompson	1	90
Nehemiah, m. Content **WOODRUFF**, Dec. 6, 1780	TM1	64
Samuel, m. Mabel **BRADLY**, Mar. 20, 1777	TM1	108
Sarah, d. Gideon & Ame, b. Dec. 16, 1773	TM1	75a
Serene, d. Gideon & Amy, b. Aug. 17, 1786	TM1	161
CANFIELD, CANFEILD, Abel, s. Abiram & Ruth, d. Mar. 13,		
1740/1	LR4	A5
Abel, s. William & Hannah, b. May 29, 1755	LR6	4
Abiel, s. Abiram & Ruth, b. May 31, 172[ ]	LR3	4
Abiel, s. Joseph & Sarah, b. Apr. 6, 1753	LR7	252
Abiel, of Derby, m. Mary **BARLOW**, of Stratford, Dec. 23, 1779	TM1	76
Abijah, s. Dr. Josiah & Naomi, b. Sept. 9, 1769	TM1	49
Abijah, s. Dr. Josiah & Noami, b. Sept. 9, 1769	TM1	82
Abiram, m. Ruth **WASHBON**, Sept. 12, 1717	LR3	9
Abraham, s. Joseph & Sarah, b. June 20, 1759	LR7	252
Ann, d. Joseph & Sarah, b. Oct. 17, 1751	LR7	252
Ann, m. Joseph **RIGGS**, 3rd b. of Derby, Nov. 13, 1775	TM1	71
Anne, w. Dr. Josiah, d. Oct. 20, 1768	TM1	49
Anne, w. Dr. Josiah, d. Oct. 20, 1768	TM1	82
Augusta B., of Derby, m. Frederic T. **BOTSFORD**, of		
Woodbury, Dec. 24, 1841, by Rev. Joseph Scott	1	189
Bette, d. John & Martha, b. Mar. 26, 1756	LR7	248
Betty, m. James **BASSIT**, b. of Derby, Mar. 28, 1780	TM1	129
Caroline, m. Treat **BOTSFORD**, Jan. 5, 18[ ], by John		
D. Smith	1	146
Charity, d. Joseph & Sarah, b. Feb. 1, 1758; d. Feb. 2, 1758	LR7	252
Charlotte, m. Peter C. **TOMLINSON**, b. of Derby, Nov. 16,		
1828, by Rev. S. Jewett	1	119
Daniel, s. Joseph & Sarah, b. Mar. 21, 1761	LR7	252
David, s. Abiram & Ruth, b. Feb. 5, 1733/4	LR4	A3
Dauid, s. Abiram & Ruth, d. Nov. 23, 1741	LR4	A5
David, s. John & Martha, b. Nov. 6, 7854	LR7	248
Eliza A., m. Sidney **DOWNS**, b. of Derby, Oct. 22, 1828,		
by Rev. Stephen Jewett	1	89
Elisabeth, w. John, d. Sept. 8, 1751	LR7	248
Emeline, of Derby, m. John K, **CLEAVELAND**, of Winsted,		
Dec. 25, 1833, by Sheldon Curtiss	1	149
Esther, m. Sheldon **KINNE**, Jan. 27, 1822, by Rev. Abner Smith	1	101
Eunice, d. John & Martha, b. Nov. 17, 1760	LR7	248
Hannah, d. William & Hannah, b. May 30, 1756	LR6	13
Horace, of New York, m. Janett **HUMPHREYS**, of		
Humphreysville, Sept. 22, 1825, by Stephen Jewett	1	105
John, s. Abiram & Ruth, b. Mar. 31, 1721	LR3	5
John, m. Elisabeth **JOHNSON**, b. of Derby, Mar. [ ], 1751, by		

	Vol.	Page
CANFIELD, CANFEILD, (cont.)		
Rev. Daniel Humphry	LR7	248
John, m. Mrs. Martha **JUDD,** b. of Derby, Nov. 20, 1753, by		
Rev. Daniel Humphry	LR7	248
Joseph, s. Abiram & Ruth, b. Oct. 1, 1719	LR3	3
Joseph, m. Sary **STILSON,** Sept. 3, 1746	LR5	4
Joseph E., m. Catharine A. **RIGGS,** b. of Derby, Oct. 18, 1848,		
by Rev. George Thatcher	1	235
[J]osiah, s. Abiram & Ruth, b. Dec. 22, 1729	LR3	15
Josiah, s. Abiram & Ruth, d. Jan. 1, 1730	LR3	12
Josiah, s. Abiram & Ruth, b. Dec. 31, 1738/9	LR4	A3
Josiah, Dr. of Derby, m. Anne **NICHOLS,** of Nutown, Jan.		
1, 1767	TM1	49
Josiah, Dr. of Derby, m. Anne **NICKOLS,** of New Town, Jan. 1,		
1767	TM1	82
Josiah, Dr., m. Naomi **DAVIS,** b. of Derby, Feb. 28, 1768	TM1	49
Josiah, Dr., m. Mrs. Naomi **DAVIS,** b. of Derby, Feb. 28, 1768	TM1	82
Josiah B, m. Jane **DAVIS,** b. of Derby, Oct. 14, 1830, by		
Rev. S. Jewett	1	95
Judson, m. Sarah **MILES,** Nov. 28, 1836, by John D. Smith	1	150
Maria, m. Joseph Harvey **REMER,** b. of Derby, Aug. 4, 1834,		
by Rev. Joseph Scott	1	177
Mary F., m. W[illia]m Leroy **CANFIELD,** b. of Derby, Dec. 20,		
1852, by Rev. Thomas T. Guion	1	236
Mary Jane, m. Charles **TOMLINSON,** b. of Derby, Nov. 10,		
1831, by Rev. Stephen Jewett	1	102
Mehitabel, m. Stephen **PERSON,** Jr., Oct. 12, 1697	2	25
Molle, d. John & Martha, b. June 1, 1758	LR7	248
Ruth, d. Joseph & Sarah, b. Feb. 20, 1750	LR7	252
Ruth, m. Ranford **WHITNEY,** Sept. 26, 1773	TM1	119
Sabra, d. Dr. Sam[ue]ll & Mary, b. Feb. 15, 1758	LR7	249
Sally, m. Sheldon **TUCKER,** b. of Derby, Aug. 5, 1835,		
by Sylvester Smith	1	181
Sam[ue]ll, s. Abiram, b. Dec. 26, 1727	LR3	15
Samuel, m. Mary **BASSIT,** Apr. 3, 1754	LR6	6
Samuel, s. Dr. Samuel & Mary, b. July 13, 1756	LR6	15
Sarah, d. Joseph & Sarah, b. Mar. 19, 1755	LR7	252
Seba, s. Dr. Sam[ue]ll & Mary, b. Jan. 2, 1762	LR7	250
Sheldon, Jr., of Derby, m. Charlotte Eliza **LUM,** of		
Camebridgeport, Mass., Nov. 10, 1831, by Rev. S. Jewett	1	103
Suze, d. Dr. Samuel & Mary, b. Nov. 6, 1759	LR7	250
William, s. Abiram & Ruth, b. Oct. 29, 1725	LR3	5
William, m. Hannah **LUMM,** May 6, 1754, by Timothy Russell	LR6	6
William, d. Sept. 30, 1761	LR7	254
William, of Derby, m. Minerviar **NETTLETON,** of Derby,		
May 9, 1822, by Bardsely Northrop	1	87
William, m. Lucy **BASSETT,** b. of Derby, Nov. 30, 1841,		
by Rev. Joseph Scott	1	154

	Vol.	Page
CANFIELD, CANFEILD, (cont.)		
W[illia]m Leroy, m. Mary F. CANFIELD, b. of Derby, Dec.		
20, 1852, by Rev. Thomas T. Guion	1	236
CARPENTER, Olive, m. Benjamin CRAWFORD, Mar. 14, 1775	TM1	92
Samuel T., Rev., of Sharon, m. Francis CHAMPLIN, of Derby,		
May 26, 1841, by Rev. D. Burhams	1	154
CARRINGTON, CARINGTON, CARRINTON, Albert, of Milford,		
m. Olive MERRIAM, of Watertown, Apr. 4, [ ]	1	106
Annah, m. Ephraim SMITH, Dec. 14, 1727	LR3	10
David, of Bethany, m. Elisabeth ROBINSON, of Bethany, Jan.		
17, 1847, by Rev. John Parves	1	234
Eliza A., m. John W. STORRS, Feb. 13, 1848, by Rev.		
W[illia]m C. Curtiss	1	440
Fanny, m. Preston LEWIS, b. of Woodbridge, Dec. 24, 1843, by		
Rev. Sylvester Smith	1	341
John, Dea., m. wid. Betsey RUSSELL, May 21, 1833, by		
Zepheniah Swift	1	149
Loly, Mrs., m. Capt. Josiah MERRICK, Dec. 10, 1843, by		
Rev. John D. Smith	1	357
CARTER, Mary A., m. Ephraim SHORT, Feb. 19, 1850, by Rev. Jno		
Morrison Reid	1	441
CARTERLINE, Horace, of Newark, N. J., m. Maria BRADLEY, of		
Derby, Oct. 15, 1835, by Zepheniah Swift	1	150
CASE, Amos B., m. Laura ROBINSON, Aug. 5, 1855, by Joseph P.		
Canfield, J. P.	1	237
CASTLE, Andrew, Dr., m. Phebe KIMBERLY, Apr. 30, 1843, by		
John D. Smith	1	233
Truman, m. Mrs. Laura C. PHELPS, Sept. 4, 1842, by Rev.		
John D. Smith	1	233
CAULKINS, David, of Lyme, m. Delia FRENCH, of Derby, Nov. 1,		
1829, by Z. Swift	1	103
CHAFFEE, Sarah M., m. Mansfield HALL, b. of Derby, Aug. 3,		
1851, by Rev. Thomas T. Guion	1	292
CHAMBERS, Jamima, d. Dec. 24, 1751	LR6	5
CHAMPLIN, Francis, of Derby, m. Samuel T. CARPENTER, Rev.		
of Sharon, May 26, 1841, by Rev. D. Burhams	1	154
CHAPIN, George W., of Hartford, m. Esther H. GAY, of Derby,		
Sept. 20, 1840, by Rev. W[illia]m Denison	1	235
CHAPMAN, Benjamin, m. Mrs. Abigail RIGGS, Jan. 8, 1756	LR6	8
Martha, m. Sam[ue]ll FRENCH, Dec. 17, 1733	LR3	10
Polly Ann, of Oxford, m. Thomas ROBINSON, of New Haven,		
Dec. 14, 1836, by Rev. John E. Bray	1	177
Rachel, m. John MURRY, b. of Derby, Feb. 17, 1766, by		
Rev. Dan[ie]ll Humphry	TM1	15
CHARLES, Betty, d. William & Margret, b. Nov. 6, 1771	TM1	73
Mary, d. William & Margret, b. Feb. 17, 1766	TM1	14
Mary, d. Feb. 27, 1826	1	513
CHATFIELD, CHATFEILD, CHATTFIELD, Abygal, d. John &		

	Vol.	Page
CHATFIELD, CHATFEILD, CHATTFIELD, (cont.)		
Annah, b. Sept. 2, 1693	2	26
Abigail, m. Gideon **JOHNSON**, Nov. 6, 1718	LR3	9
Abigail, m. Samuel **HAZELTON**, Sept. 16, 1755	LR6	8
Abigal, d. Ebenezer & Abigail, b. Jan. [ ]	LR3	16
Abijah, s. Oliver & Zeruiah, b. Oct. 8, 1767	TM1	59
Abraham, s. Sam[ue]ll & Joanna, b. Dec. 20, 1761	LR7	249
Almira, d. Joel & Ruth, b. June 23, 1791	TM1	143
Almira, m. John T. **WHEELER**, Mar. 25, 1824, by Rev.		
Stephen Jewett	1	122
Ann, had s. Gershom **BLACKMAN**, d. Sept. 14, 1751	LR6	5
Annah, d. John & Elizabeth, b. Apr. 15, 1732	LR3	16
Anne, m. David **HITCHCOCK**, b. of Derby, May 4, 1774	TM1	105
Bennet, of Oxford, m. Mary Ann **HOLBROOK**, of Derby,		
Dec. 23, 1830, by Rev. S. Jewett	1	90
Caroline, m. William Austin **LUM**, Nov. 27, 1838, by John		
D. Smith	1	164
Charles, m. Rhoda **GERARD**, b. of Derby, Jan. 3, 1841, by		
Rev. John B. Beach	1	192
Clark, of New York, m. J. A. **HOTCHKISS**, of Derby, Nov.		
22, 1852, by Rev. Thomas T. Guion	1	236
Comfort, m. Joseph **SERWOOD**, b. of Derby, Oct. 27, 1772	TM1	107
Dan, s. Oliver & Zurviah, b. Jan. 16, 1761	LR7	249
Dan, s. Oliver & Zurviah, b. Jan. 17, 1761	LR7	250
Ebenezar, s. John & Hannah, b. July 4, 1703	2	12
Ebenezar, m. Abigail **PRINGLE**, Nov. 20, 1728	LR3	10
[Ebenzer], s. Ebenezer & Abigal, b. Sept. 8, 1729	LR3	15
Ebenezer, m. Susannah **WATEROUS**, Mar. 23, 1768, by Rev.		
Richard Mansfield	TM1	17
Eli, m. Lowis **MALLERY**, Aug. 5, 1778	TM1	92
Elizabeth, d. John & Elizabeth, b. Mar. 9, 172[ ]	LR3	15
Elisabeth, m. John **SMITH**, Dec. 16, 1750	LR6	444
Elisabeth, w. Lieut. John, d. June 8, 1751	LR6	5
Elisabeth, d. Oliver & Zeruiah, b. Nov. 22, 1769	TM1	59
Easther, m. Benjamin **FOX**, Apr. 9, 1754	LR6	8
Esther, d. John & Elizabeth, b. Aug. 21, [ ]	LR3	16
Eunis, d. Solomon & Hannah, b. Feb. 6, 1742/3	LR4	A2
Hannah, m. John **COE**, b. of Derby, Sept. 8, 1755	TM1	56
Hannah, m. Abiel **FAIRCHILD**, Jr., Feb. 23, 1757	LR6	450
Isaac, s. Oliver & Zuruiah, b. Oct. 13, 1755	LR6	15
Isaac, s. Joel & Ruth, b. Jan. 15, 1787	TM1	143
Isaiah, of Oxford, m. Grace **HOLBROOK**, of Derby, Nov. 1,		
1820, by Rev. Abner Smith	1	87
Jane, of Oxford, m. Charles **HAWKINS**, of Derby, Sept. 24,		
1829, by Rev. Stephen Jewett	1	95
Joel, of Derby, m. Ruth **STODDARD**, of Woodbury, Nov. 13,		
1785	TM1	143
Joel R., m. Lucinda **HITCHCOCK**, May 7, 1826, by Rev.		

	Vol.	Page
CHATFIELD, CHATFEILD, CHATTFIELD, (cont.)		
Abner Smith	1	86
Joel R., of Derby, m. Mrs. Mary **WOOSTER,** of Oxford,		
[ ], by Rev. Joseph Scott; recorded June 26, 1837	1	150
John, m. Annah **HARGIER,** Feb. 5, 1684	2	25
John, s. John & Han[n]ah, b. Feb. 20, 1696/7	1	31
John, m. Elizabeth **JOHNSON,** Dec. 12, 1722	LR3	9
John, s. John, Jr., b. June 5, 1724	LR3	5
John, Jr., d. about Oct. 4, 1759	LR6	719
John L, of Bethany m. Mary Ann **RIGGS,** of Derby, May 1,		
1848, by Rev. George Thacher	1	234
Joseph, s. Sollomon & Hannah, b. Apr. 4, 1735	LR3	11
Joseph, of Derby, m. Dinah **PEAT,** of Stratford, Feb. 23, 1757,		
by Rev. Daniel Humphrey	LR6	8
Joseph, s. Oliver & Zerviah, b. June 29, 1772	TM1	85
Laman, s. Joel & Ruth, b. Feb. 18, 1789	TM1	143
Lemon, m. Sarah **DIBBLE,** b. of Derby, July 8, 1849, by Rev.		
S. Howland	1	235
Lemuruel, [twin with Leuy], s. Eben[ez]er & Abigal, b.		
Jan. 6, 1738	LR4	A3
Lemuel, twin with Levi, d. Sept. 30, 1758, ae 19 y. 9 m.,		
at Camp at Lake George	LR6	719
Leuy, [twin with Lemuruel], s. Eben[eze]r & Abigal, b.		
Jan. 6, 1738	LR4	A3
Leui, m. Abigail **HARGER,** b. of Derby, Jan. 30, 1758,		
by Rev. Richard Mansfield	LR6	444
Levi, s. Levi & Abigail, b. Aug. 26, 1758	LR6	719
Levi, twin with Lemuel, d. Oct. 15, 1758, ae 19 y. 9 m.	LR6	719
Levi, m. Sarah **BEARD,** b. of Derby, May 27, 1781	TM1	111
Lowis, m. Joseph **LOVELAND,** Aug. 18, 1762	TM1	75
Lucende, d. Eli & Lois, b. Oct. 10, 1784	TM1	118
Martha A., m. Andrew M. **BALDWIN,** b. of Woodbridge,		
[July] 24, 1836, by L. D. Howell	1	168
Martha A., of Bethany, m. S. Marshal **KISSAM,** of New York,		
Jan. 6, 1850, by Rev. S. Howland	1	330
Mary, d. Jno & Annah, b. Apr. 23, 1689	2	26
Mary, d. Sollomon & Hannah, b. Oct. 11, 1736	LR3	11
Mary, d. Sam[ue]ll & Ann, b. Jan. 18, 1749 /50	LR6	2
Mary, d. Sam[ue]ll & Ann, d. Sept. 18, 1751	LR6	5
Mary, d. Eli & Lois, b. Dec. 1, 1778	TM1	118
Mindwell, d. Ebenezer & Abigail, b. Sept. 9, 1735	LR3	11
Mindwell, m. Moses **WOOSTER,** June 20, 1759	LR7	248
Obedience, d. Lieut, John & Obedience, b. Dec. 11, 1755	LR6	15
Obedience, d. Eli & Lois, b. July 9, 1782	TM1	118
Olliuer, s. John & Elizabeth, b. July 23, 1730	LR3	15
Oliver, s. Oliver & Abiah, b. Oct. 16, 1758	LR6	443
Patience, d. Oliver & Zerviah, b. May 2, 1765	TM1	19
Samuel, s. John & Hannah, b. Aug. 28, 1699	2	31

	Vol.	Page
CHATFIELD, CHATFEILD, CHATTFIELD, (cont.)		
Samuel, s. Sam[ue]ll, Jr. & Joanna, b. Apr. 7, 1764	LR7	253
Sarah, d. Jno & Annah, b. Dec. 5, 1686	2	26
Sarah, m. John **DAVIS**, July 15, 1706, by Major Ebenezer Johnson	2	24
Sarah, d. John, b. Nov. 4, 1722	LR3	4
Sarah, m. John **DURAND**, June 2, 1747	LR6	450
Sarah, m. Samuel **TUCKER**, Aug. [ ], 1755, by Daniel Holbrook	LR6	445
Sarah, d. John & Sarah, b. Oct. 2, 1757	LR6	719
Sheldon, m. Catharine C. **BUNNEL**, b. of [Oxford], Jan. 4, 1835, by Rev. Samuel R. Hickcox. Witnesses: Samuel Hickox, Sarah Hickox	1	146
Sollomon, m. Hannah **PEIRSON**, June 12, [ ]	LR3	10
Solomon, s. John & Hannah, b. Aug. 13. 1708	2	23
Susan, of Derby, m. Charles E. **LASKIN**, of Stamford, Apr. 16, 1848, by Rev. W[illia]m Bliss Ashley	1	341
Sybill, d. John & Elizabeth, b. May 31, 1742	LR4	A2
---iah, d. Jno & Elizebeth, b. Oct. 2, 1737	LR3	11
CHEESMAN, George W., of Birmingham, m. Sarah Ann **DURAND**, of Derby, Mar. 7, 1847, by Rev. F. W. Smith	1	235
CHENEY, Labon C., Rev. m. Cynthia **SMITH**, Nov. 1, 1831, by Rev. Labon Clark	1	107
CHILD, CHILDS, Alexander, of Haddam, m. Eunice Francis **STANDISH**, of Bridgeport, Nov. 28, 1839, by Rev. Joseph Scott	1	153
Heman, of Hamden, m. Juliatte **WHITE**, of Derby, Dec. 31, 1834, by Rev. John E. Bray	1	149
CHILSON, Elizabeth, Mrs., m. Maxwell **BRYSON**, July 9, 1815, by Levi Tomlinson, J. P.	1	89
CHURCH, Abel, m. Betsey **HINES**, b. of Derby, Nov. 16, 1831, by Rev. Stephen Jewett	1	106
Ann, m. Isaac **KEENEY**, b. of Derby, Dec. 15, 1828	1	101
Augusta M., Mrs. of Derby, m. Francis B. **HUBBELL**, of Huntington, Nov. 22, 1835, by Bennet Lum, J. P.	1	160
Marietta, m. Sheldon **DAVIS**, b. of Derby, Mar. 22, 1840, by Rev. Joseph Scott	1	151
[CHURCHILL], CHURCHELL, CHURCHEL, Abel, s. John & Rachel, b. Feb. 10, 1774	TM1	75a
John, m. Rachel **DAVIS**, b. of Derby, Nov. 30, 1769, by Rev. Richard Mansfield	TM1	59
William, s. John & Rachel, b. Nov. 1, 1770	TM1	59
CLARK, CLARKE, CLERK, Abigail, d. Moses & Abigail **BRUSTER**, b. Dec. 24, 1776	TM1	119
Anne, m. William **WALSH**, Feb. 22, 1852, by Rev. James Lynch	1	483
Charity, d. William & Hannah, b. Mar. 26, 1752	LR6	4
Charlotte, of Milford, m. Ephraim **CURTIS**, of Huntington, Jan. 10, 1839, by Rev. Orlando Starr	1	152

	Vol.	Page
CLARK, CLARKE, CLERK, (cont.)		
Chary, d. William & Marcy, b. Sept. 25, 1784	TM1	213
Delia Helmira, of Derby, m. David **WELLS**, of Huntington,		
Apr. 4, 1833, by Rev. Stephen Jewett	1	187
Elias, of Woodbury, m. Huldah **BURR**, of Trumble, Mar. 27,		
1834, by Rev. Luther Meed	1	149
Eliza A., m. George D. **HINE**, Nov. 27, 1822, by Stephen Jewett	1	96
Elisabeth, d. William & Hannah, b. Sept. 24, 1732	LR6	4
Elizabeth, Mrs., m. Joseph **HULL**, Jr., May 3, 1750, by		
Rev. Daniel Humphry	LR6	7
Elisabeth, of Middletown, m. Joseph **RUSSELL**, of Derby,		
Sept. 25, 1764, by Rev. Mr. Huntington	TM1	6
Elizabeth, m. William **BLAKE**, Mar. 8, 1842, by John D. Smith	1	205
Eunice, d. William & Hannah, b. Apr. 15, 1746	LR6	4
Eunice, d. William & Marcy, b. Sept. 13, 1774	TM1	213
Francis, m. Mary **LARKIN**, June 22, 1851, by Rev. James		
Lynch, of Birmingham	1	236
Hannah, d. William & Hannah, b. May 22, 1739	LR6	4
Hannah, m. Oliver **CURTICE**, Apr. 2, 1754	LR6	451
Hannah, d. Ens. Thomas & Susannah, b. Nov. 2, 1766	TM1	20
Hannah, d. Sheldon & Betty, b. Mar. 5, 1769	TM1	108
Joseph, s. William & Marcy, b. May 12, 1782	TM1	213
Levi, s. Moses & Abigail **BRUSTER**, b. Dec. 17, 1774	TM1	119
Lucy, d. William & Hannah, b. Dec. 13, 1736	LR6	4
Lucey, d. Sheldon & Betty, b. Feb. 12, 1767	TM1	108
Lucy, m. John M. **WILLIAMS**, Mar. 1, 1840, by John D. Smith	1	188
Marah, of Milford, m. James **WHE[E]LER**, Jr., of Derby,		
[ ] 13, 1767, by Rev. Mr. Hawley	TM1	38
Marmre, m. Isaac **BLAKE**, Feb. 3, 1843, by John D. Smith	1	205
Mary A., of Milford, m. Henry **WARREN**, of Derby, Apr. 20,		
1840, by Rev. Joseph Scott	1	186
Mary Jane, m. Charles **THOMAS**, of West Haven, Nov. 3, 1833,		
by Zepheniah Swift	1	180
Mary Jane, m. Hiram W. **COLES**, Nov. 16, 1851, by Rev. I.		
Guernsey	1	236
Merrit, m. Charlotte D. **CAINE**, b. of Derby, Jan. 2, 1841, by		
Rev. Sylvester Smith	1	153
Moses, m. Abigail Bruster **JOHNSON**, b. of Derby, Jan. 6,		
1774, by Rev. Mr. Hawley	TM1	92
Richard M., Capt. m. Eliza A. **MERDENBROUGH**, Oct. 20,		
1822, by Rev. Stephen Jewett	1	87
Richard Newel, s. William & Marcy, b. July 6, 1787	TM1	213
Sarah, d. William & Hannah, b. Jan. 22, 1741/2	LR6	4
Sarah, of Derby, m. Austin **ALLEN**, of Woodbury, Nov. 10,		
[1839], by Rev. J. B. Beach	1	192
Sarah, m. Andrew **HARTSON**, June 15, 1844, by Rev. W[illia]m		
B. Curtiss	1	289
Shelden, s. William & Hannah, b. Feb. 10, 1743/4	LR6	4

	Vol.	Page
CLARK, CLARKE, CLERK, (cont.)		
Sheldon, m. Betty **KEENEY,** b. of Derby, Feb. 15, 1764	TM1	108
Sheldon, s. Sheldon & Betty, May 17, 1772	TM1	108
Sheldon, s. William & Marcy, b. Apr. 18, 1780	TM1	213
Smith, of Litchfield, m. Alletha **BALDWIN,** Dec. 26, 1830, by Rev. Charles Thompson	1	90
Su[s]anna, d. William & Hannah, b. Aug. 18, 1734	LR6	4
Thomas, s. Thomas & Susannah, b. Feb. 22, 1764	TM1	20
Treat Perry, of Bridgeport, m. Phebe Eliza **DIBBLE,** of Derby, Oct. 17, 1844, by Rev. George Waterbury	1	233
Waterous, s. Sheldon & Betty, b. June 20, 1774	TM1	108
Watrous, m. Mary Ann **WHITE,** b. of Derby, Sept. 6, 1832, by Charles Thompson	1	149
William, s. William & Hannah, b. Sept. 22, 1749	LR6	4
William, s. William & Hannah, d. Sept. 17, 1751	LR6	5
William, s. Sheldon & Betty, b. Jan. 11, 1765	TM1	108
William, s. William & Marcy, b. Aug. 30, 1777	TM1	213
CLEAVELAND, John K., of Winsted, m. Emeline **CANFIELD,** of Derby, Dec. 25, 1833, by Sheldon Curtiss	1	149
CLEMENS, CLEMANS, Andrew B., m. Catharine E. **GERARD,** Dec. 7, 1845, by Rev. W[illiam] B. Curtiss	1	233
Matilda N., of Huntington, m. David B. **TOMLINSON,** of Derby, Mar. 21, 1850, by Rev. Jno Morrison Reid	1	461
CLENTON, [see under **CLINTON**]		
CLINTON, CLENTON, Charlotte, of Derby, m. Thomas **ELLIS,** of Wales, Apr. 19, 1829, by Eli Bennett, Elder	1	91
Elias, m. Eliza **THOMAS,** b. of New Haven, May 10, 1837, by Rev. Stephen Jewett	1	91
Elias W., of New Haven, m. Juliette **WHEELER,** of Derby, Sept. 25, 1851, by H. N. Howknis, J. P.	1	236
Isaiah Smith, m. Mary Ann **BLAKE,** b. of Derby, Aug. 2, 1838, by Rev. Joseph Scott	1	152
Lyman Albert, m. Jennette Minnerva **BLAKE,** b. of Derby, Apr. 6, 1837, by John D. Smith	1	150
Mary, of New Haven, m. Abraham **HARGER,** of Derby, Sept. 25, 1766, by Rev. Mr. Pamer	TM1	15
COCHRANE, Emily M., of Derby, m. Charles L. **BISHOP,** of Meriden, Nov. 29, 1849, by Rev. W[illia]m Denison	1	210
COE, Denman, s. John & Hannah, b. May 25, 1759	TM1	56
Denman, of Derby, m. Mary **NORTHROP,** of Milford, Feb. 20, 1781	TM1	105
Elisabeth, d. John & Hannah, b. Dec. 10, 1774	TM1	56
Hannah, d. John & Hannah, b. Mar. 16, 1769	TM1	56
John, m. Hannah **CHATFIELD,** b. of Derby, Sept. 8, 1755	TM1	56
John, s. John & Hannah, b. Mar. 27, 1764	TM1	56
Mary, d. John & Hannah, b. Oct. 20, 1756	TM1	56
Mary, m. Philo **HINMAN,** b. of Derby, July 20, 1774	TM1	105
Ruth, of Oxford, m. W[illia]m L. **DURAND,** of Derby,		

	Vol.	Page

COE, (cont.)

Oct. 7, 1838, by Rev. Orlando Starr | 1 | 151

Sarah, d. John & Hannah, b. Feb. 5, 1762 | TM1 | 56

Sarah, d. John & Hannah, b. Feb. 5, 1762 | LR7 | 249

COGSWELL, Sarah B., of Derby, m. John William **BASSETT**, of
New York, Sept. 13, 1849, by Rev. C. S. Putman. Int. Pub. | 1 | 209

COLAHA, Mary, m. Edward **DUNNE**, Feb. 15, 1852, by Rev. James
Lynch, of Birmingham | 1 | 249

COLBURN, Susan M., m. W[illia]m J. **WHITING**, M. D., b. of
Derby, May 18, 1846, by Rev. George Thacher | 1 | 481

COLE, [see under **COLES**]

COLEMAN, Mary, m. David **GREGG**, Jan. 24, [18]52, by Rev.
James Lynch | 1 | 280

COLES, COLE, David, m. Sarah **KASSELY**, Oct. 1, 1839, by Rev.
Joseph Scott | 1 | 153

Hannah Maria, of N. Milford, m. Horace **DEMING**, of
Woodbury, Oct. 11, [1840], by Rev. John B. Beach | 1 | 192

Hiram W., m. Mary Jane **CLARK**, Nov. 16, 1851, by Rev. I.
Guernsey | 1 | 236

Julia A., of Weston Derby, m. Joseph E. **FIELD**, of South
East New York, Apr. 9, 1848, by Rev. W[illia]m Denison | 1 | 271

COLLIER, Emely, of Derby, m. Jeremiah **LORD**, of East Windsor,
Jan. 25, 1835, by Sylvester Smith | 1 | 165

COLLINS, COLLINGS, COLLENS, Abraham, m. Sarah
BOTSFORD, Nov. 2, 1847, by Rev. W[illia]m B. Curtiss | 1 | 234

Dannill, b. Feb. 8, 1677 | A1 | 9

Dannill, m. [   ], June 3, 1677 | A1 | 9

Jonathan, of Branford, m. Laura B. **BEECHER**, of N[ew]
H[aven], Nov. 17, 1852, by Rev. Thomas T. Guion | 1 | 236

Patienc[e], b. Feb. 9, 1679 | A1 | 9

Patrick, m. Catherine **BUCKLEY**, June 22, 1851, by Rev.
James Lynch | 1 | 236

CONNOLLY, Thomas, m. Jane **LARKIN**, Aug. 27, 1851, by Rev.
James Lynch, of Birmingham | 1 | 237

CONROY, Bridget, m. Edward **KIRNEON**, Nov. 27, [18]51, by Rev.
James Lynch | 1 | 330

CONVERSE, Charles E., m. Sarah **WHEELER**, Feb. 1, 1844, by
Rev. John D. Smith | 1 | 233

COOK, Mary C., m. Charles **DANIELS**, Apr. 2, 1843, by John D.
Smith | 1 | 247

Samuel, m. Charlotte **HOYT**, b. of Derby, Mar. 31, 1827,
by [   ] | 1 | 86

COOPER, Hannah, m. Jermiah **ANDREW**, b. of Derby, Sept. 13,
1840, by Rev. John B. Beach | 1 | 192

Sarah, Mrs., m. Legrand **LEWIS**, b. of Derby, Dec. 13, 1835,
by Sheldon Bassett, J. P. | 1 | 165

COREY, Fidelia G., m. Wales O. **HITCHKISS**, Nov. 27, 1842, by
John D. Smith | 1 | 289

	Vol.	Page
COSS, Anne, m. Michael McKANE, Apr. 22, 1851, by Rev. James Lynch, of Birmingham	1	358
COXHAND, John F., of Poughkeepsie, N. Y., m. Delia M. DAVIS, of Derby, June 2, 1844, by Rev. Sheldon Davis, of New York, in St. James Church	1	233
CRAFTS, Edward Blakeslee, s. Dr. Pearl & Sally, b. Jan. 13, 1814	1	5
Elisabeth Mansfield, d. Dr. Pearl & Sally, b. May 30, 1816	1	5
Pearl, Dr., m. Sally Mansfield BLAKESLEE, Dec. 24, 1812, by Rev. Richard Mansfield	1	87
CRAWFORD, [see also CROFOOT], Abigail, m Samuel PERSON, Mar. 10, 1762, by Rev. Richard Mansfield	LR7	256
Benjamin, m. Olive CARPENTER, Mar. 14, 1775	TM1	92
John, m. Sarah ADEE, Dec. 13, 1795	TM1	215
John, s. John & Sarah, b. Sept. 26, 1796	TM1	215
Sally, m. Jonas HARDEN, July 24, [1831], by John T. Wheeler, J. P.	1	92
Sarah, had d. Sarah, b. Jan. 30, 1763	TM1	4
Sarah, d. Sarah, b. Jan. 30, 1763	TM1	4
Sarah, w. John, d. Apr. 17, 1794	TM1	215
CROFOOT, [see also CRAWFORD], Samuel, m. Sarah Jane CULVER, Sept. 24, 1836, by Rev. Sam[ue]l R. Hickcox of Humphreysville. Witnesses: Stephen H. Culver, Elizabeth Wattles	1	150
CROSBY, Alonzo M., of Litchfield, m. Hannah M. BOARDMAN, of Humphreyville, July 16, 1848, by Rev. W[illia]m Denison	1	234
Samuel, m. Mary A. ROSSIN, Apr. 20, 1850, by Rev. Cha[rle]s Dickinson, of Birmingham	1	235
CULVER, Charles H., of Stratford, m. Emma SOMERS, of Milford, Oct. 10, 1847, by Rev. Ira H. Smith	1	234
Charles Harris, of Huntington, m. Jane DODD, of Monroe, Sept. 24, 1843, by Rev. Nathaniel Mead	1	233
Sarah Jane, m. Samuel CROFOOT, Sept. 24, 1836, by Rev. Sam[ue]l R. Hickcox, of Humphreysville. Witnesses: Stephen H. Culver, Elizabeth Wattles	1	150
Stephen H., m. Sarah Jane ADYE, b. of Derby, Nov. 7, 1847, by Rev. Sylvester Smith	1	234
CURTIS, CURTISS, CURTICE, Ann, m. Zacharia BOOTH, s. Joseph & Hannah, June 12, 1718 (vol. 2, page 480, Stratford Rec.)	1	214
Ann, m. John O. HOTCHKISS, b. of Derby, Jan. 5, 1849, by Rev. Thomas T. Guion	1	292
Ann, m. John O. HOTCHKISS, b. of Derby, Jan. 22, 1849, by Rev. Thomas T. Guion	1	290
Edward, m. Lucy M. MOSHIER, Dec. 24, 1840, by John D. Smith	1	154
Elisabeth, d. Oliver & Hannah, b. Feb. 28, 1756	LR6	442
Elizabeth Ann, of Derby, m. Jarius N. BENHAM, of Woodbridge, May 18, 1843, by Rev. W[illia]m Bliss Ashley	1	205

	Vol.	Page

CURTIS, CURTISS, CURTICE, (cont.)

Ephraim, of Huntington, m. Charlotte **CLARK**, of Milford,
Jan. 10, 1839, by Rev. Orlando Starr — 1 — 152

Hannah, w. Oliver, d. Oct. 3, 1803, ae 64 — TM1 — 153

Harriet, [twin with Henry], d. Sheldon & Lois, b. Jan. 4, 1796 — TM1 — 153

Harriet, d. Sheldon & Lois, d. July 3, 1835, ae 39 y. — 1 — 513

Henry, [twin with Harriet], s. Sheldon & Lois, b. Jan. 4, 1796 — TM1 — 153

Lois (Nichols), w. Sheldon, b. May 28, 1760 — TM1 — 153

Lucy Maria, d. Sheldon C. & Hannah, b. Aug. 11, 1813 — 1 — 5

Mary, m. John **MASSY**, Apr. 14, 1707, by Major Ebenezer
Johnson, J. P. — 2 — 25

Oliver, m. Hannah **CLERK**, Apr. 2, 1754 — LR6 — 451

Oliver, d. Jan. 13, 1794, ae 63 — TM1 — 153

Sally, d. Sheldon & Lois, b. May 28, 1783 — TM1 — 153

Sarah, d. Oliver & Hannah, b. Aug. 26, 1757 — LR6 — 442

Sarah, d. Oliver & Hannah, b. May 12, 1765 — TM1 — 14

Sheldon, s. Oliver & Hannah, b. Apr. 7, 1761 — TM1 — 153

Sheldon, m. Lois **NICHOLS**, Nov. 11, 1781 — TM1 — 153

Sheldon, s. Sheldon & Lois, b. Aug. 31, 1788 — TM1 — 153

Sheldon C., m. Hannah **BRADLEY**, of [Laneboro, Mass.],
Oct. 11, 1812, by Rev. Amos Pardee, of Laneboro, Mass. — 1 — 87

William, of Stratford, m. Gennett **GILBERT**, of Derby, Nov. 27,
1845, by Zephaniah Swift — 1 — 233

CUSHMAN, Oliver, of Becket, Mass., m. Sarah A. **BALDWIN**, of
Derby, Nov. 27, 1837, by Sylvester Smith — 1 — 152

DALY, Lucilla, m. Edmund B. **GILBERT**, Nov. 30, 1848, by Rev.
C. S. Putnam — 1 — 279

DAN, Alfred, of Oneida, N. Y., m. Jane **BRADLEY**, of Derby, July
8, 1832, by Charles Thompson — 1 — 180

Alfreda, of Oneida, N. Y., m. Jane **BRADLEY**, of Derby, July 8,
1832, by Rev. Charles Thompson — 1 — 149

Rockwell M., m. Julia Ann **BASSETT**, b. of Derby, Apr. 4,
1844, by Rev. Sylvester Smith — 1 — 247

DANIELS, DANULS, Caroline, m. Charles S. **SNOW**, Oct. 2, [1836],
by John D. Smith — 1 — 179

Charles, m. Mary C. **COOK**, Apr. 2, 1843, by John D. Smith — 1 — 247

Frederick D., of Bristol, m. Mary R. **JOHNSON**, of Ansonia,
Oct. 8, 1854, at Ansonia, by Rev. O. Street — 1 — 249

William, of Grove, Alegany County, N. Y., m. Betsey Jane
BALDWIN, of Woodbridge, [Oct.] 9, [1836], by Rev. L. D.
Howells — 1 — 151

DARRY, Bridget, m. Michael **FOLEY**, Feb. 14, 1852, by Rev.
James Lynch — 1 — 272

DART, Catharine, m. Ezra **SHORT**, b. of Derby, Aug. 3, 1851, by
Rev. Thomas G. Osborn — 1 — 441

Myra L., of Huntington, m. Charles I. **WARNER**, of
Humphreysville, Oct. 25, 1840, by Samuel R. Hickcox — 1 — 188

DASCOM, Cornelis, m. Mrs. Jennett **TWICHEL**, b. of New Haven,

	Vol.	Page
DASCOM, (cont.)		
Sept. 25, 1831, by Charles Thompson	1	121
DAVIS, DAVES, DAUIS, DAVIES, Abigal, d. John & Abigal,		
b. Apr. 28, 1709	2	160
Abigail, d. John & Sarah b. Nov. 20, 1713/14	LR3	2
Abigail, of Derby, m. Abel **GUNN**, of Waterbury, Dec.		
2, 1756, by Rev. Richard Mansfield	LR6	8
Elice*, d. Dan & Ruth, b. Feb. 20, 1753 *(Alice)	LR6	3
Alles, m. Nathaniel **HOLBROOK**, b. of Derby, Dec. 20, 1778	TM1	149
Anne, m. John E. **WHITE**, b. of Derby, Jan. 11, 1835, by		
John E. Bray	1	187
Anson, s. John & Mahitable, b. Sept. 5, 1785	TM1	162
Benjamin, s. Nathan & Eunice, b. Mar. 1, 1743	LR5	413
Betty, d. John, b. Oct. 11, 1719	LR3	3
Betty, Mrs., m. Ebenezer **KEENEY**, Dec. 7, 1738	TM1	7
Bette, m. Eben[e]zer **KEENEY**, Dec. 7, 1738	LR4	A4
Betty, m. Ebenezer **KENEY**, Dec. 7, 1738	LR5	4
Charles, m. Anna **HARGER**, Sept. 30, 1838, by Rev. Joseph		
Scott	1	151
Dan, s. John & Sarah, b. Jan. 10, 1709/10	2	160
Dan, m. Ruth **WOOSTER**, Dec. 6, 1738	LR4	A4
Dan, [twin with Ruben], s. Dan & Ruth, b. Sept. 17, 1745	LR5	2
Daniel, [twin with Joseph], s. Nathan & Eunice, b. Mar.		
20, 1746	LR5	413
Delia M., of Derby, m. John F. **COXHAND**, of Poughkeepsie,		
N. Y., June 2, 1844, in St. James Church, by Rev. Sheldon		
Davis, of New York	1	233
Elizabeth, d. John & Abigail, b. July 21, 1707	2	23
Elisabeth, d. Elias & Abigail, b. Jan. 12, 1748/9	LR5	413
Elisabeth, d. Elias & Abigail, [ ], Jan. 12, 1748/9	LR5	413
Ethiel, s. Dan & Ruth, b. Feb. 15, 1756	LR6	13
Eunice, d. Nathan & Eunice, b. June 20, 1740	LR5	413
Hannah, m. Beman **HALE**, b. of Derby, Nov. 11, 1779, by		
Rev. David Bronson	TM1	117
Hannah, m. John **HAWKINS**, Nov. 29, [ ]	LR3	10
Henry P., m. Mrs. Almira **HOLCOMB**, Sept. 2, 1849, by		
Rev. W[illia]m B. Curtiss	1	248
Isaac, s. Nathan & Martha, d. Oct. 1, 1781, in the 4th y. of		
his age	TM1	123
Isaac B., m. Maria A. **TUCKER**, June 19, 1842, by John D.		
Smith	1	247
Isaac H., m. Maria L. **BASSETT**, Mar. 26, 1842, by John D.		
Smith	1	247
Jabez, s. Jno & Abigail, b. July 24, 1703	2	12
Jane, m. Josiah B. **CANFIELD**, b. of Derby, Oct. 14, 1830, by		
Rev. S. Jewett	1	95
Jane, of Newtown, m. Samuel **BOTSFORD**, of Derby, Aug. 20,		
1845, by Rev. W[illia]m Bliss Ashley	1	207

	Vol.	Page

DAVIS, DAVES DAUIS, DAVIES, (cont.)

Jennette A., m. George H. **MERRICK**, Sept. 13, 1841, by		
John D. Smith	1	162
John, m. Mrs. Mary **GUN[N]**, May 12, 1691	2	25
John, m. Sarah **CHATFIELD**, July 15, 1706, by Major Ebenezer		
Johnson	2	24
John, Sr., had his ear mark for cattle recorded, Apr.		
29, 1712	2	161
John, s. Joseph & Mary, b. Feb. 2, 1748/9	LR5	413
John, Jr., m. Mahitable **THOMAS**, Apr. 10, 1782	TM1	162
John, of Naugatuck, m. Jennett **ALLEN**, of Humphreysville,		
Oct. 11, 1847, by N. L. Richardson	1	248
Joseph, m. Mary **WHE[E]LER**, Apr. 25, [ ]	LR3	10
Joseph, s. John, Jr. & Sarah, b. June 30, 1708	2	23
Jos[eph], & w. Mary had d. [ ], b. Apr. 12, 1738	LR3	11
Joseph, s. Joseph & Mary, b. July 10, 1743	LR4	A5
Joseph, [twin with Daniel], s. Nathan & Eunice, b. Mar. 20,		
1746	LR5	413
Joseph, Capt. of Derby, m. Mrs. Amy **FOOT**, of New Town, Jan.		
30, 1765, by John Beach	TM1	15
Joseph, Jr., of Derby, m. Obediance **SPERRY**, of New Haven,		
Nov. 15, 1770, by Rev. Chancey Whitelsey	TM1	65
Laura, m. David **WARNER**, [ ], by Rev. George L. Fuller,		
recorded Apr. 26, 1847	1	481
Mary, b. Aug. 2, 1693	2	26
Mary, d. Joseph & Mary, b. Oct. 15, 1740	LR4	A3
Mary, w. Capt. Joseph, d. Jan. 18, 1764, in the 50th y. of		
her age	LR7	254
Mindwell, d. John & Sary, b. Feb. 4, 1712	LR3	1
Naomy, d. Dan & Ruth, b. Jan. 1, 1742/3	LR5	2
Naomi, m. Dr. Josiah **CANFIELD**, b. of Derby, Feb. 28, 1768	TM1	49
Naomi, Mrs., m. Dr. Josiah **CANFIELD**, b. of Derby, Feb. 28,		
1768	TM1	82
Nathaniel, s. John & Abigal, b. Feb. 26, 1698/9	2	31
Rachel, d. John & Sarah, b. July 5, 1716	LR3	3
Rachel, d. Nathan & Eunice, b. Apr. [ ], 1738	LR5	413
Rachel, d. Joseph & Mary, b. July 4, 1752	LR6	2
Rachel, m. John **CHURCHEL**, b. of Derby, Nov. 30, 1769, by		
Rev. Richard Mansfield	TM1	59
Ruben, [twin with Dan], s. Dan & Ruth, b. Sept. 17, 1745	LR5	2
Sarah, w. John, d. Jan. 20, 1721	LR3	6
Sarah, d. Joseph & Mary, b. Nov. 26, 1735	LR3	11
Sarah, m. Zachariah **HAWKINS**, July 6, 1737	LR6	8
Sarah, d. Dan & Ruth, b. Nov. 1, 1747	LR5	232
Sarah, d. Nathan & Eunice, b. Oct. 6, 1756	LR6	442
Sarrah, d. Joseph & Obediance, b. Aug. 31, 1771	TM1	49
Sarah, d. John & Mahitable, b. Mar. 31, 1783	TM1	162
Sheldon, m. Marietta **CHURCH**, b. of Derby, Mar. 22, 1840,		

	Vol.	Page
DODD, (cont.)		
Samuel, s. Daniel & [E]unice, b. Nov. 4, 1779	TM1	97
DODGE, Richard T., of Boston, m. Mrs. Jerusha **WILDER**, of Ludlow, Mass., Dec. 10, 1848, by Rev. Charles Stearns	1	248
DOHERTY, Mary, m. Pat[ric]k **RENY**, Nov. 27, 1851, by Rev. James Lynch	1	426
DONALD, Sarah, m. Patrick **ROURKE**, Aug. 27, 1848, by Rev. W[illia]m B. Curtiss	1	425
DONNELLY, **DONNALLEY**, Mathew, of Derby, m. Sarah M. **HENDRIX**, of Oxford, [ ], by Rev. Joseph Scott; recorded Jan. 4, 1841	1	152
Teddy, m. Mary **MARONEY**, Jan. 25, [18]52, by Rev. James Lynch	1	249
DORMAN, **DORMAND**, James, m. Anna **HARGER**, June 9, 1779	TM1	161
Joel, s. James & Anna, b. Aug. 3, 1784	TM1	161
Lanson, s. James & Anna, b. Jan. 9, 1787	TM1	161
Laurene, d. James & Anna, b. Aug. 29, 1780	TM1	161
Mamere, d. James & Anna, b. Sept. 22, 1782	TM1	161
DOUGLAS, Lucretia, m. John **PERKINS**, Feb. 21, 1841, by John D. Smith	1	173
DOWLING, Julia, of Waterbury, m. William B. **JOYCE**, of Waterbury, Jan. 23, 1853, by Rev. Thomas G. Osborn	1	326
DOWNS, Biah, d. Abraham & Elisabeth, b. Nov. 22, 1761	LR7	250
Charry Ann, of Derby, m. Wells **HUBBELL**, of Huntington, Nov. 25, 1838, by Rev. Jos[eph] Scott	1	160
Elizabeth S., m. Robert N. **BASSETT**, b. of Derby, Oct. 5, 1842, by Rev. H. Read	1	205
Harvey, m. Caroline **MOTHROP**, Oct. 24, 1831, by Zepheniah Swift	1	151
Nelson H., m. Elisabeth **WALLACE**, b. of Derby, May 8, 1843, by Rev. W[illia]m Bliss Ashley	1	247
Sidney, m. Eliza A. **CANFIELD**, b. of Derby, Oct. 22, 1828, by Rev. Stephen Jewett	1	89
Sydney A., m. Eliza A. **BASSETT**, b. of Derby, Oct. 6, 1840, by Rev. H. Read	1	151
T. M., of Newtown, m. Ann **SCRANTON**, of Derby, Aug. 28, 1831, by Charles Thompson	1	121
William E., m. Jane Maria **HOWE**, b. of Derby, June 24, 1851, by Rev. Thomas T. Guion	1	248
DRAKE, Timothy, of Oxford, m. Olive **FREEMAN**, of Derby, (colored), Jan. 24, 1821, by Rev. Ziphaniah Swift	1	89
DRIVER, Emeline, m. Porter **HUNT**, Mar. 1, 1829, by Samuel R. Hickox. Witnesses: Jairus Driver, Russel Hurd, Nancy N. Gilyard, Welthy Miller	1	98
DRUNG, Sarah E., m. David **TUCKER**, May 15, 1848, by Rev. W[illia]m B. Curtiss	1	461
DUDLEY, Elizaabeth P., d. Josiah & Sabra, b. Apr. 4, 1801	TM1	364
Elizabeth P., m. Jeremiah **FRENCH**, May 4, 1823, by		

	Vol.	Page
DUDLEY, (cont.)		
Rev. Stephen Jewett	1	93
Henry, s. Josiah & Sabra, b. Apr. 13, 1799, in Huntington,		
Fairfield County	TM1	364
Josiah, m. Sabra DUDLEY, Jan. 20, 1798	TM1	364
Sabra, m. Josiah DUDLEY, Jan. 20, 1798	TM1	364
Sophia Maria, d. Josiah & Sabra, b. Mar. 27, 1804	TM1	364
DUNCAN, Mary E., of New York, m. Nelson **HART**, of Avon, Jan.		
27, 1850, by Rev. Jno Morrison Reid	1	210
Mary E., of New York, m. Nelson **HART**, of Avon, June 27,		
1850, by Rev. Jno Morrison Reid	1	291
DUNNE, Edward, m. Mary **COLAHA**, Feb. 15, [18]52, by Rev. James		
Lynch, of Birmingham	1	249
DURAND, DURAN, DURANT, Abigail, d. John & Elisabeth, b.		
June 2, 1716	LR3	3
Abigal, m. Abner **JOHNSON**, Aug. 9, 1738	LR4	A4
Ann, d. Joseph & Ann, b. Dec. 3, 1742	LR4	A5
Anna, m. William **McKEE**, May [ ], 1769	TM1	15
Anna, w. Joseph, d. Feb. 14, 1778, in the 65th y. of her age	TM1	209
Bryan, s. John & Desire, b. Apr. 26, 1770	TM1	92
Dameriss, of Derby, m. Abel **SOMERS**, of Milford, Jan. 16,		
1842, by Rev. Nathaniel Mead	1	185
Ebenezer, s. John & Elizabeth, b. Dec. 7, 1724	LR3	5
Ebenezer, m. Hannah **WHITE**, Dec. 17, 1754	LR6	450
Ebenezar, s. Ebenezer & Hannah, b. Feb. 24, 1755	LR6	450
Eleazer, s. Joseph & Ann, b. Oct. 4, 1754	LR6	4
Elijah, s. John & Sarah, b. Mar. 17, 1730/1	LR3	16
Elizabeth, d. John, b. Feb. 6, 1718/19	LR3	3
Elisabeth, m. Shores **UFFORD**, b. of Derby, June 10,[ ],		
by David Brounson	TM1	94
Elizabeth, d. John & Elizabeth, b. July 19, [ ]	2	13
Elisabeth, m. Joseph **JOHNSON**, Aug. 5, [ ]	LR3	10
Elizabeth, d. Samuel & Mary, b. July 29, 1743	LR4	A2
Elisabeth, d. John & Sarah, b. Feb. 17, 1751	LR6	450
Elizabeth M., m. Nelson M. **BEACH**, b. of Derby, Nov. 4,		
1838, by Rev. Orlando Starr	1	167
Elizabeth M., m. Edward A. **LUM**, Nov. 30, 1848, by Rev.		
W[illia]m B. Curtiss	1	342
Ezra, s. Sam[ue]ll & Mary, b. Feb. 11, 1747/8	LR5	413
Hannah, w. Ebenezer, d. July 26, 1752	LR6	440
[Is]aac, s. Joseph & Ann, b. Aug. 14, [ ]	LR5	2
Jeremiah, s. John, b. Aug. 8, 1749	LR6	2
Jeremiah, s. John & Sarah, b. Aug. 8, 1749	LR6	450
Jeremiah, m. Hannah **TROBRIDGE**, Nov. 21, [1773?], by		
Rev. David Bronson	TM1	87
Jeremiah, m. Maria **KEENEY**, Dec. 25, 1827, by Rev.		
Zepheniah Swift	1	89
John, s. Dr. John & Elizabeth, b. Nov. 10, 1700	2	12

	Vol.	Page
DURAND, DURAN, DURANT, (cont.)		
John, m. Sarah LUMM, Nov. 5, 1730	LR3	10
John, s. Sam[ue]ll & Mary, b. Oct. 16, 1745	LR5	2
John, m. Sarah CHATFIELD, June 2, 1747	LR6	450
John, s. John & Sarah, b. Feb. 2, 1758	LR6	450
John, Jr., m. Desire ANDRUS, b. of Derby, Oct. 3, 1769,		
by Timothy Russell	TM1	92
John, d. Mar. 8, 1773	TM1	48
Joseph, s. John & Eliezabeth, b. Dec. 20, 1709	2	160
Joseph, m. Ann TOMLINSON, Apr. 25, 1734	LR3	10
Joseph, s. John & Sarah, b. May 21, 1764	TM1	66
Joseph, d. Aug. 6, 1792, in the 82nd y. of his age	TM1	209
Marcy, d. Noah & Abigal, b. Dec. 21, [ ]	LR3	16
Mercy, d. Noah & Damaris, b. May 8, 1748	LR6	2
Nab[b]y, d. Noah, 3rd & Ruth, b. May 15, 1773	TM1	59
Nehemiah, s. John & Sarah, b. Dec. 7, 1753	LR6	450
Noah, s. John & Elizabeth, b. Aug. 27, 1707	2	23
Noah, m. Abigail RIGGS, Nov. 9, 1732	LR3	10
Noah, s. Joseph & Ann, b. May 12, 1740	LR4	A3
Noah, 3rd, of Derby, m. Ruth FOOT, Aug. 12, 1772, by		
Rev. David Brownson	TM1	76
Rachel, m. John HUMPHRYS, b. of Derby, Feb. 11, 1773	TM1	150
Samuell, s. John & Elisabeth, b. July 7, 1713	LR3	2
[S]am[ue]ll, s. Joseph & Ann, b. Feb. 28, 1734/5	LR3	11
Sarah, m. Jabish HARGER, June 24, 1748, by Rev. Jonathan		
Lyman	LR6	444
Sarah, d. John & Sarah, b. June 3, [ ]	LR3	16
Sarah Ann, of Derby, m. George W. CHEESMAN, of		
Birmingham, Mar. 7, 1847, by Rev. F. W. Smith	1	235
Susan H., m. John W. OSBORN, Jan. 18, 1835, by Rev.		
Joseph Scott	1	170
Susannah, d. John & Sarah, b. Nov. 13, 1760	TM1	66
W[illia]m L., of Derby, m. Ruth COE, of Oxford, Oct. 7, 1838,		
by Rev. Orlando Starr	1	151
Zuruiah, d. John & Sarah, b. Nov. 5, 1756	LR6	450
----ah, d. John & Sarah, b. Jan. 8, 1736/7	LR3	11
----ph, s. Joseph & Ann, b. Feb. 28, 1736/7	LR3	11
DUTTON, John, s. Osee & Elisabeth, b. Nov. 11, 1783	TM1	151
Osee, m. Elisabeth TROWBRIDGE, Jan. 19, 1783	TM1	151
Pat, m. Ellen CAMPION(?), Sept. 18, 1851, by Rev.		
James Lynch	1	248
T. S., m. Lucinda WHEELER, b. of Birmingham, Jan. 21,		
1849, by Rev. Cha[rle]s Dickinson	1	248
DYER, DIER, Eliphelet, m. Mary O'CAIN, Nov. 25, 1818	1	7
George, m. Sarah DYER, b. of Derby, Dec. 1, 1842, by H. Read	1	247
Minerva, m. Horace JOHNSON, Oct. 9, 1828, by Rev.		
Zepheniah Swift	1	98
Sarah, m. George DYER, b. of Derby, Dec. 1, 1842, by H. Read	1	247

	Vol.	Page
DYER, DIER, (cont.)		
Sarah M., Mrs. m. Joseph Harvey JOHNSON, b. of Derby, Dec. 1, 1832, by Rev. S. Jewett	1	161
William, of New Haven, m. Anna MANSFIELD, of Derby, Sept. 22, 1821, by Rev. Abner Smith	1	89
William Henry, s. Eliphalet & Mary, b. Sept. 14, 1819	1	7
EDDY, Walter B., of New Britain, m. Ann JUDSON, of Woodbridge, Nov. 30, 1837, by Rev. John E. Bray	1	153
ELDERKIN, Belinda, of Derby, m. Samuel YEMMONS, of Washington, Sept. 3, 1837	1	189
ELLIS, Thomas, of Wales, m. Charlotte CLINTON, of Derby, Apr. 19, 1829, by Eli Bennett, Elder	1	91
ENGLES, [see also ENGLISH], James S., m. Ellen Louisa STONE, Apr. 5, 1846, by Rev. Samuel R. Hickcox	1	259
ENGLISH, [see also ENGLES], Abraham, m. Hannah JOHNSON, Dec. 2, 1773?; recorded Nov. 15, 1815	1	91
Augusta Caroline, of Derby, m. Henry McNEAL, of New Haven, Oct. 18, 1835, by Rev. Zepheniah Swift	1	150
Benjamin, s. Clement & Ruth, b. Sept. 24, 1760	LR7	252
Benjamin, s. Clement & Ruth, b. Oct. 28, 1761	LR7	252
Clement, m. Ruth WIESBURY, Oct. 26, 1752	LR6	6
Clement, s. Clement & Ruth, b. June 25, 1756	LR6	441
David, s. Clement & Ruth, b. June 25, 1765	TM1	10
Dorcas, d. [Abraham & Hannah], b. Mar. 19, 1811	1	9
Dorcas, m. Augustus TOMLINSON, Apr. 18, 1830, by Samuel R. Hickox. Witnesses: Abram English, Henry English, Hannah Osborn	1	118
Grace, d. [Abraham & Hannah], b. Sept. 19, 1809	1	9
Hannah, d. [Abraham & Hannah], b. Sept. 23, 1800	1	9
Harry, s. [Abraham & Hannah], b. June 30, 1803	1	9
Harry, m. Louisa BALDWIN, Mar. 14, 1834, by Rev. Charles William Bradley	1	153
Henry, s. Clement & Ruth, b. Dec. 7, 1757	LR6	443
Isaac, s. Abraham & Hannah, b. Oct. 24, 1793	1	9
Judson, s. [Abraham & Hannah], b. Nov. 30, 1795	1	9
Judson, m. Sally GILLET, Mar. 23, 1828, by Rev. Samuel R. Hickox	1	91
Lucy, [d. Abraham & Hannah], b. Aug. 26, 1814	1	9
Maria, of Derby (Great Hill), m. George GILBERT, of New Haven, July 4, 1839, by Oliver Sykes	1	157
Mark, s. [Abraham & Hannah], b. June 7, 1808	1	9
Naomy, d. Clement & Ruth, b. June 28, 1753	LR6	441
Naomi, d. [Abraham & Hannah], b. Feb. 20, 1798	1	9
Ruth, d. Clement & Ruth, b. Oct. 22, 1754	LR6	441
FAGAN, Bridget, m. Francis FARRELL, [ ], by Rev. James Lynch, of Birmingham; recorded Mar. 3, 1852	1	272
FAIRCHILD, Abiel, Jr., m. Hannah CHATFIELD, Feb. 23, 1757	LR6	450
Abiel, m. Mrs. Mary PECK, b. of Derby, May 10, 1757	LR6	450

	Vol.	Page
FAIRCHILD, (cont.)		
Abiel, Jr., m. Zurviah **JOHNSON**, Sept. 3, 1761	LR7	248
Agur, s. Abiel & Lois, d. Nov. 26, 1755	LR6	13
Anna, w. Abiel, d. Apr. 4, 1760	LR6	719
Bille, s. Joseph & Hannah, b. Aug. 13, 1781	TM1	104
Chloe, d. Joseph & Hannah, b. Aug. 13, 1781	TM1	104
Dauid, s. Abiel & Lois, b. July 14, 1750	LR5	414
Ebenezer, s. Abiel & Lois, b. Mar. 10, 1747	LR5	414
Ebenezer, s. Abiel & Loes, b. Mar. 22, 1747	LR5	232
Ebenezer, s. Abiel & Lois, d. Sept. 8, 1751	LR6	5
Hannah, d. Abiel & Zerviah, b. Mar. 21, 1763	LR7	252
Hannah, m. Abel **PERSON**, b. of Derby, Sept. 6, 1781	TM1	119
John, s. Abial & Anne, b. Nov. 21, 1757	LR6	443
John, s. Abiel & Hannah, d. Sept. 12, 1776, in the Northern Army	TM1	86
John, s. Abiel & Zeriah, b. Apr. 11, 1777	TM1	86
Joseph, m. Hannah **WHE[E]LER**, b. of Derby, Nov. 9, 1780	TM1	104
Louis, w. Abiel, d. Dec. 9, 1755	LR6	13
Lowis, m. Samuel **WHE[E]LER**, Jr., Apr. 28, 1763, by Rev. Mr. Levenworth	TM1	31
Molly, d. Abiel & Zurviah, b. Nov. 19, 1770	TM1	59
Nathan, m. Ruth **WHE[E]LER**, July 23, 1761	TM1	9
Nathan, m. Ruth **WHE[E]LER**, b. of Derby, July 23, 1761	LR7	248
Nathan, m. Lowes **BEACHER**, Apr. 24, 1765	TM1	9
Nathan, s. Nathan & Lowes, b. July 5, 1766	TM1	9
Nehemiah, s. Abiel & Lois, d. Sept. 18, 1751	LR6	5
Ruth, d. Nathan & Ruth, b. Aug. 24, 1764	TM1	9
Ruth, w. Nathan, d. Sept. 1, 1764	TM1	9
Ruth, w. Nathan & d. of Capt. James **WHE[E]LER**, d. Sept. 1, 1764, in the 22nd y. of her age	TM1	33
Ruth, d. Nathan, d. Jan. 2, 1765	TM1	9
Ruth, d. Nathan & Lowis, b. Feb. 6, 1768	TM1	8
FARRELL, Francis, m. Bridget **FAGAN**, [ ], by Rev. James Lynch, of Birmingham; recorded Mar. 3, 1852	1	272
Franklin, m. Julia L. **SMITH**, Mar. 31, 1850, by Rev. C. S. Putnam. Int. Pub.	1	271
FELCH, Augustus, m. Henrietta **BALDWIN**, Nov. 29, 1837, by Rev. Joseph Scott	1	155
Samuel, m. Patty **BALDWIN**, May 8, 1836, by Rev. L. D. Howell	1	155
FENN, Dan, of Milford, m. Marie **BRADLEY**, of Derby, Mar. 26, 1834, by Zepheniah Swift	1	155
[FERGUSON], FURGUSON, Mary, m. Duncan **McARTHUR**, b. of Derby, Aug. 5, 1850, by Rev. Jno Morrison Reid	1	193
Mary, m. Duncan M. **ARTHUR**, b. of Derby, Aug. [ ], 1850, by Rev. Jno Morrison Reid	1	211
FIELD, FIELDS, James W., m. Betsy I. **TUCKER**, b. of Derby, June 20, 1847, by Rev. William Bliss Ashley	1	271

	Vol.	Page
FOX, (cont.)		
Benjamin, m. Easther CHATFIELD, Apr. 9, 1754	LR6	8
Comfort, d. Benjamin & Easter, b. May 25, 1754	LR6	15
Comfort, m. Noah Russel LYMAN, Feb. 13, 1771	TM1	52
Esther, of Derby, m. Ethiel PERKINS, of Derby, Oct. 26, 1767,		
by Timo[thy] Russel	TM1	65
Huldah, d. Benjamin & Easther, b. July 14, 1756	LR6	441
Hulday, m. John HOLBROOK, Jr., July 7, 1774	TM1	230
FRANCIS, Mary, m. Roswell FREEMAN (colored), b. of Derby, May		
1, 1826, by Rev. Zepheniah Swift	1	92
FREDON, Isaac, of New Preston, m. Betsey BLAKESLY, of North		
Haven, Sept. 8, 1832, by Rev. Charles Thompson	1	154
FREEMAN, Almyra, called PARSONS, m. Benjamin SEDAR, of		
Wallingford, Mar. 17, 1831, by Rev. Charles Thompson	1	90
Delia, m. Levi ALLEN, Sept. 21, 1843, by Rev. W[illia]m		
Bliss Ashely	1	193
Laura, m. Jairus JENNINGS, (colored), Dec. 24, 1822, by Rev.		
Zepheniah Swift	1	99
Olive, of Derby, m. Timothy DRAKE, of Oxford, (colored),		
Jan. 24, 1821, by Rev. Ziphaniah Swift	1	89
Roswell, m. Mary FRANCIS, (colored), b. of Derby, May 1,		
1826, by Rev. Zepheniah Swift	1	92
FRENCH, FFRENCH, Anna, w. Francis, d. Jan. 11, 17[ ]	LR5	1
Anna, d. Israel & Sarah, b. June 21, 1752	LR6	2
Asa, s. Nathan & Lucy, b. Mar. 26, 1777	TM1	118
Betty, d. Noah & Hannah, b. Feb. 11, 1759	TM1	184
Bette, d. Noah & Hannah, b. Feb. 11, 1759	LR6	440
Betty, d. Noah & Hannah, d. May 5, 1775	TM1	184
Betty, d. Noah & Hannah, b. Feb. 19, 1778	TM1	184
Bowers, s. Israel & Sarah, b. July 5, 1757	LR6	441
Charles, s. Francis & Agnes or Anna, b. Feb. 14, 1709	2	23
Charles, s. Israel & Sarah, b. Dec. 19, 1765	TM1	20
Charles, s. Francis & Anna, d. Nov. 9, 1783, in the 77th		
y. of his age	TM1	123
Charles, m. Anna WOODCOCK, Feb. 25, 1784	TM1	158
David, s. Israel & Sarah, b. Jan. 30, 1741/2	LR5	2
Delia, of Derby, m. David CAULKINS, of Lyme, Nov. 1, 1829,		
by Z. Swift	1	103
Dorcus, d. Israel & Sarah, b. Oct. 2, 1746	LR6	2
Dorcus, d. Israel & Sarah, d. May 8, 1751	LR6	5
Eliza M., of Humphreysville, m. Levi GILBERT, of New Haven,		
Nov. 8, 1827, by Rev. T. Spicer. Int. Pub.	1	94
Emeline, of Derby, m. Lemuel BLISS, of West Springfield,		
Mass., June 10, 183[ ], by Rev. John E. Bray	1	146
Emily, d. Walter, of Derby, m. Henry O. McCOY, of Branford,		
Sept. 9, 1835, by Sylvester Smith	1	149
Enoch, s. Israel & Sarah, b. May 19, 1760	LR4	250
Eunice, d. Nathan & Lucy, b. May 8, 1775	TM1	118

	Vol.	Page
FRENCH, FFRENCH, (cont.)		
Mary, d. Sam[ue]ll & Martha, b. July 26, 1743	LR4	A5
Mary, m. William **BURRETT**, Apr. 22, 1762	TM1	155
Mary, m. William **BURRITT**, b. of Derby, Apr. 22, 1762, by Rev. Richard Mansfield	LR7	256
Nathan, m. Lucy **JOHNSON**, b. of Derby, Sept. 2, 1773	TM1	118
Nathaniel, s. Frances & Anna, b. Oct. 28, 1717	LR3	3
Nathaniel, s. Francis & Anna, d. Nov. 13, [ ], ae 64 y. 5 d.	TM1	123
Noah, d. Hannah **RIGGS**, b. of Derbe, June 12, 1755, by Rev. Cyrus Marsh	LR6	7
Noah, s. Noah & Hannah, b. Jan. 14, 1767	TM1	184
Noah, d. Jan. 7, 1781	TM1	123
Pemelia, m. Isaac **BASSETT**, Jr., b. of Derby, Sept. 8, 1822, by Eli Barnett	1	87
Salle, d. Charles & Anna, b. Nov. 14, 1784	TM1	158
Samuell, s. Ffrances & Lidia, b. Jan. 6, 1672	2	2
Sa[mue]ll, d. Oct. 26, 1677	2	2
Samuell, s. Israel & Anna, b. July 23, 1704	2	12
Sam[ue]ll, m. Martha **CHAPMAN**, Dec. 17, 1733	LR3	10
Samuel, s. Noah & Hannah, b. Oct. 26, 1760	TM1	184
Samuel, s. Noah & Hannah, b. Oct. 26, 1760	LR7	249
Samuel, s. Francis & Anna, d. Feb. 2, 1783, in the 79th y. of his age	TM1	123
Sarah, m. Abraham **SMITH**, [ ]	TM1	64
Sarah, d. Sam[ue]ll & Martha, b. July 16, 1738	LR4	A3
Sarah, d. Israel & Sarah, b. Jan. 25, 1747/8	LR6	2
Sarah, d. Israel & Sarah, d. May 6, 1751	LR6	5
Sarah, m. Abraham **SMITH**, Dec. 5, 1756	LR6	451
Sarah, d. Noah & Hannah, b. Oct. 24, 1771	TM1	184
Susana, d. Ffran[ces] & Lidiah, b. June 6, 1675	2	2
Susanna, d. Francis & Olive, b. Oct. 3, 1780	TM1	130
Wales, m. Polly **ROBBINS**, Sept. 17, 1838, by Rev. John E. Bray	1	156
Warren, m. Lucinda **RIGGS**, Nov. 26, 1823, by Rev. Stephen Jewett	1	93
W[illia]m, m. Nancy **GILBERT**, b. of Derby, Mar. 22, 1823, by Eli Barnett, Elder	1	93
William, of Derby, m. Malinda **MARTIN**, of Woodbury, Dec. 24, 1823, by Rev. Stephen Jewett	1	93
William M., m. [ ] H. **HOTCHKISS**, Dec. 24, 1833, by Z. Swift	1	155
----iah, d. Ffrances & Lidia, b. Sept. 28, 1670	2	2
----h, s. Samuel & Martha, b. Oct. 31, 1736	LR3	11
FRINK, Margret, m. Nathan **SMITH**, Mar. 15, 1758, by Rev. Daniel Humphrey	LR6	445
FRISBIE, Thomas I., m. Laura (?) **SMITH**, of Humphreysville, May 31, 1846, by Rev. John Parves, of Humphreysville	1	271

	Vol.	Page

FROST, Allanson, of Cornel, N. Y., m. Mary Ann HITCHCOCK, of
New Haven, Sept. 24, 1840, by Rev. B. Y. Morse — 1 — 156

FULLER, Isaac N., of Warren, Conn., m. Frances E. SCOVILLE, of
Derby, Sept. 22, 1851, by Rev. I. Guernsey — 1 — 272

GAILER, Pacience, m. Isaak TOMLINSON, Mar. 25, 1712 — LR3 — 9

GALPIN, Phillip S., of N[ew] H[aven], m. Sarah S. HALL, of
Derby, [ ], by Rev. Thomas T. Guion; recorded
Feb. 18, 1853 — 1 — 280

GAORDON, [see under GORDON]

GARDNER, Andrew McIntyre, m. Angeline ARMITAGE, b. of
Ansonia, June 12, 1853, by Rev. Daniel W[illia]m Havens,
at Ansonia — 1 — 280

GARNER, Elizabeth, of Birmingham, m. Hiram SEALY, of New
Milford, [ ], by Rev. Thomas G. Osborn; recorded July
7, 1852 — 1 — 441

GAY, Emma M., of Derby, m. John W. BARCLIN, of Dutton, Mass.,
Sept. 20, 1840, by Rev. W[illia]m Denison — 1 — 209

Esther H., of Derby, m. George W. CHAPIN, of Hartford, Sept.
20, 1840, by Rev. W[illia]m Denison — 1 — 235

GERARD, Asahel H., m. Elsie OSBORN, Dec. 1, 1844, by Rev.
John D. Smith — 1 — 279

Catharine E., m. Andrew B. CLEMENS, Dec. 7, 1845, by Rev.
W[illia]m B. Curtiss — 1 — 233

Martha A., m. Isaiah R. SPERRY, Nov. 30, 1844, by Rev.
W. B. Curtiss — 1 — 439

Rhoda, m. Charles CHATFIELD, b. of Derby, Jan. 3, 1841,
by Rev. John B. Beach — 1 — 192

GILBERT, Agur, of Derby, m. Mary JOHNSON, of Orange, Feb. 4,
1830, by Z. Swift — 1 — 103

Catherine Sophia, m. John BASSETT, Jr., Jan. 7, 1838, by
John D. Smith — 1 — 174

Edmund B., m. Lucilla DALY, Nov. 30, 1848, by Rev. C.
S. Putnam — 1 — 279

Esther Ann, m. Dr. Thomas STODDARD, Apr. 9, 1839, by John
D. Smith — 1 — 185

Gennett, of Derby, m. William CURTISS, of Stratford, Nov. 27
1845, by Zephaniah Swift — 1 — 233

George, of New Haven, m. Maria ENGLISH, of Derby (Great
Hill), July 4, 1839, by Oliver Sykes — 1 — 157

Henrietta G., m. Charles C. BEERS, b. of Derby, Jan. 18, 1835,
by Rev. Z. Swift — 1 — 146

Levi, of New Haven, m. Eliza M. FRENCH, of Humphreysville,
Nov. 8, 1827, by Rev. T. Spicer. Int. Pub. — 1 — 94

Lucius, m. Mary L. NARAMORE, Apr. 21, 1845, by Rev.
George Thacher — 1 — 279

Lucy I., m. David T. OSBORN, Mar. 16, 1845, by Rev. George
Thacher — 1 — 393

Nancy, m. W[illia]m FRENCH, b. of Derby, Mar. 22, 1823,

	Vol.	Page
GILBERT, (cont.)		
by Eli Barnett, Elder	1	93
Phebe Ann, m. John W. HAYES, b. of Derby, Oct. 20, 1839,		
by Rev. H. Reed	1	160
Sarah E., m. Leslie BRYSON (Capt.), Aug. 25, 1844, by Rev.		
John D. Smith	1	206
GILLET, GILLETT, GILLIT, Benjamin, [twin with Joseph], s.		
Ephraim & Persis, b. Aug. 7, 1744	LR5	413
Betsey, of Roxbury, m. Henry BLAKESLEY, of Plymouth,		
Apr. 6, 1837, by Rev. John E. Bray	1	166
Caroline S., of Derby, m. Frederick P. GORHAM, of New		
Haven, Jan. 24, 1841, by Rev. Joseph Scott	1	157
Dauid, [twin with Wooster], s. Ephraim & Persis, b. Mar.		
21, 172[ ]	LR3	5
David, s. Shadrack & Mercy, b. Aug. 8, 1771	TM1	63
Ephraim, m. Peirse WOOSTER, Apr. 2, 1724	LR3	9
Ephraim, s. Ephraim, b. Jan. 8, 1724/5	LR3	5
Free Loue, d. Ephraim & Persis, b. Aug. 10, 172[ ]	LR3	15
Freeloue, d. Ephraim & Persis, b. Aug. 10, 1729	LR5	413
Isaac, m. Harriet HURD, Sept. 6, 1829, by Rev. Nathaniel		
Kellogg	1	94
Jerusha Wooster, d. Shadrack & Mercy, b. Sept. 1, 1767	TM1	30
Joseph, [twin with Benjamin], s. Ephraim & Persis, b.		
Aug. 7, 1744	LR5	413
Mary, d. Ephraim & Persis, b. Mar. 10, 1726/7	LR5	413
Mary, d. Eph[rai]m & Persis, b. Mar. 11, 1731/2	LR4	16
Mary, d. Shadrak & Mercy, b. Nov. 12, 1769	TM1	63
Mary, d. Shadrak & Mercy, d. May 1, 1770	TM1	63
Mary, m. Harris SMITH, b. of Prospect, Mar. 2, 1842, by		
Rev. John E. Bray	1	185
Sally, m. Judson ENGLISH, Mar. 23, 1828, by Rev. Samuel R.		
Hickox	1	91
Shadrack, d. Sept. 7, 1771	TM1	63
Wooster, [twin with Dauid], s. Ephraim & Persis, b. Mar.		
21, 172[ ]	LR3	5
GILYARD, Nancy, m. Glover BASSETT, b. of Derby, Oct. 21, 1839,		
by Rev. Sam[ue]l R. Hickox. Witnesses: Jared Bassett,		
Sally B. Bassett	1	167
GLOVER, Bathiah, of New Town, m. Joseph TOMLINSON, of		
Derby, Oct. 27, 1763, by Rev. Richard Mansfield	LR7	256
GOODMAN, Calvin H., of Augusta, Ga., m. Theodosia REEMER, of		
Derby, Apr. 9, 1839, by Rev. H. Read	1	157
[GORDON], GAORDON, [see also JORDON], Thomas, m. Nancy S.		
BURNS, b. of Milford, Nov. 30, 1837, by Thomas Ellis	1	127
GORHAM, Frederick P., of New Haven, m. Caroline S. GILLET,		
of Derby, Jan. 24, 1841, by Rev. Joseph Scott	1	157
GORMSBY, Edward E., of Derby, m. Mary E. THOMPSON, of		
Hartford, Nov. 26, 1848, by Rev. Charles Stearns	1	279

229

	Vol.	Page

GOULDEND, John M., m. Mahala S. PHILLIPS, b. of Derby, Oct.
 25, 1851, by Rev. Thomas T. Guion — 1 — 280
GRACY, Daniel, s. Capt. Ebenezer & Betty, b. Dec. [ ], 1783 — TM1 — 213
GRANGER, David H., m. Frances E. ALLIS, June 1, 1846, by
 Rev. W[illia]m B. Curtiss — 1 — 279
GRAY, Sarah E., of Norwalk, m. J. C. T. DeAGRELLO, of New
 York, Apr. 25, 1852, by Rev. Thomas T. Guion — 1 — 248
GREELY, Elbrige, of Meriden, m. Lucy KNAPP, of Derby, May 12,
 1844, by Rev. Nathaniel Mead — 1 — 279
GREEN, James Sheldon, of Coventry, m. Jenette BALDWIN, of
 Humphreysville, Jan. 9, 1831, by Rev. Stephen Jewett — 1 — 102
 William, of Sharon, m. Mary BLAKE, of New Preston, now
 of Derby, May 13, 1832, by Prince Hawes — 1 — 157
GREGG, David, m. Mary COLEMAN, Jan. 24, [18]52, by Rev.
 James Lynch — 1 — 280
GREGSTON, Edward, m. Laura Maria MORSE, Dec. 20, 1848, by
 Henry Whitney, J. P. — 1 — 280
GRIFFIN, GRIFFEN, Catharine, d. Charles & Catharine, b. Dec.
 30, 1753 — LR6 — 442
 Charles, m. Catharine WISEBURY, Dec. 4, 1751 — LR6 — 451
 James H., m. Nancy M. BRISTOL, Dec. 26, 1838, by Rev.
 Joseph Scott — 1 — 157
GUNN, GUNNE, GUN, Abell, s. Abell & Agnes, b. May 7, [ ] — 2 — 13
 Abell, s. Abell & Hannah, d. Mar. 14, [ ] — LR3 — 12
 Abel, m. Agnes HAWKENS, May 24, 1704, by John James — 2 — 13
 Abel, Sergt., d. Feb. 26, 1720/1 — LR3 — 6
 Abel, m. Hannah HARGER, Aug. 2, 1727 — LR3 — 10
 Abel, s. Abel & Hannah, b. July 29, 1735 — LR3 — 11
 Abel, s. Abel & Hannah, b. Jan. 15, 1747 — LR5 — 232
 Abel, of Waterbury, m. Abigail DAVIS, of Derby, Dec. 2, 1756,
 by Rev. Richard Mansfield — LR6 — 8
 Abel, Capt., d. Sept. 15, 1769 — TM1 — 48
 Abigail, d. Abell & Agnes, b. Sept. 16, 1707 — 2 — 23
 Abigail, m. John HOLLBROOK, Aug. 27, 1723 — LR3 — 9
 Abigal, m. Sam[ue]ll RIGGS, Jan. 6, 1726 — LR3 — 10
 Agnis, m. Isaac NIKOLS, Nov. 14, 1722/3 — LR3 — 9
 Agnis, [twin with Emis], d. Abell & Hannah, b. Apr. 20, 1738 — LR4 — A5
 Agniss, m. Josiah NETTLETON, Nov. [ ], 1761, by Rev.
 Richard Mansfield — TM1 — 160
 Elizabeth, of Milford, m. Joseph HAWKINS, of Derby,
 Aug. 9, 1693 — 2 — 25
 Emis, [twin with Agnis], s. Abell & Hannah, b. Apr. 20, 1738 — LR4 — A5
 Enos, s. Abel & Agnis, b. Aug. 28, 1715 — LR3 — 2
 Enos, s. Capt. Abel, d. Sept. 16, 1767, in the 30th y.
 of his age — TM1 — 38
 Hannah, d. Abel & Hannah, d. Mar. 2, 173[ ] — LR3 — 12
 Hannah, d. Abel & Hannah, b. Oct. 8, 1744 — LR5 — 232
 Hannah, w. Capt. Abel, d. Mar. 13, 1758 — LR6 — 440

	Vol.	Page
GUNN, GUNNE, GUN, (cont.)		
Hannah, wid. Capt. Abel & d. Francis & Anna **FRENCH**, d.		
Jan. 24, 1781, in the 66th y. of her age	TM1	123
Mary, Mrs., m. John **DAVIS**, May 12, 1691	2	25
Mary, d. Nathaniel & Sarah, b. Jan. 12, 1729	LR3	15
Nathaniel, s. Abel & Agnes, b. Sept. 1, 1709	2	160
Nathaniel, m. Sarah WHE[E]LER, Dec. 10, 1728	LR3	10
Sarah, d. Abel & Agnes, b. Apr. 3, 1713	LR3	2
Sarah, m. John **WASHBON**, Nov. 5, 1722	LR3	10
Sarah, of Waterbury, m. Jabez **THOMSON**, of Derby, Oct.		
25, 1748	LR5	4
Sarah, d. Abel & Abigail, b. Sept. 5, 1757	LR6	441
Sarah, d. Nathaniel & Sarah, b. Feb. 15, [ ]	LR3	16
Silas, of Oxford, m. Maria **TOMLINSON**, of Derby, Apr. 6,		
1842, by Rev. Sylvester Smith	1	279
GUSIN, Enes, d. Jan. 28, 1737	LR3	12
HALE, HAIL, HAILL, [see also HALL], Abraham, m. Martha		
SMITH, b. of Derby, Mar. 3, 1756, by Samuel Riggs	LR6	445
Beman, s. Abraham & Martha, b. Oct. 1, 1757	LR6	443
Beman, m. Hannah **DAVIS**, b. of Derby, Nov. 11, 1779, by		
Rev. David Bronson	TM1	117
Elisha, s. Samuel & Anne, b. Oct. 15, 1757	LR6	442
Hannah, d. Abraham, b. July 28, 1759	LR6	719
Hannah C., of Derby, m. John T. **STANNARD**, of New		
Marlborough, Mass., July 9, 1843, by Rev. Harman Ellis, of		
North Haven	1	439
Mary, m. Joel **BEEBEE**, Feb. 1, 1823, by Rev. Stephen Jewett,		
of St. James Church	1	84
Samuel, m. Anne **PEIRCE**, Nov. 23, 1757	LR6	451
HALL, [see also HALE & HULL], Augusta, of Derby, m. Fred A.		
PLATT, of New York, May 12, 1851, by Rev. Thomas T.		
Guion	1	407
Beach, of Trumbull, m. Amelia A. **BROOK**, of Birmingham,		
Feb. 11, 1852, by Rev. Thomas G. Osborn	1	292
Charry S., Mrs. m. Charles **NICHOLS**, b. of Derby, Feb.		
20, 1853, by Rev. O. Street	1	381
Eliza M., of Oxford, m. Joseph N. **SNELL**, of Waterbury,		
Sept. 9, 1849, by William E. Downs, J. P.	1	441
Lucretia, of Woodbury, m. Moses **SMITH**, of Derby, Feb. 28,		
1780	TM1	109
Mansfield, m. Sarah M. **CHAFFEE**, b. of Derby, Aug. 3, 1851,		
by Rev. Thomas T. Guion	1	292
Sarah S., of Derby, m. Phillip S. **GALPIN**, of N[ew] H[aven],		
[ ], by Rev. Thomas T. Guion; recorded Feb. 18, 1853	1	280
W[illia]m S., of Bristoll, m. Charlotte **SMITH**, of Derby,		
[ ], by Rev. Thomas T. Guion	1	292
Zenas M., m. Ann M. **HUMISTON**, Nov. 5, 1845, by Rev.		
Geo[rge] L. Fuller	1	407

	Vol.	Page
HALLOCK, Mary Ann, of Derby, m. John HUBBEL, of Huntington,		
Aug. 21, 1825, by Rev. Zepheniah Swift	1	101
Rebeca, m. William H. HOTCHKISS, b. of Derby, Mar. 11,		
1827, by Stephen Jewett	1	97
Sarah, m. Garred SMITH, Oct. 23, 1823, by Rev. Zepheniah		
Swift	1	116
HANSON, Elizabeth, m. Horace Augustus AUGUST, b. of New		
Haven, June 13, 1831, by Rev. Charles Thompson, of		
Humphreyville	1	121
HARD, Prudence, of New Town, m. William MOSS, of Derby, May		
30, 1751	LR7	250
HARDEN, Jonas, m. Sally CRAWFORD, July 24, [1831], by John T.		
Wheeler, J. P.	1	92
HARDYEAR, Abraham, m. Hannah RIGGS, May 19, 1703	2	13
Joseph, s. Ebenezar & Abigail, b. Oct. 13, 1704	2	12
Sally, of Derby, m. Martin BRYANT, of New York, Sept. 19,		
1824, by Rev. Stephen Jewett	1	83
HARGER, HARGIER, Abigail, m. Timothy WOOSTER, Aug. 18,		
1727	LR5	4
Abigal, m. Abyjah HULL, Nov. 30, 1727	LR3	10
Abigal, d. John & Rachel, b. Sept. 13, 1735	LR3	11
Abigail, d. John & Rachel, b. May 11, 1739	LR4	A3
Abigail, m. Leui CHATFIELD, b. of Derby, Jan. 30, 1758,		
by Rev. Richard Mansfield	LR6	444
Abraham, s. Ephraim & Mary, b. Sept. 14, 1735	LR3	11
Abraham, s. Ephraim & Mary, b. Oct. 26, 1745	LR5	2
Abraham, of Derby, m. Mary CLENTON, of New Haven, Sept.		
25, 1766, by Rev. Mr. Pamer	TM1	15
Ann, m. John TWITCHEL, Mar. 20, 1733/4	LR3	10
Annah, m. John CHATTFIELD, Feb. 5, 1684	2	25
Anna, d. Sam[ue]ll & Phebe, b. May 30, 1760	LR6	447
Anar, d. Edward & Sarah, b. Oct. 12, 1775	TM1	109
Anna, m. James DORMAN, June 9, 1779	TM1	161
Anna, m. Charles DAVIS, Sept. 30, 1838, by Rev. Joseph Scott	1	151
Beniamen, s. Jabez & Anna, b. Apr. 24, 1715	LR3	2
Benjamin, s. Ephraim & Mary, b. Dec. 22, 1743	LR4	A5
Benjamin, m. Ame TUTTLE, b. of Derby, July 4, 1768	TM1	129
Benjamin, s. Benjamin & Ame, b. Jan. 12, 1769	TM1	129
Benjamin, d. Mar. 15, 1779	TM1	129
Charlotte, d. Edward & Sarah, b. Nov. 17, 1773	TM1	109
Comfort, d. Jabish & Anna, b. Sept. 10, 1720	LR6	3
Comfort, m. Eliphelet HOCHKISS, Dec. 26, 1751	LR6	6
David, s. Jabesh & Sarah, b. Apr. 9, 1769	TM1	9
Ebenezer, m. Abigall TIBBALS, Sept. 15, 1698	2	25
Ebenezer, s. Ebenezer & Abigail, b. Feb. 11, 1706/7	2	13
Ebenezer & w. Abigal, had s. [ ], b. Nov. 3, 171[ ]	LR3	1
Ebenezer, s. Samuel & Phebe, b. Mar. 2, 1748	LR5	232
Eber, s. Edward & Susanna, b. Aug. 31, 1781	TM1	130

	Vol.	Page
HARGER, HARGIER, (cont.)		
Edward, s. Samuel & Phebe, b. Feb. 15, 1749/50	LR5	414
Edward, m. Sarah WASHBOND, b. of Derby, Sept. 9, 1771	TM1	109
Edward, of Derby, m. Susanna DICKINSON, of Stratford,		
Aug. 16, 1780	TM1	130
Elijah, s. Jabish & Sarah, b. July 14, 1764	TM1	4
Elisabeth, m. Jabez TWICHEL, b. of Derby, May 8, 1771	TM1	83
Ephraim, s. Benjamin & Ame, b. May 23, 1774	TM1	129
Gehoadan, m. Benjamin TOMLINSON, Nov. 16, 1742	LR4	A4
Hannah, m. John TIBBALS, Mar. 28, 1700	2	25
Hannah, m. Abel GUNN, Aug. 2, 1727	LR3	10
Hannah, d. Edward & Sarah, b. Dec. 29, 1771	TM1	109
Jabiz, s. Jabiz & Annah, b. Feb. 24, 173[ ]	LR3	16
Jabez, s. Jabish & Sarah, b. Nov. 25, 1766	TM1	4
Jabiah, m. Sarah DURAND, Jan. 24, 1758, by Rev. Jonathan		
Lyman	LR6	444
Jehoaddan, d. Jabez & Anna, b. Mar. 11, 1717/18	LR3	3
John, s. Ebenezer & Abigal, b. Sept. 22, 1710	LR3	0
John & w. Rachil had s. [ ], b. June 6, 1737	LR3	11
John, m. Rachel STEPHENS, Dec. 24, [ ]	LR3	10
Joseph, s. Samuel & Hannah, b. Apr. 20, 1694	2	26
Joseph, s. Samuel & Hannah, d. July 30, 1698	2	27
Joseph, s. Ebenezer & Abigail, d. Dec. 27, 170[ ]?	2	27
Joseph, s. Ebenezer & Abigail, d. Aug. 6, 1714	LR3	6
Joseph, s. Benjamin & Ame, b. Apr. 19, 1779	TM1	129
Laria, m. James HUMPHREYS, Jr., Apr. 18, 1824, by Rev.		
Stephen Jewett	1	96
Luseney, d. Benjamin & Amey, b. Sept. 17, 1776	TM1	129
Luseney, d. Benjamin & Ame, d. July 4, 1778	TM1	129
Margret, d. Samuel & Hannah, b. Dec. 6, 1695	2	26
Margret, m. Joseph JOHNSON, Jan. 24, 1717	LR3	9
Margret, d. Jabiz & Annah, b. Apr. 23, 1725	LR3	15
Margret, d. Ephr[ai]m & Mary, b. Nov. 26, 1741	LR3	a5
Naomi, d. Samuel & Phebe, b. June 13, 1767	TM1	19
Patience, d. Sam[ue]ll & Phebe, b. May 20, 1754	LR6	4
Philo, s. Samuel & Phebe, b. Sept. 16, 1769	TM1	63
Sally, m. Daniel M. JOHNSON, May [ ], 1822, by Rev.		
Zepheniah Swift	1	99
Samuel, of Derby, m. Han[n]ah STILES, of Stratford,		
May 9, 1693	2	25
Samuel, d. Feb. 18, 1697	2	27
Samuel, s. Samuel & Hannah, b. Sept. 24, 1697/8	2	31
Samuel, s. Jabez, b. Mar. 11, 1722/3	LR3	4
Samuel, m. Phebe WOOSTER, Dec. 9, 1747	LR5	4
Sarah, d. Ephr[ai]m & Mary, b. Dec. 24, 1739	LR4	A3
Sarah, d. Ephraim & Mary, b. Dec. 24, 1739	LR4	A5
Sarah, d. Jabish & Sarah, b. Aug. 5, 1760	LR7	249
Sarah, m. Josiah WASHBOND, b. of Derby, June 2, 1767,		

	Vol.	Page
HARGER, HARGIER, (cont.)		
by Rev. Richard Mansfield	TM1	86
Sarah, d. Benjamin & Ame, b. Jan. 23, 1771	TM1	129
William, of Derby, m. Jane Lavinia THOMAS, of East Haven,		
Mar. 19, 1829, by S. Jewett	1	98
William, m. Deborah Ann SAMPSON, June 14, 1849, by		
Rev. W[illia]m B. Curtiss	1	291
---nnah, d. John & Rachel, b. Dec. 8, 1744	LR5	2
HARRIS, John, m. Rachel MOSS, Feb. 5, 1739/40	LR5	4
John, s. [ ] & Rachel, b. Mar. 5, 1744	LR5	2
Mary, m. Benjamin TOMLINSON, b. of Derby, Nov. 15, 1768	LR5	31
Rachel, had s. John, b. Mar. 5, 1744	LR5	2
Timothy, s. John & Rachel, b. Oct. 6, 1742	LR5	2
HARRISON, Eliza, of Derby, m. Perry WILLIAMS, of Plymouth,		
Aug. 24, 1828, by Rev. A. M. Train, of Milford	1	124
HART, George L., Capt. of Huntington, m. Hannah LOTTEREGES,		
of Kinderhook, N. Y., Aug. 29, 1825, by Stephen Jewett	1	105
Nelson, of Avon, m. Mary E. DUNCAN, of New York, Jan. 27,		
1850, by Rev. Jno Morrison Reid	1	210
Nelson, of Avon, m. Mary E. DUNCAN, of New York, June 27,		
1850, by Rev. Jno Morrison Reid	1	291
Thomas Albert, m. Sarah Grace MORSE, Nov. 26, 1838, by		
Rev. Joseph Scott	1	160
HARTSHORN, HARTSON, Andrew, m. Emily BOUGHTON, Jan.		
5, 1840, by John D. Smith	1	158
Andrew, m. Sarah CLARK, June 15, 1844, by Rev. W[illia]m B.		
Curtiss	1	289
HAWKINS, HAWKENS, HAWKINGS, Abygail, b. Feb. 2, 1672	2	1
Abigal, m. John PRINGIL, Mar. 1, 1696/7	2	25
Abigal, d. Joseph & Elizabeth, b. July 31, 1698	2	31
Abigail, m. Thomas SMITH, Dec. 20, 1727	LR3	10
Abijah, m. Hannah BARTHOLOMEW, b. of Derby, [Feb.] 16,		
1823, by Rev. Stephen Jewett	1	96
Abraham, s. Moses, b. Apr. 22, 1725	LR3	5
Abraham, m. Elisabeth BASSIT, Apr. 20, 1748	LR5	4
Abraham, s. Abraham & Elisabeth, d. [ ], 29, 1760	LR7	249
Abraham, s. Abraham & Elisabeth, d. Apr. 29, 1760	LR7	250
Abram, Jr., of Derby, m. Betsey BRUNSON, of New Milford,		
Jan. 17, 1836, by Rev. Joseph Scott	1	160
Agnes, m. Abel GUNNE, May 24, 1704, by John James	2	13
Agnes, [twin with Loes], d. Jos[eph], b. [ ]	2	1
Ann, wid., Capt. Moses, d. May 9, [ ], in the 78th y.		
of her age	TM1	49
Ann, d. Moses & Ann, b. Aug. 1, 1731	LR3	16
Ann, m. Elijah SMITH, May 3, 1748	LR5	4
Ann, d. Abraham & Elisabeth, b. Mar. 21, 1753	LR6	5
Ann, d. Abraham & Elisabeth, d. Mar. 16, 1766, in the		
13th y. of her age	TM1	11

	Vol.	Page
HAWKINS, HAWKENS, HAWKINGS, (cont.)		
Ann, d. Abraham & Elisabeth, b. Sept. 6, 1768	TM1	63
Ann, wid. Capt. Moses, d. May 9, 1782, in the 78th y. of her age	TM1	210
Annah, d. Moses & Anne, b. Feb. 4, 1737/8	LR4	A3
Army (?), d. Zachariah & Mary, b. Apr. 4, 1750	LR6	441
Berth (?), d. Moses & Ann, b. Dec. 20, 1735	LR3	11
Birth, d. Capt. Moses & Ann, d. Sept. 30, 1751, in the 16th y. of her age	LR6	5
Bearth, d. Abraham & Elisabeth, b. Aug. 25, 1755	LR6	13
Betsey, m. John RIGGS, Mar. 8, 1829, by Rev. Stephen Jewett	1	114
Betsey, of Derby, m. Agur HUBBELL, of Huntington, Mar. 28, 1841, by John B. Beach	1	289
Betsey, of Derby, m. Cyrus NORTON, of Salem, Aug. 15, 1841, by Rev. T. Sparks	1	169
Betty, d. Abraham & Elisabeth, b. Feb. 3, 1750/1	LR6	2
Charles, of Derby, m. Jane CHATFIELD, of Oxford, Sept. 24, 1829, by Rev. Stephen Jewett	1	95
Charlotte C., m. Ely BURRITT, Nov. 7, 1841, by John D. Smith	1	174
Clarinah, d. Lieut. Samuel & Sarah, b. Oct. 19, 1759	LR6	443
Daniel, s. Daniel & Ann, b. Apr. 3, 1727	LR3	15
Daniel, m. Anne WOOSTER, Jan. 6, 172[ ]	LR3	10
Daniel, s. Joseph & Elizabeth, b. [ ] 9, [ ]	2	13
David, s. Abraham & Elisabeth, b. Feb. 11, 1763	LR7	252
Decline, d. Moses & Ann, b. Feb. 26, 1742/3	LR4	A2
Durand, m. Mary M. WOOSTER, Nov. 25, 1822, by Rev. Abner Smith	1	97
Edward, s. Lieut. Sam[ue]ll & Sarah, b. Aug. 6, 1760	LR6	451
Edward, s. Lieut. Sam[ue]ll & Sarah, b. Aug. 6, 1760	LR6	719
Eleazer, b. Dec. 12, 1670	2	1
Eleazar, b. May last day, 1701	2	12
Eleazer, s. Joseph & Elizabeth, d. June 7, 1702 (Entry reads "s. of Joseph HAWKINS & sister Elizabeth HAWKINS his wife")	2	27
Eleazar, s. Joseph & Elizabeth, b. Nov. 27, 1706	2	23
Eleazier, m. Damarus WOOSTER, Dec. 13, 1727	LR3	10
Eliezor, s. Moses & Ann, b. Oct. 5, 1733	LR3	16
Eleazer, m. Ruth BOTCHFORD, Jan. 7, 1762	LR7	248
Elijah, s. John & Hannah, b. Nov. 8, 1734	LR3	11
Elijah, s. Zachariah & Mary, b. Feb. 2, 1748	LR6	441
Elizabeth, d. Joseph & Elizabeth, b. Apr. 11, 1694	2	26
Elizabeth (?), d. Joseph & sister of Eleazer, d. June 7, 1702 (Entry reads "Eleazer ye son of Joseph HAWKINS, & sister Elizabeth HAWKINS his wife deceased")	2	27
Elisabeth, m. John MUNSON, Dec. 25, 1718	LR3	9
Elisabeth, d. John & Hannah, b. Feb. 14, 1736	LR4	A5
Elisabeth, [twin with John], d. Zachariah & Mary, b. Jan. 10, 1746	LR6	441

	Vol.	Page
HAWKINS, HAWKENS, HAWKINGS, (cont.)		
Elisabeth, w. Abraham, d. Aug. 9, 1789, in the 62nd y.		
of her age	TM1	210
Elizabeth, m. Charles REYNOLDS, Mar. 17, 1834, by Zepheniah		
Swift	1	159
Eunice, d. Capt. Moses & Ann, b. June 14, 1750	LR5	414
Eunice, m. Thomas HORSEY, Feb. 12, 1771	TM1	208
Gallord, s. Zachariah & Mary, b. Apr. 2, 1752	LR6	441
Gracy, Mrs., m. Richard HOLBROOK, Oct. 6, 1799	TM1	229
Hannah, m. Edward LEWIS, July 26, 1731	LR3	10
Hannah, 3rd, m. John L. TOMLINSON, Jan. 29, 1811, by		
Rev. Abner Smith	1	119
Horatio Nelson, of Long Island, N. Y., m. Sally HUBBLE,		
of Derby, Nov. 10, 1823, by Jeremiah French, J. P.	1	103
Irene, m. Curtiss JOHNSON, b. of Derby, Mar. 18, 1821, by		
Rev. Abner Smith	1	99
Isaac, s. Abraham & Elisabeth, b. Apr. 10, 1760	LR7	249
Isaac, s. Abraham & Elisabeth, b. Apr. 10, 1760	LR7	250
Isaac, s. Capt. Zachariah & Mary, b. June 26, 1766	LR6	441
Jane, of Derby, m. Burr BEECHER, of Oxford, Nov. 10, 1830,		
by Rev. Stephen Jewett	1	91
John, m. Hannah DAUIS, Nov. 29, [ ]	LR3	10
John, b. Sept. 28, 1679	2	1
John, d. Dec. 5, 1679	2	1
John, s. Joseph & Eleazbeth, b. July 5, 1710	2	160
John, [twin with Elisabeth], s. Zachariah & Mary, b. Jan.		
10, 1746	LR6	441
Joseph, b. Feb. 14, 1668	2	1
Joseph, m. [ ], Apr. 8, 1668	2	1
Joseph, of Derby, m. Elizabeth GUN[N], of Milford, Aug.		
9, 1693	2	25
Joseph, s. Joseph & Elizabeth, b. Jan. 1, 1696/7	2	31
Joseph, m. Sarah BUSTER, Nov. 17, 1720	LR3	9
Joseph, s. Joseph & Sarah, b. Apr. 30, 1724	LR3	5
Joseph, m. Mery RIGGS, Jan. 1, 1749/50	LR5	4
Joseph, s. Capt. Zachariah & Mary, b. July 26, 1759	LR6	441
Joseph, s. Zachariah & Mary, b. July 26, 1759	LR6	719
Joseph, d. May 31, 1767	TM1	33
Joseph, Jr., m. Grace HOLBROOK, b. of Derby, Nov. 27, 1828,		
by S. Jewett	1	98
Joseph, Sr., m. Elizabeth WOOSTER, b. of Derby, June 10,		
1829, by Rev. S. Jewett	1	101
Julia, m. David SCRANTON, Nov. 6, 1825, by Rev. Abner		
Smith	1	115
Julia Ann, of Derby, m. William HINE, of Oxford, Feb. 11,		
1834, by Rev. Stephen Jewett	1	159
Loes, [twin with Agnes], d. Jos[eph], b. [ ]	2	1
Lois, d. Elieazor & Damarus, b. July 5, 1728	LR3	15

	Vol.	Page
HAWKINS, HAWKENS, HAWKINGS, (cont.)		
Lois, m. Thomas WOOSTER, Jr., Jan. 21, 1746/7	LR5	4
Martha, of Birmingham, m. William KINNIE, of Derby, Dec.		
25, 1851, by Rev. Thomas Osbom	1	330
Mary, b. June 11, 1677	2	1
Mary, d. Joseph & Elizabeth, b. Apr. 1, 1700	2	31
Mary, m. Moses WOOSTER, Apr. 5, 1720, by Rev. Joseph		
Moss	LR3	9
Mary, d. Joseph, b. Sept. 5, 1721	LR3	4
Mary, d. Zachariah & Mary, b. May 7, 1744	LR6	441
Mary, w. Capt. Zachariah, d. Aug. 18, 1773	TM1	92
Mary, m. Isaac TOMLINSON, Dec. 19, 1775	TM1	154
Mary Minnerva, m. Walter SMITH, May 28, 1837, by Rev.		
John D. Smith	1	179
Mercy, d. Zachariah & Sarah, b. June 26, 1740	LR6	441
Mercy, d. Jos[eph] & Mercy, b. Aug. 21, 1750	LR5	414
Mercy, d. Jos[eph] & Mercy, d. Sept. 19, 1750	LR5	1
Mercy, m. Joshua PERRY, Nov. [ ], 1759, by Timothy Russell	LR7	249
Miriam, d. Joseph & Elizabeth, b. Dec. 1, 171[ ]	LR3	2
Moses, s. Joseph & Elizabeth, b. Aug. 23, 1703	2	12
Moses, & w. Ann had s. [ ]li, b. Apr. 21, 1729	LR3	15
Moses, s. Moses & Ann, b. Dec. 19, 1739	LR4	A3
Moses, s. Moses & Ann, d. Dec. 25, 1739	LR4	A5
Moses, s. Moses & Ann, b. Feb. 14, 1740/1	LR4	A3
Moses, s. Moses & Ann, d. Jan. 6, 1741/2	LR4	A5
Moses, s. Zachariah & Mary, b. Aug. 12, 1761	LR6	441
Moses, m. Betsey M. PATCHIN, b. of Derby, May 24, 1841, by		
Rev. John E. Bray	1	175
Naomi, d. Abraham & Elisabeth, b. Apr. 26, 1765	TM1	11
Robert, b. July 4, 1675	2	1
Robert, d. [July] [ ], 1675	2	1
Robart, s. Eliezer & Damirus, b. Oct. 15, 1729	LR3	15
Ruth, d. Zachariah & Mary, b. June 22, 1754	LR6	441
Samuel, Ens., m. Sarah SMITH, b. of Derby, Mar. 16, 1758, by		
Rev. Richard Mansfield	LR6	444
Samuel, s. Eleazer & Ruth, b. June 4, 1762	TM1	14
Sarah, d. Joseph & Elizabeth, b. May 23, 1695	2	26
Sarah, m. Thomas WO[O]STER, Dec. 25, 1718	LR3	9
Sarah, d. Moses, b. Feb. 11, 1726/7	LR3	5
Sarah, m. Bennajah JOHNSON, Oct. 10, 1728	LR3	10
Sarah, d. Zachariah & Sarah, b. Aug. 12, 1739	LR6	441
Sarah, w. Zachariah, d. Feb. 12, 1741	LR6	440
Sarah, m. Joseph BASSIT, Nov. 16, 1748	LR5	4
Sarah, m. Daniel WOOSTER, May 11, 1780	TM1	130
Silas, s. Zachariah & Mary, b. Sept. 22, 1756	LR6	13
Silas, s. Zachariah & Mary, b. Sept. 22, 1756	LR6	441
Susan Caroline, of Derby, m. John T. JACKSON, of		
Huntington, Feb. 6, 1831, by Rev. S. Jewett	1	100

	Vol.	Page

HAWKINS, HAWKENS, HAWKINGS, (cont.)

Suse, m. Abram SMITH, Mar. 18, 1778 — TM1 151

Thomas, s. Zadock & Lydia, b. Oct. 11, 1771 — TM1 17

Truman, Jr., m. Betsey HOLBROOK, b. of Derby, June 5, 1831,
    by Bennet Lewis, J. P. — 1 102

Zechariah, s. Joseph & Elisabeth, b. Feb. 8, 1716/17 — LR3 3

Zachariah, m. Sarah DAVIS, July 6, 1737 — LR6 8

Zachariah, m. Mary TOMLINSON, June 31, 1743 — LR6 8

Zachariah, Capt., m. Mrs. Rachel PERRY, b. of Derby,
    Feb. 16, 1774, by Rev. David Brownson — TM1 92

Zacheriah, s. Capt. Zacheriah & Rachel, b. Apr. 14, 1777 — LR6 441

Zadock, m. Lydia WILLMOOT, Aug. 4, 1754 — LR6 7

----, [sister of Eleazer & d.], of Joseph & Elizabeth,
    d. June 7, 1702 — 2 27

HAWLEY, HAWLY, Elizabeth, m. Mordecai PRINDLE, July 28,
    1839, by Rev. Joseph Scott — 1 173

Emily, of Derby, m. Thomas JAMES, of Wales, Nov. 17, [1839],
    by Rev. J. B. Beach — 1 192

Hannah, Mrs. of Stratford, m. Jedediah MILLS, of Derby,
    Feb. 24, 1756, by Rev. [ ] Mills, of Ripton — LR6 444

Mary Ann, m. Nathan BRISTOL, b. of Derby, Dec. 2, 1838,
    by Rev. Orlando Starr — 1 171

HAYDEN, George W., of Westbrook, m. Nancy MALLORY, of
    Birmingham, Feb. 29, 1852, by Rev. Thomas G. Osborn — 1 291

HAYES, John W., m. Phebe Ann GILBERT, b. of Derby, Oct. 20,
    1839, by Rev. H. Reed — 1 160

Michael, m. Mary RYAN, Feb. 24, [18]52, by Rev. James Lynch — 1 292

HAZELTON, Samuel, m. Abigail CHATFIELD, Sept. 16, 1755 — LR6 8

HEALY, Bridget, m. Jones WOLFE, Sept. 7, 1848, by Rev. William
    B. Curtis, at Humphreysville — 1 482

Margaret, m. William HOLLARAN, Apr. 27, 1851, by Rev.
    James Lynch — 1 291

HEARD, James, s. James & Elizabeth, b. Jan. 8, 1694/5 — 2 31

HEATER, Mary Ann, m. Patrick BOYLE, Jan. 28, 1844, by George
    Thacher — 1 206

HEAZELTIN, David, s. Samuel & Abigail, b. May 17, 1757 — LR6 441

Lydia, d. Samuel & Abigail b. Mar. 22, 1756 — LR6 441

HECOCK, [see under HITCHCOCK]

HENDRIX, Sarah M., of Oxford, m. Mathew DONNALLEY, of
    Derby, [ ], by Rev. Joseph Scott: recorded Jan. 4, 1841 — 1 152

HENRIETTA, HENRIETTEE, Sarah, m. John S. MIDWINTER,
    Oct. 7, 1832, by Nath[aniel] W. Taylor — 1 166

Sarah F., of Huntington, m. Hiram B. SMITH, of N[ew] H[aven],
    Oct. 25, 1852, by Rev. Thomas T. Guion — 1 442

HIFFENAS, Ann, m. James PLUNKET, Nov. 27, 1851, by Rev.
    James Lynch — 1 408

HIGGINS, S. B. P., of New York, m. Sarah ATWOOD, of Derby,
    May 7, 1851, by Rev. Thomas T. Guion — 1 292

	Vol.	Page
HILL, Enock, s. Jonathan & Hannah, b. Oct. 13, 1719	LR3	3
Huldah, d. Jonath[a]n & Hannah, b. Apr. 28, 1718	LR3	3
Jonathan, m. Hannah **TWITCHEL**, Sept. 19, 1717	LR3	9
HINE, HINES, Abigail, m. Benjamin **BATES**, Apr. 2, 1751	LR6	450
Betsey, m. Abel **CHURCH**, b. of Derby, Nov. 16, 1831, by Rev. Stephen Jewett	1	106
David, of Derby, m. Mary **BRIGDEN**, of New Haven, Dec. 29, 1820, by Rev. Zephaniah Swift	1	97
Elisabeth, m. Ens. Ebenezer **JOHNSON**, Feb. 19, 1718/19	LR3	9
George D., m. Eliza A. **CLARK**, Nov. 27, 1822, by Stephen Jewett	1	96
Mary, m. Samuel **ROSELL**, Jan. 16, 1833, by Charles Thompson	1	177
Mercy, m. Siluester **WOOSTER**, Feb. 20, 1737/8	LR5	4
Robert, of Derby, m. Ann **LEWIS**, of Oswego, N. Y., June 15, 1829, by Stephen Jewett	1	100
Samuel, m. Anna Addaline **CAN**[ ], b. of Oxford, Jan. 20, 1828, by Rev. Stephen Jewett	1	122
William, of Oxford, m. Julia Ann **HAWKINS**, of Derby, Feb. 11, 1834, by Rev. Stephen Jewett	1	159
HINMAN, HENMAN, Charity, d. Philo & Mary, b. Oct. 30, 1783	TM1	107
Charles, m. Rachel **RUSSEL**, Jan. 1, 1835, by John D. Smith	1	159
Esther E., of Derby, m. William L. **UPSON**, of Roxbury, Sept. 9, 1838, by Oliver Sykes at John B. Hinmans	1	183
Hannah, m. Sam[ue]ll **TWITCHEL**, Dec. 13, 1739	LR4	A4
Hannah, d. Philo & Mary, b. Sept. 13, 1777	TM1	105
John, s. Philo & Mary, b. Sept. 16, 1775	TM1	105
John, m. Abigail **POOL**, b. of Derby, June 2, 1796	TM1	215
Mary, d. Philo & Mary, b. Aug. 26, 1779	TM1	107
Molly, m. Joseph **BASSIT**, Mar. 18, 1779	TM1	156
Nelson, of Southbury, m. Nancy **WOOSTER**, of Derby, Mar. 19, 1823, by Rev. Abner Smith	1	96
Philo, m. Mary **COE**, b. of Derby, July 20, 1774	TM1	105
Rebecah, of Woodbury, m. Isaac **NICHOLS**, of Derby, Feb. 10, 1756	LR6	450
HITCHCOCK, HICKCOCK, HICHCOCK, HECOCK, Abigail, d. Jonathan & Abigail, b. July 15, 1751	LR6 TM1	A2
Abigail, d. Jonathan & Abigail, b. July 15, 1751		58
Abigail N., m. Noyes **HOTCHKISS**, Nov. 20, 1843, by Rev. John D. Smith	1	289
Ann, w. Sam[ue]ll, d. Apr. 14, 1760	LR6	440
Anne, d. Jonathan & Abigail, b. Dec. 1, 1747	TM1	58
Anne, d. Jonathan & Abigail, b. Dec. 1, 1747	LR5	232
Anne, m. Daniel **HOLBROOK**, Jr., Oct. 8, 1766, by Rev. Daniel Humphry	TM1 LR6	15
David, s. Jonathan & Abigail, b. Oct. 1, 1753	TM1	4
David, s. Jonathan & Abigail, b. Oct. 1, 1753	TM1	58
David, m. Anne **CHATFIELD**, b. of Derby, May 4, 1774	LR6	105
Elisabeth, d. Sam[ue]ll & Ann, b. July 11, 1752		3

	Vol.	Page
HITCHCOCK, HICKCOCK, HICHCOCK, HECOCK, (cont.)		
Eunice, m. Daniel **TODD**, Jr., b. of Derby, Mar. 27, [ ],		
by Rev. Mr. Humphry	TM1	76
Eunice, d. Jonathan & Abigail, b. Jan. 27, 1758	TM1	58
Eunice, m. Daniel **TODD**, Jr., b. of Derby, Mar. 27, 1775	TM1	104
Harriet, m. John W. **FRENCH**, Sept. 22, 1831, by Rev.		
Herman Bangs	1	92
Jonathan, m. Abigail **BEACHER**, Jan. 21, 1746/7	LR5	4
Jonathan, m. Abigail **BEACHER**, Jan. 21, 1746/7	TM1	58
Jonathan, s. Jonathan & Abigail, b. Jan. 4, 1761	TM1	58
Jonathan, s. Jonathan & Abigail, b. Jan. 4, 1761	LR7	249
Luceane, d. Jonathan & Abigail, b. Aug. 9, 1763	TM1	58
Lucinda, m. Joel R. **CHATFIELD**, May 7, 1826, by Rev.		
Abner Smith	1	86
Lucy, of Waterbury, m. Moses **WHE[E]LER**, of Derby, Dec. 26,		
1770, by Rev. Mark Leavenworth	TM1	87
Mary, d. Samuel & Ann, b. Mar. 12, 1760	LR6	442
Mary Ann, of New Haven, m. Allanson **FROST**, of Cornel,		
N. Y., Sept. 24, 1840, by Rev. B. Y. Morse	1	156
Meliscent, d. Jonathan & Abigail, b. Sept. 29, 1749	LR5	413
Melesent, d. Jonathan & Abigail, b. Sept. 29, 1749	TM1	58
Melecent, d. Jonathan & Abigail, d. Apr. 28, 1766, in the		
17th y. of her age	TM1	17
Melecent, d. Apr. 28, 1766, in the 17th y. of her age	TM1	58
Phebe, d. Jonathan & Abigail, b. Dec. 11, 1755	TM1	58
Phebe, d. Jonathan & Abigail, b. Dec. 11, 1755	LR6	15
Robert, of Springfield, Mass., m. Jane **BLANNETT**, of		
Humphreysville, Mar. 24, 1850, by Rev. S. Howland	1	291
Samuel, m. Ann **JOHNSON**, Jan. 20, 1747/8	LR6	6
Samuel, s. Samuel & Ann, b. June 8, 1750	LR6	2
Samuel, of Derby, m. Elizabeth D. **SPENCER**, of Suffield,		
Jan. 5, 1840, by Rev. Sylvester Smith	1	160
Timothy, m. Miranda **BASSETT**, b. of Derby, Aug. 2, 1843, by		
Rev. Sylvester Smith	1	289
HOADLEY, Levi M., m. Mrs. Sally **RANDALL**, June 10, 1835, by		
John D. Smith	1	158
HOBARD, Mary, of Guilford, m. James **BEARD**, of Derby, Dec. 10,		
1781, by Rev. Mr. Ells, of Branford	TM1	36
HODGE, Robert T., m. Mary A. **JOHNSON**, Apr. 6, 1845, by Rev.		
W[illia]m B. Curtiss	1	289
HOLBROOK, HOLEBROOK, Abel, m. Tabitha **WOOSTER**, Jan.		
29, 1723	LR3	9
Abel, s. Abel, b. July 28, 1723	LR3	4
Abel, Dea., d. May 30, 1747, in the 94th y. of his age	LR5	1
Abel, s. John & Esther, b. Dec. 4, 1762	TM1	74a
Abel, s. John & Esther, b. Dec. 4, 1762	LR7	252
Abigal, d. Abel & Hannah, b. Nov. 25, 1694	2	26
Abigal, d. May 5, 1709, in the 15th y. of her age	2	27

	Vol.	Page
HOLBROOK, HOLEBROOK, (cont.)		
Abigal, d. John & Abigal, b. July 27, 1729	LR3	15
Abigal, d. Jno & Abigal, d. June 29, [ ]	LR3	12
Abigail, d. John & Easther, b. Dec. 19, 1754	LR6	4
Abigail, d. John & Esther, b. Dec. 19, 1754	TM1	74a
Abigail, d. John & Easther, d. Sept. 13, 1757	TM1	74a
Abigail, d. John & Esther, d. Sept. 13, 1757	LR6	440
Abigail, d. John & Easther, d. Sept. 13, 1757	LR6	441
Abigail, d. John & Esther, b. Dec. 9, 1764	TM1	14
Abigail, d. John & Esther, b. Dec. 9, 1764	TM1	74a
Abijah, s. Philo & An[n]ah, b. May 2, 1786	TM1	102
Ann, d. Daniel & Elisabeth, b. Feb. 16, 1739	LR6	440
Ann, m. Samuel SMITH, b. of Derby, Mar. 16, 1758, by		
Rev. Daniel Humphry	LR6	444
Ann, d. Capt. John & Esther, b. Jan. 22, 1769	TM1	40
Ann, d. Capt. John & Esther, b. Jan. 22, 1769	TM1	74a
Austin, s. John & Esther, b. Nov. 17, 1766	TM1	20
Austin, s. John & Esther, b. Nov. 17, 1766	TM1	74a
Austin, s. Richard & Gracy, b. Jan. 21, 1804	TM1	229
Benjamin, s. John & Hulday, b. Oct. 26, 1780	TM1	230
Betsey, m. Josiah SMITH, Jr., July 30, 1795	TM1	156
Betsey, m. Truman HAWKINS, Jr., b. of Derby, June 5, 1831,		
by Bennet Lewis, J. P.	1	102
Cyrus, s. Nathaniel & Alles, b. Jan. 1, 1782	TM1	149
Dan, s. Nathaniel & Alles, b. Mar. 28, 1780	TM1	149
Dannil, m. Elizabeth RIGGS, Jan. 22, 1728/9	LR3	10
Daniel, s. Daniel & Elisabeth, b. Sept. 21, 1747	LR6	440
Daniel, Jr., of Derby, m. Anne HITCHCOCK, Oct. 8, 1766, by		
Rev. Daniel Humphry	TM1	15
Daniel, s. Daniel & Anne, b. Apr. 30, 1769	TM1	49
Daniel Lum, s. Richard & Sarah, b. Nov. 21, 1798	TM1	229
Dauid, s. Abel, Jr. & Tabitha, b. Apr. 8, 173[ ]	LR3	16
David, s. John & Hulday, b. Dec. 27, 1782	TM1	230
David, m. Cynthia SMITH, b. of Derby, Nov. 25, 1847, by		
Rev. Sylvester Smith	1	290
David B., m. Henrietta WHITE, Jan. 2, 1848, by Rev.		
W[illia]m B. Curtiss	1	290
Eliza A., m. Clement A. SEARGEANT, b. of Derby, Nov. 5,		
1848, by Rev. W[illia]m Denison	1	440
Elisabeth, d. Daniel & Elisabeth, b. Aug. 3, 1735	LR6	440
Ester, d. Nov. 23, 1712	LR3	6
Esther, d. John & Esther, b. Sept. 18, 1760	TM1	74a
Esther, d. John & Esther, b. Sept. 18, 1760	LR7	249
Esther, d. Nathaniel & Alles, b. Sept. 7, 1783	TM1	149
Esther, w. Capt. John, d. Feb. 5, 1795, ae 63 y.	TM1	230
Esther, d. Richard & Grace, b. Feb. 26, 1812	1	15
Esther, m. Ephraim SMITH, b. of Derby, Nov. 26, 1829	1	106
Eunice, d. Philo & Anar, b. Jan. 15, 1782	TM1	128

	Vol.	Page
HOLBROOK, HOLEBROOK, (cont.)		
Grace, w. Rich[ar]d, d. Feb. 26, 1812	1	523
Grace, of Derby, m. Isaiah CHATFIELD, of Oxford, Nov. 1, 1820, by Rev. Abner Smith	1	87
Grace, m. Joseph HAWKINS, Jr., b. of Derby, Nov. 27, 1828, by S. Jewett	1	98
Hannah, w. Dea. Abel, d. Oct. 20, 1740, in the 73rd y. of her age	LR5	1
Hannah, d. John & Hulday, b. Jan. 6, 1775	TM1	230
Hulday, w. John, Jr., d. Apr. 1, 1796	TM1	230
Israel, s. Abel & Hannah, d. Mar. 11, 1693	2	27
Jane M., m. William P. BEERS, Mar. 15, 1848, by Rev. W[illia]m B. Curtiss	1	208
John, s. Abell & Hannah, b. Oct. 19, 1699	2	31
John, m. Abigail GUNN, Aug. 27, 1723	LR3	9
John, s. John & Abigal, b. Aug. 12, 1725	LR3	5
John, of Derby, m. Easther NICKOLS, of Newtown, Nov. 4, 1750	LR5	4
John, of Derby, m. Esther NICKOLS, of New Town, Nov. 4, 1750, by Rev. John Beach	TM1	74a
John, s. John & Easther, b. Oct. 2, 1751	LR6	2
John, s. John & Esther, b. Oct. 2, 1751	TM1	74a
John, d. June 5, 1752, in the 53rd y. of his age	LR6	5
John, s. John & Easther, d. Aug. 17, 1752	LR6	5
John, s. John & Esther, d. Aug. 17, 1752	TM1	74a
John, s. John & Esther, b. Mar. 13, 1753	LR6	3
John, s. John & Esther, b. Mar. 13, 1753	TM1	74a
John, Jr., m. Huldy FOX, July 7, 1774	TM1	230
John, s. John & Hulday, b. Apr. 29, 1777	TM1	230
John, Capt., d. Jan. 28, 1801, ae 74 y.	TM1	230
Mary Ann, of Derby, m. Bennet CHATFIELD, of Oxford, Dec. 23, 1830, by Rev. S. Jewett	1	90
Melissee, d. Daniel & Anne, b. June 28, 1767	TM1	31
Nabby, d. John & Hulday, b. Jan. 24, 1785	TM1	230
Nancy, m. Eli TYREL, June 17, 1832, by Rev. John Bayden, Jr.	1	180
Nancy M., m. Asahel M. WILLIAMS, Dec. 11, 1842, by John D. Smith	1	481
Nathaniel, s. John & Esther, b. Oct. 1, 1758	TM1	74a
Nathaniel, m. Alles DAVIS, b. of Derby, Dec. 20, 1778	TM1	149
Patty, of Derby, m. Joseph PLATT, of Southbury, Dec. 19, 1820, by Rev. Abner Smith	1	111
Philo, s. John & Ester, b. Nov. 23, 1756	TM1	74a
Philo, s. John & Esther, b. Nov. 23, 1756	LR6	450
Philo, m. Annah WOOSTER, b. of Derby, June 3, 1779	TM1	118
Philo, s. Richard & Gracy, b. Mar. 12, 1802	TM1	229
Philo, Capt., m. Amelia TOMLINSON, b. of Derby, July 31, 1831, by Rev. S. Jewett	1	107
Richard, m. Esther NICHOLS, June 9, 1708, by Rev. Joseph		

	Vol.	Page
HOLBROOK,HOLEBROOK, (cont.)		
Moss	2	24
Richard, d. May 3, 1709, in the 25th y. of his age	2	27
Richard, s. Abel & Tabitha, b. Feb. 16, 1726/7	LR3	5
Richard, s. Capt. John & Esther, b. Oct. 29, 1771	TM1	74a
Richard, s. Capt. John & Esther, d. Oct. 30, 1771	TM1	74a
Richard, s. Capt. John & Esther, b. Aug. 1, 1775	TM1	75a
Richard, m. Mrs. Sarah LUM, Sept. 13, 1797	TM1	229
Richard, m. Mrs. Gracy HAWKINS, Oct. 6, 1799	TM1	229
Richard, s. Richard & Grace, b. Nov. 19, 1805	TM1	229
Richard, s. Richard & Grace, b. Mar. 4, 1808	TM1	403
Ruth, d. Daniel & Elisabeth, b. Oct. 19, 1737	LR6	440
Ruth, Mrs., m. James BEARD, Oct. 31, 1754	LR6	7
Ruthan, d. Nathaniel & Alles, b. Jan. 29, 1786	TM1	149
Sabra, d. Philo & An[n]ah, b. May 2, 1784	TM1	102
Sally, d. John & Hulday, b. June 9, 1787	TM1	230
Sally, d. John & Hulday, d. May 27, 1788	TM1	230
Samuel, s. Daniel & Elizabeth, b. Feb. 6, [ ]	LR3	16
Samuel, s. Daniel & Elisabeth, b. Feb. 6, 1733	LR6	440
Samuel, s. Dea. Daniel & Elisabeth, d. Dec. 29, 1752	LR6	440
Sarah, d. Capt. John & Easther, b. Mar. 30, 1773	TM1	74A
Sarah, d. Capt. John & Esther, d. Mar. 21, [ ]	TM1	75A
Sarah, d. Philo & Annah, b. Aug. 11, 1780	TM1	118
Sarah, w. Richard, d. Nov. 21, 1798, ae 22 y.	TM1	229
Sarah, d. Richard & Gracy, b. July 30, 1800	TM1	229
Sarah, m. Stephen D. RUSSELL, Oct. 28, 1844, by Rev. John D. Smith	1	425
----ard, s. Abell, b. Dec. 24, 1684	2	2
---iel, s. Abell & Tabitha, b. Aug. 15, [ ]	LR3	15
HOLCOMB, Almira, Mrs., m. Henry P. DAVIS, Sept. 2, 1849, by Rev. W[illia]m B. Curtiss	1	248
John, m. Almira STEEL, b. of Derby, Nov. 23, 1834, by Rev. John E. Bray	1	159
HOLGATE, Charlotte, m. Joseph TIFFANY, Jan. 21, 1849, by Rev. C. S. Putman. Int. Pub.	1	461
HOLLARON, HOLLARAN, James, m. Margaret CAMPION, Aug. 3, 1851, by Rev. James Lynch	1	292
William, m. Margaret HEALY, Apr. 27, 1851, by Rev. James Lynch	1	291
HOPKINS, Edwin A., m. Grace Ann SMITH, Mar. 30, 1845, by Rev. George Thacher	1	289
Lowis, of Waterbury, m. Isaac JOHNSON, of Derby, Jan. 24, 1758	LR7	248
Lowis, of Waterbury, m. Isaac JOHNSON, of Derby, Jan. 24, 1758, by Rev. Mark Leavenworth	LR6	444
HOPSON, Oliver, Rev., m. Caroline ALLIS, Sept. 9, 1833, by Rev. S. Jewett	1	161
HORSEY, Eunice, [d. Thomas & Eunice], b. June 19, 1773	TM1	208

	Vol.	Page

HORSEY, (cont.)

Nancy, [d. Thomas & Eunice], b. Sept. 26, 1782	TM1	208
Ralph, s. Thomas & Eunice, b. Nov. 27, 1771	TM1	208
Sam[ue]ll W[illia]m, [s. Thomas & Eunice], b. July 8, 1778	TM1	208
Sarah, [d. Thomas & Eunice,], b. Oct. 31, 1780	TM1	208

Thomas, father of Capt. Thomas, was s. Ralph of Dunyatt
  in County, of Somerset Shire & his w. Margery mother of
  Capt. Thomas, was d. of Richard WALTER, of Wadford,
  near said Coomb St., Nickless, near Chard   TM1   208

Thomas, m. Eunice HAWKINS, Feb. 12, 1771   TM1   208

Thomas, Capt., s. Thomas & Margery, b. Comb St., Neckless,
  Somersett Shire, Old England, [   ], d. June 19, 1789, ae
  about 46 years   TM1   208

Thomas Walter, [s. Thomas & Eunice], b. Mar. 10, 1784   TM1   208

HORTON, Betsey Ann, m. Philander S. MORGAN, b. of Bethel,
  Nov. 7, 1847, by Rev. Nathan E. Shailer   1   358

Deborah, m. Janes H. BARNUM, b. of Bethel, Nov. 7, 1847,
  by Rev. Nathan E. Shailer   1   208

Hellen A., of Bethel, m. John K. LYON, of Danbury, Nov. 8,
  1847, by Rev. Nathan E. Shailer   1   341

HOTCHKISS, HOCHKISS, Amelia, of Derby, m. Benjamin
  WELLS, of Huntington, Apr. 8, 1849, by W[illia]m
  Denison, of Humphreysville   1   482

Cyrus, s. Elijah & Mehethabel, b. July 16, 1774   TM1   51

David, s. Lieut. Eliphalet & Comfort, b. Dec. 30, 1759   LR6   719

David, s. Eliphalet & Comfort, d. Aug. 30, 1776, in the 17th
  y. of his age   TM1   75a

Eli, m. Susannah KIMBERLY, Dec. 24, 1833, by Z. Swift   1   159

Elijah, of Derby, m. Mehethabel HOTCHKISS, of New Haven,
  Nov. 11, 1761, by Rev. Chancy Whitelsey   TM1   51

Elijah, of Derby, m. Metithabel HOTCHKISS, of New Haven,
  Nov. 11, 1761, by Rev. Chancey Whitelsey   LR7   248

Elijah, s. Elijah & Mehethebel, b. Nov. 16, 1766   TM1   51

Eliphelet, s. Daniel & Susannah, b. Nov. 1, 1727   LR6   3

Eliphelet, m. Comfort HARGER, Dec. 26, 1751   LR6   6

Eliphelet, s. Dea. Eliphelet & Comfort, d. Feb. 24, 1775,
  in the 19th y. of his age   TM1   75a

Elisabeth, d. Elijah & Mehethabel, b. June 17, 1769   TM1   51

Elisabeth, m. David JOHNSON, Jr., b. of Derby, June 23, 1776   TM1   109

Elizabeth, of Derby, m. Denzel ALLEN, of Orange, June 21,
  1829, in Humphreysville   1   106

Eunice, m. Sheldon NOTHROP, b. of Derby, Sept. 24, 1830,
  by Rev. Charles Thompson   1   106

Eunice I., m. Willis P. SPERRY, b. of Derby, Oct. 31, 1842, by
  Rev. H. Read   1   439

George Bryant, of Derby, m. Almira S. SUTLIFF, of Haddam,
  Nov. 25, 1847, by Rev. W[illia]m Bliss Ashley   1   290

Harriet, of Derby, m. Lucius ALLEN, of Woodbridge, Nov. 12,

	Vol.	Page
HOTCHKISS, HOCHKISS, (cont.)		
1829, by P. Jewett	1	82
Harvey, m. Augusta **KIMBERLY**, Apr. 9, 1849, by Rev. C. S. Putman. Int. Pub.	1	290
J. A., of Derby, m. Clark **CHATFIELD**, of New York, Nov. 22, 1852, by Rev. Thomas T. Guion	1	236
Jane, of Bethany, m. Thomas **SANFORD**, of Oxford, Sept. 9, 1835, by Rev. John E. Bray	1	179
Jane Eliza, m. Augustus **PARKER**, b. of Derby, Feb. 23, [1841], by Rev. John B. Beach	1	192
John, m. Betsey **RIGGS**, Oct. 16, 1796	TM1	215
John O., m. Ann **CURTISS**, b. of Derby, Jan. 5, 1849, by Rev. Thomas T. Guion	1	292
John O., m. Ann **CURTISS**, b. of Derby, Jan. 22, 1849, by Rev. Thomas T. Guion	1	290
Leavrett, s. Elijah & Mehethebell, b. Oct. 6, 1762	TM1	51
Leaveret, s. Elijah & Mehethabel, b. Oct. 6, 1762	LR7	252
Leveret, m. Sarah **BURRITT**, Aug. 14, 1785, by Rev. Martin Tuller	TM1	164
Leui, s. Eliphelet & Comfort, b. May 2, 1754	LR6	4
Mary Ann, of Derby, m. David L. **PARMELEE**, of Oxford, Dec. 24, 1828, by Rev. Stephen Jewett	1	110
Mary Elizabeth, m. Lyman **TUCKER**, Oct. 19, 1834, by Zepheniah Swift	1	181
Mehethabel, of New Haven, m. Elijah **HOTCHKISS**, of Derby, Nov. 11, 1761, by Rev. Chancy Whitelsey	TM1	51
Mehithabel, of New Haven, m. Elijah **HOTCHKISS**, of Derby, Nov. 11, 1761, by Rev. Chancey Whitelsey	LR7	248
Mehethabel, d. Elijah & Mehethabel, b. July 22, 1772	TM1	51
Merritt, m. Esther Ann **SMITH**, Dec. 25, 1836, by Rev. L. D. Howell	1	158
Moses, s. Lieut. Eliphelet & Comfort, b. Dec. 28, 1757	LR6	443
Nabbe, d. Elijah & Mehetebel, b. Aug. 30, 1777	TM1	51
Nancy, m. Peter **MALLET**, Mar. 2, 1834, by Zepheniah Swift	1	166
Noyes, m. Abigail N. **HITCHCOCK**, Nov. 20, 1843, by Rev. John D. Smith	1	289
Phebe, d. Elijah & Mehithebel, b. Aug. 2, 1764	TM1	51
Phebe, m. Ira **PHELPS**, June 8, 1834, by Zepheniah Swift	1	172
Sally L, of Bethany, m. Walter C. **WOOSTER**, of Naugatuc, Sept. 9, 1841, by Rev. John E. Bray	1	190
Sarah M., m. William **BALDWIN**, b. of Derby, Nov. 22, 1835, by Rev. John E. Bray	1	148
Susan, m. W[illia]m W. **STARR**, Mar. 22, 1847, by Rev. George Thacher	1	440
Susannah, d. Eliphelet & Comfort, b. Jan. 6, 1753	LR6	3
Susanna, m. Dan **TOMLINSON**, b. of Derby, June 13, 1774, by Rev. Daniel Humphry	TM1	76
Wales O., m. Fidelia G. **COREY**, Nov. 27, 1842, by John D.		

	Vol.	Page
HOTCHKISS, HOCHKISS, (cont.)		
Smith	1	289
William H., m. Rebeca **HALLOCK,** b. of Derby, Mar. 11, 1827, by Stephen Jewett	1	97
Wyllys, s. Leveret & Sarah, b. Apr. 25, 1788	TM1	164
Wyllys, m. Mary Ann **KIMBERLY,** b. of Derby, Dec. 24, 1828, by Rev. S. Jewett	1	98
----h, m.mWilliam M. **FRENCH,** Dec. 24, 1833, by Z. Swift	1	155
HOWD, HOUDE, Betty, d. John & Molle, b. Sept. 6, 1743	LR6	3
Betty, d. John, b. Sept. 6, 1743	LR5	232
Hesther, d. John & Molle, b. Mar. 5, 1746	LR6	3
John, m. Hannah **SMITH,** b. of Darby, Mar. 1, 1764, by Rev. Richard Mansfield	TM1	15
Sarah, d. John & Nabbe, b. June 4, 1752	LR6	3
HOWE, Jane Maria, m. William E. **DOWNS,** b. of Derby, June 24, 1851, by Rev. Thomas T. Guion	1	248
HOYS, Alice, m. Charles **McCARTHY,** Dec. 1, [18]51, by Rev. James Lynch, of Birmingham	1	359
HOYT, Charlotte, m. Samuel **COOK,** b. of Derby, Mar. 31, 1827	1	86
Mary Elizabeth, of Huntington, m. Ezra Wakeley **DAYTON,** Mar. 26, 1837, by Rev. Joseph Scott	1	151
HUBBARD, Edward C., m. Sarah M. **HUMPHREYS,** June 20, 1849, by Rev. C. S. Putnam. Int. Pub.	1	290
Hannah E., m. David S. **STILSON,** b. of New Haven, Apr. 29, 1839, by Rev. I. B. Beach	1	185
Stephen, m. Amelia S. **ROOT,** Nov. 21, 1850, by Rev. Jno Morrison Reid	1	291
Susan Jane, m. Everett O. **SHIPMAN,** Sept. 13, 1848, by Rev. C. L. Putnam	1	440
HUBBELL, HUBBEL, HUBBLE, Agur, of Huntington, m. Betsey **HAWKINS,** of Derby, Mar. 28, 1841, by John B. Beach	1	289
Angeline, m. Uriah M. **BEACH,** Sept. 5, 1827, by Rev. Zepheniah Swift	1	86
Benjamin, of Huntington, m. Mrs. Maria **NORTHROP,** of Derby, Nov. 22, 1835, by Bennet Lum, J. P.	1	160
Betsey Ann, of Derby, m. Stephen **BALDWIN,** of Oxford, Dec. 16, 1820, by Rev. Zephaniah Swift	1	85
Francis B., of Huntington, m. Mrs. Augusta M. **CHURCH,** of Derby, Nov. 22, 1835, by Bennet Lum, J. P.	1	160
John, of Huntington, m. Mary Ann **HALLOCK,** of Derby, Aug. 21, 1825, by Rev. Zepheniah Swift	1	101
Lucy, Mrs. of Derby, m. Lyman **MANSFIELD,** of Hamden, Mar. 27, 1842, by Rev. H. Read	1	162
Lucy Cornelia, of Huntington, m. Abner **LANE,** of Huntington, Oct. 27, 1839, by Rev. J. B. Beach	1	192
Normon, m. Susan **MUNSON,** June 15, 1822, by Rev. Zephaniah Swift	1	101
Pearl, of Derby, m. Maria **BOUGHTON,** of Waterbury, Nov. 27,		

	Vol.	Page
HUBBELL, HUBBEL, HUBBLE, (cont.)		
1834, by Sylvester Smith	1	159
Polly Maria, m. Marcus A. **BLAKEMAN,** Apr. 13, 1851, by		
Rev. Ja[me]s M. Mershon	1	211
Sally, of Derby, m. Horatio Nelson **HAWKINS,** of Long Island,		
N. Y., Nov. 10, 1823, by Jeremiah French, J. P.	1	103
Wells, of Huntington, m. Charry Ann **DOWNS,** of Derby, Nov.		
25, 1838, by Rev. Jos[eph] Scott	1	160
HUGHS, Margaret, m. Daniel **BROOKS,** Feb. 26, 1837, by Rev.		
Joseph Scott	1	168
HULL, HULLS, [see also **HALL,** Abijah, s. Joseph & Mary, b. Dec.		
[ ]	2	13
Abyjah, m. Abigal **HARGER,** Nov. 30, 1727	LR3	10
Abijah, of Natchez, m. Betsey **THOMPSON,** of Derby, Aug. 19,		
1822, by Rev. Stephen Jewett	1	97
Alfred, s. Sarah, b. Oct. 25, 1785	TM1	112
[Andrew], s. John, b. July 15, 1685	2	2
Andrews, s. Joseph & Mary, b. Jan. 13, 1697/8	2	31
Annah, d. Joseph & Sarah, b. June 9, 1736	LR3	11
Anna, Mrs., m. Rev. Richard **MANSFIELD,** Oct. 10, 1751, in		
Christ Church, by Rev. Samuel Johnson, of Stratford	LR6	8
Avery, m. Elizabeth A. **NORTHROP,** b. of Derby, May 13,		
1838, by Rev. John E. Bray	1	158
Betsey, m. Augustus **ROSSEBY,** aug. 22, 1830, by Rev. Stephen		
Jewett	1	114
Calep. s. Joseph & Mary, b. Feb. 4, 1695/6	2	26
Caroline, m. George **BRISTOL,** b. of Derby, Sept. 30, [1835], by		
Rev. Joseph Scott	1	148
Daniel, s. Daniel & Elizebeth, b. Dec. 26, [ ]	LR3	16
Daniel, s. Daniel & Elizebeth, d. Feb. 8, [	LR3	12
Dannel, s. John & Mary, b. Mar. 15, 1699/1700	2	25
Daniel, m. Elizabeth **LUMM,** Mar. 2, 173[ ]	LR3	10
David, s. Joseph & Elisabeth, b. Mar. 27, 1765	TM1	3
Deborah, d. John & Mary, b. Dec. 26, 1691	2	26
Deborah, Mrs., d. Feb. 17, 1772, in the 81st y. of her age	TM1	17
Ebenezer, s. John, b. Mar. 16, 1677/8	2	2
Ebenezer, s. John & Mary, b. July 8, 17[ ]	2	160
Ebenezer, s. Daniel & Elizebeth, b. Dec. 22, 1741	LR4	A2
Ebenezer, d. Jan. 18, 1764	LR7	254
Eli, s. Samuel & Betty, b. Feb. 18, 1763	LR7	252
Elijah, s. John & Mary, b. Mar. 25, 1707	2	23
Elijah, s. John & Mary, d. July 23, 1709	2	161
Elijah, [twin with Elisabeth], s. Daniel & Elisebeth, b.		
Nov. 7, 1738	LR4	A3
Elizebeth, d. Jo[seph] & Sarah, b. Sept. 18, 1731	LR3	11
Elisabeth, [twin with Elijah], d. Daniel & Elisebeth, b.		
Nov. 7, 1738	LR4	A3
Elisabeth, d. Joseph & Elisabeth, b. Jan. 27, 1759	TM1	3

	Vol.	Page
HULL, HULLS, (cont.)		
Elisabeth, m. Wooster **TWICHEL**, b. of Derby, Oct. 11, 1764, by Rev. Humphry	TM1	38
Elisabeth, Mrs., m. Sergt. Joseph **TOMLINSON**, Oct. 14, 1776	TM1	116
Esther, d. Abijah & Abigal, b. Sept. 13, 172[ ]	LR3	5
Eunice, d. Sam[ue]ll & Ann, b. Nov. 19, 172[ ]	LR3	15
Eunice, m. John **WOOSTER**, June 18, 1746	LR6	7
Hannah, d. Sam[ue]ll & Ann, b. May 11, 1726	LR3	15
Harriet, m. Sheldon **BASSETT**, Mar. 4, 1827, by Rev. Zepheniah Swift	1	86
Isaac, s. Joseph & Elisabeth, b. Dec. 28, 1760	TM1	3
Jereme, s. Daniel & Elisabeth, b. Oct. 22, 1752	LR6	3
[Jer]emiah, s. John, b. Sept. 28, 1679	2	2
John, s. John & Mary, b. Jan. 9, 1693/4	2	26
John, d. Nov. 9, 1714	LR3	6
John, s. Daniel & Elizabeth, b. June 7, 1744	LR4	A5
John, d. May 25, 1753	LR6	5
Jos[eph], Capt., m. Mrs. Hannah **PRINGLE**, Nov. [ ]	LR3	10
Joseph, m. Mary **NICKELS**, Jan. 20, 1691	2	25
Joseph, s. Joseph & Mary, b. May 28, 1694	2	26
Joseph, s. Joseph & Sarah, b. Feb. 18, 1727/8	LR3	11
Joseph, s. Joseph & Sarah, b. Feb. 7, 1727/8	LR3	15
Joseph, Capt., d. Oct. 5, 1744, in the 75th y. of his age	LR5	1
Joseph, Jr., m. Mrs. Elizabeth **CLARK**, May 3, 1750, by Rev. Daniel Humphry	LR6	7
Joseph, s. Joseph & Elisabeth, b. Oct. 27, 1750	TM1	3
Joseph, s. Joseph, Jr. & Elisabeth, b. Oct. 27, 1750	LR6	15
Joseph, Capt., m. Mrs. Freelove **NICHOLS**, b. of Derby, Feb. 8, 1821, by Rev. Abner Smith	1	97
Lemmuel, s. Daniel & Elizabeth, b. Nov. 7, 1735	LR3	11
Lemuel, s. Daniel & Elisebeth, d. Feb. 15, [ ]	LR3	12
Levi, s. Joseph & Elisabeth, b. Apr. 29, 1771	TM1	3
Mary, m. John **PRINGLE**, Dec. 23, 1685	2	25
Mary, d. John & Mary, b. July 16, 1696	2	26
Mary, d. Joseph & Mary, b. Sept. 13, 1699	2	31
Mary, m. Timothy **RUSSELL**, Nov. 2, 1721	LR3	9
Mary, w. Capt. Joseph, d. Apr. 5, 1730	LR3	12
Miles, s. John & Mary, b. July 6, 1704	2	12
Morrison C., m. Eliza S. **BEECHER**, Sept. 7, 1847, by Rev. W[illia]m Bliss Ashley	1	289
Nathan, s. Joseph & Mary, b. Nov. 26, 17[ ]	2	160
Priscilla, d. Jno & Mary, b. June 3, 1702	2	12
[R]ichard, s. John, b. Oct. 16, 1674	2	2
Sam[ue]ll, m. Ann **RIGGS**, Jan. 15, [ ]	LR3	15
Samuel, s. Joseph & Mary, b. Nov. 15, 1692	2	26
Sam[ue]ll], [& w. Ann] had 1st child, b. Jan. 25, 1725	LR3	15
Samuel, s. Joseph & Elisabeth, b. Aug. 5, 1755	TM1	3
Samuel, s. Joseph, Jr. & Elisabeth, b. Aug. 5, 1755	LR6	15

	Vol.	Page
HULL, HULLS, (cont.)		
Sarah, d. Joseph & Mary, b. Aug. 13, 1701	2	31
Sarah, d. Joseph & Sarah, b. Sept. 7, 172[ ]	LR3	15
Sarah, d. Joseph & Sarah, b. Sept. 7, 1726	LR3	11
Sarah, d. Joseph & Elisabeth, b. Jan. 6, 1769	TM1	3
Sarah, had s. Alfred, b. Oct. 25, 1785	TM1	112
Sarah, m. John J. **RIDER,** b. of Derby, Sept. 15, 1841, by		
Rev. John E. Bray	1	184
Susan, of Oxford, m. David M. **NETTLETON,** of Derby, Feb.		
12, 1829, by Rev. S. Jewett	1	107
William, s. Joseph, Jr. & Elisabeth, b. June 24, 1752	LR6	15
William, s. Joseph & Elisabeth, b. June 24, 1753	TM1	3
William, m. Lucy Ann **FRENCH,** Oct. 24, 1837, by Rev.		
Joseph Scott	1	158
----er, d. Jan. 19, 1722/3 "Drowned in Naugatuck River"	LR5	1
HUMISTON, Ann M., m. Zenas M. **HALL,** Nov. 5, 1845, by Rev.		
Geo[rge] L. Fuller	1	407
Ann Maria, m. Capt. Zenas M. **PLATT,** Nov. 5, 1845, by		
Rev. Geo[rge] L. Fuller	1	207
HUMPHREY, HUMPHREYS, HUMPHRIS, HUMPHRYS,		
HUMPHRY, Anna, d. Elijah & Anna, b. Sept. 14, 1775	TM1	207
Anne, d. John & Rachel, b. Dec. 9, 1781	TM1	150
Betsy, d. Elijah & Anna, b. Oct. 10, 1781	TM1	207
Bille, s. John & Rachel, b. May 16, 1788	TM1	150
Daniel, Rev., m. Mrs. Sarah **BOWERS,** Apr. 18, 1739	LR4	A4
Daniel, s. Daniel & Sarah, b. May 18, 1740	LR4	A3
Daniel, s. John & Rachel, b. Mar. 4, 1779	TM1	150
Daniel, Rev., d. Sept. 2, 1787	TM1	206
Daniel, s. John & Rachel, d. Apr. 2, 1807, ae 27 y.	1	523
Daniel & w. Sarah had s. [ ], b. Apr. 27, [ ]	LR5	2
David, s. Daniel & Sarah, b. July 10, 1752	LR6	3
David, s. Elijah & Anna, b. Feb. 26, 1784	TM1	207
David, s. John & Rachel, b. Jan. 28, 1786	TM1	150
Elijah, m. Anna **MANSFIELD,** Oct. 22, 1774	TM1	207
Elijah, s. Elijah & Anna, b. Oct. 12, 1779	TM1	207
Elijah, Maj., s. Rev. Daniel & Sarah, d. July 2, 1785, on		
his passage to the West Indies, bd. in the Island of		
Martineco, ae 40 y.	TM1	207
James, s. James, b. Nov. 10, 1715	LR3	4
James, m. Submitt **STEVENS,** Mar. 15, 1749/50	LR6	6
James, s. James & Submit, b. Dec. 10, 1752	LR6	443
James, Jr., m. Laria **HARGER,** Apr. 18, 1824, by Rev.		
Stephen Jewett	1	96
Janett, of Humphreysville, m. Horace **CANFIELD,** of New		
York, Sept. 22, 1825, by Stephen Jewett	1	105
John, s. Rev. Daniel & Sarah, b. Jan. 3, 1743/4	LR4	A5
John, s. James & Submit, b. Mar. 25, 1761	LR7	248
John, m. Rachel **DURAND,** b. of Derby, Feb. 11, 1773	TM1	150

	Vol.	Page
HUMPHREY, HUMPHREYS, HUMPHRIS, HUMPHRYS,		
HUMPHRY, (cont.)		
John, s. John & Rachel, b. Dec. 30, 1773	TM1	150
John C., m. Thirsa RIGGS, b. of Derby, Dec. 24, 1829, by		
S. Jewett	1	95
Laura, m. William WOOSTER, Mar. 24, 1842,by John D. Smith	1	481
Mary, d. James, b. Dec. 10, 1716	LR3	4
Mary, d. James & Submit, b. Dec. 23, 1750	LR6	2
Mary, d. James & Submit, b. Dec. 23, 1750	LR6	443
Polly, d. John & Rachel, b. Feb. 1, 1777	TM1	150
Sally, d. John & Rachel, b. Apr. 19, 1775	TM1	150
Sally, d. Elijah & Anna, b. Dec. 26, 1777	TM1	207
Sally, d. John & Rachel, d. May 12, 1812, ae 37	1	523
Samuel, s. James, b. Dec. 24, 1711	LR3	4
Samuel, of Derby, m. Susannah THOMAS, of Woodbury, Aug.		
18, 1735	LR6	7
Samuel, s. James & Submit, b. May 8, 1755	LR6	443
Sarah, d. James, b. Aug. 1, 1719	LR3	4
Sarah, m. Ephraim ANDRUS, Mar. 21, 1745	LR5	4
Sarah, w. [Rev. Daniel], d. July 29, 1787	TM1	206
Sarah, of Derby, m. Hon. Moses AUSTIN, of Durham, N. Y.,		
Feb. 26, 1829, by Rev. P. Jewett	1	82
Sarah M., m. Edward C. HUBBARD, June 20, 1849, by Rev.		
C. S. Putnam. Int. Pub.	1	290
Susan, d. John & Rachel, d. Sept. 2, 1811, ae 26 y.	1	523
Suse, d. John & Rachel, b. Dec. 24, 1783	TM1	150
Thirza, m. Joshua KENDALL, M. D., b. of Derby, May 17,		
1836, by John D. Smith	1	163
HUMFREVILLE, UMFREVILLE, Nabbe, d. Eliphelet & Martha, b.		
Aug. 4, 1766	TM1	10
Sarah, d. Eliphalet & Martha, b. Oct. 1, 1764	TM1	6
HUNT, Porter, m. Emeline DRIVER, Mar. 1, 1829, by Samuel R.		
Hickox. Witnesses: Jairus Driver, Russel Hurd, Nancy N.		
Gilyard, Welthy Miller	1	98
HUNTEY, Almira A., m. Willis B. BALDWIN, Aug. 18, 1850, by		
Rev. Jno Morrison Reid	1	211
HURD, Edward B., m. Mary Jane SMITH, b. of Derby, Oct. 4, 1847,		290
by W[illia]m Bliss Ashely	1	
Harriet, m. Isaac GILLETT, Sept. 6, 1829, by Rev. Nathaniel		94
Kellogg	1	279
Mary, m. Munroe SCRANTON, Dec. 15, 1844, by Rev. John D.		
Smith	1	439
Mary, m. Munroe SCRANTON, Dec. 15, 1844, by Rev. John D.		
Smith	1	175
HUTCHINS, Lyman D., of Fairfield, m. Harriet F. JOHNSON, of		
Derby, Sept. 5, 1841, by Rev. John E. Bray	1	175
HYDE, Charles L., of Oxford, m. Harriet E. WHITE, of Derby,		
Mar. 24, 1842, by Rev. John E. Bray	1	289

JOHNSON, (cont.)

	Vol.	Page
her age	TM1	52
Abigail Bruster, m. Moses CLARK, b. of Derby, Jan. 6, 1774, by Rev. Mr. Hawley	TM1	92
[Ab]ijah, s. Israel & Elisabeth, b. Mar. 5, 1745	LR5	2
Abner, s. Jeremiah & Elizabeth, b. Apr. 10, 1709	2	160
Abner, m. Abigal DURAND, Aug. 9, 1738	LR4	A4
Abner, s. Abner & Abigail, b. Feb. 22, 1751/2	LR6	2
Abraham, s. John & Mary, d. Jan. 18, 1712	LR3	6
Abram, s. John & Mary, b. Dec. 6, 1694	2	26
Agnis, d. Peter & Mary, b. June 29, 1727	LR3	5
Amus, s. Benajah & Sarah, b. Aug. 13, 1743	LR4	A2
Amos, s. Nathaniel & Susanna, b. Jan. 17, 1759	TM1	95
Amos Hawkins, s. Isaac & Lowis, b. Mar. 26, 1771	TM1	43
Amos Hawkins, s. Isaac & Lowis, d. Sept. 26, 1772	TM1	48
Andrew, s. Nathaniel & Susanna, b. Apr. 3, 1765	TM1	95
Andrew, m. Rebecca BLOOMFIELD, b. of Derby, Sept. 15, 1821, by Rev. Abner Smith	1	99
Ann, d. Ebenezer & Elisabeth, b. June 26, 1727	LR3	5
Ann, m. Samuel HICHCOCK, Jan. 20, 1747/8	LR6	6
Annah, d. Moses & Sary, b. Mar. 1, 1704	LR3	1
Anne, d. Gideon & Lydia, b. Jan. 28, 1748/9	LR6	3
Anne, d. Isaac & Lowis, b. Mar. 22, 1779	TM1	86
Asael, s. Joseph & Elizabeth, b. Aug. 15, 1739	LR4	A3
Asahel, of Derby, m. Lowis WILLIAMS, of Fairfield, May 19, 1756, by Rev. Richard Mansfield	TM1	61
Asahel, of Derby, m. Meriam FOWLER, of Middletown, Apr. 6, 1783	TM1	60
Benaja, s. Jer[emiah] & Elizabeth, b. July 24, 1704	2	13
Bennajah, m. Sarah HAWKINS, Oct. 10, 1728	LR3	10
Bennajah, s. Bennajah & Sarah, b. Aug. 20, 1732	LR3	16
Benajah, d. Apr. 13, 1763, in the 59th y. of his age	LR7	254
Benony, s. Peter & Abigail, b. May 2, 1763	LR7	252
Benony, s. Peter & Abigail, d. May 13, 1763	LR7	252
Betsey, m. John D. SCOTT, Sept. 26, 1847, by Rev. W[illia]m B. Curtiss	1	440
Betty, d. Peter & Abigail, b. June 18, 1756	LR6	15
Betty, d. Ebenezer & Thankfull, b. Feb. 5, 1768	TM1	40
Briant, s. Asahel & Lowis, b. Sept. 5, 1772	TM1	61
Charity, d. Jeremiah & Hannah, b. Sept. 24, 1772	TM1	103
Charles, s. Capt. [ ] & Hannah, b. Dec. 29, 1696/7	2	31
Charl[e]s, s. Timo[thy] & Abigal, b. Apr. 19, 1739	LR4	A3
[Ch]arles, s. Israel & Elisabeth, b. June 27, 1741	LR5	2
Charles, [s. Israel & Elisabeth], d. Oct. 28, 1763, in the 23rd y. of his age	LR7	254
Charles, m. Sarah WOOSTER, Aug. 16, [ ]	LR3	10
Chauncy, s. Isaac & Lowis, b. Apr. 19, 1777	TM1	96
Chauncey, s. Jesse & Hepzibah, b. Jan. [ ], 1823	1	17

	Vol.	Page
JOHNSON, (cont.)		
Comfort, d. Peter & Abigail, b. Jan. 8, 1761	LR7	249
Curtiss, m. Irene HAWKINS, b. of Derby, Mar. 18, 1821, by		
Rev. Abner Smith	1	99
Daniel, s. Israel & Elisabeth, b. Apr. 13, 1747	LR5	413
Daniel M., m. Sally HARGER, May [ ], 1822, by Rev.		
Zepheniah Swift	1	99
Dauid, s. Left. Ebenezer & Elisabeth, b. Jan. 7, 1724/5	LR3	5
David, m. Esther RIGGS, May 6, 1755	LR6	7
David, s. David & Easther, b. Dec. 21, 1755	LR6	15
David, s. Lieut. Nathaniel & Susanna, b. June 21, 1771	TM1	95
David, Jr., m. Elisabeth HOTCHKISS, b. of Derby, June 23,		
1776	TM1	109
David, d. Aug. 14, 1777, ae 21 y. 8 m., wanted 7 das	TM1	117
David, m. Sarrah THOMPSON, b. of Derby, Mar. 18, 1778	TM1	92
David, of Derby, m. Ruth Ann SCOTT, of Oxford, May 17,		
1840, by Rev. John E. Bray	1	176
David T., of Ansonia, m. Sarah LINDLEY, of Humphreysville,		
Apr. 20, 1846, by Rev. John Parvies	1	325
Ebenezar, m. Nov. 23, 1676	2	1
Ebenezer, Ens., m. Elisabeth HINE, Feb. 19, 1718/19	LR3	9
Ebenezer, s. Ens. Ebenezer, b. July 1, 1723	LR3	4
Ebenezer, Lieut., d. Sept. 10, 1751, in the 65th y. of		
his age	LR6	5
Ebenezer, of Derby, m. Mrs. Lucy BARNS, of Waterbury, Mar.		
19, 1754, by M. Leuenworth	LR6	6
Edwin C., of Birmingham, m. Lydia LOOMIS, of Franklin,		
July 2, 1848, by Rev. W[illia]m Denison	1	326
Elenor, Mrs. of Oxford, m. Isaac Noyes ALLEN, Mar. 1,		
1832, by Rev. Stephen Jewett	1	108
Elijah, [s. Israel & Elisabeth], d. Nov. 11, [ ], in		
the 19th y. of his age	LR7	254
Eliflet, s. Joseph & Marget, b. Apr. 1, 1725	LR3	5
Eliphalet, s. Joseph & Eliz[a]beth, Jr., b. Aug. 22, 1743	LR4	A2
Eliphelet, s. Samuel & Mary, b. Feb. 2, 1763	TM1	20
Eliphlet, s. Samuel & Mary, b. Feb. 2, 1763	TM1	43
Elisha, s. Joseph & Elizebeth, b. Apr. 10, 1741	LR4	A2
Elisha, s. Asahel & Lowis, b. Oct. 27, 1767	TM1	9
Elisha, s. Asahel & Lowis, b. Oct. [ ], 1767	TM1	61
Elezabeth, d. Jer[emiah], [Sr., b.[ ] 2, 1684	2	2
Elizabeth, d. Gidion, b. Aug. 25, 1722	LR3	4
Elizabeth, m. John CHATFIELD, Dec. 12, 1722	LR3	9
Elizebeth, m. Daniel TUCKER, July 9, 1741	LR4	A4
Elizebeth, d. Sam[ue]ll & Mary, b. Feb. 25, 1742	LR4	A5
Elisabeth, m. John CANFIELD, b. of Derby, Mar. [ ], 1751, by		
Rev. Daniel Humphry	LR7	248
Elisabeth, d. Joseph & Elisabeth, b. Mar. 14, 1753	LR6	3
Elisabeth, [d. Israel & Elisabeth], d. Nov. 15, 1763, in		

JOHNSON, (cont.)

	Vol.	Page
the 3rd year of her age	LR7	254
Elisabeth, w. Joseph, d. Oct. 1, 1784, in the 66th y. of her age	TM1	159
Elisabeth, d. Hezekiah & Rebecca, d. Dec. 6, 1785	TM1	163
Elisabeth, d. Hezekiah & Rebecca, b. Dec. 6, 1785	TM1	163
Elisabeth, d. Hezekiah & Rebecca, b. Nov. 26, 1786	TM1	163
Emeline, of Derby, m. John LEWIS, of Oxford, Nov. 27, 1836, by Rev. John E. Bray	1	164
Esther, d. Asahel & Lowis, b. May 3, 1757	TM1	61
Esther, w. David, d. May 22, 1766, in the 30th y. of her age	TM1	17
Eunes, b. Aug. 22, 1678	2	1
Eunice, twin with Lowis, d. Asahel & Lowis, b. Mar. 11, 1766	TM1	9
[E]unice, [twin with Lowis], d. Asahel & Lowis, b. Mar. 11, 1766	TM1	61
Eunice, d. Peter & Abigail, b. July 2, 1767	TM1	33
Eunice, m. John THOMAS, Aug. 29, 1841, by John D. Smith	1	191
Ezra, s. Jeremiah & Hannah, b. Nov. 6, 1768	TM1	103
Fanny, m. Rev. Samuel BASSETT, Oct. 6, 1828, by Sam[ue]l R. Hickcox. Witnesses: Isaac Bassett, Joseph Johnson, Isaac Bassett, Jr.	1	88
Gideon, m. Abigail CHATFIELD, Nov. 6, 1718	LR3	9
Gedion, s. Gedion & Abigal, b. Jan. 3, 1724/5	LR3	5
Gideon, of Derby, m. Lydia BEACHER, of New Haven, Mar. 24, 1749	LR6	6
Gideon, s. Gideon & Lydia, b. Sept. 3, 1752	LR6	3
Hannah, m. John RIGGS, Oct. 29, [ ]	LR3	10
Hannah, d. Ebenezer, [ ], Dec. 6, 1680	2	1
Hannah, d. Ens. Ebenezer, b. Nov. 17, 1719	LR3	3
Hannah, m. Sam[ue]ll WOOSTER, May 22, 1725	LR3	10
Hannah, d. Joseph & Margrit, b. Feb. 16, 1729	LR3	15
Hannah, d. Timothy & Abigal, b. Dec. 4, 172[ ]	LR3	15
Hannah, d. Sam[ue]ll & Mary, b. Feb. 12, 1749/50	LR5	414
Hannah, d. Israel & Elisabeth, b. Oct. 26, 1750	LR5	414
Hannah, m. Jeremiah JOHNSON, b. of Derby, Dec. 3 or 4, 1767	TM1	103
Hannah, d. Jeremiah & Hannah, b. Oct. 12, 1769	TM1	103
Hannah, d. Alexander & Hannah, b. Jan. 26, 1772	TM1	66
Hannah, m. Abraham ENGLISH, Dec. 2, 1773?; recorded Nov. 15, 1815	1	91
Hannah, m. John ADEE, Mar. 22, 1775	TM1	108
Hannah, m. Newton TIBBILS, b. of Derby, Aug. 25, 1824, by Rev. Abner Smith	1	119
Harriet F., of Derby, m. Lyman D. HUTCHINS, of Fairfield, Sept. 5, 1841, by Rev. John E. Bray	1	175
Harvey, b. Mar. 30, 1805	TM1	433
Henry, m. Abby Jane TREADWELL, Sept. 6, 1846, by Rev. W[illia]m Bliss Ashley	1	325

	Vol.	Page
JOHNSON, (cont.)		
Hepzibah, b. Jan. 25, 1803	TM1	433
Hezekiah, s. Joseph & Elisabeth, b. Oct. 25, 1748	LR5	232
Hezekiah, m. Rebecca JORDAN, Dec. 12, 1784	TM1	163
Horace, m. Minerva DYER, Oct. 9, 1828, by Rev. Zepheniah Swift	1	98
Icabod, s. Gedion & Abigal, b. Mar. 3, 1726/7	LR3	5
Isaac, s. Benajah & Sarah, b. Oct. 6, 1735	LR3	11
Isaac, of Derby, m. Lowis HOPKINS, of Waterbury, Jan. 24, 1758, by Rev. Mark Leavenworth	LR6	444
Isaac, of Derby, m. Lowis HOPKINS, of Waterbury, Jan. 24, 1758	LR7	248
Isaac, s. Isaac & Lowis, b. July 2, 1769	TM1	30
Isaac, s. Isaac & Lowis, d. Dec. 4, 1774	TM1	48
Isaac, s. Isaac & Lowis, d. July 3, 1777	TM1	48
Isaac, [b.] Apr. 2, 1799	TM1	433
Israel, s. Ebenezer & Hannah, b. Apr. 13, 1689	2	26
Israill, Lieut., d. Jan. 31, 1712/13	LR3	6
Israiel, s. Peter & Martha, b. Jan. 12, 1714	LR3	2
Israel, m. Elisabeth WAKLING, May 28, 1740	LR5	4
James D., of Weston, m. Jane KEENEY, of Humphreysville, Nov. 26, 1829	1	106
Jerimiah, s. Moses & Sary, b. Sept. 20, 1711	LR3	1
Jeremiah, s. Joseph, b. Apr. 1, 1722	LR3	4
[J]eremiah, s. Abner & Abigail, b. Mar. 21, 174[ ]	LR5	2
Jeremiah, s. Joseph & Elisabeth, b. Dec. 29, 1745	LR5	2
Jeremiah, m. Hannah JOHNSON, b. of Derby, Dec. 3 or 4, 1767	TM1	103
Jeremiah, s. Jeremiah & Hannah, b. Nov. 17, 1775	TM1	103
Jeremiah, [ ]	TM1	87
Jesse, s. Isaac & Lowis, b. July 28, 1773	TM1	65
Jesse, Jr., b. Mar. 28, 1801	TM1	433
Joel, s. Asahel & Lowis, b. May 1, 1759	TM1	61
Joel, s. Asahel & Lowis, d. Aug. 23, 1777, at King's Bridge	TM1	61
Johanah, d. Peter & Martha, b. May 17, 1710	2	160
John, m. Mary WASHBONE, Sept. 24, 1694	2	25
Joseph, m. Margret HARGER, Jan. 24, 1717	LR3	9
Joseph, s. Joseph & Margret, b. Nov. 29, 1717	LR3	3
Joseph, d. June 15, 1787, in the 70th y. of his age	TM1	159
Joseph, d. June 25, 1818	TM1	428
Joseph, m. Elisabeth DURAND, Aug. 5, [ ]	LR3	10
Joseph Harvey, m. Mrs. Sarah M. DIER, b. of Derby, Dec. 1, 1832, by Rev. S. Jewett	1	161
Laura, d. Jesse & Hepzibah, b. June 2, 1819	1	17
Lowis, d. Peter & Abigail, b. July 15, 1753	LR6	15
Lowis, twin with Eunice, d. Asahel & Lowis, b. Mar. 11, 1766	TM1	9
Lowis, [twin with [E]unice], d. Asahel & Lowis, b. Mar. 11, 1766	TM1	61
Lowis, w. Asahel, d. Jan. 28, 1783, in the 49th y. of her age	TM1	61

JOHNSON, (cont.)

	Vol.	Page
Louis, of Oxford, m. Peter **VADER**, of Mammaronick, N. Y., Nov. 13, 1836, by Sylvester Smith	1	185
Lois Emily, b. Feb. 24, 1810	TM1	433
Lucinda, m. Charles Denison **MERRICK**, Dec. 24, 1825, by Stephen Jewett, at Humphreysville	1	104
Lucey, d. Asahel & Lowis, b. Aug. 25, 1763	TM1	61
Lucy, d. Asahel & Lois, b. Aug. 25, 1763	LR7	252
Lucy, m. Nathan **FRENCH**, b. of Derby, Sept. 2, 1773	TM1	118
Lucy, d. Capt. Nathaniel & Susanna, b. Sept. 9, 1774	TM1	95
Luranah, m. Jeremiah **OCAIN**, Sept. 18, 1765, by Rev. Richard Mansfield	TM1	43
Lydia, d. Gideon & Lydia, b. May 31, 1754	LR6	4
Lydia, d. Gideon & Lydia, b. May 31, 1754	LR6	442
Mabel, d. Moses & Sary, b. Oct. 18, 1707	LR3	1
Mabel, d. Gidion & Abigail, b. Aug. 24, 1719	LR3	3
Mabel, m. Joseph **RIGGS**, Feb. 20, 1739	TM1	225
Mabel, d. Abner & Abigal, b. May 23, 1739	LR4	A3
Mabel, m. Joseph **RIGGS**, Feb. 20, 1739/40	LR4	A4
Mabel, d. Gideon & Lydia, b. Sept. 22, 1756	LR6	442
Mabel, m. James **PERRY**, Apr. [ ], 1760	TM1	19
Mabel, d. Isaac & Lois, b. Nov. 27, 1766	TM1	20
Margret, d. Joseph & Elisabeth, b. Dec. 7, 1750	LR6	3
Margret, d. Joseph & Elisabeth, d. Feb. 20, 1751	LR6	5
Margrat, d. Joseph & Elisabeth, b. June 16, 1756	LR6	441
Margret, d. Sam[ue]ll & Mary, b. Apr. 21, 1765	TM1	20
Margret, d. Sam[ue]ll & Mary, b. Apr. 21, 1766	TM1	43
Margret, m. David **TWITCHEL**, Dec. [ ], 1773	TM1	96
Martha, d. Peter & Martha, b. May 6, 1717	LR3	3
Martha, w. Peter, d. May 7, 1720	LR3	6
Mary, d. John & Mary, b. Nov. 7 ?, 1696	2	26
Mary, d. Peter & Mary, b. Dec. 3, 1724	LR3	5
Mary, d. Peter & Abigail, b. Dec. 23, 1757	LR6	440
Mary, d. Peter & Abigail, b. Dec. 23, 1757	LR6	443
Mary, of Orange, m. Agur **GILBERT**, of Derby, Feb. 4, 1830, by Z. Swift	1	103
Mary, m. Stiles **BALDWIN**, June 2, 1834, by Zepheniah Swift	1	147
Mary A., m. Robert T. **HODGE**, Apr. 6, 1845, by Rev. W[illia]m B. Curtiss	1	289
Mary R., of Ansonia, m. Frederick D. **DANIELS**, of Bristol, Oct. 8, 1854, by Rev. O. Street, at Ansonia	1	249
Mellee, d. Asahel & Lowis, b. Oct. 5, 1769	TM1	61
Mercy, d. Sam[ue]ll & Mary, b. June 21, 1747	LR5	232
Molly, d. Isaac & Lois, b. Apr. 4, 1759	LR6	440
Molly, m. Abram **SMITH**, Aug. 4, 1782	TM1	151
Moses, m. Sarah **ADAMS**, Apr. 15, 1703	2	13
Nathan C., m. Martha I. **LASEE**, May 9, 1847, by Rev. W[illia]m B. Curtiss	1	326

	Vol.	Page
JOHNSON, (cont.)		
Nathaniel, s. Timothy & Abigail, b. Mar. 6, 1726	LR3	5
Nathaniel, s. Joseph & Margret, b. Feb. 11, 1731/2	LR3	16
Nathaniel, m. Susanna SMITH, Jan. 30, 1753	LR6	6
Nathaniel, s. Lieut. Nathaniel & Susanna, b. July 21, 1769	TM1	95
Newel, s. Hezekiah & Rebecka, b. May 22, 1789	TM1	163
Peter, s. Ebenezer, b. Oct. 9, 1684	2	2
Peter, had his ear mark for cattle, recorded Feb. 25, 1709/10	2	161
Peter, Jr., m. Abigail JOHNSON, Nov. 9, 1749	LR6	8
Peter, s. Peter, b. [ ]	LR3	4
Phebe, w. David, d. Aug. 6, 1777	TM1	117
Philene, d. Asahel & Lowis, b. Oct. 5, 1761	TM1	61
Philo, s. Nathaniel & Susanna, b. May 3, 1754	TM1	95
Philo, s. Nathaniel & Susanna, b. May 4, 1754	LR6	4
Philo, s. Nathaniel & Susanna, b. May 4, 1754	LR6	5
Polle, d. Jeremiah & Hannah, b. Aug. 29, 1778	TM1	103
Polly, b. July 12, 1807	TM1	433
Polly, of Humphreysville, m. Elam NICKOLS, of Bridgeport, Dec. 11, 1836, by Rev. Sam[ue]l R. Hickcox	1	169
Rachell, d. Moses & Sary, b. Mar. 13, 1712	LR3	1
Ruth, d. Alexander & Hannah, b. Nov. 21, 1769	TM1	63
Ruth, d. Timothy & Abigal, b. Apr. 28, [ ]	LR3	16
Saberah, d. Nathanael & Susana, b. June 12, 1756	LR6	15
Sabra, d. Nathaniel & Susanna, b. June 12, 1756	TM1	95
Sabra, d. Nathaniel & Susanna, d. Oct. 8, 1763	TM1	95
Sabra, d. Lieut. Nathaniel & Susanna, b. July 8, 1767	TM1	95
Sally B., d. Jesse & Hepzibah, b. Sept. 6, 1797	TM1	433
Samuel, s. Joseph, b. Dec. 23, 1719	LR3	3
Sarah, d. Ens. Ebenezer, b. July 14, 1721	LR3	4
Sarah, of Derby, m. James WHE[E]LER, of Stratford, May 19, 1736	TM1	32
Sarah, d. Sam[ue]ll & Mary, b. Aug. 22, 1752	LR6	3
Sarah, [twin with Susse], d. Nathaniel & Susannah, b. July 15, 1762	TM1	95
Sarah, wid., d. May 7, 1773	TM1	48
Sarah, m. John WHE[E]LER, Nov. 19, 1777	TM1	85
Sheldon C., m. Susan H. STODDARD, May 19, 1828, by Rev. Stephen Jewett	1	99
Sheldon N., m. Eliza PATCHEN, b. of Derby, Sept. 1, 1833, by S. Jewett	1	161
Sylas, s. John & Mary, b. July 18, 1713 (Silas)	LR3	2
Stiles, s. Isaac & Lowis, b. Dec. 4, 1781	TM1	111
Stiles, had adopted s. Stiles JOHNSON, s. Jesse, b. May 14, 1813	1	17
Stiles, s. Jesse & adopted s. of Stiles JOHNSON, b. May 14, 1813	1	17
Stiles, b. May 14, 1813	TM1	433
Susanna, d. Isaac & Lowis, b. Sept. 3, 1760	LR7	250

	Vol.	Page
JUDSON, (cont.)		
Oct. 12, 1851, by Rev. Thomas T. Guion	1	342
KASSELY, Sarah, m. David **COLE,** Oct. 1, 1839, by Rev. Joseph Scott	1	153
KEENEY, KENEY, KEENNEY, [see also **KENNEY & KINNEY**],		
Abigail, d. Ebenezer & Betty, b. Feb. 11, 1753	TM1	7
Betsey, m. Lyman **SMITH,** July 26, 1824, by Stephen Jewett	1	118
Betty, d. Ebenezer & Betty, b. Sept. 20, 1745	LR5	2
Betty, d. Ebenezer & Betty, b. Sept. 20, 1745	TM1	7
Betty, m. Sheldon **CLARK,** b. of Derby, Feb. 15, 1764	TM1	108
Comfort, d. Ebenezer & Bette, b. Oct. 11, 1741	LR4	A5
Comfort, d. Ebenezer & Betty, b. Oct. 11, 1741	TM1	7
Comfort, d. Ebenezer & Betty, b. Oct. 11, 1741	TM1	74
Comfort, m. Judson **BURTON,** Nov. 23, 1758, by Rev. Daniel Humphry	TM1	74
Comfort, m. Judson **BURTON,** Nov. 23, 1758	LR7	248
Eben[e]zer, m. Bette **DAUIS,** Dec. 7, 1738	LR4	A4
Ebenezer, m. Betty **DAVIS,** Dec. 7, 1738	LR5	4
Ebenezer, m. Mrs. Betty **DAVIS,** Dec. 7, 1738	TM1	7
Ebenezer, s. Ebenezer & Betty, b. Oct. 27, 1750	TM1	7
Ebenezer, s. Ebenezer & Betty, b. Oct. 27, 1750	LR5	414
Eithiel, s. Ebenezer & Betty, b. Mar. 17, 1755	LR6	4
Eunis, d. Ebenezer & Bette, b. Aug. 31, 1743	LR4	A5
Eunice, d. Ebenezer & Betty, b. Aug. 31, 1743	TM1	7
Eunice, m. Stephen **WHITNEY,** Nov. 5, 1764	TM1	84
Isaac, m. Ann **CHURCH,** b. of Derby, Dec. 15, 1828, by [ ]	1	101
Jane, m. Enos B. **MILES,** Aug. 9, 1829, by Rev. Stephen Jewett	1	104
Jane, of Humphreysville, m. James D. **JOHNSON,** of Weston, Nov. 26, 1829	1	106
Lockwood, m. Maria **SHIPMAN,** b. of Derby, Oct. 17, 1830, by Rev. Zepheniah Swift	1	107
Lusee, d. Ebenezer & Betty, b. Dec. 3, 1739	LR4	A2
Lucy, d. Ebenezer & Betty, b. Dec. 3, 1739	TM1	7
Lucy, d. Ebenezer & Betty, b. Sept. 20, 1761	TM1	7
Maria, m. Jeremiah **DURAND,** Dec. 25, 1827, by Rev. Zepheniah Swift	1	89
Medad, s. Ebenezer & Betty, b. May 31, 1759	TM1	7
Medad, s. Ebenezar & Betty, b. May 31, 1759	LR7	249
Sarah, d. Ebenezer & Betty, b. Oct. 3, 1748	TM1	7
Sarah, d. Ebenezer & Beaty, b. Oct. 3, 1748	LR5	413
Sarah Grace, m. Isaac **WHITE,** Jr., b. of Derby, Jan. 11, 1835, by Rev. John E. Bray	1	187
William, s. Ebenezer & Betty, b. July 16, 1757	TM1	7
William, s. Ebenezer & Betty, b. July 16, 1757	LR6	443
KELBOURNE, Hiram G., m. Lelia E. **BARNES,** July 2, 1851, by Rev. Jno Morrison Reid	1	330
KENDALL, Joshua, M. D., m. Thirza **HUMPHREYS,** b. of Derby, May 17, 1836, by John D. Smith	1	163

	Vol.	Page
KNAPP, (cont.)		
by Rev. J. B. Beach	1	192
LACY, LASEE, LOSEE, Augusta Jennette, m. Thomas		
THOMPSON, (colored), June 29, 1840, by John D. Smith	1	182
Harriet, of Derby, m. Abel **BEERS**, of Newtown, Sept. 11, 1836,		
by Rev. John E. Bray	1	168
Isaac, m. Jane E. **BUNNELL**, b. of Humphreysville, Oct. 15,		
1848, by Rev. Charles Stearns, at Humphreysville.	1	342
Martha I., m. Nathan C. **JOHNSON**, May 9, 1847, by Rev.		
W[illia]m B. Curtiss	1	326
LAKE, Ann Augusta, m. Julius **BASSETT**, Sept. 13, 1841, by John		
D. Smith	1	189
Walker, of Oxford, m. Hepzibah **BASSETT**, of Derby, Apr. 4,		
1838, by Rev. David Miller	1	164
LAMBERT, Deborah, m. John **SMITH**, Dec. 9, 1719, by Rev.		
Sam[ue]ll Andrew, at Milford	LR3	9
LANE, Abner, of Huntington, m. Lucy Comelia **HUBBELL**, of		
Huntington, Oct. 27, 1839, by Rev. J. B. Beach	1	192
David B., of Monroe, m. Phebe A. **JUDSON**, of Huntington,		
Oct. 12, 1851, by Rev. Thomas T. Guion	1	342
Jane, Mrs. of Derby, m. Roger N. **WHITTLESEY**, of New		
Preston, Aug. 19, 1838, by Rev. David Miller	1	188
John, of Huntington, m. Jane **TOMLINSON**, of Derby, Nov. 24,		
1831, by Rev. Heman Bangs	1	112
LARKIN, Jane, m. Thomas **CONNOLLY**, Aug. 27, 1851, by Rev.		
James Lynch, of Birmingham	1	237
Mary, m. Francis **CLARK**, June 22, 1851, by James Lynch, of		
Birmingham	1	236
LASEE, [see under **LACY**]		
LASKIN, Charles E., of Stamford, m. Susan **CHATFIELD**, of Derby,		
Apr. 16, 1848, by Rev. W[illia]m Bliss Ashely	1	341
LATHON, Elizabeth, of Bridgeport, m. Mark A. **NORTHRUP**, of		
Sherman, July 4, 1843, by Rev. Sylvester Smith	1	381
LEAVENWORTH, LEVENWORTH, LEUENSWORTH, Caroline		
Elizabeth, m. Daniel Sterling **JOICE**, Nov. 27, 1836, by		
John D. Smith	1	161
Edmund S., m. Ellen E. **THOMAS**, Feb. 25, 1841, by John D.		
Smith	1	184
George, m. Mabel **STEPHENS**, May 28, 1848, by Rev.		
W[illia]m B. Curtiss	1	342
Hannah, m. Nichol **MOSS**, Mar. 23, 1740	LR4	A4
John, of Derby, m. Mary **WALESTOWN**, of Guilford, Oct. 20,		
1844, by Rev. Sylvester Smith	1	341
Maria, m. Harris B. **MONSON**, July 23, 1843, by Rev. John D.		
Smith	1	357
LEDDLE, Hannah, m. William **BROOKS**, Oct. 3, 1844, by Rev.		
W[illia]m Bliss Ashley, in Birmingham	1	206
LEE, LEES, Cyrus, m. Emily Maria **FISHER**, Jan. 27, 1835, by		

	Vol.	Page
LOVELAND, (cont.)		
Joseph, s. Joseph & Hannah, b. Feb. 8, 1739	TM1	75
Joseph, m. Lowis **CHATFIELD**, Aug. 18, 1762	TM1	75
Lowis, d. Joseph & Lowis, b. July 17, 1763	TM1	75
Sarah, m. Israel **FRENCH**, Sept. 11, 1739	LR5	4
Sarah, d. Joseph & Lowis, b. Dec. 2, 1770	TM1	75
Treat, s. Joseph & Lowis, b. Sept. 6, 1767	TM1	75
LOYD, Gay, of New Haven, m. Laura **SMITH**, of Woodbridge, Oct.		
30, 1836, by Rev. Joseph Scott	1	165
LUM, LUMM, LUME, Adam, s. Jonathan & Elisabeth, b. Nov. 11,		
1753	LR6	3
Ann, m. Eleazer **LEWIS**, Feb. 16, 1757, by Rev. Richard		
Mansfield	LR6	445
Charlotte Eliza, of Camebridgeport, Mass., m. Sheldon		
CANFIELD, Jr., of Derby, Nov. 10, 1831, by Rev. S.		
Jewett	1	103
Clark, of New Haven, m. Miranda E. **KINNEY,** of Derby, Sept.		
25, 1836, by Rev. John E. Bray	1	165
David, s. Joseph & Sarah, b. Apr. 6, 1742	LR6	441
David, m. Sally **THOMPSON**, June 8, 1837, by Rev. Joseph		
Scott	1	164
Edward A., m. Elizabeth M. **DURAND**, Nov. 30, 1848, by Rev.		
W[illia]m B. Curtiss	1	342
Edward C., m. Mary Jane **BASSETT**, b. of Derby, Mar. 2, 1845,		
by Rev. W[illia]m Bliss Ashley	1	341
Elisabeth, d. Jonathan & Sarah, b. Mar. 15, 1712/13	LR3	2
Elizabeth, m. Daniel **HULL**, Mar. 2, 173[ ]	LR3	10
Elizebeth, d. Jonathan & Eliz[e]beth, b. June 7, 1739	LR4	A3
Eunice, d. Joseph & Sarah, b. Sept. 6, 1746	LR6	441
Freelove, m. Josiah **NETTLETON**, July 18, 1776, by Rev.		
Richard Mansfield	TM1	160
Hannah, d. Joseph & Sarah, b. May 2, 1744	LR6	441
Hannah, m. William **CANFIELD**, May 6, 1754, by Timothy		
Russell	LR6	6
Henry, s. Jonathan & Elisabeth, b. June 1, 1748	LR5	232
Jane, m. Rev. John D. **SMITH**, June 21, 1835, by Rev. Joseph		
Scott	1	158
John, s. Johnathan & Sarah, b. July 17, 1703	2	12
John, s. Jonathan & Elizebeth, b. Sept. 5, 1743	LR4	A5
John, of Derby, m. Freelove **LYNES,** of Litchfield, Oct. 18,		
1769, by Timothy Russell	TM1	87
John, s. John & Freelove, b. Mar. 29, 1770	TM1	87
John, d. Aug. 18, 1771	TM1	87
John, Jr., m. Augusta **WOOSTER**, Feb. 26, 1828, by Rev.		
Stephen Jewett	1	111
Jonathan, m. Sarah **RIGGS**, Oct. 10, 1700	2	25
Jonathan & w. Elisabeth had d. [ ], b. Mar. 22, 1737	LR3	11
Jonathan, Jr., m. Elisabeth **TOMLINSON**, Mar. 13, [ ]	LR3	10

	Vol.	Page
LUM, LUMM, LUME, (cont.)		
Joseph, s. Jonathan & Sarah, b. Jan. 14, [ ]	LR3	2
Joseph, m. Sarah WASHBOND, Apr. 29, 1741	LR4	A4
Joseph, s. Joseph & Sarah, b. Mar. 17, 1750	LR6	441
Lemuel, s. Jonath[a]n & Elizebeth, b. Mar. 2, 1741/2	LR4	A2
Mary, m. Robert S. TREAT, Apr. 25, 1841, by John D. Smith	1	182
Mary Augusta, of Derby, m. Liester KIMBERLY, of West Haven, Nov. 20, 1842, by Rev. William Bliss Ashely	1	333
Olive, d. Jonathan & Elisabeth, b. Dec. 9, 1758	LR6	719
Ruben, s. Joseph & Sarah, b. Mar. 22, 1754	LR6	441
Samuel & w. Hannah had s. [ ], b. Feb. 19, [ ]	LR3	16
Sam[ue]ll, m. Hannah [TID ?], Dec. 7, 1730	LR3	10
Sarah, d. Jonathan & Sarah, b. Nov. 29, 1701	2	12
Sarah m. John DURAND, Nov. 5, 1730	LR3	10
Sarah, d. Jonathan & Elisabeth, b. Nov. 21, 1745	LR5	2
Sarah, Mrs., m. Richard HOLBROOK, Sept. 13, 1797	TM1	229
Sarah, m. William SMITH, b. of Derby, Apr. 24, 1823, by Rev. Stephen Jewett	1	116
Sarah J., m. W[illia]m B. ACKLEY, of N. Y., Oct. 13, 1852, by Rev. Thomas T. Guion	1	194
William Austin, m. Caroline CHATFIELD, Nov. 27, 1838, by John D. Smith	1	164
William D., m. Mary TIBBLES, Jan. 6, 1833, by Rev. S. Jewett	1	165
----e, d. Jonathan & Elizebeth, b. Mar. 7, 1734/5	LR3	11
LYMAN, Abigail, m. Isaa[c] NICKOLS, b. of Derby, Dec. 24, 1769	TM1	128
Adaline E., m. Burritt TUTTLE, of Plymouth, May 15, 1851, by Rev. Jno Morrison Reid	1	462
Nab[b]e, d. Noah Russel & Comfort, b. Nov. 25, 1772	TM1	52
Noah Russel, m. Comfort FOX, Feb. 13, 1771	TM1	52
LYONS, LYON, Daniel M., of Derby, m. Maria BOTSFORD, of Woodbridge, May 9, 1847, by Rev. Sylvester Smith	1	341
John K., of Danbury, m. Hellen A. HORTON, of Bethel, Nov. 8, 1847, by Rev. Nathan E. Shailer	1	341
LYNES, [see under LINES]		
McARTHUR, Duncan, m. Mary FURGUSON, b. of Derby, Aug. 5, 1850, by Rev. Jno Morrison Reid	1	193
McCARTHY, Charles, m. Alice HOYS, Dec. 1, [18]51, by Rev. James Lynch, of Birmingham	1	359
McCOY, Henry O., of Branford, m. Emily FRENCH, d. of Walter, of Derby, Sept. 9, 1835, by Sylvester Smith	1	149
McKANE, Michael, m. Anne COSS, Apr. 22, 1851, by Rev. James Lynch, of Birmingham	1	358
McKEE, [see also MACKEY], Anne, w. William d. Mar. 1, 1773	TM1	52
Samuel, s. William & Anne, b. July 31, 1772	TM1	52
William, m. Anna DURAND, May [ ], 1769	TM1	15
William, s. William & Anne, b. [ ], 1770	TM1	52
MACKEY, [see also McKEE], Bridget, m. Michael BURK, July 13, 1851, by Rev. James Lynch, of Birmingham	1	213

	Vol.	Page
McMANN, James M., of New York, m. Susan A. WHITNEY, of Derby, Apr. 17, [1843], by Rev. W[illia]m Bliss Ashley	1	357
McNEAL, Henry, of New Haven, m. Augusta Caroline ENGLISH, of Derby, Oct. 18, 1835, by Rev. Zepheniah Swift	1	150
MAGUIRE, Pat[ric]k, m. Mary REGAN, Sept. 8, 1851, by Rev. James Lynch, of Birmingham	1	359
MALLET, MALLETT, Nancy, m. Luther ROOT, Nov. 27, 1848, by Rev. J. Guernsey	1	426
Nancy, m. Luther ROOT, Nov. 27, 1849, by Rev. Jesse Guernsey	1	210
Peter, m. Nancy HOTCHKISS, Mar. 2, 1834, by Zepheniah Swift	1	166
MALLEY, Rose, m. Thomas PATTERSON, June 24, 1849, by Rev. Cha[rle]s Dickinson	1	407
MALLORY, MALLERY, Fanny E., m. Chipman S. JACKSON, Nov. 5, 1843, by Rev. Joseph P. Wakeley	1	325
Hannah, of West Haven, m. Joseph SMITH, 3rd, of Derby, Aug. 21, 1753	LR6	444
Lowis, m. Eli CHATFIELD, Aug. 5, 1778	TM1	92
Mary Jane, of Derby, m. Ely SMITH, of Naugatuck, July 22, 1849, by Bishop Cha[rle]s Dickinson, of Birmingham	1	235
Mary L., of Derby, m. Ely SMITH, of Naugatuck, July 22, 1849, by Bishop Cha[rle]s Dickinson	1	441
Nancy, of Birmingham, m. George W. HAYDEN, of Westbrook, Feb. 29, 1852, by Rev. Thomas G. Osborn	1	291
Prentice A., of Woodbury, m. Mary Ann PATCHEN, of Derby, Dec. 5, 1830, by Rev. S. Jewett	1	104
MANN, Josiah, of New York City, m. Maria Brower WHITNEY, of Derby, Dec. 1, 1840, by Rev. Hollis Read	1	169
MANSFIELD, Abba Ann, m. Samuel SHERWOOD, Sept. 8, 1833, by Rev. S. Jewett	1	161
Ann Hull, m. Eleazer PECK, Sept. 9, 1833, by Rev. S. Jewett	1	172
Anna, m. Elijah HUMPHREYS, Oct. 22, 1774	TM1	207
Anna, of Derby, m. William DYER, of New Haven, Sept. 22, 1821, by Rev. Abner Smith	1	89
Betse, d. Nathan & Anna, b. Dec. 1, 1777	TM1	105
Charles, m. Laura LINDLEY, Dec. 13, 1846, by Rev. W[illia]m B. Curtiss	1	357
Elisa A., m. Abraham FOWLER, Apr. 28, 1844, by Rev. John D. Smith	1	271
Elisabeth, d. Richard & Anna, b. Sept. 15, 1754	LR6	15
Jered, s. Nathan & Anna, b. July 11, 1775	TM1	105
Lyman, of Hamden, m. Mrs. Lucy HUBBELL, of Derby, Mar. 27, 1842, by Rev. H. Read	1	162
Nathan, m. Anna TOMLINSON, Mar. 5, 1775	TM1	105
Richard, Rev., m. Mrs. Anna HULL, Oct. 10, 1751, by Rev. Samuel Johnson, of Stratford, in Christ Church	LR6	8
Richard, s. Richard & Anna, b. Aug. 23, 1752, O. S. [N. S. Sept. 3, 1752]	LR6	15

	Vol.	Page

MANSFIELD, (cont.)

Stephen, m. Caroline OATMAN, b. of Derby, Mar. 4, 1830, by
Rev. Stephen Jewett ... 1 ... 104

MANSON, [see also MUNSON], Joseph B., of Huntington, m. Sarah
A. JACKSON, of Derby, Oct. 3, 1847, by Rev. Charles
Stearns ... 1 ... 357

MARDENBROUGH, MERDENBROUGH, Eliza A., m. Capt.

Richard M. CLARK, Oct. 20, 1822, by Rev. Stephen Jewett ... 1 ... 87

Jane, m. Calvin WHITE, Jan. 9, 1828, by Rev. Stephen Jewett ... 1 ... 122

MARKS, Abraham, s. Mordicai, b. Oct. 19, 1748 ... LR6 ... 4

Elizebeth, d. Mordica & Eliz[a]beth, b. Apr. 3, 1742 ... LR4 ... A2

Mary, d. Mordecai & Elizebeth, b. Sept. 5, 1732 ... LR4 ... A2

Mordica, s. Mordica & Eliz[a]beth, b. May 30, 1739 ... LR4 ... A2

Nehemiah, s. Mordicai, b. Oct. 9, 1746 ... LR6 ... 4

Zachariah, s. Mordicai & Elizebeth, b. June 28, 1734 ... LR4 ... A2

MARONEY, Mary, m. Teddy DONNELLY, Jan. 25, [18]52, by Rev.
James Lynch ... 1 ... 249

MARTIN, Malinda, of Woodbury, m. William FRENCH, of Derby,
Dec. 24, 1823, by Rev. Stephen Jewett ... 1 ... 93

Margaret, m. William O'NEILE, May 27, 1851, by Rev. James
Lynch ... 1 ... 381

MASSY, John, m. Mary CURTISS, Apr. 14, 1707, by Major Ebenezer
Johnson, J. P. ... 2 ... 25

MATHEWS, Lucy T., of Derby, m. Ezekiel D. BRYANT, of
Sheffield, Mass., Sept. 5, 1841, by Rev. Nathaniel Mead, of
Birmingham ... 1 ... 189

MAY, Robert, of Apilachicola, Fla., m. Maria BASSETT, of Derby,
Oct. 3, 1839, by Rev. Hollis Reed ... 1 ... 167

MEAD, John, of Albany, N. Y., m. Maria BURGES, of Derby, Sept.
16, 1838, by Rev. Joseph Scott ... 1 ... 167

MERDENBROUGH, [see under MARDENBROUGH]

MEROL, Ellen, m. Robert WALLIS, Dec. 24, 1840, by John D.
Smith ... 1 ... 190

MERRIAM, Olive, of Watertown, m. Albert CARRINGTON, of
Milford, Apr. 4, [ ] ... 1 ... 106

MERRICK, [see also MYRICK], Charles Denison, m. Lucinda
JOHNSON, Dec. 24, 1825, by Stephen Jewett, at
Humphreysville ... 1 ... 104

George H., m. Jennette A. DAVIS, Sept. 13, 1841, by John
D. Smith ... 1 ... 162

Josiah, Capt., m. Mrs. Loly CARRINGTON, Dec. 10, 1843, by
Rev. John D. Smith ... 1 ... 357

Walter I., m. Harriet BROADWELL, b. of Derby, Mar. 3, 1847,
by Rev. Sylvester Smith ... 1 ... 357

MIDWINTER, John S., m. Sarah HENRIETTA, Oct. 7, 1832, by
Nath[aniel] W. Taylor ... 1 ... 166

MILES, [see also MILLS], Betsey, d. Jonathan & Lucy, b. Feb.
17, 1774 ... TM1 ... 85

	Vol.	Page
MITCHELL, (cont.)		
Derby, Aug. 21, 1850, by Rev. Thomas T. Guion	1	359
MIX, John, of Waterbury, m. Anna **LINES,** of Oxford, Apr. 15, 1834,		
by Rev. Samuel R. Hickcox	1	166
MONSON, [see under **MUNSON]**		
MOORE, Jesse, m. Ellen **BENTLY,** b. of Ansonia, Nov. 27, 1851,		
by David Osborn	1	358
MORGAN, Lewis, of Wilton, m. Susan **THOMAS,** of Derby, Jan. 21,		
1821, by Rev. Zephaniah Swift	1	105
Philander S., m. Betsey Ann **HORTON,** b. of Bethel, Nov. 7,		
1847, by Rev. Nathan E. Shailer	1	358
Samuel, m. Louisa **BEACH,** b. of Woodbridge, Apr. 27, 1840, by		
Rev. John E. Bray	1	167
MORRISS, Anna Ritta, of Derby, m. Richard **ATWATER,** of New		
Haven, July 12, 1829, by Rev. Stephen Jewett	1	124
MORSE, [see also **MOSS],** Laura Maria, m. Edward **GREGSTON,**		
Dec. 20, 1848, by Henry Whitney, J. P.	1	280
Sarah Grace, m. Thomas Albert **HART,** Nov. 26, 1838, by		
Rev. Joseph Scott	1	160
MOSES, John C., of Patterson, N. Y., m. Charlotte G. **WILCOXSON,**		
of Derby, May 5, 1853, by Rev. S. Hanson Cox, of		
Birmingham	1	359
Stephen, d. Mar. 27, 1713	LR3	6
MOSHIER, MOSHER, John H., of Derby, m. Rebecca L.		
NORTHROP, of Bethany, Nov. 1, 1840, by Rev. Joseph		
Scott	1	169
Lucy M., m. Edward **CURTISS,** Dec. 24, 1840, by John D.		
Smith	1	154
Margaret Ana, m. David Thompson **WELLS,** Jan. 7, 1838,		
by John D. Smith	1	186
Sally Maria, m. Philo **BEECHER,** Jan. 27, 1840, by John D.		
Smith	1	189
MOSS, [see also **MORSE],** Abigal, m. Elisha **KENT,** Apr. 3, 17[ ]	LR3	10
Abigail, d. Joseph & Abigail b. Sept. [ ]	LR3	2
Ann, m. Sam[ue]ll **WOOSTER,** Jr., Oct. 28, 1731	LR3	10
Barbra, Mrs., d. Sept. 8, 1745	LR5	1
Deborah, d. William & Abigail, b. Feb. 10, 1714/15	LR3	2
Dorcas, Mrs., d. Sept. 2, 1715	LR3	6
Edward, s. William & Rachel, b. Apr. 26, 1765	TM1	30
Elizabeth, d. William & Abigail, b. June 23, 1718	LR3	3
Elizabeth, d. William, b. Apr. 30, 1721	LR3	4
Isaac, s. William & Rachel, b. June 30, 1761	LR7	250
Israeil, m. Lidia **BOW[E]RS,** Dec. 31, 1717	LR3	9
John, s. Israel, b. May 10, 1721	LR3	4
Jonathan, s. Samuell & Barbary, b. May 10, 1718	LR3	3
Joseph, m. Mrs. Docus **ROSWELL,** Feb. 10, 1714	LR3	9
Joseph, m. Mrs. Abigail **RUSSEL,** Oct. 3, 1716	LR3	9
Mary, Mrs., d. Feb. 28, 1714	LR3	6

	Vol.	Page
MOSS, (cont.)		
Mary, d. Samuell & Barbara, b. Dec. 20, 1715	LR3	2
Mary, d. Joseph, b. Aug. 28, 1721	LR3	3
Mary, m. Jonah TOMLINSON, [ ], 26, [ ]	LR3	10
Nathaniel, s. Israel & Lidia, b. Dec. 14, 1722	LR3	11
Nemiah, s. Nickols & Hannah, b. Aug. 18, 1741	LR4	A2
Nicolls, s. William & Abigail, b. Apr. 28, 1716	LR3	3
Nichol, m. Hannah LEUENSWORTH, Mar. 23, 1740	LR4	A4
Prudence, d. William & Prudence, b. Mar. 27, 1754	LR7	250
Prudence, w. William, d. Apr. 6, 1754	LR7	250
Rachil, d. Isarail & Lidia, b. Jan. 24, 1719	LR3	3
Rachel, m. John HARRIS, Feb. 5, 1739/40	LR5	4
Samuell, m. Barbery BOWERS, Dec. 3, 1713	LR3	9
Sam[ue]ll, d. Dec. 28, 1721; "shot by Sam[ue]ll Perry"	LR3	6
Samuell, his ear mark for cattle, recorded [ ]	2	161
Sarah, d. William & Prudence, b. May 2, 1752	LR7	250
William, m. Abigail RIGGS, Mar. 18, 1714	LR3	9
William, s. William & Abigal, b. Mar. 14, 172[ ]	LR3	5
William, Sergt., d. Aug. 26, 1749, in the 69th y. of his age	LR5	1
William, of Derby, m. Prudence HARD, of New Town, May 30, 1751	LR7	250
William, of Derby, m. Rachel BEARDSLEY, of Stratford, Sept. 20, 1759	LR7	250
William, s. William & Rachel, b. July 31, 1766	TM1	30
MOTHROP, Caroline, m. Harvey DOWNS, Oct. 24, 1831, by Zepheniah Swift	1	151
Huldah, of Humphreysville, m. Isaac ROE, of Oxford, Apr. 4, 1824, by Rev. Labon CLARK, at Humphreysville	1	115
Luther, m. Jennett CANDEE, Dec. 19, 1830, by Rev. Charles Thompson	1	90
MOULTON, Sophia, Mrs. of Derby, m. Nathaniel BACON, of New Haven, Apr. 11, 1838, by Rev. Lewis D. Howell	1	168
MOWREN, Charles R., m. Mary S. BOTSFORD, Feb. 10, 1840, by John D. Smith	1	167
MOWRY, Henry, m. Sarah SNIDER, b. of Humphreysville, Sept. 1, 1849, by Rev. W[illia]m Denison	1	358
MUNN, Ledusky, m. Mary SPARK, b. of Derby, Oct. 12, 1835, by Rev. Joseph Scott	1	166
MUNSON, MUNSEN, MONSON, Aaron, of Southbury, m. Emeline JACKSON, of Derby, Apr. 4, 1837, by John D. Smith	1	167
Daniel, s. John & Elizabeth, b. Mar. 4, 1736	LR4	A5
Daniel, s. John & Elisabeth, d. Aug. 2, 1756, at Fort Edward	LR6	13
David H., m. Huldah BALDWIN, b. of Woodbridge, Sept. 18, 1836, by Rev. S. D. Howell	1	166
Ester, d. John & Elizabeth, b. Nov. 5, 1727	LR3	16
Hannah, d. John, b. Mar. 7, 1721	LR3	4
Hannah, m. Stephen PIERSON, Jr., June 15, 1738	LR4	A4
Harris B., m. Maria LEAVENWORTH, July 23, 1843, by		

	Vol.	Page
MUNSON, MUNSEN, MONSON, (cont.)		
Rev. John D. Smith	1	357
John, s. John & Hannah, of Brook Haven, L. I., b. Apr. 24, 1690	LR3	0
John, b. Apr. 24, 1690	LR3	0
John, m. Elisabeth HAWKINS, Dec. 25, 1718	LR3	9
John, had d. [ ]ty, b. Jan. 7, 1722/3	LR3	3
John, s. John & Elizebeth, b. Jan. 1, 1738/9	LR4	A5
Joseph, s. John & Elizabeth, b. Oct. 27, 1731	LR3	16
Joseph, s. John & Elizebeth, b. Oct. 27, 1731	LR4	A5
Marcus J., m. Nancy NICHOLS, b. of Humphreysville, Jan. 1, 1842, by Rev. T. Sparks	1	162
Ransom R., m. Nancy A. BRADLEY, b. of Naugatuck, Mar. 13, 1850, by Rev. Sylvester Smith	1	358
Sarah, d. John & Elisabeth, b. Mar. 2, 1725	LR3	5
Susan, m. Normon HUBBEL, June 15, 1822, by Rev. Zepheniah Swift	1	101
Willis E., of Hamden, m. Betsey M. RIGGS, of Oxford, May 10, 1836, by Rev. John E. Bray	1	166
MURPHY, Orrin H., m. Julia LEECH, Aug. 10, 1845, by Rev. W[illia]m B. Curtiss, at Humphreysville	1	357
MURRY, John, m. Rachel CHAPMAN, b. of Derby, Feb. 17, 1766, by Rev. Dan[ie]ll Humphry	TM1	15
Rachel, m. John BOTCHFORD, b. of Derby, Sept. 1, 1774	TM1	76
MYRICK, [see also **MERRICK**], Martha E., of Derby, m. Harris SANFORD, of Oxford, Dec. 28, 1829, by S. Jewett	1	95
NARAMORE, Mary L., m. Lucius GILBERT, Apr. 21, 1845, by Rev. George Thacher	1	279
NATHAN, NATHANS, David, of Derby, m. Jane E. BALDWIN, of Woodbridge, Sept. 16, 1841, by Rev. Joseph Scott	1	170
David, m. Caroline BIRDSEYE, Mar. 24, 1850, by Rev. Cha[rle]s Dickinson	1	358
David, m. Caroline BIRDSEYE, Mar. 24, 1850, by Rev. Cha[rle]s Dickinson	1	381
NATHANIEL, Isaac, m. Lucretia BEACH, b. of Derby, Oct. 8, 1837, by Rev. Abraham Brown	1	169
NETTLETON, NETTELTON, Agness, d. Josiah & Agness, b. Sept. 24, 1763	TM1	160
Agnis, d. Josiah & Agnis, b. Sept. 24, 1763	LR7	253
Agness, w. Josiah, d. Jan. 16, 1774	TM1	160
Agnis, w. Josiah, d. Jan. 23, 1774	TM1	92
Agusta M., m. William E. TREAT, Jan. 2, 1842, by John D. Smith	1	182
David M., of Derby, m. Susan HULL, of Oxford, Feb. 12, 1829, by Rev. S. Jewett	1	107
Enos Gunn, s. Josiah & Agnis, b. Sept. 9, 1767	TM1	38
Enos Gun[n], s. Josiah & Agness, b. Sept. 9, 1767	TM1	160
Eunice, d. Josiah & Freelove, b. July 19, 1777	TM1	160
Eunice, d. Josiah & Freelove, d. July 9, 1783	TM1	160-1

	Vol.	Page
NETTLETON, NETTELTON, (cont.)		
Freelove, [twin with Josiah], d. Josiah & Freelove, b.		
May 6, 1779	TM1	160
Josiah, m. Agniss GUN[N], Nov. [ ], 1761, by Rev.		
Richard Mansfield	TM1	160
Josiah, m. Freelove LUM[M], July 18, 1776, by Rev. Richard		
Mansfield	TM1	160
Josiah, [twin with Freelove], s. Josiah & Freelove, b.		
May 6, 1779	TM1	160
Mary Ann, d. Josiah & Freelove, b. Dec. 26, 1782	TM1	160
Mary Ann, m. Nathan WOOSTER, Apr. 8, 1824, by Rev.		
Stephen Jewett	1	122
Minerviar, m. William CANFIELD, b. of Derby, May 9,		
1822, by Bardsley Northrop	1	87
Sarah, d. Josiah & Freelove, b. July 3, 1781	TM1	160
NEWCOMB, Charlotte P., m. James FISHER, Oct. 4, 1840, by John		
D. Smith	1	156
John L., m. Emily H. SMITH, Nov. 21, 1841, by John D. Smith	1	170
John Lee, s. Silas & Betsey, b. Dec. 12, 1814	1	25
Robert Palmer, s. Silas & Betsey, b. Mar. 13, 1813	1	25
NEWELL, Emily, of New Haven, m. Star BALDWIN, of Derby, June		
28, 1835, by Rev. Zepheniah Swift	1	146
NICHOLS, NICKOLS, NICKOLLS, NIKOLS, NICCOLLS,		
Abigail, m. Edward RIG[G]S, Jan. 5, 1708, by Rev. Charles		
(Cheney?)	2	24
Agnis, d. Isaac & Rebeckah, b. Dec. 10, 1757	LR6	441
Anne, of Nutown, m. Dr. Josiah CANFIELD, of Derby, Jan.		
1, 1767	TM1	49
Anne, of New Town, m. Dr. Josiah CANFIELD, of Derby, Jan.		
1, 1767	TM1	82
Benjamin, m. Minerva TOMLINSON, Mar. 24, 1839, by John D.		
Smith	1	169
Charles, m. Mrs. Charry S. HALL, b. of Derby, Feb. 20, 1853,		
by Rev. O. Street	1	381
Elam, of Bridgeport, m. Polly JOHNSON, of Humphreysville,		
Dec. 11, 1836, by Sam[ue]l R. Hickcox	1	169
Elizabeth, of Stratford, m. Joseph WEBB, July 8, 1691, by		
by Capt. William Curtiss, at Stratford	2	25
Esther, m. Richard HOLBROOKE, June 9, 1708, by Rev.		
Joseph Moss	2	24
Ester, d. Jan. 15, 1716/17	LR3	6
Easther, of Newtown, m. John HOLBROOK, of Derby, Nov. 4,		
1750	LR5	4
Esther, of New Town, m. John HOLBROOK, of Derby, Nov. 4,		
1750, by Rev. John Beach	TM1	74a
Freelove, Mrs., m. Capt. Joseph HULL, b. of Derby, Feb.		
8, 1821, by Rev. Abner Smith	1	97
Grace, d. Isaac & Hester, d. Mar. 2, 1701/2	2	27

	Vol.	Page
NICHOLS, NICKOLS, NICKOLLS, NIKOLS, NICCOLLS, (cont.)		
Isaak, Dea., d. Dec. 20, 1713	LR3	6
Isaac, m. Agnis GUNN, Nov. 14, 1722/3	LR3	9
Isaac, s. Isaac & Agness, b. Nov. 25, 1723	LR3	5
Isaac, d. Apr. 12, 1733	LR3	12
Isaac, m. Sarah TOMLINSON, July 22, 1747	LR5	4
Isaac, s. Isaac & Sarah, b. May 8, 1748	LR5	413
Isaac, of Derby, m. Rebecah HENMAN, of Woodbury, Feb. 10, 1756	LR6	450
Isaa[c], m. Abigail LYMAN, b. of Derby, Dec. 24, 1769	TM1	128
Isaac, s. Isaac & Abigail, b. Oct. 21, 1770	TM1	128
Jonathan Lyman, s. Isaac & Abigail, b. Aug. 17, 1772	TM1	128
Lowis, d. Isaac & Sarah, b. May 27, 1760	LR6	447
Lois, see Lois (NICHOLS), CURTISS	TM1	153
Lois, m. Sheldon CURTIS, Nov. 11, 1781	TM1	153
Mary, m. Joseph HUL[L]S, Jan. 20, 1691	2	25
Mary, Mrs., d. June 9, 1736	LR3	12
Merrit, m. Elizabeth ANDREWS, b. of Waterbury, Apr. 26, 1837, by Rev. John E. Bray	1	169
Nancy, m. Marcus J. MUNSON, b. of Humphreysville, Jan. 1, 1842, by Rev. T. Sparks	1	162
Rebecah, w. Isaac, d. June 30, 1757	LR6	440
Samuell, m. Mrs. Mary BOW[ ], May [ ], 1682, by Major Trea[ ]	2	1
Sarah, d. Isaac & Sarah, b. Feb. 12, 1750/1	LR6	2
Sarah, d. Isaac & Sarah, b. Feb. 12, 1751	LR6	441
Sarah, w. Isaac, d. Nov. 23, 1754	LR6	440
Susanna, of Huntington, m. Cyrus TREADWELL, of Trumbull, Apr. 28, 1839, by Rev. Joseph Scott	1	191
Timothy Russell, s. Isaac & Abigail, b. Nov. 30, 1776	TM1	128
NICHOLSON, Margaret, m. John ASKNITH, b. of Derby, Apr. 1, 1851, by Rev. Thomas T. Guion	1	193
NORTH, Emma, of Birmingham, m. Burwell A. BRADLEY, of New York, Oct. 11, 1852, by Rev. Thomas G. Osbom, of Birmingham	1	211
NORTHROP, NORTHROUP, NOTHROP, Eliza, of Woodbridge, m. John UMBERFIELD, of Derby, Oct. 9, 1831, by Rev. Stephen Jewett	1	106
Elizabeth A., m. Avery HULL, b. of Derby, May 13, 1838, by Rev. John E. Bray	1	158
Hannah, w. Isaac, d. Mar. 6, 1765	TM1	17
Isaac, m. Hannah WHE[E]LER, b. of Derby, Sept. 27, 1764, by Rev. David Brunson	TM1	15
Jane, of Sherman, m. Joseph BAGLEY, of Humphreysville, Apr. 19, 1840, by Rev. Sylvester Smith	1	189
Maria, Mrs. of Derby, m. Benjamin HUBBELL, of Huntington, Nov. 22, 1835, by Bennet Lum, J. P.	1	160
Mark A., of Sherman, m. Elizabeth LATHON, of Bridgeport,		

	Vol.	Page
OSBORN, OSBURN, ORSBORN, (cont.)		
Elsie, m. Asahel H. **GERARD,** Dec. 1, 1844, by Rev. John D. Smith	1	279
John W., m. Susan H. **DURAND,** Jan. 18, 1835, by Rev. Joseph Scott	1	170
Lois, d. Tho[ma]s & Elizebeth, b. Feb. 23, 1744	LR4	A5
Lowis, of Waterbury, m. Edward **RIGGS,** of Derby, May 17, 1759, by Rev. Mr. Mansfield	LR7	256
Walter, of New Haven, m. Mary Jane **REMER,** Sept. 17, 1833, by Zepheniah Swift	1	170
Welthy, m. Truman **TOMLINSON,** Jan. 9, 1831, by Sam[ue]ll H. Hickox	1	102
OVIATT, OUIEAT, Esther, m. Josiah **SMITH,** Aug. 21, 172[ ]	LR3	10
Mary J., m. Robert **BUCHANAN,** Oct. 27, 1851, by Rev. J. Guernsey	1	211
Susanna, d. John & Abigail, b. Apr. 15, 1754	LR6	4
PARKER, Augustus, m. Jane Eliza **HOTCHKISS,** b. of Derby, Feb. 23, [1841], by Rev. John B. Beach	1	192
PARMELEE, PARMLEE, Abner, m. Georgianna **ROWE,** b. of Derby, May 8, 1842, by Rev. Nathaniel Mead	1	407
David L., of Oxford, m. Mary Ann **HOTCHKISS,** of Derby, Dec. 24, 1828, by Rev. Stephen Jewett	1	110
Lucretia, of Woodbury, m. Elliott **SMITH,** of Waterbury, Oct. 19, [1840], by Rev. John B. Beach	1	192
PARRIOTT, Frederick W., m. Lucretia Ann **BURNES*,** Apr. 8, 1827, by Rev. Zepheniah Swift *(Perhaps "BURNER")	1	111
PARSONS, [see also **PIERSON**], Almyra, see Almyra **FREEMAN**	1	90
PATCHEN, PATCHIN, Betsey M., m. Moses **HAWKINS,** b. of Derby, May 24, 1841, by Rev. John E. Bray	1	175
Eliza, m. Sheldon N. **JOHNSON,** b. of Derby, Sept. 1, 1833, by S. Jewett	1	161
Jane, m. David **LOUNSBURY,** Apr. 15, 1832, by Stephen Jewett	1	92
Mary Ann, of Derby, m. Prentice A. **MALLORY,** of Woodbury, Dec. 5, 1830, by Rev. S. Jewett	1	104
Mary J., of Derby, m. Charles L. **JORDAN,** of Newtown, Sept. 12, 1841, by Rev. John E. Bray	1	161
Sally Maria, m. Alva **DEER,** Aug. 18, 1822, by Rev. Abner Smith	1	89
William J., of Danbury, m. Mary J. **BRONSON,** of Derby, Sept. 15, 1839, by Sam[ue]l R. Hickox. Witnesses: Samuel Hickcox, Hannah Osborn	1	173
PATTERSON, Thomas, m. Rose **MALLEY,** June 24, 1849, by Rev. Cha[rle]s Dickinson	1	407
PEASE, Mary Jane, m. Daniel B. **VAMOSBURG,** June 13, 1824, by Stephen Jewet	1	118
PEAT, Dinah, of Stratford, m. Joseph **CHATFIELD,** of Derby, Feb. 23, 1757, by Rev. Daniel Humphrey	LR6	8
PECK, PECKE, Beniamen, m. Mary **SPERRY,** [of] New Haven, May		

	Vol.	Page
PECK, PECKE, (cont.)		
2, 1700	2	25
Eleazer, m. Ann Hull **MANSFIELD,** Sept. 9, 1833, by Rev. S. Jewett	1	172
Eliza, of Woodbridge, m. Merrit P. **BALDWIN,** Apr. 18, 1830, by Rev. Stephen Jewett	1	88
Friend, of Hamden, m. Sarah **SPERRY,** of Woodbridge, Jan. 30, 1831, by Rev. Stephen Jewett	1	102
Mary, Mrs. m. Abiel **FAIRCHILD,** b. of Derby, May 10, 1757	LR6	450
Mary, m. Gilbert **THOMAS,** b. of Woodbridge, Nov. 27, 1836, by Sam[ue]l R. Hickox. Witnesses: Smith Clark, Olney Streeter	1	181
Rachel, m. Ebinezer **RIGGS,** July 4, [ ]	LR3	10
Rachel, of Waterbury, m. Ebenezer **RIGGS,** of Derby, July 5, 1733	LR7	256
William, of Newtown, m. Nancy C. **AUGUSTUS,** of New Haven, May 15, 1838, by Rev. Joseph Scott	1	172
PENFIELD, Nicholas, m. Diana **BURNS,** Oct. 12, 1840, by John D. Smith	1	156
PERKINS, PURKINS, Anna, d. Ethiel & Esther, b. July 21, 1776	TM1	96
Athiel, s. Roger & Ann, b. Jan. 10, 1733/4	LR3	16
Benjamin, s. Ruben & Lucey, b. May 1st Monday, 1769	TM1	4
David, s. Ethiel & Esther, b. Apr. 20, 1771	TM1	73
David, s. Ethiel & Esther, b. Apr. 20, 1771	TM1	96
Ethiel, of Derby, m. Esther **FOX,** of Derby, Oct. 26, 1767, by Timo[thy] Russel	TM1	65
Eunise, d. Roger & Mary, b. June 22, 1749	LR6	441
Fanny, of Derby, m. Asa **SPERRY,** of Orange, Apr. 1, 1835, by Rev. John E. Bray	1	178
John, m. Lucretia **DOUGLAS,** Feb. 21, 1841, by John D. Smith	1	173
John Hawkins, s. Elias & Elisabeth, b. Jan. 2, 1768	TM1	38
Joseph, s. Ethiel & Esther, b. Oct. 30, 1773	TM1	96
Laura, of Derby, m. Lyman **WATERS,** of Oxford, Feb. 8, 1823, by Rev. Abner Smith	1	123
Roger, s. Ethiel & Esther, b. Apr. 5, 1769	TM1	65
Sand, m. Clarine **SHERWOOD,** b. of Danbury, Apr. 15, 1835, by Zepheniah Swift	1	172
Sarah, d. Roger & Mary, b. Oct. 7, 1748	LR6	441
Sarah, d. Elias & Elisabeth, b. Oct. 27, 1765	TM1	20
Thomas, s. Ruben & Lucey, b. Dec. 7, 1766	TM1	33
PERRY, An[n]ah, m. Timothy **WO[O]STER,** May 23, 1699	2	25
Anna, d. Josiah & Anna, b. Feb. 18, 1732	LR7	253
Benjamin, of Oxford, m. Laura **WEBSTER,** of Derby, Mar. 11, 1827, by Rev. Abner Smith	1	111
Betty, d. Caleb & Hannah, b. Oct. 14, 1736	LR5	414
Betty, d. James & Mabel, b. Jan. 5, 1761	TM1	19
Caleb, s. Caleb & Hannah, b. Jan. 19, 1729/30	LR5	414
Ezekiel, s. Josiah & Anna, b. Feb. 6, 1734	LR7	253

	Vol.	Page
PERRY, (cont.)		
Gideon, s. Caleb & Hannah, b. June 10, 1732	LR5	414
Hannah, d. Caleb & Hannah, b. June 14, 1728	LR5	414
James, m. Mabel JOHNSON, of Derby, Apr. [ ], 1760	TM1	19
James, s. James & Mabel, b. June 15, 1767	TM1	40
John, s. Caleb & Hannah, b. Sept. 3, 1722	LR5	414
Joseph, s. Caleb & Hannah, b. Nov. 30, 1726	LR5	414
Joshua, s. Josiah & Anna, b. Nov. 16, 1735	LR7	253
Joshua, m. Mercy HAWKINS, Nov. [ ], 1759, by Timothy Russel	LR7	249
Josiah, s. Josiah & Anna, b. Feb. 28, 1748	LR7	253
Lucey, d. James & Mabel, b. Feb. 2, 1763	TM1	19
Mary, d. Josiah & Anna, b. May 7, 1741	LR7	253
Mary Ann, d. Joshua & Mercy, b. June 4, 1760	LR7	249
Nathaniel, s. Caleb & Hannah, b. Jan. 4, 1723/4	LR5	414
Olive, d. James & Mabel, b. Mar. 28, 1765	TM1	19
Prudance, d. Caleb & Hannah, b. Dec. 5, 1733	LR5	414
Rachel, Mrs., m. Capt. Zachariah HAWKINS, b. of Derby, Feb. 16, 1774, by Rev. David Brownson	TM1	92
Tabatha, d. Josiah & Anna, b. Sept. 3, 1737	LR7	253
Yeluerton, s. Caleb & Hannah, b. Feb. 24, 1738/9	LR5	414
PERSON, [see under PIERSON]		
PETTIT, PETTITT, Catharine, d. Sam[ue]ll & Elizebeth, b. June 25, 1744	LR4	A5
Cyrenius, s. Sam[ue]ll & Elizebeth, b. Jan. 20, 1741/2	LR4	A2
Sam[ue]ll & w. Elizebeth had s. [ ], b. July 19, 1737	LR3	11
Sam[ue]ll, m. Elizebeth TOMLINSON, Nov. 1, [ ]	LR3	10
PHELPS, Caroline S., m. Edwin C. WHEELER, b. of Derby, Jan. 30, 1840, by Rev. Sylvester Smith	1	188
Ira, m. Phebe HOTCHKISS, June 8, 1834, by Zepheniah Swift	1	172
Laura C., Mrs., m. Truman CASTLE, Sept. 4, 1842, by Rev. John D. Smith	1	233
Peter P., m. Ann Eliza WHITNEY, [Nov.] 23, [1836], by L. D. Howell	1	172
Sarah, of Derby, m. William TALMAGE, of Meriden, July 1, 1838, by Rev. Orlando Starr	1	191
PHILLIPS, Mahala S., m. John M. GOULDEND, b. of Derby, Oct. 25, 1851, by Rev. Thomas T. Guion	1	280
PIERCE, PEIRCE, Anne, m. Samuel HAILL, Nov. 23, 1757	LR6	451
Nancy H., of Derby, m. F. W. ROWE, of Ill., Sept. 9, 1850, by Rev. Thomas T. Guion	1	426
PIERSON, PEARSON, PERSON, [see also PARSONS], Abel, s. Nathan & Amy, b. Sept. 19, 1757	LR6	443
Abel, m. Hannah FAIRCHILD, b. of Derby, Sept. 6, 1781	TM1	119
Abraham, s. Abraham & Sarah, b. July 28, 1707	2	23
Abraham, Jr., m. Susanah WOOSTER, Apr. 10, 1731	LR3	10
Abraham, s. Abraham & Susanna, b. Feb. 1, 1745/6	LR5	232
Abraham, Sergt., d. May 12, 1758, in the 78th y. of his age	LR6	440

	Vol.	Page
PIERSON, PEARSONS, PERSON, (cont.)		
Sarah, m. Thomas BASSIT, Aug. 24, 1727	LR3	10
Sarah, d. Oliver & Hannah, b. Sept. 20, 1753	LR6	3
Sarah, d. David & Lowis, b. Oct. 28, 1767	TM1	39
Stephen, Jr., m. Mehitabel CANFEILD, Oct. 12, 1697	2	25
Stephen, s. Abraham, b. Mar. 4, 1719/20	LR3	3
Stephen, Jr., m. Hannah MUNSON, June 15, 1738	LR4	A4
Stephen, Sr., d. May 14, 1739	LR3	12
Susannah, d. Abraham & Keziah, b. Mar. 10, 1768	TM1	73
Thompson, s. David & Lowis, b. Sept. 9, 1775	TM1	102
PITCHET, [see under **PRITCHARD**]		
PLANT, Ebenezer, m. Esther BASSIT, b. of Derby, Aug. 17, 1774	TM1	82
PLATT, Fred A., of New York, m. Augusta HALL, of Derby, May 12, 1851, by Rev. Thomas T. Guion	1	407
Joseph, of Southbury, m. Patty HOLBROOK, of Derby, Dec. 19, 1820, by Rev. Abner Smith	1	111
Zenas M., Capt., m. Ann Maria HUMISTON, Nov. 5, 1845, by Rev. Geo[rge] L. Fuller	1	207
PLUMB, PLUM, David W., m. Clarissa ALLEN, Mar. 14, 1841, by Rev. Joseph Scott	1	173
Jared, s. Sam[ue]ll & Mary, b. Mar. 18, 1748/9	LR5	413
[Jo]shua, s. Sam[ue]ll & Mary, b. June 22, 1734	LR3	16
Mary, d. Sam[ue]ll & Mary, b. Feb. 27, 1737/8	LR5	413
Mary, Mrs., m. Silas BALDWIN, Feb. 12, 1755	LR6	7
Sam[ue]ll, s. Sam[ue]ll & Mary, b. Apr. 12, 1729	LR3	15
Samuel & w. Mary had s. [ ], b. Jan. 15, 1735/6	LR3	11
Samuel, s. Sam[ue]ll & Mary, b. Apr. 18, 1741	LR5	413
Susanna, d. Sam[ue]ll & Mary, b. Apr. 23, 1744	LR5	413
Zuriel, s. Sam[ue]ll & Mary, b. Apr. 8, 1731	LR3	15
PLUMMER, William H., of New Haven, m. Eugenia H. ALLING, of Ansonia, Oct. 11, 1852, by Rev. Owen Street	1	407
PLUNKET, James, m. Ann HIFFENAS, Nov. 27, 1851, by Rev. James Lynch	1	408
POOL, Abigail, m. John HINMAN, b. of Derby, June 2, 1796	TM1	215
Anna, d. John & Abigail, b. Dec. 24, 1783	TM1	162
Betty, d. Micah & Mary, b. Aug. 20, 1768	TM1	82
Isaac, s. Micah & Mary, b. Jan. 4, 1767	TM1	30
Isaac, s. Micah & Mary, b. Jan. 4, 1767	TM1	82
John, s. Micah & Mary, b. June 13, 1761	TM1	30
John, s. Micah & Mary, b. June 13, 1761	TM1	82
John, m. Abigail BASSIT, [ ], 1783	TM1	162
Joseph, s. Micah & Mary, b. July 1, 1778	TM1	128
Mary Ann, d. Micah & Mary, b. July 30, 1770	TM1	40
Mary Ann, d. Micah & Mary, b. July 30, 1770	TM1	82
Micah, s. Micah & Mary, b. June 25, 1772	TM1	82
Nabby, d. Micah & Mary, b. May 26, 1774; d. Oct. 30, 1774	TM1	82
Neomy, d. John & Abigail, b. June 6, 1786	TM1	162
Ruth, d. Micah & Mary, b. Apr. 20, 1763	TM1	30

	Vol.	Page
POOL, (cont.)		
Ruth, d. Micah & Mary, b. Apr. 20, 1763	TM1	82
Ruth, d. Micah & Mary, b. Apr. 20, 1763	LR7	252
Samuel, s. Micah & Mary, b. Feb. 28, 1765	TM1	30
Samuel, s. Micah & Mary, b. Feb. 28, 1765	TM1	82
POPE, Mary, wid., m. Josiah SMITH, Sr., Nov. [ ], 1825, by Rev.		
Zepheniah Swift	1	116
POWE, Nancy M., m. Thomas V. WHITNEY, Mar. 13, 184[ ], by		
Rev. Jos[eph] Scott	1	190
PRATT, Edwin A., m. Mary A. BRADLEY, Apr. 14, 1845, by Rev.		
George Thacher	1	407
PRINDLE, PRINDEL, PRINGDELL, PRINGEL, PRINGELL,		
PRINGLE, Abigal, w. John d. July 1, 1698	2	27
Abigail, d. Jno & Hannah, b. Oct. 17, 1704	2	12
Abigail, m. Ebenezer CHATFIELD, Nov. 20, 1728	LR3	10
Anne, d. Enos & Deborah, b. Feb. 23, 1762	TM1	47
David, s. Enos & Deborah, b. Oct. 26, 1767	TM1	47
Ebenezer, s. John & Mary, b. July 15, 1693	2	26
Ebenezer, s. Enos & Deborah, b. June 26, 1760	TM1	47
Edman, s. John & Deborah, b. Feb. 28, 1709	2	160
Edmon, d. Sept. 22, 1734	LR3	12
Elisabeth, d. Enos & Deborah, b. May 16, 1752	TM1	47
Elnathan, s. Jno & Hannah, b. July 13, 1702	2	12
Elnathan, d. May 11, 1721	LR3	6
Enos, m. Deborah JONES, b. of Milford, Jan. 16, 1750, by		
Rev. Samuel Whittelsey	TM1	47
Enos Jones, s. Enos & Deborah, b. Nov. 23, 1750	TM1	47
Hannah, Mrs., m. Capt. Jos[eph] HULL, Nov. [ ]	LR3	10
Hannah, d. Jno & Hannah, b. Dec. 4, 1700	2	12
John, m. Mary HULL, Dec. 23, 1685	2	25
John, m. Abigal HAWKINS, Mar. 1, 1696/7	2	25
John, m. Hannah BOXFORD, Dec. 21, 1699	2	25
John, of Derby, m. Deborah BOOTH, of Stratford, May 31,		
1709, by Joseph Curtiss	3	451
John, Jr., d. Dec. 4, 1712	LR3	6
John, d. Nov. 25, 1735	LR3	12
John, s. Enos & Deborah, b. Sept. 7, 1755	TM1	47
Joseph, s. Enos & Deborah, b. Sept. 3, 1764	TM1	47
Lucey, d. Enos & Deborah, b. Nov. 23, 1766	TM1	47
Mary, d. John, b. Sept. (6th?), or 5, 1696	2	26
Mary, w. John, d. Sept. 5, 1696	2	27
Mary, d. John & Mary, d. Dec. 26, 1696	2	27
Mary, d. John & Han[n]ah, b. Sept. 20, 1708	2	160
Mary, m. Edward WASHBOND, Dec. 31, 1730	LR3	10
Mary, d. Enos & Deborah, b. Dec. 17, 1756	TM1	47
Mordecai, m. Elizabeth HAWLEY, July 28, 1839, by Rev.		
Joseph Scott	1	173
Nathanill, s. John, Jr. & Debrah, b. Aug. 23, 1711	LR3	1

	Vol.	Page

PRINDLE, PRINDEL, PRINGDELL, PRINGEL, PRINGELL, PRINGLE, (cont.)

	Vol.	Page
Nathaniel, s. John, Jr., d. Jan. 8, 172[ ]	LR3	6
Samuell, s. John & Mary, b. July 18, 1691	2	26
Sarah, d. Enos & Deborah, b. Aug. 10, 1758	TM1	47
William M.*, m. Betsey A. SMITH, July 1, 1821, by Rev. Zepheniah Swift (*William Nelson corrected in margin)	1	111
------el, s. John, b. Oct. 1, 1686	2	2

PRITCHARD, PRICHARD, PITCHET, Charlotte, of Derby, m. Isaac **LINDSLEY,** of Oxford, Oct. 16, 1834, by Rev. John Smith | 1 | 172

	Vol.	Page
David, m. Ruth SMITH, b. of Derby, Dec. 20, 1757	LR6	451
Jabez, of Derby, m. Eunice BOTCHFORD, of Derby, Oct. 31, 1764, by Rev. Daniel Humphry	TM1	71
Jabez, Lieut., d. Dec. [ ], 1777, at New York	TM1	71
Jabez, Lieut., d. Dec. [ ]*, 1777, at New York *last day	TM1	111
Jabez E., m. Lucretia MILES, b. of Derby, Nov. 26, 1828, by S. Jewett	1	110
James, Jr., m. Rachel WARREN, Nov. 1, 1773	TM1	92
Joseph, d. Dec. 10, 1712	LR3	6
Levret, s. Jabez & Eunice, b. Sept. 16, 1765	TM1	71
Lydia, d. James & Abigail, b. Aug. 11, 1757	LR6	442
Nathaniel, s. Philo & Sabara, b. Aug. 25, 1787	TM1	164
Sally, m. Hiram RANDALL, Jan. 4, 1829, by Rev. S. Jewett	1	114
Sarah, d. James & Abigail, b. Nov. 15, 1759	LR6	440

PUTNAM, Oliver Crosby, m. Francis **WHEELER,** Nov. 9, 1837, by John D. Smith | 1 | 172

RAFERTY, John, m. Mary **TRACY,** Sept. 24, 1851, by Rev. James Lynch | 1 | 426

RANDALL, Hiram, m. Sally **PRICHARD,** Jan. 4, 1829, by Rev. S. Jewett | 1 | 114

Sally, Mrs., m. Levi M. **HOADLEY,** June 10, 1835, by John D. Smith | 1 | 158

RANFORD, Horace, of Derby, m. Eliza **BOUGHTON,** of Waterbury, Nov. 9, 1834, by Sylvester Smith | 1 | 177

RECTOR, Samuel H., m. Susan **LEWIS,** Nov. 25, 1847, by Rev. Geo[rge] Thacher | 1 | 407

REDFIELD, Grace Ann, m. Josiah W. **SMITH,** Apr. 25, 1841, by Rev. Joseph Scott | 1 | 185

Sylvester, m. Clarissa **BRONSON,** Jan. 23, 1837, by Sheldon Bassett, J. P. Witnesses: Jos[eph] P. Canfield, Isaac S. Gilbert, Elisha Hotchkiss | 1 | 176

REGAN, Mary, m. Pat[ric]k **MAQUIRE,** Sept. 8, 1851, by Rev. James Lynch, of Birmingham | 1 | 359

REMER, REEMER, REME, Ammiline, of Derby, m. Enoch F. **SPENCER,** of Barry, N. Y., Apr. 4, 1824, by Rev. Zepheniah Swift | 1 | 116

Joseph Harvey, m. Maria **CANFIELD,** b. of Derby, Aug. 4,

	Vol.	Page
REMER, REEMER, REME, (cont.)		
1834, by Rev. Joseph Scott	1	177
Lewis G., m. Sarah **WALLACE**, Oct. 24, 1850, by Cha[rle]s Dickinson	1	210
Lewis G., m. Sarah **WALLACE**, Oct. 24, 1850, by Cha[rle]s Dickinson	1	426
Mary Jane, m. Walter **OSBORN**, of New Haven, Sept. 17, 1833, by Zepheniah Swift	1	170
Sarah M., of Derby, m. Edward T. **STANLEY**, of New Haven, Nov. 4, 1834, by Zepheniah Swift	1	178
Theodosia, of Derby, m. Calvin H. **GOODMAN**, of Augusta, Ga., Apr. 9, 1839, by Rev. H. Read	1	157
RENODE, Jarvis, m. Jane **BOICE**, June 29, 1841, by Rev. Joseph Scott	1	184
RENY, Pat[ric]k, m. Mary **DOHERTY**, Nov. 27, 1851, by Rev. James Lynch	1	426
REYNOLDS, Charles, m. Elizabeth **HAWKINS**, Mar. 17, 1834, by Zepheniah Swift	1	159
Charles, m. Mary A. **SHORT**, Nov. 23, 1853/4, by Rev. William B. Curtiss, at Humphreysville	1	425
Delia, m. George **WASBORN**, b. of Derby, Oct. 3, 1832, by Charles Thompson	1	187
Joseph, of New Haven, m. Harriet **ANDREW**, of Bethany, June 26, 1843, by Rev. Sylvester Smith	1	425
Julia, m. Levi R. **LOUNDSBURY**, b. of Derby, Sept. 24, 1837, by Rev. John E. Bray	1	164
Mary A., m. Clark **MILES**, b. of Derby, Dec. 28, 1829, by S. Jewett	1	95
RIDER, John J., m. Sarah **HULL**, b. of Derby, Sept. 15, 1841, by Rev. John E. Bray	1	184
RIGGS, RIGS, Abigal, d. Edward & Abigall, b. Feb. 5, 1710/11	LR3	0
Abigail, m. William **MOSS**, Mar. 18, 1714	LR3	9
Abigal, d. Sam[ue]ll & Abigal, b. Mar. 3, 1728	LR3	15
Abigail, m. Noah **DURAND**, Nov. 9, 1732	LR3	10
Abigail, Mrs., m. Benjamin **CHAPMAN**, Jan. 8, 1756	LR6	8
Abigail, d. John & Abigail, b. July 16, 1765	TM1	11
Abner, s. John & Abigail, b. Dec. 24, 1760	TM1	109
Ann, d. John & Hannah, b. June 14, 1741	LR5	232
Ann, m. Sam[ue]ll **HULL**, Jan. 15, [ ]	LR3	15
Anne, d. Jno & Elizabeth, b. June 10, 1704	2	12
Anson, of Oxford, m. Catharine **UMBERFIELD**, of Humphreysville, July 1, 1832, by Charles Thompson	1	180
Betsee, d. Joseph & Ann, b. Jan. 26, 1777	TM1	71
Betsey, m. John **HOTCHKISS**, Oct. 16, 1796	TM1	215
Betsey M., of Oxford, m. Willis E. **MUNSON**, of Hamden, May 10, 1836, by Rev. John E. Bray	1	166
Bettee, d. Philo & Elisabeth, b. Mar. 6, 1760	LR6	719
Catharine A., m. Joseph E. **CANFIELD**, b. of Derby, Oct. 18,		

	Vol.	Page
RIGGS, RIGS, (cont.)		
1848, by Rev. George Thacher	1	235
Charlotte, m. Linsen **DeFOREST**, Sept. 27, 1849, by Rev.		
Charles Dickinson, of Birmingham	1	248
David, s. Edward & Lowis, b. May 20, 1764	TM1	10
David, s. Edward & Lowis, d. Oct. 2, 1764	TM1	10
David, s. Edward & Lowis, b. Aug. 14, 1765	TM1	10
David Johnson, s. Joseph & Ann, b. May 23, 1779	TM1	128
Ebenezer, s. Sa[mue]l, b. [ ], 1678	2	1
Ebenezer, s. Ebenezer & Lois, b. Apr. 15, 1707	2	23
Ebenezer, d. May 11, 1712	LR3	6
Ebenezer, of Derby, m. Rachel **PECK**, of Waterbury, July		
5, 1733	LR7	256
Ebin[ez]er, & w. Rachil had d. [ ], b. July 24, 1736	LR3	11
Ebenezer, s. Ebenezer & Rachel, b. Nov. 17, 1738	LR7	256
Ebenezer, s. Ebenezer & Rachel, d. May 29, 1740	LR7	256
Ebenezer, s. Ebenezer & Rachel, b. Jan. 22, 1748	LR7	256
Ebinezer, m. Rachel **PECK**, July 4, [ ]	LR3	10
Edward, s. Sa[mue]l, b. Oct. [2], 1680	2	1
Edward, m. Abigail **NICKOLLS**, Jan. 5, 1708, by Rev.		
Charles (Cheney?)	2	24
Edward, d. Nov. 25, 1712	LR3	6
Edward, s. John & Hannah, b. Apr. 24, 1737	LR4	A3
Edward, of Derby, m. Lowis **ORSBORN**, of Waterbury, May 17,		
1759, by Rev. Mr. Mansfield	LR7	256
Edward, s. Edward & Lowis, b. Jan. 24, 1762	LR7	256
Eli, of Oxford, m. Susan L. **BRONSON**, of Derby, Sept. 31,		
1835, by Rev. John E. Bray	1	177
Eliza, m. J. J. **LINES**, b. of Derby, Mar. 29, 1843, by		
Rev. H. Read	1	341
Elezabeth, d. Sa[mue]l, [b.] June [ ], 1668	2	1
Elizabeth, d. John & Elizabeth, b. June 17, 1706	2	13
Elizabeth, m. Dannil **HOLBROOK**, Jan. 22, 1728/9	LR3	10
Elizebeth, d. Sam[ue]ll & Abigal, b. Nov. 21, 1733	LR3	16
Elisabeth, Mrs., m. Philo **MILLS**, Mar. 19, 1755, by Rev.		
Daniel Humphry	LR6	8
Elizabeth, d. Sam[ue]ll & Abigal, d. May 27, [ ]	LR3	12
Ester, d. wid., Abigail, b. Feb. 10, 1712/13	LR3	2
Esther, d. Ebenezer & Rachel, b. July 24, 1736	LR7	256
Esther, m. David **JOHNSON**, May 6, 1755	LR6	7
Eunice, d. Ebenezer & Rachel, b. Oct. 14, 1745	LR7	256
Grace, d. Edward & Abigal, b. Oct. 24, 1708	2	160
Grace, m. [ ] **SMITH**, Mar. 22, 1726	LR3	9
Hannah, m. Abraham **HARDYEAR**, May 19, 1703	2	13
Hannah, d. Jno & Hannah, b. Nov. 7, 1738	LR4	A3
Hannah, d. Joseph & Mabel, b. Dec. 21, 1740	LR6	2
Hannah, d. Joseph & Mabel, b. Dec. 21, 1740	TM1	225
Hannah, m. Noah **FRENCH**, b. of Derbe, June 12, 1755, by		

	Vol.	Page
RIGGS, RIGS, (cont.)		
Rev. Cyrus Marsh	LR6	7
Harpin, m. Harriett UPSON, b. of Derby, May 17, 1840, by		
Rev. John E. Bray	1	176
Henry, m. Mary Ann BRADLEY, Sept. 24, 1837, by John D.		
Smith	1	176
Jabish, s. John & Hannah, b. June 28, 1744	LR5	232
Jeremiah, s. Ebenezer & Rachel, b. July 1, 1750	LR7	256
John, s. Sam[ue]l, b. about Apr. [ ], 1676	2	1
John, m. Hannah JOHNSON, Oct. 29, [ ]	LR3	10
John, s. Ebenezer & Loess, b. Dec. 27, [ ]	LR3	1
John, m. Elezabeth TOMLINSON, Feb. 23, 1699/1700	2	25
John, s. Jno & Hannah, b. Aug. 31, 1735	LR4	A3
John, s. Joseph & Mabel, b. Apr. 10, 1742	LR6	2
John, s. Joseph & Mabel, b. Apr. 10, 1742	TM1	225
John, d. Sept. 24, 1755, in the 80th y. of his age	LR6	440
John, m. Betsey HAWKINS, Mar. 8, 1829, by Rev. Stephen		
Jewett	1	114
Joseph, d. Oct. 22, 1707, in the 21st y. of his age	2	27
Joseph, s. John & Elizabeth, b. Feb. [ ], 1709/10	2	160
Joseph, m. Mabel JOHNSON, Feb. 20, 1739	TM1	225
Joseph, m. Mabel JOHNSON, Feb. 20, 1739/40	LR4	A4
Joseph, s. Joseph & Mabel, b. July 20, 1746	LR6	2
Joseph, s. Joseph & Mabel, b. July 21, 1746	TM1	225
Joseph, s. Ebenezer & Rachel, b. Aug. 17, 1753	LR7	256
Joseph, 3rd, m. Ann CANFIELD, b. of Derby, Nov. 13, 1775	TM1	71
Joseph N., of Oxford, m. Julia E. BEECHER, of New Haven,		
Apr. 2, 1835, by Zepheniah Swift	1	177
Lois, d. Ebenezer & Lois, b. July 10, 1709	LR3	0
Lowis, d. Ebenezer & Rachel, b. July 25, 1743	LR7	256
Lowis, d. Ebenezer & Rachel, d. Aug. [ ], 1751	LR7	256
Lucinda, m. Warren FRENCH, Nov. 26, 1823, by Rev. Stephen		
Jewett	1	93
Lucinda, m. Elizur TALMAGE, b. of Oxford, Dec. 21, 1834,		
by Rev. John E. Bray	1	181
Mabel, d. Joseph & Mabel, b. May 5, 1759	TM1	225
Mabel, d. Lieut. Joseph & Mabel, b. May 5, 1759	LR7	253
[M]arcy, d. Sam[ue]ll & Abigail, b. Dec. 6, 1730	LR3	15
Mary, m. Joseph HAWKINS, Jan. 1, 1749/50	LR5	4
Mary Ann, of Derby, m. John L. CHATFIELD, of Bethany, May		
1, 1848, by Rev. George Thacher	1	234
Moses, s. John & Hannah, b. May 26, 1740	LR5	232
Moses, s. Edward & Lowis, b. Apr. 10, 1760	LR7	256
Moses, m. Harriet O'CAIN, Dec. 21, 1828, by John F.		
Wheeler, J. P.	1	114
Rachel, d. Ebenezer & Rachel, b. May 31, 1734	LR7	256
Rachel, d. Ebenezer & Rachel, d. May 25, 1740	LR7	256
Rachel, d. Ebenezer & Rachel, b. Jan,. 23, 1741	LR7	256

	Vol.	Page
RIGGS, RIGS, (cont.)		
Samuell, s. Sa[mue]l, b. [ ] 8, 1670	2	1
Samuel, s. Jno & Elizabeth, b. Jan. [ ], 1700/1	2	12
Sam[ue]ll, Ens., m. Mrs. Sarah **WASBON**, May 6, 1713	LR3	9
Sam[ue]ll, m. Abigal **GUNN**, Jan. 6, 1726	LR3	10
Samuel, s. Joseph & Mabel, b. Nov. 21, 1750	TM1	225
Samuel, s. Joseph & Mabel, b. Nov. 21, 1750	LR6	2
Samuel, s. Joseph & Mabel, d. Sept. 21, 1766	TM1	225
Samuel, m. [ ] **BALDWIN**, June 14, [ ]	2	1
Samuel Edward, of Derby, m. Amelia Elizabeth **SHUTE**, of Woodbridge, Jan. 20, 1829, by Rev. Zepheniah Swift	1	115
Sarah, d. Sam[ue]ll, b. Jan. [ ], [16]72; d. Jan. [ ], [16]72	2	1
Sarah, m. Jonathan **LUM**, Oct. 10, 1700	2	25
Sarah, d. John & Elizebeth, b. Dec. 17, 171[ ]	LR3	1
Sarah, Mrs., d. May 14, 1712	LR3	6
Sarah, m. John **BOWERS**, Nov. 22, 1732	LR3	10
Sarah, d. Sa[meu]l, b. [ ] 3, [ ]	2	1
Thirsa, m. John C. **HUMPHREYS**, b. of Derby, Dec. 24, 1829, by S. Jewett	1	95
----ah, d. Samuell, b. Feb. 24, 1683	2	2
----bil, d. Ebin[ez]er & Rachel, b. May 31, 1734	LR3	11
----les, s. John & Hannah, d. July 26, 1740	LR5	1
ROATH, James, of Norwich, m. MInerva **SILES**, of Humphreysville, June 6, 1827, by Smith Dayton, Elder	1	114
ROBBINS, Polly, m. Wales **FRENCH**, Sept. 17, 1838, by Rev. John E. Bray	1	156
ROBINSON, ROBBINSON, Elisabeth, of Bethany, m. David **CARINGTON**, of Bethany, Jan. 17, 1847, by Rev. John Parves	1	234
George B., of Derby, m. Grace A. **SMITH**, of Oxford, Feb. 8, 1846, by Rev. N. S. Richardson	1	425
Laura, m. Amos B. **CASE**, Aug. 5, 1855, by Joseph P. Canfield, J. P.	1	237
Marietta, m. Abijah **THOMPSON**, b. of Derby, Nov. 27, 1845, by Rev. W[illia]m Bliss Ashely	1	461
Thomas, of New Haven, m. Polly Ann **CHAPMAN**, of Oxford, Dec. 14, 1836, by Rev. John E. Bray	1	177
ROCHE, Catherine, m. John **BLONCY**, Feb. 15, [18]52, by Rev. James Lynch, of Birmingham	1	213
ROCKWELL, Francis, of Ridgefield, m. Martha **TUCKER**, of Derby, Dec. 23, 1847, by Rev. W[illia]m Bliss Ashley	1	425
ROE, [see under **ROWE**]		
ROODE, Isaac, of Milford, m. Sally M. **BUCKINGHAM**, of Derby, Jan. 22, 1843, by Rev. Nathaniel Mead	1	425
ROOT, Amelia S., m. Stephen **HUBBARD**, Nov. 21, 1850, by Rev. Jno Morrison Reid	1	291
Emerette, m. George B. **BOUTWELL**, Apr. 4, 1852, by Rev. J. Guernsey	1	210

	Vol.	Page
ROOT, (cont.)		
Luther, m. Nancy MALLETT, Nov. 27, 1849, by Rev. Jesse Guernsey	1	210
Luther, m. Nancy MALLETT, Nov. 27, 1848, by Rev. J. Guernsey	1	426
ROSSEBY, Augustus, m. Betsey HULL, Aug. 22, 1830, by Rev. Stephen Jewett	1	114
ROSSIN, Mary A., m. Samuel CROSBY, Apr. 20, 1850, by Rev. Cha[rle]s Dickinson, of Birmingham	1	235
ROSWELL, [see also RUSSELL], Docus, Mrs., m. Joseph MOSS, Feb. 10, 1714	LR3	9
ROURKE, Patrick, m. Sarah DONALD, Aug. 27, 1848, by Rev. W[illia]m B. Curtiss	1	425
ROWE, ROE, F. W., of Ill., m. Nancy H. PIERCE, of Derby, Sept. 9, 1850, by Rev. Thomas T. Guion	1	426
Georgianna, m. Abner PARMLEE, b. of Derby, May 8, 1842, by Rev. Nathaniel Mead	1	407
Hepsibah M., m. Thomas JAMES, June 19, 1843, by Rev. Joseph B. Wakeley	1	325
Huldah, m. John BODGE, b. of Humphreysville, Sept. 10, 1845, by Samuel R. Hickcox	1	207
Isaac, of Oxford, m. Huldah MOTHROP, of Humphreysville, Apr. 4, 1824, by Rev. Labon Clark, at Humphreyville	1	115
Keziah, m. Amos BASSETT, Sept. 7, 1845, by Rev. John D. Smith	1	207
RUSSELL, ROSELL, RUSSEL, [see also ROSWELL], Abigail, Mrs., m. Joseph MOSS, Oct. 3, 1716	LR3	9
Betsey, wid., m. Dea. John CARRINGTON, May 21, 1833, by Zepheniah Swift	1	149
Betsey, m. William Albert SMITH, Nov. 30, 1837, by John D. Smith	1	178
Betsey, Mrs. of Derby, m. Edward RUSSEL, of Waterbury, Dec. 17, 1849, by Rev. Sylvester Smith	1	425
Edward, of Waterbury, m. Mrs. Betsey RUSSEL, of Derby, Dec. 17, 1849, by Rev. Sylvester Smith	1	425
Eunice Ellis, of Derby, m. Nathaniel B. BOOTH, of Stratford, Nov. 25, 1829, by William A. Curtiss	1	82
Harriet, of Derby, m. Stephen WARNER, of Watertown, Dec. 1, 1830, by Rev. S. Jewett	1	124
Joseph, s. Timothy & Mary, b. Feb. 3, 1729/30	LR3	15
Joseph, of Derby, m. Elisabeth CLARK, of Middletown, Sept. 25, 1764, by Rev. Mr. Huntington	TM1	6
Mary, d. Timothy, b. Oct. 16, 1726	LR3	5
Polly, m. Horace OATMAN, Oct. 5, 1825, by Rev. Abner Smith	1	105
Rachel, m. Charles HINMAN, Jan. 1, 1835, by John D. Smith	1	159
Ruth Ann, m. Thomas Vose WOOSTER, b. of Derby, Jan. 18, 1831, by Rev. Stephen Jewett	1	124
Sally, of Derby, m. George BASSETT, of Oxford, Nov. 2,		

	Vol.	Page
RUSSSELL, ROSELL, RUSSEL, (cont.)		
1824, by Rev. Abner Smith	1	83
Sam[ue]ll, s. Timo[thy] & Mary, b. Dec. 3, 1738	LR4	A3
Samuel, m. Mary HINE, of Derby, Jan. 16, 1833, by Charles Thompson	1	177
Sarah I., of Derby, m. John M. JENNINGS, of New Milford, Mar. 27, 1842, by Rev. John C. Bray	1	325
Stephen D., m. Sarah HOLBROOK, Oct. 28, 1844, by Rev. John D. Smith	1	425
Sibilla, d. Timothy, b. Feb. 11, 1723/4	LR3	4
Sibillah, m. Isaac TOMLINSON, Jr., Jan. 17, 1749/50	LR6	6
Sibbilah, m. Isaac TOMLINSON, Jan. 17, 1749/50	LR6	7
Timothy, m. Mary HULLS, Nov. 2, 1721	LR3	9
----gail, d. Timothy, b. Sept. 29, 1722	LR3	3
RYAN, Mary, m. Pat KIRBY, Jan. 22, 1852, by Rev. James Lynch	1	330
Mary, m. Michael HAYES, Feb. 24, [18]52, by Rev. James Lynch	1	292
SALSBURY, Angeline C., of Long Meadow, Mass., m. Charles L. BASSETT, of Derby, Oct. 30, 1848, by Rev. Joseph Scott	1	209
SAMPSON, Deborah Ann, m. William HARGER, June 14, 1849, by Rev. W[illia]m B. Curtiss	1	291
SANFORD, Harriet, m. Ebenezer SILEY, b. of Oxford, Jan. 4, 1825, by Rev. Abner Smith	1	99
Harris, of Oxford, m. Martha E. MYRICK, of Derby, Dec. 28, 1829, by S. Jewett	1	95
Mary L., of Naugatuck, m. Timothy SQUIRE, of Roxbury, Nov. 30, 1848, by Rev. Charles Stearns, at Humphreysville	1	441
Nathan, m. Polly TALMAGE, b. of Oxford, Feb. 7, 1836, by John E. Bray	1	179
Thomas, of Oxford, m. Jane HOTCHKISS, of Bethany, Sept. 9, 1835, by Rev. John E. Bray	1	179
SATCHEN, Albia, m. Caroline SMITH, Feb. 4, 1828, by Rev. Zepheniah Smith	1	111
SCOTT, John, of Warsing, Ulster Co., N. Y., m. Elizabeth H. BROADWELL, of Derby, Mar. 23, 1843, by Rev. Sylvester Smith	1	439
John D., m. Betsey JOHNSON, Sept. 26, 1847, by Rev. W[illia]m B. Curtiss	1	440
Marietta, m. William L. BOADMAN, Apr. 2, 1840, by John D. Smith	1	189
Ruth Ann, m. William Elliot WHEELER, June 19, 1836, by Rev. John D. Smith	1	188
Ruth Ann, of Oxford, m. David JOHNSON, of Derby, May 17, 1840, by Rev. John E. Bray	1	176
Sarah T., m. Lorenzo M. BASSETT, b. of Derby, May 7, 1848, by Rev. Sylvester Smith	1	208
Susan, d. Andrew G. & Susan, b. Aug. 9, 1803	TM1	368
SCOVILLE, SCHOVIL, Frances E., of Derby, m. Isaac N. FULLER,		

	Vol.	Page

SCOVILLE, SCHOVIL, (cont.)

of Warren, Conn., Sept. 22, 1851, by Rev. I. Guernsey	1	272
Leverett, m. Lucinda **BOTSFORD**, Mar. 11, 1822, by Rev. Abner Smith	1	117
Timothy, of Oxford, m. Experience **BOTSFORD**, of Derby, Dec. 3, 1820, by Rev. Abner Smith	1	117

SCRANTON, Ann, of Derby, m. T. M. **DOWNS**, of Newtown, Aug. 28, 1831, by Charles Thompson — 1 — 121

David, m. Julia **HAWKINS**, Nov. 6, 1825, by Rev. Abner Smith	1	115
Munroe, m. Mary **HURD**, Dec. 15, 1844, by Rev. John D. Smith	1	279
Munroe, m. Mary **HURD**, Dec. 15, 1844, by Rev. John D. Smith	1	439

SEALY, [see also **SILEY**], Hiram, of New Milford, m. Elizabeth **GARNER**, of Birmingham, [ ], by Rev. Thomas G. Osborn; recorded July 7, 1852 — 1 — 441

SEARGEANT, Clement A., m. Eliza A. **HOLBROOK**, b. of Derby, Nov, 5, 1848, by Rev. W[illia]m Denison — 1 — 440

SEDAR, Benjamin, of Wallingford, m. Almyra **FREEMAN**, called **PARSONS**, Mar. 17, 1831, by Rev. Charles Thompson — 1 — 90

SELBY, SILBY, Betty, d. Thomas & Anne, b. July 29, 1757 — LR6 — 440

David Meluel, s. Thomas & Anne, b. Mar. 22, 1759	LR6	440
Thomas, m. Anne **BLACKMAN**, Oct. 12, 1756	LR6	445

SERWOOD, Joseph, m. Comfort **CHATFIELD**, b. of Derby, Oct. 27, 1772, by [ ] — TM1 — 107

SHAIN, Eliza, of New York, m. Major H. **FISHER**, of Humphreysville, Jan. 21, 1830, by Rev. Stephen Jewett — 1 — 95

SHARP, Maria O., m. Albert **LOUNSBURY**, b. of Humphreysville, Aug. 20, [1848], by Rev. Charles Stearns, at Humphreysville — 1 — 342

SHEFFIELD, Elizabeth, late of Stonington, d. Oct. 31, 1812 — 1 — 543

SHELTON, Frances M., m. Francis **STILES**, b. of Southbury, Mar. 1, 1846, by Rev. Sylvester Smith — 1 — 439

SHERWOOD, Clarine, m. Sand **PERKINS**, b. of Danbury, Apr. 15, 1835, by Zepheniah Swift — 1 — 172

Delia, m. Benjamin S. **WHEELER**, Sept. 2, 1827, by Rev. Zepheniah Swift — 1 — 123

Samuel, of Derby, m. Phebe **JENNINGS**, of Fairfield, Mar. 10, 1821, by Rev. Zephaniah Swift — 1 — 117

Samuel, m. Abba Ann **MANSFIELD**, Sept. 8, 1833, by Rev. S. Jewett — 1 — 161

Sheldon, s. Joseph & Comfort, b. Sept. 7, 1777 — TM1 — 107

SHEY, Jane, m. Nicholas **BROCKWAY**, Jan. 8, [18]52, by Rev. James Lynch, of Birmingham — 1 — 213

SHIPMAN, Maria, m. Lockwood **KEENNEY**, b. of Derby, Oct. 17, 1830, by Rev. Zepheniah Swift — 1 — 107

Everett O., m. Susan Jane **HUBBARD**, Sept. 13, 1848, by Rev. C. L. Putnam — 1 — 440

SHORT, Ephraim, m. Mary A. **CARTER**, Feb. 19, 1850, by Rev. Jno Morrison Reid — 1 — 441

Vol. Page

SHORT, (cont.)

Ezra, of Derby, m. Catharine **DART**, of Derby, Aug. 3, 1851,
  by Rev. Thomas G. Osbom   1   441

Isaac, s. Joseph & Abigail, b. May 16, 1771   TM1   66

Mary A., m. Charles **REYNOLDS**, Nov. 23, 1853/4, by Rev.
  William B. Curtiss, at Humphreysville   1   425

Peter, s. Joseph & Abigail, b. July 17, 1773   TM1   87

SHUTE, Amelia Elizabeth, of Woodbridge, m. Samuel Edward
  RIGGS, of Derby, Jan. 20, 1829, by Rev. Zepheniah Swift   1   115

SILBY, [see under **SELBY**]

SILES, [see under **STILES**]

SILEY, [see also **SEALY**], Ebenezer, m. Harriet **SANFORD**, b. of
  Oxford, Jan. 4, 1825, by Rev. Abner Smith   1   99

SIMPSON, Elisabeth, m. Eli **DEWHURST**, b. of Derby, Dec. 25,
  1845, by Rev. W[illia]m Bliss Ashley   1   247

SISSON, Ann Eliza, m. George **BARTHOLOMEW**, Oct. 14,
  1829, by P. Jewett   1   82

SIZER, Sarah, of Middletown, m. Joseph **PERSON**, of Derby,
  June 4, 1775   TM1   92

SLATER, Sarah, m. Thomas **WALLACE**, Jr., Nov. 25, 1852, by
  Bishop Cha[rle]s Dickinson, of Birmingham   1   483

SMITH, Abigal, d. Tho[ma]s & Abigal, b. Oct. 21, 1739   LR4   A3

Abigail, d. Joseph & Hannah, b. Oct. 16, 1757   LR6   443

Abijah, s. Abraham & Sarah, b. Oct. 3, 1764   TM1   64

Abraham, m. Sarah **FRENCH**, Dec. 5, 1756   LR6   451

Abraham, s. Abraham & Sarah, b. Oct. 1, 1759   TM1   64

Abraham, m. Sarah **FRENCH**, [   ]   TM1   64

Abram, m. Suse **HAWKINS**, Mar. 18, 1778   TM1   151

Abram, m. Molly **JOHNSON**, Aug. 4, 1782   TM1   151

Almira, d. Josiah & Betsey, b. Oct. 5, 1797   TM1   156

Almira, of Derby, m. Lucius G. **OLMSTEAD**, of Huntington,
  Mar. 30, 1840, by Rev. Jos[eph] Scott   1   171

Almond, s. Josiah & Betsey, b. Apr. 19, 1796   TM1   156

Amy, m. Nathan **PERSON**, Nov. 17, 1756, by Daniel Hoolbrook LR6   8

Andrew, m. Sarah **TOMLINSON**, May 21, 1696   2   25

Andrew, s. Andrew & Sarah, b. Oct. 3, 1711   LR3   3

Andrew, s. Nathan & Margret, b. Aug. 31, 1761   LR7   252

Andrew, s. Nathan & Margret, d. Jan. 20, 1765   TM1   11

Andrew, s. John & Abigail, b. June 10, 1766   TM1   4

Betsy, d. Josiah & Betsy, b. Oct. 30, 1799   TM1   156

Betsey A., m. William M.* **PRINDLE**, July 1, 1821, by Rev.
  Zepheniah Swift. *(William Nelson* **PRINDLE** hand
  written in margin)   1   111

Betty, d. John & Elisabeth, b. Apr. 25, 1757   LR6   443

Caroline, m. Albia **SATCHEN**, Feb. 4, 1828, by Rev.
  Zepheniah Smith   1   111

Charity, d. Isaac & Lucy, b. Dec. 22, 1757   LR7   249

Charlotte, of Derby, m. W[illia]m S. **HALL**, of Bristoll,

	Vol.	Page

SMITH, (cont.)

[ ], by Rev. Thomas Guion	1	292
Christopher, m. Lucinda BUNNEL, Jan. 4, 1823, by Rev.		
Abner Smith	1	117
Clark, s. Josiah & Ester, b. Nov. 10, 1776	TM1	153
Clark, of New Milford, m. Eliza Ann FOOT, of Derby, Sept.		
8, 1824, by Rev. Abner Smith	1	86
Cynthia, m. Rev. Labon C. CHENEY, Nov. 1, 1831, by Rev.		
Labon Clark	1	107
Cynthia, m. David HOLBROOK, b. of Derby, Nov. 25, 1847, by		
Rev. Sylvester Smith	1	290
Dameras, of Derby, m. Elisha OATMAN, of Oxford, Jan. 7,		
1836, by Rev. Jonah Bowen	1	170
Daniel, m. Hannah STYLES, Nov. 25, [ ]	LR3	10
David, m. Harriet JUDD, Nov. 8, 1832, by Rev. Samuel R.		
Hickox	1	178
Deborah, d. John, b. May 16, 1721	LR3	4
Ebb, s. John & Abigail, b. Mar. 15, 1775	TM1	109
Edward, s. Jonah & Grace, b. Apr. 25, 1748	LR5	413
Edward, s. Jonah & Grace, b. Apr. 25, 1748	LR5	414
Eleamy, s. Joseph & Hannah, b. May 16, 1756	LR6	443
Eleanor, m. William TAYLOR, Sept. 6, 1846, by Rev.		
W[illia]m Bliss Ashley	1	461
Eleanor, m. Chauncey BALL, b. of Derby, Nov. 28, 1852, by		
Rev. Thomas T. Guion	1	212
Eli, s. Elnathan & Abigail, b. Sept. 12, 1750, in		
Elisabeth Town in the Jarsyes	LR6	13
Elijah, m. Ann HAWKINS, May 3, 1748	LR5	4
Elijah Fitch, m. Mary Jane FINLEY, Mar. 22, 1830, by		
Z. Swift	1	103
Eliza, of Derby, m. Frisbie J. JACKSON, of Watertown,		
Nov. 18, 1838, by Rev. Joseph Scott	1	161
Elisabeth, d. Ephraim & Elisabeth, b. Sept. 27, 1748	LR5	232
Elisabeth, of Derby, m. Samuel Tillotson BABBIT, of		
Huntington, Apr. 17, 1821, by Rev. Abner Smith	1	85
Elizabeth I., of Derby, m. Jeremiah S. STEVEN, of		
Burlington, Conn. Aug. 10, 1845, by Rev. W[illia]m Bliss		
Ashley	1	439
Ellender, m. David ALLIEN, Dec. 27, 1769, by Richard		
Mansfield	TM1	40
Elliott, of Waterbury, m. Lucretia PARMLEE, of Woodbury,		
Oct. 19, [1840], by Rev. John B. Beach	1	192
Elnathan, s. Nathan & Hannah, b. May 10, 1723	LR3	4
Ely, of Naugatuck, m. Mary Jane MALLERY, of Derby, July		
22, 1849, by Bishop Cha[rle]s Dickinson, of Birmingham	1	235
Ely, of Naugatuck, m. Mary L. MALLORY, of Derby, July		
22, 1849, by Bishop Cha[rle]s Dickinson	1	441
Emily H., m. John L. NEWCOMB, Nov. 21, 1841, by John D.		

	Vol.	Page
SMITH, (cont.)		
Smith	1	170
Enos, s. John & Abigail, b. Feb. 16, 1760	LR7	252
Ephraim, m. Annah CARRINTON, Dec. 14, 1727	LR3	10
Ephraim, m. Esther HOLBROOK, b. of Derby, Nov. 26, 1829	1	106
Easther, d. Isaac & Leucy, b. Feb. 4, 1756	LR7	249
Ester, m. Josiah SMITH, b. of Derby, Sept. 8, 1773	TM1	153
Ester, d. Josiah & Ester, b. Feb. 4, 1775	TM1	153
[E]sther, d. Jonah & Grace, b. Dec. 18, [ ]	LR5	2
Esther Ann, m. Merritt HOTCHKISS, Dec. 25, 1836, by Rev. L. D. Howell	1	158
Eunice, d. Nathan & Sarah, b. Mar. 31, 1755	LR6	443
Eurenia, m. Ralph LEWIS, July 22, 1847, by George L. Fuller	1	341
Fitch, s. Abraham & Sarah, b. May 14, 1772	TM1	64
Garom Seth, s. Epharim & Hannah, b. Jan. 11, 1738/9	LR4	A3
Garred, m. Sarah HALLOCK, Oct. 23, 1823, by Rev. Zapheniah Swift	1	116
Gideon, s. John & Elisabeth, b. Sept. 16, 1754	LR6	443
Gipson, s. Samuel & Anna, b. Jan. 17, 1781	TM1	215
Grace A., of Oxford, m. George B. ROBINSON, of Derby, Feb. 8, 1846, by Rev. N. S. Richardson	1	425
Grace, Ann, m. Edwin A. HOPKINS, Mar. 30, 1845, by Rev. George Thacher	1	289
Hanna, d. Andrew & Sarah, b. May 12, 1[ ]	2	13
Hannah, m. Sam[ue]ll BOTCHFORD, July 27, [ ]	LR3	10
Hannah, d. Joseph & Martha, b. Aug. 18, [ ]	LR3	4
Hannah, d. Nov. 28, 1712	LR3	6
Hannah, d. Elnathan & Abigail, b. June 23, 1754, in Derby	LF6	13
Hannah, of Milford, m. Ebenezer BASSIT, of Derby, Mar. 17, 1756	LR6	450
Hannah, d. Joseph & Martha, d. May 3, 1757, in the 34th y. of her age	LR6	13
Hannah, m. John HOWD, b. of Derby, Mar. 1, 1764, by Rev. Richard Mansfield	TM1	15
Harris, m. Mary GILLET, b. of Prospect, Mar. 2, 1842, by Rev. John E. Bray	1	185
Henry L., m. Maria LINES, b. of Derby, Dec. 24, 1841, by Rev. H. Read	1	185
Hiram B., of N[ew] H[aven], m. Sarah F. HENRIETTEE, of Huntington, Oct. 25, 1852, by Rev. Thomas T. Guion	1	442
Horatio Goodwin, s. Almon & Fanny, b. Nov. 12, 1820	1	35
Isaac, s. Abraham & Sarah, b. July 8, 1757	TM1	64
Isaac, s. Abraham & Sarah, b. July 8, 1757	LR6	451
Isaac, s. Abraham & Sarah, d. Mar. 24, 1775	TM1	64
Isaac, s. Abram & Suse, b. Oct. 24, 1779	TM1	151
[I]ssaac, s. Jonah & Grace, b. Mar. 18, 17[ ]	LR5	2
James, s. Abraham & Sarah, b. Sept. 14, 1767	TM1	64
James, Jr., m. Martha UPSON, Dec. 24, 1846, by W[illia]m		

	Vol.	Page
SMITH, (cont.)		
B. Curtiss	1	234
James, Jr., m. Martha **UPSON**, Dec. 24, 1846, by Rev.		
William B. Curtiss	1	440
Jeremiah, s. Joseph & Hannah, b. May 26, 1754	LR6	443
John, m. Deborah **LAMBERT**, Dec. 9, 1719, by Rev. Sam[ue]ll		
Andrew, at Milford	LR3	9
John, s. Thomas & Abigail, b. Jan. 14, 172[ ]	LR3	15
John, s. John, Jr., b. Apr. 21, 1723	LR3	4
John, d. May 31, 1749, in the 75th y. of his age	LR5	1
John, m. Elisabeth **CHATFIELD**, Dec. 16, 1750	LR6	444
John, s. John & Abigail, b. Sept. 9, 1777	TM1	117
John, s. Abraham & Sarah, b. Apr. 22, 1781	TM1	64
John, of New York, m. Mrs. Aseneth **BARNS**, of Woodbury,		
Nov. 17, 1830, by Bennet Lum, J. P.	1	112
John D., Rev., m. Jane **LUM**, June 21, 1835, by Rev. Joseph		
Scott	1	158
John French, s. Abraham & Sarah, b. Mar. 20, 1762	TM1	64
John French, s. Abraham & Sarah, d. Apr. 20, 1781	TM1	64
Jonas, s. Andrew & Sarah, b. Sept. 29, 1699	2	31
Jonathan, s. John & Mary, b. May 21, 1716	LR3	3
Jonathan, m. Rachel **TOMLINSON**, Mar. 12, 1745/6	LR5	4
Joseph, s. Andrew & Sarah, b. July 20, 1715	LR3	3
Joseph, m. Martha **BEMAN**, Oct. 11, 1722	LR3	9
Joseph, 3rd, of Derby, m. Hannah **MALLERY**, of West Haven,		
Aug. 21, 1753	LR6	444
Josiah, s. Andrew & Sarah, b. June 13, 17[ ]	2	13
Josiah, m. Esther **OUIEAT**, Aug. 21, 172[ ]	LR3	10
[Jos]iah, s. Josiah & Ester, b. June 28, 1729	LR3	15
Josiah, s. Eliah & Ann, b. Dec. 12, 1748	LR5	413
Josiah, s. Abraham & Sarah, b. Oct. 23, 1769	TM1	64
Josiah, m. Ester **SMITH**, b. of Derby, Sept. 8, 1773	TM1	153
Josiah, s. Josiah & Ester, b. Sept. 11, 1778	TM1	153
Josiah, Jr., m. Betsey **HOLBROOK**, July 30, 1795	TM1	156
Josiah, Sr., m. wid. Mary **POPE**, Nov. [ ], 1825, by Rev.		
Zepheniah Swift	1	116
Josiah, m. Betsey **ALLEN**, Nov. 7, 1836, by Rev. L. D. Howell	1	179
Josiah W., m. Grace Ann **REDFIELD**, Apr. 25, 1841, by		
Rev. Joseph Scott	1	185
Julia Ann, m. Gilbert **WHEELER**, b. of Derby, Dec. 24, 1835,		
by Rev. Josiah Bowen	1	186
Julia L., m. Franklin **FARRELL**, Mar. 31, 1850, by Rev.		
C. S. Putnam. Int. Pub.	1	271
Laura, of Woodbridge, m. Gay **LOYD**, of New Haven, Oct. 30,		
1836, by Rev.Joseph Scott	1	165
Laura (?), of Humphreysville, m. Thomas I. **FRISBIE**, May 31,		
1846, by Rev. John Parves, of Humphreysville	1	271
Lavinia, m. Abiram **STODDARD**, 2nd, b. of Derby, Dec. 14,		

	Vol.	Page
SMITH, (cont.)		
1834, by Rev. Joseph Scott	1	178
Levi, s. Abraham & Sarah, b. Sept. 25, 1774	TM1	64
Lockwood W., m. Sarah LEWIS, b. of Derby, Apr. 15, 1822, by		
Rev. Stephen Jewett	1	117
Lowis, d. John & Abigail, b. Sept. 20, 1768	TM1	40
Lucy, d. Isaac & Lewey, b. Dec. 22, 1754	LR7	249
Lucy, of Glasenbury, m. Jonathan MILES, of Derby, Feb. 17,		
1768	TM1	85
Lyman, m. Betsey KEENEY, July 26, 1824, by Stephen Jewett	1	118
Manoah, s. Jonathan & Lucy, b. Mar. 22, 1769	TM1	85
Margret, w. Nathan, d. Nov. 9, 1765	TM1	11
Martha, d. Joseph & Martha, b. Jan. 30, 1725/6	LR3	5
Martha, m. Abraham HALE, b. of Derby, Mar. 3, 1756, by		
Samuel Riggs	LR6	445
Marven, s. Ens. Nathan & Taphenes, b. Aug. 13, 1768	TM1	63
Mary, d. Andrew & Sarah, b. Feb. 12, 1705	LR3	3
Mary, d. Thomas & Abigail, b. Sept. 19, 1728	LR3	15
Mary, d. Ephr[ai]m & Hannah, b. Aug. 4, 1740	LR4	A3
Mary, w. John, d. June 11 or 12, 1745, in the 68th y.		
of her age	LR5	1
Mary, d. Nathan & Sarah, b. Sept. 1, 1751	LR6	2
Mary, m. Dickerman M. BASSETT, Nov. 17, 1852, by Rev.		
Cha[rle]s Dickinson	1	212
Mary, w. Ephraim, d. May 5, [ ]	LR3	6
Mary Jane, m. Edward B. HURD, b. of Derby, Oct. 4, 1847, by		
Rev. W[illia]m Bliss Ashley	1	290
Moses, of Derby, m. Lucretia HALL, of Woodbury, Feb. 28,		
1780	TM1	109
Myra, of Derby, m. Daniel BLAKESLEE, of Roxbury, June 19,		
1844, by Rev. George Thacher	1	206
Nancy, m. William BUCKINGHAM, b. of New Haven, Nov. 10,		
1835, by Rev. Zepheniah Swift	1	148
Nathan, s. Andrew & Sarah, b. Feb. 14, 1696/7	2	31
Nathan, s. Nathan & Hannah, b. Sept. 19, 1724	LR3	5
Nathan, d. June 27, 1725	LR3	6
Nathan, of Derby, m. Sarah NORTHRUP, of Milford, Nov. 4,		
1747	LR6	6
Nathan, s. Elnathan & Abigail, b. July 25, 1752, in Elisabeth		
Town in the Jerseys	LR6	13
Nathan, m. Margret FRINK, Mar. 15, 1758, in Rev. Daniel		
Humphrey	LR6	445
Nathan, s. Nathan & Margret, b. Sept. 30, 1763	TM1	11
Nathan Galard, s. Moses & Lucretia, b. Feb. 25, 1781	TM1	109
Rachel, d. Andrew & Sarah, b. Mar. 24, 1708	LR3	3
Rachil, m. Benjamin STRONG, Sept. 7, 1729	LR3	10
Rachel, m. Benjamin L. WALKER, Mar. 31, 1850, by Rev.		
Jno Morrison Reid	1	210

	Vol.	Page

SMITH, (cont.)

Rachel, m. Benjamin L. **WALKER**, Mar. 31, 1850, by Rev.
Jno Morrison Reid — 1 — 482
Ransom, m. Elisabeth **BASSETT**, b. of Derby, Apr. 7, 1844,
by Rev. Ezra Jagger — 1 — 439
Rebecca, m. David W. **BOYD**, b. of Derby, Nov. 20, 1848, by
Rev. Thomas T. Guion — 1 — 212
Rebecca, m. David Willis **BOYD**, b. of Derby, Nov. 30, 1848,
by Rev. Tho[ma]s T. Guion — 1 — 209
Richard, s. John & Deborah, b. Apr. 29, 1725 — LR3 — 5
Ruamee, m. John **TWICHEL**, Jr., b. of Derby, June 3, 1773 — TM1 — 109
Ruth, m. Benjamin **BUNNEL**, Jr., b. of Derby, Oct. 10, 1752, by
Rev. Jonathan Lyman — LR6 — 444
Ruth, m. David **PRITCHARD**, b. of Derby, Dec. 20, 1757 — LR6 — 451
Sam[ue]ll, s. Ephraim & Mary, b. Aug. 17, 172[ ] — LR3 — 4
Samuel, m. Ann **HOLBROOK**, b. of Derby, Mar. 16, 1758,
by Rev. Daniel Humphry — LR6 — 444
Samuel Josiah, s. Almon & Fanny, b. Jan. 19, 1822 — 1 — 35
Sarah, d. Andrew & Mary, b. Aug. 5, 1744 — LR4 — A2
Sarah, d. Nathan & Sarah, b. Apr. 18, 1750 — LR6 — 2
Sarah, d. Andrew & Mary, d. Oct. 5, 1751, in the 9th y.
of her age — LR6 — 5
Sarah, d. Andrew & Mary, b. July 28, 1752 — LR6 — 2
Sarah, w. Nathan, d. June 25, 1757 — LR6 — 440
Sarah, m. Ens. Samuel **HAWKINS**, b. of Derby, Mar. 16, 1758,
by Rev. Richard Mansfield — LR6 — 444
Sarah, d. John & Abigail, b. Jan. 29, 1762 — LR7 — 252
Sheldon, s. Josiah & Ester, b. Dec. 13, 1780 — TM1 — 153
Sterling, of Kingston, N. Y., m. Lucy G. **WHEELER**, of
Derby, Sept. 4, 1849, by Rev. Thomas T. Guion — 1 — 442
Susanna, m. Nathaniel **JOHNSON**, Jan. 30, 1753 — LR6 — 6
Suse, d. Abram & Suse, b. Mar. 5, 1780 — TM1 — 151
Suse, w. Abram, d. July 7, 1781 — TM1 — 151
Sylvester T., of Birmingham, m. Sarah **BASSETT**, of
Humphreysville, Sept. 21, 1845, by Rev. John Parvies — 1 — 440
Thomas, m. Abigail **HAWKINS**, Dec. 20, 1727 — LR3 — 10
Thomas, d. Apr. 13, 1762 — LR7 — 254
Timothy Wheaton, s. Moses & Lucresey, b. Sept. 6, 1782 — TM1 — 104
Walter, m. Mary Minnerva **HAWKINS**, May 28, 1837, by Rev.
John D. Smith — 1 — 179
William, m. Sarah **LUM**, b. of Derby, Apr. 24, 1823, by Rev.
Stephen Jewett — 1 — 116
William Albert, m. Betsey **RUSSEL**, Nov. 30, 1837, by John
D. Smith — 1 — 178
Zerviah, m. Nison **FOOTE**, Sept. 19, 1812 — 1 — 93
----, m. Grace **RIGGS**, Mar. 22, 1726 — LR3 — 9
---auid, s. John & Deborah, b. Feb. 26, 1727/8 — LR3 — 15
----ah, d. Daniel & Hannah, b. Aug. 14, 1737 — LR3 — 11

Vol.   Page

SMITH, (cont.)

---rah, d. Jonah & Grace, b. July 1, [   ]   LR5   2

---naah, d. Jonah & Grace, b. July 15, [   ]   LR5   2

SNELL, Joseph N., of Waterbury, m. Eliza M. HALL, of Oxford,
    Sept. 9, 1849, by William E. Downs, J. P.   1   441

SNIDER, Sarah, m. Henry MOWRY, b. of Humphreysville, Sept. 1,
    1849, by Rev. W[illia]m Denison   1   358

SNOW, Charles S., m. Caroline DANIELS, Oct. 2, [1836], by John D.
    Smith   1   179

SOMERS, Abel, of Milford, m. Dameriss DURAND, of Derby, Jan.
    16, 1842, by Rev. Nathaniel Mead   1   185

Emma, of Milford, m. Charles H. CULVER, of Stratford, Oct.
    10, 1847, by Rev. Ira H. Smith   1   234

SPARKS, SPARK, Elisabeth, of Derby, m. Henry B. JOY, of
    Danbury, July 28, 1845, by Rev. N. S. Richardson   1   325

Emily, of Derby, m. Merrit SPERRY, of Meriden, Dec. 23, 1839,
    by Rev. Joseph Scott   1   185

Mary, m. Ledusky MUNN, b. of Derby, Oct. 12, 1835, by Rev.
    Joseph Scott   1   166

SPENCE, [see also SPENCER], Thomas, of Oxford, m. Calsina
    Jennet BASSETT, of Derby, Nov. 15, 1835, by Rev. Joseph
    Scott   1   179

SPENCER, [see also SPENCE], Abigail, of Suffield, m. Charles
    OATMAN, of Derby, Dec. 20, 1840, by Rev. Sylvester
    Smith   1   170

Bille, s. Jehiel & Anne, b. Apr. 11, 1777   TM1   130

Elisabeth Ann, m. Charles R. JUDSON, Nov. 25, 1847, by
    Rev. George Thacher   1   326

Elizabeth D., of Suffield, m. Samuel HICKOX, of Derby,
    Jan. 5, 1840, by Rev. Sylvester Smith   1   160

Enoch F., of Barry, N. Y., m. Ammiline REMER, of Derby,
    Apr. 4, 1824, by Rev. Zepheniah Swift   1   116

Hannah, d. Jehiel & Anne, b. Apr. 9, 1779   TM1   130

Jehiel, m. Anne Patience TOMLINSON, b. of Derby, Nov.
    6, 1775   TM1   130

Lewis, of Derby, m. Lucy BOUGHTON, of Waterbury, Dec. 28,
    1835, by Sylvester Smith   1   179

SPERRY, Adaline, of North Milford, m. Sharon BEACH, of North
    Haven, Oct. 3, 1832, by Rev. C. Thompson   1   179

Asa, of Orange, m. Fanny PERKINS, of Derby, Apr. 1, 1835,
    by Rev. John E. Bray   1   178

Fanny, m. Horace BUNNEL, Nov. 16, 1840, by John D. Smith   1   189

Isaiah R., m. Martha A. GERARD, Nov. 30, 1844, by Rev.
    W. B. Curtiss   1   439

Lucy A., of Woodbridge, m. Lyman L. LOOMER, of South
    Hadley, Mass., Mar. 31, 1836, by Rev. John E. Bray   1   165

Mary, [of] New Haven, m. Beniamen PECK, May 2, 1700   2   25

Merrit, of Meriden, m. Emily SPARKS, of Derby, Dec. 23,

	Vol.	Page

SPERRY, (cont.)

1839, by Rev. Joseph Scott — 1 — 185

Obediance, of New Haven, m. Joseph **DAVIS**, Jr., of Derby,
Nov. 15, 1770, by Rev. Chauncey Whitelsey — TM1 — 65

Sarah, of Woodbridge, m. Friend **PECK**, of Hamden, Jan. 30,
1831, by Rev. Stephen Jewett — 1 — 102

Willis P., m. Eunice I. **HOTCHKISS**, b. of Derby, Oct. 31, 1842,
by Rev. H. Read — 1 — 439

SQUIRE, Timothy, of Roxbury, m. Mary L. **SANFORD**, of
Naugatuck, Nov. 30, 1848, by Rev. Charles Stearns, at
Humphreysville — 1 — 441

STANDISH, Eunice Francis, of Bridgeport, m. Alexander **CHILDS**,
of Haddam, Nov. 28, 1839, by Rev. Joseph Scott — 1 — 153

STANLEY, Edward T., of New Haven, m. Sarah M. **REMER**, of
Derby, Nov. 4, 1834, by Zepheniah Swift — 1 — 178

STANNARD, John T., of New Marlborough, Mass., m. Hannah C.
HALE, of Derby, July 9, 1843, by Rev. Harman Ellis, of
North Haven — 1 — 439

STARR, W[illia]m W., m. Susan **HOTCHKISS**, Mar. 22, 1847, by
Rev. George Thacher — 1 — 440

STED, Albert J., m. Julia M. **JONES**, b. of Derby, Feb. 11, 1835, by
Rev. John E. Bray — 1 — 178

STEEL, Almira, m. John **HOLCOMB**, b. of Derby, Nov. 23, 1834, by
Rev. John E. Bray — 1 — 159

STEPHENS, [see under **STEVENS**]

STEPHENSON, Emma, of Ansonia, m. Amos O. N. **BUNNELL**, of
Plainville, Sept. 12, 1852, by Rev. Owen Street — 1 — 212

Emma, of Ansonia, m. Amos N. **BUNNEL**, of Plainville, Sept.
12, 1852, by Rev. Owen Street, in Ansonia — 1 — 213

Mary Ann, of Ansonia, m. James H. **LOTHER**, of Ansonia,
Sept. 15, 1852, by Rev. Thomas G. Osbom, of Birmingham — 1 — 342

STEUCKMAN, Conrad, m. Sarah M. **BEERS**, b. of Derby, Oct. 15,
1848, by Rev. W[illia]m Denison — 1 — 441

STEVENS, STEPHENS, Jeremiah S., of Burlington, Conn., m.
Elizabeth I. **SMITH**, of Derby, Aug. 10, 1845, by Rev.
W[illia]m Bliss Ashely — 1 — 439

Mabel, m. George **LEAVENWORTH**, May 28, 1848, by Rev.
W[illia]m B. Curtiss — 1 — 342

Rachel, m. John **HARGER**, Dec. 24, [ ] — LR3 — 10

Submitt, m. James **HUMPHRIS**, Mar. 15, 1749/50 — LR6 — 6

STILES, STYLES, SILES, Francis, m. Frances M. **SHELTON**, b. of
Southbury, Mar. 1, 1846, by Rev. Sylvester Smith — 1 — 439

Han[n]ah, of Stratford, m. Samuel **HARGER**, of Derby, May
9, 1693 — 2 — 25

Hannah, m. Daniel **SMITH**, Nov. 26, [ ] — LR3 — 10

Harriet L., of Southbury, m. Abram **BASSETT**, of Oxford,
Feb. 27, 1831, by Rev. John Lovejoy — 1 — 100

Minerva*, of Humphreysville, m. James **ROATH**, of Norwich,

	Vol.	Page
STILES, STYLES, SILES, (cont.)		
June 6, 1827, by Smith Dayton, Elder *(Minerva		
STILES?)	1	114
Nathan T., s. Nathan & Phebe, b. Feb. 27, 1796	TM1	433
STILSON, David S., m. Hannah E. HUBBARD, b. of New Haven,		
Apr. 29, 1839, by Rev. I. B. Beach	1	185
Sarah M., m. Clark WEBSTER, b. of Derby, Nov. 7, 1830,		
by Stephen Jewett	1	91
Sary, m. Joseph CANFIELD, Sept. 3, 1746	LR5	4
STODDARD, Abiram, 2nd, m. Lavinia SMITH, b. of Derby, Dec. 14,		
1834, by Rev. Joseph Scott	1	178
Oliver, m. Aurelia SUTTON, b. of Derby, June 17, 1830, by		
Rev. S. Jewett	1	119
Ruth, of Woodbury, m. Joel CHATFIELD, of Derby, Nov. 13,		
1785	TM1	143
Susan H., m. Sheldon C. JOHNSON, May 19, 1828, by Rev.		
Stephen Jewett	1	99
Thomas, Dr., m. Esther Ann GILBERT, Apr. 9, 1839, by John		
D. Smith	1	185
STONE, Ellen, of Derby, m. Frederick W[illia]m STONE, of New		
York, May 17, 1824, by Rev. Stephen Jewett	1	100
Ellen, of Derby, m. Frederick W[illia]m STONE, of New York,		
May 17, 1824, by Rev. Stephen Jewett	1	118
Ellen Louisa, m. James S. ENGLES, Apr. 5, 1846, by Rev.		
Samuel R. Hickcox	1	259
Frederick W[illia]m, of New York, m. Ellen STONE, of Derby,		
May 17, 1824, by Rev. Stephen Jewett	1	100
Frederick W[illia]m, of New York, m. Ellen STONE, of		
Derby, May 17, 1824, by Rev. Stephen Jewett	1	118
Jane E., m. Charles BASSETT, Oct. 22, 1843, by Rev.		
John D. Smith	1	206
STORRS, John W., m. Eliza A. CARRINGTON, Feb. 13, 1848, by		
Rev. W[illia]m C. Curtiss	1	440
STRONG, Anne, d. Adino & Eunice, b. Oct. 23, 1702	2	12
Benjamin, m. Rachil SMITH, Sept. 7, 1729	LR3	10
Ebenezer, s. Adino & [E]unis, b. Sept. 21, 17[ ]	2	13
----n, d. Benjamin & Rachil, b. Dec. 27, 1729	LR3	15
SUTLIFF, Almira S., of Haddam, m. George Bryant HOTCHKISS,		
of Derby, Nov. 25, 1847, by Rev. W[illia]m Bliss Ashley	1	290
SUTTON, Aurelia, m. Oliver STODDARD, b. of Derby, June 17,		
1830, by Rev. S. Jewett	1	119
SWIFT, Mary, of Derby, m. Samuel BEACH, M. D., of Stanford,		
Apr. 13, 1829, by Rev. Zephiniah Swift	1	82
TALMAGE, Elizur, m. Lucinda RIGGS, b. of Oxford, Dec. 21, 1834,		
by Rev. John E. Bray	1	181
Polly, m. Nathan SANFORD, b. of Oxford, Feb. 7, 1836, by		
John E. Bray	1	179
William, of Meriden, m. Sarah PHELPS, of Derby, July 1,		

	Vol.	Page
TALMAGE, (cont.)		
1838, by Rev. Orlando Starr	1	191
TAYLOR, William, m. Eleanor **SMITH**, Sept. 6, 1846, by Rev. W[illia]m Bliss Ashley	1	461
TEFFT, TEFFTE, TIFFE, TIFT, Benjamine, s. John & Sarah, b. Aug. 11, 1738	LR4	A3
John, s. John & Sarah, b. Oct. 8, 1732	LR3	16
Joseph, s. John & Sarah, b. Jan. 5, [ ]	LR3	16
Joseph, s. Jno & Sarah, d. Feb. 21, 1737/8	LR3	12
Joseph, s. John & Sarah, b. Mar. 4, 1740/1	LR5	232
TERRILL, TERREL, TYREL, TYRREL, Eli, m. Nancy HOLBROOK, June 17, 1832, by Rev. John Bayden, Jr.	1	180
Eli, m. Betsey **WOOSTER**, Oct. 7, 1838, by John D. Smith	1	180
Elizabeth, of Bethany, m. Atwater **TREAT**, of Oxford, Oct. 31, 1835, by Sylvester Smith	1	181
Elizabeth, m. John A. **BLAND**, Dec. 2, 1841, by John D. Smith	1	190
Grace, m. Hiram **ANDREWS**, b. of Bethany, Sept. 17, 1837, by Sylvester Smith	1	145
Henry, m. Jennett **WOOSTER**, b. of Derby, Mar. 29, 1837, by Rev. Lewis D. Howell	1	182
Isaac H., of Newtown, m. Harriet **BLAKE**, of Derby, Dec. 5, 1830, by Rev. S. Jewett	1	104
Laura Minerva, of Southbury, m. John **WOODRUFF**, of Orange, Mar. 25, 1824, by Rev. Zepheniah Swift	1	123
Philo, m. Fanny **UMBERFIELD**, Dec. 1, 1839, by John D. Smith	1	180
TERRY, Theodore P., of Terrysville, m. Sophronia A. **BARTHOLOMEW**, of Ansonia, Nov. 6, 1854, by Rev. O. Street, at Ansonia	1	249
Theodore P., of Terrysville, m. Sophronia A. **BARTHOLOMEW**, of Ansonia, Nov. 6, 1854, by Rev. O. Street, at Ansonia	1	461
THOMAS, Charles, of West Haven, m. Mary Jane **CLARK**, Nov. 3, 1833, by Zepheniah Swift	1	180
Eliza, m. Elias **CLINTON**, b. of New Haven, May 10, 1837, by Rev. Stephen Jewett	1	91
Ellen E., m. Edmund S. **LEVENWORTH**, Feb. 25, 1841, by John D. Smith	1	184
Gilbert, m. Mary **PECK**, b. of Woodbridge, Nov. 27, 1836, by Sam[ue]l R. Hickox. Witnesses: Smith Clark, Olney Streeter	1	181
Jane Lavinia, of East Haven, m. William **HARGER**, of Derby, Mar. 19, 1829, by S. Jewett	1	98
John, m. Eunice **JOHNSON**, Aug. 29, 1841, by John D. Smith	1	191
Mahitable, m. John **DAVIS**, Jr., Apr. 10, 1782	TM1	162
Susan, of Derby, m. Lewis **MORGAN**, of Wilton, Jan. 21, 1821, by Rev. Zepheniah Swift	1	105
Susannah, of Woodbury, m. Samuel **HUMPHRIS**, of Derby,		

	Vol.	Page
TIFT, [see under TEFFT]		
TODD, TOOD, Daniel, Jr., m. Eunice HITCHCOCK, b. of Derby, Mar. 27, 1775	Tm1	104
Daniel, Jr., m. Eunice HITCHCOCK, b. of Derby, Mar. 27, [ ], by Rev. Mr. Humphry	TM1	76
Daniel, s. Daniel & Eunice, b. Dec. 24, 1777	TM1	104
Joseph, s. Daniel & Sibill, b. Jan. 4, 1771	TM1	49
Sibbel, m. John WHE[E]LER, b. of Derby, July 10, 1776	TM1	85
TOLLES, Mary A., m. Milo BEECHER, b. of Bethany, May 5, 1833, by Rev. Stephen Jewett	1	147
Nehemiah, m. Polly BEECHER, Dec. 4, 1836, by John D. Smith	1	181
TOMLINSON, TOMLENSON, TOMOMLINSON, Abigail, d. Caleb & Mary, b. Mar. 30, 1750	TM1	4
Abigail, d. Caleb & Mary, b. Mar. 30, 1750	LR6	442
Abigail, d. John & Elisbeth, b. [ ] 18, [ ]	LR3	4
Abraham, s. Abraham & Mary, b. Sept. 2, 1712	LR3	3
[Abr]aham, s. Jonah & Mary, b. July 20, 1738	LR5	2
Abraham, s. Jonah & Mary, b. July 20, 1738	LR6	442
Agur, s. Abraham & Mary, b. Nov. 10, 1713	LR3	2
Agur, of Huntington, m. Polly TOMLINSON, of Derby, Mar. 31, 1828, by Eli Barnett, Elder	1	119
Agar, m. Sarah BOWERS, Dec. 4, [ ]	LR3	10
Amarilous, d. Noah & Abigail, b. June 28, 1748	TM1	88
Ammorillus, d. Noah & Abigail, b. June 28, 1748	LR5	413
Ammorilous, d. Noah & Abigail, d. July 9, 1748	TM1	88
Amelia, d. Levi & Amelia, b. Dec. 3, 1777	TM1	149
Amelia, m. Philo HOLBROOK, b. of Derby, July 31, 1831, by Rev. S. Jewett	1	107
Amon, s. Isaac & Mary, b. July 23, 1784	TM1	154
Ann, m. Joseph DURAND, Apr. 25, 1734	LR3	10
Ann, d. Caleb & Mary, b. Sept. 7, 1752	LR6	442
Anna, d. Benjamin & Jehoadan, b. July 1, 1747	LR5	232
Anna, m. Nathan MANSFIELD, Mar. 5, 1775	TM1	105
Anna M., m. Birdseye BLAKEMAN, Jan. 29, 1850, by Cha[rle]s Dickinson, Bishop	1	211
Anne, d. Caleb & Mary, b. Sept. 7, 1753	TM1	4
Anne Patience, d. Jonah & Mary, b. Sept. 1, 1753	LR6	4
Anne Patience, d. Jonah & Mary, b. Sept. 1, 1753	LR6	442
Anne Patience, m. Jehiel SPENCER, b. of Derby, Nov. 6, 1775	TM1	130
Augustus, m. Dorcas ENGLISH, Apr. 18, 1830, by Samuel R. Hickox. Witnesses: Abram English, Henry English, Hannah Osbom	1	118
Bathsheba, d. John & Elisabeth, b. Dec. 24, 1714	LR3	2
Bears, s. Noah & Abigail, b. Mar. 13, 1755	TM1	88
Bears, s. Noah & Abigail, b. Mar. 18, 1755	LR6	15
Benjamin, m. Gehoadan HARGER, Nov. 16, 1742	LR4	A4
Benjamin, s. John & Hannah, b. Sept. 30, 1745	LR5	232
Benj[amin] & w. Jehodan had d. [ ], d. Jan. 8, 1748/9	LR6	1

	Vol.	Page
TOMLINSON, TOMLENSON, TOMOMLINSON, (cont.)		
Benjamin, s. Benjamin & Jehoadin, b. Aug. 30, 1752	LR6	2
Benjamin, m. Mary HARRIS, b. of Derby, Nov. 15, 1768	TM1	31
Betsey, d. John & Sarah, b. Mar. 30, 1800	1	37
Beatty, d. Joseph & Sarah, b. Mar. 23, 1743/4	LR5	232
Bette, d. Levi & Amelia, b. Nov. 30, 1775	TM1	149
Caleb, s. Sam[ue]ll & Anna, b. Mar. 30, 1723	LR3	4
Caleb, s. Jonah & Mary, b. Sept. 11, 1749	LR6	442
Caleb, d. June 28, 1764	TM1	11
Charles, m. Mary Jane CANFIELD, b. of Derby, Nov. 10, 1831, by Rev. Stephen Jewett	1	102
Comfort, d. Benj[amin] & Jehoadan, b. May 13, 1749	LR5	413
Damaras, d. John & Deborah, b. May 11, 1749	LR6	450
Dan, s. Noah & Abigail, b. July 30, 1749	TM1	88
Dan, m. Susanna HOTCHKISS, b. of Derby, June 13, 1774, by Rev. Daniel Humphry	TM1	76
Daniel, s. John & Deborah, b. May 20, 1759	LR6	450
David, s. Benj[ami]n & Jehoadan, b. Aug. 16, 1762	LR7	252
David B., of Derby, m. Matilda N. CLEMANS, of Huntington, Mar. 21, 1850, by Rev. Jno Morrison Reid	1	461
Deborah, d. Levi & Amelia, b. Nov. 20, 1782	TM1	149
Elezabeth, m. John RIGGS, Feb. 23, 1699/1700	2	25
Elisabeth, d. Samuell & Hannah, b. Oct. 10, 1713	LR3	2
Elisabeth, d. John & Elisabeth, b. Dec. 9, 1720	LR3	5
Elisebeth, m. Joseph TWITCHEL, May 14, 1739	LR4	A4
Elisabeth, m. Jonathan LUMM, Jr., Mar. 13, [ ]	LR3	10
ElizEbeth, m. Sam[ue]ll PETTIT, Nov. 1, [ ]	LR3	10
Eunice, d. Henry & Patience, b. Feb. 27, 1745/6	LR5	2
Gedion, s. Benjamin & Jehoadan, b. Oct. 27, 1743	LR4	A5
Gideon, s. Benjamin & Mary, b. Mar. 18, 1777	TM1	109
Hannah, d. Samuel & Anna, b. Sept. 2, 1718	LR3	3
Hannah, d. Henrey & Patience, b. Dec. 16, 1742/3	LR4	A2
Hannah, d. Benj[ami]n & Jehoadan, b. Apr. 26, 1757	LR6	440
Henery, s. Samuell & Hannah, b. Apr. 18, 1712	LR3	2
Henry, m. Patience TOMOMLINSON, Dec. 12, 1737	LR4	A4
Henry, s. Henry & Patience, b. Oct. 20, 1752	LR6	3
Isaak, & w. Pacience, had [d.] [ ], b. Mar. 8, 17[ ]	LR3	1
Isaak, m. Pacience GAILER, Mar. 25, 1712	LR3	9
Isaac, s. Isaac & Patience, b. Oct. 16, 1723	LR3	5
Isaac, s. John & Hannah, b. Apr. 7, 1749	LR5	413
Isaac, s. John & Hannah, b. Apr. 7, 1749	LR5	414
Isaac, Jr., m. Sibillah RUSSELL, Jan. 17, 1749/50	LR6	6
Isaac, m. Sibbilah RUSSELL, Jan. 17, 1749/50	LR6	7
Isaac, s. Isaac & Sibbilah, b. Aug. 31, 1752	LR6	4
Isaac, d. Jan. 27, 1754	LR6	13
Isaac, m. Mary HAWKINS, Dec. 19, 1775	TM1	154
Isaac, s. Isaac & Mary, b. Apr. 2, 1778	TM1	154
Jabez, s. Benjamin & Jehoadan, b. Dec. 1, 1754	LR6	15

	Vol.	Page
TOMLINSON, TOMLENSON, TOMOMLINSON, (cont.)		
James, of New Haven, m. Phila Amelia MILES, of Derby,		
Jan. 23, 1825, by Rev. S. Jewett	1	119
Jane, of Derby, m. John LANE, of Huntington, Nov. 24, 1831,		
by Rev. Heman Bangs	1	112
[Je]remiah, s. Benjamin & Jehiodan, b. May 8, 1745	LR5	2
Jeremiah, s. Benjamin & Mary, b. Apr. 15, 1774	TM1	109
John, m. Elisabeth WO[O]STER, Mar. 27, 1712	LR3	9
John, s. John & Elisbeth, b. Sept. 23, 1725	LR3	5
John, m. Deborah BASSIT, Apr. 28, 1748	LR5	4
John, m. Deborah BASSIT, Apr. 28, 1748	LR6	450
John, d. Nov. 18, 1756, in the 71st y. of his age	LR6	13
John, s. John & Deborah, b. Jan. 24, 1757	LF6	450
John L., s. John & Sarah, b. Aug. 9, 1785	1	37
John L., m. Hannah HAWKINS, 3rd, Jan. 29, 1811, by Rev.		
Abner Smith	1	119
Jonah & Mary had d. [ ], b. Sept. 26, 1740	LR5	2
Jonah, m. Mary MOSS, [ ] 26, [ ]	LR3	10
Jonas, s. Abraham & Mary, b. Apr. 6, 1712	LR3	2
Jonas, d. Oct. 2, 1796	TM1	209
Joseph, s. John & Elizabeth, b. Dec. 27, 1716	LR3	3
Joseph, m. Sarah BEERS, May 24, 1743	LR4	A4
Joseph, s. Benjamin & Jehoadan, b. Nov. 9, 1758	LR6	440
Joseph, of Derby, m. Bathiah GLOVER, of New Town, Oct.		
27, 1763, by Rev. Richard Mansfield	LR7	256
Joseph, Sergt., m. Mrs. Elisabeth HULL, Oct. 14, 1776	TM1	116
Julia Ann, m. George BLACKMAN, Jan. 6, 1823, by Rev.		
Zephinah Swift	1	84
Laura, d. John & Sarah, b. June 10, 1804	1	37
Laura, m.George BASSETT,Dec. 24,1844,by Rev. John D. Smith	1	206
Lemme, s. Jonah & Mary, b. Apr. 25, 1745	LR6	442
Lemuel, s. Jonah & Mary, b. Apr. 26, 1745	LR5	2
Levi, s. John & Deborah, b. Feb. 15, 1752	LR6	2
Leui, s. John & Deborah, b. Feb. 15, 1752	LR6	450
Levi, m. Amelia BEARD, b. of Derby, Dec. 29, 1774, by Rev.		
Daniel Humphrys	TM1	101
Levi, s. John & Sarah, b. July 21, 1797	1	37
Levi, m. wid. Laura WARDIN, Feb. 14, 1830, by Z. Swift	1	103
Lewis, s. John & Sarah, b. July 30, 1791	1	37
Lois, Mrs., mother of Capt. James WHE[E]LER, d. Sept.		
11, 1767, in the 87th y. of her age	TM1	33
Lusendee, d. Benjamin & Mary, b. Aug. 11, 1769 (Lucinda)	TM1	31
Lucy, d. Noah & Abigail, b. July 19, 1767	TM1	88
Lucy, d. Noah & Abigail, d. Sept. 16, 1767	TM1	88
Lucy, d. Noah & Abigail, b. July 18, 1769	TM1	88
Luthene, d. John & Deborah, b. Jan. 27, 1755	LR6	450
Luthenia, d. John, Jr. & Sarah, b. Dec. 27, 1783	1	37
Maria, of Derby, m. Silas GUNN, of Oxford, Apr. 6, 1842,		

	Vol.	Page
TOMLINSON, TOMLENSON, TOMONLINSON, (cont.)		
by Rev. Sylvester Smith	1	279
Maria M., m. Rev. Sheldon **DIBBLE**, of the Sandwich Island,		
Oct. 31, 1830, by Z. Swift	1	90
Martha, d. Abraham, b. Sept. 22, 1719	LR3	3
[Mara]tha, d. Jonah & Mary, b. May 13, 1743	LR5	2
Martha, d. Jonah & Mary, b. May 13, 1743	LR6	442
Mary, d. Isaac, b. Feb. 18, 1720/21	LR3	4
Mary, d. Abraham, b. Dec. 18, 1721	LR3	4
Mary, d. Jonah & Mary, b. Sept. 26, 1740	LR6	442
Mary, m. Zachariah **HAWKINS**, June 31, 1743	LR6	8
Mary, d. Isaac & Mary, b. Mar. 17, 1782	TM1	154
Mary, m. Joseph D. **WOOSTER**, b. of Derby, Jan. 6, 1831, by		
Rev. Stephen Jewett	1	121
Mary Jane, m. John W[illia]m **FLOWERS**, b. of Derby, Jan.		
22, 1849, by Rev. Thomas T. Guion	1	271
Mary Jane, m. John W[illia]m **FLOWERS**, b. of Derby, Jan.		
22, 1849, by Rev. T. Guion	1	290
Mary Jane, m. John W. **FLOWERS**, b. of Derby, Jan. 27, 1849,		
by Rev. Thomas T. Guion	1	272
Minerva, m. Benjamin **NICKOLS**, Mar. 24, 1839, by John D.		
Smith	1	169
Nabbe, d. Jonah & Mary, b. Apr. 21, 1747	LR6	442
Nab[b]y, d. Noah & Abigail, b. Oct. 22, 1751	TM1	88
Nabby, d. Benjamin & Mary, b. Aug. 12, 1771	TM1	65
Nab[b]y, d. Noah & Abigail, d. Apr. 22, 1773	TM1	88
Nab[b]e, m. David **BASSIT**, b. of Derby, Oct. 21, 1773, by		
John Davis	TM1	94
Nathan, s. Noah & Abigail, b. Aug. 4, 1760	TM1	88
Nathan, s. Noah & Abigail, b. Aug. 4, 1760	LR7	249
Nathaniel, s. Agur & Sarah, b. Apr. 9, 1736	LR3	11
Noah, s. Isaac & Patience, b. Mar. 6, 1727	LR3	15
Noah, m. Abigail **BEARS**, July 2, 1747	LR5	4
Noah, s. Noah & Abigail, b. June 8, 1753	LR6	3
Noah, s. Noah & Abigail, b. June 8, 1753	TM1	88
Noah, s. Noah & Abigail, d. June 16, 1753	LR6	5
Noah, s. Noah & Abigail, d. June 16, 1753	TM1	88
Noah, s. Noah & Abigail, b. Aug. 3, 1757	TM1	88
Noah, s. Noah & Abigail, b. Aug. 3, 1757	LR6	440
Patience, d. Isaak & Patience, b. Sept. 6, 1715	LR3	2
Patience, m. Henry **TOMLINSON**, Dec. 12, 1737	LR4	A4
Peter C., of Derby, m. Charlotte **CANFIELD**, of Derby, Nov.		
16, 1828, by Rev. S. Jewett	1	119
Phebe, d. John & Elisabeth, b. Jan. 27, 1712/13	LR3	2
Phebee, d. John & Deborah, b. Sept. 23, 1750	LR6	2
Phebe, d. John & Deborah, b. Sept. 23, 1750	LR6	450
Philo, s. Dan & Susanna, b. May 15, 1778	TM1	128
Polly, of Derby, m. Agur **TOMLINSON**, of Hungtington, Mar.		

	Vol.	Page
TOMLINSON, TOMLENSON, TOMOMLINSON, (cont.)		
31, 1828, by Eli Barnett, Elder	1	119
Rachel, d. Isaak & Patience, b. Feb. 2, 1718	LR3	3
Rachel, m. Jonathan SMITH, Mar. 12, 1745/6	LR5	4
Rebecah, d. Caleb & Mary, b. Nov. 14, 1760	TM1	4
Russell, s. Isaac & Sibbilah, b. Dec. 23, 1754	LR6	4
Ruth, d. Levi & Amelia, b. Mar. 11, 1780	TM1	149
Sally, d. John & Sarah, b. Apr. 25, 1789	1	37
Same Lord Moss, s. Jonah & Mary, b. Dec. 15, 1757	LR6	447
Samuel, s. Samuel, b. Dec. 13, 1720	LR3	4
Sam[ue]ll, s. Henry & Patience, b. Jan. 4, 1739	LR4	A3
Sam[ue]ll, s. Henry & Patience, d. Sept. 13, 1742	LR4	A5
Samuel, s. Caleb & Mary, b. Oct. 18, 1747	TM1	4
Samuel, s. Caleb & Mary, b. Oct. 18, 1747	LR6	442
Samuel, s. John & Sarah, b. Feb. 25, 1787	1	37
Sarah, m. Andrew SMITH, May 21, 1696	2	25
Sarah, d. Sam[ue]ll & Annah, b. Feb. 11, 1725/6	LR3	5
Sarah, m. Ebenezer BASSIT, Feb. 2, 1742/3	LR4	A4
Sarah, d. Henry & Patience, b. June 4, 1747	LR5	232
Sarah, m. Isaac NICKOLS, July 22, 1747	LR5	4
Sarah, w. Sergt. Joseph, d. Feb. 22, 1776	TM1	116
Sarah Ann, d. Weeb & Jerusha, b. Mar. 1, 1772	TM1	61
Sibilla, d. Henry & Patience, b. Apr. 11, 1738	LR4	A3
Sibillah, d. Isaac & Sibillah, b. Sept. 10, 1750	LR6	2
Sibbilah, d. Isaac, b. Sept. 12, 1750	LR6	4
Sibbillah, m. Stephen BURWELL, Aug. 12, 1754	LR6	451
Silas, s. Isaac & Mary, b. Sept. 19, 1776	TM1	154
Susan Caroline, d. John L. & Hannah, b. Sept. 13, 1813	1	37
Suse, d. Dan & Susannah, b. June 11, 1776	TM1	96
Truman, s. Isaac & Mary, b. July 7, 1780	TM1	154
Truman, m. Welthy OSBORN, Jan. 9, 1831, by Sam[ue]ll H.		
Hickox	1	102
William, Sr., d. Dec. 8, 1711	LR3	6
Zachariah, s. Isaac & Mary, b. Aug. 16, 1787	TM1	154
Zachariah, s. Isaac & Mary, d. Aug. 1, 1789	TM1	154
Zachariah, s. Isaac & Mary, d. Aug. 1, 1789	TM1	154
----on, s. William, b. Sept. 19, [16]86	2	2
----illus, s. Noah & Abigail, d. July 11, 1748	LR5	1
TOWNER, Elizabeth*, d. John & Jen, b. Mar. 23, 1710 *(Written		
"Elizabeth FOWNER")	2	160
Eunice, d. John, b. May 16, 1720	LR3	4
Isaac, s. John & Sarah, b. July 28, 1745	LR5	2
Jane, w. John, d. May 4, 175[ ]	LR5	1
Jeane, d. John & Jeane, d. Mar. 23, 1739	LR5	1
John, m. Jaine FRENCH, Aug. 13, 1707	LR3	9
John, s. John & Jaine, b. June 29, 1714	LR3	2
John, Jr., m. Sarah WILDMAN, Nov. 5, 1741	LR5	4
John, s. John & Sarah, b. Feb. 22, 1749/50	LR5	413

	Vol.	Page
TOWNER, (cont.)		
John, s. John & Sarah, b. Feb. 22, 1750	LR5	413
John, m. Mrs. Hannah **CAINE**, June 26, 1759	LR6	445
Joseph, s. John & Jan[e], b. Apr. 22, 1712	LR3	1
Joseph, m. Abigail **BIZELL**, Jan. 4, 1743/4	LR5	4
Phineas, s. John & Jain, b. Apr. 28, 1708	2	23
Rebeckah, d. John & Jane, b. Mar. 27, 1718	LR3	3
Rebeckah, d. John & Jeane, d. Aug. 17, 1738	LR5	1
Rebeckah, d. John & Sarah, b. Jan. 8, 1742	LR5	2
Sarah, d. John & Sarah, b. Jan. 1, 1753	LR6	3
TOWNSEND, Phebe Ann, of Fishkill, N. Y., m. George **BIRCH** (colored & transients), [ ]. by Rev. N. S. Richardson; recorded Dec. 2, 1845	1	207
TRACY, Mary, m. John **RAFERTY**, Sept. 24, 1851, by Rev. James Lynch	1	426
TREADWELL, Abby Jane, m. Henry **JOHNSON**, Sept. 6, 1846, by Rev. W[illia]m Bliss Ashley	1	325
Cyrus, of Trumbull, m. Susanna **NICHOLS**, of Huntington, Apr. 28, 1839, by Rev. Joseph Scott	1	191
TREAT, Atwater, of Oxford, m. Elizabeth **TERREL**, of Bethany, Oct. 31, 1835, by Sylvester Smith	1	181
Robert S., m. Mary **LUM**, Apr. 25, 1841, by John D. Smith	1	182
William E., m. Agusta M. **NETTLETON**, Jan. 2, 1842, by John D. Smith	1	182
TROWBRIDGE, TROBRIDGE, Abigail, d. Israel & Mary, b. Nov. 9, 1748	LR6	442
An[n]e, d. Israel & Mary, b. Aug. 28, 1765	TM1	33
David, s. Israel & Mary, b. Mar. 7, 1755	LR6	442
Ebenezer, s. Israel & Mary, b. May 18, 1763	TM1	33
Elisabeth, d. Israel & Mary, b. Mar. 15, 1757	LR6	442
Elisabeth, m. Osee **DUTTON**, Jan. 19, 1783	TM1	151
Hannah, d. Israel & Mary, b. Feb. 9, 1751	LR6	442
Hannah, m. Jeremiah **DURAND**, Nov. 21, [1773?], by Rev. David Bronson	TM1	87
Leui, s. Israel & Mary, b. May 25, 1753	LR6	442
TRUESDALE, Lorenzo, m. Caroline E. **BUNNELL**, b. of Derby, Nov. 10, 1844, by Rev. Samuel R. Hickox, of Humphreysville	1	461
TUCKER, Almira, of Oxford, m. Willis G. **THOMAS**, of Waterbury, Jan. 6, 1832, by Rev. Charles Thompson	1	180
Anne, d. Joseph & Eunice, d. Oct. 19, 1775, in the 3rd y. of her age	TM1	48
Betsy I., m. James W. **FIELDS**, b. of Derby, June 20, 1847, by Rev. William Bliss Ashley	1	271
Betty, d. Zepheniah & Sarah, b. Nov. 17, 1767	TM1	33
Byram, of Oxford, m. Eunice **BROWN**, of Bethany, Apr. 23, 1837, by Rev. John E. Bray	1	182
Daniel, m. Elizebeth **JOHNSON**, July 9, 1741	LR4	A4

	Vol.	Page
TUCKER, (cont.)		
Daniel, s. Daniel & Elizebeth, b. May 1, 1742/3	LR4	A2
David, m. Sarah E. **DRUNG,** May 15, 1848, by Rev. W[illia]m		
B. Curtiss	1	461
Francis, m. Caroline **BROWN,** Jan. 12, 1851, by Rev. Cha]rle]s		
Dickinson	1	462
Gedion, s. Daniel & Elisabeth, b. Apr. 17, 1746	LR5	232
Gedion, s. Daniel & Elizabeth, b. Apr. 17, 1746	LR5	295
Grace, m. Edward E. **BRADLEY,** b. of Derby, Nov. 18, 1838,		
by Rev. Orlando Starr	1	171
Jerome, of Oxford, m. Mary **BOUGHTON,** of Waterbury, July		
30, 1837, by Sylvester Smith	1	182
Joseph, s. Daniel & Elisabeth, b. July 1, 1748	LR6	15
Joseph, d. Nov. 10, 1775, in the 28th y. of his age	TM1	48
Lyman, m. Mary Elizabeth **HOTCHKISS,** Oct. 19, 1834,		
by Zepheniah Swift	1	181
Maria A., m. Isaac B. **DAVIS,** June 19, 1842, by John D. Smith	1	247
Martha, of Derby, m. Francis **ROCKWELL,** of Ridgefield, Dec.		
23, 1847, by Rev. W[illia]m Bliss Ashley	1	425
Mary, Mrs. of Derby, m. John W. **FRENCH,** of Derby, Sept.		
15, 1838, by Rev. David Miller, of Humphreysville	1	155
Medad K., m. Esther A. **KENNEY,** b. of Derby, Dec. 6, [1842],		
by Rev. H. Read	1	247
Oliver, s. Zepheniah & Sarah, b. Mar. 11, 1765	TM1	6
Rubin, s. Daniel & Elizebeth, b. Mar. 7 (?), 1743/4	LR4	A5
Rubin, s. Daniel & Elisabeth, b. Mar. 1, 1744/5	LR6	15
Samuel, m. Sarah **CHATFIELD,** Aug. [ ], 1755, by Daniel		
Holbrook	LR6	445
Samuel, s. Samuel & Sarah, b. Feb. 10, 1756	LR6	440
Sarah, d. Samuel & Sarah, b. Mar. 26, 1772	TM1	43
Sarah, m. Philo C. **BIRDSEYE,** Dec. 25, 1843, by Rev.		
W[illia]m Bliss Ashley	1	205
Sheldon, m. Sally **CANFIELD,** b. of Derby, Aug. 5, 1835, by		
Sylvester Smith	1	181
Susannah, d. Samuel & Sarah, b. Nov. 6, 1761	TM1	20
William, s. Samuel & Sarah, b. Nov. 20, 1757	LR6	440
Zepheniah, s. Daniel & Elisabeth, b. Oct. 28, 1759	LR6	719
TUTTLE, Ame, d. Joseph & Hannah, b. Oct. 30, 1767	TM1	9
Ame, m. Benjamin **HARGER,** b. of Derby, July 4, 1768	TM1	129
Burritt, of Plymouth, m. Adaline E. **LYMAN,** Mar. 15, 1851, by		
Rev. Jno Morrison Reid	1	462
Henry, of New Haven, m. Esther **BLAKE,** of Derby, Dec. 25,		
1832, by Rev. S. Jewett	1	181
Jane E., of Derby, m. Vinas **WOODWARD,** of Hamden, Dec.		
27, 1840, by Rev. Jos[eph] Scott	1	188
Maria, of Humphreysville, m. Nelson B. **WILLIAMS,** of		
Woodbury, Dec. 2, 1832, by Rev. S. Jewett	1	187
TWICHEL, TWITCHELL, TWITCHILL, TWITCHEL, Abijah, s.		

	Vol.	Page
TWICHEL, TWITCHELL, TWITCHILL, TWITCHEL, (cont.)		
David & Margret, b. June 11, 1776	TM1	96
Ame, d. Sam[ue]ll & Hannah, b. July 23, 1741	LR4	A2
Amy, d. Joseph & Elisabeth, b. Aug. 18, 1762; d. Aug. 30, 1762	LR7	251
Amey, d. Joseph & Elisabeth, b. Sept. 26, 1766	TM1	33
Annes, d. John & Ann, b. Feb. 5, 1733/4	LR3	16
Benjamin, s. John & Ann, b. July 10, 1748	LR5	414
Clare, d. Jabez & Elisabeth, b. Aug. 8, 1771	TM1	83
Dauid, s. Joseph & Elisabeth, b. Feb. 12, 1746/7	LR5	414
David, s. Joseph & Elisabeth, b. Feb. 10, 1747	LR7	250
David, s. Joseph & Elisabeth, b. June 10, 1757	LR7	250
David, m. Margret **JOHNSON**, Dec. [ ], 1773	TM1	96
Ebenezer, s. Wooster & Elisabeth, b. July 30, 1765	TM1	38
Edward, s. Jno & Sarah, b. Mar. 28, 1700/1	2	12
Elizabeth, d. John & Sarah, b. June 22, 1707	2	23
Elisabeth, d. John & Ann, b. Dec. 7, 1742	LR5	414
Elisabeth, [twin with Mary], d. Joseph & Elisabeth, b. Feb. 10, 1760	LR7	250
Elisabeth, d. Joseph & Elisabeth, b. Feb. 10, 1760	LR6	719
Elisabeth, w. Joseph, d. Feb. 7, 1789, in the 68th y. of her age	TM1	159
Enoch, s. Joseph & Elisabeth, b. Jan. 18, 1754	LR7	250
Eunice, d. John & Ann, b. Sept. 30, 1745	LR5	414
Hannah*, d. John & Sarah, b. Aug. 21, 1699 *(Written "Hannah **TWICHER**")	2	31
Hannah, m. Jonathan **HILL**, Sept. 19, 1717	LR3	9
Hannah, d. John & Ann, b. Mar. 18, 1741	LR5	414
Isaac, s. Joseph & Elizebeth, b. Dec. 20, 1741	LR4	A2
Isaac, s. Joseph & Elisabeth, b. Dec. 19, 1742	LR7	250
Jabez, m. Elisabeth **HARGER**, b. of Derby, May 8, 1771	TM1	83
Jabish, s. John & Ann, b. Mar. 18, 1750	LR5	414
Jennett, Mrs., m. Cornelis **DASCOM**, b. of New Haven, Sept. 25, 1831, by Charles Thompson	1	121
John, m. Sarah **PEARSON**, Jan. 21, 1698/9	2	25
John, s. John & Sarah, b. June 1, 1713	LR3	2
John, s. John & Sarah, b. Feb. 15, 1717	LR3	3
John, m. Ann **HARGER**, Mar. 20, 1733/4	LR3	10
John, s. John & Ann, b. Oct. 11, 1746	LR5	414
John, Jr., m. Ruamee **SMITH**, b. of Derby, June 3, 1773	TM1	109
Joseph, m. Elisebeth **TOMLINSON**, May 14, 1739	LR4	A4
Joseph, s. Joseph & Elisabeth, b. Sept. 6, 1751	LR6	3
Joseph, s. Joseph & Elisabeth, b. Sept. 16, 1752	LR7	250
Mary, d. Joseph & Elisabeth, b. May 21, 1749	LR5	414
Mary, d. Joseph & Elisabeth, b. May 23, 1750	LR7	250
Mary, d. Joseph & Elisabeth, b. Feb. 10, 1760	LR6	719
Mary, [twin with Elisabeth], d. Joseph & Elisabeth, b. Feb. 10, 1760	LR7	250
Patience, d. John & Ann, b. Mar. 23, 1736	LR5	414
Patience, d. John & Ann, b. Mar. 24, 1736	LR3	11

	Vol.	Page
TWICHEL, TWITCHELL, TWITCHILL, TWITCHEL, (cont.)		
Patience, d. John & Ann, d. June 28, 1752, in the 17th y.		
of her age	LR6	5
Patience, d. John & Ruamee, b. Jan. 3, 1775	TM1	109
Phebe, d. Joseph & Elisabeth, b. May 19, 1744	LR7	250
Samuell, s. John & Sarah, b. Feb. 15, 1710/11	LR3	0
Sam[ue]ll, m. Hannah HINMAN, Dec. 13, 1739	LR4	A4
Sam[ue]ll, s. John & Ann, b. Feb. 17, 1744	LR5	414
Sarah, d. Jno & Sarah, b. Sept. 10, 1703	2	12
Sarah, w. Jno, d. Mar. 14, 1738/9	LR3	12
Sarah, d. John & Ann, b. Sept. 4, 1739	LR5	414
Wooster, s. Joseph & Elizebeth, b. Jan. 12, 1739	LR4	A2
Wooster, s. Joseph & Elisabeth, b. Jan. 12, 1740	LR7	250
Wooster, m. Elisabeth HULL, b. of Derby, Oct. 11, 1764,		
by Rev. Humphry	TM1	38
----id, s. John & Ann, b. Oct. 10, 1737	LR3	11
----be, d. Joseph & Elizebeth, b. [ ]	LR5	2
TYLER, Thomas, d. Mar. 12, 1703/4	2	27
William, m. Mary LOTHRUP, June 3, 1692	2	25
TYREL, TYRREL, [see under TERRILL]		
UFFORD, Abigail, d. Thomas & Mabel, b. Feb. 1, 1741/4	LR5	232
Mehethebel, d. Tho[ma]s & Mabel, b. Apr. 27, 1743	LR5	232
Samuel, s. Shores & Elisabeth, b. Oct. 31, 1773	TM1	94
Shoars, s. Thomas & Mabel, b. May 17, 1745	LR5	232
Shores, m. Elisabeth DURAND, b. of Derby, June 10, [ ],		
by David Bronson	TM1	94
UMBERFIELD, Catharine, of Humphreysville, m. Anson RIGGS, of		
Oxford, July 1, 1832, by Charles Thompson	1	180
Fanny, m. Philo TERRILL, Dec. 1, 1839, by John D. Smith	1	180
John, of Derby, m. Eliza NORTHROP, of Woodbridge, Oct. 9,		
1831, by Rev. Stephen Jewett	1	106
Mary E., m. Henry BRADLEY, Apr. 17, 1848, by Rev.		
W[illia]m B. Curtiss	1	209
Willis, m. Harriet LOUNSBURY, b. of Oxford, Feb. 1, 1836, by		
Rev. John E. Bray	1	183
UMFREYVILLE, [see under HUMFREYVILLE]		
UPSON, Harriett, m. Harpin RIGGS, b. of Derby, May 17, 1840, by		
Rev. John E. Bray	1	176
Martha, m. James SMITH, Jr., Dec. 24, 1846, by W[illia]m		
B. Curtiss	1	234
Martha, m. James SMITH, Jr., Dec. 24, 1846, by Rev. William		
B. Curtiss	1	440
William L., of Roxbury, m. Esther E. HINMAN, of Derby,		
Sept. 9, 1838, by Oliver Bykes at John B. Hinmans	1	183
UYANT, Wilson, m. Vilette NORTHROP, b. of Sherman, Mar. 14,		
1841, by Rev. Sylvester Smith	1	188
VADER, Peter, of Mammaronick, N. Y., m. Louis JOHNSON, of		
Oxford, Nov. 13, 1836, by Sylvester Smith	1	185

	Vol.	Page

VAMOSBURG, Daniel B., m. Mary Jane PEASE, June 13, 1824, by
   Stephen Jewet — 1 — 118

VOSE, Charity, of Oxford, m. James BEARDSLEY, of Huntington,
   Sept. 7, 1822, by Rev. Abner Smith — 1 — 85

WADSWORTH, Elizabeth Ann, of Hartford, m. Harvey D.
   BRONSON, of Derby, Jan. 26, 1842, by Joseph Scott — 1 — 174

WAITH, Peter, m. Mary Ann ANDREWS, b. of Humphreysville, July
   1, 1849, by Rev. W[illia]m Denison — 1 — 482

WAKELEE, WAKELEY, Catherine, m. Menzier WAKELEE, b. of
   Huntington, Dec. 27, 1852, by Rev. Thomas G. Osborn — 1 — 483

   Julia N., m. David A. BANKS, b. of Derby, Mar. 3, 1845, by
   Rev. W[illia]m Bliss Ashley — 1 — 207

   Menzier, of Huntington, m. Catherine WAKELEE, of
   Huntington, Dec. 27, 1852, by Rev. Thomas G. Osborn — 1 — 483

WAKLING, Elisabeth, m. Israel JOHNSON, May 28, 1740 — LR5 — 4

WALESTOWN, Mary, of Guilford, m. John LEAVENWORTH, of
   Derby, Oct. 20, 1844, by Rev. Sylvester Smith — 1 — 341

WALKER, Benjamin L., m. Rachel SMITH, Mar. 31, 1850, by Rev.
   Jno Morrison Reid — 1 — 210

   Benjamin L, m. Rachel SMITH, Mar. 31, 1850, by Rev.
   Jno Morrison Reid — 1 — 482

WALLACE, WALLIS, Agnes, m. Charles Chester JACKSON, b. of
   Derby, Dec. 25, 1847, by Rev. W[illia]m Bliss Ashley — 1 — 326

   Elisabeth, m. Nelson H. DOWNS, b. of Derby, May 8, 1843, by
   Rev. W[illia]m Bliss Ashley — 1 — 247

   Elisabeth, m. Robert R. WOOD, b. of Derby, June 30, 1847,
   by Rev. William B. Ashley — 1 — 482

   John, m. Cosis Ann JACKSON, b. of Derby, Dec. 12, 1843,
   by Rev. Zepheniah Swift — 1 — 481

   Priscilla, of Derby, m. Edward BEARDSLEY, of Stratford,
   Dec. 31, 1852, by Rev. Thomas T. Guion — 1 — 212

   Robert, m. Ellen MEROL, Dec. 24, 1840, by John D. Smith — 1 — 190

   Sarah, m. Lewis G. REME, Oct. 24, 1850, by Cha[rle]s
   Dickinson — 1 — 210

   Sarah, m. Lewis G. REMER, Oct. 24, 1850, by Cha[rle]s
   Dickinson — 1 — 426

   Thomas, Jr., m. Sarah SLATER, Nov. 25, 1852, by Bishop
   Cha[rle]s Dickinson, of Birmingham — 1 — 483

   William, m. Sarah MILLS, b. of Derby, Sept. 16, 1849, by
   Rev. Jno Morrison Reid — 1 — 482

WALSH, William, m. Anne CLARKE, Feb. 22, 1852, by Rev. James
   Lynch — 1 — 483

WARD, Hezekiah, s. John & Easther, b. Mar. 28, 1756 — LR6 — 15

   Joseph, s. Stephen & Abigail, b. Nov. 29, 1753 — LR6 — 442

   Mary, d. Stephen & Abigail, b. Feb. 28, 1756 — LR6 — 442

   Rhodee, d. Stephen & Abigail, b. Dec. 11, 1758 — LR6 — 440

   Ruth, d. Jeams & Elizabeth, b. Feb. 10, 1704/5 — 2 — 13

   Stephen, of Derby, m. Abigail JOHNSON, of Wallingford,

	Vol.	Page
WARD, (cont.)		
Nov. 22, 1752	LR6	451
WARDIN, Laura, wid. m. Levi **TOMLINSON,** Feb. 14, 1830, by Z. Swift	1	103
WARNER, Catharine, d. Preston B. & Catharine, b. Mar. 4, 1829	1	217
Charles I., of Humphreysville, m. Myra L. **DART,** of Huntington, Oct. 25, 1840, by Samuel R. Hickox	1	188
David, m. Laura **DAVIS,** [ ], by Rev. George L. Fuller; recorded Apr. 26, 1847	1	481
Eliza, d. Preston B. & Catharine, b. Dec. 11, 1822	1	217
Emily, d. Preston B. & Catharine, b. Nov. 12, 1826	1	217
Emily, m. Lucius **ALLIS,** b. of Derby, [ ], by Rev. N. S. Richardson; recorded Dec. 2, 1845	1	193
Emily, m. Lucius **ALLIS,** b. of Derby, [ ], by Rev. N. S. Richardson; recorded Dec. 2, 1845	1	325
Eunice, m. Miles L. **BRONSON,** b. of Derby, Dec. 3, 1843, by Rev. Zephaniah Swift	1	205
George, s. Preston B. & Catharine, b. Aug. 20, 1832; d. Oct. 8, 1850	1	217
Harriett, d. Preston B. & Catharine, b. June 26, 1834	1	217
Marvin, s. Preston B. & Catharine, b. Oct. 14, 1824	1	217
Marvin, m. Elisabeth S. **BOYCE,** b. of Derby, May 16, 1847, by Rev. W[illia]m Bliss Ashley	1	481
Myra, d. Preston B. & Catharine, b. Mar. 20, 1821	1	217
Myra, d. Preston B., d. July 18, 1837	1	217
Newel, m. Eunice M. **BUTLER,** Aug. 2, 1840, by Rev. Sam[ue]l R. Hickox	1	186
Preston B., s. Asahel & Rhoda, b. Dec. 22, 1790; m. Catherine **LEWIS,** d. Nathan & Charity, May 14, 1818	1	217
Preston B., m. Catherine **LEWIS,** d. Nathan & Charity (BOOTH), May 14, 1818. Witnesses: Nathan Lewis, Elizabeth M. Squires. Affidavit made June 8, 1853 to Christopher N. Shelton, J. P. of Huntington	1	216-7
Preston B., made affidavit Apr. 19, 1855, to Foster P. Abbott, J. P., of his marriage	1	217
Stephen, of Watertown, m. Harriet **RUSSEL,** of Derby, Dec. 1, 1830, by Rev. S. Jewett	1	124
Teresa, of Derby, m. Clark **FORD,** of Bethany, Dec. 10, 1848, by Rev. Charles Stearns, at Humphreysville	1	271
WARREN, Henry, of Derby, m. Mary A. **CLARK,** of Milford, Apr. 20, 1840, by Rev. Joseph Scott	1	186
Rachel, m. James **PRITCHARD,** Jr., Nov. 1, 1773	TM1	92
WASHBOND, WASHBON, WASBORN, WASHBONE, WASBON, WASHBAND, WASHBAN, Abel, s. Edward & Mary, b. Oct. 17, 1753	LR6	1
Ann, d. John & Sarah, b. Feb. 19, 1732/3	LR3	16
Anne, d. Gideon & Easther, b. Jan. 30, 1748	LR6	2
Aszel, s. Gideon & Esther, b. Mar. 30, 1746	LR5	232

	Vol.	Page
WASHBOND, WASHBON, WASBORN, WASHBONE, WASBON,		
WASHBAND, WASHBAN, (cont.)		
Benjamin, [twin with Joseph], s. Ephr[aim] & Meriam, b.		
July 5, [ ]	LR3	16
Benjamin, s. Ephraim, d. Nov. 4, 1737	LR3	12
Benjamin, s. Ephraim & Meriaham, b. June 6, 1747	LR5	232
Benjamin, s. Ephraim & Meriam, b. June 6, 1747	LR6	2
Bowers, s. Ephraim & Meriam, b. June 18, 1745	LR5	232
Dorcus, d. Ephraim & Meriam, d. Nov. 13, 1737	LR3	12
Dorcus, d. Ephraim & Meriam, b. Mar. 22, 1742	LR5	232
Edmon, s. Timothy & Hannah, b. Nov. 27, 1747	LR6	2
Edward, s. William & Hannah, b. June 17, 1708	2	23
Edward, m. Mary PRINGLE, Dec. 31, 1730	LR3	10
Eli, s. Sam[ue]ll & Sarah, b. Sept. 19, 1758	LR7	253
Elijah Woolsey, s. Ebenezer, b. Jan. 8, 1814	1	17
Ephraim, s. William & Hannah, b. [ ], 1701	LR6	2
Ephraim, m. Merriam BOWERS, Oct. 7, 1722	LR3	9
Eunis, d. Edward & Mary, b. Apr. 14, 1742	LR4	A2
Eunice, d. Gedion & Esther, b. May 20, 1755	LR6	13
George, m. Delia REYNOLDS, b. of Derby, Oct. 3, 1832,		
by Charles Thompson	1	187
Gedion, m. Esther ALLIN, Oct. 6, 1743	LR4	A4
Gedion, m. Esther ALLIEN, Oct. 6, 1743	LR5	4
Hannah, d. Eph[raim] & Meriam, b. May 2, [ ]	LR3	16
Hannah, d. Ephraim & Meriam, d. Oct. 30, 1737	LR3	12
Hannah, d. Ephraim & Merriam, b. Aug. 23, 1740	LR5	232
Hope, s. Edward & Mary, b. Mar. 1, 1750	LR6	1
John, m. Sarah GUNN, Nov. 5, 1722	LR3	10
John, s. John & Sarah, b. [ ]	LR3	16
Joseph, [twin with Benjamin], s. Ephr[aim] & Meriam, b.		
July 5, [ ]	LR3	16
Joseph, s. Ephraim & Meriam, d. Oct. 28, 1737	LR3	12
Joseph, s. Timothy & Hannah, b. May 12, 1750	LR6	2
Josiah, m. Sarah HARGER, b. of Derby, June 2, 1767, by		
Rev. Richard Mansfield	TM1	86
Josiah, s. Josiah & Sarah, b. Jan. 9, 1769	TM1	86
Lemuel, s. Edward & Mary, b. Nov. 28, 1744	LR5	2
Luera, d. Gideon & Esther, b. Sept. 5, 1750	LR6	3
Mabel, d. Gideon & Esther, b. Sept. 16, 1752	LR6	3
Mary, m. John JOHNSON, Sept. 24, 1694	2	25
Mary, wid., d. Jan. 11, 1712	LR3	6
Mary, d. Edward & Mary, b. Mar. 20, 1740	LR4	A2
Mary, d. Samuel & Sarah, b. Dec 4, 1744	LR5	2
Mary, d. Samuel & Sarah, b. Aug. 15, 1749	LR5	414
Mary, d. Sam[ue]ll & Sarah, d. Dec. 5, 1749	LR5	1
Mary, d. Josiah & Sarah, b. Feb. 5, 1774	TM1	96
Philene, d. Gedion & Esther, b. July 6, 1744	LR5	232
Ruth, d. William & Hannah, b. July 6, 1697	2	31

	Vol.	Page
WASHBOND, WASHBON, WASBORN, WASHBONE, WASBON, WASHBAND, WASHBAN, (cont.)		
Ruth, m. Abiram CANFIELD, Sept. 12, 1717	LR3	9
Samuell, m. Susanna WO[O]STER, Nov. 30, 1714	LR3	9
Samuell, s. Samuell & Susanah, b. May 4, 1717	LR3	3
Samuel, m. Sarah BEACH, May 19, 1741	LR5	4
Samuel, s. Sam[ue]ll & Sarah, b. Jan. 6, 1751	LR7	253
Samuel, d. Oct. 24, 1760, in the Army	LR7	254
Sarah, Mrs., m. Ens. Sam[ue]ll RIGGS, May 6, 1713	LR3	9
Sarah, m. Joseph LUM, Apr. 29, 1741	LR4	A4
Sarah, d. Timothy & Hannah, b. June 11, 1746	LR6	2
Sarah, d. Sam[ue]ll & Sarah, b. Feb. 4, 1755	LR7	253
Sarah, d. Gideon & Esther, b. Oct. 16, 1760	LR7	252
Sarah, m. Edward HARGER, b. of Derby, Sept. 9, 1771	TM1	109
Seth Staples, m. Sylvia C. DAVIS, Mar. 19, 1843, by John D. Smith	1	481
Timothy, s. Ephraim & Merrian, b. Jan. 20, 1724/5	LR3	5
William, m. Han[n]ah WOOSTER, of Derby, Aug. 20, 1696	2	25
William, s. Samuel & Sarah, b. Aug. 28, 1742	LR5	2
William, s. Gideon & Esther, b. May 1, 1751	LR6	443
WATEROUS, Andrew, s. Richard & Susanna, b. Mar. 27, 1759	TM1	66
Anne, d. Richard & Susanna, b. Dec. 3, 1761	TM1	66
Charety, d. Richard & Susanna, b. Sept. 19, 1753	TM1	66
Charty, d. May 24, 1760	TM1	66
Isaac*, s. Richard & Susanna, b. Mar. 27, 1757 *(Written "Isaac WATERS")	TM1	66
Richard, s. Richard & Susana, b. May 26, 1751	TM1	66
Susanna, d. Richard & Susanna, b. May 21, 1755	TM1	66
Susannah, m. Ebenezer CHATFIELD, Mar. 23, 1768, by Rev. Richard Mansfield	TM1	17
WATERS, John, of New York, m. Mrs. Lydia DEPLANK, of Derby, Oct. 10, 1756, by [ ]	LR6	450
Lyman, of Oxford, m. Laura PERKINS, of Derby, Feb. 8, 1823, by Rev. Abner Smith	1	123
WATTLES, Clarissa, of Derby, m. David S. WEBSTER, of Bethleham, Oct. 31, 1827, by Rev. Abner Smith	1	123
WEBB, Joseph, m. Elizabeth NICKOLLS, of Stratford, July 8, 1691, by Capt. William Curtiss, at Stratford	2	25
WEBSTER, Clark, m. Sarah M. STILSON, b. of Derby, Nov. 7, 1830, by Rev. Stephen Jewett	1	91
David, m. Anne BUNNEL, Mar. 13, 1826, by Rev. Abner Smith	1	122
David S., of Bethleham, m. Clarissa WATTLES, of Derby, Oct. 31, 1827, by Rev. Abner Smith	1	123
Laura, of Derby, m. Benjamin PERRY, of Oxford, Mar. 11, 1827, by Rev. Abner Smith	1	111
WEED, Abel, s. Samuel & Sarah, b. Nov. 5, 1744	LR5	2
Andrew, s. John, b. Sept. 27, 1721	LR3	4
Caleb, s. John & Mary, b. Dec. 27, 1714	LR3	2

	Vol.	Page
WEED, (cont.)		
Dan, s. Sam[ue]ll & Sarah, b. Mar. 10, 1738/9	LR4	A2
Dauid, s. Sam[ue]ll & Sarah, b. Jan. 16, 1733/4	LR4	A2
Elijah, s. George & Esther, b. Feb. 17, 1739	LR4	A3
George, s. John & Mary, b. Mar. 20, 1717	LR3	3
Joannah, d. John & Mary, b. Apr. 22, 1724	LR3	5
John, m. Mary BEAMANT, Dec. 17, 1702	2	13
John, s. John & Mary, b. Sept. 29, 1706	2	13
John & w. Mary had s. [ ], b. Apr. 6, 1711	LR3	0
John, d. about May 2, 1739	LR3	12
John, s. Sam[ue]ll & Sarah, b. May 9, 1742	LR4	A2
Joseph, s. John & Mary, b. Nov. 2, 1708	2	22
Mary, wid., d. Oct. 27, 1743	LR3	12
Nath[anie]ll, s. Sam[ue]ll & Sarah, b. June 3, 1736	LR4	A2
Ruben, s. Sam[ue]ll & Sarah, b. Oct. 16, 1740	LR4	A2
Samuell, s. John & Mary, b. July 18, 1704	2	12
Samuel, s. John & Mary, b. July 18, 170[ ]	2	13
Sam[ue]ll, s. Sam[ue]ll & Sarah, b. Mar. 4, 1731/2	LR4	A2
----nry, d. John & Mary, b. Mar. 25, 1719	LR3	3
WELLS, Benjamin, of Huntington, m. Amelia HOTCHKISS, of		
Derby, Apr. 8, 1849, by Rev. W[illia]m Denison, of		
Humphreysville	1	482
Columbus, of Fairfield, m. Rhoda NORTON, of Waterbury, Dec.		
31, 1835, by Rev. Joseph Scott	1	187
David, of Huntington, m. Delia Helmira CLARK, of Derby,		
Apr. 4, 1833, by Rev. Stephen Jewett	1	187
David Thompson, m. Margaret Ana MOSHIER, Jan. 7, 1838, by		
John D. Smith	1	186
WELTON, Andrew, s. Moses & Elisabeth, b. Jan. 29, 1774	TM1	92
Eleazer, s. Moses & Elisabeth, b. Jan. 26, 1776	TM1	65
Moses, m. Elisabeth WOOSTER, Dec. 17, 1772	TM1	52
WESTON, Anson, m. Margaret MILLER (colored), May 21, 1843,		
by John D. Smith	1	481
Nelson, m. Lois BAGDEN, Sept. 30, 1834, by Rev. Joseph Scott	1	187
WHEELER, WHEALER, WHEELAR, WHELER, Abel, s. Samuel		
& Lowis, b. Dec. 18, 1765	TM1	31
Abigail, m. John BRINSMEAD, July 28, 1703	2	13
Abigail, m. Samuel WHE[E]LER, Dec. 2, 1739	LR5	4
Abigal, d. Sam[ue]ll & Abigal, b. Jan. 17, 1743/4	LR4	A5
Agnes, d. Sam[ue]ll & Abigail, b. Sept. 26, 1748	LR5	414
Ann, d. James & Sarah, b. Aug. 10, 1752	LR6	2
Ann, d. James & Mary, b. Sept. 12, 1771	TM1	43
Ann, d. Sam[ue]ll & Lowis, b. Sept. 9, 1773	TM1	31
Anne, d. James & Sarah, b. Aug. 10, 1752	TM1	32
Asa, s. Moses & Lucy, b. Jan. 23, 1785	TM1	87
Benjamin S., m. Delia SHERWOOD, Sept. 2, 1827, by Rev.		
Zepheniah Swift	1	123
Bette, d. Moses & Lucy, b. Feb. 20, 1775	TM1	87

	Vol.	Page
WHEELER, WHEALER, WHEELAR, WHELER, (cont.)		
Chearry, [twin with Clarry], d. Moses & Lewse, b. May 3, 1777	TM1	51
Clarry, [twin with Chearry], d. Moses & Lewse, b. May 3, 1777	TM1	51
Daniel, s. Samuel & Lowis, b. May 28, 1769	TM1	31
Daniel, s. Samuel & Lowis, d. Jan. 7, 1770	TM1	31
Daniel, s. Moses & Lucy, b. Mar. 14, 1782	TM1	87
Daniel H., of Huntington, m. Mary C. BOYCE, of Derby, Apr. 2, 1843, by Rev. I. B. Beach	1	481
David, s. James & Sarah, b. May 14, 1754	LR6	4
David, s. Ens. James & Sarah, b. May 14, 1754	TM1	32
David, s. Moses & Lucy, b. Sept. 7, 1779	TM1	87
Edwin C. m. Caroline S. PHELPS, b. of Derby, Jan. 30, 1840, by Rev. Sylvester Smith	1	188
Elijah, s. Capt. James & Sarah, b. Dec. 22, 1758	TM1	32
Elijah, s. Capt. James & Sarah, b. Dec. 22, 1758	LR6	451
Elijah, d. May 5, 1775	TM1	32
Elijah, s. John & Sarah, b. Dec. 4, 1778	TM1	112
Elisha, s. Robert & Ruth, b. Jan. 29, 1771	TM1	73
Elizabeth, m. Henry Martin JACKSON, Nov. 25, 1852, by Cha[rle]s Dickinson, Elder	1	326
Eunice, d. Samuel & Lowis, b. Oct. 26, 1767	TM1	31
Francis, m. Oliver Crosby PUTNAM, Nov. 9, 1837, by John D. Smith	1	172
Gilbert, m. Julia Ann SMITH, b. of Derby, Dec. 24, 1835, by Rev. Josiah Bowen	1	186
Hannah, d. Capt. James & Sarah, b. May 25, 1761	TM1	32
Hannah, d. Capt. James & Sarah, b. May 25, 1761	LR7	249
Hannah, m. Isaac NORTHROP, b. of Derby, Sept. 27, 1764, by Rev. David Brunson	TM1	15
Hannah, d. James & Mary, b. Jan. 30, 1776	TM1	48
Hannah, d. Sam[ue]ll & Lowis, b. Sept. 6, 1777	TM1	52
Hannah, d. Sam[ue]ll & Lowis, b. Sept. 6, 1777	TM1	104
Hannah, m. Joseph FAIRCHILD, b. of Derby, Nov. 9, 1780	TM1	104
James & w. Sarah had d. [ ], b. Dec. 27, 173[ ]	LR3	11
James, of Stratford, m. Sarah JOHNSON, of Derby, May 19, 1736	TM1	32
[J]ames, s. James & Sarah, b. Apr. 6, 1745	LR5	2
James, s. James & Sarah, b. Apr. 6, 1745	TM1	32
James & Sarah had d. [ ], s. b. Mar. 1, 1747	TM1	32
James, Jr., of Derby, m. Marah CLARK, of Milford, [ ] 13, 1767, by Rev. Mr. Hawley	TM1	38
James, Capt. d. July 9, 1768, in the 53rd y. of his age	TM1	32
James, s. James & Mary, b. Mar. 1, 1781	TM1	108
John, s. Capt. James & Sarah, b. June 2, 1756	LR6	13
John, s. Capt. James & Sarah, b. June 2, 1756	TM1	32
John, m. Sibbel TOOD, b. of Derby, July 10, 1776	TM1	85
John, s. John & Sibbel, b. May 4, 1777	TM1	85
John, m. Sarah JOHNSON, Nov. 19, 1777	TM1	85

	Vol.	Page
WHEELER, WHEALER, WHEELAR, WHELER, (cont.)		
Sam[ue]ll, s. James & Sarah, b. Sept. 24, 1739	LR4	A3
Samuel, s. James & Sarah, b. Sept. 24, 1739	TM1	32
Samuel, m. Abigail WHE[E]LER, Dec. 2, 1739	LR5	4
Samuel, Jr., m. Lowis FAIRCHILD, Apr. 28, 1763, by Rev.		
Mr. Levenworth	TM1	31
Samuel, s. Robert & Ruth, b. July 2, 1769	TM1	39
Samuel, d. Aug. 23, 1778	TM1	104
Samuel, s. John & Sarah, b. Jan. 17, 1781	TM1	112
Sarah, m. Nathaniel GUNN, Dec. 10, 1728	LR3	10
Sarah, d. James & Sarah, b. Dec. 27, 1737	TM1	32
Sarah, d. Capt. James & Sarah, b. Apr. 15, 1764	LR7	253
Sarah, d. Capt. James & Sarah, b. Apr. 15, 1764	TM1	32
Sarah, of Stratford, m. Joseph WHE[E]LER, of Derby,		
Apr. 11, 1771, by Rev. Jedidiah Mills	TM1	65
Sarah, w. Joseph, d. Apr. 10, 1772	TM1	65
Sarah, d. Simeon & Sarah, b. Feb. 21, 1774	TM1	73
Sarah, m. Charles E. CONVERSE, Feb. 1, 1844, by Rev.		
John D. Smith	1	233
Sarah, see Sarah WHITNEY	TM1	33
Simeon, s. James & Sarah, b. Apr. 15, 1741	LR4	A2
Simeon, s. James & Sarah, b. Apr. 15, 1741	TM1	32
Simeon, m. Sarah BALDWIN, b. of Derby, Oct. 10, 1764, by		
Rev. Mr. Humphry	TM1	31
Simeon, s. Simeon & Sarah, b. Nov. 13, 1771	TM1	73
Sibbel, w. John, d. May 11, 1777	TM1	85
Sybil, d. John & Sarah, b. Apr. 14, 1783	TM1	112
Timothy, s. Simeon & Sarah, b. Feb. 16, 1771	TM1	73
Whittelsey, s. Joseph & Lucy, b. Sept. 19, 1784	TM1	212
William, s. Joseph & Lucy, b. Apr. 3, 1779	TM1	212
William Elliot, m. Ruth Ann SCOTT, June 19, 1836, by		
Rev. John D. Smith	1	188
WHITE, Abner, m. Electa BASSETT, b. of Derby, Dec. 2, 1849, by		
Rev. S. Howland	1	482
Calvin, m. Jane MARDENBROUGH, Jan. 9, 1828, by Rev.		
Stephen Jewett	1	122
Hannah, m. Ebenezer DURAND, Dec. 17, 1754	LR6	450
Harriet E., of Derby, m. Charles L. HYDE, of Oxford, Mar.		
24, 1842, by Rev. John E. Bray	1	289
Henrietta, m. David B. HOLBROOK, Jan. 2, 1848, by Rev.		
W[illia]m B. Curtiss	1	290
Isaac, Jr., m. Sarah Grace KEENEY, b. of Derby, Jan. 11,		
1835, by Rev. John E. Bray	1	187
John E., m. Anne DAVIS, b. of Derby, Jan. 11, 1835, by		
Rev. John E. Bray	1	187
Juliatte, of Derby, m. Heman CHILD, of Hamden, Dec. 31, 1834,		
by Rev. John E. Bray	1	149
Mary Ann, m. Watrous CLARK, b. of Derby, Sept. 6, 1832,		

	Vol.	Page
WHITE, (cont.)		
by Charles Thompson	1	149
WHITING, W[illia]m J., M. D., m. Susan M. **COLBURN**, b. of		
Derby, May 18, 1846, by Rev. George Thacher	1	481
WHITMORE, Elias, m. Rachel **WISEBURY**, Feb. 21, 1755	LR6	451
Elisabeth, d. Elias & Rachel, b. Sept. 21, 1757	LR6	442
Sarah, d. Elias & Rachel, b. Oct. 13, 1760	LR7	249
WHITNEY, Abigail, d. Stephen & Eunice, b. June 17, 1769	TM1	84
Abigail, d. Stephen & Eunice, d. Sept. 13, 1769	TM1	84
Ann Eliza, m. Peter P. **PHELPS**, [Nov.] 28, [1836], by		
L. D. Howell	1	172
Betsey Ann, m. Henry Beers **BEECHER**, Sept. 27, 1840, by		
John D. Smith	1	171
Isaac, s. Stephen & Sarah, b. Nov. 17, 1761	TM1	84
James, s. Stephen & Sarah, b. Mar. 23, 1764	TM1	84
Joseph Lyman, s. Ranford & Ruth, b. Sept. 1, 1775	TM1	119
Lusida, d. Stephen & Eunice, b. Apr. 2, 1768	TM1	84
Lusinda, d. Stephen & Eunice, d. Sept. 18, 1769	TM1	84
Lucenda, [twin with Stephen], d. Stephen & Eunice,		
by Mar. 24, 1772	TM1	84
Maria Brower, of Derby, m. Josiah **MANN**, of New York		
City, Dec. 1, 1840, by Rev. Hollis Read	1	169
Nabbe, d. Stephen & Eunice, b. Apr. 4, 1774	TM1	84
Ranford, m. Ruth **CANFIELD**, Sept. 26, 1773	TM1	119
Samuel, s. Stephen & Sarah, b. Mar. 15, 1759	LR6	719
Samuel, s. Stephen & Sarah, b. Mar. 24, 1769*		
*(Probably 1759)	TM1	84
Sarah, w. Stephen & d. of Capt. James **WHE[E]LER**, d. Mar.		
31, 1764, in the 27th y. of her age	TM1	33
Sarah, w. Stephen, d. Mar. 31, 1764	TM1	84
Sarah, [twin with Stephen], d. Stephen & Eunice, b.		
Aug. 11, 1765	TM1	84
Sarah, d. Ranford & Ruth, b. Apr. 3, 1774	TM1	119
Stephen, m. Eunice **KEENEY**, Nov. 5, 1764	TM1	84
Stephen, [twin with Sarah], s. Stephen & Eunice, b.		
Aug. 11, 1765	TM1	84
Stephen, [twin with Lucenda], s. Stephen & Eunice, b.		
Mar. 24, 1772	TM1	84
Stephen, s. Stephen & Eunice, d. Apr. 9, 1772	TM1	84
Stephen, m. Charlotte **LEWIS**, Oct. 6, 1822, by Rev. Stephen		
Jewett	1	123
Susan A., of Derby, m. James M. **McMANN**, of New York,		
Apr. 17, [1843], by Rev. W[illia]m Bliss Ashley	1	357
Thomas V., m. Nancy M. **POWE**, Mar. 13, 184[ ], by Rev.		
Jos[eph] Scott	1	190
WHITTLESEY, Roger N., of New Preston, m. Mrs. Jane **LANE**,		
of Derby, Aug. 19, 1838, by Rev. David Miller	1	188
WILCOXSON, Caroline, m. Charles H. **MITCHELL**, b. of Derby,		

	Vol.	Page
WOOSTER, WOSTER, WORSTER, (cont.)		
31st y. of her age	LR5	1
Abigail, d. Henry, 3rd & Rebecca, b. June 28, 1789	TM1	187
Abraham, s. Abr[aha]m & Martha, b. Sept. 20, 1740	LR4	A5
Amy, d. David & Mary, b. Dec. 9, 1754	LR6	4
An[n], d. Timothy & Anna, b. Jan. 7, 1704	LR3	3
Ann, d. John & Eunice, b. Apr. 13, 1747	LR5	414
Annah, m. Philo HOLBROOK, b. of Derby, June 3, 1779	TM1	118
Anne, m. Daniel HAWKINS, Jan. 6, 172[ ]	LR3	10
Anne, d. John & Eunice, b. Apr. 13, 1747	LR6	4
Anne, d. John & Eunice, d. Aug. 3, 1751	LR6	13
Anne, d. John & Eunice, b. Nov. 13, 1754	LR6	4
Anne, d. Henry & Elisabeth, b. Nov. 10, 1781	TM1	64
Apame, d. Daniel & Sarah, b. Dec. 26, 1782	TM1	226
Asher, s. Timothy & Anna, b. Mar. 26, 1713	LR3	3
Augusta, m. John LUM, Jr., Feb. 26, 1828, by Rev. Stephen Jewett	1	111
Bennet, m. Elsie Louiza WILLIAMS, Nov. 5, 1837, by John D. Smith	1	186
Betsey, d. Henry & Elisabeth, b. July 26, 1778	TM1	18
Betsey, m. Eli TERRILL, Oct. 7, 1838, by John D. Smith	1	180
Damares, d. Timothy & Anna, b. Feb. 20, 1708	LR3	3
Damarus, m. Eleazier HAWKINS, Dec. 13, 1727	LR3	10
Danniel, s. Thommas & Sarah, b. July 14, 1729	LR3	15
Daniel, m. Sarah HAWKINS, of Derby, May 11, 1780	TM1	130
Daniel, s. Daniel & Sarah, b. Mar. 14, 1786	TM1	226
Dauid, s. Tho[ma]s & Sarah, b. Jan. 5, 1734/5	LR3	16
David, s. Joseph & Hannah, b. Dec. 1, 1774	TM1	104
David Daniel, 2nd, m. Carroline BASSETT, b. of Derby, Apr. 9, 1835, by Sylvester Smith	1	186
Dorcus, d. Timo[thy] & Abigail, b. Apr. [ ], 1731	LR5	413
Dorcus, d. Timothy & Abigal, d. Apr. [ ], 17[ ]	LR5	1
Dorcus, d. Timo[thy] & Sarah, b. Mar. 25, 1738	LR5	413
Edward, s. Timothy & Anna, b. Sept. 17, 1702	LR3	3
Edward, s. Timothy & Anna, b. Sept. 17, 1702	2	12
Edward, s. Timo[thy] & Sarah, b. Feb. 18, 1740	LR5	413
Edward, S. Timo[thy] & Sarah, d. Oct. 15, 1746	LR5	1
Edward, s. Timo[thy] & Sarah, b. Sept. 28, 1747	LR5	413
Edward, m. Sarah JUDD, June 30, 1760	LR7	248
Edward Hawley, s. Thomas A. & Nancy, b. Aug. 7, 1850; recorded Nov. 19, 1860	1	484
Eliezer, s. Timothy & Anna, b. Oct. 16, 1715	LR3	3
[E]lisha, s. Sam[ue]ll & Ann, b. July 5, 1732	LR3	16
Elisabeth, m. John TOMLINSON, Mar. 27, 1712	LR3	9
Elisabeth, d. John & Eunice, b. Nov. 26, 1748	LR5	414
Elisabeth, d. John & Eunice, b. Nov. 28, 1748	LR6	4
Elisabeth, d. John & Eunice, d. Aug. 8, 1751	LR6	13
Elisabeth, m. Moses WELTON, Dec. 17, 1772	TM1	52

	Vol.	Page
WOOSTER, WOSTER, WORSTER, (cont.)		
Elisabeth, w. Henry, d. Sept. 23, 1786, in the 43rd y.		
of her age	TM1	159
Elizabeth, m. Joseph HAWKINS, Sr., b. of Derby, June 10,		
1829, by Rev. S. Jewett	1	101
Emma E., d. Thomas A. & Nancy, b. Mar. 2, 1844; recorded		
Nov. 19, 1860	1	484
Enoch, s. Henry & Elisabeth, b. May 7, 1765	TM1	14
Enoch, s. Henry & Elisabeth, d. Dec. 8, 1785, in the 21st y.,		
of her age	TM1	159
Grace, d. Edward, b. Feb. 16, 1726/7	LR3	15
Han[n]ah, m. William WASHBUN, Aug. 20, 1696	2	25
Hannah, d. Siluester & Mercy, b. May 10, 1739	LR5	232
Hannah, d. John & Eunice, b. July 8, 1750	LR5	414
Hannah, d. John & Eunice, b. July 8, 1750	LR6	4
Hannah, d. John & Eunice, b. Sept. 14, 1758	LR7	253
Harriett, m. George KIRTLAND, b. of Derby, Nov. 25, 1830, by		
Rev. John Lovejoy	1	102
Henry, s. Timothy & Anna, b. Feb. 19, 1710	LR3	3
Henry, s. Henry & Elisabeth, b. Oct. 25, 1762	LR7	252
Hinman, s. Abr[aha]m & Martha, b. Apr. 26, 1735	LR4	A5
Isaac, s. Daniel & Sarah, b. July 24, 1781	TM1	130
Isaac, s. Daniel & Sarah, b. Dec. 26, 1782	TM1	226
Jabez, s. Tim[othy] & Abigail, b. Oct. 15, 1728	LR5	413
Jennett, m. Henry TYREL, b. of Derby, Mar. 29, 1837, by		
Rev. Lewis D. Howell	1	182
Jesse, s. Timo[thy] & Sarah, b. May 4, 1743	LR5	413
John, s. Thomas & Sarah, b. Dec. 22, 1719	LR3	5
John, m. Eunice HULL, June 18, 1746	LR6	7
John, s. John & Eunice, b. Oct. 11, 1752	LR6	3
John, s. Ens. John & Eunice, b. May 31, 1763	LR7	253
Joseph, s. Thomas & Sarah, b. June 30, 1732	LR3	16
Joseph, s. Daniel & Sarah, b. Mar. 22, 1790; d. June 14, 1790	TM1	226
Joseph D., m. Mary TOMLINSON, b. of Derby, Jan. 6, 1831, by		
Rev. Stephen Jewett	1	121
Julia A., d. Thomas A. & Nancy, b. Oct. 17, 1841; recorded Nov.		
19, 1860	1	484
Lemuel, s. Moses & Mindwell, b. June 23, 1760	LR7	249
Lois, d. Siluester & Mercy, b. Feb. 17, 1743	LR5	232
Marcy, d. Siluester & Mercy, b. Mar. 28, 1745	LR5	232
Mary, d. Abr[aha]m & Martha, b. May 10, 1733	LR4	A5
Mary, Mrs. of Oxford, m. Joel R. CHATFIELD, of Derby,		
[ ], by Rev. Joseph Scott; recorded June 26, 1837	1	150
Mary M., m. Durand HAWKINS, Nov. 25, 1822, by Rev. Abner		
Smith	1	97
Merrit, of Oxford, m. Harriet BALDWIN, of Derby, Jan. 28,		
1829, by Eli Barnett, Elder	1	124
Miles, s. Abr[aha]m & Martha, b. June 10, 1738	LR4	A5

	Vol.	Page
WOOSTER, WOSTER, WORSTER, (cont.)		
Moses, m. Mary HAWKINS, Apr. 5, 1720, by Rev. Joseph Moss	LR3	9
Moses, m. Mindwell CHATFIELD, June 20, 1759	LR7	248
Nancy, of Derby, m. Nelson HINMAN, of Southbury, Mar. 19, 1823, by Rev. Abner Smith	1	96
Naomi, m. John BASSIT, Dec. 15, 1746	LR5	4
Nathan, m. Mary Ann NETTLETON, Apr. 8, 1824, by Rev. Stephen Jewett	1	122
Persis, d. David & Mary, b. May 30, 1704	2	23
Peirse*, m. Ephraim GILLIT, Apr. 2, 1724 *(Persis)	LR3	9
Phebe, m. Samuel HARGER, Dec. 9, 1747	LR5	4
Phebe, d. Tho[ma]s & Sarah, b. Mar. [ ]	LR3	5
Roene, d. Daniel & Sarah, b. Nov. 11, 1784	TM1	226
Ruth, d. Thomas & Sarah, b. Mar. 30, 1722	LR3	5
Ruth, m. Dan DAUIS, Dec. 6, 1738	LR4	A4
Ruth, d. Siluester & Mercy, b. Aug. 5, 1749	LR5	414
Ruth, d. Ens. John & Eunice, b. Jan. 26, 1761	LR7	253
Ruth, m. [ ]ell BOWERS, b. of [ ]	2	2
Sally, d. Daniel & Sarah, b. Apr. 20, 1788	TM1	226
Samuell, s. Timothy & Anna, b. Apr. 17, 1706	LR3	3
Sam[ue]ll, m. Hannah JOHNSON, May 22, 1725	LR3	10
Sam[ue]ll, Jr., m. Ann MOSS, Oct. 28, 1731	LR3	10
Sarah, d. Sam[ue]ll & Hannah, b. Nov. 28, 1725	LR3	5
Sarah, d. Thomas & Lois, b. Feb. 2, 1748/9	LR5	413
Sarah, w. Timothy, d. Oct. 23, 1749, supposed in the 43rd y. of her age	LR5	1
Sarah, wid. Thomas, d. Dec. 10, 1785, ae 92	TM1	159
Sarah, w. Daniel, d. Oct. 13, 1790	TM1	226
Sarah, m. Charles JOHNSON, Aug. 16, [ ]	LR3	10
Susanna, d. Susanna, b. July 23, 1713	LR3	2
Susanna, had d. Susanna, b. July 23, 1713	LR3	2
Susanna, m. Samuell WASBON, Nov. 30, 1714	LR3	9
Susanah, m. Abraham PEIRSON, Jr., Apr. 10, 1731	LR3	10
Sylvester, had his ear mark for cattle recorded, Dec. 10, 1711	2	161
Syluestor, d. Nov. 16, 1712	LR3	6
Siluester, m. Mercy HINE, Feb. 20, 1737/8	LR5	4
Tabitha, d. Timothy & Anna, b. May 3, 1701	LR3	3
Tabitha, d. Timothy & Anna, b. May 3, 1701	2	12
Tabitha, m. Abel HOLBROOK, Jan. 29, 1723	LR3	9
Tamar, d. David & Mary, b. June 16, 1707	2	23
Thankful, d. Thomas & Phebee, b. Nov. 7, 1695	2	26
Thankfull, d. Lef. Thomas, d. Nov. 18, 1706	2	27
Thomas, s. Thomas & Phebe, b. Feb. 18, 1692	2	26
Thomas, Lieut., d. Jan. 9, 1712/13	LR3	6
Thomas, m. Sarah HAWKENS, Dec. 25, 1718	LR3	9
Thomas, s. Thomas & Sarah, b. Oct. 11, 1724	LR3	5
Thomas, Jr., m. Lois HAWKINS, Jan. 21, 1746/7	LR5	4